This book covers all recent developments and brings you fully abreast of the latest technological advances in the highly important analog-computer field.

The book's purpose is threefold:

(1) To introduce research and development workers to modern electronic analog computers, and especially to the new iterative differential analyzers

(2) To present up-to-date design information on hybrid analog-digital computing devices and systems— including circuits for instrumentation, control, and data processing as well as for general-purpose problem solving

(3) To introduce improved computing techniques made possible by new, ultra-fast hybrid analog-digital computers, especially in connection with optimization and statistical studies

Part I of this volume introduces "classical" electronic analog computation and tried programming and scaling procedures. The second part of the book deals with the actual design of modern analog computing elements, emphasizing the new, high-speed solid-state computing elements.

Part III covers the design of complete analog and hybrid analog-digital computing systems. The last section of the book introduces some of the new mathematical techniques brought about by the new iterative differential analyzers.

Among the topics treated in these pages are: preparation of practical computer setups; design of networks, coefficient potentiometers, and operational amplifiers; D-c amplifier design; vacuum-tube D-c amplifiers; transistor D-c amplifiers; limits; switching circuits; electronic function generators; electronic multipliers, dividers, and resolvers; computer servomechanisms; vector resolvers; special analog-digital circuits for instrumentation, control, and simulation; integrator-mode control; analog memory; and iterative computation.

This volume is illustrated with more than 800 computer circuits, block diagrams, and photographs to facilitate your understanding of the material under discussion. In addition, the book gives you convenient access to the ever-growing literature on computers by listing over 900 bibliographical references.

In short, here is complete, authoritative, and practical coverage of electronic analog and hybrid computers— a book that will be welcomed by electrical and electronic engineers, computer designers, research and development engineers, computer programmers, and all others wishing to be brought up-to-date on the many recent developments in the analog-computer field.

ELECTRONIC ANALOG AND HYBRID COMPUTERS

ELECTRONIC ANALOG AND HYBRID COMPUTERS

GRANINO A. KORN, Ph.D.

Professor of Electrical Engineering, University of Arizona

THERESA M. KORN, M.S.

 McGRAW-HILL BOOK COMPANY

New York   San Francisco   Toronto   London

ELECTRONIC ANALOG AND HYBRID COMPUTERS

35360

To the memory of Dean Roland George Dwight Richardson
of Brown University, who has contributed so much to the development
of applied mathematics in the United States,
this book is respectfully dedicated.

PREFACE

Electronic analog computers are now firmly established as "live mathematical models" for scientists and engineers. Analog simulation helps to close the gap between physical intuition and exact analysis, and this benefits almost every designer or research worker, no matter what his special field is. Quite lately, a veritable two-headed revolution has added memory, automatic program control, and digital operations to the familiar analog computer, and all-solid-state circuits have increased computing speed and reliability by two orders of magnitude. Automatic iteration with hybrid analog-digital differential analyzers has contracted month-long statistical and optimization studies into hours. Nor is this all, for problem solving is only one of many computer applications in an increasingly automatic world. New hybrid analog-digital computing devices, large and small, handle live instrumentation and control data in industry, in communications, in weapons, and in space.

The purpose of this new volume, then, is threefold:

1. To introduce research and development workers to modern electronic analog computers, and especially to the new iterative differential analyzers.
2. To present up-to-date design information on hybrid analog-digital computing devices and systems; this includes circuits for instrumentation, control, and data processing as well as for general-purpose problem solving.
3. To introduce improved computing techniques made possible by new, ultra-fast hybrid analog-digital computers, especially in connection with optimization.

This book, which includes much previously unpublished information, will, we hope, be useful to research workers and engineers. The subject matter should be readily accessible to seniors in electrical engineering or physics. Lecture notes based on the same material have served as a text for a series of special senior-elective and graduate courses involving research participation rather than term examinations.* A study guide, problem collection and laboratory manual for these courses are in preparation.

With well over 800 computer circuits, block diagrams, and photographs, this is truly a picture book, and the reader will be able to form a fair preliminary idea of the text material by a first look at the illustrations. Circuit diagrams are presented in related groups to permit convenient comparisons. We have also attempted to give the reader convenient access to the ever-growing computer literature by listing over 900 bibliographical references, by topics and subtopics, at the end of related chapters; a special author index provides alphabetical access to this bibliography.

Chapters 1 and 2, comprising Part I of this volume, introduce "classical" electronic analog computation and tried programming and scaling procedures, with many simple examples. In particular, Chap. 2 also treats computer setups for linear transfer operators and introduces the computation of impulse responses for use in more advanced calculations.

The second part of the book, comprising Chaps. 3 through 9, deals with the actual design of modern analog computing elements, with emphasis on the new high-speed solid-state computing elements. Chapter 3 presents a detailed error analysis for linear computing networks and operational amplifiers and discusses errors in computer solutions of linear differential equations.

Chapters 4 and 5 describe the design of vacuum-tube and transistor d-c amplifiers and treat stage design, automatic balancing, frequency response, feedforward amplifiers, and test circuits. Special emphasis is given to the design of drift-compensated transistor differential amplifier stages and feedforward circuits permitting computation from d-c to above 20 Mc. Many practical circuits are shown.

Chapters 6 and 7 deal similarly with function generators and electronic multipliers, with three special sections devoted to the design of the latest diode and transistor switches. Chapter 8 discusses computer servomechanisms and servo and electronic resolvers.

Chapter 9 is concerned with special analog-digital circuits useful for instrumentation, control, and simulation, including precision limiters, selectors, extreme-value holding circuits, voltage-to-time converters, precise oscillators and their applications to the simulation of nonlinear dynamical systems.

Part III (Chaps. 10 and 11) deals with the design of complete analog and hybrid analog-digital computing systems. Starting with the design of circuits for integrator mode control, Chap. 10 dwells on track-hold

* G. A. Korn, Analog Computers in the Electrical Engineering Department, *Instruments and Control Systems*, September, 1959; and G. A. Korn, Hybrid Computer Teaching Aid, *Instruments and Control Systems*, August, 1963.

circuits, analog point storage and function memory, comparator design, and introduces the modern iterative differential analyzer comprising fast analog computing elements and digital control circuits. Flow diagrams are used to detail iterative subroutines.

Chapter 11 describes the design of complete analog and hybrid computer systems, including patchbays, power supplies, recorders, and checking circuits. We next turn to analog-to-digital and digital-to-analog converters and combined simulation with analog and digital computers; the chapter closes with a description of operational digital computation and of more exotic hybrid computing systems.

Part IV, comprising the final chapter, introduces some of the new mathematical techniques opened up by the new iterative differential analyzers. Chapter 12 begins with accurate perturbation methods for space-vehicle-trajectory computation and steepest-descent methods for continuous optimization and improvement of computing accuracy. The major part of this chapter is devoted to circuits for automatic parameter optimization; the chapter ends with a brief account of analog/hybrid techniques for solving partial differential equations and integral equations.

An appendix presents a number of tables of special computer circuits for reference; shorter tables are located in the text proper.

We originally intended to include two additional chapters describing analog/hybrid computer applications to random-process simulation and measurements. In particular, Monte-Carlo-type simulation of control, communication, and detection systems is a striking application of the modern high-speed iterative differential analyzer. Computer techniques for noise generation and statistical measurements are widely useful. For better or for worse, however, our account of these techniques (which have been the subject of most of our research at the University of Arizona) proved to be too extensive for inclusion in this book. Since, too, this material is not directly related to other topics treated in this volume and also involves some additional mathematics, it will be published as a separate monograph (see also ref. 111, Chap. 10).

The writers are grateful to the University of Arizona, to Dr. T. L. Martin, Jr., and to Dr. P. E. Russell for their encouragement of our hybrid-computer research; and to the National Science Foundation, the Air Force Office of Scientific Research, and the National Aeronautics and Space Administration for their support of the APE and ASTRAC II hybrid-computer projects. We would like to thank the many students whose term papers and thesis work contributed to our research, and especially the present and former assistants and research associates in the University's Analog/Hybrid Computer Laboratory:

| T. Brubaker | H. Eckes | R. Hampton | J. Hartmann |
| B. Conant | C. Foiles | H. Handler | H. Koerner |

R. Mangels   B. Mitchell   J. Wait
R. Maybach   E. O'Grady   R. Whigham

Last, but not least, we are, once again, grateful to our friends in the computer industry for contributing their know-how in the form of reports, circuits, photographs, and discussions. We are, in particular, indebted to the following individuals and organizations:

Applied Dynamics, Inc.   Mr. J. D. Kennedy
Ann Arbor, Michigan   Mr. G. Graber

Beckman/Berkeley Division   Mr. J. A. Brussolo
Richmond, California

Bell Telephone Laboratories   Mr. F. D. Waldhauer
Murray Hill, N.J.

Brush Instruments   Mr. E. F. Crafts
Cleveland, Ohio

Burr-Brown Research Corporation   Mr. H. Koerner
Tucson, Arizona   Mr. D. Ozdes

Comcor, Inc.   Mr. R. G. Wieneke
Denver, Colorado

Computer Instruments Corporation   Mr. M. Butensky
Hempstead, L.I., N.Y.

Computer Products, Inc.   Mr. R. C. Lonick
South Belmar, N.J.

Computer Systems, Inc.   Mr. R. Haskins
Richmond, Virginia

Electronic Associates, Inc.   Mr. R. R. Favreau
Long Branch, N.J.   Mr. R. W. Olmstead
                                               Mr. W. Brunner

Embree Electronics   Mr. J. Embree
West Hartford, Conn.

General Electric Company   Mr. G. M. Kirkpatrick
Syracuse, N.Y.   Mr. K. C. Cummings

Hitachi Central Research Laboratory   Dr. T. Miura
Tokyo, Japan

Massachusetts Institute of Technology   Mr. M. E. Connelly
Cambridge, Massachusetts

McGraw-Hill Publishing Company   Mr. W. MacDonald
Electronics Magazine
New York, N.Y.

F. L. Moseley Company   Mr. B. G. Hall
Pasadena, California

G. A. Philbrick Researches, Inc.   Mr. D. H. Sheingold
  Boston, Massachusetts

Reeves Instrument Corporation   Mr. B. D. Loveman
  Garden City, L.I., N.Y.

Simulation Councils, Inc.   Mr. J. McLeod
  La Jolla, California   Mr. S. Rogers

Stevens-Arnold, Inc.   Mr. E. F. Stevens
  South Boston, Mass.

Systron-Donner Corporation   Mr. F. W. Jenkinson
  Concord, California

University of California   Dr. W. J. Karplus
  Los Angeles, California

University of Southern California   Dr. G. A. Bekey
  Los Angeles, California

University of Wisconsin   Dr. V. C. Rideout
  Madison, Wisconsin

General Electric Company   Mr. H. Schmid
  Johnson City, New York

Special thanks are due the editor and publishers of *Simulation* for
their permission to use material from an article on iterative-differential-
analyzer control by H. R. Eckes and G. A. Korn.

                                        GRANINO A. KORN
                                        THERESA M. KORN

CONTENTS

Preface vii

PART I. PRINCIPLES OF ELECTRONIC
ANALOG COMPUTATION

Chapter 1. Introduction to Electronic Analog Computers . . . 3

Analog Computers
1-1. Introduction 3
The Electronic Analog Computer
1-2. Introduction 4
1-3. Machine Variables and Computing Elements 6
1-4. Time Dependence of Variables. Integration 7
1-5. Solution of Differential Equations: Classical Differential-analyzer
    Technique 8
1-6. Operation of "Slow" Electronic Differential Analyzers 10
1-7. "Fast" (Repetitive) Electronic Analog Computers 11
1-8. Analog-computer Solution of Problems Other Than Ordinary Differ-
    ential Equations: Survey 11
How the Basic Computing Elements Work
1-9. Coefficient-setting Potentiometers 12
1-10. Operational Amplifiers: The Phase Inverter 13
1-11. Summing Networks and Summing Amplifiers 14
1-12. Integration 15
    (a) Integrating Circuits. Accuracy Limitations 15
    (b) Electronic Integration: The Parallel-feedback Integrator . . . 17
    (c) Initial Conditions 19
1-13. Multipliers and Function Generation 19
    (a) Computer Servomechanisms 19
    (b) Electronic Function Generators and Multipliers 20
    (c) Division 21
More General Computing Networks and Operational Amplifiers
1-14. Direct-analog Networks and Operational Amplifiers 21
1-15. Practical Design Considerations 27
1-16. Differentiating Circuits 29
Analog-computer Systems
1-17. The Analog-computer System 30
1-18. Accuracy and Computing Speed 30

xiii

CONTENTS

1-19. Computing Devices as Components of Instrumentation, Control, and Data-handling Systems 31
References and Bibliography 34

Chapter 2.   Preparation of Practical Computer Setups 37

Introduction
2-1. Introductory Remarks 37
Amplitude-scaling Procedure.   Examples of Scaled Relations
2-2. Amplitude Scaling: The Choice of Scale Factors 37
2-3. Amplitude Scaling: Machine Equations and Block Diagram . . . 39
2-4. Examples of Scaled Relations.   Block-diagram Symbols. 41
  (a) Algebraic Sums 41
  (b) Multiplication, Division, and Square Roots.   How to Avoid Division 41
  (c) Proper Use of Function Generators 45
Changing the Time Scale
2-5. Time Scaling 46
2-6. Choice of Time Scale 47
Ordinary Differential Equations
2-7. Solution of Differential Equations 48
  (a) Scaling First-order Equations and Systems 48
  (b) Equations of the Second and Higher Order 48
  (c) Generation of Forcing Functions 50
  (d) Generalized Integration 50
2-8. Checking and Rescaling 52
Examples of Scaling and Computer Solutions
2-9. The Damped Harmonic Oscillator.   Scale-factor Estimation . . . 53
2-10. Mathieu's and Legendre's Differential Equations 54
2-11. Solution of Nonlinear Second-order Differential Equations: Two Typical Oscillation Problems 57
  (a) Van der Pol's Differential Equation 57
  (b) Rayleigh's Differential Equation.   Accurate Use of Diode Function Generators. 58
Linear Operations: Simple Transfer Operators and Impulse-response Functions
2-12. Introduction 62
2-13. Differential-analyzer Techniques 64
2-14. Scaling and Initial Conditions for Transfer-operator Setups. . . . 67
  (a) Amplitude Scaling 67
  (b) Time Scaling 68
  (c) Initial Conditions. 68
2-15. Factored and Partial-fraction Representation of Complicated Linear Operators 69
2-16. The Impulse Response.   Weighting-function Techniques for Computing Step Response, Ramp Response, and Frequency Response . . . 69
Summary of Scaling and Setup Procedure.   Special Precautions
2-17. Review and Summary 71
2-18. Some Special Precautions. 72
References and Bibliography 73

PART II.   DESIGN OF THE BASIC COMPUTING ELEMENTS

Chapter 3.   Computer Accuracy.   Design of Networks, Coefficient Potentiometers, and Operational Amplifiers 77

Computer Accuracy and Other Design Specifications
3-1. A Discussion of Analog-computer Accuracy 77
3-2. Component Accuracy: Static and Dynamic Errors 78
   (a) Static Accuracy, Step Response, and Small-signal Frequency
      Response 78
   (b) Phase Errors 79
   (c) Rate-limit Specifications and Switch-timing Errors 80
3-3. Other Design Specifications 81
Coefficient-setting Potentiometers
3-4. Specifications and Construction 81
3-5. Loading Considerations and Potentiometer Setting 85
3-6. Dynamic Errors and Capacitor Compensation 87
Computing Resistors and Capacitors. Parasitic-impedance Effects
3-7. Computing Resistors 91
   (a) Resistance Stability. Wirewound Computing Resistors . . . 91
   (b) Parasitic Inductance and Capacitance. Carbon-film Resistors . 92
3-8. Computing Capacitors: Stability 92
3-9. Capacitor Leakage and Dielectric Absorption 93
   (a) Resistive Leakage 93
   (b) Dielectric Absorption. Capacitor Models 94
   (c) Effects of Dielectric Absorption 96
The Parallel-feedback Operational Amplifier
3-10. Introduction 96
3-11. Operational-amplifier Performance with Finite Gain and Loading . . 98
3-12. Error Calculations 99
3-13. Effect of Amplifier Internal Impedance and Loading 100
3-14. Operational Amplifiers with Two-terminal Computing Impedances.
    Input-source Loading 100
3-15. Effects of D-c Offsets and Noise 101
3-16. Effects of Gain Changes and Distortion 102
3-17. Summary of Error Analysis 102
Design of Phase Inverters, Summing Amplifiers, and Integrators
3-18. Introduction 103
3-19. Design of Phase Inverters and Summing Amplifiers 103
   (a) Static Accuracy 103
   (b) Dynamic Accuracy and Phase-equalizing Capacitors 104
3-20. Electronic Integrators: Effects of Finite Gain, Loading, and Parasitic
    Impedances on the Integrator Frequency Response 106
3-21. Electronic Integrators: Errors Due to Calibration, D-c Offset, and
    Noise 109
Errors in Solutions of Linear Differential Equations with Constant Coefficients.
System-design Considerations
3-22. Introduction 110
3-23. First-order Mode-error Calculations 111
3-24. Errors in Sinusoidal Modes. Circle Test and System Design . . . 114
   (a) The Circle Test 114
   (b) Examples and System-design Considerations 117
References and Bibliography 119

Chapter 4. Vacuum-tube D-c Amplifiers **122**

Introduction
4-1. Requirements and Specifications 122
4-2. Survey of Design Procedure 124

CONTENTS

Design of Vacuum-tube D-c Amplifier Stages

4-3. Choice of Vacuum-tube Operating Points 125
4-4. Linear Equivalent Circuits 126
4-5. Use of Resistance-coupled-amplifier Tables 128
4-6. Differential-amplifier Stages 129
4-7. Output-stage Design 131
4-8. Totem-pole Output Stages 134
4-9. Regenerative D-c Amplifier Stages 135

Drift, Noise, and Chopper Stabilization

4-10. Effects of Drift and Noise 137
4-11. Causes of D-c Amplifier Drift 138
4-12. Low-drift Circuit Design 139
4-13. Improved D-c Amplifier Design: Automatic-balancing Circuits. . . 140
4-14. Chopper-stabilizer Design 144
    (a) Chopper Construction and Operation 144
    (b) The A-c Amplifier 145
    (c) Stabilizer-channel Filters and Frequency Response 145
    (d) Overload Recovery and Error Lights 147
4-15. Frequency Response and Stability of Feedback Amplifiers . . . 147
4-16. High-frequency Equivalent Circuits. Miller Effect 151
4-17. Frequency-response Shaping with Stabilizing Networks 153
    (a) Interstage Lead Capacitors 153
    (b) "Submerging" the Effect of High-frequency Poles . . . 153
    (c) Rolloff Networks 154
    (d) Load-capacitance Effects. 157
    (e) Experimental Procedure for Rolloff-network Design . . . 158
4-18. External Stabilizing Networks 158
4-19. Design of Wideband D-c Amplifiers by Feedforward Techniques . . 160
4-20. Frequency Response of Regenerative and Degenerative D-c Amplifier
    Stages 163
4-21. Practical Frequency-response Measurements 165

Examples of Vacuum-tube Computer-amplifier Design

4-22. Representative Amplifier Specifications. 167
4-23. Examples 167
    (a) Plug-in Utility D-c Amplifiers 167
    (b) High-quality D-c Amplifiers for Conventional "Slow" Electronic
        Analog Computers 172
    (c) Wideband D-c Amplifiers 173

References and Bibliography 173

**Chapter 5. Transistor D-c Amplifiers and Miscellaneous Practical
Considerations** 176

Introduction

5-1. Transistor vs. Vacuum-tube D-c Amplifiers 176

Simple Transistor D-c Amplifier Stages

5-2. The Common-emitter Stage 177
5-3. Emitter-follower Stages, Current-source Loads, and Output-stage
    Circuits 179

Transistor Differential-amplifier Stages. Low-drift Design

5-4. Low-frequency Performance 180
5-5. Operating Points and Voltage Drift 182
5-6. Some Circuit Improvements 184
5-7. Current Drift and Current-drift Cancellation 187

Chopper-stabilized Transistor Amplifiers and Solid-state Choppers
    5-8. General Remarks. Transistor-chopper Circuits 189
    5-9. Switching Spikes. Double-chopper Circuit 190
    5-10. Other Electronic Choppers 192
Amplifier Design
    5-11. Frequency Response, Noise, and General Design Considerations . . 192
    5-12. Typical Amplifier Specifications and Examples. Voltage and Current
        Balancing 198
Miscellaneous Practical Considerations
    5-13. Construction of D-c Amplifiers. Choice of Components 201
    5-14. D-c Amplifier Ground Connections 202
    5-15. Differential Amplifiers and Unity-gain Followers 204
References and Bibliography 204

Chapter 6. Limiters, Switching Circuits, and Electronic Function
Generators 207

Introduction
    6-1. Function Generators and Switches 207
Limiter and Selector Circuits
    6-2. Diode Characteristics and Diode Models 208
    6-3. The Basic Diode Limiter Circuits 210
    6-4. Low-frequency Analysis of Diode Circuits 213
    6-5. High-frequency Performance of Diode Circuits 214
    6-6. Diode-bridge Limiters 218
    6-7. Other Limiter Circuits 219
Analog Switching Circuits
    6-8. Analog Switches and Comparators 219
    6-9. Operational Relays 222
    6-10. Diode Switches 223
    6-11. Transistor Switches 226
        (a) Static Characteristics 226
        (b) The Inverted Transistor as a Switch 227
        (c) Practical Switching Circuits 228
Electronic Function Generators
    6-12. Introduction 233
    6-13. Diode Function Generators 235
        (a) Special-purpose Function Generators. Smoothing Oscillators . 235
        (b) General-purpose Function Generators 236
        (c) Multiple-function Generation 238
        (d) Function Setting and Storage 238
    6-14. Varistor Function Generators 240
    6-15. Cathode-ray-tube Function Generators 241
Functions of Two or More Variables
    6-16. Introduction. Interpolation Schemes 243
    6-17. Diode Function Generators 245
        (a) Simple Limiter Circuits 245
        (b) Use of General-purpose Diode Function Generators . . . 245
        (c) Special Diode Function Generators 247
    6-18. Comparator/Switch-type Function Generators 247
    6-19. Cathode-ray-tube Function Generators 248
References and Bibliography 249

Chapter 7. Electronic Multipliers and Dividers. **254**

Introduction

7-1. Survey 254
7-2. Multiplication of Positive and Negative Quantities 255
7-3. Voltage-controlled Variable-gain Devices. Modulation Schemes . . 255

Feedback Control of Multiplier Gain

7-4. The Basic Feedback Scheme. 258
7-5. Design Problems 259
7-6. Examples of Feedback Multipliers 260
  (a) Servomultipliers 260
  (b) Step Multipliers 260
  (c) Heat-transfer Multipliers 262
  (d) Hall-effect and Magnetoresistance Multipliers 263
  (e) Sampling Multipliers 264
7-7. AM/FM Multipliers and Other Feedback Multipliers Employing Dual Modulation. 265
7-8. Time-sharing and Frequency-sharing Schemes. 267

Time-division Multipliers

7-9. Principle of Operation 268
7-10. Externally Excited Time-division Multipliers 268
7-11. Self-excited Time-division Multipliers 269
  (a) Basic Four-quadrant Multiplier. 269
  (b) Four-quadrant Operation with Simple Electronic Switches . . . 272
  (c) A Modified Circuit 273
7-12. Electronic Switching Circuits 274
7-13. Static vs. Dynamic Accuracy in Multipliers Employing Ripple Filters. Ripple-filter Design 277

Quarter-square Multipliers and Triangle-averaging Multipliers

7-14. Electronic Quarter-square Multipliers 281
7-15. Diode Squaring Circuits 283
7-16. Triangle-averaging Multipliers 290

Other Electronic Multiplication Circuits

7-17. Logarithmic Multipliers 293
7-18. Electron-beam Multipliers 293
7-19. Generation of Products as Functions of Two Variables 296

Electronic Multipliers: General Design Considerations, Testing, and Division Circuits

7-20. Multiplier Adjustment and Testing. 296
7-21. Comparative Performance, Cost, and Reliability of Different Electronic Multipliers 298
7-22. Improved Electronic Multipliers Employing Coarse and Fine Channels 299
7-23. Electronic Division 301

References and Bibliography 302

Chapter 8. Computer Servomechanisms and Vector Resolvers. . **307**

Computer Servomechanisms

8-1. Introduction. Performance Specifications and Tests. 307
8-2. Small-signal Performance Analysis and Servo Equalization 311
8-3. Motors, Amplifiers, and Gear Trains 315
  (a) Motors and Amplifiers 315
  (b) Gears and Limit Stops 317

8-4. Servo-design Considerations 318
Servo-driven Potentiometers
8-5. Potentiometer Specifications. 320
8-6. Function Potentiometers 322
8-7. Potentiometer-loading Errors 323
8-8. Tapped-potentiometer Function Generators 325
Vector Resolution and Composition. Resolver Servos
8-9. Vector Resolution and Composition. 328
8-10. Resolver Servos Using Sine-Cosine Potentiometers 330
8-11. Induction Resolvers. Modulation and Demodulation 331
8-12. Quadrant Switching and Rate Resolvers 333
8-13. Inverse Resolvers. Automatic Gain Control 334
Electronic Resolvers
8-14. Introduction. Combination of Function Generators and Multipliers . 336
8-15. Use of Sampling and Comparator Circuits. 337
8-16. Implicit-computation Schemes 339
References and Bibliography 341

Chapter 9. Special Analog-Digital Circuits for Instrumentation, Control, and Simulation **344**

Introduction
9-1. Introductory Remarks 344
Precision Limiters, Selectors, and Timers
9-2. Precision Limiters, and Some Related Circuits 344
9-3. Accurate Selectors, Extreme-value Holding Circuits, and Peak Detectors 352
9-4. Simple Voltage-to-time Converters and Digital Voltmeters . . . 353
Bistable Operational-amplifier Circuits, Special Signal Generators, and Communication-system Simulation
9-5. Bistable Operational-amplifier Circuits 354
9-6. Accurate Sine-wave Oscillators 357
Simulation of Special Control-system Nonlinearities
9-7. Saturation, Limit Stops, and Backlash 360
9-8. Simulation of Static and Coulomb Friction 364
9-9. Other Common Nonlinearities 365
References and Bibliography 368

PART III. ANALOG MEMORY, HYBRID ANALOG-DIGITAL COMPUTATION, AND COMPUTER-SYSTEM DESIGN

Chapter 10. Integrator-mode Control, Analog Memory, and Iterative Computation **373**

Introduction
10-1. Survey. 373
Integrator-mode Control and Track-hold Memory
10-2. Integrator-control Relays 373
10-3. Control Systems for "Slow" Electronic Differential Analyzers. . . 375
    (a) Requirements. The POT SET Mode 375
    (b) A Simple Control System 375
    (c) A Practical Pushbutton Control System 376
10-4. Track-hold Circuits 378

(a) Basic Track-hold Circuits 378
(b) Track-hold Performance 379
(c) Improved Track-hold Circuits. 383
10-5. Electronically Switched Integrators and Other Operational Amplifiers 385
(a) Integrator Circuits 385
(b) Switched Operational Amplifiers 386
Iterative Differential Analyzers: Operation and Control
10-6. Introduction. Subroutines and Flow Charts 387
(a) Iterative Differential Analyzers 387
(b) Subroutines and Control Variables 387
(c) Flow Charts 388
(d) Applications 389
10-7. Block-diagram Notation. 391
10-8. Analog Point Storage and Memory-pair Operation 392
(a) Point-storage Requirements 392
(b) Memory Pairs 392
(c) The INITIAL RESET Mode 396
(d) Accumulator Circuits 396
10-9. Fast Analog Comparators 396
10-10. Digital Operations 399
(a) Module Logic 399
(b) Digital Clock-gated Logic 402
(c) Relay Logic 402
10-11. Design of a Digital Control Unit. Oscilloscope Displays 404
(a) Introduction 404
(b) Basic Digital Clock and Sample Timer 405
(c) Auxiliary Timer and Scanning Readout 409
(d) Subroutine Counter and REPEAT Switch 410
(e) Starting, Two-time-scale Operation, and External Control . . 410
(f) Multitrace Oscilloscope Displays 411
10-12. Two Simple Applications 416
(a) Double Integration 416
(b) Simulation of Semielastic Impact 416
Track-hold Operations with Sampled Data and Simulation of Digital Computers
10-13. Sampled-data Sequences and Solution of Difference Equations . . 416
10-14. Linear Operations on Sampled Data 420
10-15. Conversion to and from Sampled-data Representations. 422
(a) Sampling 422
(b) Data Reconstruction 422
10-16. Application to Iterative Computation 423
Time-delay Simulation and Function Storage
10-17. Problem Statement and General Remarks 424
10-18. Operational-amplifier and Network Approximations. 424
(a) Introduction 424
(b) All-pass Approximations 426
(c) Low-pass Approximations 428
(d) Practical Considerations. Treatment of Variable Time Delays . 429
(e) Passive-network Delay Lines 430
10-19. Switched-capacitor Memories 430
10-20. Other Storage Techniques 431
(a) Magnetic Storage of Analog Data. 431
(b) Digital Storage 432
(c) Delay-line Storage and Pulse Modulation 433
References and Bibliography 433

Chapter 11. Analog and Hybrid Analog-Digital Computer Systems 439

The Man/Machine Interfaces: Programming, Readout, and Checking Systems
11-1. Patchbays and Other Programming Systems. 439
    (a) Patchbay Construction and Layout 439
    (b) Relay-circuit Patching. Control-variable Patchbays and Pin-
        boards. 442
    (c) Simulation Boards 444
11-2. Potentiometer and Function-generating Setting 444
11-3. Readout Systems. 447
    (a) Analog-computer Readout 447
    (b) Strip-chart Recorders 448
    (c) Servo Plotting Boards and Curve Followers 449
    (d) Amplifier-readout Switching 449
11-4. Calibration and Program Checks. Programming Automation . . 451
    (a) Calibration and Amplifier-balance Checks 451
    (b) Overload-alarm Systems and Minimum-excursion Indicators . . 451
    (c) Static Checks, Rate Tests, and Time-scale Check 452
    (d) Checkout, Scaling, and Setup Automation 453
11-5. Analog-computer Accuracy Checks and Maintenance Procedures. . 454
Design of Complete Electronic Differential Analyzers
11-6. Analog-computer Systems 455
    (a) Introduction 455
    (b) Small Analog Computers. Educational-computer Systems . . 455
    (c) General-purpose Analog Computers 456
11-7. A Fast Iterative Differential Analyzer 461
11-8. Computer Power Supplies 463
11-9. Noise and Ground Systems 466
Conversion Circuits and Combined Analog-Digital Computation
11-10. D/A Converters and D/A Multipliers. 468
11-11. A/D Converters 471
    (a) Introduction 471
    (b) Ramp/comparator Converters. 471
    (c) A/D Converters with D/A Converter Feedback 471
    (d) A/D Converters with Multiple Comparators 473
11-12. Combined Simulation 473
    (a) Introduction 473
    (b) Complete Conversion Linkages 475
    (c) Choice of Digital Computer 476
11-13. A Complete Hybrid System 477
*Digital-computer Solution of Differential Equations, and Miscellaneous Hybrid
Computing Techniques*
11-14. Truncation Errors and Frequency Response of Digital Integrators . 478
11-15. Digital Computers with Special Assembler Programs. Digital Simu-
    lation 480
11-16. Digital Computers with Fast Analog Subroutines 482
11-17. Operational Digital Computers. 483
    (a) Introduction 483
    (b) Parallel Digital Differential Analyzers 483
11-18. Pulse-modulation Representation of Variables 485
11-19. Hybrid-code Computing Elements and Differential Analyzers . . . 489
    (a) Hybrid-code Representation of Variables 489
    (b) Analog-to-hybrid-code Converters and Extended-scale Integrators 491

(c) Hybrid-code Differential Analyzers 492
(d) Accuracy/Bandwidth Limitations. 494
11-20. Hybrid Analog-Digital Function Generators 495
References and Bibliography 497

PART IV.   ADVANCED COMPUTER UTILIZATION

Chapter 12.   More Advanced Computing Techniques **505**

Introduction and Survey
12-1. Requirement for Advanced Computing Techniques 505
Gauging and Improving Computer Accuracy: Perturbations, Parameter Sensitivity, Resubstitution, and Automatic Scaling
12-2. Perturbations and Linearization 506
12-3. Example: Earth-satellite Orbit and Reentry Computation 507
12-4. Parameter-influence Coefficients and Parameter-sensitivity Studies . 509
12-5. Resubstitution Checks 510
12-6. Special Scaling Problems and Automatic Scaling 510
Continuous Optimization, Equation Solvers, Constraints, and Model Matching
12-7. Maxima and Minima 511
    (a) Introduction 511
    (b) Automatic Optimization: Continuous Steepest Descent . . . 513
12-8. Solution of Equations 514
    (a) Algebraic and Transcendental Equations. 514
    (b) Simultaneous Linear Equations 515
    (c) Hybrid Iteration. 516
12-9. Steepest Descent and Dynamical Constraints 516
    (a) Dynamical Constraints 516
    (b) Steepest-descent Methods for Improving Differential-analyzer Accuracy 518
12-10. Linear Programming and Related Problems 520
12-11. Optimization by Parameter Perturbation 524
12-12. Continuous Optimization and Model Matching 525
Iterative Optimization
12-13. Parameter Optimization of Functionals.   Examples 527
12-14. Iterative-differential-analyzer Techniques. 530
    (a) Introduction 530
    (b) Automatic Iteration. 530
    (c) Use of Parameter-influence Coefficients 532
    (d) Gradient Methods 533
    (e) Termination of the Iteration.   Step-size Determination . . . 535
    (f) Other Optimization Routines 538
12-15. Optimization by Sequential Random Perturbations 538
12-16. True Functional Optimization 539
Solution of Partial Differential Equations and Integral Equations
12-17. Introduction 540
12-18. Separation of Variables and Integral-transform Methods 541
12-19. Space-variable Differencing. 541
12-20. Time-variable Differencing 544
12-21. Iteration Methods 544
12-22. Transformation to a System of Equations 546

12-23. Solution of Integral Equations 546
References and Bibliography 547

Appendix: Tables of Special Computer Circuits **553**

Table A-1.   Short-circuit Transfer Impedances for Operational Amplifiers . . 553
Fig. A-1.   Design Nomograph for Analog-computer Representation of Mass-
spring-dashpot Systems 560
Table A-2 and Figs. A-2 and A-3.   Generation of Functions with Linear
Potentiometers 561

Author Index 565

Subject Index 573

PART I

PRINCIPLES OF
ELECTRONIC ANALOG
COMPUTATION

CHAPTER 1

INTRODUCTION TO ELECTRONIC ANALOG COMPUTERS

ANALOG COMPUTERS

1-1. Introduction. In the most general sense, *an analog computer is any physical system which establishes definite prescribed relations between continuously variable physical quantities.* These quantities (*machine variables*) can be furnished by almost any kind of measurable phenomenon, but the most frequently employed machine variables are voltages, currents, and shaft rotations. Note that definite relationships between variables are necessarily stated in terms of *mathematical relations.*

Every analog computer, then, implements a requirement for approximate *physical realization of a mathematical model.* Thus analog computers serve as easily manipulated "live" models for problem solving. Perhaps even more important, if less spectacular, is the direct engineering application of analog computing devices as building blocks of instrumentation and control systems. Here, nicely packaged computing units can often force at least parts of a physical system to approximate a designer's mathematical model, and thus permit practical application of powerful mathematical synthesis techniques.

Analog computers used to solve problems represent each problem variable by a corresponding physical quantity (voltage, shaft displacement) on a convenient scale (*problem scaling*). These machine variables are made to obey mathematical relations corresponding to those of the given problem; most analog computing systems are combinations of *analog computing elements* which establish elementary mathematical relations (e.g., addition, multiplication, integration).

3

THE ELECTRONIC ANALOG COMPUTER

1-2. Introduction.   In an *electronic analog computer* (*d-c analog computer*), the machine variables are instantaneous values of voltages, measured with respect to a ground reference (*signal ground*).   Such machines use readily available electronic components and permit flexible interconnections by electrical wiring or patchcords.   Electronic analog computers

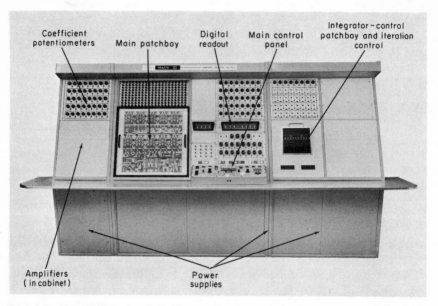

Fig. 1-1. A typical analog/hybrid-computer console permitting expansion to over 200 d-c amplifiers, electronic multipliers, and function generators.   Special coefficient-setting potentiometers can be either hand-set or servo-set.   A separate patchbay controls individual integrators for moderate-speed iterative operation (Chap. 10) and can accommodate digital modules.   An accessory linkage unit permits combined analog-digital simulation with an external digital computer.   (*Computer Products, Inc.*)

range all the way from large multipurpose machines and desk-top computers (Figs. 1-1 and 1-2) to specialized calculators and control devices, such as antiaircraft fire-control computers and the maximum-acceleration sensor in a manned satellite.

The problems solved by analog computers usually deal with the behavior of a number of variables $x_1, x_2, \ldots , x_n$.   One such problem may be to find the values of these variables under certain conditions by solving a set of equations.   Another problem may be to determine how the variables change with time, or with another independent variable t, under given conditions.

The variables $x_1, x_2, \ldots , x_n$ are represented in the d-c analog com-

FIG. 1-2a. This 24-amplifier table-top analog computer has a static component accuracy within 0.1 per cent of half-scale and can be expanded with additional computing-element strips. (*Applied Dynamics, Inc.*)

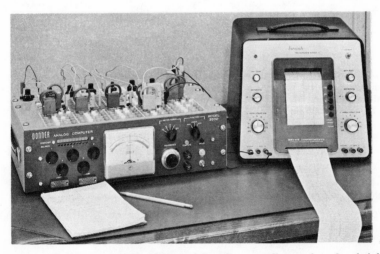

FIG. 1-2b. A complete 10-amplifier differential analyzer small enough to fit a briefcase. One-per-cent plug-in computing resistors and capacitors are used. Such a portable unit is also useful as a test-signal generator (Secs. 9-6 and 9-7) and can pinch-hit as an industrial controller or instrumentation-data processor. Price is of the order of $2,000. (*Systron-Donner Corporation.*)

puters by corresponding voltages X_1, X_2, . . . , X_n. In general, these machine variables are simply proportional to the corresponding original variables on a convenient scale:

$$X_1 = a_1 x_1 \qquad X_2 = a_2 x_2 \qquad \cdots \qquad X_n = a_n x_n$$

The given relations between the problem variables are, then, expressed by an analogous set of relations between the machine variables.   A straightforward, generally applicable method of obtaining convenient scale factors will be discussed in detail in Chap. 2.

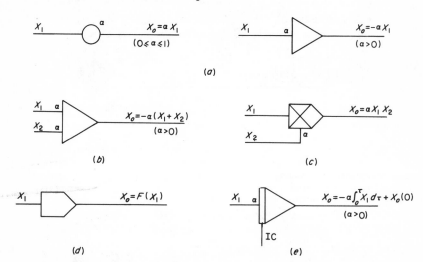

Fig. 1-3. Basic computing elements of an electronic analog computer.   Input voltages and initial-condition voltages are obtained from accurate reference power supplies. (a) Multiplication   by   constant   coefficients.   (b) Addition.   (c) Multiplication. (d) Generation of functions.   (e) Integration.

1-3. Machine Variables and Computing Elements.   The voltages

serving as machine variables in electronic analog computers are most frequently measured in volts and are permitted to vary between limits of ± 100 volts, ± 50 volts, or ± 10 volts.   As a rule, one realizes most mathematical operations on the computer voltages through combinations of a limited number of *basic computing elements*, which can perform the following operations (Fig. 1-3):

1. *Multiplication* of a machine variable (voltage) by constant coefficients
2. *Addition* of two or more machine variables
3. *Multiplication* of two machine variables
4. *Generation of functions* of machine variables
5. *Integration* of a machine voltage with respect to real time

The first four of these computing elements may be regarded as black boxes producing the desired output voltages

$$X_o = \alpha X_1 \qquad X_o = \alpha(X_1 + X_2) \left.\vphantom{\begin{matrix}a\\b\end{matrix}}\right\}$$
$$X_o = \alpha X_1 X_2 \qquad X_o = F(X_1) \qquad\qquad (1\text{-}1)$$

when input voltages X_1, X_2 are applied to the input terminals. Figure 1-4 shows how such computing elements may be *combined* to produce more complex relations, say

$$X_o = 0.02 X_1 X_2 - 100 \sin 3X_2 = F(X_1, X_2)$$

In each case, voltages X_1, X_2, . . . appear as input voltages to a *block of computing elements* producing the output voltage X_o. This output

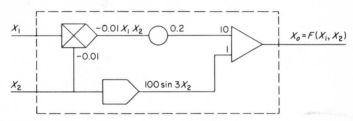

Fig. 1-4. The electronic analog computer combines simple mathematical operations to produce more complicated functions of input voltages. Here, a block of computing elements produces the output voltage

$$X_o = 0.02 X_1 X_2 - 100 \sin 3X_2 = F(X_1, X_2)$$

voltage will be the desired function of the input voltages if the correct combination of computing elements has been used. Note that, in general, the relation produced by the block in Fig. 1-4 is "unilateral": while changes in the input voltages will produce the correct changes in the output voltage X_o, the converse is not true unless additional connections and computing elements are used.

1-4. Time Dependence of Variables. Integration. In many problems, one desires to observe changes of the machine variables as functions of the time (real time, *computer time* τ, measured in seconds), which plays the part of the *independent variable* in the computer. For example, the relations

$$X_1 = X_2 \qquad X_2 = \sin \tau$$

describe the variations of two machine variables, X_1 and X_2, with the time τ. Physical time τ here serves as an input to certain computing elements which produce voltages as functions of time. Examples of such devices are potentiometers driven by a clock motor, and circuits containing charging or discharging capacitors. The machine variables can thus be made to vary with time in the prescribed manner and may be recorded by means of a recording milliammeter or oscillograph.

In many important applications, one is required to relate *rates of change* of time-dependent machine variables, so that these voltages are made to vary in accordance with given *differential equations*. It will be practical to introduce the notation

$$\frac{d}{d\tau} \equiv P \qquad \text{thus} \qquad \frac{dX}{d\tau} \equiv PX \qquad \frac{d^2X}{d\tau^2} \equiv P^2X \qquad \cdots \qquad (1\text{-}2)$$

We require computing elements relating the time-variable voltages $X, PX, P^2X, \ldots$.

An electrical analog *integrator* relates a voltage $X_o(\tau)$ to its time derivative PX_o; specifically, the integrator input voltage $X_1(\tau)$ and output voltage $X_o(\tau)$ are related by

$$\left.\begin{array}{l} X_1(\tau) = \dfrac{1}{\alpha}\dfrac{d}{d\tau}X_o(\tau) = \dfrac{1}{\alpha}PX_o \\[2ex] \text{or} \qquad X_o(\tau) = \alpha \displaystyle\int X_1(\tau)\,d\tau = \alpha\dfrac{1}{P}X_1 = \alpha\displaystyle\int_0^\tau X_1(\tau)\,d\tau + X_o\,(0) \end{array}\right\} \quad (1\text{-}3)$$

(Fig. 1-3e). Note carefully that (1) the integrator integrates its input $X_1(\tau)$ *with respect to the computer time* τ, and (2) this relationship requires a given *initial condition* $X_o(0) = X_o\big]_0$ to be established at the integrator output at the start of the computation.

1-5. Solution of Differential Equations: Classical Differential-analyzer Technique.
A given *ordinary differential equation*, such as

$$\frac{dx}{dt} = -x \tag{1-4}$$

is *solved* when $x = x(t)$ is found as a function of the independent variable t. Thus, the differential equation (4) is satisfied by

$$x = Ce^{-t} \tag{1-5}$$

where C is an arbitrary constant (value of x for $t = 0$).

An electronic analog computer represents the independent variable t by a proportional number of seconds of computer time τ, while x is represented by a voltage proportional to x. For simplicity, assume $1:1$ scaling, so that t is numerically equal to τ, and x problem units correspond to (x) volts. *If we now succeed in making the voltage (x) vary with the computer time τ so as to satisfy the differential equation (machine equation)*

$$\frac{d}{d\tau}(x) = -(x) \qquad \text{or} \qquad -P(x) = (x) \tag{1-6}$$

then a record of the voltage (x) vs. time will describe a solution of the given differential equation.

Figure 1-5a shows how the electronic analog computer enforces the desired relationship (6). The negative derivative $-P(x)$ of the voltage (machine variable) (x) is itself a voltage; this voltage is treated as though it were known and is fed to a sign-inverting integrator to produce the

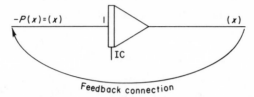

Fig. 1-5a. Electronic-analog-computer setup implementing the differential equation $P(x) = -(x)$ (Sec. 1-5). The physical feedback action is easily traced around the loop: if the machine is started at the time $\tau = 0$ with a given positive initial value $x(0)$ of the integrator output voltage, say, $x(0) = a > 0$, the negative-feedback voltage (x) at the integrator input forces the output to integrate down at an exponentially decreasing rate, as required by the correct solution $x = x(0)e^{-\tau}$.

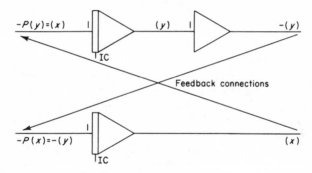

Fig. 1-5b. Computer setup for the system

$$P(x) = (y) \qquad P(y) = -(x)$$
or
$$P^2(x) = -(x)$$

with given initial values $x(0)$, $y(0)$. The physical feedback action is again easily traced around the loop. The computer circuit simulates a mechanical or electrical harmonic oscillator.

voltage (x). In this case, the integrator output $(x) = -P(x)$ happens to be precisely the voltage needed at the integrator input. The resulting *feedback connection* forces the voltage (x) to vary in accordance with the given mathematical relation (6). The arbitrary constant C in the solution (5) is determined by the given initial value $x(0)$ of x set into the integrator, so that the voltage (x) starts with the correct value at the beginning of the computation.

Figure 1-5b similarly illustrates the analog-computer setup for a *system of two first-order differential equations*

$$P(x) = (y) \qquad P(y) = -(x) \qquad \left(P \equiv \frac{d}{d\tau}\right) \tag{1-7}$$

relating two time-variable voltages (x) and (y).

The voltages $-P(x) = -(y)$ and $-P(y) = (x)$ are treated as though they were known and are fed to integrators producing the machine variables (x) and (y); one again has a feedback loop enforcing the given differential equations.   The resulting computer solution

$$x = C \sin (\tau + \varphi) \qquad y = C \cos (\tau + \varphi) \tag{1-8}$$

contains *two* arbitrary constants C and φ, which are uniquely determined if the x and y integrators in Fig. 1-5*b* are set to given initial conditions $x = x(0)$, $y = y(0)$ at the start of the computer "run."

Note that *differential equations of order greater than one* can always be reduced to systems of first-order equations.   Thus the second-order machine equation

$$\frac{d^2}{d\tau^2}(x) = P^2(x) = -(x) \tag{1-9}$$

reduces to the system (7) if one introduces $P(x) = y$ as a new variable. Two initial conditions (initial values of x and its first derivative) are again needed for a definite solution.   The practical analog-computer solution of many types of differential equation will be treated in detail in Chap. 2.

Analog computers capable of solving ordinary differential equations are called *differential analyzers*.

1-6. Operation of "Slow" Differential Analyzers.   Electronic analog computers are particularly useful as differential-equation solvers in many scientific and engineering applications.   The solution of a set of differential equations—or the computer representation of a physical process described in terms of differential equations—proceeds as follows:

1. With the machine connected up to solve the given problem, one sets the machine variables (voltages) to the given initial conditions by forcing all integrator output voltages to assume their correct initial values (RESET *condition of the computer*).
2. The computing elements are then made operative and force the voltages in the machine to vary in a manner prescribed by the given differential equations.   The voltage variations with time are recorded and constitute solutions of the given problem (OPERATE *or* COMPUTE *condition*).
3. The machine is stopped at a time chosen by the operator; there may be a maximum allowable computing time determined by limitations

of the computing elements. The machine is then returned to the RESET condition and is ready for the next run with changed coefficients, initial conditions, etc.

The usual "slow" electronic analog differential-equation solvers admit signal frequencies up to about 50 cps; this is sufficient for simulation of most dynamical systems on a 1:1 time scale. Solutions may be recorded by direct-writing strip-chart recorders and/or by servo-operated plotting boards, which permit one to record one machine variable against another machine variable. Both types of recorders afford an instantly available, permanent record of computer solutions.

1-7. "Fast" (Repetitive) Electronic Analog Computers. In an increasingly important alternative scheme, the steps of the solution procedure outlined above are repeated automatically at a rapid rate (10 to 1,000 cps) by means of an electromechanical or electronic switching system. During each cycle, each machine variable varies in the prescribed manner and is then reset to its initial value. The results can now be presented on an ordinary cathode-ray oscillograph whose sweep frequency equals the computer repetition rate. *The rapid operation of such machines permits immediate observation of the effects of parameter changes on the solution;* modern electronic analog computers also combine repetitive operation with automatic program changes to permit very sophisticated computing techniques. On the other hand, the requirements for rapid switching and greatly increased frequency response make the design of accurate computing elements for repetitive operation a rather formidable problem (Chaps. 3 and 10).

1-8. Analog-computer Solution of Problems Other Than Ordinary Differential Equations: Survey. Electronic analog computers are, basically, devices for solving systems of ordinary differenial equations, using the computer time τ as the independent variable. Such machines can also be adapted to other problems which can be related to differential-equation solutions, e.g., *solution of equations, integral equations, partial differential equations, Fourier analysis,* and *location of maxima and minima,* especially in connection with *linear programming* (Chap. 12). More recently, the development of new accurate electronic switching and analog-storage techniques has given electronic analog computers the ability to change their own programs, to make decisions, and to introduce results of earlier computer runs into later runs. The resulting automatic-programming features, combined with increased computing speeds (repetitive operation), have greatly enlarged the scope of analog computation (Chaps. 10 to 12).

Statistical applications of electronic analog computers include special techniques for convenient determination of the effects of linear transducers on statistical parameters of random inputs, such as noise. In addition, the extraordinarily high computing speeds of modern repetitive computers make such machines especially suitable for *Monte-Carlo-type studies* of random processes. In such studies, random inputs and initial conditions are applied to a computer model of the process under consideration, and the computer takes statistics on samples of the output functions.[20]

HOW THE BASIC COMPUTING ELEMENTS WORK

1-9. Coefficient-setting Potentiometers. Figure 1-6a shows how a simple voltage divider or potentiometer is used to multiply a voltage by a constant positive coefficient α $(0 \leq \alpha \leq 1)$:

$$X_o = \alpha X_1 \qquad (1\text{-}10)$$

Figure 1-3a shows the corresponding block-diagram symbol.

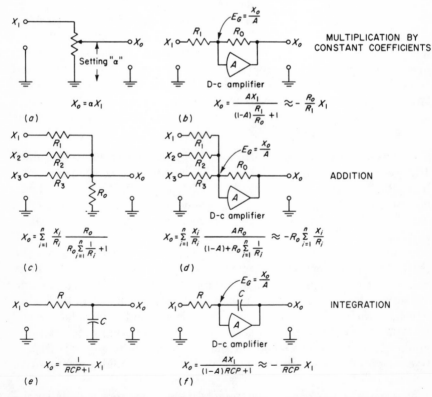

FIG. 1-6. Passive networks and operational-amplifier circuits for multiplication by constant coefficients, addition, and integration.

1-10. Operational Amplifiers: The Phase Inverter.   A d-c amplifier can multiply d-c voltages by a constant numerically greater than one; note that the amplifier output voltage must be capable of negative as well as positive excursions, and that the output has to be zero when the input voltage is zero.   In practice, the requirement of keeping the amplifier free from any voltage "offset" (finite d-c output for zero input due to amplifier *drift*) is a major design problem (Chaps. 4 and 5).   In order to make the amplifier gain independent of vacuum-tube or transistor parameters, practical computer amplifiers combine degenerative feedback with high gain (10^3 to 10^8) over the range of operating frequencies, so that the amplifier transfer function is essentially determined by the feedback network.   Most computer amplifiers used for multiplication by constants multiply by *negative* constants; i.e., they act as *phase inverters* or *sign changers*.

Consider the circuit of Fig. 1-6b, where A is the d-c amplifier forward gain.   Assuming that the feedback circuit is stable and that the amplifier output is, say, between -100 and $+100$ volts, the voltage $E_G = X_o/A$ at the amplifier input terminal (*summing point* or *summing junction*) will be quite small if the absolute gain $|A|$ is between 10^3 and 10^8.   If no appreciable current (such as grid current or base current) flows into the amplifier proper, the currents through R_1 and R_o will necessarily add up to zero; if E_G can be regarded as negligible, the resulting node equation at the summing point is

$$\frac{X_1}{R_1} + \frac{X_o}{R_o} = 0 \tag{1-11}$$

The amplifier output voltage X_o is then given by the simple relation

$$X_o = -\frac{R_o}{R_1} X_1 \tag{1-12}$$

If $E_G = X_o/A$ is *not* neglected, the node equation (11) is replaced by

$$\left(\frac{X_o}{A} - X_o\right)\frac{1}{R_o} + \left(\frac{X_o}{A} - X_1\right)\frac{1}{R_1} = 0 \tag{1-13}$$

so that

$$X_o = X_1 \frac{A}{(1 - A)(R_1/R_o) + 1} = -\left(1 - \frac{1}{1 - A\beta}\right)\frac{R_o}{R_1} X_1 \tag{1-14}$$

with

$$\beta = \frac{R_1}{R_o + R_1} = \left(1 + \frac{R_o}{R_1}\right)^{-1} \tag{1-15}$$

In most practical cases, the amplifier gain is so high that $|A\beta|$ is very large compared with unity, and Eq. (14) reduces again to the simple form (12). The significance of the quantity $A\beta$ (idealized loop gain) and the validity of the approximation (12) are discussed in detail in Sec. 3-11.   Feedback amplifiers of the type shown in Fig. 1-6 are widely employed to implement various operations on voltages and are known as *operational amplifiers*.

1-11. Summing Networks and Summing Amplifiers. *Summing or averaging networks* of the type shown in Fig. 1-6c may be used to obtain a voltage proportional to the sum of several input voltages. The sum of all currents flowing to the output terminal must be zero, i.e.,

$$(X_o - X_1)\frac{1}{R_1} + (X_o - X_2)\frac{1}{R_2}$$
$$+ \cdots + (X_o - X_n)\frac{1}{R_n} + X_o\frac{1}{R_o} = 0 \quad (1\text{-}16)$$

so that

$$X_o = \left(\frac{X_1}{R_1} + \frac{X_2}{R_2} + \cdots + \frac{X_n}{R_n}\right)\frac{1}{1/R_1 + 1/R_2 + \cdots + 1/R_n + 1/R_o}$$
$$(1\text{-}17)$$

Such networks can be used for addition, but it is seen from Eq. (17) that the performance changes appreciably with the load resistance R_o, and that there is considerable attenuation in this circuit.

The *summing amplifier* circuit of Fig. 1-6d permits the addition of several voltages or machine variables, as well as multiplication by constants and phase inversion, without attenuation or loading effects. The voltage at the summing point is, as before, equal to X_o/A. The nodal equation for this point becomes

$$\left(\frac{X_o}{A} - X_1\right)\frac{1}{R_1} + \left(\frac{X_o}{A} - X_2\right)\frac{1}{R_2} + \cdots$$
$$+ \left(\frac{X_o}{A} - X_n\right)\frac{1}{R_n} + \left(\frac{X_o}{A} - X_o\right)\frac{1}{R_o} = 0$$

so that

$$X_o = -\left(1 - \frac{1}{1 - A\beta}\right)R_o\left(\frac{X_1}{R_1} + \frac{X_2}{R_2} + \cdots + \frac{X_n}{R_n}\right) \quad (1\text{-}18)$$

with

$$\beta = \left(1 + \frac{R_o}{R_1} + \frac{R_o}{R_2} + \cdots + \frac{R_o}{R_n}\right)^{-1} \quad (1\text{-}19)$$

In most applications, the amplifier gain is, again, so high that $|A\beta|$ is very large compared with unity, and Eq. (18) reduces to

$$X_o = -R_o\left(\frac{X_1}{R_1} + \frac{X_2}{R_2} + \cdots + \frac{X_n}{R_n}\right) \quad (1\text{-}20)$$

The validity of this approximation is discussed in detail in Secs. 3-11 to 3-17. Equation (20) is particularly useful for establishing relations of the form

$$X_o = -(a_1 X_1 + a_2 X_2 + \cdots + a_n X_n) \quad (1\text{-}21)$$

with

$$a_1 = \frac{R_o}{R_1} \qquad a_2 = \frac{R_o}{R_2} \qquad \cdots \qquad a_n = \frac{R_o}{R_n}$$

A practical summing amplifier might employ the arrangement of Fig. 1-6d with the resistance values

$$R_o = 1\text{M}$$
$$R_1 = R_2 = R_3 = R_4 = 1\text{M}$$
$$R_5 = R_6 = 0.2\text{M}$$
$$R_7 = 0.1\text{M}$$

so that Eq. (21) becomes

$$X_o = -(X_1 + X_2 + X_3 + X_4 + 5X_5 + 5X_6 + 10X_7) \quad (1\text{-}22)$$

Seven input terminals corresponding to the coefficients 1, 1, 1, 1, 5, 5, and 10 are available.

1-12. Integration. (a) Integrating Circuits. Accuracy Limitations. One of the more significant features of electronic analog computers is their ability to implement accurate integration of a machine variable (voltage) with respect to the computer time τ by means of relatively inexpensive circuits. The physical

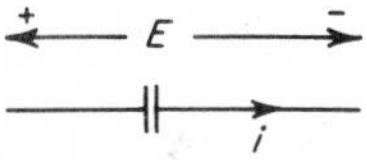

FIG. 1-7. Basic property of capacitance.

basis of most electrical integrating (and differentiating) devices is the well-known fact that *the current through a capacitor* (Fig. 1-7) *is proportional to the time derivative of the capacitor voltage:*

$$i = C\frac{d}{d\tau}E = CPE \quad (1\text{-}23a)$$

or

$$E = \frac{1}{CP}i = \frac{1}{C}\int i\,dt = \frac{1}{C}\int_0^\tau i\,dt + E(0) \quad (1\text{-}23b)$$

In the simple *integrating network* of Fig. 1-8a, the input voltage X_1 will tend to cause a current through the resistance R and thus to charge the capacitor in a manner approximating integration. Unfortunately, any voltage X_o built up on the capacitor will affect the charging current, so that the latter is proportional to $X_1 - X_o$ rather than to the input voltage; this prevents exact integration. Quantitatively, the sum of all currents flowing to the output terminal must be zero, so that

$$(X_o - X_1)\frac{1}{R} + CPX_o = 0 \quad (1\text{-}24a)$$

or, in operator notation,*

$$X_o = \frac{1}{RCP+1}X_1 \quad (1\text{-}24b)$$

* NOTE. Equation (24b) should be considered as a rewritten form of the differential equation (24a); i.e., $1/(RCP + 1)$ is an *operator* (*transfer operator*) representing the action of the network on an input voltage X_1. The *operator* $P \equiv d/d\tau$ must not be confused with the Laplace-transform variable s, which is a complex *number*.

The performance equation (24) of the simple integrating network is of the form

$$X_o = \frac{a}{TP + 1} X_1 = \frac{a}{TP}\left(1 - \frac{1}{TP + 1}\right) X_1 \qquad (1\text{-}25)$$

which is typical of many electrical integrating circuits; a/T is called the *rate gain*, and T is the *time constant* of the integrating circuit. Equation (25) is seen to approximate exact integration, or

$$X_o = \frac{a}{TP} X_1 \qquad (1\text{-}26)$$

whenever the time constant T is sufficiently large to make the error term

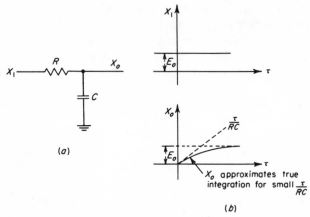

Fig. 1-8. Simple integrating network (a), and approximate integration of a step input (b).

in Eq. (25) as small as required.   Specifically, if the input voltage X_1 is a positive voltage step,

$$X_1 = \begin{cases} 0 \ (\tau \le 0) \\ V \ (\tau > 0) \end{cases}$$

then Eq. (25) yields the integrator output voltage

$$X_o = aV(1 - e^{-\tau/T})$$
$$= aV\frac{\tau}{T}\left[1 - \frac{1}{2!}\left(\frac{\tau}{T}\right) + \frac{1}{3!}\left(\frac{\tau}{T}\right)^2 \mp \cdots\right] \qquad (\tau \ge 0) \quad (1\text{-}27)$$

(Fig. 1-8b).   Equation (27) is seen to approximate the ideal integrator output $aV\tau/T$ within ϵ per cent for

$$\tau \le \frac{T}{50}\epsilon \qquad (1\text{-}28)$$

The frequency-response function

$$H(j\omega) = \frac{a}{j\omega T + 1} = \frac{a}{j\omega T}\left(1 - \frac{1}{j\omega T + 1}\right) \qquad (1\text{-}29)$$

corresponding to Eq. (25) approximates the frequency response $a/j\omega T$ of a true integrator within ϵ per cent for

$$\omega \geq \frac{100}{\epsilon T} \qquad (1\text{-}30)$$

Note that ideal integration would require $H(j\omega)$ to be infinitely large (have a pole) at zero frequency.

Since *every* integrator input voltage $X_1(\tau)$ can be regarded as due to superposition of step-function or sinusoidal inputs, the integrator error criteria (28) and (30) apply quite generally. Specifically, for any input voltage $X_1(\tau)$ lasting less than τ sec or containing only components of circular frequency greater than ω, the percentage error ϵ may be estimated from

$$\epsilon \leq 50\frac{\tau}{T} \qquad \text{or} \qquad \epsilon \leq \frac{100}{\omega T} \qquad (1\text{-}31)$$

The error criteria (28), (30), and (31) are practically useful mainly for estimating errors in simple integration. In differential-analyzer loops (like those in Fig. 1-5), integration errors may partially cancel or be compounded.

(b) Electronic Integration: The Parallel-feedback Integrator. The simple RC integrating network of Fig. 1-8a can yield a large integrator time constant $T = RC$ only at the expense of low rate gain $a/T = 1/RC$; and both time constant and rate gain are further decreased by any resistive load connected to the output. These serious disadvantages are readily overcome by the operational-amplifier circuit of Fig. 1-6f (*parallel-feedback integrator*). This circuit can use reasonable values of resistance and capacitance to yield excellent integration without attenuation; and the output can drive a load without impairing the quality of the integration.

As in other operational-amplifier circuits, the summing-point voltage $E_G = X_o/A$ in Fig. 1-6f will be quite small for frequencies exceeding, say, 0.005 cps if the absolute gain $|A|$ is large in absolute value (typically 10^7 at d-c, 50,000 at 5 cps). Since, here, only the small voltage E_G opposes the capacitor-charging current, the amplifier will charge the capacitor at a rate closely proportional to X_1. The output voltage X_o will, then, be closely proportional to the time integral of input voltage X_1. The transfer function of the electronic integrator is derived in the same manner as that of other operational amplifiers. The node equation for the input grid is

$$\left(\frac{X_o}{A} - X_1\right)\frac{1}{R} + CP\left(\frac{X_o}{A} - X_o\right) = 0 \tag{1-32}$$

if amplifier input current and capacitor leakage can be neglected (see also Sec. 3-20). It follows that

$$X_o = \frac{A}{(1-A)RCP + 1}\,X_1$$

$$= -\frac{1}{RCP}\left[1 - \frac{RCP+1}{(1-A)RCP+1}\right]X_1 \tag{1-33}$$

which approximates true integration within ϵ per cent for

$$\tau \leq \frac{|A|RC}{50}\,\epsilon \quad \text{or} \quad \omega \geq \frac{100}{|A|RC\epsilon} \quad (|A| \gg 1) \tag{1-34}$$

In high-quality multipurpose electronic analog computers, the integrator errors given by Eq. (34), together with any errors due to d-c

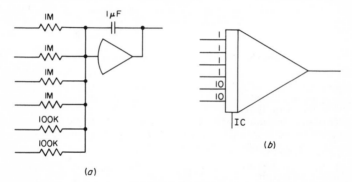

FIG. 1-9. Summing integrator (a), and block-diagram symbol (b). Special relay circuits permit charging of the integrating capacitor to the desired initial-condition voltage applied through the IC jack (Fig. 10-1).

amplifier drift (Chap. 4), can be made so small that errors due to capacitor dielectric absorption may constitute the principal limit on integration accuracy at low frequencies. Refer to Secs. 3-20 and 3-21 for a more detailed error analysis, including the effects of high-frequency gain limitations.

Figure 1-9 shows an electronic *summing integrator* with the performance equation

$$X_o = \sum_{k=1}^{n}\frac{X_k}{R_k}\,\frac{A}{(1-A)CP + \sum\limits_{k=1}^{n}(1/R_k)} \approx -\frac{1}{CP}\sum_{k=1}^{n}\frac{X_k}{R_k} \tag{1-35}$$

The error criteria based on Eq. (34) still apply if one substitutes

$$R = \left(\frac{1}{R_1} + \frac{1}{R_2} + \cdots + \frac{1}{R_n} \right)^{-1} \tag{1-36}$$

(c) Initial Conditions. Before every computer run, the integrating capacitor C in each integrating circuit must be charged to the correct initial value $X_o(0)$ of the integrator output voltage $X_o = X_o(\tau)$. The design of practical *integrator-control-relay circuits* which accomplish this charging operation and then release all integrators simultaneously is treated in detail in Sec. 10-2; the simplified circuit of Fig. 1-10 will

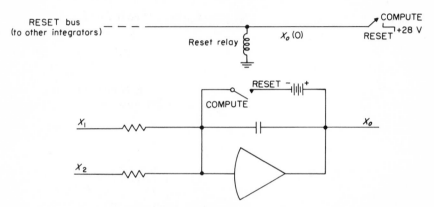

FIG. 1-10. This simplified initial-condition circuit employs a low-impedance d-c source ("volt box") to disable the integrator and to charge the integrator capacitor C to a desired initial-condition voltage $X_o(0)$ in RESET. The requirement for accurate voltage sources floating with respect to ground is a serious disadvantage; refer to Sec. 10-2 for more practical integrator-reset circuits.

illustrate the principle. Here, a low-impedance d-c source disables each integrator and charges the integrator capacitors in RESET. To start a computer run, the operator deenergizes (opens) the reset relays of all integrators by means of a COMPUTE-RESET switch. Most modern computers do not use "floating" initial-condition voltage sources in the manner of Fig. 1-9; instead, the initial-condition voltage is applied between an *initial-condition (IC) input terminal* on the integrator and ground (Sec. 10-2). Figure 1-9*b* shows the block-diagram symbol for the summing integrator of Fig. 1-9*a*, including the initial-condition input terminal.

1-13. Multiplication and Function Generation. **(a) Computer Servomechanisms.** To generate a voltage proportional to the product of two machine variables (voltages) X_1, X_2 (as contrasted to multiplication by a mere constant coefficient), one must apply X_1 to a transducer whose gain can be varied in accordance with a second input X_2. The *servomultiplier* of Fig. 1-11*a* positions the slider of a linear potentiometer so that its transfer function is accurately proportional to the servo input voltage X_2, which must be greater than zero; X_1 can be of either sign (*two-quadrant multiplication*).   Figure 1-11*b* shows a servomultiplier capable of multiplying two input voltages of arbitrary sign (*four-quadrant multiplier*).

With suitably tapered and/or tapped potentiometer cards (Sec. 8-8), the potentiometer transfer function can be made a specified nonlinear function of the shaft setting, and hence of the servo input voltage X_2, so that

$$X_o = X_1 F(X_2) \qquad (1\text{-}37)$$

Note that a single computer servomechanism can position several potentiometers, and thus generate several products and functions (Fig. 1-11*c*).

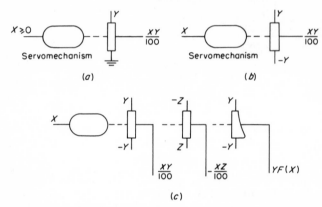

(*a*)

(*b*)

(*c*)

Fig. 1-11. Two-quadrant servomultiplier (*a*), four-quadrant servomultiplier (*b*), and simultaneous multiplication by several variables and functions (*c*).

In practice, the servo frequency response will limit the rate at which the servo input X_2 can be allowed to vary, and careful attention must be paid to potentiometer loading effects (Secs. 8-6 to 8-8).

(b) Electronic Function Generators and Multipliers.   Almost all *electronic function generators* in common use employ resistive networks or operational-amplifier circuits containing vacuum or silicon-junction diodes as voltage-sensitive switches.   The output voltage X_o of such a device will be a piecewise-linear function of the input voltage X_1 and can be made to approximate a wide range of arbitrary functions by piecewise-linear approximations (Chap. 6).   Practical multipurpose diode function generators are designed to permit simple function setup with a minimum of interaction of controls.   Special diode circuits can also implement logical and decision functions, timing circuits, amplitude selectors, comparators, and analog-to-digital converters and permit very sophisticated automatic programming of analog computers (Chaps. 9 and 10).

Electronic multipliers generate the product of two input voltages by various modulation schemes, by implementing the relation

$$xy = \tfrac{1}{4}[(x + y)^2 - (x - y)^2] \tag{1-38}$$

with the aid of function generators and summing amplifiers (*quarter-square multipliers*), or (less frequently) by employing special nonlinear physical relationships. Electronic multipliers have reached a high level of development and are discussed in detail in Chap. 7.

(c) **Division.** A voltage X_o proportional to the quotient X_1/X_2 of two machine variables can be obtained through multiplication of X_1 by the function α/X_2 of X_2. More frequently, division is accomplished by "implicit computation" involving a multiplier in a feedback loop (division loop) similar to that shown in Fig. 1-12. If the feedback loop is stable, the summing-point voltage $E_G = X_o/A$ is again negligibly small, so that the summing-point node equation

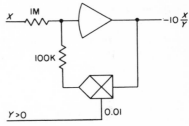

Fig. 1-12. Division by implicit computation.

$$\frac{X_1}{R_1} + \frac{1}{R_o}\frac{X_o Y}{100} = 0 \tag{1-39}$$

yields the desired relation

$$X_o = -100\,\frac{R_o}{R_1}\frac{X_1}{Y} \qquad (Y > 0) \tag{1-40}$$

Note that negative values of the divisor Y would result in instability; division circuits capable of division by both positive and negative quantities will be discussed in Chaps. 2 and 12.

MORE GENERAL COMPUTING NETWORKS AND OPERATIONAL AMPLIFIERS

1-14. Direct-analog Networks and Operational Amplifiers. (a) Many control and instrumentation applications, as well as simulation problems, require one to relate an input voltage $X(\tau)$ and an output voltage $Y(\tau)$ by a linear differential equation of the form

$$\frac{d^n Y}{d\tau^n} + a_{n-1}\frac{d^{n-1}Y}{d\tau^{n-1}} + \cdots + a_0 Y$$
$$= b_m\frac{d^m X}{d\tau^m} + b_{m-1}\frac{d^{m-1}X}{d\tau^{m-1}} + \cdots + b_0 X \tag{1-41a}$$

where the a_i, b_k are given constant coefficients. One requires, in other words, a computing device implementing the linear operation

$$Y(\tau) = H(P)X(\tau)$$

$$H(P) \equiv \frac{b_m P^m + b_{m-1} P^{m-1} + \cdots + b_0}{P^n + a_{n-1} P^{n-1} + \cdots + a_0} \qquad \left(P \equiv \frac{d}{d\tau} \right) \qquad (1\text{-}41b)$$

(Fig. 1-13; see also Sec. 2-12).*

If $n \geq m$, which is true in many practical applications, the relation (41) is readily implemented by the classical differential-analyzer technique of Sec. 1-5, as discussed in detail in Secs. 2-12 to 2-16. The resulting computer setups will require at least n integrators and, in general, a number of summing amplifiers, phase inverters, and/or coefficient-setting potentiometers. Particularly in special-purpose control or instrumentation

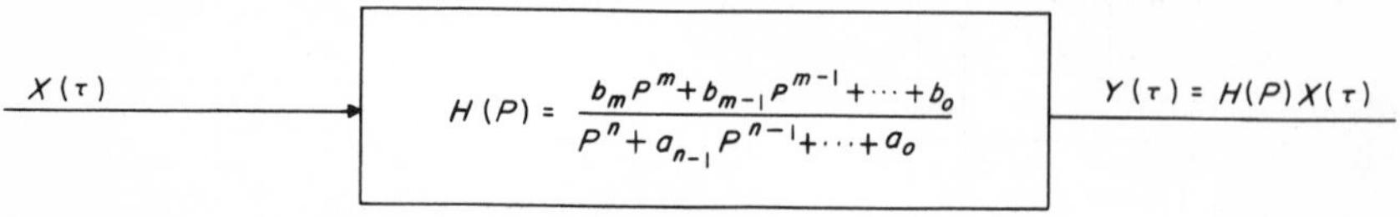

$$X(\tau) \longrightarrow \boxed{H(P) = \frac{b_m P^m + b_{m-1} P^{m-1} + \cdots + b_0}{P^n + a_{n-1} P^{n-1} + \cdots + a_0}} \longrightarrow Y(\tau) = H(P)X(\tau)$$

Fig. 1-13. Block representation of a linear operation implementing the relation (1-41).

computers, it is often desirable to implement a relation (41) less expensively. One may, thus, attempt to construct a relatively simple network or feedback amplifier which implements the desired operation directly without recourse to elementary mathematical operations; such a circuit constitutes a *direct-analog representation* of $H(P)$. Networks and feedback amplifiers can also represent "blocks" having more than one input variable. Direct-analog representations are most useful in applications where the system response to forcing functions, rather than to initial conditions, is of interest, so that initial values of most variables can be regarded as equal to zero (see also Sec. 2-14).

(b) As a simple example, Fig. 1-14 shows differential-analyzer and network representations of the differential equation

$$T_0 \frac{dY}{d\tau} + Y = kX \qquad \text{or} \qquad Y = \frac{k}{T_0 P + 1} X \qquad (T_0 > 0) \qquad (1\text{-}42)$$

which is of importance in many problems dealing with damping and decay phenomena. The simple network can save two amplifiers (and thus also

---

* The linear *operator* $H(P)$ is commonly represented by the *transfer function* $H(s)$ or by the *frequency-response function* $H(j\omega)$ respectively defined by

$$\mathcal{L}\{Y(\tau);s\} = H(s)\mathcal{L}\{X(\tau);s\} \qquad \overrightarrow{Y} = H(j\omega)\overrightarrow{X} \qquad (1\text{-}41c)$$

where $\mathcal{L}\{f(\tau);s\}$ is the Laplace transform of $f(\tau)$, and $\overrightarrow{E}$ is the complex number (phasor) representing a sinusoidal function $|\overrightarrow{E}| \sqrt{2} \cos (\omega\tau + \arg \overrightarrow{E})$.[1]

drift, phase shift, and output range limitations). Such circuits are particularly useful in special-purpose computers.

(c) The *parallel-feedback operational amplifiers* of Fig. 1-15 are generalizations of the phase inverters, summers, and integrators introduced in Secs. 1-10 to 1-12. As indicated in Fig. 1-16a, each complex two-terminal impedance $Z_k(j\omega)$ implements a differential equation

$$i_k(\tau) = \frac{1}{Z_k(P)} X(\tau) \qquad \left(P \equiv \frac{d}{d\tau}; k = 0,1,2, \ldots \right) \qquad (1\text{-}43)$$

relating the current i_k through the impedance to the voltage X_k across the impedance. Assuming sufficient feedback loop gain to make the

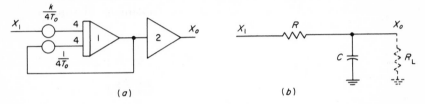

(a)   (b)

FIG. 1-14a, b. Two possible computer setups implementing

$$X = \frac{1}{k} (T_o P + 1) Y \qquad (T_o > 0)$$

In Fig. 1-14b, $k = \dfrac{R_L}{R + R_L}$, $T_o = \dfrac{R R_L C}{R + R_L}$.

summing-point voltage $E_G = X_o/A$ negligible, the summing-point node equation for Fig. 1-15a is then

$$\frac{1}{Z_o(P)} X_o + \frac{1}{Z_1(P)} X_1 = 0 \qquad (1\text{-}44)$$

so that we have the important performance equation

$$X_o(\tau) = - \frac{Z_o(P)}{Z_1(P)} X_1(\tau) \qquad (1\text{-}45)$$

In Fig. 1-15b, the summing-point node equation

$$\frac{1}{Z_o(P)} X_o + \frac{1}{Z_1(P)} X_1 + \frac{1}{Z_2(P)} X_2 + \cdots = 0 \qquad (1\text{-}46)$$

similarly yields the basic performance equation

$$X_o(\tau) = -Z_o(P) \left[\frac{1}{Z_1(P)} X_1(\tau) + \frac{1}{Z_2(P)} X_2(\tau) + \cdots \right] \qquad (1\text{-}47)$$

(d) The more general operational-amplifier circuits of Fig. 1-15c and d employ passive linear *four-terminal networks* in their input and feedback

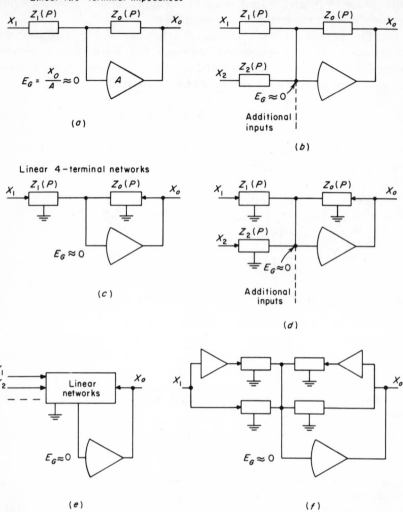

FIG. 1-15. Parallel-feedback operational amplifiers. Each circuit is assumed to be stable; assuming sufficient feedback loop again, each summing-point voltage E_G will be small throughout the working-frequency range.

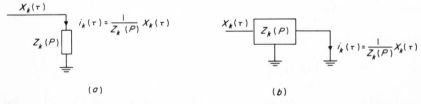

FIG. 1-16. A two-terminal impedance (a) and the short-circuit transfer impedance of a network (b) as linear operators.

circuits.   The *short-circuit transfer impedance* $Z_k(j\omega)$ or $Z_k(P)$ of such a network will be defined by the differential equation

$$i_k(\tau) = \frac{1}{Z_k(P)} X_k(\tau) \qquad \left(P \equiv \frac{d}{d\tau}; k = 0,1,2, \ldots \right) \qquad (1\text{-}48)$$

where X_k is the input voltage, and i_k is the current drawn from the network output terminal short-circuited to ground (or to a summing point), as shown in Fig. 1-16.   It follows that the summing-point node equations (44) and (46), and hence the performance equations (45) and (47), apply to Fig. 1-15c, d for sufficiently high loop gain; each $Z_k(P)$ is now the short-circuit transfer impedance of a network.   The simple impedances of Fig. 1-15a, b are clearly special cases of such short-circuit transfer impedances.

The assumption of practically infinite loop gain is often reasonable, since low-frequency amplifier gains as high as several million are readily available.   Note, however, that the infinite-loop-gain assumption, and hence the idealized performance equations (45) and (47), will apply only to a restricted range of working frequencies.   The validity of the approximations made here is further discussed in Secs. 3-10 to 3-17, where a detailed error analysis is presented.

The operational-amplifier technique can be generalized still further. The infinite-gain performance equation (47) applies to the circuits of the type shown in Fig. 1-15e if one defines each short-circuit transfer impedance as the operational ratio of X_k and the corresponding short-circuit current i_k into the summing point when all other network terminals are grounded.   In general, it is, however, simpler to derive the circuit performance directly from node equations.

The circuit of Fig. 1-15f permits the representation of complex transfer functions having zeros in the positive as well as in the negative half-plane. Note that, while such an operational amplifier circuit may not be stable by itself, it may well be stable when placed in an external degenerative feedback loop.

(e) Table 1-1 lists some examples of operational-amplifier circuits. The design of operational amplifiers of the types shown in Fig. 1-15a to d is made especially convenient by widely available *tables of transfer impedances* for various networks (Table A-1).   Figure 1-17a illustrates the design procedure with the aid of the table; in this case,

$$Z_1 = 2R \left(\frac{RC}{2} P + 1 \right) \qquad Z_o = \frac{1}{C_oP}$$

$$\frac{X_o}{X_1} = -\frac{Z_o}{Z_1} = -\frac{1}{2RC_oP[(RC/2)P + 1]}$$

If no table is available, or in the case of more general circuits (Fig. 1-15e), operational amplifiers are best designed with the aid of the usual node

Table 1-1. Examples of Parallel-feedback-type Operational Amplifiers for a Number of Transfer Functions $\dfrac{X_o}{X_1} = -\dfrac{Z_o(P)}{Z_1(P)}$ **(Sec. 1-14)**

Additional circuits may be designed with the aid of Table C-2.
Set potentiometers in No. 6 with the load connected.

	Transfer operator X_o/X_1	Circuit		Transfer operator X_o/X_1	Circuit
1	$-\dfrac{R_o}{R_1}\dfrac{1}{R_oCP+1}$		4	$-\dfrac{R_o}{R_1}\dfrac{R_1C_1P+1}{R_oC_oP+1}$	
2	$-\dfrac{R_o}{R_1}(R_1CP+1)$		5*	$-\dfrac{1}{4(RC)^2P^2}$	
3	$-\dfrac{R_oCP+1}{R_1CP}$		6	$-\dfrac{a_1R_o\,\frac{1}{a_1}R_1C_1P+1}{a_oR_1\,\frac{1}{a_o}R_oC_oP+1}$	

* Accurate double integration with this circuit requires very close matching of resistance and capacitance values.

equations, together with the assumption that $E_G \approx 0$ whenever this assumption is justified (Sec. 3-11).

Figure 1-17b illustrates the node-equation design of a practical circuit using only one amplifier to implement the important second-order differential equation

$$\frac{d^2Y}{d\tau^2} + 2\xi\omega_n\frac{dY}{d\tau} + \omega_n^2 Y = -\omega_n^2 X \tag{1-49a}$$

or

$$Y = -\frac{1}{(1/\omega_n^2)P^2 + (2\xi/\omega_n)P + 1}X \tag{1-49b}$$

which describes damped mass-spring systems such as accelerometers, rate gyros, valves, and many spring- or servo-restrained transducers and measuring devices.[3] Referring to Fig. 1-17b, note that the integrator input voltage must be $-RCPY$ if high loop gain is assumed; one requires, then, only one node equation, that for the integrator-input node, to derive Eq. (49) with

$$\omega_n = \sqrt{\frac{1}{R_1 R_2 C_1 C_2}} \qquad \xi = \left(\frac{R_1}{2} + R_2\right)\sqrt{\frac{C_2}{C_1}\frac{1}{R_1 R_2}} \qquad (1\text{-}50)$$

The price paid for circuit simplicity is the interaction of adjustments of the natural circular frequency ω_n and the damping ratio ξ; but design is simplified by nomographs of the type given in the Appendix (Fig. A-1).

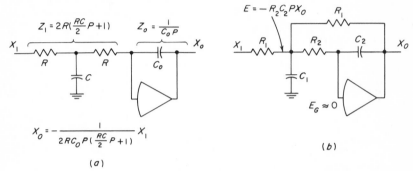

FIG. 1-17. Examples showing operational-amplifier design with the aid of Table A-1 (a), and using node equations (b), assuming practically infinite loop gain (see text).

1-15. Practical Design Considerations. The physical analogies inherent in direct-analog representations appeal to many system designers and may result in especially simple and accurate computer setups, particularly if several linear-operator blocks are to be cascaded. On the other hand, circuit simplifications tend to cause interaction between the various parameter adjustments (Fig. 1-17), so that the direct-analog approach is most useful where most parameters are fixed, as in special-purpose computers. In spite of the attractive simplicity of all-passive networks, operational-amplifier circuits are often preferred, because

1. Operational amplifiers can have high input impedances and low output impedance without attenuation. Their transfer functions are, thus, largely independent of the load; source and load are effectively isolated.
2. The performance equation (47) of a high-gain operational amplifier depends in a simple manner on the impedances Z_k, so that calibration is relatively simple.

Networks, special operational amplifiers, and differential-analyzer techniques can, of course, be used in combination.

The d-c amplifiers used for electronic analog computation should have *high d-c gain* (500 to 300 $\times$ 10^6), *low drift* (offset voltages vary between 2 mV and 2 μV referred to the input), and *low noise* (less than 15 mV referred to the input).   The reference levels of both input and output voltages are zero, and the amplifier must be stable in the required

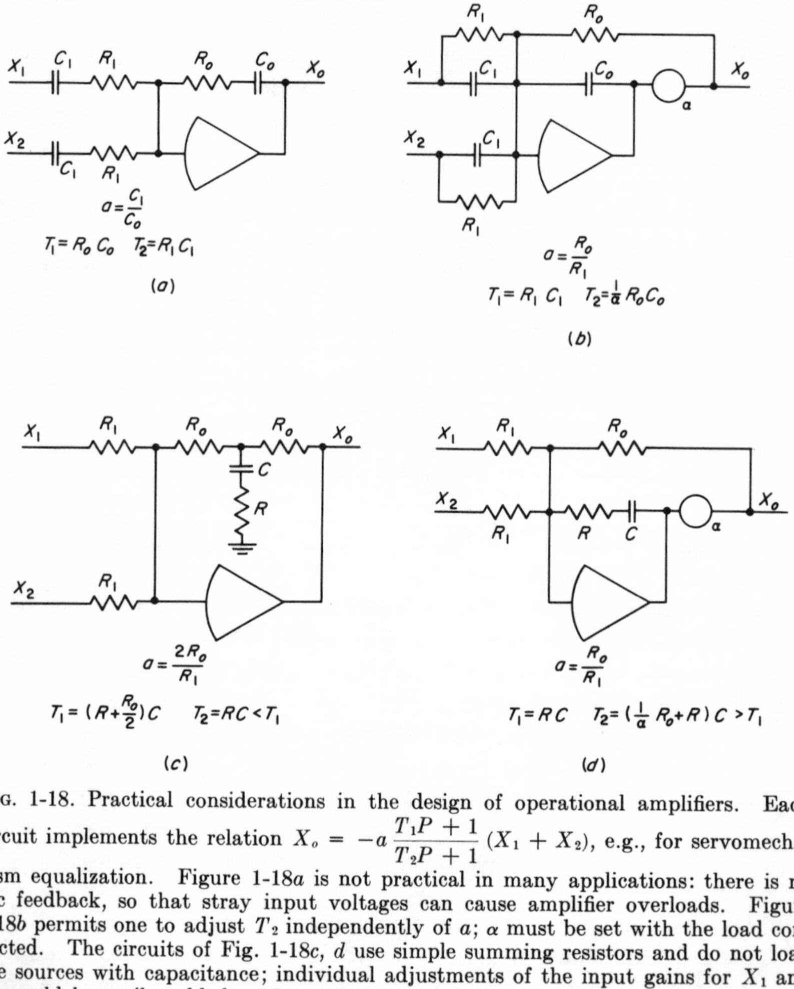

$$a = \frac{C_1}{C_o}$$
$$T_1 = R_o C_o \quad T_2 = R_1 C_1$$

(a)

$$a = \frac{R_o}{R_1}$$
$$T_1 = R_1 C_1 \quad T_2 = \frac{1}{a} R_o C_o$$

(b)

$$a = \frac{2 R_o}{R_1}$$
$$T_1 = (R + \frac{R_o}{2}) C \quad T_2 = RC < T_1$$

(c)

$$a = \frac{R_o}{R_1}$$
$$T_1 = RC \quad T_2 = (\frac{1}{a} R_o + R) C > T_1$$

(d)

Fig. 1-18. Practical considerations in the design of operational amplifiers.   Each circuit implements the relation $X_o = -a \dfrac{T_1 P + 1}{T_2 P + 1} (X_1 + X_2)$, e.g., for servomechanism equalization.   Figure 1-18a is not practical in many applications: there is no d-c feedback, so that stray input voltages can cause amplifier overloads.   Figure 1-18b permits one to adjust T_2 independently of a; α must be set with the load connected.   The circuits of Fig. 1-18c, d use simple summing resistors and do not load the sources with capacitance; individual adjustments of the input gains for X_1 and X_2 could be easily added.   Many similar circuits can be designed with the aid of Table A-1.

feedback circuits.   The design of amplifiers meeting these requirements is treated in detail in Chaps. 4 and 5.

A choice between different possible operational-amplifier circuits yielding the same idealized performance equation (47) will be made on the basis of the error analysis detailed in Secs. 3-10 to 3-17 together with the following practical considerations (see also Fig. 1-18):

1. To minimize noise and high-frequency attenuation, impedance levels should be as low as amplifier power permits.
2. Convenient implementation of variable parameters; adjustment of each parameter by a single variable resistance or potentiometer is best.
3. As many circuit parameters as possible should have conveniently obtainable values (especially capacitances).
4. Circuits with d-c (zero-frequency) feedback are preferable to circuits without d-c feedback to minimize effects of d-c offset voltages.
5. Capacitor (a-c) coupling to a preceding or succeeding circuit may reduce drift effects or obviate the need for drift stabilization.
6. Simple resistive summing networks are usually preferable to reactive summing networks; the latter are more expensive, more difficult to match, and they place reactive loads on the voltage sources.

The use of four-terminal feedback networks often affords extra design flexibility at the expense of some feedback loop gain.

1-16. Differentiating Circuits. While the usual differential-analyzer setups generate derivatives of machine variables by implicit computation (Secs. 2-12 and 2-13), direct differentiation is needed in various instrumentation and control applications, e.g., derivative control of servomechanisms. The ideal differentiation transfer operator P would require

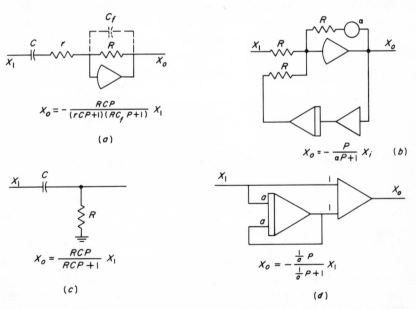

$$X_o = - \frac{RCP}{(rCP+1)(RC_f P+1)} X_i$$

(a)

$$X_o = - \frac{P}{aP+1} X_i \quad (b)$$

$$X_o = \frac{RCP}{RCP+1} X_i$$

(c)

$$X_o = - \frac{\frac{1}{a}P}{\frac{1}{a}P+1} X_i$$

(d)

Fig. 1-19. Practical differentiating circuits. In practice, circuit (d) may be less noisy than (b) and (c) (see also refs. 1 and 19).

an unlimited increase in gain with frequency and is not physically realizable, but realizable operators like $aP/(T_oP + 1)$ or $aP/(T_1P + 1)(T_2P + 1)$ implement differentiation with any desired accuracy over a range of working frequencies sufficiently low compared with $1/T_o$, $1/T_1$, and $1/T_2$. Such approximate differentiators have the added advantage of "smoothing" spurious high-frequency noise pulses, which might be unduly amplified by an ideal differentiator.   Figure 1-19 shows some practical circuits.

ANALOG-COMPUTER SYSTEMS

1-17. The Analog-computer System.   By judiciously combining basic computing elements, one can design complete d-c analog computers for a wide range of applications.   Besides a set of operational amplifiers (phase inverters, summers, and integrators) and other computing elements, a complete electronic analog-computer installation will comprise

1. Permanent wiring or flexible means for *interconnecting* the computing elements as required by each application.   Multipurpose computers typically comprise a *patchbay* with computing-element terminations and *patchcords* to set up (program) problems.   *Removable patchboards* permit problems to be set up away from the computer and also allow for problem storage (Sec. 11-1).
2. Regulated *power supplies* for the computing elements (Sec. 11-8).
3. *Reference power supplies* to furnish accurate *reference voltages* (e.g., ± 100 volts) to be used as computing and initial-condition voltages; one of the reference power supplies may serve as a *secondary voltage standard* for the computer installation (Sec. 11-8).
4. *Control switches and relays* to place initial conditions on all integrators (RESET condition) and to make the computing elements operative (COMPUTE or OPERATE condition), to set potentiometers, to select circuits for metering, etc. (Secs. 10-2 to 10-3).
5. *Readout devices*, such as strip-chart recorders, xy recorders, digital voltmeters, and printers (Fig. 1-20; see also Secs. 11-3 and 11-6).

The practical design of complete electronic analog-computer systems will be discussed in Chap. 11.

1-18. Accuracy and Computing Speed.   The *component accuracies* of individual electronic and electromechanical analog computing elements for addition, multiplication, integration, etc., vary between 3 *and* 0.005 *per cent of full scale* (note that "full scale" has come to mean 200 volts for a ± 100-volt machine).   Costs increase rapidly if component accuracies better than 0.2 per cent are desired.   Accuracies obtainable in solving a complete problem depend critically on the problem and on the computer setup as well as on the component accuracies, since errors may cancel or be compounded.   In electronic analog computers, the overall accuracy is essentially equal to the component accuracy in problems involving linear differential equations with constant coefficients if the solutions comprise only well-damped modes (see also Sec. 3-1).

Computing speeds vary between 1 msec for the solution of a typical system of differential equations on an all-electronic repetitive computer to several minutes for a "slow" d-c analog computer, which may be restricted by the frequency response of mechanical components (computer servomechanisms). The latter computing speed is sufficient for real-time simulation of most dynamical systems.

FIG. 1-20. Multiple-channel strip-chart recorders can plot several variables against time and are the most generally used analog-computer readout devices. (*Brush Instrument Co.*)

In electronic analog computers, integrator drift and phase shift may also limit the *maximum permissible computing time* to a few minutes, depending on the problem to be solved.

1-19. Computing Devices as Components of Instrumentation, Control, and Data-handling Systems.[4-18] Since most instrumentation and control systems measure and/or control continuously variable physical quantities, analog computing elements are well suited as accurate and easily calibrated system components for performing various operations on analog data. Drift-stabilized solid-state d-c amplifiers serve as convenient plug-in building blocks which can simplify the design of precise instrumentation. Modern diode/amplifier circuits permit sophisticated control and decision functions (amplitude comparison and selection,

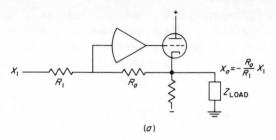

(a)

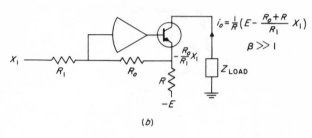

(b)

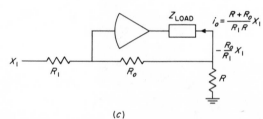

(c)

FIG. 1-21. Voltage regulator (a) and current regulators (b), (c) using operational amplifiers. In each case, either vacuum-tube or transistor output stages can be used; a suitable power output stage may be added to an existing d-c amplifier. In Fig. 1-21b, E must be a stable reference voltage; ordinary transistors or vacuum-tube cathode followers yield current in one direction only (reverse the signs of E and i_o if a pnp transistor is used). Substitution of a symmetrical transistor could permit bidirectional operation. The current generators (b), (c) are useful for driving special networks, electronic switches (Sec. 7-12), and electromagnets requiring accurate control of magnetomotive force, e.g., oscillographs and cathode-ray-tube deflection yokes. Relatively large currents (0.5 amp) have been regulated by such circuits. Note that the power-transistor output stages required for such large currents must themselves be driven by power amplifiers; so that a cascade of emitter followers may be required.[4,5]

timing, sampling, analog/digital/analog conversion, statistical measurements; see also Chaps. 9 to 11).

Small, portable multipurpose electronic analog computers can be extraordinarily useful during breadboarding, installation, or modification of various control systems and data-handling devices. A small computer of this type (Fig. 1-2a and b) permits plug-in setup of very accurate voltage and current regulators (Figs. 1-21 and 1-22), unloading circuits (Fig.

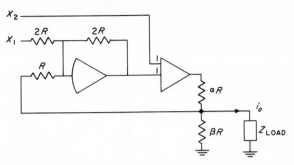

Fig. 1-22. Two-amplifier current generator. The output current i_o and the source impedance Z_S are given by

$$i_o = \frac{X_1 - X_2}{\alpha R} \frac{1}{1 + Z_L/Z_S} \qquad Z_S = \frac{\alpha \beta R}{\alpha \beta + \alpha - \beta}$$

if d-c amplifier gain is practically infinite. The source impedance becomes infinite if $\alpha\beta + \alpha - \beta = 0$, or if $\beta = \infty$, $\alpha = 1$.

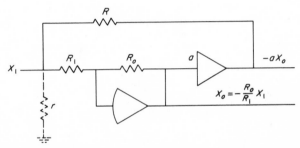

Fig. 1-23. In this *bootstrap unloading circuit*, the "bootstrap current" through R accurately balances the current drawn from the input-voltage source by r and R_1 if

$$R = \frac{r}{r + R_1}(aR_o - R_1)$$

so that the source sees an infinite impedance. r may be a load external to the bootstrap circuit; if $r = \infty$, one must have $R = aR_o - R_1$ for infinite-impedance input. (If R is decreased beyond the finite-impedance condition in Fig. 1-23, the source sees a *negative resistance;* in practice, circuit stability will now depend on the source impedance. Substitution of reactive network components for r, R_1, R_o, and R yields unloading circuits for reactive loads, and circuits simulating negative reactances; see also ref. 8.) Practically attainable input impedances exceed 1,000M; the low-impedance outputs X_o and $-aX_o$ can drive measuring or computing devices.

1-23), and easily synthesized filters, controllers, and phase shifters for many control and audio-frequency applications (Figs. 1-18 and 1-24). Simple electronic multipliers and function generators may be used for on-the-spot synthesis of automatic-gain-control circuits and other nonlinear transfer characteristics such as limiters and dead-space controllers, and for linearization of the transfer characteristics associated with control-system components such as flow valves.[8] All-solid-state versions of

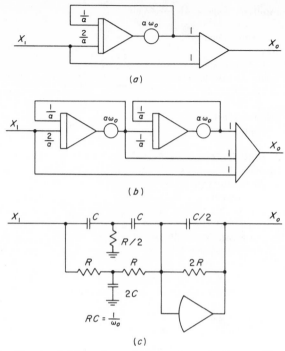

Fig. 1-24. Operational-amplifier phase shifter and notch filters. The phase shifter (a) implements $X_o = \dfrac{\omega_o - P}{\omega_o + P} X_1$; for steady-state sinusoidal input, X_o lags X_1 by 2 arctan (ω/ω_o). The notch filters (b) and (c) implement $X_o = -\dfrac{P^2 + \omega_o^2}{(P + \omega_o)^2} X_1$.

similar circuits can later be permanently incorporated into the finished system. Plug-in analog-computer setups also serve as accurate signal generators for a variety of test signals (Secs. 9-6 and 9-7).

REFERENCES

1. Korn, G. A., and T. M. Korn: *Mathematical Handbook for Scientists and Engineers*, McGraw-Hill, New York, 1961.
2. Mathews, M. V., and W. W. Seifert: Transfer-function Synthesis with Computer Amplifiers and Passive Networks, *Proc. Western Joint Computer Conf.*, 1955; see also R. Beck, *Project Cyclone Symposium* 1, Reeves Instrument Corp., New York, 1950.
3. Smith, G. W., and R. C. Wood: *Principles of Analog Computation*, McGraw-Hill, New York, 1959.
4. Eklund, K.: Use of Operational Amplifiers in Precision Current Regulators, *Rev. Sci. Instr.*, **30**: 328 (May, 1959).
5. ———: Use of Operational Amplifiers in Accelerator Beam Control Systems, *Rev. Sci. Instr.*, **30**: 331 (May, 1959).
6. Michaelis, T. D.: Transfer-function Simulation by Network Synthesis on GEDA

Analog Computers, *Report* GER-6867, Goodyear Aircraft Corp., Akron, Ohio, July, 1956.
7. Katell, E.: Positive Feedback Provides Infinite Input Impedance, *Electronics*, Nov. 18, 1960.
8. Karplus, W. J.: Synthesis of Non-physically-realizable Driving-point Impedance Functions Using Analog-computer Units, *IRE Trans. PGCT*, **4:** 170 (1957).
9. Bickart, T. A.: Suppressing a Single Interference Frequency, *Electronic Inds.*, May, 1961.
10. McGregor, W. K.: Electronic Analog Computers as Control-system Components, in Huskey, H., and G. A. Korn, *Computer Handbook*, McGraw-Hill, New York, 1962.
11. Nelson, J. K.: Missile Rate Simulator Provides Sinusoidal Motion for Guidance Systems, *Automatic Control*, **9** (December, 1958).
12. Blum, N. A.: Recording Optical Pyrometer, *Rev. Sci. Instr.*, **30:** 251 (April, 1959).
13. Vosteen, R. E.: Problems and Solutions, *Electronic Products*, June, 1961.
14. Vander Schmidt, G. F.: Vacuum-tube Electrometers Using Operational Amplifiers, *Rev. Sci. Instr.*, **31:** 1004 (September, 1960).
15. Reece, J. M.: Subaudio Tunable Amplifier, *Electronics*, Nov. 6, 1959.
16. Brog, K. C., and F. J. Milford: High-precision Large-current Generator, *Rev. Sci. Instr.*, **31:** 321 (March, 1960).
17. Schwent, G. V., W. K. McGregor, D. W. Russell, and L. F. Burns: A New Approach to Control-system Design, *ISA Journal*, July–December, 1956.
18. McGregor, W. K.: Linearization Functions in Process-control Systems, ISA paper 56-33-3, presented in New York, September, 1956.
19. Diamantides, N. D.: Improved Electronic Differentiator, *Electronics*, July 27, 1962.
20. Korn, G. A.: *Random-process Simulation and Measurements*, McGraw-Hill, New York, 1965.

BIBLIOGRAPHY

Ernst, D.: *Elektronische Analogrechner*, Oldenbourg, Munich, 1960.
Eterman, I. I.: *Analog Computers*, translated by G. Segal, Pergamon Press, New York, 1960.
Feldbaum, A. A.: *Rechengeräte in automatischen Systemen*, translated by R. R. Herschell, Oldenbourg, Munich, 1962.
Fifer, S.: *Analogue Computation* (4 vols.), McGraw-Hill, New York, 1961.
Giloi, W., and R. Lauber: *Analogrechnen*, Springer, Berlin, 1963.
Goode, H. H., and R. E. Machol: *System Engineering*, McGraw-Hill, New York, 1957.
Grabbe, E. M., S. Ramo, and D. E. Wooldridge: *Handbook of Automation, Computation, and Control*, vol. 2, Wiley, New York, 1959.
Howe, R. M.: *Design Fundamentals of Analog Computer Components*, Van Nostrand, Princeton, N.J., 1961.
Huskey, H., and G. A. Korn: *Computer Handbook*, McGraw-Hill, New York, 1962.
Jackson, A. S.: *Analog Computation*, McGraw-Hill, New York, 1960.
Johnson, C. L.: *Analog Computer Techniques*, 2d ed., McGraw-Hill, New York, 1963.
Karplus, W. J.: *Analog Simulation*, McGraw-Hill, New York, 1958.
——— and W. W. Soroka: *Analog Methods*, 2d ed., McGraw-Hill, New York, 1959.
Kogan, B. Y.: *Electronic Analog Computers*, Fismatgis, Moscow, 1963.
Korn, G. A.: *Random-process Simulation and Measurements*, McGraw-Hill, New York, 1965.
Levine, L.: *Methods for Solving Engineering Problems Using Analog Computers*, McGraw-Hill, New York, 1964.

MacKay, D. M., and M. E. Fisher: *Analogue Computing at Ultra-high Speed*, Wiley, New York, 1962.

Rogers, A. E., and T. W. Connolly: *Analog Computation in Engineering Design*, McGraw-Hill, New York, 1960.

Scott, N. R.: *Analog and Digital Computer Technology*, McGraw-Hill, New York, 1960.

Smith, G. W., and R. C. Wood: *Principles of Analog Computation*, McGraw-Hill, New York, 1959.

Tomović, R.: *Calculateurs analogiques electroniques*, Masson et Cie, Paris, 1959.

——— and W. J. Karplus: *High-speed Analog Computers*, Wiley, New York, 1962.

Truitt, T. D., and A. E. Rogers: *Basics of Analog Computers*, John F. Rider, New York, 1960.

Warfield, J. N.: *Electronic Analog Computers*, Prentice-Hall, Englewood Cliffs, N.J., 1959.

Wass, C. A.: *Introduction to Electronic Analogue Computers*, Pergamon Press, New York, 1955.

Winkler, H.: *Elektronische Analogieanlagen*, Akademie-Verlag, Berlin, 1961.

Periodical Literature on Analog Computation

The most important periodical sources are:

1. *Simulation Council Newsletter*, in *Instruments and Control Systems*, describes current analog-computer work in the United States of America. Replaced by *Simulation* (magazine) after 1963.
2. *IRE* (IEEE since 1963) *Transactions on Electronic Computers* (*IRETEC*, *IEEETEC* since 1963; contains bibliographies and abstracts).
3. *Automatika i Telemekhanika* (translated by Instrument Society of America; also contains periodical bibliographies on analog computation).
4. *Annales de l'Association Internationale pour le Calcul Analogique* (*AICA*), Presses Académiques Européennes, Brussels, Belgium; contains bibliographies. See also the *Proceedings of AICA Conferences* published every 3 years.
5. *Automation Express* (excerpts from Russian periodical literature).

Consult also current issues of *Electronics*, *Electronic Engineering* (*London*), *Trans. AIEE*, *Proc. IEEE*, *Instruments and Control Systems*, *Review of Scientific Instruments*, *Rechentechnik*, and *Control Engineering*.

CHAPTER 2

PREPARATION OF PRACTICAL COMPUTER SETUPS

INTRODUCTION

2-1. Introductory Remarks. When an electronic analog computer is to solve a given system of differential equations, specific voltages in the machine must be made to vary with time in a manner prescribed by these differential equations. The computer is "set up" for the given problem when a suitable arrangement of computing elements establishes the correct relationships between computer voltages.

AMPLITUDE-SCALING PROCEDURE. EXAMPLES OF SCALED RELATIONS

2-2. Amplitude Scaling: The Choice of Scale Factors. (a) It is important to remember that an analog computer will establish mathematical relations between voltages (machine variables) *representing* the variables of a given problem, rather than between the problem variables as such. The machine variables (voltages) associated with electronic computing elements such as amplifiers must necessarily stay within specified limits (typically ± 100 volts, ± 50 volts, or ± 10 volts) to prevent overloads or saturation, which would cause incorrect computation. Multipurpose analog computers are equipped with *overload indicators* to warn the operator of overload conditions (Sec. 11-4*b*). Within the permissible operating range, on the other hand, it is desirable to have each machine variable assume as large absolute values as possible, so as to minimize fractional errors due to d-c offset voltages, noise, and the like.

Accordingly, electronic analog computers represent the "problem

37

variables" x, y, . . . of a given problem by voltages

$$X = (a_x x) \qquad Y = (a_y y) \qquad \cdots \tag{2-1}$$

where a_x, a_y, . . . are dimensional *scale factors* chosen so that the absolute value of each machine variable X, Y, . . . becomes as large as practical without exceeding its maximum permissible excursion (± 100 volts, ± 50 volts, or ± 10 volts).

If one desires to scale a given problem for an electronic analog computer working, say, over a ± 100-volt range, there are some advantages in measuring X, Y, . . . in 100-volt *machine units*, but *scaling in volts* is almost universally accepted and will be adopted throughout this book. In this case each scale factor, say a_x, must satisfy the relation

$$a_x \leq \frac{100}{|x|_{\max}} \frac{\text{volts}}{\text{unit of } x} \tag{2-2}$$

where $|x|_{\max}$ is the largest expected excursion of the problem variable x. In special-purpose computers, a_x might be chosen to be as large as permitted by the basic relation (2). In general-purpose problem solutions, *the choice of scale factors is usually restricted to convenient round numbers of the form* 10^n, 2×10^n, or 5×10^n ($n = 0, \pm 1, \pm 2$, . . .), and possibly also 2.5×10^n and 4×10^n.

Note that the choice of scale factors requires one to estimate the expected maximum excursions of the problem variables. These maximum excursions may be immediately evident from the physical context or from approximate computations, or the estimate may require more insight and/or more sophisticated considerations. This information need not be accurate, since it is relatively easy to change scale factors after one or more trial runs. It is better to use such a trial-and-error approach than to use excessively small scale factors; some modern analog computers have special warning lights which indicate voltages remaining within an excessively small range of values (*minimum-excursion indicators*, Sec. 11-4b).

(b) Machine Units and Volts.   The maximum permissible voltage of either sign usable in a given type of electronic analog computer is defined as the *machine unit* for this type of machine; thus one machine unit would equal 100 volts for a ± 100-volt machine, 50 volts for a ± 50-volt repetitive computer, and 10 volts for a ± 10-volt transistor computer. In each case, the scale factors a_x must satisfy the same relation

$$a_x \leq \frac{1}{|x|_{\max}} \frac{\text{machine unit}}{\text{unit of } x} \tag{2-3}$$

Scaling in machine units has some decided advantages: all machine variables will range between -1 and $+1$ machine unit, and *scale factors, as well as block diagrams and computer setups, will be identical for all types of electronic analog computers.* In particular, the machine-unit method simplifies the scaling of products (Fig. 2-3) and of hybrid analog-digital representations of variables (Sec. 11-19).

On the other hand, the smaller scale factors resulting from machine-unit scaling appear to annoy many engineers, while scaling in volts frequently permits the use of unity or simple integral-valued scale factors. In addition, many (although by no means all) computer readout devices are calibrated in volts, which also have an intuitive appeal to many electrical engineers. These advantages of scaling in volts, however, are largely lost in the case of, say, the widely used ± 10-volt transistor machines.

In the writers' opinion, a simple and practical way out of this controversy is to scale consistently in terms of *per-cent machine units.* In the common case of ± 100-volt machines, one per-cent machine unit equals precisely one volt, so that the usual American scaling procedure applies without any change whatsoever. Each computer setup and scale factor derived in this manner still applies to, say, ± 50-volt or ± 10-volt computers with a per-cent machine unit corresponding to 0.5 volt or 0.1 volt, respectively.

Conventional scaling in volts—or per-cent machine units—is therefore adopted throughout this book, and accepted American scaling practice is employed. All computer setups and scale factors presented here still apply without change to analog computers operating over ± 10 volts or any other range, if the voltage units given in each case are simply interpreted as per-cent machine units.

2-3. Amplitude Scaling: Machine Equations and Block Diagrams.
Once the scale factors have been chosen, one obtains the correct machine equations relating the voltages $(a_x x)$, $(a_y y)$, . . . , simply by writing

$$x \text{ as } \frac{1}{a_x} (a_x x) \qquad y \text{ as } \frac{1}{a_y} (a_y y) \qquad \cdot \cdot \cdot$$

in each given problem equation. Then one proceeds to set up a computer block diagram, leaving terms like $(a_x x)$, $(a_y y)$, . . . intact: *the parentheses indicate that these terms will appear as voltages whose absolute values cannot exceed the computer operating range.*

In addition, it is important to realize that *the output voltage of every operational amplifier or function generator must be regarded as a separate machine variable, which may require separate scaling.* It is easy to deal with terms like $-(a_x x)$, $(a_x x) + (a_y y)$, $(a_x x)(a_y y)$, or $F[(a_x x)]$ (Secs. 2-4 and 2-7); but note also that *derivatives of x, like $\dot{x}$, $\ddot{x}$, . . . are new machine voltages with separate and distinct scale factors* (Sec. 2-7).

The examples of Secs. 2-4 to 2-11 will illustrate the general scaling and

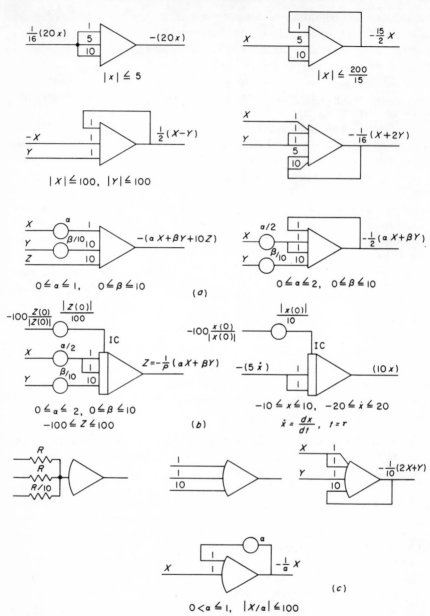

Fig. 2-1. Use of summing amplifiers, potentiometers, and summing integrators to produce scaled algebraic sums. Note how summing amplifiers with paralleled inputs and/or feedback yield accurate integral and integral-fraction coefficients. Figure 2-1c shows two different notations for high-gain amplifiers (frequently, these are summers or integrators with feedback connection removed).

setup procedure. Note that *each scaled machine equation is easily checked directly against the corresponding problem equation by cancellation of all scale factors.*

2-4. Examples of Scaled Relations. Block-diagram Symbols. (a) Algebraic Sums. Figure 2-1 shows representative computer setups yielding scaled algebraic sums $\alpha_1 X_1 + \alpha_2 X_2 + \cdots$. Summing amplifiers with parallel inputs and/or feedback connections can be used to produce accurate integral and integral-fraction coefficients α_1, α_2, ... (Figs. 2-1a and c); note that integral-fraction feedback is *not* possible with summing *integrators* (Fig. 2-1b).

(b) Multiplication, Division, and Square Roots. How to Avoid Division. Figures 2-2 and 2-3 illustrate multiplication with servomultipliers and with electronic multipliers, respectively. Note that most analog multipliers are scaled so that they will not overload as long as neither input exceeds the computer overload limits; multipliers are, therefore, rarely equipped with overload indicators.

To minimize the effect of multiplication errors, it is usually wise to reduce expressions of the form $X(Y + a)$ to the form $XY + aX$, especially when Y is small compared with a (see also Fig. 2-4d).

Figure 2-4 shows how one obtains scaled quotients $Z = X/\alpha Y$ and square roots by using a servo or electronic multiplier to vary the feedback around a high-gain d-c amplifier. Note that the divisor Y must not change sign, and that we must scale so that Z does not overload. The feedback ratio of our division loop is seen to depend on Y, and loop stability is a problem in some computer setups (Sec. 7-23). Many electronic multipliers have a *division mode* which connects the multiplier output amplifier into a properly equalized internal division loop producing $X/\alpha Y$. The transition from multiplication to the division mode is made by a front-panel switch or (preferably) by a relay actuated through a patchbay connection (Fig. 2-3g and Sec. 7-23).

The static and dynamic accuracy of a division loop is not usually quite as good as that of the multiplier used (see also Sec. 7-23). The division-loop gain, and hence the division accuracy, decreases with the absolute value of the divisor Y. Again, the latter must not change sign, even though the quotient X/Y may remain finite as X and Y go through zero together. These disadvantages of simple division loops can be avoided, at the cost of a somewhat more complicated computer setup, by the steepest-descent technique described in Sec. 12-9b. One can also quite often avoid the actual generation of quotients altogether through a transformation of the given problem.[3,4] Thus, the differential equation

$$\frac{dy}{dx} = \frac{f(x,y)}{g(x,y)} \tag{2-4}$$

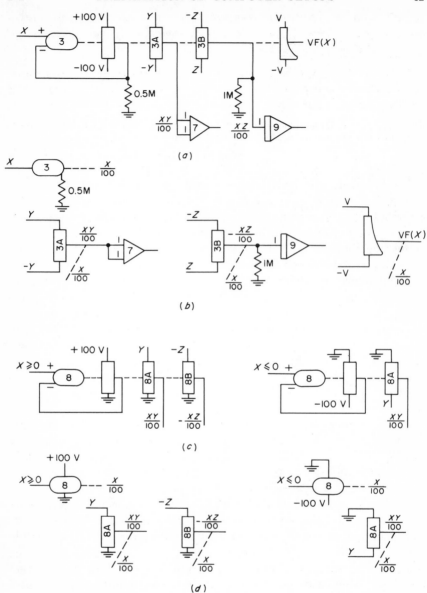

FIG. 2-2a to d. Four-quadrant multiplication (a, b), and two-quadrant multiplication (c, d) with computer servomechanisms, showing two different systems of notation. Potentiometer-load-equalizing resistors used with linear follow-up and multiplying potentiometers are indicated in Fig. 2-2a, b (see also Sec. 8-7).

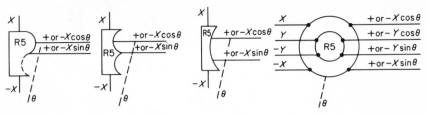

Fig. 2-2e. Four different block-diagram symbols for servo-driven sine-cosine potentiometers (resolver servos, Sec. 8-10).

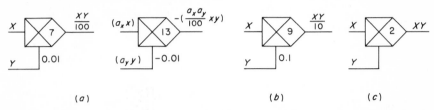

Fig. 2-3a, b, c. Machine relations for an electronic multiplier in terms of *volts* for a ±100-volt machine (a), for a ±10-volt machine (b), and in terms of *machine units* for all three types of machines (c). Figure 2-3a also applies to all three types of machines if scaling is understood to be in *per-cent machine units*.

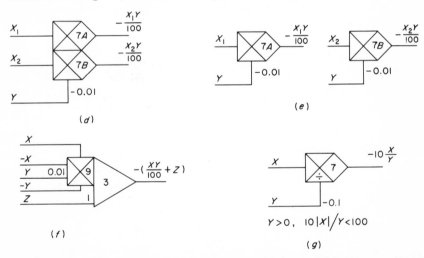

Fig. 2-3d, e, f, g. Notation for electronic multipliers having multiple "slave sections" (d), (e), for diode quarter-square-multiplier networks used with existing summing amplifiers (f), and for an electronic multiplier with built-in decision mode (g).

is equivalent to the system

$$\frac{dx}{dt} = ag(x,y) \qquad \frac{dy}{dt} = af(x,y) \qquad (2\text{-}5)$$

where t is a new independent variable, and a is a constant; we have $y = y(0)$ and $x = 0$ for $t = 0$. Problems in which $f = g = 0$ for some

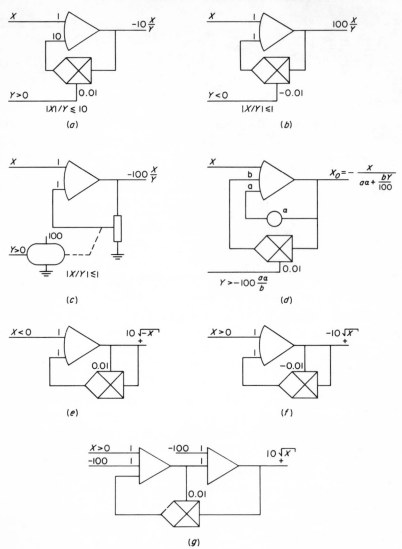

FIG. 2-4. Scaled division and square-root loops. The circuit of Fig. 2-4d is preferable to direct division by $a\alpha + bY/100$, especially when $bY/a\alpha$ is small (Sec. 12-3). The circuit of Fig. 2-4g is based on ref. 23.

value of t may or may not lead to difficulties; refer to Sec. 2-10b for an example.

More generally, systems expressible in the form

$$\frac{dy_i}{dx} = \frac{f_i(x,y_1,y_2, \ldots ,y_n)}{g_i(x,y_1,y_2, \ldots ,y_n)} \qquad (i = 1,2, \ldots ,n) \qquad (2\text{-}6)$$

are transformed into

$$
\left.\begin{array}{l}
\dfrac{dx}{dt} = a \displaystyle\prod_{k=1}^{n} g_k(x, y_1, y_2, \ldots, y_n) \\[2em]
\dfrac{dy_i}{dt} = a f_i(x, y_1, y_2, \ldots, y_n) \displaystyle\prod_{k \neq i}^{n} g_k(x, y_1, y_2, \ldots, y_n)
\end{array}\right\} \tag{2-7}
$$

with $x = 0$ for $t = 0$. Note also that many differential equations

$$
\frac{dy_i}{dx} = F_i(x, y_1, y_2, \ldots, y_n)
$$

where F_i is an unbounded function, can be rewritten in the form (6).[3,4]

(c) **Proper Use of Function Generators.**[1,2]   A general function $y = f(x)$ will be represented in the computer by the scaled function-generator output

$$
Y = (a_y y) = a_y f\left[\frac{1}{a_x}(a_x x)\right] = F[(a_x x)] = F(X) \tag{2-8}
$$

corresponding to the function-generator input $(a_x x) = X$. If, for example, $|x| < 5$, $y = x^3 + x$ can be represented by

$$
(0.5y) = \frac{1}{16,000}(20x)^3 + \frac{1}{40}(20x)
$$

Arbitrary-function generators, such as diode function generators, tapped potentiometers, or curve followers (Secs. 6-13, 8-8, and 11-3c), are usually less accurate than linear computing elements and multipliers. To minimize the effects of function-generator errors,

1. Attempt to scale function-generator input and output voltages so as to utilize the full voltage range available.
2. Whenever possible, arbitrary-function generators should supply only *corrections* to analytic (most frequently linear) approximations of the desired function.

In Fig. 2-5, a typical function is generated as the sum of a linear approximation $mx + b$ and a correction function; note how the function-generator output, and hence the function-generator error, is divided by a factor of 10. Many diode function generators (Sec. 6-13) already comprise accurate linear network components for generating $mx + b$, so that their diode networks generate only the correction function.

If accurate multipliers are available, function generators can generate corrections to second- or third-order polynomials. A different analytic approximation is needed for functions of the form $f(x) = Ae^{b/x}$, which occur frequently in chemical-reaction problems. $Ae^{b/x}$ is often small over much of the range of x but increases rapidly for small x. Reference 2 suggests generation of $Ae^{b/x}$ in the form

$$f(x) = Ae^{b/x} = \frac{g(x) + c}{(x + a)^2}$$

with $g(x) = Ae^{b/x}(x + a)^2 - c \qquad g(0) = g(100) = 0$ (2-9)

$g(x)$ is a bell-shaped function of relatively small dynamic range, which is easily set up on a tapped-potentiometer function generator. If the exponent can become very large, one may express $Ae^{b/x}$ in the alternative form

$$f(x) = Ae^{b/x} = \frac{g(x)}{(a - x)^2}$$

with $g(x) = Ae^{b/x}(a - x)^2 \qquad g'(100) = 0$ (2-10)

so that $g(x)$ becomes a "semi-bell"-shaped function.

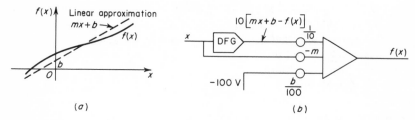

(a)   (b)

Fig. 2-5. A typical function $f(x)$ (a), and generation of $f(x)$ as the sum of a linear approximation $mx + b$ and a small correction function (b). Note that all function-generator errors are divided by 10. (*From H. D. Huskey and G. A. Korn, Computer Handbook, McGraw-Hill, New York, 1962.*)

CHANGING THE TIME SCALE

2-5. Time Scaling. In analog-computer solutions of ordinary differential equations, the computer time τ represents the problem independent variable t; in many representations of dynamical systems, t is the problem time. One-to-one representation of the problem time t by the computer time τ ($\tau = t$) will result in simulation of a dynamical system on a $1:1$ *time scale* (*real-time scale*) and give a realistic idea of the physical progress of a simulated process. Real-time operation is, for instance, required whenever physical system components or human operators are to be included in a computer setup (*partial system tests*). Frequently, though, real-time simulation would result in inconveniently long or short computer runs or involves frequencies not reproducible in a given computer. In such cases, we relate the problem time (or other independent variable) t to the computer time τ by a simple "time-scale transformation"

$$t = \frac{1}{\alpha_t}\tau$$ (2-11)

The coefficient α_t is the *time-scale factor;* note that $\alpha_t > 1$ for a *slow* time scale where t sec of problem time are represented by a *longer* period τ of computer time. $\alpha_t < 1$ corresponds to a *fast* time scale.

To produce a suitably time-scaled computer setup, *we must substitute the expression* (11) *for t throughout the (scaled or unscaled) problem equations;* in particular, note that now

$$\frac{d}{dt} = \alpha_t \frac{d}{d\tau} \equiv \alpha_t P \tag{2-12}$$

The substitutions (11) and (12) rescale the independent variable t like any other problem variable. *If, as is usually the case, each derivative operator* $P \equiv d/d\tau$ *is implemented by an integrator or network capacitor, then we can also time-scale an electronic-analog-computer setup simply by increasing each network capacitor in the ratio* $\alpha_t : 1$. *This will, in particular, decrease each integrator input gain in the same ratio and thus slow the computation if* $\alpha_t > 1$. Signal generators or timing devices external to the computer setup proper will require separate time scaling.

Note very carefully that time-scale changes do not affect the maximum or minimum values of any problem variable in any way, so that amplitude scale factors are completely unaffected by time scaling (Fig. 2-12b).

To check our time scaling, we note that resubstitution of $\tau = \alpha_t t$, $P = (1/\alpha_t)(d/dt)$ in our time-scaled equations must return us to the original $1:1$ time scale.

EXAMPLE: A $1:1,000$ (fast) time scale transforms the problem equations

$$\frac{d^2 y}{dt^2} = -y \quad \text{or} \quad \frac{d\dot{y}}{dt} = -y \quad \frac{dy}{dt} = \dot{y}$$

(harmonic oscillator, Secs. 1-5 and 2-9) into

$$10^{-6} \frac{d^2 y}{d\tau^2} = -y \quad \text{or} \quad \frac{d\dot{y}}{d\tau} = P\dot{y} = -1,000y \quad \frac{dy}{d\tau} = 1,000y$$

for solution by a repetitive analog computer yielding 50 solutions per second (Sec. 1-7). Note (1) each integrator input is multiplied by $1/\alpha_t = 1,000$, and (2) solution amplitudes are completely unaffected by the time-scale change.

2-6. Choice of Time Scale. Where a $1:1$ time scale is not required for real-time simulation or partial-system tests, the choice of the time scale will be a compromise between a desire for fast computation and the frequency range yielding optimum accuracy of computing elements and readout devices. Computer runs of 5 to 200 sec are usually best for "slow" electronic differential analyzers. Computer runs longer than 300 sec may degrade integration accuracy (Secs. 3-20 and 3-21), while large voltage excursions at frequencies higher than 1 to 5 cps tend to cause servo errors (Sec. 8-1); all-electronic multipliers and function generators permit faster operation. Repetitive analog computers (Sec. 1-7) employ solution times between 2 sec and 0.3 msec (0.3- to 3,000-cps repetition rates), which ordinarily require fast time scales. Communication-system simulation (Sec. 9-6) ordinarily employs a $10^4:1$ to $10^6:1$ (slow) time scale in order to bring carrier or intermediate frequencies down into the audio-frequency range.

ORDINARY DIFFERENTIAL EQUATIONS

2-7. Solution of Differential Equations (see also Sec. 1-5). **(a) Scaling First-order Equations and Systems.** To solve a differential equation expressible in the form

$$\frac{dx}{dt} = f(t,x) \tag{2-13}$$

on an $\alpha_t:1$ time scale ($t = \tau/\alpha_t$, $d/dt = \alpha_t d/d\tau = \alpha_t P$, Sec. 2-5), we rewrite the given relation (13) as a scaled machine equation

$$P(a_x x) = \frac{a_x}{\alpha_t} f\left[\frac{\tau}{\alpha_t}, \frac{(a_x x)}{a_x}\right] \tag{2-14}$$

where a_x is a suitably chosen scale factor (Sec. 2-2). Figure 2-6 shows the corresponding scaled computer setup.

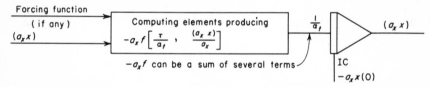

Fig. 2-6. Scaled computer setup for the first-order differential equation

$$\frac{dx}{dt} = f(t,x)$$

Similarly, a *system* of first-order equations

$$\frac{dx_i}{dt} = f_i(t;x_1,x_2, \ldots ,x_n) \qquad (i = 1,2, \ldots ,n) \tag{2-15}$$

becomes

$$P(a_i x_i) = \frac{a_i}{\alpha_t} f\left[\frac{\tau}{\alpha_t}; \frac{(a_1 x_1)}{a_1}, \frac{(a_2 x_2)}{a_2}, \ldots , \frac{(a_n x_n)}{a_n}\right] \quad (i = 1,2, \ldots ,n) \tag{2-16}$$

where a_i is the scale factor assigned to $x_i = x_i(t)$ (Fig. 2-7).

Note that each integrator output $(a_x x)$ or $(a_i x_i)$ in Figs. 2-6 and 2-7 must be assigned a properly scaled initial value (Sec. 1-5).

(b) Equations of the Second and Higher Order. Differential equations of the second or higher order will also be assumed to permit solution for the highest derivative, so that we have

$$\frac{d^r y}{dt^r} = f\left(t; y, \frac{dy}{dt}, \frac{d^2 y}{dt^2}, \ldots , \frac{d^{r-1} y}{dt^{r-1}}\right) \tag{2-17}$$

It is best to reduce each such equation to a set of r first-order equations by introducing the first $r - 1$ derivatives as new variables:

$$\frac{dy}{dt} = \dot{y} \qquad \frac{d\dot{y}}{dt} = \ddot{y} \qquad \cdots \qquad \frac{dy^{(r-1)}}{dt} = f(t;y,\dot{y},\ddot{y}, \ldots ,y^{(r-1)}) \qquad (2\text{-}18)$$

The system (18) is set up in the manner of Fig. 2-7. Each of the problem variables $y, \dot{y}, \ldots , y^{(r-1)}$ will be represented by an integrator output; it is usually convenient to obtain voltages proportional to $y, -\dot{y}, \ddot{y}, \ldots$ or $-y, \dot{y}, -\ddot{y}, \ldots$ from a string of integrators without intervening phase inverters. Note that we shall have to supply scale factors and initial values for each one of the variables $y, \dot{y}, \ldots , y^{(r-1)}$.

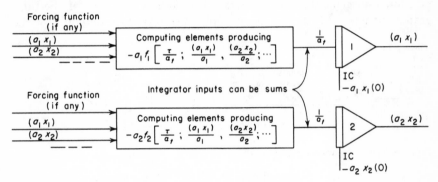

FIG. 2-7. Solution of a system of first-order equations

$$\frac{dx_i}{dt} = f_i(t;x_1,x_2, \ldots ,x_n) \qquad (i = 1,2, \ldots ,n)$$

In particular, a *second-order equation* (e.g., an equation of motion in mechanics)

$$\frac{d^2y}{dt^2} = f\left(t; y, \frac{dy}{dt}\right) \qquad (2\text{-}19)$$

becomes

$$\frac{d\dot{y}}{dt} = f(t;y,\dot{y}) \qquad \frac{dy}{dt} = \dot{y} \qquad (2\text{-}20)$$

The corresponding scaled machine equations on an $\alpha_t:1$ time scale $(t = \tau/\alpha_t, d/dt = \alpha_t d/d\tau = \alpha_t P$, Sec. 2-5) are

$$P(a_{\dot{y}}\dot{y}) = \frac{a_{\dot{y}}}{\alpha_t} f\left[\frac{\tau}{\alpha_t}; \frac{(a_y y)}{a_y}, \frac{(a_{\dot{y}}\dot{y})}{a_{\dot{y}}}\right] \qquad P(a_y y) = \frac{a_y}{\alpha_t a_{\dot{y}}} (a_{\dot{y}}\dot{y}) \qquad \left(P \equiv \frac{d}{d\tau}\right) \tag{2-21}$$

which yields the general type of computer setup shown in Fig. 2-8 (see Secs. 2-9 to 2-11 for examples).

Similarly, introduction of derivatives $\dot{y}_k, \ddot{y}_k, \ldots$ as new variables quite simply reduces every set of differential equations expressible in the form

$$\frac{d^{r_i}y_i}{dt^{r_i}} = f_i(t;y_1,y_2, \ldots ,y_N;\dot{y}_1,\dot{y}_2, \ldots ,\dot{y}_N; \ldots) \quad (i = 1,2, \ldots ,N) \quad (2\text{-}22)$$

to an equivalent first-order system (15). The resulting computer setup will again have the form of Fig. 2-7.

(c) **Generation of Forcing Functions.** In our differential-equation-solver setups (Figs. 2-6 to 2-8), each integrator input must add up to a specified function of the integrator output voltages and of the computer time τ. Suitable combinations of summers, potentiometers, multipliers, and function generators will generate the desired functions of the integrator outputs; but, in general, we must also introduce functions of the

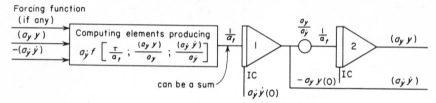

Fig. 2-8. Scaled computer setup for the second-order equation

$$\frac{d^2y}{dt^2} = f\left(t; y, \frac{dy}{dt}\right)$$

computer time τ (*forcing functions*) explicitly into our computer setup. As an example, the machine equation

$$P(5x) = -2(5x) + 50 \sin \tau$$

requires us to generate a voltage $-50 \sin \tau$, which must be fed into a summing integrator together with twice the integrator output $(5x)$.

Forcing functions are sometimes obtained from external signal generators, which may have to be synchronized with the start of the computer run. More frequently, one lets the analog computer generate its own forcing-function inputs as solutions of known differential equations, as shown in Fig. 2-9 and Sec. 2-10a. In this case, all computer input voltages are ultimately derived from the computer reference power supplies, which supply constant inputs and initial-condition inputs.

(d) **Generalized Integration.** Operational-amplifier integrators integrate the sum of their input voltages with respect to the computer time τ (real time), which serves as the independent machine variable. It is, however, possible to obtain integrals of a voltage $Y = Y(\tau)$ with respect to a dependent machine variable $X = X(\tau)$ in the form

$$Z = \int_0^\tau Y\,dX + Z(0) = \int_0^\tau \left(Y\frac{dX}{d\tau}\right)d\tau + Z(0) \quad (2\text{-}23)$$

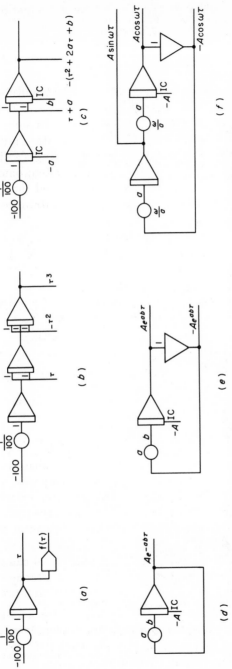

FIG. 2-9. Generation of various functions of the computer time τ as solutions of differential equations.

51

if a voltage proportional to the time derivative $dX/d\tau$ of X is available in the computer (*generalized integration*, Fig. 2-10). Substitution of "generalized integrators" like that of Fig. 2-10 in Fig. 2-9 yields functions of X (see also Sec. 8-16).

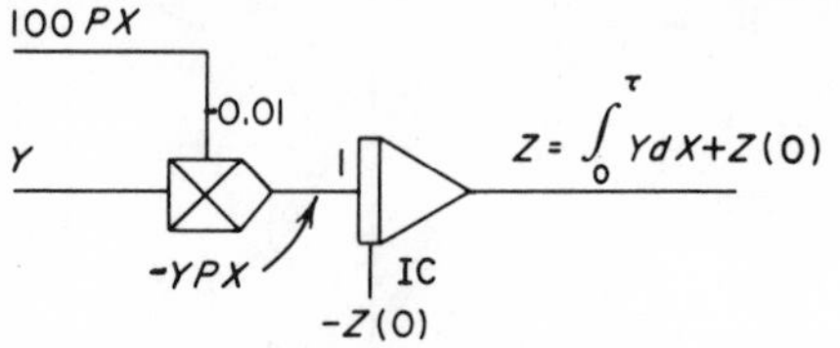

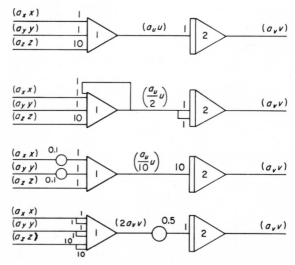

FIG. 2-10. Integration with respect to a machine variable X when a voltage proportional to the time derivative $dX/d\tau = PX$ is available in the computer. Substitution of such "generalized integrators" in Fig. 2-9 yields functions of X.

2-8. Checking and Rescaling. Note carefully that the relations implemented by each analog-computer setup (e.g., Figs. 2-6 to 2-9) can be read off the block diagram, and that cancellation of all scale factors must yield the correct original problem equation. *This is a convenient and practical check on our computer setups.*

More often than not, it will be necessary to revise preliminary scale-factor estimates, and/or to change scale factors, in the course of a computation. Frequently, only a portion of the computer setup needs to be

FIG. 2-11. Rescaling (see text).

rescaled. Since multiplier and function-generator outputs will, in general, not overload unless an input is overloaded, we need to consider only rescaling of summers and integrators (or other operational amplifiers). Referring to Fig. 2-11, simple multiplication of all amplifier input gains (and initial-value settings in integrators!) by a desired factor b will change the scaled amplifier output $(a_x x)$ to $(ba_x x)$, so that ba_x is the new scale factor. Since the problem equations are to remain unchanged, we shall have to multiply each output $(ba_x x)$ of our amplifier by $1/b$ farther ahead in the computer setup; note that this may or may not necessitate rescaling of another amplifier or amplifiers. Sometimes, it is possible to rescale a string of cascaded computing elements together.

2-9. The Damped Harmonic Oscillator.   Scale-factor Estimation.
The linear differential equation

$$\frac{d^2y}{dt^2} + r\frac{dy}{dt} + ky = 0 \qquad (r > 0, k > 0) \qquad (2\text{-}24a)$$

or
$$\frac{d\dot{y}}{dt} = -r\dot{y} - ky \qquad\qquad \frac{dy}{dt} = \dot{y} \qquad (2\text{-}24b)$$

with
$$y(0) = y_0 \qquad\qquad \dot{y}(0) = 0 \qquad (2\text{-}25)$$

describes an oscillatory damped, critically damped, or overdamped oscillation if the *damping ratio* $\xi = r/2\sqrt{k}$ is, respectively, less than, equal to, or greater than unity; for $\xi < 1$, the oscillation frequency is $\omega_1/2\pi = \sqrt{k(1 - \xi^2)}/2\pi$.[5] The analog-computer setup for Eq. (24) is frequently used for demonstration.

To scale Eq. (24), we note that the maximum excursions of $y(t)$ and $\dot{y}(t)$ will surely be at most as large as they would be without damping $(r = 0)$, i.e.,

$$y \leq y_0 \qquad \dot{y} \leq \omega_1 y_0 \leq y_0\sqrt{k} \qquad (2\text{-}26)$$

Suppose that y is measured in feet and t in seconds, and we are given

$$1 \text{ sec}^{-1} \leq r \leq 5 \text{ sec}^{-1} \qquad 250 \text{ sec}^{-2} \leq k \leq 350 \text{ sec}^{-2} \qquad y_0 = 9 \text{ ft}$$

Then $a_y = 10$ volts/ft, $a_{\dot{y}} = 0.5$ volt/ft will be reasonable scale factors ensuring that $|y|$ and $|\dot{y}|$ cannot exceed 100 volts. If we employ an α_t:1 time scale $(t = \tau/\alpha_t,\ d/dt = \alpha_t d/d\tau = \alpha_t P)$, the machine equations become

$$P(0.5\dot{y}) = -\frac{1}{\alpha_t}\left[r(0.5)\dot{y} - \frac{k}{20}(10y)\right] \Bigg\}$$
$$P(10y) = \frac{1}{\alpha_t}20(0.5\dot{y}) \qquad\qquad\qquad\qquad (2\text{-}27)$$

Figure 2-12a shows a scaled computer setup, and Fig. 2-12b shows computer solutions for two different time scales recorded at the same paper speed; note again that *solution amplitudes are not affected by the time scale.* Equation (27) may be checked against Eq. (24) through cancellation of scale factors.

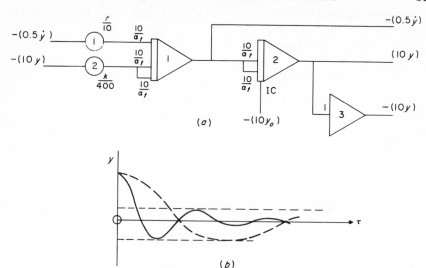

(a)

(b)

FIG. 2-12. Scaled computer setup for the differential equation

$$\frac{d^2y}{dt^2} + r\frac{dy}{dt} + k = 0$$

(a), and solutions computed on two different time scales reproduced at the same recorder-paper speed (b). Note that solution amplitudes are not affected by time-scale changes.

2-10. Mathieu's and Legendre's Differential Equations. (a) *Mathieu's differential equation*

$$\frac{d^2y}{dt^2} + \omega_0^2(1 + \epsilon \cos \omega_m t)y = 0 \qquad (2\text{-}28a)$$

or
$$\frac{d\dot{y}}{dt} = -\omega_0^2(1 + \epsilon \cos \omega_m t) \qquad \frac{dy}{dt} = \dot{y} \qquad (2\text{-}28b)$$

with given constant parameters ϵ, ω_0, and ω_m describes an oscillator having a time-variable "stiffness" coefficient. Assuming that

$$y(0) = 2 \qquad \dot{y}(0) = 0 \qquad \omega_0 = 20 \qquad 0 < \omega_m \le 100 \qquad 0 < \epsilon \le 1$$

and that solutions will be of interest for $0 \le t \le 15$, we will slow the time scale by a factor of 10, so that

$$t = \frac{\tau}{10} \qquad \frac{d}{dt} = 10\frac{d}{d\tau} = 10P \qquad (2\text{-}29)$$

Since we should like to display unstable as well as stable solutions $y(t)$

generated by the parametric excitation in Eq. (28), we choose a fairly small scale factor for y, say, $a_y = 10$ volts/unit of y; as in Sec. 2-9, we let $a_{\dot{y}} = a_y/\omega_0 = 0.5$ volt/unit of $\dot{y}$; our scale-factor estimation is quite

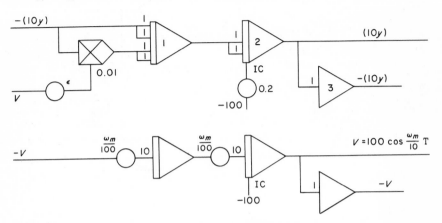

FIG. 2-13a. Computer setup for Mathieu's differential equation

$$\frac{d^2y}{dt^2} + \omega_0^2(1 + \epsilon \cos \omega_m t)y = 0$$

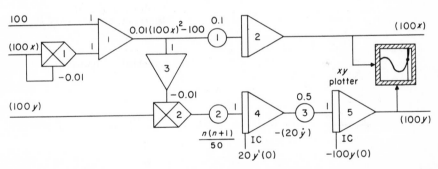

FIG. 2-13b. Scaled computer setup for Legendre's differential equation (31) in the form (35) (see text).

rough and, as usual, subject to revision. The resulting machine equations corresponding to Eq. (28) are

$$\left. \begin{array}{l} P(0.5\dot{y}) = -2\left(1 + \epsilon \cos \dfrac{\omega_m}{10}\,\tau\right)(10y) \\ P(10y) = 2(0.5\dot{y}) \end{array} \right\} \qquad (2\text{-}30)$$

The computer setup of Fig. 2-13a implements these relations and generates the required time-variable voltage

$$V = 100 \cos \frac{\omega_m}{10}\,\tau$$

with a three-amplifier sine-generating loop solving the differential equations

$$P\dot{V} = -\frac{\omega_m}{10}V \qquad PV = \frac{\omega_m}{10}\dot{V}$$

with $V(0) = 100$ volts, $\dot{V}(0) = 0$ in the manner of Fig. 2-9f. We check our machine equation (30) by resubstituting $\tau = 10t$, $P = \frac{1}{10}d/dt$ and canceling all scale factors to obtain the original equation (28).

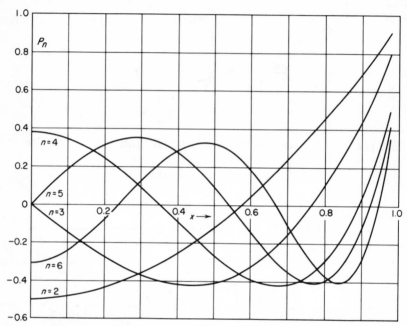

FIG. 2-13c. The first six Legendre polynomials $y = P_n(\dot{x})$.

(**b**) Solution of *Legendre's differential equation*

$$(1 - x^2)\frac{d^2y}{dx^2} - 2x\frac{dy}{dx} + n(n + 1)y = 0 \qquad (n = 0,1,2, \ldots) \qquad (2\text{-}31)$$

subject to the initial conditions

$n =$	0	1	2	3	4	5	6
$y(0) =$	1	0	$-\frac{1}{2}$	0	$\frac{3}{8}$	0	$-\frac{5}{16}$
$\dfrac{dy}{dx}\bigg]_0 =$	0	1	0	$-\frac{3}{2}$	0	$\frac{15}{8}$	0

yields the first six of the well-known Legendre polynomials[5] and furnishes an interesting example of the division-avoiding technique described in

Sec. 2-4*b*.   We replace Eq. (31) by the first-order system

$$\frac{dy'}{dx} = \frac{2xy' - n(n+1)y}{1 - x^2} \qquad \frac{dy}{dx} = y' \qquad (2\text{-}32)$$

To avoid the division by $1 - x^2$ (which becomes zero for $x = 1$), we introduce a new independent variable t and solve the system

$$\frac{dx}{dt} = 1 - x^2 \qquad \frac{dy'}{dt} = 2xy' - n(n+1)y \qquad \frac{dy}{dt} = (1 - x^2)y' \quad (2\text{-}33)$$

with $x = 0$ for $t = 0$.   If we do not require an explicit output proportional to $y'(t)$, a further simplification results if we introduce

$$\dot{y} = (1 - x^2)y'$$

as a new variable[4] and solve

$$\frac{dx}{dt} = 1 - x^2 \qquad \frac{d\dot{y}}{dt} = -n(n+1)(1 - x^2)y \qquad \frac{dy}{dt} = \dot{y} \quad (2\text{-}34)$$

with $x = 0$, $\dot{y} = y'(0)$ for $t = 0$.

$a_y = 100$ volts/unit of y and $a_{\dot{y}} = 20$ volt-sec/unit of $\dot{y}$, $a_x = 100$ volts will be reasonable scale factors for $n \leq 6, 0 \leq x \leq 1$.   With a 10:1 (slow) time scale useful for servo-table plots of y against the original independent variable x, the machine equations corresponding to Eq. (34) become

$$\left.\begin{aligned}
P(100x) &= 0.1 \left[100 - \frac{(100x)^2}{100} \right] \\
P(20\dot{y}) &= -2 \times 10^{-4} n(n+1) \left[100 - \frac{(100x)^2}{100} \right](100y) \\
P(100y) &= 0.5(20\dot{y})
\end{aligned}\right\} \quad (2\text{-}35)$$

which is set up in Fig. 2-13*b*.   References 6 and 7 describe more conventional analog-computer setups for Legendre's equation.

2-11. Solution of Nonlinear Second-order Differential Equations: Two Typical Oscillation Problems.   (a) Van der Pol's Differential Equation.   *Van der Pol's differential equation*

$$\frac{d^2y}{dt^2} + \mu(y^2 - 1)\frac{dy}{dt} + y = 0 \qquad (2\text{-}36a)$$

or

$$\frac{d\dot{y}}{dt} = -y - \mu(y^2 - 1)\dot{y} \qquad \frac{dy}{dt} = \dot{y} \qquad (2\text{-}36b)$$

where μ is a given constant, is typical of an important class of differential equations describing the buildup of oscillations in nonlinear electrical and mechanical systems.   The Van der Pol equation (36) resembles the performance equation of a damped harmonic oscillator, but has a nonlinear damping term which tends to increase the amplitude of the oscillations for small values of y and to decrease the amplitude for large values of y. If an oscillator of this type is given a small initial displacement $y(0)$, periodic oscillations of constant amplitude will result after an initial transient.[8] While such nonlinear oscillation problems yield only to rather cumbersome graphical or numerical approximation methods, relatively simple analog-computer setups yield accurate records of $y(t)$ and $\dot{y}(t)$; moreover, *phase-plane plots* of $\dot{y}$ or $-\dot{y}$ vs. y, which often give considerable insight into the nature of the oscillations, are easily obtained with the aid of an oscilloscope or xy plotter. The mathematical theory of nonlinear oscillations is discussed in detail in refs. 8 and 9.

At least for small values of μ, $y = A \cos t$ will be an approximate solution. The solution will be stable at a *limit-cycle amplitude* A such that the energy dissipation per cycle is zero, i.e.,

$$\int_0^{2\pi} \mu(y^2 - 1)\dot{y}^2 \, dt \approx A^2\mu\pi \left(\frac{A^2}{4} - 1\right) = 0 \qquad (2\text{-}37)$$

so that $A \approx 2$. Since it is interesting to study convergence to the limit cycle for initial values $y(0)$ larger as well as smaller than the limit-cycle amplitude $A = 2$, we assume $|y| < 4$ so that also $|\dot{y}| < 4$. We take $a_y = a_{\dot{y}} = {}^{10}\!\%_4 = 25$ volts/unit, so that the machine equations for a $1:1$ time scale ($t = \tau$, $d/dt = d/d\tau = P$) become

$$\begin{array}{l} P(25\dot{y}) = -(25y) - \mu[0.0016(25y)^2 - 1](25\dot{y}) \\ P(25y) = (25\dot{y}) \end{array} \right\} \qquad (2\text{-}38)$$

where $(25y)$ and $(25\dot{y})$ are measured in volts.

Figure 2-14a shows a practical computer setup using electronic multipliers. A single coefficient-setting potentiometer permits adjustment of the parameter μ to any desired value between 0 and 1. With such an all-electronic computer setup, one can speed up the time scale by simply replacing the 1-μF integrating capacitors with 0.1-μF capacitors. The solutions of Fig. 2-14c were obtained in this manner and illustrate the convergence to a limit cycle for small and large initial values of y.

Although modern computer servomechanisms and servo plotting tables can follow the real-time solution of Eq. (38), a time-scale increase will be advisable for use with older machines. The computer setup of Fig. 2-14b employs servomultipliers to implement the machine equation (38) on a $10:1$ (slow) time scale; each integrator input has been attenuated by a factor of 10 as compared with Fig. 2-14a.

(b) **Rayleigh's Differential Equation. Accurate Use of Diode Function Generators.** If a new dependent variable z is introduced into Eq. (37) through the transformation

$$\frac{dz}{dt} = y \qquad (2\text{-}39)$$

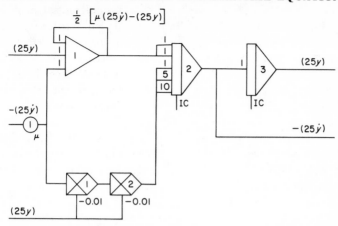

FIG. 2-14a. This simple all-electronic computer setup also permits speeded-up computation (1:10 time scale) if the 1-μF integrating capacitors are replaced by 0.1-μF capacitors, so that each integrator input is multiplied by 10. With sufficiently fast computing elements, one may also use 0.01-μF capacitors (1:100 time scale) for repetitive operation.

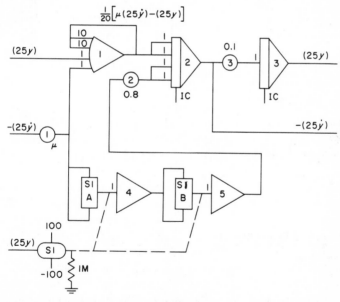

FIG. 2-14b. A slowed-down (10:1 time scale) computer setup for use with older servo-multipliers and recorders. The linear center-tapped potentiometers S1A, S1B are connected to multiply by $0.01|(25y)|$ (Table A-2) to save amplifiers. All servo-driven potentiometers are equally loaded if the servo follow-up potentiometer is loaded by 1M as shown. Note also the use of parallel integrator inputs and the connection of amplifier 1 for accurate multiplication by constant coefficients.

FIG. 2-14. Analog-computer solution of Van der Pol's differential equation

$$\frac{d^2y}{dt^2} = -y - \mu(y^2 - 1)\frac{dy}{dt}$$

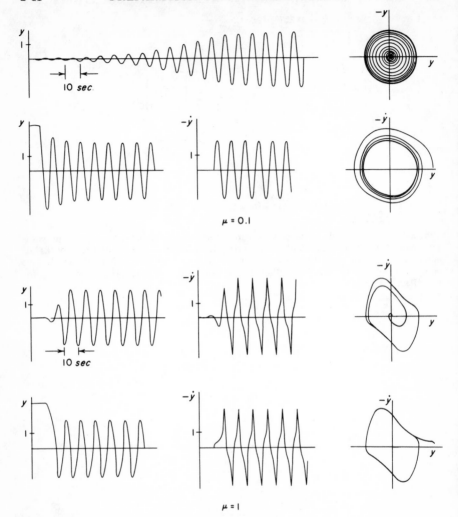

FIG. 2-14c. Analog-computer solutions $y(t)$ and phase-plane plots ($-\dot{y}$ vs. y) for Van der Pol's equation obtained from the computer setup of Fig. 2-14a with 0.1-μF integrating capacitors.

FIG. 2-14. (*Continued*).

one obtains *Rayleigh's differential equation*

$$\frac{d^2z}{dt^2} + \mu\left[\frac{1}{3}\left(\frac{dz}{dt}\right)^3 - \frac{dz}{dt}\right] + z = 0 \tag{2-40a}$$

or
$$\frac{dz}{dt} = -z - \mu\left(\frac{1}{3}\dot{z}^3 - \dot{z}\right) \qquad \frac{dz}{dt} = \dot{z} \tag{2-40b}$$

which was originally introduced in acoustics. We may assume $0.1 \leq \mu \leq 1$.

The analog-computer solution of the Rayleigh equation (40) is not only of interest for its own sake but will also yield the solution of the Van der Pol equation (37) by virtue of Eq. (39).   This can be useful because the analog-computer solution of Eq. (40) requires only a single function generator and no multipliers.

In view of Eq. (39) and the approximate limit-cycle solution $y \approx 2 \cos t$ derived in Sec. 2-11a, it is again reasonable to assume $|z| < 4$, $|\dot{z}| < 4$ and

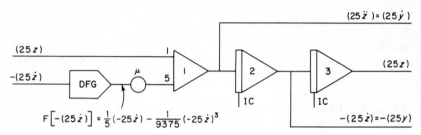

Fig. 2-15. Scaled computer setup for Rayleigh's differential equation

$$\frac{d^2z}{dt^2} + \mu\left[\frac{1}{3}\left(\frac{dz}{dt}\right)^3 - \frac{dz}{dt}\right] + z = 0$$

This computer setup also yields solutions $y(t)$ of Van der Pol's equation (see text).

to take $a_z = a_{\dot{z}} = 25$ volts/unit, so that the scaled machine equations for a 1:1 time scale ($t = \tau$, $d/dt = d/d\tau = P$) are

$$P(25\dot{z}) = -(25z) - \mu\left[\frac{1}{1{,}875}(25\dot{z})^3 - (25\dot{z})\right] \Bigg\}$$
$$= -(25z) - \mu f[(25\dot{z})] \qquad \qquad (2\text{-}41)$$
$$P(25z) = (25\dot{z})$$

Figure 2-15 shows a suitable computer setup and serves as an interesting illustration of the principles stated in Sec. 2-4c regarding the use of diode function generators.   First, the desired function

$$f[(25\dot{z})] = \frac{1}{1{,}875}(25\dot{z})^3 - (25\dot{z}) \qquad (2\text{-}42)$$

must be scaled.   Since $|\dot{z}| < 4$, $|f| < 500$, so that we can write

$$f[(25\dot{z})] = 5\{\tfrac{1}{5}f[(25\dot{z})]\} = 5F[-(25\dot{z})] \qquad (2\text{-}43)$$

and the scaled function $F[-(25\dot{z})]$ can be generated with a diode function generator (Fig. 2-15).   The parameter μ is again set on a single coefficient potentiometer.

As noted earlier, the Rayleigh-equation setup of Fig. 2-15 can also be used to yield the solution y of the Van der Pol equation (37) and its derivative $\dot{y}$ with the aid of the transformation

$$y = \dot{z} \qquad \dot{y} = \ddot{z} = -z - \mu(\tfrac{1}{3}\dot{z}^3 - \dot{z}) \qquad (2\text{-}44)$$

These relations can be solved for z and $\dot{z}$ to determine the suitably scaled initial values of z and $\dot{z}$ from given initial values of y and $\dot{y}$:

$$z = -\dot{y} - \mu(\tfrac{1}{3}y^3 - y) \qquad \dot{z} = y \qquad (2\text{-}45)$$

The judicious use of variable transformations is seen to be useful for machine solution as well as for analytical and numerical solution of differential equations; this is especially true if only a limited number or choice of computing elements is available.

LINEAR OPERATIONS: SIMPLE TRANSFER OPERATORS AND IMPULSE-RESPONSE FUNCTIONS

2-12. Introduction. In many problems involving transducers or energy conversion, a mechanical, electrical, or thermodynamic "input" variable (stimulus) $x(t)$ produces an "output" (response) $y(t)$ related to $x(t)$ by a linear differential equation

$$\frac{d^n y}{dt^n} + a_{n-1}\frac{d^{n-1}y}{dt^{n-1}} + \cdots + a_0 y$$

$$= b_m \frac{d^m x}{dt^m} + b_{m-1}\frac{d^{m-1}x}{dt^{m-1}} + \cdots + b_0 x \qquad (2\text{-}46a)$$

where the a_i, b_k are given *constant* coefficients. The more general case of *time-variable* coefficients is discussed in ref. 25. The dynamic input-output relationship expressed by Eq. (46a) is brought out more clearly if we rewrite it in terms of a time-invariant linear transfer operator $H(p)$, i.e.,

$$y(t) = H(p)x(t)$$

$$= \frac{b_m p^m + b_{m-1}p^{m-1} + \cdots + b_0}{p^n + a_{n-1}p^{n-1} + \cdots + a_0} x(t) \qquad \left(p \equiv \frac{d}{dt}\right) \quad (2\text{-}46b)$$

Such transfer operators represent the action of physical devices or system "blocks" on their input variables; linear transfer operators can be *added* (paralleled), *multiplied* (cascaded), and combined into feedback loops corresponding to the block-diagram notation of Fig. 2-16, which is familiar especially to control engineers. In addition, *time-invariant* linear operators *commute;* i.e., the order of cascaded operators can be reversed without effect on the output (Fig. 2-16; see also Sec. 2-16).

An electronic analog computer will represent each physically realizable transfer operator by a corresponding block of computing elements whose input voltage X and output voltage Y represent x and y on convenient

scales.   Such computer blocks can be interconnected precisely in the
manner of the block diagrams of Fig. 2-16; so that the relation of inputs,
operators, and responses is conveniently implemented by a "live mathematical model."

(a) Transfer–operator notation

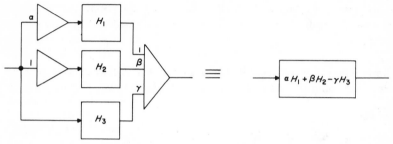

(b) Addition and multiplication by constants

(c) Multiplication (cascading) of linear transfer operators.
In general $H_1 H_2 \neq H_2 H_1$ unless H_1 and H_2 are both time-invariant

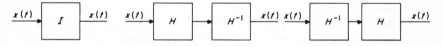

(d) Identity operator and inverse (reciprocal) operators

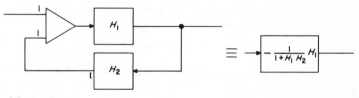

(e) Feedback

FIG. 2-16. Representation of the differential equation (46) by a linear transfer operator (a), and block-diagram representation of operator algebra (b) to (e).

As already noted in Sec. 1-14, a time-invariant linear transfer operator $H(p)$ is
represented by the corresponding transfer *function* $H(s)$ or by the corresponding frequency-response function $H(j\omega)$ in Laplace- and Fourier-transform analyses.   The
reader should distinguish carefully between $H(p)$, $H(s)$, and $H(j\omega)$.
Note also that, unless we can assume zero initial values for the output y and its

derivatives, it is *not* in general correct to cancel common factors in the numerator and denominator of Eq. (46b).

2-13. Differential-analyzer Techniques.[10-15] Direct-analog representations of relations of the form (46) by means of computing networks and special operational amplifiers have already been discussed in Secs. 1-14 to 1-16. Such direct-analog representations can save much equipment and are, thus, especially useful in special-purpose computers used, say, in control and instrumentation systems. On the other hand, the more compact direct-analog representations frequently do not permit flexible parameter adjustments without interaction between parameters; besides, introduction of specified initial conditions other than zero may be difficult, since one would require a special charging circuit for each network capacitance. The differential-analyzer techniques outlined in the following simplify setup problems at the expense of added equipment. The resulting computer setups employ only integrators, summer/phase inverters, and coefficient-setting potentiometers and do not require explicit differentiation as long as $n \geq m$.

Let us now leave the problem of scaling to Sec. 2-14 and represent $x, \dot{x}, \ldots$ and $y, \dot{y}, \ldots$ directly by numerically corresponding voltages; this will be possible at least for sufficiently small inputs $x(t)$. Let us assume $n \geq m$. We want to operate on the input voltage x so as to produce the output voltage y. Our usual differential-analyzer technique of introducing $\dot{y}, \ddot{y}, \ldots, y^{(n-1)}$ as new variables related by first-order differential equations (Sec. 2-5) will not work without explicit differentiation, since the derivatives $\dot{x}, \ddot{x}, \ldots$ of the input voltage x are not directly available.

Method 1 ("Successive-integration Method"). Remembering that the a_i, b_k are constants and that $n \geq m$, rewrite the given differential equation (46a) as

$$y = b_n x + \frac{1}{p}(b_{n-1}x - a_{n-1}y) + \frac{1}{p^2}(b_{n-2}x - a_{n-2}y) + \cdots$$
$$+ \frac{1}{p^n}(b_0 x - a_0 y) \qquad \left(p \equiv \frac{d}{dt}\right) \quad (2\text{-}46c)$$

where $b_i = 0$ for $i > m$. Introduce the n new variables

$$\left.\begin{aligned}
v_1 &= y - b_n x \\
v_2 &= a_{n-1}y - b_{n-1}x + \frac{dv_1}{dt} \\
v_3 &= a_{n-2}y - b_{n-2}x + \frac{dv_2}{dt} \\
&\cdots\cdots\cdots\cdots\cdots \\
v_n &= a_1 y - b_1 x + \frac{dv_{n-1}}{dt}
\end{aligned}\right\} \qquad (2\text{-}47)$$

The given differential equation (46) is equivalent to the system of n first-order equations

$$\left.\begin{aligned}
\frac{dv_n}{dt} &= b_0 x - a_0 y \\
\frac{dv_{n-1}}{dt} &= v_n + b_1 x - a_1 y \\
\frac{dv_{n-2}}{dt} &= v_{n-1} + b_2 x - a_2 y \\
&\cdots \cdots \cdots \cdots \cdots \\
\frac{dv_1}{dt} &= v_2 + b_{n-1} x - a_{n-1} y
\end{aligned}\right\} \qquad (2\text{-}48a)$$

together with

$$y = v_1 + b_n x \qquad (2\text{-}48b)$$

These relations are implemented by successive operational amplifiers 1, 2, . . . , $n + 1$ in Fig. 2-17a on a 1:1 time scale ($t = \tau$, $d/dt = P$).

Method 2.   Introduce a new variable $z = z(t)$ related to the unknown output y by

$$y = b_m \frac{d^m z}{dt^m} + b_{m-1} \frac{d^{m-1} z}{dt^{m-1}} + \cdots + b_0 z \qquad (2\text{-}49a)$$

so that

$$z = \frac{1}{p^n + a_{n-1} p^{n-1} + \cdots + a_0} x \qquad \left(p \equiv \frac{d}{dt}\right)$$

must satisfy the differential equation

$$\frac{d^n z}{dt^n} + a_n \frac{d^{n-1} z}{dt^{n-1}} + \cdots + a_0 z = x \qquad (2\text{-}49b)$$

which does not involve explicit differentiation of the input x. With suitable scaling, a conventional n-integrator computer setup for Eq. (49b) yields voltages proportional to z, $\dot{z}$, $\ddot{z}$, . . . , $z^{(m)}$ ($n \geq m$); and simple algebraic combination of these voltages produces the desired output y in accordance with Eq. (49a) (Fig. 2-17b).   Coefficients a_i, b_k exceeding unity in absolute value are dealt with as before.   This method is particularly useful if we have to set up two or more operators (46b) with identical denominators.[7]

Figure 2-18 illustrates the application of both setup methods to the same specific example.   In each case, each given coefficient A_i or B_k is set on one and only one potentiometer, a useful feature.   Either method necessarily requires n integrators.   Method 1 frequently produces simpler computer setups than Method 2, but the latter may yield simpler scaling, initial-condition setup, or impulse-function computation (Secs.

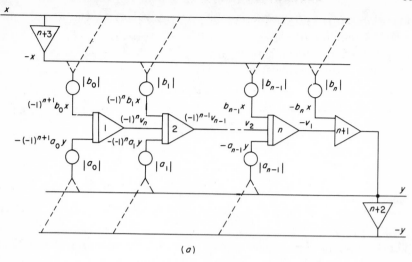

(a)

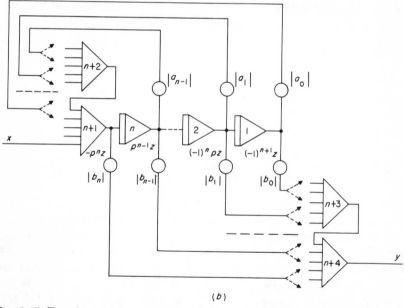

(b)

Fig. 2-17. Transfer-operator setups by Method 1 (a), and by Method 2 (b). Each setup procedure requires n integrators; in general, Method 1 requires three summer/ phase inverters, and Method 2 requires four summer/phase inverters. Each coefficient A_i or B_k is set on one and only one potentiometer; coefficients exceeding unity in absolute value are obtained through combinations of potentiometers and amplifier input gains, as in Fig. 2-1 [e.g., $a_k = 10(a_k/10)$].

2-14 and 2-16).   Either type of setup can often be simplified through judicious circuit rearrangement.   The two general transfer-operator setup procedures shown here are by no means the only possible ones,[10-15] but other setup methods do not seem to offer particular advantages.

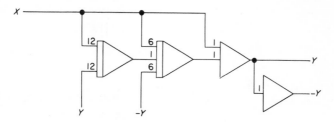

FIG. 2-18a. To produce a computer setup for $Y = -\dfrac{P^2 - 6P + 12}{P^2 + 6P + 12} X$, method 1 implements $Y = -X + \dfrac{6}{P}(X - Y) - \dfrac{12}{P^2}(X + Y)$.

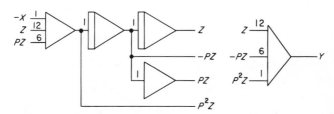

FIG. 2-18b. Method 2: $(P^2 + 6P + 12)Z = X$ is solved for Z, $-PZ$, and P^2Z. These voltages are combined to produce $Y = -(P^2 - 6P + 12)Z$.

2-14. Scaling and Initial Conditions for Transfer-operator Setups.
(a) **Amplitude Scaling.**   As a rule, it is not difficult to estimate the ranges of the input variable x and the output variable y in Sec. 2-13, so that suitable scale factors for these quantities are readily obtained (Sec. 2-2).   In general, however, the various amplifier output voltages in Fig. 2-17 will depend not only on x and y but also on the derivatives $\dot{x}$, $\ddot{x}$, . . . , $x^{(m-1)}$ and $\dot{y}$, $\ddot{y}$, . . . , $y^{(n-1)}$ $(n \geq m)$.   In particular, the amplifier output voltages in Fig. 2-17a (Method 1) are related to x, y, and their derivatives by the recursion formulas (47), which can be used to scale v_n, v_{n-1}, . . . , v_1 in the usual manner.   Similar relations can be derived for Fig. 2-17b.   Unfortunately, range estimates for all derivatives of x and y needed for complete scaling are seldom readily available, and we must employ the trial-and-error procedure of Sec. 2-8 to rescale individual amplifiers as required.

In the special case of transfer-operator problems of the form

$$\left.\begin{aligned}
a_n \frac{d^n z}{dt^n} + a_{n-1} \frac{d^{n-1} z}{dt^{n-1}} + \cdots + a_0 z &= x(t) \\
z = \dot{z} = \ddot{z} = \cdots = z^{(n-1)} &= 0 \qquad \text{for } t = 0
\end{aligned}\right\} \qquad (2\text{-}50)$$

where $x(t)$ contains no periodic terms which might cause resonance, Jackson[6] suggests that the following "equal-coefficient rule" often approximates favorable scaling:
The ranges of z and its derivatives $\dot{z}$, $\ddot{z}$, . . . , $z^{(n)}$ are assumed to satisfy

$$|z|_{\max} \approx \frac{2}{|a_0|} |x|_{\max} \qquad |z^{(k)}|_{\max} \approx \frac{1}{|a_k|} |x|_{\max} \qquad (k = 1, 2, \ldots, n) \qquad (2\text{-}51)$$

subject to the restriction that the sequence $|z|_{\max}$, $|\dot{z}|_{\max}$, . . . must either increase or decrease (this avoids trouble due to vanishing coefficients a_i). Tentative scale factors are, then, chosen in accordance with

$$a_x \le \frac{100}{|x|_{\max}} \qquad a_z \le \frac{50}{|x|_{\max}} |a_0| \qquad a_{z^{(k)}} \le \frac{100}{|x|_{\max}} |a_k| \qquad (k = 1, 2, \ldots, n) \qquad (2\text{-}52)$$

so that the coefficients of $(a_{\dot{z}}\dot{z})$, $(a_{\ddot{z}}\ddot{z})$, . . . in the resulting machine equation

$$\frac{a_n}{a_{z^{(n)}}} (a_{z^{(n)}} z^{(n)}) + \frac{a_{n-1}}{a_{z^{(n-1)}}} (a_{z^{(n-1)}} z^{(n-1)}) + \cdots + \frac{a_0}{a_z} (a_z z) = \frac{1}{a_x} (a_x x)$$

are all roughly equal to 1.
This rule, when applicable, will also help to scale transfer-operator problems of the more general form (46) when setup method 2 of Sec. 2-13 is used.

(b) Time Scaling. The computer time scale can be slowed down or speeded up by explicit time-scale transformation $[t = \tau/\alpha_t, \; d/dt = \alpha_t(d/d\tau) = \alpha_t P]$ as in Sec. 2-5, without effect on the amplitude scaling.

(c) Initial Conditions. The integrator output voltages in each transfer-operator setup of Fig. 2-17 are, as noted, linear functions of x, $\dot{x}$, $\ddot{x}$, . . . , $x^{(m-1)}$ and y, $\dot{y}$, $\ddot{y}$, . . . , $y^{(n-1)}$, and the initial values of these quantities are required for complete problem specification. In many applications, all variables can, fortunately, be assumed to start from zero, so that all integrators are simply reset to zero. If this is not the case, the correct initial-value setting for each integrator output is related explicitly to the given initial values of x, y, $\dot{x}$, $\dot{y}$, . . . by a set of formulas such as Eq. (47).

One can, instead, reset all integrators to zero and replace the initial conditions by an equivalent "complementary function" added to the "normal response" obtained with zero initial integrator outputs. As an example, application of the one-sided Laplace transformation[5] to the relation

$$a_2 \frac{d^2 y}{dt^2} + a_1 \frac{dy}{dt} + a_0 y = b_1 \frac{dx}{dt} + b_0 x \qquad (2\text{-}53)$$

with given initial values $y(0 + 0) = y(0)$, $\dot{y}(0 + 0) = \dot{y}(0)$, $x(0 + 0) = x(0)$ yields

$$Y(s) = \frac{b_1 s + b_0}{a_2 s^2 + a_1 s + a_0} X(s) + \frac{a_2 y(0) s + a_1 y(0) + a_2 \dot{y}(0) - b_1 x(0)}{a_2 s^2 + a_1 s + a_0} \qquad (2\text{-}54)$$

where $X(s)$ and $Y(s)$ are the respective Laplace transforms of $x(t)$ and $y(t)$. It follows that

$$y(t) = \frac{b_1 p + b_0}{a_2 p^2 + a_1 p + a_0} x(t) + \frac{a_2 y(0) p + [a_1 y(0) + a_2 \dot{y}(0) - b_1 x(0)]}{a_2 p^2 + a_1 p + a_0} \delta_+(t) \qquad (t > 0)$$

$$(2\text{-}55)$$

where $\delta_+(t)$ is the (asymmetrical) unit-impulse function.[5] The second term is the impulse response of a new operator of the form $\dfrac{c_1 p + c_0}{a_2 p^2 + a_1 p + a_0}$ and can be obtained in the manner of Sec. 2-16 (see also ref. 7).

2-15. Factored and Partial-fraction Representation of Complicated Linear Operators.

The setup methods of Sec. 2-13 will, in general, result in computer setups involving feedback around loops of n or more amplifiers. Although the spurious phase shift per summer or integrator (Secs. 3-19 and 3-20) may be well within reasonable component-accuracy specifications, accumulation of phase shift in loops of four or more amplifiers can sometimes cause increased errors or even high-frequency instability. As a rule, such trouble will be experienced only with especially unfavorable combinations of the given parameters A_i, B_k. If, as is often the case, we can rewrite a given transfer operator $H(p)$ as a product of simpler factors such as $\dfrac{T_1 p + 1}{T_2 p + 1}$, $\dfrac{T_1 p + 1}{\alpha_2 p^2 + \alpha_1 p + \alpha_0}$, each having a "stable" (decaying) impulse response, then it is advisable to represent $H(p)$ as a cascade (product) of the simpler operators.

Another possibility is to represent a complicated operator $H(p)$ as a sum of partial fractions $\dfrac{\beta}{T_2 p + 1}$, $\dfrac{\gamma_1 p + \gamma_0}{\alpha_2 p^2 + \alpha_1 p + \alpha_0}$, etc., in the manner of Fig. 2-16b. Note that each term can be scaled and checked separately.

2-16. The Impulse Response. Weighting-function Techniques for Computing Step Response, Ramp Response, and Frequency Response.

(a) It is often convenient to express the response $y(t)$ of a time-invariant linear transfer operator $H(p)$ to an input $x(t)$ as a convolution integral

$$y(t) = \int_{-\infty}^{\infty} h(t - \lambda) x(\lambda)\, d\lambda \qquad (2\text{-}56)$$

In the practically important cases where $m < n$ in Eq. (46), the *weighting function* $h(t - \lambda)$ exists and is bounded; $h(t)$ is related to the given frequency-response function $H(j\omega)$ by

$$h(t) = \int_{-\infty}^{\infty} H(j\omega) e^{j\omega t} \frac{d\omega}{2\pi} \qquad (2\text{-}57)$$

For physical realizability, the integral (56) for $y(t)$ must not depend on future values of $x(t)$, so that $h(t) = 0$ for $t < 0$. $h(t - \lambda)$ can be interpreted as the response (56) to a symmetrical unit impulse (Dirac delta function)[5] $\delta(t - \lambda)$ applied at the time $t = \lambda$ (*symmetrical-impulse response*).

In the case of initial-value problems with $x(t) = 0$ for $t \leq 0$, it is customary to replace Eq. (56) by

$$y(t) = \int_{0}^{\infty} h_+(t - \lambda) x(\lambda)\, d\lambda + y_T(t) \qquad (t > 0) \qquad (2\text{-}58)$$

where $y_T(t)$ is the zero-input transient response due to given nonzero initial values of $y, \dot{y}, \ldots,$ and/or $y^{(n-1)}$. $h_+(t)$ is the response to an *asymmetrical* unit impulse[5] $\delta_+(t)$ applied at (i.e., immediately after) $t = 0$; for physical realizability, $h_+(t) = 0$ for $t \leq 0$. While $h(t)$ and $h_+(t)$ are identical wherever they are continuous, they must not be confused if we are to avoid serious errors in Laplace-transform calculations; note that the unilateral Laplace transform of $\delta_+(t)$ is 1, while that of $\delta(t)$ is $\frac{1}{2}$.[5]

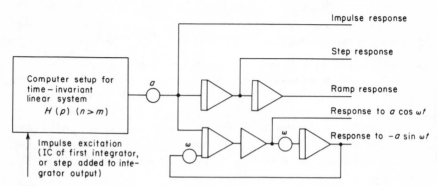

Fig. 2-19. Weighting-function method for producing the impulse response, step response, ramp response, and sinusoidal response of a time-invariant linear system, all in a single computer run (based on ref. 17).

(**b**) Physical generation of true impulse voltages is manifestly impossible, although one can approximate impulse functions through approximate electrical differentiation (Sec. 1-16) of sharply switched voltage steps. *The unit-impulse response*

$$h_+(t) = (p^n + a_{n-1}p^{(n-1)} + \cdots + a_0)^{-1}\delta_+(t) \qquad (n \neq 0)$$

with
$$y(0+0) = y(0+0) = \cdots = y^{(n-1)}(0+0) = 0 \qquad \left(p \equiv \frac{d}{dt}\right) \Bigg\} \qquad (2\text{-}59)$$

is, however, bounded and is easily obtained as the analog-computer solution of the zero-input initial-value problem

$$(p^n + a_{n-1}p^{n-1} + \cdots + a_0)h_+(t) = 0$$

with
$$y(0+0) = y(0+0) = \cdots = y^{(n-2)}(0+0) = 0$$
$$y^{(n-1)}(0+0) = 1 \qquad \left(p \equiv \frac{d}{dt}\right) \Bigg\} \qquad (2\text{-}60)$$

This fact is made evident by Laplace transformation of Eqs. (59) and (60).

It follows that *the impulse response of a more general time-invariant linear operator,*

$$y(t) = h_+(t) = \frac{b_m p^m + b_{m-1}p^{m-1} + \cdots + b_0}{p^n + a_{n-1}p^{n-1} + \cdots + a_0}\delta_+(t)$$

with $n > m$, $y(0+0) = \dot{y}(0+0) = \cdots = y^{(n-1)}(0+0) = 0 \qquad \left(p \equiv \frac{d}{dt}\right) \Bigg\} \qquad (2\text{-}61)$

is also bounded and is readily obtained from the analog-computer setup of Fig. 2-17*b* (Method 2, Sec. 2-13) *with zero input* and

$$z(0+0) = \dot{z}(0+0) = \cdots = z^{(n-2)}(0+0) = 0 \qquad z^{(n-1)}(0+0) = 1 \quad (2\text{-}62)$$

(**c**) A number of test waveforms $h_{\text{TEST}}(t)$ useful, e.g., for control-system studies are conveniently generated as impulse responses of simple time-invariant linear operators $H_{\text{TEST}}(p)$. Particularly useful examples are

$$
\begin{aligned}
&h_{\text{TEST}}(t) = aU_+(t) = \begin{cases} 0 \ (t \leq 0) \\ a \ (t > 0) \end{cases} && H_{\text{TEST}}(p) = \frac{a}{p} && \text{(STEP VOLTAGE)} \\[2mm]
&h_{\text{TEST}}(t) = \begin{cases} 0 \ (t \leq 0) \\ at \ (t > 0) \end{cases} && H_{\text{TEST}}(p) = \frac{a}{p^2} && \text{(RAMP VOLTAGE)} \\[2mm]
&h_{\text{TEST}}(t) = \begin{cases} 0 \ (t \leq 0) \\ a \cos \omega t \ (t > 0) \end{cases} && H_{\text{TEST}}(p) = \frac{ap}{p^2 + \omega^2} && \text{(COSINE VOLTAGE)} \\[2mm]
&h_{\text{TEST}}(t) = \begin{cases} 0 \ (t \leq 0) \\ a \sin \omega t \ (t > 0) \end{cases} && H_{\text{TEST}}(p) = \frac{a\omega}{p^2 + \omega^2} && \text{(SINE VOLTAGE)}
\end{aligned} \tag{2-63}
$$

To find the response $y(t)$ of a given computer-simulated time-invariant linear operator $H(p)$ to the test input $h_{\text{TEST}}(t)$, we can implement

$$
y(t) = H(p)h_{\text{TEST}}(t) = H(p)[H_{\text{TEST}}(p)\delta_+(t)] \tag{2-64}
$$

At this point, we note that *time-invariant linear operators commute* (Sec. 2-12), *so that we can just as well obtain the desired response* $y(t)$ *from*

$$
y(t) = H(p)h_{\text{TEST}}(t) = H_{\text{TEST}}(p)[H(p)\delta_+(t)] = H_{\text{TEST}}(p)h_+(t) \tag{2-65}
$$

We can therefore operate on the impulse response $h_+(t)$ of the given operator $H(p)$ to obtain its step response, ramp response, sinusoidal response, etc., *all in a single computer run* (Fig. 2-19).[17]

SUMMARY OF SCALING AND SETUP PROCEDURE.
SPECIAL PRECAUTIONS

2-17. Review and Summary. Assuming that we are given a problem whose mathematical representation makes analog-computer solution reasonable, we shall employ the following general procedure:

Step 1. Obtain a written problem statement for the record. This statement should include

> *A clear indication of the study objective*
> *Given mathematical relations (differential equations, etc.)*
> *Given numerical values of parameters, initial values of variables, given functions*
> *Parameters to be varied in the course of the study*
> *Estimated ranges of variables and derivatives*
> *Any available solutions or checks*

Step 2. Rewrite all differential equations as first-order equations of the form (15), introducing new variables as necessary.

Step 3. Choose the time scale, and determine tentative scale factors for each variable and function (Secs. 2-2 and 2-6). Write scaled machine equations (Secs. 2-3 to 2-7); do not forget to scale initial conditions, limiting levels, etc.

Step 4. Draw a tentative computer-setup block diagram corresponding to the scaled machine equations (Secs. 2-4 to 2-7). Review and simplify this block diagram, then check whether the computer setup correctly imple-

ments the given mathematical relations (Sec. 2-8). *Consider the possibility of overloading an amplifier by connecting its output to too many potentiometers and/or other computing elements.*

At this point, we are ready to patch the actual computer setup; some computer laboratories first use the block diagrams to prepare *setup sheets* listing input and output connections for each computing element together with the settings of coefficient potentiometers and function generators.

Step 5. Interconnect the various computing elements with patchcords, following the revised block diagram, equation by equation. Do this with a view to short, convenient connections. Carefully note the number of each actual computing element on the block diagram for reference.

Step 6. Set potentiometers, initial values, limiting levels, and function generators. Set or check recorder calibration.

Step 7. Check the entire setup. If at all possible, have a second person check steps 2 to 6 independently. A good check is, again, to rederive the machine equations from the computer setup.

The machine is now ready for a *static check* of amplifier output voltages in RESET and for trial runs. Sometimes, parts of a computer setup will be checked separately. Revise the setup and rescale where necessary (Sec. 2-8). *Be sure to keep a careful record of all setup and scale-factor changes.* Colored dummy plugs may be used to indicate temporarily removed patchcords.

Every block diagram should be carefully inspected for possible setup simplifications, redundant phase inverters, etc.; simplified setups not only conserve equipment but also remove possible error sources. The most useful setup improvements may be obtained by mathematical transformation of the problem equations rather than by computer-setup changes as such (Secs. 2-4b, 2-10b, and 2-11b). A roughly systematic matrix notation for specification and simplification especially of linear analog-computer setups exists[18-21] but seems to have few practical advantages; such a notation might, however, be of interest for automatic analog-computer setup by a digital-computer program.

2-18. Some Special Precautions.   It is advisable to avoid, insofar as possible,

Feedback loops which do not contain an integrator or integrators ("algebraic loops").

Summing-amplifier gains in excess of 30.

Analog-computer setups involving more integrators than are actually required.

Computer setups in which more than a single amplifier output represents the same variable. In the latter case, it is advisable to test the sensitivity of the solution to a small gain change in one of the channels generating the variable. Similar precautions apply when a coefficient must be set by more than one coefficient-setting potentiometer.

A number of *methods for checking solutions* and *methods for checking the operating condition of the machine* are discussed in Secs. 3-1, 11-4, and 12-5.

REFERENCES AND BIBLIOGRAPHY

General

1. Rubin, A. I.: Analog-computer Programming, Scaling, and Problem Preparation, in Huskey, H. D., and G. A. Korn, *Computer Handbook*, McGraw-Hill, New York, 1962.
2. ———: Function Generators, *PCC Rept.* 116, Electronics Associates, Inc., Computing Center, Princeton, N.J., 1959.
3. Fisher, M. E.: Avoiding the Need for Dividing Units, *J. Sci. Instr.*, August, 1957.
4. Hausner, A.: Parametric Techniques for Eliminating Division and Treating Singularities in Computer Solutions of Ordinary Differential Equations, *IRETEC*, February, 1962.
5. Korn, G. A., and T. M. Korn: *Mathematical Handbook for Scientists and Engineers*, McGraw-Hill, New York, 1961.
6. Jackson, A. S.: *Analog Computation*, McGraw-Hill, New York, 1960.
7. Fifer, S.: *Analogue Computation*, McGraw-Hill, New York, 1961.
8. Minorski, N.: *Nonlinear Mechanics*, Van Nostrand, Princeton, N.J., 1963.
9. Kuntze, K.: Lösung von Schwingungsproblemen, *Ann. AICA*, October, 1960.

Computer Setups for Linear Transfer Operators

10. Beck, C.: A Method for Solving Problems on the REAC by the Use of Transfer Functions without Passive Networks, *Project Cyclone Symposium* I, Reeves Instrument Corp., Garden City, N.Y., March, 1951.
11. ———: Treating Transfer Functions on Analog Computers, *Elec. Mfg.*, October, 1958.
12. Kogan, B. Y.: Methods of Simulating Rational-fraction Functions without the Use of Differentiating Elements, *Automatika i Telemekhanika*, January, 1960.
13. Harbert, F. C.: The Simulation of Transfer Functions on the Analog Computer, *Electronic Eng.*, June, 1960.
14. Matyaš, J.: Letter to the Editor, *Automatika i Telemekhanika*, October, 1960.
15. Miller, K. S., and J. B. Walsh: Initial Conditions in Computer Simulation, *IRETEC*, March, 1961.

Weighting-function Techniques

16. Aseltine, J. A., and R. R. Favreau: Weighting Functions for Time-varying Feedback Systems, *Proc. IRE*, October, 1954.
17. Rogers, A. E., and T. W. Connolly: *Analog Computation in Engineering Design*, McGraw-Hill, New York, 1960.

Matrix Programming Techniques

18. Horn, R. E., and P. M. Honnell: Matrix Programming of Electronic Analog Computers, *Trans. AIEE (Communications and Electronics)*, September, 1958.
19. ———: Matrices in Analog Mathematical Machines, *J. Franklin Inst.*, September, 1955.
20. ———: Analog-computer Synthesis and Error Matrices, *Trans. AIEE*, **75** (1): 26 (March, 1956); see also *Electronic Eng.*, February, 1957.
21. ———: Electronic Network Synthesis of Linear Algebraic Matrix Equations, *Trans. AIEE*, **78** (1): 1028 (January, 1960).

22. Robichaud et al.: *Signal-flow Graphs and Applications*, Prentice-Hall, Englewood Cliffs, N.J., 1962.

Special Circuits for Roots, Division, etc.
(See also Chap. 12)

23. Abrahanian, V. V.: An Improved Square-root Circuit, *Instruments and Control Systems*, April, 1963.
24. Witsenhausen, H.: Utilization optimum des multiplieurs electromécaniques, *Proc. 2d AICA Conf.*, Strasbourg, France, 1958, Presses Académiques Euopéennes, Brussels, 1959.

Simulation of Time-variable Linear Systems

25. Korn, G. A.: *Random-process Simulation and Measurements*, McGraw-Hill, New York, 1965.

PART **II**

DESIGN OF THE BASIC
COMPUTING ELEMENTS

CHAPTER 3

COMPUTER ACCURACY. DESIGN OF NETWORKS, COEFFICIENT POTENTIOMETERS, AND OPERATIONAL AMPLIFIERS

COMPUTER ACCURACY AND OTHER DESIGN SPECIFICATIONS

3-1. A Discussion of Analog-computer Accuracy. Electronic analog computers can produce true solution accuracies varying all the way between 0.05 and 15 per cent; and, in each case, such results may or may not be entirely satisfactory. True solution accuracies can, in general, be specified only for special-purpose computers performing a precisely circumscribed class of operations. General-purpose analog computers are applied to a very wide class of problems, and solution accuracies depend so radically on the specific problem solved that one is restricted to the specification of *component accuracies* for individual computing elements. Since some computing-element errors, such as those due to noise and d-c offsets, exist even when the component output voltages are zero, it is customary to specify analog-computer component errors in per cent of half-scale (i.e., in volts for ± 100-volt analog computers).*

The effects of component accuracies on the computer solution of, say, a system of differential equations are not easy to predict in general and will depend strongly on the problem under investigation. Although a general theory of differential-analyzer errors exists,[1] mathematical error prediction for even moderately complex problems is usually more difficult

---

* The questionable practice of specifying analog-computer component accuracies in per cent of *full scale* (i.e., of 200 volts for ± 100-volt analog computers) is meaningful only after division by 2 and is being gradually discarded.

to obtain than, say, a precise solution of the problem by a digital computer. Hence, many analog-computer centers rely on digital check solutions of every tenth to thirtieth analog-computer solution unless, as is often the case, the investigator can rely on his professional knowledge of the behavior of the simulated systems, components, or subsystems. Checks on known solutions for special parameter values are often helpful (e.g., omission of air resistance and perturbations in ballistic-trajectory computations).

A perhaps more interesting approach to error estimation is the use of the analog computer itself for the prediction of component-error effects on the final solution. Methods of this type should disclose, for instance, whether or not a given analog-computer solution is "stable" in the sense that small changes in coefficients or component accuracies will not generate large departures from a given solution. Basically, such methods involve the introduction of artificial errors such as bias voltages, phase shift, increased or decreased coefficients, and added step or impulse functions in selected computing elements, and comparison of the resulting changed solutions with the original analog-computer solution.[30] Judicious use of such methods permits an investigator to decide whether suspected or real component inaccuracies can produce serious changes in the analog-computer solution. As an example, a d-c drift voltage added to the output of a simulated servomotor will be naturally decreased if the simulated motor forms part of a simulated high-gain position-servo loop. On the other hand, initial-condition or forcing-function errors in the open-loop integration of a ballistic trajectory may cause substantial errors in the solution. Even more serious error effects are found in solutions of nonlinear oscillation problems, where small changes in initial conditions or coefficients can lead to a mode jump with radically changed solution behavior. In problems of the latter type, no single analog-computer solution can be relied on. It is necessary to show the mode-change behavior through an entire family of solutions with different values of the critical parameter.

More sophisticated versions of this approach have led to various perturbation techniques and to the theory of parameter-influence coefficients (Secs. 12-2 and 12-4). The effects of insufficient computing bandwidth are similarly investigated through repetition of solutions on different time scales (*time-scale check*, Sec. 11-4c).

Solution checks by *resubstitution* of computer solutions into the given differential equations have been suggested[2,31] and may become increasingly practical in combined analog-digital computer systems (Sec. 12-5).

3-2. Component Accuracy: Static and Dynamic Errors. (a) **Static Accuracy, Step Response, and Small-signal Frequency Response.** Analog computing elements are, in general, most accurate for constant input or inputs (specified *static or d-c component accuracy*) and exhibit increasing *dynamic errors* as the output changes more rapidly. The *response to small and large input-voltage steps* is generally of interest, especially in the case of iterative differential analyzers, where frequent switching is required (Sec. 10-6).   Step-response specifications indicate how quickly a computing-element output settles to within a stated percentage of the correct static value after a step disturbance and also specify per cent overshoot, ringing, etc.

To describe dynamic errors for small input changes (up to, say, 10 per cent of half-scale), we note that a small sinusoidal variation of one of the inputs of operational amplifiers, of multipliers, and of certain function generators will produce a roughly sinusoidal output variation.   It is then possible to plot output amplitude and phase for constant input amplitude against frequency (*small-signal frequency response* to the input in question).

Honest component specifications will identify error percentages measured immediately after component adjustments and after a reasonable period of time, say, 8 hours or 1 week.   This is especially true for electronic analog computers comprising solid-state components subject to drift with time and/or with temperature changes.

Whenever possible, both static and dynamic accuracy measurements are made by *difference or null methods;* i.e., the difference between actual and desired computing-element outputs for specified inputs is displayed and/or recorded (see Secs. 4-21, 7-20, and 8-1 for examples).

(b) Phase Errors. The small-signal sinusoidal-error frequency response of many computing elements takes the form shown in Fig. 3-1*a*. We note that *the phase error becomes appreciable long before the amplitude error can even be measured.*   Figures 3-1*b* and *c* indicate that such phase-shift errors can cause considerable computing errors in spite of the practically ideal amplitude response; for small errors, the true absolute percentage error due to pure phase error is $\epsilon = 100\delta$, where δ is the phase error measured in radians, or about 1.8 per cent per degree of phase error.

For the typical frequency response $a/(j\omega/2\pi f_1 + 1)(-3$ db point at f_1 cps), the low-frequency phase shift (lag) is arctan $f/f_1 \approx f/f_1$ radians at f cps; *note that we already have 0.57 deg lag or 1 per cent error at $0.01f_1$ cps.* A slightly underdamped second-order frequency-response function causes less phase shift at very low frequencies but produces step-response overshoot or "ringing."

The usual computing voltages are rarely sinusoidal; typically, their *high-frequency components are smaller in amplitude than low-frequency components.*   For instance, in the case of a *symmetrical square wave* with peak-to-peak amplitude $2A$ and period T_0,

$$f(t) = \frac{4}{\pi} A \left(\cos \omega_0 t - \frac{1}{3} \cos 3\omega_0 t + \frac{1}{5} \cos 5\omega_0 t - \cdots \right) \qquad \left(\omega_0 = \frac{2\pi}{T_0} \right)$$

the individual sinusoidal components contribute roughly equal absolute phase-shift errors, assuming that phase-shift errors are small and proportional to frequency. In this example, some of the individual phase-shift errors cancel partially; but *a conservative if somewhat arbitrary rule of thumb ensuring adequate step response might be to specify less than p deg component phase error for 50/T cps, where p is the specified static component accuracy in per cent of half-scale, and T is the duration of a typical computer run.* This rule is, generally speaking, satisfied by the phase inverters of existing analog computers, but less often by their multipliers.

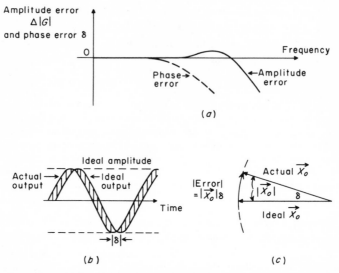

FIG. 3-1. Typical small-signal frequency response of an analog computing element to steady-state sinusoidal input (*a*), and comparison of ideal and actual output sinusoids (*b*) and phasors (*c*). Note that phase shift can cause substantial dynamic errors while the amplitude response is still essentially ideal.

(c) Rate-limit Specifications and Switch-timing Errors. Even with adequate small-signal frequency response, the working-frequency range of most analog computing elements is limited by *output-voltage rate limiting*, a nonlinear phenomenon usually associated with the currents drawn by load or circuit capacitances, or with servo velocity limiting (Secs. 4-7 and 8-3). A given output-rate limit of, say, r volts/sec necessarily restricts the frequency f of an undistorted sinusoidal output waveform $b \sin 2\pi f \tau$ to $r/2\pi b$ cps, where b is the sine-wave amplitude. Note, however, that the absolute output-voltage rate of any conventional integrator is never required to exceed $100a$ per-cent machine units (or volts) per second, where a is the sum of all integrator input gains, since no input can exceed one machine unit in absolute value. This fact determines, for instance, the maximum output rate ever required of a servomultiplier driven by an integrator. Integrator input variables, however, may require much faster rates of change and may, in particular, comprise stepwise changes.

The maximum *timing error* due to a switching delay T_D in integrator mode-control switches or relays, operational relays, or electronic switches and sample-hold readout devices is rT_D, where r is the maximum absolute rate of the voltage being switched. We note here that *timing errors rather than computing-element bandwidths may constitute the ultimate speed limitation for fast analog computation.* If, for example, a group of ± 100-volt computing elements producing the 10-cps output

$$X_o = 100 \sin 2\pi(10\tau) \text{ volts} \qquad (\tau > 0) \qquad (3\text{-}1)$$

are switched into COMPUTE only 0.1 msec too early, the resulting voltage error is $2\pi/10$ volts, or over 0.6 per cent of half-scale. Again, in a ± 10-volt iterative analog computer producing the 5-Kc waveform

$$X_o = 10 \sin 2\pi(5,000\tau) \text{ volts} \qquad (\tau > 0) \qquad (3\text{-}2)$$

a switching delay of only 0.25 μsec can produce an error of $\pi/40$ volts, or almost 0.8 per cent of half-scale.

3-3. Other Design Specifications. Data needed to determine the suitability of computing equipment for a given application (including its compatibility with other system components) include specifications such as size, weight, and power-supply requirements, and design limits on temperature, humidity, shock, etc., required to maintain a specified or suitably derated performance.

In the writers' opinion, *maintenance-free operation* (few or no periodic adjustments) ranks in importance with accuracy and frequency response, and frequently ahead of cost. Generally speaking, solid-state devices show smaller aging effects than vacuum tubes but are more sensitive to temperature variations. High-accuracy computing-element designs may place limiter or switching diodes and transistors into small temperature-controlled ovens, employ compensation by temperature-sensitive resistors, or mount solid-state devices in assemblies of high thermal inertia and well away from heat-generating vacuum tubes.

COEFFICIENT-SETTING POTENTIOMETERS

3-4. Specifications and Construction (see also Sec. 8-5). A *potentiometer* is an adjustable resistive voltage divider consisting of a fixed resistance with a movable sliding contact. In a *simple coefficient-setting potentiometer (scale-factor potentiometer, attenuator)*, one end of the potentiometer resistance (LO *terminal*) is grounded; the input voltage X_1 is applied to the other end (HI *terminal*), so that the slider (ARM *terminal*) produces the adjustable output voltage $X_o = \alpha X_1$, where $0 \leq \alpha \leq 1$

(Fig. 3-2a; see also Sec. 1-9). In a *three-terminal coefficient-setting potentiometer*, two input voltages X_1, X_2 are applied to the HI and LO terminals, so that the ARM terminal produces an adjustable output of the form

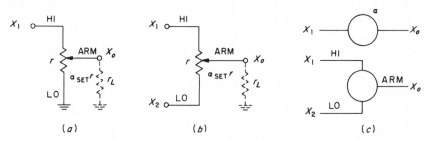

(a) (b) (c)

FIG. 3-2. Two-terminal coefficient-setting potentiometer (a), three-terminal coefficient-setting potentiometer (b), and block-diagram symbols (c). The true coefficient α indicated in the block diagram includes the effect of the load (Sec. 3-5). The load resistance r_L is most frequently due to the input resistor of an operational amplifier.

$$X_o = k[\alpha X_1 + (1 - \alpha)X_2], \quad \text{where} \quad 0 \leq \alpha \leq 1, \quad 0 < k \leq 1 \quad \text{(Fig. 3-2b;}$$
see also Sec. 3-5).

In the most common types of potentiometers, a wirewound resistance wound on a flat card or on a cylindrical mandrel is bent into circular shape, with the sliding contact mounted on a revolving arm (Fig. 3-3).

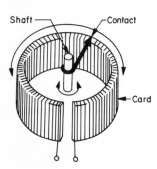

FIG. 3-3. Rotary potentiometer with a wirewound resistance element wound on a flat card. The actual slider contact can be a precious-metal knob or bar, or a single- or multiple-spring finger.[3-6] (*Copyright HELIPOT Corporation, reprinted by permission.*)

Resistance elements consisting of carbon or metal films deposited on ceramic are also employed. Slider contacts can be spring-mounted precious-metal buttons or bars, or single or multiple wire contacts.[3-6] Potentiometer *resistance* varies between 1,000 and 100,000 ohms and must be determined by a compromise between available amplifier power and potentiometer resolution, which favor high resistance, and resistance stability, phase-shift, and/or loading considerations (Secs. 3-5 and 3-6), which favor lower potentiometer resistance. The resistance of a coefficient-setting potentiometer is usually specified within 0.5 per cent and should remain stable within 0.01 to 0.1 per cent in a given environment. Most practical coefficient-setting potentiometers exhibit *end resistances* (about 3 ohms at the HI end and 30 ohms at the LO end for a 30K potentiometer), which interfere with precise realization of coefficients equal to one and zero.

Computing potentiometers are usually rated between 2 and 5 watts to reduce self-heating effects, even though much less power is actually dissipated. It is wise to fuse the potentiometer-arm connection in order to avoid potentiometer failure due to faulty patching (grounding of the potentiometer arm at high coefficient settings); $\frac{1}{32}$-amp fuses adequately protect 30,000-ohm 5-watt potentiometers, which have current ratings of about 13 mA.

The conformity of the actual coefficient set with a (usually) linear *dial calibration* is of interest in special applications (e.g., comparison potentiometers, Sec. 3-5). In electronic analog computers, however, most coefficient-setting potentiometers are set by actual measurement of their output voltages (Sec. 3-5); so that potentiometer conformity and linearity will be more properly discussed in Sec. 8-7 in connection with servo-driven potentiometers used for multiplication and function generation. The static accuracy of a coefficient-setting potentiometer is, then, essentially determined by its *setting stability* (ability to maintain set coefficients), and its *resetting precision*, which involves dial readability and backlash as well as potentiometer setting stability. Both these specifications are quoted in per cent of the total potentiometer scale; 0.01 to 0.1 per cent are obtainable. Some potentiometer applications require *mechanical ruggedness* to maintain settings in spite of vibrations and shock. In addition, *freedom from microphonism and electrical noise* is desirable.

The resetting precision of a potentiometer cannot be better than its *resolution*. In wirewound potentiometers, resolution is limited by the resistance of one wire turn on a card or mandrel. For increased resolution, the potentiometer-arm contact may slide along a single resistance wire (*slide-wire potentiometer*). More frequently, the resistance wire is wound on a helical mandrel having 2 to 20 turns; so that the potentiometer arm must be capable of axial displacement as well as rotation (*helical potentiometer*, Fig. 3-4). This method of construction is the one most commonly used for coefficient-setting potentiometers and permits better than 0.01 per cent resolution for a 30,000-ohm potentiometer. Figure 3-5 shows two types of *multiturn dials* used with such potentiometers.

Another type of potentiometer has a rectilinear resistance element with a sliding contact positioned by a lead screw turned by a multiturn dial. *Deposited-film potentiometers* have practically infinite resolution. If the resolution of a given potentiometer is not sufficient for a given application, one may add variable series resistances at the top or bottom of the potentiometer to permit fine adjustment; special dials permit alternate fine and coarse adjustments. Inexpensive computers also use one-turn carbon- or metal-film potentiometers with friction drives; it is difficult to adjust a one-turn potentiometer to within better than about 0.25 per cent without some sort of reduction drive.

Fig. 3-4. Ten-turn potentiometer with helical resistance element and precious-metal contacts (HELIPOT precision potentiometer). (*Copyright HELIPOT Corporation, reprinted by permission.*)

(*a*)   (*b*)

Fig. 3-5. Typical dials for multiple-turn coefficient-setting potentiometers: Type RB DUODIAL turn-counting dial (*a*) and Borg Model 1301 MICRODIAL (*b*). Note the dial-lock levers. Such dials can be read and set to 1 part in 10,000 or better, corresponding to the resolution and linearity attainable with high-quality helical potentiometers. (*a, Copyright HELIPOT Corporation, reprinted by permission; b, courtesy of the George W. Borg Corporation.*)

3-5. Loading Considerations and Potentiometer Setting. Referring to Fig. 3-2a, let α_{SET} be the nominal setting or fraction of the total potentiometer resistance r between the ARM terminal and the grounded LO terminal of a potentiometer connected to a load resistance r_L. The node equation for the ARM terminal is readily solved for the output voltage

$$X_o = \alpha X_1$$
$$= \alpha_{\text{SET}} X_1 \left[1 - \frac{\alpha_{\text{SET}}(1 - \alpha_{\text{SET}})(r/r_L)}{1 + \alpha_{\text{SET}}(1 - \alpha_{\text{SET}})(r/r_L)} \right] \quad (0 \le \alpha_{\text{SET}} \le 1) \quad (3\text{-}3)$$

The effect of the load tends to make the true coefficient α set on the potentiometer smaller than the nominal setting α_{SET}; specifically,

$$\alpha_{\text{SET}} - \alpha = \frac{\alpha_{\text{SET}}^2(1 - \alpha_{\text{SET}})(r/r_L)}{1 + \alpha_{\text{SET}}(1 - \alpha_{\text{SET}})(r/r_L)}$$
$$\left[\approx \alpha_{\text{SET}}^2(1 - \alpha_{\text{SET}})\frac{r}{r_L} \approx \alpha^2(1 - \alpha)\frac{r}{r_L} \text{ for } \frac{r}{r_L} \ll 1 \right] \quad (3\text{-}4)$$

Equation (4) yields exact or approximate *loading corrections* to be added to the desired coefficient α so as to produce the correct nominal potentiometer setting α_{SET} (Fig. 3-6).

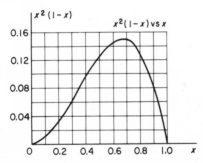

FIG. 3-6. This approximate potentiometer-loading correction chart, based on the relation $\alpha_{\text{SET}} - \alpha \approx \alpha^2(1 - \alpha)(r/r_L)(r/r_L \ll 1)$, is useful for $r/r_L \ll 0.3$ and setting accuracies down to 0.1 per cent. To use the chart, multiply the ordinate corresponding to the desired coefficient α by r/r_L and add the resulting correction to α to obtain α_{SET}. (EXAMPLE: for $r = 20$K, $r_L = 100$K, $\alpha = 0.4$, we find $\alpha_{\text{SET}} = 0.4 + 0.02 = 0.42$.) For greater accuracy, one requires separate tables based on the exact formula (3-4) for each value of r/r_L.

In the case of the *three-terminal potentiometer* of Fig. 3-2b, the nodal equation for the ARM terminal yields

$$X_o = [\alpha_{\text{SET}} X_1 + (1 - \alpha_{\text{SET}}) X_2]$$
$$\left[1 - \frac{\alpha_{\text{SET}}(1 - \alpha_{\text{SET}})(r/r_L)}{1 + \alpha_{\text{SET}}(1 - \alpha_{\text{SET}})(r/r_L)} \right] \quad (0 \le \alpha_{\text{SET}} \le 1) \quad (3\text{-}5)$$

Note that the load reduces the output voltage without affecting the ratio of the coefficients of X_1 and X_2.

Potentiometer loading effects prevent the use of linear dial calibrations without loading corrections depending on the specific potentiometer load in each problem. In general-purpose electronic analog computers, one prefers to set coefficients by *direct measurement of the potentiometer output corresponding to a reference-voltage input, with the load (succeeding computing elements) connected;* this does away with the nuisance of loading charts and, incidentally, with the necessity for adjusting a possibly large number of potentiometer-dial zeros accurately. The dial calibration is

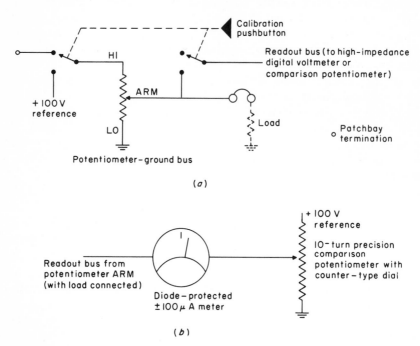

Fig. 3-7. Pushbutton potentiometer-setting circuit (*a*), and comparison potentiometer (*b*). It is customary to disconnect and ground all amplifier summing junctions during the potentiometer-setting operation to prevent amplifier overloads (POT SET mode, Sec. 10-3).

needed only for rough settings and, possibly, for resetting coefficients used earlier.

Figure 3-7*a* shows how a simple double-pole/double-throw pushbutton switch associated with each potentiometer connects its input to the computer reference power supply and the output to a measuring device (readout bus) without disconnecting the load. The operator can depress the readout button and set the dial with one hand. The simple pushbutton readout system is much more convenient and foolproof than potentiometer-setting schemes employing selector buttons and stepping relays to connect potentiometers to the readout bus; in the writers' opinion, stepping-relay systems are justified only if automatic logging of coefficients by a printer or tape punch is contemplated, or if the potentiometers are to be set by an automatic servosystem (Sec. 11-2).

Unquestionably, the most convenient voltage-readout device for potentiometer setting is a *digital voltmeter*, which can also serve for setting initial conditions, static checks, and general readout (see also Secs. 11-2 to 11-4). In inexpensive analog computers, potentiometers are set, again with the load connected, by null comparison with a precision *comparison potentiometer* having an accurately calibrated dial (Fig. 3-7b). After the desired coefficient is first set on the comparison potentiometer, the operator depresses the potentiometer-readout button and rotates the dial of the coefficient-setting potentiometer until the meter indicates zero current; note that the comparison potentiometer is not loaded at this point. Accurately linear multiturn helical wirewound potentiometers with counter-type dials (Fig. 3-5b) are useful as comparison potentiometers and permit coefficient settings to within better than 0.05 per cent.

Very small potentiometer settings (below 0.1) are advantageously set by means of *two* cascaded coefficient-setting potentiometers, with the one closer to the output adjusted first to avoid changes of the load on the first one. *Three-terminal potentiometers* can be set with the LO terminal temporarily grounded, or by an output-voltage measurement depending on the specific application.

Servo setting of coefficient-setting potentiometers will be discussed in connection with semiautomatic and automatic programming systems in Sec. 11-2.

3-6. Dynamic Errors and Capacitor Compensation. With increasing computing frequencies, the high-frequency phase shift in coefficient-setting potentiometers may greatly exceed phase shift in other computing elements and can introduce serious dynamic errors into computations (see also Sec. 3-24). Potentiometer phase shift is mainly due to the capacitive load produced by computer circuits and wiring, and by the distributed capacitances of the potentiometer resistance, housing, and/or copper mandrel. With wirewound potentiometer resistance elements wound on flat cards or small-diameter mandrels, the effects of potentiometer *inductance* are not ordinarily felt at computing frequencies below 1 Mc.

Potentiometer and load capacitances cause both lag and lead effects. Figure 3-8 shows a simplified equivalent circuit which matches the frequency-response characteristics of helical-copper-mandrel potentiometers quite accurately;[9,13,14] Fig. 3-9 shows typical phase shift vs. frequency for a 30K potentiometer of this type. While an ideal voltage divider would not introduce any phase changes at all, the wirewound potentiometer is seen to introduce a lag at high potentiometer settings and a lead at low potentiometer settings.

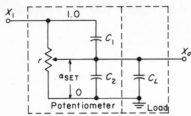

FIG. 3-8. Simplified equivalent circuit for a 10-turn copper-mandrel potentiometer (Beckman Helipot), useful for potentiometer settings α_{SET} between 0.05 and 0.95, r between 10K and 100K, and frequencies below $1/24\pi r C_1$. For type A Helipots, C_1 equals C_2 and varies between 200 pF ($r = 10K$) and 225 pF ($r = 100K$). C_L is the load capacitance, including wiring capacitance. The potentiometer phase shift is

$$\delta_P = \omega r C_1 (1 - \alpha_{\text{SET}})$$
$$\cdot \left(1 - \alpha_{\text{SET}} \frac{C_1 + C_2 + C_L}{C_1}\right)$$

(*Based on ref. 14.*)

Potentiometer phase shift decreases with the potentiometer resistance, but this cannot be reduced below a minimum value determined by amplifier power and, in wirewound potentiometers, by the required resolution. For fast (repetitive) analog computers which do not require setting stability below 0.1 per cent, the best type of coefficient-setting potentiometer might be a type with a linear deposited-film resistance element with the slider positioned by a multiturn dial turning a lead screw. Such potentiometers have negligible inductance and distributed capacitance; note, though, that potentiometer construction can do nothing about the effects of capacitive loading due to computer circuits and wiring.

Capacitor compensation permits the use of high-stability wirewound helical potentiometers at frequencies as high as 20 Kc. Suitably chosen compensating capacitors are switched, patched, or plugged between the ARM and HI terminals for high potentiometer settings, and between the ARM and LO terminals for low settings. The correct capacitance values

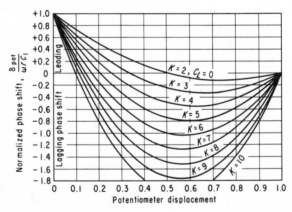

FIG. 3-9. Normalized potentiometer phase shift $\delta_P/\omega r C_1 \approx (1 - \alpha_{\text{SET}})(1 - K\alpha_{\text{SET}})$, where $K = \dfrac{C_1 + C_2 + C_L}{C_1} = 2 + \dfrac{C_L}{C_1}$ and $r_L \gg \alpha_{\text{SET}}(1 - \alpha_{\text{SET}})r$. The approximate formula for $\delta_P/\omega r C_1$ is valid up to 6.6 Kc for $r = 10K$ and up to 600 cps for $r = 100K$. (*From ref. 14.*)

for different potentiometer settings, load resistances, and load capacitances may be tabulated for each type of potentiometer.   One can also select compensating capacitors with the aid of an oscilloscope displaying the potentiometer output for a square-wave test input; conceivably, such test circuits could be combined with the potentiometer-setting system.

If the resistive and capacitive loads on the coefficient-setting potentiometers are known or can be standardized, compensating capacitors could be switched simply in accordance with the potentiometer setting. As a perhaps more practical alternative, Figs. 3-10 and 3-11 show the *application of compensating capacitors to potentiometer taps* and illustrate

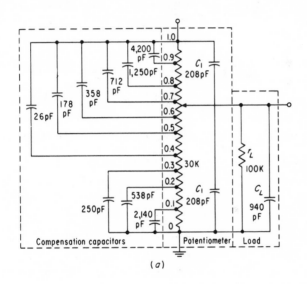

(a)

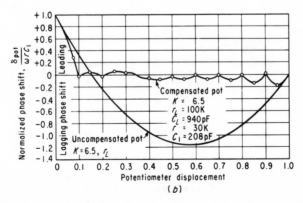

Fig. 3-10a, b. Phase compensation of a potentiometer (a), and effect on phase shift (b).   Phase compensation is designed for a specific resistance-capacitance load.[14]

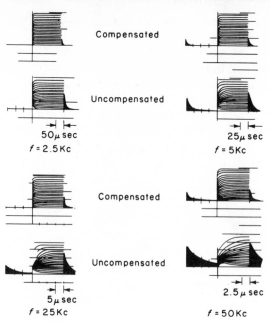

FIG. 3-10c. Effect of phase compensation on potentiometer step response.[14]

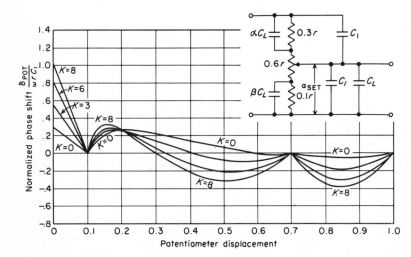

FIG. 3-11. This simple two-tap compensation circuit compares nicely with the 10-tap circuit of Fig. 3-10; note the nonuniform tap spacing.[13]

the remarkable frequency-response improvement obtainable by this method.[8,9,13,14]

COMPUTING RESISTORS AND CAPACITORS.
PARASITIC-IMPEDANCE EFFECTS

3-7. Computing Resistors. (a) Resistance Stability. Wire-wound Computing Resistors. *Resistance stability* is the ability of a resistor to maintain its nominal resistance value. Note that many committed summing amplifiers and electronic multipliers require accurate resistance *ratios*, which are easier to establish and maintain than individually accurate resistance values. References 10 to 12 describe detailed practical methods for precision measurement or matching of resistances or resistance ratios.

Most computing resistors are *wirewound resistors* noninductively wound on ceramic or thermosetting-plastic rods. The resistance winding undergoes a temperature- and current-recycling process to eliminate instability (relaxation effects due to stresses in the wire). The initially intentionally high resistance is then trimmed to its nominal value. To obtain a stable resistor, one must carefully maintain the insulation between windings, which are usually separated into individual subwindings or pies; prolonged baking and immediate impregnation or encapsulation with plastic or ceramic keeps out moisture.

Wirewound resistors stable to within 50 to 1,000 ppm at constant temperature are commercially available; and suitable resistance-wire alloys yield *temperature coefficients* less than 25 ppm/deg C. Resistors should, of course, be trimmed at or near their typical operating temperature. One attempts to minimize the effects of *self-heating* due to the current in the resistor by using the largest power rating (wire diameter and radiating surface) practical for a given physical size, and by providing suitable air circulation. Resistance changes due to self-heating may vary between 3 and 3,000 ppm/watt at rated current and constant ambient temperature. Plastic encapsulation tends to increase the thermal inertia of a resistor, but may aggravate self-heating effects. Resistor installation should also guard against generation of spurious voltages due to thermal gradients and contact potentials.

Constant-temperature ovens used with some larger analog computers maintain resistance values within ± 15 ppm for ambient temperature changes of ± 20 deg C (see also Sec. 3-8). Resistors for electronic analog computers operating in a reasonable indoor environment will, in the writers' opinion, not really require constant-temperature ovens; but such ovens are often provided in any case for computing capacitors, and the use of an oven may permit the designer to specify slightly less expensive resistance wire.

Resistors used to make up resistance *ratios* are often encapsulated together in plastic or installed in a common oil bath, so that some temperature effects are effectively canceled out.

(b) Parasitic Inductance and Capacitance.   Carbon-film Resistors.   Figure 3-12 shows a simple a-c equivalent circuit for a physical resistor.   The equivalent impedance $Z_R(j\omega)$ of the resistor is given by

$$Z_R(j\omega) = R_{DC} \frac{j\omega(L_R/R_{DC}) + 1}{j\omega R_{DC}C_R + 1 - \omega^2 L_R C_R} \qquad (3\text{-}6)$$

where $R_{DC} = Z_R(0)$ is the nominal (d-c) resistance value.   The physical resistor effectively constitutes a low-Q resonant circuit, which can be tested by pulse excitation.

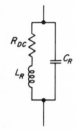

Wirewound computing resistors should have noninductive windings, not just to minimize the parasitic inductance L_R but also to reduce inductive pickup and crosstalk at high frequencies.   For noninductively wound wirewound resistors, the values of parasitic inductance L_R will be below $100R_{DC}$ mH, if R_{DC} is measured in megohms.   For $R_{DC} > 25\text{K}$, the effect of the inductance L_R is essentially negligible at signal frequencies below 1 Mc, in which case

FIG. 3-12. High-frequency equivalent circuit for a wirewound resistor.

$$Z_R(j\omega) \approx \frac{R_{DC}}{j\omega R_{DC}C_R + 1} \qquad (3\text{-}7)$$

Typical values of the resistor distributed capacitance C_R range between $1/2R_{DC}$ and $4/R_{DC}$ pF, if R_{DC} is measured in megohms. Resistor distributed capacitance has no adverse effect in properly designed summing amplifiers at computing frequencies up to 1 Mc (Sec. 3-19).   In integrators, however, errors due to resistor distributed capacitance prevent the use of wirewound resistors greater than 10^5 ohms already at about 100 cps (Sec. 3-20),[11,12] and carefully sealed *carbon-film computing resistors* are most frequently employed in fast electronic integrators.   The distributed capacitance of such resistors is essentially due to the resistor terminal caps and is independent of the resistance; 0.5 pF is a typical value for a $\frac{1}{2}$-watt carbon-film resistor.   The inductance of carbon-film resistors is essentially negligible (≤ 0.01 μH); their stability is better than 500 ppm/year at constant temperature, with a temperature coefficient less than 400 ppm/deg C.

3-8. Computing Capacitors: Stability.   The nominal capacitance value for a given capacitor depends somewhat on the method of measurement (Sec. 3-9).   Assuming that a capacitance-measurement method suitable for definition of computing capacitances is agreed on, one finds that capacitance values not only vary with temperature but are affected by their recent history with respect to temperature changes and mechanical stresses. Table 3-1 lists temperature coefficients of capacitance for various types of capacitors. If one desires to maintain nominal capacitance value within 0.05 per cent, a constant-temperature oven, maintained at a temperature somewhat above room temperature, may be required; a fast-cycling oven will stabilize capacitor temperatures within a narrower range than a slow-cycling oven.[12] In addition, any appreciable temperature transient will necessitate capacitor readjustment (*temperature-retrace error*).[14] Retrace accuracy for one to five temperature

Table 3-1. Properties of Dielectrics Used for Computing Capacitors (Typical Values)

Dielectric	Dissipation coefficient D (at 10 cps and 25 deg C)	Insulation resistance r_{DC} (megohms/μF)	Temperature coefficient of capacitance
Mylar........	8×10^{-4} to 14×10^{-4}	2×10^5 (20 deg C) 10^3 (100 deg C)	$+250$ ppm/deg C (20 to 80 deg C; larger at high and low temperatures)
Polystyrene...	1.4×10^{-4} to 2×10^{-4} (decreases from this figure with increasing frequency up to about 70 Kc, then increases again)	2×10^6 (20 deg C) 2×10^5 (60 deg C)	-50 to -100 ppm/deg C (-60 to $+60$ deg C)
Teflon........	0.7×10^{-4} to 1.2×10^{-4}	10^6 (0 deg C) 100 (160 deg C)	-250 ppm/deg C (-60 to $+160$ deg C)

cycles between -70 and $+120$ deg C can be within 0.03 per cent for high-quality plastic-film capacitors, with a maximum capacitance change below 0.1 per cent. Adjustment of capacitors located in an oven must be made without temperature transients after adjustment. It may be best to locate trimmer capacitors outside the capacitor oven. Ovens *refrigerated* to just below room temperature are also an attractive possibility (Sec. 11-1).

3-9. Capacitor Leakage and Dielectric Absorption (see also Secs. 3-20 and 3-24). (a) **Resistive Leakage.** The effects of *resistive leakage* shunting a computing capacitance can be reduced completely to leakage in the capacitor dielectric proper through installation of grounded conductors surrounding all capacitance terminations ("insulation with metal"; see also Sec. 5-13). The remaining leakage resistance r_{DC} in high-quality polystyrene capacitors will exceed 5×10^5 M/μF at 100 deg F.* The time constant of the resulting parallel resistance-capacitance combination will, then, exceed 5×10^5 sec, so that purely resistive leakage will affect computer accuracy noticeably only for relatively long computing or holding times or low frequencies (see also Fig. 3-14).

(b) Dielectric Absorption. Capacitor Models. Unfortunately, resistive leakage does not cause the only energy loss in capacitors. Activation-energy thresholds delay the dielectric polarization associated with capacitor-voltage changes, and thus cause frequency-dependent energy dissipation commonly referred to as *capacitor dielectric absorption.* This

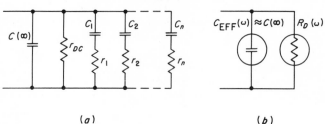

(a)   *(b)*

FIG. 3-13. Linear capacitor model (a), and nonlinear model (b). For a typical 1-μF 200-volt polystyrene computing capacitor, refs. 13 and 14 give $C(\infty) = 1$ μF. $r_{DC} = 10^6$M with the r_k, C_k combinations 60 pF, 2.65×10^6M; 132 pF, 1.21×10^5M; 204 pF, 7.80×10^3M; 216 pF, 737M; 219 pF, 72.7M; 234 pF, 6.80M. The resulting linear model is valid between 0 and 100 cps.

"relaxation" effect can be represented to a good approximation by a set of fixed leakage resistances $r_1, r_2, \ldots, r_n$ respectively in series with small capacitances $C_1, C_2, \ldots, C_n$ (Dow's capacitor model, Fig. 3-13a); values of n between 1 and 10 have been used.[10,13–18] The capacitor impedance operator given by the equivalent circuit of Fig. 3-13a can still be written in the form $Z_C(P) = 1/C(P)P$, where the "capacitance" $C(P)$ is no longer a constant but an operator

$$C(P) = C(\infty) + \frac{1}{r_{DC}P} + \sum_{k=1}^{n} \frac{C_k}{1 + r_k C_k P} \qquad (3\text{-}8)$$

For steady-state sinusoidal voltages and currents, one has the complex impedance $Z_C(j\omega) = 1/j\omega C(j\omega)$, where $C(j\omega)$ is the *complex capacitance*

$$C(j\omega) = C(\infty) + \frac{1}{j\omega r_{DC}} + \sum_{k=1}^{n} \frac{C_k}{1 + j\omega r_k C_k}$$

$$= C(\infty) + \frac{1}{j\omega r_{DC}} + \sum_{k=1}^{n} \frac{1 - j\omega r_k C_k}{1 + \omega^2 r_k^2 C_k^2} C_k = |C(j\omega)| e^{-jD(\omega)} \quad (3\text{-}9)$$

where $\qquad D(\omega) = -\arg C(j\omega) = \dfrac{1}{2\pi} \dfrac{\text{energy loss per cycle}}{\text{peak energy stored}} \qquad (3\text{-}10)$

* Leakage tends to increase with temperature. Where capacitor ovens are used, their temperatures should not greatly exceed room temperature; 100 deg F is a reasonable value.

is the *capacitor dissipation coefficient,* which measures both dielectric absorption and resistive leakage. In properly installed polystyrene capacitors, resistive leakage is negligible compared with dielectric absorption above 0.001 cps, so that $D(\omega)$ is essentially identical with the *coefficient of dielectric absorption* at higher frequencies.

One may also write the admittance $Y_C(j\omega) = 1/Z_C(j\omega)$ of the physical capacitor as

$$Y_C(j\omega) = \frac{1}{Z_C(j\omega)} = j\omega C(j\omega) = \frac{1}{R_D(\omega)} + j\omega C_{\text{EFF}}(\omega) \qquad (3\text{-}11)$$

in terms of the real but frequency-dependent resistance $R_D(\omega)$ and capacitance $C_{\text{EFF}}(\omega)$ of an *equivalent resistance-capacitance shunt circuit* (Fig. 3-13b), where

$$\left.\begin{aligned} \frac{1}{R_D(\omega)} &= -\omega \operatorname{Im} C(j\omega) = \frac{1}{r_{DC}} + \sum_{k=1}^{n} \frac{\omega^2 r_k C_k^2}{1 + \omega^2 r_k^2 C_k^2} \\ C_{\text{EFF}}(\omega) &= \operatorname{Re} C(j\omega) = C(\infty) + \sum_{k=1}^{n} \frac{C_k}{1 + \omega^2 r_k^2 C_k^2} \end{aligned}\right\} \qquad (3\text{-}12)$$

so that

$$C(j\omega) = C_{\text{EFF}}(\omega) + \frac{1}{j\omega R_D(\omega)} = C_{\text{EFF}}(\omega)[1 - jD(\omega)] \qquad (3\text{-}13)$$

with
$$D(\omega) = -\arg C(j\omega) = \frac{1}{\omega R_D(\omega) C_{\text{EFF}}(\omega)}$$

$$= \frac{1}{\omega r_{DC} C_{\text{EFF}}(\omega)} + \sum_{k=1}^{n} \frac{\omega r_k C_k}{1 + \omega^2 r_k^2 C_k^2} \frac{C_k}{C_{\text{EFF}}(\omega)} \qquad (3\text{-}14)$$

$C_{\text{EFF}}(\omega)$ is the "effective" capacitance actually measured by bridge or oscillator test circuits with sinusoidal excitation at the circular frequency ω; note that $C_{\text{EFF}}(\omega)$ is a function of frequency. For all high-quality capacitors, $\sum_{k=1}^{n} C_k \ll C(\infty)$, so that $C_{\text{EFF}}(\omega) \approx C(\infty)$ varies only slightly with frequency (about -0.02 per cent per decade of frequency increase for polystyrene between 0.1 and 100 cps).

With suitably chosen parameters $C(\infty)$, r_{DC}, C_k, r_k, Dow's capacitor model matches actual phase-shift measurements very accurately (Fig. 3-14). For practical dielectrics, one finds that the dissipation coefficient $D(\omega)$ is practically constant between 0.1 and 1,000 cps. Table 3-1 lists dissipation coefficients for various dielectrics; dielectric absorption in actual plastic films will depend mainly on the dielectric grains and impurities obtained in each specific manufacturing process.[15,18] Polystyrene capacitors are most commonly used in high-quality electronic analog computers. Production of improved polyethylene and Teflon films is still experimental but holds promise for the future. Mylar is a reasonable substitute for polystyrene in low-cost applications.

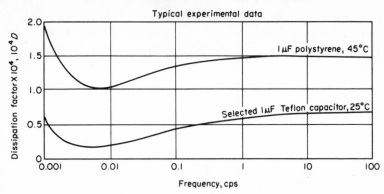

Fɪɢ. 3-14. Capacitor dielectric absorption vs. frequency for polystyrene and Teflon capacitors.   (*From ref.* 14.)

(c) Effects of Dielectric Absorption.   The capacitor model of Fig. 3-13a correctly accounts for the following effects of dielectric absorption in physical capacitors:

1. Sinusoidal current leads voltage by $\pi/2 - D(\omega)$ radians, as compared with the $\pi/2$ lead angle of ideal capacitors.
2. An initially charged and discharged capacitor will gradually recover a fraction of its earlier charge; the linear model reproduces this effect as the various capacitor charges redistribute themselves in a manner depending on the past charging history (*"soakage" or memory effect* of dielectric absorption).
3. Results of accurate capacitance measurements will depend on the method of measurement.   In particular, the results of bridge and oscillator measurements depend on the frequency components of the test signals used (see also Sec. 3-20); and capacitance measurements based on timed charging or discharging are affected by the past charging history of the capacitor under test.[10]

For purposes of analog computation, Single[14] suggests successive adjustment of three similar integrating capacitors in an accurately timed computer setup for $d^2x/dt^2 = -\omega^2 x$ (Sec. 2-9) with accurately known computing resistors; ω^2 is a power of 10 chosen so as to yield a sinusoidal frequency $\omega/2\pi$ near the center of the computer working-frequency range. $\omega^2 = 1$ would be a suitable choice for a "slow" electronic analog computer.

THE PARALLEL-FEEDBACK OPERATIONAL AMPLIFIER

3-10. Introduction.   The general parallel-feedback operational amplifier circuit of Fig. 3-15 is usually designed with the aid of the "ideal" performance equation

$$X_o = -Z_o(P) \left[\frac{X_1}{Z_1(P)} + \frac{X_2}{Z_2(P)} + \cdots + \frac{X_n}{Z_n(P)} \right] \quad \left(P \equiv \frac{d}{d\tau} \right) \quad (3\text{-}15)$$

already derived in Sec. 1-14c on the assumption of infinite loop gain. Here, Z_o, Z_1, Z_2, . . . , Z_n are short-circuit transfer impedances computed for each four-terminal network as the operational ratio between input voltage and short-circuit output current, as in Fig. 1-16; expressions

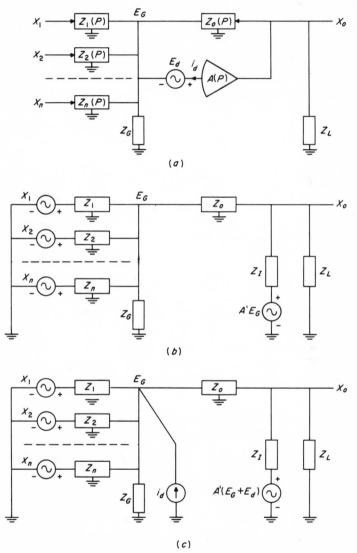

(a)

(b)

(c)

Fig. 3-15. Operational amplifier (a), and equivalent circuits (b), (c).

for the transfer impedances of many networks are available in published tables like Table A-1.

The performance equation (15) neglects d-c offset and noise effects and holds, in any case, exactly only if the feedback loop gain is sufficiently large to make the summing-point voltage E_G practically negligible. In this case, Eq. (15) follows from the summing-point node equation. It is the purpose of the following sections to derive more exact performance equations, which will permit the designer to estimate errors due to the use of Eq. (15) in the more realistic case of finite loop gain. The effect of the output load on the loop gain will also be investigated. In addition, Secs. 3-15 and 3-16, respectively, treat d-c offset and noise effects and the effects of gain changes and distortion. Errors due to parasitic impedances in the computing networks are discussed in Secs. 3-18 to 3-21.

3-11. Operational-amplifier Performance with Finite Gain and Loading.[19]

Since any output due to d-c offset and noise in Fig. 3-15a will be simply added to the output due to the given input voltages X_1, X_2, . . . , X_n, we can leave a discussion of these effects safely for Sec. 3-15 and start by neglecting the offset/noise voltage E_d and current i_d. This results in the simplified equivalent circuit of Fig. 3-15b, while Fig. 3-15c includes sources introducing E_d and i_d. Referring to Fig. 3-15b, elimination of all node voltages except for X_1, X_2, . . . , X_n, E_G, and X_o will yield the node equations for the summing point and for the output terminal in the respective forms

$$E_G = \alpha_1(P)X_1 + \alpha_2(P)X_2 + \cdot \cdot \cdot + \alpha_n(P)X_n + \beta(P)X_o \quad (3\text{-}16)$$

and
$$X_o = a_I(P)A'(P)E_G + a_T(P)E_G = A(P)E_G \quad (3\text{-}17a)$$

where $A'(P)$ is the open-loop/open-circuit gain of the amplifier used, and

$$A = A' \left(a_I + \frac{a_T}{A'} \right) \quad (3\text{-}17b)$$

Combination of Eqs. (16) and (17) yields the exact performance equation

$$X_o = \frac{A\beta}{1 - A\beta} \frac{\alpha_1 X_1 + \alpha_2 X_2 + \cdot \cdot \cdot + \alpha_n X_n}{\beta} \quad (3\text{-}18)$$

or, since Eqs. (15) and (18) must agree as $|A'(j\omega)| \to \infty$ with $a_I\beta \neq 0$,

$$X_o = \frac{A\beta}{1 - A\beta} Z_o \left(\frac{X_1}{Z_1} + \frac{X_2}{Z_2} + \cdot \cdot \cdot + \frac{X_n}{Z_n} \right)$$
$$= - \left(1 - \frac{1}{1 - A\beta} \right) Z_o \left(\frac{X_1}{Z_1} + \frac{X_2}{Z_2} + \cdot \cdot \cdot + \frac{X_n}{Z_n} \right) \quad (3\text{-}19)$$

In practice, the transfer impedances Z_o, Z_1, Z_2, . . . , Z_n can be found in published tables (Table A-1). The transfer operators β, a_I, and a_T must be obtained for each specific operational amplifier from the explicit node equations (16), (17). β, a_I, and a_T admit an intuitively suggestive interpretation:

β is the *feedback ratio* (output terminal to summing point), so that $A\beta$ is the *loop gain* of the operational amplifier.

a_I is the attenuation of the open-circuit forward gain A' due to amplifier loading by computing networks and load ($a_I = 1$ if $Z_I = 0$).

a_T is the "feedforward" transfer function from summing point to output; a_T/A' measures an undesirable lack of isolation between inputs and output.

In certain transistor amplifiers, the output voltage X_o is proportional to the current into Z_G, and Z_G is small compared with the computing impedances. In this case, $A' = K/Z_G$, $\beta \approx bZ_G$, and $A'\beta \approx Kb$ is practically independent of Z_G (current amplifier).

3-12. Error Calculations. The exact performance equation (19) permits convenient separation and estimation of the error or difference

$$e = \frac{1}{1 - A\beta} Z_o \left(\frac{X_1}{Z_1} + \frac{X_2}{Z_2} + \cdots + \frac{X_n}{Z_n} \right) \qquad (3\text{-}20)$$

between the actual amplifier output (19) and the output predicted by the approximate performance equation (15), which is commonly used to design the amplifier circuit. Substitution of $j\omega$ for P in Eq. (19) yields the *phase error* $\delta(\omega)$ for steady-state sinusoidal inputs at the circular frequency ω:

$$\delta(\omega) = \arg \frac{-A\beta}{1 - A\beta} = -\arg \left(1 - \frac{1}{A\beta} \right) \qquad \text{radians} \qquad (3\text{-}21)$$

For the usual large values of $|A| = |A(j\omega)|$ and $|A\beta| = |A(j\omega)\beta(j\omega)|$, one has

$$e \approx -\frac{1}{A\beta} Z_o \left(\frac{X_1}{Z_1} + \frac{X_2}{Z_2} + \cdots + \frac{X_n}{Z_n} \right) \qquad (3\text{-}22)$$

and the absolute percentage dynamic error $|\epsilon(\omega)|$ for steady-state sinusoidal inputs may be estimated from

$$|\epsilon(\omega)| \approx 100 \frac{1}{|A(j\omega)\beta(j\omega)|} \qquad (3\text{-}23)$$

Equations (19) to (23) specify the error arising from the use of the simplified design equation (15) in the face of finite gain and amplifier loading. Equation (20) or (23) may be used to define the working frequency range of the operational amplifier for a given percentage error $|\epsilon(\omega)|$. Near the limits of the working frequency range, $|\epsilon(\omega)|$ is often numerically practically equal to $100|\delta(\omega)|$; i.e., most of the dynamic error is due to phase shift (see also Secs. 3-1, 3-6, 3-19, and 3-20).

Quite frequently, $|a_T/A'|$ can be neglected compared with a_I, so that the steady-state absolute fractional dynamic error $100|\epsilon(\omega)|$ is simply the reciprocal of the absolute loop gain $|A'a_I\beta|$ and can be studied very conveniently by means of the open-loop Bode plot for the operational amplifier (see also Secs. 3-19 and 3-20).

3-13. Effect of Amplifier Internal Impedance and Loading.   The equivalent-generator impedance (source impedance) $Z_S(P)$ of the operational amplifier, as seen by the load, is given by

$$X_o = \frac{Z_L}{Z_S + Z_L}\bar{X}_o \tag{3-24}$$

where X_o is given by Eq. (19), and $\bar{X}_o$ is the same expression with $Z_L = \infty$ (no-load output voltage).   Equations (19) and (24) yield

$$Z_S = \left(\frac{\bar{X}_o}{X_o} - 1\right)Z_L = \left(\frac{1 - 1/A\beta}{1 - 1/\bar{A}\beta} - 1\right)Z_L \tag{3-25}$$

where barred terms refer to the no-load condition ($Z_L = \infty$).   Introducing Eq. (17b) and neglecting terms of higher order in $1/A'$, one finds

$$Z_S \approx \frac{1}{A'\beta}\left(\frac{1}{\bar{a}_I} - \frac{1}{a_I}\right)Z_L, \text{ where}$$

$$a_I = \frac{Z_LZ_F}{Z_LZ_F + Z_LZ_I + Z_IZ_F} \qquad \bar{a}_I = \frac{Z_F}{Z_I + Z_F}$$

if Z_F is the load due to the feedback network.   It follows that

$$Z_S \approx -\frac{Z_I}{A'\beta} \tag{3-26}$$

3-14. Operational Amplifiers with Two-terminal Computing Impedances. Input-source Loading.   (a) In the important special case of operational amplifiers with simple two-terminal computing impedances Z_o, Z_1, Z_2, . . . , Z_n (Fig. 1-15b), the transfer impedances are ordinary impedances.   The summing-point node equation (16) becomes

$$\frac{1}{Z_o}(E_G - X_o) + \frac{1}{Z_1}(E_G - X_1) + \frac{1}{Z_2}(E_G - X_2) + \cdots$$

$$+ \frac{1}{Z_n}(E_G - X_n) + \frac{1}{Z_G}E_G = 0 \tag{3-27}$$

and the output-terminal node equation (17) is now

$$\frac{1}{Z_o}(X_o - E_G) + \frac{1}{Z_I}(X_o - A'E_G) + \frac{X_o}{Z_L} = 0 \tag{3-28}$$

By comparison of Eqs. (16), (17) and (27), (28), it follows that

$$\left. \begin{array}{c} \beta = \dfrac{1}{Z_o}\left(\dfrac{1}{Z_o} + \dfrac{1}{Z_1} + \dfrac{1}{Z_2} + \cdots + \dfrac{1}{Z_n} + \dfrac{1}{Z_G}\right)^{-1} = \dfrac{Z_A}{Z_o} \\[2mm] a_I = \dfrac{Z_o Z_L}{Z_I Z_o + Z_I Z_L + Z_o Z_L} = \dfrac{Z_B}{Z_I} \\[2mm] a_T = \dfrac{Z_I Z_L}{Z_I Z_o + Z_I Z_L + Z_o Z_L} = \dfrac{Z_B}{Z_o} \end{array} \right\} \quad (3\text{-}29)$$

$$Z_S = \dfrac{Z_o Z_I}{(1 - A'\beta)Z_o + (1 - \beta)Z_I} \quad \left[\approx -\dfrac{Z_I}{A'\beta} \text{ if } |A'(j\omega)\beta(j\omega)| \gg 1\right]$$

$$(3\text{-}30)$$

where Z_A is the combined parallel impedance of all branches terminating at the summing point (Z_o, Z_1, Z_2, . . . , Z_n, and Z_G), and Z_B is the combined parallel impedance of the branches terminating at the output terminal (Z_o, Z_I, and Z_L). The expressions (29) and (30) must be substituted into the design equations (19) to (26).

(b) **Input-source Loading.** If Z_1 (but not necessarily Z_o, Z_2, Z_3, . . . , Z_n) is a two-terminal impedance, then the source of the input voltage X_1 "sees" the impedance Z_1 grounded in series with the voltage $E_G = X_o/A$, or an equivalent input impedance

$$Z_1' = -\dfrac{Z_1}{1 - \dfrac{\beta}{1 - A\beta}\dfrac{Z_o}{Z_1}} \quad (3\text{-}31)$$

grounded in series with the voltage $\dfrac{\beta}{1 - A\beta} Z_o \left(\dfrac{X_2}{Z_2} + \dfrac{X_3}{Z_3} + \cdots + \dfrac{X_n}{Z_n}\right)$. For sinusoidal components such that $|A(j\omega)\beta(j\omega)| \gg 1$, the X_1 source "sees" essentially the grounded impedance Z_1; the summing point of a high-gain parallel-feedback operational amplifier acts as a "virtual ground" which effectively isolates each input from all others and from the amplifier output.

3-15. Effects of D-c Offsets and Noise. In Fig. 3-15a, the voltage E_d represents the combined effect of *d-c unbalance* due to initial unbalance or drift and/or *noise* due to vacuum tubes, transistors, resistors, choppers, and stray pickup, all referred to the amplifier input. The current i_d represents similar effects described in terms of currents into the amplifier summing point; i_d is mainly direct offset current due to grid or base current in the amplifier input stage, and leakage from various terminals into the summing point. The latter effect can be eliminated by grounded conductors surrounding all summing-point terminations (see also Sec. 5-13).

The effects of E_d and i_d must be added to the output (19) computed in Sec. 3-11. Referring to the equivalent circuit of Fig. 3-15c, we repeat the

analysis of Sec. 3-11 to find that Eq. (19) for the amplifier output voltage
is now replaced by

$$X_o = -\left(1 - \frac{1}{1 - A\beta}\right) Z_o \left(\frac{X_1}{Z_1} + \frac{X_2}{Z_2} + \cdots + \frac{X_n}{Z_n}\right)$$
$$+ \frac{a_I A'}{1 - A\beta} E_d + \frac{A\beta}{1 - A\beta} Z_o i_d \quad (3\text{-}32)$$

By virtue of the superposition principle, the absolute error due to E_d
and i_d, viz.,

$$e_d = \frac{a_I A'}{1 - A\beta} E_d + \frac{A\beta}{1 - A\beta} Z_o i_d \quad (3\text{-}33)$$

is simply added to the error (20) due to finite gain and loading.   For d-c
offset, and for low-frequency noise, one has usually $|A(j\omega)\beta(j\omega)| \gg 1$,
$a_I A' \approx A$, so that

$$e_d \approx -\frac{1}{\beta} E_d - Z_o i_d \quad (3\text{-}34)$$

3-16. Effects of Gain Changes and Distortion.   The inverse feedback inherent in the operational-amplifier circuit helps to reduce the
effects of gain changes in the d-c amplifier on the output voltage X_o; the
range of permissible gain changes may be investigated with aid of Eqs.
(19) and (22).

For pure sinusoidal voltages, the fractional effect of a steady-state gain
change $dA(j\omega)$ on the output amplitude is reduced in the ratio $1:|1 - A(j\omega)\beta(j\omega)|$.   A similar reduction applies to the fractional amplitude
of each separate sinusoidal distortion and intermodulation component
originating in the d-c amplifier, but the effect of feedback on the *total* distortion error depends on the vector sum of the distortion components and
is not so easily computed.

3-17. Summary of Error Analysis.   The analysis of Secs. 3-10 to 3-16
indicates that, with ideal network components, all operational-amplifier
errors other than d-c offset are, for all practical purposes, inversely pro-
portional to the absolute feedback loop gain $|A(j\omega)\beta(j\omega)|$.   With modern
high-gain low-offset d-c amplifiers, computing accuracy is therefore
limited essentially by calibration errors and by parasitic-impedance
effects, which will be further investigated in Secs. 3-18 to 3-20.

An additional consideration is the accumulation of errors due to phase
shift, distortion, d-c offset, and noise in cascaded strings or loops of
operational amplifiers.   As a rough general rule, one obtains the best
results by keeping the absolute loop gains $|A(j\omega)\beta(j\omega)|$ (and hence the
closed-loop forward gains, assuming similar d-c amplifiers) of the various
amplifiers approximately equal near the most typical working frequencies.

DESIGN OF PHASE INVERTERS, SUMMING AMPLIFIERS,
AND INTEGRATORS

3-18. Introduction. The design of specific operational amplifiers such as summers or integrators requires us to combine the design criteria of Secs. 3-10 to 3-17 with due consideration of parasitic impedances in physical networks (Secs. 3-7 to 3-9). The designer is, furthermore, constrained by system considerations, such as amplifier power and potentiometer loading (Sec. 3-24).

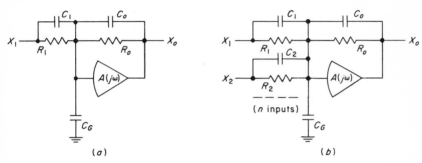

FIG. 3-16. Phase-inverting amplifier (a), and summing amplifier (b).

3-19. Design of Phase Inverters and Summing Amplifiers. (a) **Static Accuracy.** For a phase inverter or summing amplifier (Fig. 3-16), the d-c feedback ratio is

$$\beta(0) = \left(\frac{R_o}{R_1} + \frac{R_o}{R_2} + \cdots + \frac{R_o}{R_n} + \frac{R_o}{R_G} + 1\right)^{-1} \leq \frac{1}{a+1} \quad (3\text{-}35)$$

where a is simply the absolute phase-inverter gain, or the total absolute summer gain (phase-inverter gain with all summer inputs connected together) at d-c. Referring to Eq. (20), we see that *absolute static accuracy within ϵ per cent requires a d-c gain $|A(0)|$ exceeding*

$$|A(0)|_{\text{MIN}} = (a+1)\left(\frac{100}{\epsilon} - 1\right) \approx \frac{100}{\epsilon}(a+1) \quad (3\text{-}36)$$

in addition to correspondingly accurate matching of the resistance ratios R_o/R_i and low amplifier drift. Modern chopper-stabilized d-c amplifiers exceed the low-frequency gain requirement (36) by a wide margin and have very low drift (Sec. 4-13). The static accuracy of phase inverters and summers in general-purpose analog computers is, then, essentially determined by resistance-ratio accuracy.

EXAMPLE: For absolute static accuracy within 0.01 per cent, a summing amplifier with 1, 1, 1, 10, 10, 10 inputs ($a = 33$) requires a d-c gain $|A(0)| \geq 34 \times 10^4$. $|A(0)| \geq 10^7$ and d-c offset below 100 μV (i.e., 3.4 mV at the amplifier output, Sec. 3-15) are easy to obtain.

(b) Dynamic Accuracy and Phase-equalizing Capacitors. Figure 3-17a shows the open-loop frequency response of a typical computer d-c amplifier (see also Chap. 4). *Although the newer amplifiers maintain open-loop gains $|A(j\omega)|$ above 1,000 well beyond 10 Kc (Secs. 4-23 and 5-12), phase shift due to the parasitic capacitances C_G, C_o, C_1, C_2, . . . , C_n indicated in Fig. 3-16 affects phase-inverter or summer accuracy at much lower*

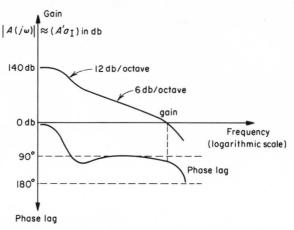

Fig. 3-17a. Open-loop frequency response of a computer d-c amplifier. In the low-frequency region, stabilizer-channel filters and rolloff networks shape a more or less conservative amplitude and phase response. In the intermediate-frequency region, rolloff networks and/or feedforward circuits reduce slope and phase shift. Circuit and load capacitances cause the response to drop sharply after unity gain (0 db) is reached (see also Chap. 4).

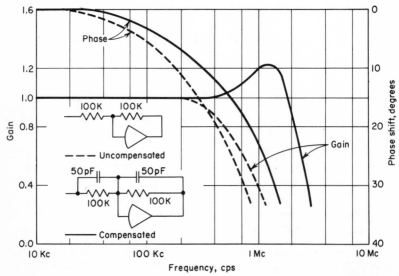

Fig. 3-17b. Unity-gain phase-inverter response with and without phase-compensating capacitors. (*University of Arizona; ASTRAC I data from ref. 28.*)

frequencies. In the following, we can restrict explicit analysis to the case of the phase inverter, since the summing-amplifier performance will be, essentially, that of a phase inverter with the input resistance

$$\left(\frac{1}{R_1} + \frac{1}{R_2} + \cdots + \frac{1}{R_n}\right)^{-1}$$

paralleled by the capacitance $C_1 + C_2 + \cdots + C_n$.

Referring to Fig. 3-16, we write the amplifier open-loop gain as

$$A(j\omega) = -\frac{A_0}{1 + j\delta_A(\omega)} \tag{3-37}$$

where A_0 is the absolute d-c gain; $\delta_A(\omega)$ is, in general, complex, but most frequently real and approximately proportional to ω over a wide frequency range (Fig. 3-17a). The shunt capacitance C_G is due to wiring and inter-electrode capacitances, including Miller effect (Secs. 4-16 and 5-11). C_1 and C_o are resistor capacitances (Sec. 3-7) combined with added equalizing capacitances.

Figure 3-16 yields the phase-inverter (or summer) frequency response

$$\frac{\overrightarrow{X_o}}{\overrightarrow{X_1}} = -\frac{R_o}{R_1}\frac{j\omega R_1 C_1 + 1}{j\omega R_o C_o + 1}\left[1 - \frac{1}{1 - A(j\omega)\beta(j\omega)}\right] \tag{3-38a}$$

with

$$\beta(j\omega) = \frac{1}{R_o/R_1 + 1}\frac{j\omega R_o C_o + 1}{j\omega \dfrac{R_o}{1 + R_o/R_1}(C_o + C_1 + C_G) + 1} \tag{3-38b}$$

either directly or by reference to Sec. 3-14. The desired response is $-R_o/R_1$. We expand Eq. (38) with the aid of the relation

$$\frac{1 + \lambda}{1 + \mu} = (1 + \lambda)(1 - \mu + \mu^2 \mp \cdots) \qquad (|\mu| < 1) \tag{3-39}$$

At frequencies sufficiently low for us to neglect higher-order terms,

$$\frac{\overrightarrow{X_o}}{\overrightarrow{X_1}} \approx -\frac{R_o}{R_1}\left\{1 + \omega^2 R_o C_o(R_1 C_1 - R_o C_o) - \frac{1}{A_0}\left(\frac{R_o}{R_1} + 1\right)\right.$$

$$+ j\omega\left[R_1 C_1 - R_o C_o + \frac{R_o}{A_0 R_1}(R_o C_o - R_1 C_1 - R_1 C_G)\right.$$

$$\left.\left. - \left(\frac{R_o}{R_1} + 1\right)\frac{\delta_A(\omega)}{\omega A_0}\right]\right\} \tag{3-40}$$

This analysis yields important and practical design information:

1. Dynamic as well as static errors increase with the closed-loop gain $a = R_o/R_1$. This applies, in particular, to the output amplifiers of electronic function generators and multipliers.

2. *We can often extend phase-inverter or summer frequency response by at least a decade if we pad the resistor shunt capacitances C_o, C_1 so as to cancel error terms in Eq. (40) (Fig. 3-17).*

We shall try to make R_1C_1 slightly larger than R_oC_o to partially compensate the effects of C_G and $\delta_A(\omega)$. $R_1C_1 - R_oC_o$ is reduced to the order of magnitude of $1/A_0$, so that Eq. (40) is replaced by

$$
\frac{\vec{X}_o}{\vec{X}_1} \approx -\frac{R_o}{R_1}\left\{ 1 - \frac{1}{A_0}\left(\frac{R_o}{R_1} + 1\right)\right.
$$
$$
\left. + j\omega\left[R_1C_1 - R_oC_o - \frac{R_oC_G}{A_0} - \left(\frac{R_o}{R_1} + 1\right)\frac{\delta_A(\omega)}{\omega A_0}\right]\right\} \quad (3\text{-}41a)
$$

The corresponding phase error is

$$
\delta_S(\omega) = \arg\left(-\frac{\vec{X}_o}{\vec{X}_1}\right) \approx \omega\left(R_1C_1 - R_oC_o - \frac{R_oC_G}{A_0}\right)
$$
$$
- \frac{1}{A_0}\left(\frac{R_o}{R_1} + 1\right)\delta_A(\omega) \quad (3\text{-}41b)
$$

where $\delta_S > 0$ signifies phase *lead*.

Padding of C_o, C_1 can benefit older existing computers as well as new designs.[13,14] In general, both C_o and C_1 must be increased; note that the resulting pole-zero cancellation in the feedback ratio (38b) also benefits amplifier *stability* (Sec. 4-18) and may thus permit increased gain. Single[13,14] recommends about 40 pF shunt capacitance for 1M resistors in "slow" analog computers. The corresponding 400 pF shunt capacitance for 100K resistors is already a rather uncomfortable load on preceding amplifiers and especially on coefficient-setting potentiometers (Sec. 3-6). In wideband computing amplifiers operating above 1 Kc, frequency response depends so critically on shunt-capacitance adjustments that individual trimmer capacitors and/or (preferably) lower computing-resistance values are a practical necessity. Resistances in series with C_1 and C_o can be useful for "stopping" the capacitive loading at high frequencies. Such frequency-dependent loads, however, cannot usually be connected to coefficient-setting potentiometers.

3-20. Electronic Integrators: Effects of Finite Gain, Loading, and Parasitic Impedances on the Integrator Frequency Response.

Figure 3-18a shows an electronic-integrator model without many of the idealizing assumptions made in Sec. 1-12b:

1. A suitably given expression for the amplifier gain $A = A(P)$ will account for effects of *finite gain* and can be written in the form (37) to account for the effect of the *amplifier load*.

2. The "capacitance" $C = C(P)$ is not a constant, but is given by the capacitor model of Sec. 3-9 as

$$C(P) = C(\infty) + \frac{1}{r_{DC}P} + \sum_{k=1}^{n} \frac{C_k}{1 + r_k C_k P} \qquad (3\text{-}42a)$$

or $\quad C(j\omega) = C_{\text{EFF}}(\omega) + \dfrac{1}{j\omega R_D(\omega)} = C_{\text{EFF}}(\omega)[1 - jD(\omega)] \qquad (3\text{-}42b)$

to account for both *resistive leakage* and *dielectric absorption*.

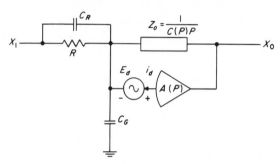

FIG. 3-18a. Electronic integrator with finite gain, loading, parasitic impedances, and d-c offset.

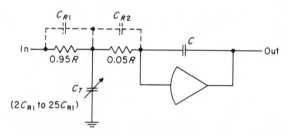

FIG. 3-18b. A simple way to reduce integrator phase error due to the parasitic capacitance C_R is to use a series combination of two or three carbon-film resistors for R. For more precise phase compensation, a trimmer C_T is added; C_{R2} is of the same order of magnitude as C_{R1} (typically 0.5 to 2 pF), so that $0.05 R C_{R2} \ll R C_{R1}$.

3. The *distributed capacitance* C_R *of the integrating resistor* and the *summing-point capacitance* C_G are explicitly included. Resistor inductance can safely be neglected below 200 Kc (Sec. 3-7).

The purely additive effects of d-c offset and noise (E_d and i_d in Fig. 3-18a) will again be considered separately (Sec. 3-21). And, as in Sec. 3-19, our frequency-response analysis also applies to summing integrators (Sec. 1-12) if R is regarded as the parallel combination of all summing resistors, and C_R is the sum of their shunt capacitances.

For $E_d = i_d = 0$, Fig. 3-18a yields the summing-point node equation

$$\left(\frac{1}{R} + C_R P\right)\left[\frac{1}{A(P)} X_o - X_1\right]$$
$$+ \frac{C_G P}{A(P)} X_o + C(P)P\left[\frac{1}{A(P)} X_o - X_o\right] = 0 \quad (3\text{-}43)$$

and hence the *integrator performance equation*

$$X_o = -\frac{RC_R P + 1}{RC(P)P - [RP/A(P)][C(P) + C_G + C_R] - [1/A(P)]} \quad (3\text{-}44a)$$

We can substitute the proper expressions for $C(P)$ and $A(P)$ into this equation to compare our integrator performance with ideal integration ($X_o = \text{const}/P$).

For steady-state sinusoidal signals, we introduce

$$C(j\omega) = C_{\text{EFF}}(\omega)[1 - jD(\omega)]$$

where $C_{\text{EFF}}(\omega)$ is the "effective" or "nominal" integrating capacitance measured with sinusoidal signals at the circular frequency ω. Substitution of $j\omega$ for P in Eq. (44a) yields the *integrator frequency-response function*

$$\frac{\vec{X}_o}{\vec{X}_1} = -\frac{1}{j\omega RC_{\text{EFF}}}$$
$$\frac{j\omega RC_R + 1}{1 - jD(\omega) - \dfrac{1}{A(j\omega)}\left[1 - jD(\omega) + \dfrac{C_G + C_R}{C_{\text{EFF}}} + \dfrac{1}{j\omega RC_{\text{EFF}}}\right]} \quad (3\text{-}44b)$$

which must be compared with the frequency response $-1/j\omega RC_{\text{EFF}}$ of an ideal integrator whose capacitance equals the "effective" capacitance $C_{\text{EFF}} = C_{\text{EFF}}(\omega)$ at the frequency in question. At this point, it is again expedient to write the amplifier gain $A(j\omega)$ in the form (37). For reasonably small errors, we can now expand the frequency-response function (44b) with the aid of the relation (39) and find

$$\frac{\vec{X}_o}{\vec{X}_1} \approx -\frac{1}{j\omega RC_{\text{EFF}}}\left\{1 + j\left[\frac{1}{\omega A_0 RC_{\text{EFF}}} + D(\omega) + \omega RC_R\right.\right.$$
$$\left. - \frac{\delta_A(\omega)}{A_0}\left(1 + \frac{C_G}{C_{\text{EFF}}}\right)\right] - \frac{1}{A_0}\left[1 + \frac{C_G + C_R}{C_{\text{EFF}}} + D(\omega)\delta_A(\omega)\right.$$
$$\left.\left. + \frac{\delta_A(\omega)}{\omega RC_{\text{EFF}}} - jD(\omega) + j\delta_A(\omega)\frac{C_R}{C_{\text{EFF}}}\right]\right\} \quad (3\text{-}45)$$

The terms obtained from the last bracket can be conservatively neglected compared with the other error terms in Eq. (45) for essentially every practical integrator circuit; this fact should be checked in each particular case (Sec. 3-24).   *The frequency response of a practical electronic integrator is, then, given by*

$$\frac{\overrightarrow{X_o}}{\overrightarrow{X_1}} \approx -\frac{1}{j\omega RC_{\text{EFF}}} \left\{ 1 + j\left[\frac{1}{\omega A_0 RC_{\text{EFF}}} + D(\omega) \right.\right.$$
$$\left.\left. + \omega RC_R - \frac{\delta_A(\omega)}{A_0}\left(1 + \frac{C_G}{C_{\text{EFF}}}\right) \right]\right\} \quad (3\text{-}46)$$

throughout the integrator working frequency range.   The resulting *integrator phase error* is

$$\delta_I(\omega) = \arg\frac{\overrightarrow{X_o}}{\overrightarrow{X_1}} - \frac{\pi}{2} \approx \frac{1}{\omega A_0 RC_{\text{EFF}}} + D(\omega)$$
$$+ \omega RC_R - \frac{\delta_A(\omega)}{A_0}\left(1 + \frac{C_G}{C_{\text{EFF}}}\right) \quad (3\text{-}47)$$

(phase *lead* for $\delta_I > 0$) and the absolute percentage error for sinusoidal components at the circular frequency ω is $|\epsilon_I(\omega)| = 100|\delta_I(\omega)|$ (see also Sec. 3-2).   The error in Eq. (46) is seen to be a sum of terms respectively due to *finite amplifier gain* (at d-c or at the computer repetition rate), *capacitor leakage and dielectric absorption*, *distributed capacitance of the integrating resistor*, and *amplifier high-frequency bandwidth limitations.*

In practice, C_G/C_{EFF} is small for all but very fast integrators.   The capacitor dissipation coefficient $D(\omega)$ is usually almost constant except at very low frequencies,where it is given by $1/\omega r_{DC}C(\infty)$ (Sec. 3-9).   The phase shift due to C_R precludes the use of 1M integrating resistors above about 50 cps;[13,14] Fig. 3-18b shows a possible compensation scheme.   Table 3-2 illustrates the relative importance of the various error sources with two numerical examples.

3-21. Electronic Integrators: Errors Due to Calibration, D-c Offset, and Noise.   In addition to the dynamic errors discussed in Sec. 3-20, integrators exhibit a constant-percentage *calibration error* mainly due to changes in the effective capacitance C_{EFF} with temperature (and also with frequency, Secs. 3-8 and 3-9).   Finally, *d-c offset voltage and/or current* (Fig. 3-18a) produce an additive error output

$$X_o = -\frac{\tau}{RC}(E_D + Ri_D) \quad (3\text{-}48)$$

where τ is the computing time.   Effects of high-frequency noise are largely "integrated out."

For modern high-quality d-c amplifiers, E_D will be between 10 and 100 μV, while i_D is of the order of nanoamperes even in the case of transistor amplifiers (Chap. 5).   The integrator drift error (48) is, then, usually appreciable only in instrumentation applications requiring long integration times; in general-purpose analog computers, integrator accuracy is most frequently limited by capacitance calibration and dielectric absorption (see also Table 3-2).

Table 3-2. Examples of Error Sources in Electronic Integration

(Secs. 3-20 and 3-21.)   For comparison purposes note that *unity-gain phase-inverter errors* are usually readily made less than integrator errors (Sec. 3-19), while *errors due to potentiometer phase shift* might exceed the figures quoted for $100\omega R C_R$ per cent by a factor of 10 without careful phase compensation (Sec. 3-6).

Source	A typical "slow" integrator		A low-cost repetitive-computer integrator		A high-quality wideband (transistor) integrator	
Half-scale..........	10 or 100 volts		10 or 100 volts		10 volts	
Calibration error.....	0.025 per cent		0.5 per cent		0.3 per cent	
$C,\ R$...............	1 μF, 1 M		0.001 μF, 50K		0.005 μF, 2 K	
$A_0,\ \delta_A(\omega)$............	10^7, 10ω		10^4, $\omega/100$		10^6, $\omega/100$	
D...................	2×10^{-4}		$<10^{-3}$		$<10^{-3}$	
C_R.................	4 pF		2 pF		1 pF	
C_G.................	500 pF		20 to 100 pF		20 to 50 pF	
$E_d,\ i_d$.............	50 μV		200 μV, 20 nA*		100 μV, 10 nA*	
Frequency..........	0.01 cps†	100 cps	100 cps†	10 Kc	1 Kc†	100 Kc
$\dfrac{100}{\omega A_0 R C}$ (per cent).....	1.6×10^{-4}	1.6×10^{-8}	3.2×10^{-2}	3.2×10^{-4}	1.6×10^{-3}	1.6×10^{-5}
$-100\ \dfrac{\delta_A(\omega)}{A_0}$ (per cent)	-6.3×10^{-6}	-6.3×10^{-2}	-6.3×10^{-2}	-6.3	-6.3×10^{-3}	-0.63
$100D$ (per cent)......	2×10^{-2}	2×10^{-2}	<0.1	<0.1	<0.1	<0.1
$100\omega R C_R$ (per cent)...	2.5×10^{-5}	0.25	6.3×10^{-3}	0.63	1.25×10^{-3}	0.125
$\dfrac{E_d}{RC}\tau$ (per cycle).....	5 mV	0.5 μV	4 mV	40 μV	10 mV	100 μV
$\dfrac{i_d}{C}\tau$ (per cycle).......	0	0	200 mV	2 mV	2 mV	20 μV

* From electronic switch and/or transistor amplifier.

† One cycle at this frequency is one typical computer run with the R, C values quoted.

ERRORS IN SOLUTIONS OF LINEAR DIFFERENTIAL EQUATIONS WITH CONSTANT COEFFICIENTS. SYSTEM-DESIGN CONSIDERATIONS

3-22. Introduction.   Consider a set of potentiometers, summer/phase inverters, integrators, and/or more general operational amplifiers interconnected to solve a linear homogeneous differential equation with constant coefficients,

$$F(P)Y \equiv (a_n P^n + a_{n-1} P^{n-1} + \cdots + a_0)Y = 0 \qquad \left(P \equiv \frac{d}{d\tau}\right) \quad (3\text{-}49)$$

To assess the effects of errors in the various computing elements, we replace their idealized performance equations by the corresponding more realistic relations from Secs. 3-6, 3-11, 3-19, and 3-20. The analog-computer setup will, then, implement a linear differential equation

$$\bar{F}(P)\bar{Y} \equiv (\bar{a}_{\bar{n}}P^{\bar{n}} + \bar{a}_{\bar{n}-1}P^{\bar{n}-1} + \cdots + \bar{a}_0)\bar{Y} = 0 \qquad \left(P \equiv \frac{d}{d\tau}\right) \quad (3\text{-}50)$$

different from the desired given differential equation (49) and, in general, of higher order than the given equation ($\bar{n} \geq n$). In particular, the n roots $s_1, s_2, \ldots, s_n$ of the characteristic equation

$$F(s) \equiv a_n s^n + a_{n-1}s^{n-1} + \cdots + a_0 = 0 \quad (3\text{-}51)$$

which determine the normal modes of the correct solution $Y = Y(\tau)$ are replaced by the $\bar{n}$ roots $\bar{s}_1, \bar{s}_2, \ldots, \bar{s}_{\bar{n}}$ of the new characteristic equation

$$\bar{F}(s) \equiv \bar{a}_{\bar{n}}s^{\bar{n}} + \bar{a}_{\bar{n}-1}s^{\bar{n}-1} + \cdots + \bar{a}_0 = 0 \quad (3\text{-}52)$$

associated with the actual computer setup. Small phase and amplitude errors in the various linear computing elements tend to produce a twofold effect:

1. n of $\bar{n}$ roots of Eq. (52), say $\bar{s}_1, \bar{s}_2, \ldots, \bar{s}_n$, will correspond to the n correct roots $s_1, s_2, \ldots, s_n$, but will be slightly shifted; this expresses errors in the corresponding normal modes of the computer solution $\bar{Y} = \bar{Y}(\tau)$.

2. The $\bar{n} - n$ remaining roots $\bar{s}_{n+1}, \bar{s}_{n+2}, \ldots, \bar{s}_{\bar{n}}$ represent *spurious modes* due to parasitic energy-storage elements and have no counterpart in the correct solution.

The spurious modes are usually caused by high-frequency phase shift. In practice, the spurious-mode roots often have large negative real parts, so that the corresponding false-solution modes damp out very quickly and will not affect the solution appreciably. But in certain high-gain computing loops, or in "algebraic" feedback loops without integrators, phase shifts of cascaded amplifiers may add and cause spurious high-frequency oscillatory modes which render the computer setup useless. A suitable setup modification can often remedy such a situation by effectively damping the spurious high-frequency modes.

3-23. First-order Mode-error Calculations (see also Sec. 3-24). Although formulas permitting explicit computation of mode errors and spurious modes exist,[22-24] they are based on none-too-realistic standard computer setups and on greatly simplified formulations of computing-element frequency-response functions. The following simplified procedures often permit approximate mode-error calculations without restriction to a standard computer setup. In particular, the method of Sec.

3-23b permits comparisons of mode errors in different computer setups for the same problem.

(a) **Low-frequency Errors.**[22]   In low-frequency computations, especially with inexpensive (low-gain) integrators, phase-shift errors are essentially due to imperfect integration at low frequencies (Secs. 1-12 and 3-20).   Reference to Sec. 3-20 indicates that at low frequencies the transfer operator $-1/RCP$ of an ideal integrator is approximately replaced by $-1/RC(P + \lambda)$ with $\lambda = 1/r_{DC}C + 1/A_0RC$.   The given differential equation (49) is, then, replaced by

$$F(P + \lambda)\bar{Y} \equiv [a_n(P + \lambda)^n + a_{n-1}(P + \lambda)^{n-1}$$
$$+ \cdots + a_0]\bar{Y} = 0 \qquad \left(P \equiv \frac{d}{d\tau}\right) \quad (3\text{-}53)$$

so that each real or complex root s_k of Eq. (49) is simply reduced by the same real quantity λ.   The computer solution $\bar{Y}(\tau)$ is related to the desired correct solution $Y(\tau)$ by

$$\bar{Y}(\tau) = e^{-\lambda\tau}Y(\tau) \qquad (3\text{-}54)$$

The resulting error could be corrected through multiplication by $e^{\lambda\tau}$ prior to recording of solutions.

(b) Assuming that the spurious modes can be neglected, the following procedure[25] permits approximate calculation of the mode changes.   Let $\bar{F}(s) = F(s) + \Delta F(s)$ and $\bar{s}_k = s_k + \Delta s_k$, where $\Delta F(s)$ and the Δs_k are small.   Then, since $F(s_k) = \bar{F}(\bar{s}_k) = 0$,

$$\bar{F}(s_k) = \Delta F(s_k) \approx -\bar{F}'(\bar{s}_k)\Delta s_k \qquad (3\text{-}55)$$

so that the error Δs_k in the kth root s_k is approximately given by

$$\Delta s_k \approx -\frac{\Delta F(s_k)}{\bar{F}'(\bar{s}_k)} \approx -\frac{\Delta F(s_k)}{F'(s_k)} \qquad (3\text{-}56)$$

Consider, for example, the computer setup of Fig. 3-19a for the differential equation

$$F(P)Y \equiv (P^3 + a_2P^2 + a_1P - a_0)Y = 0 \qquad (3\text{-}57)$$

In Fig. 3-19b, the ideal integrator, summer, and potentiometer transfer operators $-1/P$, -1, and a_k have been replaced by the corresponding more realistic operators

$$-\frac{1}{P}[1 + b_I(P)] \qquad -[1 + b_S(P)] \qquad a_k[1 + b_k(P)]$$

where $b_I(P)$, $b_S(P)$, and $b_k(P)$ are small error terms respectively obtained from Secs. 3-20, 3-19, and 3-6.   The actual differential equation imple-

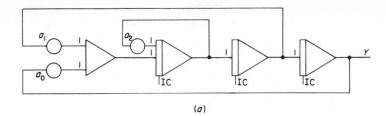

(a)

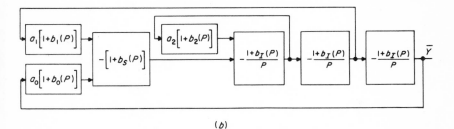

(b)

FIG. 3-19. Analog-computer setup for the differential equation

$$(P^3 + a_2 P^2 + a_1 P - a_0)Y = 0$$

(a), and a block diagram showing the effects of small linear errors (b).

mented by the computer setup of Fig. 3-19 is

$$\bar{F}(P)\bar{Y} \equiv \left\{ \frac{P^3}{(1 + b_I)^3} + a_2(1 + b_2) \frac{P^2}{(1 + b_I)^2} \right.$$
$$\left. + (1 + b_S) \left[a_1(1 + b_1) \frac{P}{1 + b_I} - a_0(1 + b_0) \right] \right\} \bar{Y} = 0 \quad (3\text{-}58)$$

If terms of the second and higher order in the various $b(P)$'s can be neglected, we have

$$\bar{F}(s) = F(s) + \Delta F(s) \approx F(s) - sb_I(s)F'(s) + b_S(s)(a_1 s - a_0)$$
$$+ a_2 b_2(s)s^2 + a_1 b_1(s)s - a_0 b_0(s)$$

and our first-order error estimate (56) for the root s_k is

$$\Delta s_k \approx s_k b_I(s_k) - \frac{b_S(s_k)(a_1 s_k - a_0) + a_2 b_2(s_k)s_k^2 + a_1 b_1(s_k)s_k - a_0 b_0(s_k)}{3s_k^2 + 2a_2 s_k + a_1}$$

$$(3\text{-}59)$$

An analogous procedure yields the root shifts Δs_k for every computer setup implementing a given differential equation (49) with integrators, summer/phase inverters, and coefficient potentiometers. *In each case, the first-order contribution of the integrator-frequency-response error to Δs_k will be $+s_k b_I(s_k)$, provided that the same error factor $[1 + b_I(P)]$ applies to every integration.*

3-24. Errors in Sinusoidal Modes. Circle Test and System Design. (a) The Circle Test. Mode-shift errors are most notice-able* when Re $s_k = 0$ and Δs_k is real, i.e., when component errors cause a decay or increase in a supposedly sinusoidal (or constant) computer solution. The well-known computer setup for the harmonic-oscillator equation

$$F(P)Y \equiv (P^2 + \omega^2)Y = 0 \tag{3-60}$$

(Fig. 3-20a) demonstrates such a situation and serves as a sensitive test for

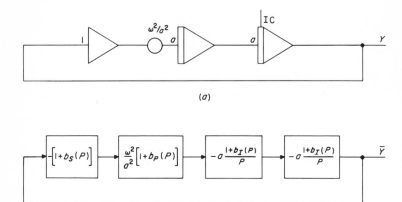

(a)

(b)

FIG. 3-20. A circle-test setup implementing $(P^2 + \omega^2)Y = 0$ (a), and a block diagram showing the effects of small linear errors (b).

phase shift in the computing elements used (*circle test*). Since $s_1 = j\omega$, $s_2 = -j\omega$, the correct solution for $Y(0) = B$, $\dot{Y}(0) = 0$ is

$$Y = B \cos \omega\tau \tag{3-61}$$

Referring to Fig. 3-20b, the actual computer setup solves the machine equation

$$\bar{F}(P)\bar{Y} \equiv \left\{ \frac{P^2}{[1 + b_I(P)]^2} + \omega^2[1 + b_S(P)][1 + b_P(P)] \right\} \bar{Y} = 0 \tag{3-62}$$

where $b_I(P)$, $b_S(P)$, and $b_P(P)$ are small error terms due, respectively, to the integrator, phase inverter, and coefficient potentiometer, as in

---

* This does *not* mean that similar component errors necessarily cause larger per-centage errors in sinusoidal solutions. In the computer solution corresponding to Eq. (53), for instance, percentage errors are constant and the same for all modes; absolute errors increase or decrease with the solution. Errors in sinusoidal or constant solutions are simply easier to see, especially since such solutions can usually be observed for longer periods of time than increasing or decaying solutions.

Sec. 3-23.   Our first-order approximation leads to

$$\bar{F}(s) = F(s) + \Delta F(s) \approx F(s) - 2s^2 b_I(s) + \omega^2[b_S(s) + b_P(s)]$$
$$F'(s) = 2s$$

and, using Eq. (56),

$$\Delta s_k \approx s_k b_I(s_k) - \frac{\omega^2}{2s_k}[b_S(s_k) + b_P(s_k)] \tag{3-63}$$

where $s_k = \pm j\omega$.   Since $b_I(P)$, $b_S(P)$, and $b_P(P)$ are real transfer operators, we must have $b(-j\omega) = -b(j\omega)$ for each b in Eq. (63), so that

$$\Delta s_k = j\omega \left[b_I(j\omega) + \frac{b_S(j\omega) + b_P(j\omega)}{2} \right] \tag{3-64}$$

for both $s_1 = j\omega$ and $s_2 = -j\omega$.

Expressions for $b_I(j\omega)$, $b_S(j\omega)$, and $b_P(j\omega)$ in terms of circuit parameters are readily obtained from Secs. 3-20, 3-19, and 3-6; these quantities can also be obtained directly from frequency-response data as complex (phasor) fractional component errors for sinusoidal excitation.   Assuming accurate gain calibration, component errors will be practically entirely due to phase shift at all frequencies where our first-order analysis applies, so that

$$b_I(j\omega) = j\delta_I(\omega) \qquad b_S(j\omega) = j\delta_S(\omega) \qquad b_P(j\omega) = j\delta_P(\omega) \quad (3\text{-}65)$$

where $\delta_I(\omega)$, $\delta_S(\omega)$, and $\delta_P(\omega)$ are simply the component phase errors (obtained from Secs. 3-20, 3-19, and 3-6, or measured; see also Sec. 3-24b). Hence the root shift

$$\Delta s_k = -\omega \left[\delta_I(\omega) + \frac{\delta_S(\omega) + \delta_P(\omega)}{2} \right] = -\omega\delta(\omega) \tag{3-66}$$

is real and equals $-\omega$ times one-half the total phase shift $2\delta(\omega)$ around our computer loop.   The resulting shifted roots $\bar{s}_k$ obtained from our first-order theory are

$$\bar{s}_{1,2} = \pm j\omega - \omega \left[\delta_I(\omega) + \frac{\delta_S(\omega) + \delta_P(\omega)}{2} \right] = \pm j\omega - \omega\delta(\omega) \quad (3\text{-}67)$$

The correct solution $Y(\tau) = B \cos \omega\tau$ *of Eq.* (60) *is, then, replaced by the actual computer solution*

$$\bar{Y}(\tau) = Be^{-\omega\delta(\omega)\tau} \cos \omega\tau \tag{3-68}$$

The solution amplitude decays exponentially with time for a positive net phase error $2\delta(\omega) = 2\delta_I(\omega) + \delta_S(\omega) + \delta_P(\omega)$ *(lead), while a negative net phase error (lag) will cause the amplitude to increase.*   The fractional error in the nth maximum $(\tau = 2\pi n/\omega, n = 1,2, \ldots)$ of $\bar{Y}(\tau)$, i.e.,

$$\frac{1}{B}\left[B - \bar{Y}\left(\frac{2\pi n}{\omega}\right) \right] = 1 - e^{-2\pi n\delta(\omega)} \approx 2\pi n\delta(\omega) \qquad (n = 1,2, \ldots) \quad (3\text{-}69)$$

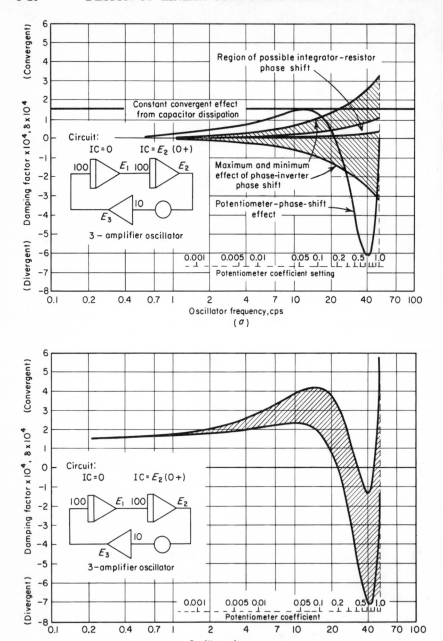

Fig. 3-21. Individual effects (a) and combined effect (b to e) of various sources of phase shift on circle-test damping (based on refs. 13 and 14). Note that δ = 8 × 10⁻⁴ corresponds to approximately 0.5 per cent amplitude decay per oscillation cycle.

is easy to measure and permits convenient study of the various sources of phase shift.

(b) Examples and System-design Considerations. Reference to Secs. 3-6, 3-19, and 3-20 shows that for suitably small errors (component phase errors below 10 deg < 0.2 radian are reasonable)

$$\delta(\omega) = \delta_I(\omega) + \frac{1}{2}\,\delta_S(\omega) + \frac{1}{2}\,\delta_P(\omega) \approx \frac{1}{\omega A_0 R C_{\text{EFF}}} + D(\omega)$$

$$+\ \omega R C_R - \frac{\delta_A(\omega)}{A_0}\left(1 + \frac{C_G}{C_{\text{EFF}}}\right) + \frac{1}{2}\,\delta_S(\omega) + \frac{1}{2}\,\delta_P(\omega) \quad (3\text{-}70)$$

where A_0 and $\delta_A(\omega)$ are assumed to be the same for all three amplifiers. The potentiometer phase shift $\delta_P(\omega)$ can be found from Fig. 3-9 for the correct potentiometer setting α.

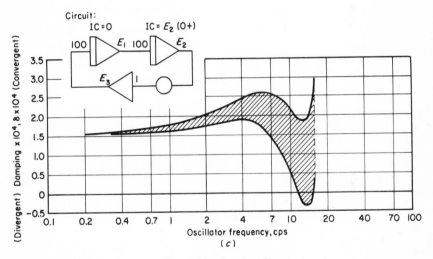

Fig. 3-21. (*Continued*).

Note that the sum (70) for the damping ratio $\delta(\omega)$ can contain negative as well as positive terms. Figure 3-21a illustrates the individual contributions of various error sources for a typical circle-test setup as the oscillation frequency $\omega/2\pi$ is changed by the potentiometer setting, and Fig. 3-21b indicates their combined effect. Figure 3-22 shows similar plots of $\delta(\omega)$ for different combinations of integrator input gain and phase-inverter gain. Finally, Table 3-2 summarizes the effects of various error sources in "slow" and wideband electronic integrators.

Circle-test data taken over a suitable frequency range appear to give a fairly conservative indication of combined error effects on computer solutions of linear if not nonlinear differential equations. The data of

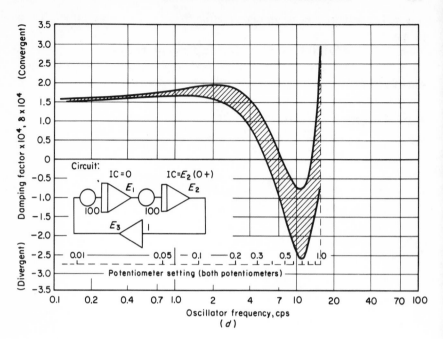

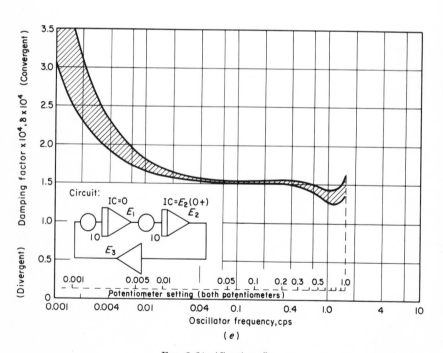

FIG. 3-21. (*Continued*).

Figs. 3-21 and 3-22 cover an intermediate frequency range (0.1 to 100 cps) of particular interest for real-time simulation, and Fig. 3-22 applies to moderate-speed repetitive computation. Below 0.1 cps, $\delta(\omega) \approx 1/r_{DC}C + 1/A_0RC$. With high-quality equipment ($r_{DC}C > 5 \times 10^5$ sec, $A_0 \geq 10^7$), the resulting one-cycle decay is between 0.05 and 0.1 per cent. At higher frequencies (100 cps to 1 Mc, repetitive/iterative and hybrid computation), errors begin to be affected by d-c-amplifier frequency response

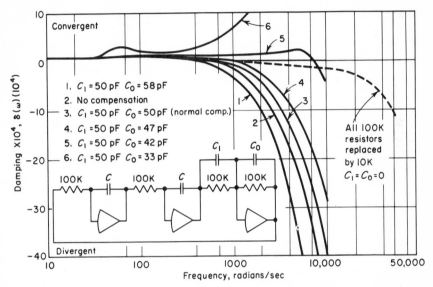

FIG. 3-22. Effect of phase-inverter compensation and computing-impedance level on circle-test damping at higher frequencies. Note the striking effect of lower computing impedances. *(ASTRAC I data from ref. 28.)*

(δ_A/A_0 terms), but this effect is usually masked or compensated by phase shift determined by C_R, C_o, and C_1, and especially by potentiometer phase shift (Table 3-2). Figure 3-22 shows clearly that, at these higher frequencies, phase inverters, summers, and potentiometers must employ lower resistance values and be carefully phase-compensated, and *distributed capacitances to ground* can become critical. These problems suggest the use of low-impedance, high-current transistor amplifiers and miniaturized construction with short wiring runs (Sec. 11-7).

REFERENCES AND BIBLIOGRAPHY

1. Miller, K. S., and F. J. Murray: The Mathematical Basis for the Error Analysis of Differential Analyzers (2 parts), *J. Math. Phys.*, nos. 2 and 3, 1953.
2. Meissinger, H. F.: Substitution Methods for the Verification of Analog Solutions, *Proc. Natl. Simulation Conf.*, Dallas, Tex., 1956, Simulation Councils, Inc., La Jolla, Calif.

3. Fifer, S.: *Analogue Computation*, McGraw-Hill, New York, 1961.

4. Blackburn, J. F.: *Components Handbook*, MIT Radiation Laboratory Series, vol. 17, chap. 8, McGraw-Hill, New York, 1949.

5. Nettleton, L. A., and F. E. Dole: Potentiometers, *Rev. Sci. Instr.*, **17**: 356 (1946).

6. Loveman, B. D.: Coefficient-setting Potentiometers, in Huskey, H. D., and G. A. Korn, *Computer Handbook*, McGraw-Hill, New York, 1962.

7. Gilbert, J.: Shortcut in Compensating Potentiometer Loading Errors, *Control Eng.*, February, 1955.

8. ————: Compensating Functions Potentiometers for Loading Errors, *Control Eng.*, March, 1955.

9. Single, C. H., and J. A. Brussolo: Copper-mandrel Potentiometer Dynamic Error and Compensation, *IRETEC*, September, 1961.

10. Single, C. H.: Precision Components for Analog Computers, *ISA Convention Record*, paper 56-21-2, September, 1956.

11. Sykes, R. P.: Calibration of High-resistance Padded Resistors, *Instruments and Control Systems*, October, 1959.

12. ————: Calibrating Analog-computer Integrators, *Instruments and Control Systems*, September, 1960.

13. Single, C. H., and E. M. Billinghurst: Optimization of Analog-computer Linear System Dynamic Characteristics, *Proc. Western Joint Computer Conf.*, Los Angeles, Calif. May, 1961.

14. ————: Linear-element Error Sources and Effects, in Huskey, H. D., and G. A. Korn, *Computer Handbook*, McGraw-Hill, New York, 1962.

15. Dow, P. C.: Capacitor Dielectric Absorption, *IRETEC*, March, 1958.

16. Howe, R. M.: *Design Fundamentals of Analog-computer Components*, Van Nostrand, Princeton, N.J., 1961.

17. Brussolo, J., and C. H. Single: Transient Analysis of Capacitor Equivalent Circuit, *Beckman/Berkeley Eng. Rept.* CRD 59-5, 1959.

18. Miura, T., et al.: Some Considerations of the Error Due to Absorption Phenomena in Integrating Capacitors, *Proc. 2d AICA Conf.*, Strasbourg, France, 1958, Presses Académiques Européennes, Brussels.

19. Korn, G. A.: Exact Design Equations for Operational Amplifiers with Four-terminal Computing Networks, *IRETEC*, February, 1962.

20. Hubaut, E. E.: Stabilité et précision des cellules linéaires du calcul analogique, *Proc. 3d AICA Conf.*, Opatija, Yugoslavia, 1961, Presses Académiques Européennes, Brussels.

21. Miura, T., et al.: On Computing Errors of an Integrator, *Proc. 2d AICA Conf.*, Strasbourg, France, 1958, Presses Académiques Européennes, Brussels.

22. MacNee, A. B.: Some Limitations on the Accuracy of Electronic Differential Analyzers, *Proc. IRE*, **40**: 303 (March, 1950).

23. Marsocci, V. A.: An Error Analysis of Electronic Analog Computers, *IRETEC*, December, 1956.

24. Dow, P. C.: An Analysis of Certain Errors in Electronic Differential Analyzers (2 parts), *IRETEC*, December, 1957; March, 1958.

25. Miura, T., and M. Nagata: Theoretical Considerations of Computing Errors of a Slow-type Electronic Analog Computer, *IRETEC*, December, 1958.

26. Sosenskii, N. L.: On the Determination of Certain Errors in Analog Computers, *Automatika i Telemekhanika*, Oct. 20, 1959.

27. Kogan, B. Y.: On the Steady-state Operational-amplifier Errors Due to the Pass-band Limitations, *Ann. AICA*, Apr. 4, 1962.

28. Brubaker, T. A.: Design, Development, and Applications of ASTRAC I, Ph.D. Thesis, Electrical Engineering Department, University of Arizona, 1963; see also *Ann. AICA*, April, 1964.

29. Western Simulation Council, Committee on Specifications of General-purpose
    Analog Computers, *Interim Rept.*, July 17, 1962, Simulation Councils, Inc.,
    La Jolla, Calif.
30. Korn, G. A.: Parameter-perturbation Generator for Analog-computer Error and
    Optimization Studies, *Ann. AICA*, April, 1963.
31. Tomovič, R., and W. J. Karplus: *High-speed Analog Computers*, Wiley, New York,
    1962.

CHAPTER **4**

D - C AMPLIFIER DESIGN

INTRODUCTION AND SURVEY

4-1. Requirements and Specifications. *Direct-current* or *d-c ampli-fiers* capable of finite gain at zero frequency are the key active elements of electronic analog computers. The operational-amplifier theory presented in Chap. 3 indicates the following design requirements for computer d-c amplifiers:

1. The requirement for zero-frequency (d-c) gain usually* implies direct (conductive) coupling between amplifier stages (Fig. 4-1), as opposed to capacitor or transformer coupling. The amplifier output is sensitive to changes in the input d-c level.
2. Computing and feedback connections require zero amplifier output voltage for zero input voltage. It follows that a computer d-c amplifier will require at least two high-voltage power supplies (Fig. 4-1) unless floating supplies are used (which is rarely practical). A variable bias-voltage adjustment somewhere in the amplifier permits one to set the output voltage accurately to zero for zero input (*balancing of d-c amplifiers*). As time passes, d-c offset voltages due to changes in components and/or supply voltages cause the amplifier to *drift* out of balance, so that periodic rebalancing may be necessary. The design of d-c amplifier circuits having low drift is a paramount requirement for successful electronic analog computation (Secs. 4-10 to 4-14 and 5-4 to 5-10).
3. The computer amplifier must have a specified forward gain $A(j\omega)$ at

* The definition of d-c amplifiers is usually taken to include also amplifiers employing modulation, a-c amplification, and demodulation (Secs. 4-13 and 5-8), which are not "direct-coupled."

122

d-c and over a specified frequency range.   The designer must control amplifier gain and phase shift well beyond the actual working
frequency range in order to maintain stability in operational-amplifier feedback circuits (Secs. 4-15 to 4-19).   In addition to these

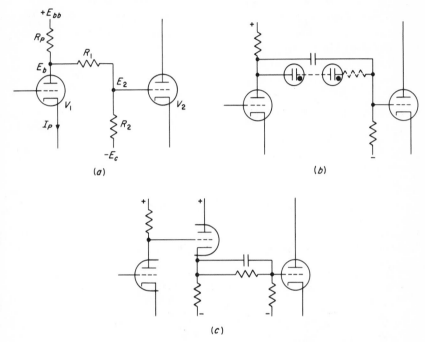

FIG. 4-1. Conductive coupling of d-c amplifier stages.   To establish a desired quiescent
level E_2 at the grid of V_2 in Fig. 4-1a, one must have

$$R_1 = \frac{E_b - E_2}{E_{bb} - E_b - I_P R_P} R_P \qquad R_2 = \frac{E_2 + E_c}{E_{bb} - E_b - I_P R_P} R_P$$

To minimize the resulting signal attenuation $\left(\dfrac{R_2}{R_1 + R_2} \text{ at d-c}\right)$, R_1/R_2 should be as
small as possible, so that a large bias voltage E_c is desirable.   The circuit of Fig.
4-1b replaces R_1, or part of R_1, by the relatively low incremental resistance of a *neon
bulb or bulbs* (5 to 10K each).   Neon bulbs are painted with radioactive jeweler's
paint for good ionization and are bypassed by a noise-reducing capacitor.   A *zener
diode* can replace the neon bulbs and has even lower incremental resistance (about
100 ohms); note that the circuit design must provide the rated minimum operating
current for either zener diode or neon bulbs.   In Fig. 4-1c, a *cathode follower* inserted
between two triode stages minimizes the Miller effect (Sec. 4-15); the dual triode
shown permits very short wiring to the cathode-follower input.

small-signal gain requirements, the amplifier must supply its full
rated output voltage to a specified resistive and capacitive load over
a specified frequency range (Sec. 4-16).   Low amplifier output
impedance is desirable (Secs. 4-16 and 4-17).

Many multipurpose electronic analog computers in current use employ vacuum-tube amplifiers with their familiar advantages of high input impedance, high output-voltage capabilities, and good frequency response. It appears, however, that all-transistor amplifiers can meet all specifications of the best vacuum-tube amplifiers, if cost is no object.   With a continuing trend to price reductions in mass-produced solid-state devices, the smaller size and power dissipation and greater reliability of transistor amplifiers will cause them to replace vacuum-tube amplifiers in more and

Table 4-1. Specifications for Computer D-c Amplifiers

1. *Rated d-c output voltage vs. current*
2. *Maximum open-loop* output voltage with specified total harmonic distortion vs. frequency* (*brief specifications* should state maximum frequency for full rated output voltage); at rated output current and at a specified fraction of rated output current
3. *Open-loop gain and phase shift vs. frequency* for small-signal (5 per cent of rated max amplitude) sinusoidal output
   a. No load
   b. With specified resistance-capacitance loads (*brief specifications* should state −3-db frequency, 0-db frequency, phase shift at 0 db, and maximum phase shift with gain above 0 db)
4. *Open-loop* step response* (rise and fall times, per cent overshoot) for positive and negative steps of 5 and 80 per cent of max rated output amplitude
   a. No load
   b. With specified resistance-capacitance loads
5. *Maximum offset voltage* (referred to input) 10 min, 8 hr, and 1 week after balancing. For transistor amplifiers, specify temperature range and offset voltage and current change per deg C.   Specify power-supply voltage tolerances
6. *RMS and peak-to-peak noise* (referred to input); give amplitude of line-frequency components separately
7. *Overload-recovery time* after specified overload condition
8. *Power-supply and environmental requirements, physical dimensions,* etc.
9. *Input impedance* (Z_G) *and output impedance* (Z_I)

---

* Manufacturers also often specify frequency response and step response for a unity-gain inverter with specified feedback circuit, specified resistance-capacitance load, and specified summing-point shunt capacitance, as in a computer.

more applications, as they already have in practically all airborne analog computers.   Miniaturized solid-state amplifiers with their low impedance levels and low heat dissipation open new horizons of system design with decreased wiring-capacitance effects, a feature of the greatest importance for fast iterative and hybrid analog-digital computation.

Table 4-1 summarizes recommended specifications for computer d-c amplifiers.   Table 4-2 and Secs. 4-23 and 5-12 illustrate amplifier design principles by a number of practical examples.

4-2. Survey of Design Procedure.   Amplifier design frequently starts with the choice of an *output stage* on the basis of required output, available power supplies, and environment (Secs. 4-7, 4-8, and 5-3).

The type and number of voltage-amplifier stages are next determined through consideration of successive trial designs; one would like to implement the required amplifier specifications as simply and economically as possible.

The design of *d-c voltage-amplifier stages* (Secs. 4-3 to 4-9, 5-3 to 5-7) is not essentially different from the usual design procedure for a-c amplifiers, except for the fact that vacuum-tube or transistor electrode voltages will be related by conductive interconnections; in addition, the quiescent voltages at the amplifier input and output terminals must be zero. The d-c amplifier input stage, usually the most critical with respect to drift and noise effects (Sec. 4-10), is very frequently a difference-amplifier stage (Secs. 4-6 and 5-1) and permits simple addition of chopper stabilization (Secs. 4-13, 4-14, and 5-8) to reduce amplifier drift and to increase the low-frequency gain.   Since amplifier design is a well-developed art, the development of a new amplifier will frequently draw on possible modifications of an existing proved design (Secs. 4-23 and 5-12).

A proposed combination of d-c amplifier stages yielding sufficient d-c gain will have to be analyzed, and usually modified, with a view to meeting frequency-response and feedback-stability specifications (Secs. 4-15 to 4-21 and 5-11).   The final amplifier circuit must be carefully reviewed to ensure acceptable worst-case performance with respect to the effects of specified component tolerances.

DESIGN OF VACUUM-TUBE D-C AMPLIFIER STAGES

4-3. Choice of Vacuum-tube Operating Points.   The basic procedure for designing amplifier stages with the aid of published vacuum-tube characteristics is described in detail in texts on electronics, such as ref. 5. Figure 4-2 shows typical vacuum-tube characteristics and load lines drawn for a particular value of the plate-load resistor R_P.

The operating point for a voltage-amplifier stage will be selected for high gain without excessive distortion, usually about 5 per cent without feedback.   As a rule of thumb, one selects operating voltages so that the quiescent plate voltages E_b of all tubes except for low-level input stages equal about one-half of the available supply voltage, so as to permit sufficient plate-voltage swings.[13]   Some cathode potentials can be negative with respect to ground to yield suitable voltage relations.   The quiescent plate currents, determined by plate-load, cathode, and/or screen resistors, are next selected so that vacuum-tube transconductances are as high as practicable (1,000 to 15,000 μmhos); note that this will affect the total power-supply current, and a compromise may be necessary.   A rough value for the plate-load resistance R_P (Fig. 4-2a) yielding a desired plate current is $R_P \approx (E_{bb} - E_b)/I_b$.

Proper amplifier design must allow for operating-point changes due

to resistor and vacuum-tube tolerances (*worst-case design*); note that some
of these effects can be amplified in succeeding stages.   Resistor tolerances
of 10 per cent are usually specified.   One can usually compensate for the
effects of vacuum-tube changes by placing the amplifier balance control
into the input stage.

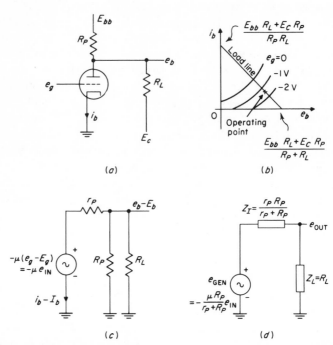

(a)   (b)

(c)   (d)

Fig. 4-2. Simple vacuum-tube (triode or pentode) amplifier (a), plate characteristics
with load lines (b), small-signal equivalent circuit (c), and equivalent-generator
circuit (d).   For *pentodes*, $r_P \gg R_P$, so that

$$e_{\text{GEN}} \approx -\frac{\mu R_P}{r_P} e_{\text{IN}} = -g_m R_P e_{\text{IN}} \qquad Z_I \approx R_P$$

4-4. Linear Equivalent Circuits.   For purposes of amplifier design,
vacuum-tube characteristics can be considered as piecewise linear;[5]
minor nonlinear distortion, even in output stages, is usually greatly
reduced in operational-amplifier feedback circuits (Sec. 3-16).   It is,
then, sufficient to obtain the incremental vacuum-tube parameters

$$r_P = \frac{\partial e_b}{\partial i_b} \qquad \text{(PLATE RESISTANCE)}$$

$$g_m = \frac{\partial i_b}{\partial e_g} \qquad \text{(GRID-PLATE TRANSCONDUCTANCE)} \qquad \Big\} \quad (4\text{-}1)$$

$$\mu = \frac{\partial e_b}{\partial e_g} = g_m r_P \qquad \text{(AMPLIFICATION FACTOR)}$$

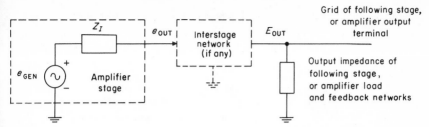

FIG. 4-3a. General equivalent-generator representation of vacuum-tube amplifier stages.

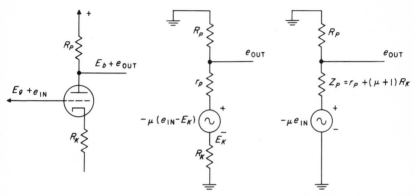

FIG. 4-3b. Cathode-biased amplifier stage and linear equivalent circuits, with

$$e_{GEN} = -\frac{\mu R_P}{r_P + (1 + \mu)R_K} e_{IN} \qquad Z_I = \frac{R_P}{1 + \{R_P/[r_P + (1 + \mu)R_K]\}}$$

Cathode degeneration decreases the gain and increases the internal impedance; note that the vacuum tube with cathode feedback has the equivalent (incremental) impedance $Z_P = r_P + (1 + \mu)R_K$.

from the published tube characteristics for the desired operating points (quiescent grid voltage E_g and quiescent plate and screen voltages and currents E_b, E_s, I_b, I_s).

For piecewise-linear vacuum-tube characteristics, the output voltage e_b of the basic amplifier stage of Fig. 4-2 is given by

$$\frac{e_b - E_b}{e_g - E_g} = \frac{e_{OUT}}{e_{IN}} = -\mu \frac{R_P}{R_P + r_P} \frac{1}{1 + [R_P r_P/(R_P + r_P)R_L]} \qquad (4\text{-}2)$$

and the small input voltage $e_{IN} = e_g - E_g$ and output voltage

$$e_{OUT} = e_b - E_b$$

are conveniently related by the *linear equivalent circuit* of Fig. 4-2c. Application of Thévenin's theorem to this equivalent circuit results in the *equivalent-generator circuit* of Fig. 4-2d, which yields the small-signal output e_{OUT} for any load impedance $Z_L = Z_L(j\omega)$ in the form

$$e_{\text{OUT}} = \frac{1}{1 + Z_I/Z_L}\, e_{\text{GEN}} \qquad (4\text{-}3)$$

The *no-load d-c gain* $e_{\text{GEN}}/e_{\text{IN}}$ and the *equivalent-generator impedance* Z_I of a vacuum-tube stage can usually be regarded as real and independent of frequency, so that the equivalent-generator representation is particularly convenient for frequency-response calculations (Fig. 4-3a, Secs.

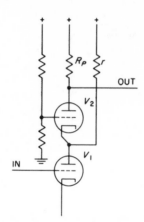

FIG. 4-3c. A cascode amplifier stage, with

$$e_{\text{GEN}} = \frac{-\mu_1(1 + \mu_2)R_P}{(1 + r_{P1}/r)(r_{P2} + R_P) + (1 + \mu_2)r_{P1}}\, e_{\text{IN}}$$

$$Z_I = \frac{(1 + r_{P1}/r)r_{P2} + (1 + \mu_2)r_{P1}}{(1 + r_{P1}/r)(r_{P2} + R_P) + (1 + \mu_2)r_{P1}}\, R_P$$

has relatively high gain and low Miller effect (Sec. 4-16) and may be useful, for example, for replacing a pentode with two triodes. Resistor r supplies extra current to V_1 for a more favorable operating point.

4-16 and 4-17). Figures 4-3b, 4-5, and 4-6 give equivalent-generator data for the most important types of vacuum-tube stages. These formulas will be found useful in gain and frequency-response calculations (see also Sec. 4-16).

4-5. Use of Resistance-coupled-amplifier Tables. The design of d-c voltage-amplifier stages is greatly simplified if one can adopt vacuum-tube operating conditions similar to those given in published *resistance-coupled-amplifier tables*. Such tables usually refer to an a-c voltage-amplifier stage of the type shown in Fig. 4-4a with bypassed cathode and screen resistors. The tabulated data may be used to design an "equivalent" d-c amplifier, shown in Fig. 4-4b. This d-c amplifier will have approximately the same operating point as the original a-c amplifier if the resistance of the load connected to it is high; this is usually the case for voltage-amplifier stages. The equivalent d-c amplifier stage has fixed bias and, in the case of pentodes, a fixed screen voltage. The gain will, in general, be slightly higher than that given in the tables, since the plate-load resistance is higher and also because the resistance of the load connected to the d-c amplifier stage often will be higher than the resistance R_g specified in the tables.

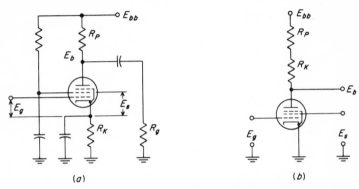

FIG. 4-4. Development of a d-c amplifier stage from a known resistance-coupled a-c amplifier stage. Disregard screen and suppressor grid in case of triodes.

4-6. Differential-amplifier Stages.

Differential-amplifier stages (Fig. 4-5) are frequently employed, especially in the input stages of computer amplifiers, because of the following significant features:

1. Possibility of mixing two input voltages or an input and a feedback voltage.
2. Output of either sign, with or without phase inversion can be obtained; if desired, one can obtain push-pull output as well as push-pull input.
3. The quiescent levels of input and output voltages can be chosen with relative freedom.
4. Self-biasing operation permits wide input-voltage swings (up to ± 50 volts) without overload.
5. No Miller effect (Sec. 4-16) occurs on the cathode-follower-input side.
6. Drift and noise reduction through subtraction of the effects of cathode-emission changes, grid-current pickup, etc., in two similar tubes (common-mode rejection).

On the other hand, the gain of a differential-amplifier stage is necessarily less than that of a similar amplifier stage using the worse of the two tubes alone; if both difference-amplifier tubes are of the same type, the stage gain will be, at most, one-half of that obtainable with a single tube for the operating point and same load circuit.

If the output is to be accurately proportional to $e_2 - e_1$ (common-mode rejection), one requires $\mu_1 \gg 1$, $\mu_2 \gg 1$, $\mu_2 R_K \gg r_{P2}$; one employs high-μ

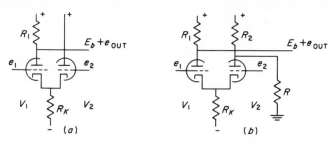

FIG. 4-5. Differential-amplifier stages. The following formulas are derived for the circuit of Fig. 4-5a but apply to the push-pull circuit of Fig. 4-5b if r_{P2} is replaced by $r_{P2} + \dfrac{R_2 R}{R_2 + R}$.

$$e_{\text{GEN}} = \frac{R_1}{\dfrac{(1 + \mu_1)R_K r_{P2}}{r_{P2} + (1 + \mu_2)R_K} + R_1 + r_{P1}} \left[\frac{\mu_2(1 + \mu_1)R_K}{r_{P2} + (1 + \mu_2)R_K} e_2 - \mu_1 e_1 \right]$$

$$Z_I = R_1 \frac{\dfrac{(1 + \mu_1)r_{P2}R_K}{r_{P2} + (1 + \mu_2)R_K} + r_{P1}}{\dfrac{(1 + \mu_1)r_{P2}R_K}{r_{P2} + (1 + \mu_2)R_K} + r_{P1} + R_1}$$

In most practical situations, these relations can be simplified:

1. For $\mu_1 \gg 1$, $\mu_2 \gg 1$, $\mu_2 R_K \gg r_{P2}$, $r_{P1} \gg R_1$ (V_1 is a pentode),

$$e_{\text{GEN}} \approx \frac{g_{m1}g_{m2}}{g_{m1} + g_{m2}} R_1(e_2 - e_1) \qquad Z_I \approx R_1$$

2. For $\mu_1 = \mu_2 = \mu$, $r_{P1} = r_{P2} = r_P$ (Fig. 4-5a with two similar tubes),

$$e_{\text{GEN}} = \frac{\mu R_1}{\dfrac{r_P}{1 + \dfrac{r_P}{(1 + \mu)R_K}} + R_1 + r_P} \left[\frac{1}{1 + \dfrac{r_P}{(1 + \mu)R_K}} e_2 - e_1 \right]$$

If, in addition, $\mu \gg 1$ and $\mu R_K \gg r_P$, then

$$e_{\text{GEN}} \approx \frac{\mu}{R_1 + 2r_P} (e_2 - e_1) \qquad Z_I \approx \frac{2r_P}{1 + 2r_P/R_1}$$

tubes and returns R_K to the negative high-voltage supply, so that R_K can be as large as possible (see also Figs. 4-26 to 4-31). R_K can also be replaced by the high incremental impedance of a vacuum tube with current feedback (see also Sec. 4-8).

4-7. Output-stage Design. (a) The amplifier output stage must supply a specified output voltage (usually either ± 100 volts or ± 50 volts for vacuum-tube amplifiers) to a rated load. Load specifications should include the load capacitance due to computing networks and unavoidable circuit and wiring capacitances. Low open-loop amplifier output impedance (output-stage source impedance) Z_I is desirable to minimize gain deterioration, phase shift, and possible instability at high frequencies (see also Secs. 4-17 and 5-12). In addition, output stages supplying more than a fraction of a watt should be designed so as to dissipate as little power as possible, especially at zero output current, in order to minimize power consumption, heat dissipation, and tube-size requirements. Output-stage distortion is usually greatly reduced by the feedback loop gain of the operational amplifier.

Two basic types of vacuum-tube output stages may be distinguished:

1. *Cathode-follower Output Stages* (Figs. 4-6a and c). A cathode follower produces no voltage gain, but it has low output impedance and requires only two high-voltage power supplies. Cathode-follower output stages are used in most wideband computer amplifiers (zero-db bandwidth in excess of 100 Kc) and in small computing and instrumentation systems where the cost of an extra power supply would be spread over only a few amplifiers.

2. *Amplifier-type Output Stages* (Figs. 4-6b and d). Output stages producing voltage gain have higher output impedances than cathode-follower output stages and necessarily require two negative supply voltages as well as a positive supply. The second negative power supply can, however, simply take the form of a capacitor-bypassed power zener diode in the cathode lead. Output-stage gain may save the cost and phase shift of an added voltage-amplifier stage; in addition, the design of the voltage amplifier driving the output stage becomes less critical because of the reduced voltage swing required. Amplifier-type output stages are, therefore, commonly employed in "slow" electronic analog computing systems, where the cost of the extra power supply required can be spread over 10 or more amplifiers.

Output-stage tubes and operating points are chosen with the aid of published vacuum-tube characteristics in the conventional manner.[5] The use of high-g_m tubes is advisable in cathode-follower circuits requiring a low output impedance.

(b) Figure 4-7a illustrates the currents and power dissipation in a typical *cathode-follower output stage* as its output varies between $+100$ volts and -100 volts. For $X_o = E_{\text{MIN}} = -100$ volts, essentially the entire output current i_L is supplied through the cathode resistor R_K, so

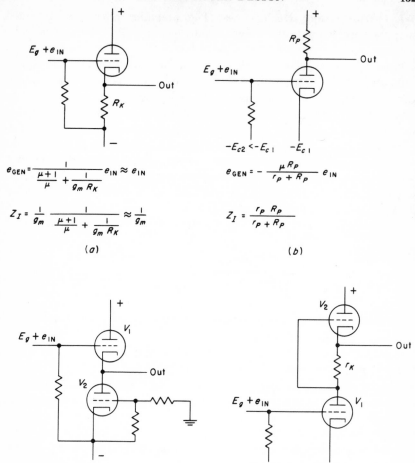

FIG. 4-6. Cathode-follower and amplifier-type output stages for operational amplifiers, and equivalent-generator data. Each amplifier output operates at zero d-c level.

that the maximum output current for linear operation is limited by

$$R_K = \frac{E_c + E_{\text{MIN}}}{|i_{\text{MAX}}|} \tag{4-4}$$

But the value of R_K also determines the maximum plate dissipation

P_1 in V_1, which is largest for the positive output voltage

$$X_o = E_{MAX} = +100 \text{ volts}$$

so that a compromise must be made for each given tube type.   General-purpose computer amplifiers should be able to supply equal load currents at $+E_{MAX}$ and $-E_{MAX}$, but some special-purpose amplifiers can be designed for different output currents at positive and negative output

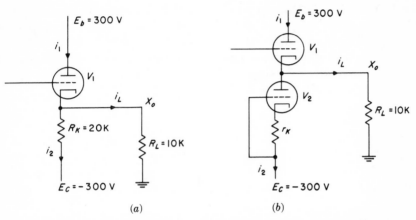

(a)   (b)

FIG. 4-7. Comparison of currents and power dissipation in a cathode-follower output stage (a) and a totem-pole cathode-follower stage (b).   The incremental imped-ance $R'_K = \Delta X_o/\Delta i_2$ of the cathode circuit is $Z_P = r_P + (\mu + 1)r_K$; for $\mu = 20$, $r_K = 15\text{K}$, and $Z_P > 300\text{K}$. i_2 changes by less than 0.35 mA as X_o varies from 0 to $+100$ or -100 volts.

	$X_o = 0$	$X_o = -100$ volts	$X_o = +100$ volts	$X_o = 0$	$X_o = -100$ volts	$X_o = +100$ volts
i_L	0	-10 mA	10 mA	0	-10 mA	10 mA
i_2	15 mA	10 mA	20 mA	10 mA	≈ 10 mA	≈ 10 mA
i_1	15 mA	0 (V_1 just cut off)	30 mA	10 mA	0 (V_1 just cut off)	20 mA
P_L	0	1 watt	1 watt	0	1 watt	1 watt
P_2	4.5 watts	2 watts	8 watts	3 watts	2 watts	4 watts
P_1	4.5 watts	0	6 watts	3 watts	0	4 watts
P_{total}	9 watts	3 watts = $3P_L$	15 watts = $15P_L$	6 watts	3 watts = $3P_L$	9 watts = $9P_L$

voltages.   Since the usual amplifier loads comprise some parallel capaci-tance, the load current at a given output voltage will increase with fre-quency, and proper amplifier specifications should include the maximum frequency at which full rated output into a specified load is required (see also Sec. 4-16).

(c) In an *amplifier-type output stage* (Fig. 4-6b), the output current at the maximum positive output voltage E_{MAX} is essentially determined by the plate resistor R_P; the choice of R_P again affects the maximum power dissipation in vacuum tube V_1, which will now take place at *negative* output voltages.

(**d**) To save power and heat dissipation when the amplifier is lightly loaded, the output-stage load resistors R_K or R_P of some computer amplifiers are deliberately made larger than permissible for maximum plate dissipation, and external *booster resistors* are wired or patched across R_K or R_P to supply extra load current when needed.

4-8. Totem-pole Output Stages.   (**a**) If the power dissipated in the output stage exceeds $\frac{1}{2}$ watt, it is customary to replace the resistor R_K or R_P by a vacuum tube with cathode feedback (Figs. 4-6c, d, and 4-7b). Although such a circuit easily passes as much current as the 2K to 50K resistors it replaces, its *incremental* impedance $Z_P = \partial e/\partial i$ can be made large.   Specifically, for $r_K = 15\text{K}$, and $\mu = 20$,

$$Z_P = r_P + (\mu + 1)r_K \tag{4-5}$$

exceeds 300K.   It follows that the current drawn through such a "constant-current" branch changes by only a fraction of a milliampere from its design value (set by the choice of r_K) as the output voltage X_o varies through its full range.   By comparison, the cathode-resistor current in Fig. 4-7a is seen to vary between 10 and 20 mA under the same conditions.   As a result, both the total quiescent power and the maximum power dissipated in the totem-pole output stage are very substantially reduced (Fig. 4-7b), and cooler and more efficient operation is achieved.

Figure 4-8a illustrates another constant-current circuit which permits the use of a smaller vacuum tube, frequently a half-triode left over in some other part of the amplifier, as the cathode resistance.   In Fig. 4-8b, *feedback to the grid of the dynamic-load tube* further decreases the output impedance.

(**b**) In the *totem-pole-amplifier output stage*, the plate-load resistor is replaced by a constant-current tube with substantially the same results as in the case of the totem-pole cathode-follower output circuit.   In practice, the output is taken at the cathode of V_2 rather than at the plate of V_1, because this appreciably reduces the output impedance (Fig. 4-6d).

(**c**) A vacuum tube used as a "dynamic load resistor" in the manner of Fig. 4-6c and d has the desired high incremental resistance and still supplies sufficient plate current to the amplifier tube to realize the full transconductance available from modern high-transconductance tubes.   This feature can be useful in *voltage-amplifier stages* as well as in output stages.   Note that biasing circuits for the dynamic-load tube must not introduce significant attenuation between the cathode-resistor voltage and the grid.

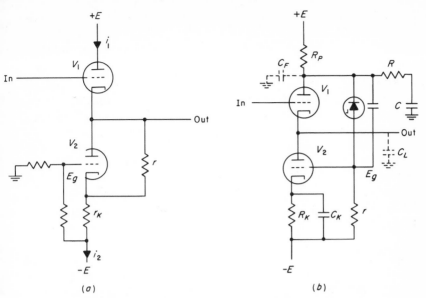

FIG. 4-8. (a) Cathode-follower output stage with a modified constant-current circuit of incremental impedance $R'_K = \dfrac{[r_P + (\mu + 1)r_K]r + r_P r_K}{r + r_P}$. Since r carries part of i_2, V_2 can be a smaller vacuum tube than V_1, e.g., a half-triode left over in another part of the amplifier. With $V_1 = $ 6AQ5, $V_2 = \frac{1}{2}$6U8, $E = 300$ volts, $E_g = -250$ volts, $r = 25\text{K}$, and $R_K = 3\text{K}$, this circuit yields 15 mA at ± 100 volts.[9]

(b) A cathode follower with feedback to lower the output impedance Z_I at high frequencies. At high frequencies, the parallel impedance of R_K, C_K is negligible, and the parallel impedance of R_P and R, C is $R_P R/(R_P + R) = R_F$. We must consider the stray capacitance C_F and find (assuming identical tubes)

$$Z_I = \frac{1}{g_m} \frac{j\omega + \alpha/R_F C_F}{j\omega + \beta/R_F C_F} \qquad \alpha = 1 + \frac{R_F}{r_P} \qquad \beta = 1 + g_m R_F$$

We vary R (and thus R_F, α, and β) to obtain a favorable frequency-response function $Z_L/(Z_I + Z_L)$. For a given capacitive load $Z_L \approx 1/j\omega C_L$,

$$\left(\frac{\alpha}{R_F C_F} + \frac{g_m}{C_L}\right)^2 \approx \frac{4\beta g_m}{R_F C_L C_F}$$

yields wideband flat response with a 12 db/octave rolloff. An output impedance as low as 30 ohms at 1 Mc has been measured, as compared with $Z_I \approx g_m^{-1} = 125$ ohms without feedback.[35] The zener diode can often be replaced by a capacitor.

4-9. Regenerative D-c Amplifier Stages (see also Sec. 4-20).

Regeneration (positive feedback) in one stage of a multistage amplifier enclosed within an overall degenerative loop offers the attractive possibility of increasing the feedback-loop gain so as to reduce finite-gain errors and to reduce the amplifier low-frequency output impedance together with the effects of phase shift, distortion, and gain changes in *other* stages of the amplifier. In Fig. 4-9a, the overall forward gain is

$$A = \frac{A_1 A_2}{1 - A_1 \beta_1} \tag{4-6}$$

so that $A_1 \beta_1 > 0$ will increase the amplifier loop gain in the ratio $(1 - A_1 \beta_1):1$. Regeneration around one amplifier stage will, then, decrease operational-amplifier errors due to finite gain, gain changes, and distortion (Secs. 3-10 to 3-16). In particular, small stage-gain changes dA_1,

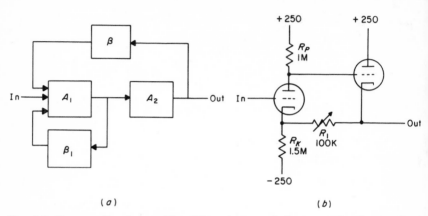

(a)   (b)

Fig. 4-9. Regenerative d-c amplifier (a), and a practical regenerative d-c amplifier stage (b) (see also ref. 13 and Fig. 4-26).

dA_2 due to circuit-element variations or distortion will produce the fractional forward-gain change

$$\frac{dA}{A} = \frac{1}{1 - A_1 \beta_1} \frac{dA_1}{A_1} + \frac{dA_2}{A_2} \tag{4-7}$$

The corresponding fractional change in the operational-amplifier output (3-19) is $dA/A(1 - A\beta)$ or, for the usual case of $|A\beta| \gg 1$,

$$\frac{1}{1 - A\beta} \frac{dA}{A} \approx -\frac{1}{A\beta} \frac{dA}{A} = -\frac{1}{A_1 A_2 \beta} \left[\frac{dA_1}{A_1} + (1 - A_1 \beta_1) \frac{dA_2}{A_2} \right] \tag{4-8}$$

Note that *regeneration in a d-c amplifier stage will reduce the effects of gain changes in the other amplifier stages without affecting the results of gain changes in the regenerative stage itself.*

Although one could, in principle, obtain conditional stability with infinite d-c loop gain by critical regeneration $(1 - A_1 \beta_1 = 0)$ at zero frequency,[5] this would make amplifier performance excessively dependent on $A_1 \beta_1$, and thus on possible component changes or tolerances in the regenerative stage. Amplifiers relying on regeneration for a major portion of their gain may require periodic regeneration adjustments, something to be avoided. In practice, regenerative d-c amplifier stages are used to increase the low-frequency gain by a factor of 2 to 10 and, especially, to cancel degeneration due to cathode-bias or screen-dropping resistors. Most commonly used regenerative circuits increase the amplifier gain only at relatively low frequencies and do not affect high-frequency stability adversely (Sec. 4-20).

Figure 4-9b shows a practical regenerative circuit used in several low-cost d-c amplifiers to save a voltage-amplifier stage (see also Fig. 4-26). Regeneration can also be introduced into difference-amplifier grids or into pentode screens.[26]

In symmetrical push-pull differential-amplifier stages (Fig. 4-5b), common-mode cancellation can be enhanced by regenerative feedback through crossed plate-to-grid resistors (see Sec. 5-6).

DRIFT, NOISE, AND CHOPPER STABILIZATION

4-10. Effects of Drift and Noise. Even if a d-c amplifier is initially balanced (zero output for zero input, Sec. 4-1), physical changes in amplifier and environment will cause addition of slowly varying unbalance voltages to the correct amplifier output, so that periodic rebalancing may be required. This d-c amplifier *drift* may be considered as a variety of very low-frequency noise, and like other additive amplifier noise, can be regarded as due to a set of voltage or current generators adding *error*

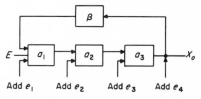

Fig. 4-10. Effect of d-c offset and noise voltages in different amplifier stages.

voltages e_1, e_2, . . . to the various stage inputs or outputs (Fig. 4-10). The combined effect of these unbalance or noise sources is best described in terms of the *equivalent offset (or noise) voltage E referred to the amplifier input*, defined as the input voltage required to cancel the effects of e_1, e_2, ... Thus, in Fig. 4-10, the output

$$X_o = a_1a_2a_3e_1 + a_2a_3e_2 + a_3e_3 + e_4 + a_1a_2a_3\beta X_o + a_1a_2a_3E$$
$$= \frac{a_1a_2a_3e_1 + a_2a_3e_2 + a_3e_3 + e_4 + a_1a_2a_3E}{1 - a_1a_2a_3\beta} \tag{4-9}$$

will be brought back to zero if

$$E = -\left(e_1 + \frac{1}{a_1}e_2 + \frac{1}{a_1a_2}e_3 + \frac{1}{a_1a_2a_3}e_4\right) \tag{4-10}$$

Note that the equivalent offset (or noise) E is completely independent of the feedback ratio β used, say, in an operational amplifier, since E is defined by $X_o = 0$ in Eq. (9).

Our equations (9) and (10) express the plausible idea that *low-drift and/or low-noise design is most important in the earlier amplifier stages* (*notably the input stage*), since errors will be amplified by succeeding stages.

Proper d-c amplifier specifications state the maximum value of the equivalent offset E during two or more time intervals after balancing, say during a typical computer run and during an 8-hr, 24-hr, or 7-day period.

Other spurious voltage or current sources in computer amplifiers are line-frequency and high-frequency pickup (Sec. 5-14), chopper noise (Sec. 4-14), and random vacuum-tube, semiconductor, and resistor noise. In general-purpose analog computers, amplifier output rms noise levels below 0.01 per cent of half scale are usually tolerable; note that this figure must be divided by the closed-loop gain to yield the rms noise referred to the amplifier input. Higher noise levels can cause objectionable offsets through rectification in multipliers or function generators. Instrumentation-type d-c amplifiers employ low-noise components together with special differential input circuits and shielding to achieve substantially lower noise levels than computer-type amplifiers.

4-11. Causes of D-c Amplifier Drift. Drift in d-c amplifier stages is mainly due to the following effects (see also Secs. 4-14 and 5-2):

1. Changes in the various amplifier *supply voltages*. Effects of filament-current changes in vacuum-tube input stages* are particularly serious, since they would contribute to e_1 in Fig. 4-10.
2. Effects of *temperature changes* on resistance values and especially on semiconductors.
3. *Aging* of vacuum tubes (especially cathode-emission changes in input stages), resistors, and semiconductors.
4. *Grid-current changes* in vacuum-tube stages. Although the bias due to a constant or steady-state grid current is readily balanced out, *changes* in grid current cause voltage drops leading to drift.†

---

* For most vacuum tubes with oxide-coated unipotential cathodes, a 20 per cent change in filament voltage is approximately equivalent to a grid-voltage change of 0.2 volt.

† 0.01 μA of grid current in a 1M input resistor causes a d-c input of 10 mV. For constant plate current, grid current in a vacuum triode increases with grid voltage from an initial negative value to a positive value (Fig. 4-11). The current into the grid is negative for sufficiently negative grid bias, because positive ions of the residual gas in the tube are attracted to the negative grid. The latter may even emit electrons if some of the oxide coating from the cathode should be deposited on the grid. For constant plate and filament currents, the amount of the negative grid current will depend mainly on the amount of the residual gas in the tube type in question. Typical negative grid currents vary between 10^{-3} and 10^{-5} μA for controlled-quality tubes like type 5691 or 5814 but may exceed 10^{-2} μA for ordinary receiving-type tubes. Cathode followers using high-quality tubes operating at low plate currents (plate-to-cathode voltage 25 volts, $i_b = 50$ μA, $R_K = 5$M) can have grid currents as low as 10^{-6} μA.

In addition to d-c amplifier drift in the strict sense of the word, changes in *spurious d-c input voltages* due to *d-c leakage* (from adjacent high-voltage points) and to *d-c ground currents* can contribute appreciably to the total unbalance voltage (see also Secs. 5-13 and 5-14). *Internal leakage currents* across amplifier circuit boards, connectors, or capacitor dielectrics must be guarded against as additional possible drift sources (Sec. 5-13).

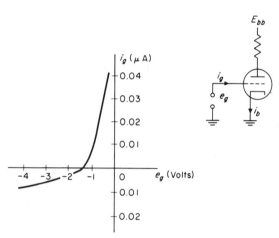

Fig. 4-11. Grid current vs. grid voltage for constant plate current in a triode.

4-12. Low-drift Circuit Design (see also Secs. 4-14 and 5-4 to 5-7). One can minimize drift due to resistance changes by choosing resistors of reasonable quality and operating them well below their power ratings. Circuit layout should permit a measure of ventilation, with critical resistors placed well away from hot vacuum tubes. Well-regulated power supplies reduce drift due to supply-voltage changes. Some computer installations supply regulated filament current at least to the amplifier input stages.

One can reduce input-stage grid current by using quality-controlled low-grid-current tubes and by operating the vacuum tubes with low plate, screen, and filament voltages to minimize ionization. One can also precede the amplifier with a low-grid-current cathode follower whose low output impedance makes the grid current of the succeeding stage harmless.

D-c leakage from high-voltage points, an elusive source of drift, must be avoided by good circuit layout (Sec. 5-13). The effects of supply-voltage changes, filament emission, and grid-voltage changes can be reduced by a factor of 4 to 7 through common-mode cancellation in difference-amplifier stages (Secs. 4-6 and 4-23) and similar symmetrical circuit arrangements (Fig. 4-12).

Drift in carefully designed vacuum-tube d-c amplifiers without chopper stabilization can be made as low as 2 to 10 mV referred to the input after a warmup period of about 1 hr; lower drift is possible with transistor amplifiers (Secs. 5-4 to 5-7). Very substantially reduced drift is obtained with automatic-balancing circuits.

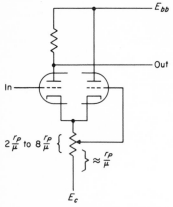

4-13. Improved D-c Amplifier Design: Automatic-balancing Circuits. The development of *automatic-balancing circuits* for d-c amplifiers represents a real breakthrough not only in the design of multipurpose electronic analog computers but in the entire related art of scientific and control instrumentation. Modern automatic-balancing circuits

1. Reduce d-c amplifier drift by a factor of 20 to 300.
2. Increase d-c amplifier gain at low frequencies by a factor of 500 to 5,000 for greatly improved static accuracy or integration accuracy.
3. Eliminate the necessity for frequent manual balancing. In certain applications, amplifier balance controls can be eliminated entirely.

FIG. 4-12. The *Miller compensator circuit*[1] can reduce drift due to filament-current and cathode-emission changes in the two similar half-triodes by a factor of 7 to 9. The tube should be aged and cycled through the expected extremes of heater voltage; the tap adjustment is best made so as to minimize effects of artificial heater-voltage changes. Designed for d-c amplifiers without chopper stabilization, this circuit lacks the two inputs and wide overload-free input swing of a difference-amplifier stage.

Figure 4-13 illustrates the operation of a *carrier-type* or *modulator/demodulator d-c amplifier* employing a single *synchronous vibrator* or *chopper* for both modulation and demodulation. The d-c (low-frequency) input voltage is interrupted periodically by the vibrating chopper relay. The resulting modulated a-c is amplified by a conventional a-c amplifier whose output is then rectified synchronously by the same vibrator; the d-c (low-frequency) output voltage is smoothed by a filter network. The waveforms of Fig. 4-13b indicate that both modulation and demodulation are *phase-sensitive;* i.e., both the a-c carrier phase and the d-c output polarity reverse with the sign of the input voltage. Note that the overall gain of the carrier-type amplifier in Fig. 4-13 is *negative* if the a-c amplifier gain is *positive* (even number of conventional vacuum-tube stages).

The striking feature of carrier-type d-c amplifiers employing electromechanical choppers or equivalent rotating switches is their very low

drift. Even for relatively inexpensive circuits (Fig. 4-15), 1-hr offset is
below 100 μV referred to the input, and substantially better results are
possible. Note, however, that modulated-carrier operation restricts the
use of such d-c amplifiers to frequencies below about one-twentieth of
the carrier frequency. Since electromechanical choppers cannot be
operated consistently at frequencies much above 400 cps, wideband
carrier-type d-c amplifiers require electronic chopping at relatively high
frequencies, with an attendant increase in the amplifier drift (Sec. 5-8).

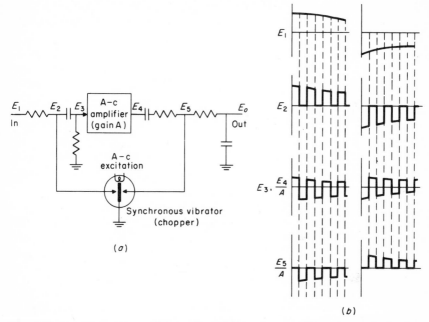

Fig. 4-13. Carrier-type or modulator/demodulator d-c amplifier using a single electromechanical chopper (*a*), and waveforms (*b*).

Figure 4-14*a* shows how a low-offset carrier-type d-c amplifier (*chopper-
stabilizer channel*) is combined with a conventional d-c amplifier to
improve its drift and low-frequency gain without any bandwidth reduction. While high-frequency signal components can enter the main d-c
amplifier directly through the blocking capacitor C_B, low-frequency components are seen to pass first through the chopper-stabilizer channel.
Referring to our discussion of Sec. 4-10, the stabilizer channel is seen to
act as a low-frequency preamplifier, so that *drift originating in the main
amplifier is effectively divided by the absolute d-c gain* $|A_2|$ *of the stabilizer
channel,* typically 1,000 to 4,000. As a result, practically the entire
remaining drift of the chopper-stabilized d-c amplifier is due to

1. Chopper-frequency pickup, including ground currents, in the stabilizer channel
2. Small offset voltages originating in the chopper itself
3. Leakage into summing-point or stabilizer-input connections (see also Secs. 5-13 and 11-1)
4. D-c offset voltages in the ground circuits

(see also Secs. 4-14 and 5-8). In typical computer installations, the remaining long-term (8-hr) offset voltages are within 20 to 200 μV,

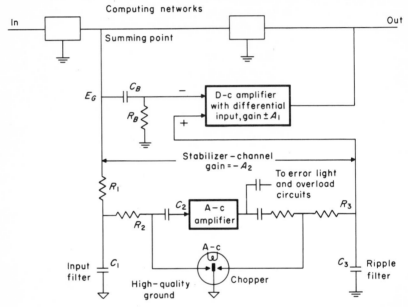

FIG. 4-14a. Operational d-c amplifier with chopper stabilization. The grid-blocking circuit C_B, R_B can be omitted to speed overload recovery if the main d-c amplifier has a low-grid-current input stage. Capacitors C_1, C_2, C_3, and C_B must have low dielectric absorption.

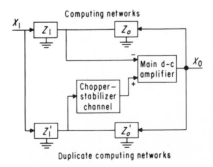

FIG. 4-14b. This alternative chopper-stabilization scheme reduces drift due to grid current or transistor base current in the main amplifier and does not require a grid-blocking capacitor, but all computing networks must be duplicated; $Z_o'/Z_1' = Z_o/Z_1$.

although much smaller offsets can be obtained in instrument-type amplifiers.

In addition to the drift reduction afforded by the stabilizer channel, the extreme-low-frequency gain of the main amplifier is multiplied by $|A_2|$; thus, for $A_1 = 50,000$, $|A_2| = 2,000$, we obtain the phenomenal d-c gain $|A| = |A_1A_2| = 100,000,000$ combined with low drift, so that excellent low-frequency computing accuracy becomes possible.

The alternative chopper-stabilization scheme of Fig. 4-14b[20] reduces the effects of offset currents at the main amplifier input (grid current, transistor base current) without a grid-blocking capacitor. Since this circuit requires duplicate computing networks, it is rarely used in general-purpose analog computers.

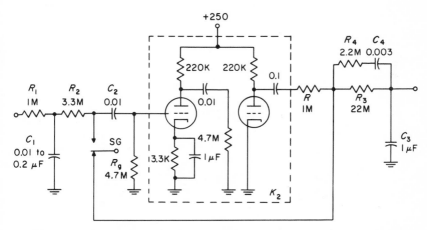

FIG. 4-15. A practical chopper-stabilizer channel for use with a 60-cps chopper. A 12AX7 tube may be used. (*From H. D. Huskey and G. A. Korn, Computer Handbook, McGraw-Hill, New York, 1962.*)

Commutator Stabilization. A *commutator-type automatic balancing circuit*[21] time-shares a single stabilizing pulse amplifier among up to 85 d-c amplifiers by means of ganged rotating switches (commutators with rotating brushes), which replace the input and output choppers in Fig. 4-14. The input switch rotates at 180 rpm and samples the summing-point d-c unbalance on each capacitor C_1 three times per second. The sample pulses are successively amplified by the stabilizer amplifier and are then applied to the stabilizer output filter of the correct d-c amplifiers by the second or output section of the commutator switch. An extra pair of commutator sections permits a continuous check of the stabilizer amplifier. The relatively low 3-cps sampling rate makes the commutator stabilizer less effective in increasing d-c amplifier low-frequency gain than a 60- or 94-cps chopper stabilizer, but automatic balancing to within 100 to 400 μV is achieved.

After initial difficulties due to pulse crosstalk, hum pickup, and electrostatic charges (electret and hysteresis effects) in the cables needed to connect the individual d-c amplifiers, commutator stabilizers were used with excellent results in large and small analog computers.[12] In the writers' opinion, however, commutator stabilization has been made obsolete by the development of relatively low-cost, high-quality choppers whose estimated life of about 9,000 hr compares favorably with commutator-brush life. The actual equipment savings are, at best, marginal; and commutator stabilization compromises computer system design, not so much by its somewhat inferior performance as by the necessity of tying many amplifiers by critical cabling into a single switch rotating at fairly high speed.

4-14. Chopper-stabilizer Design.   (a) Chopper Construction and Operation.   Figure 4-16 shows the mechanical construction of a high-quality chopper.   Since any a-c pickup at a chopping frequency is equivalent to a d-c offset error, careful electromagnetic shielding isolates the signal circuit not only from outside fields, but also from the chopper a-c coil.   Chopper contacts carrying different signals must be similarly isolated from each other.   The exciting a-c may or may not be supplied through a top connector for further isolation.   The potential accuracy of modern chopper circuits is so great that attention has to be paid to

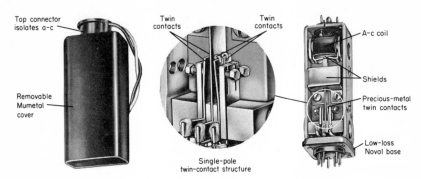

Fig. 4-16. Mechanical construction of a high-quality electromechanical chopper. (*Stevens-Arnold, Inc., So. Boston, Mass.*)

minute d-c offset voltages generated by electrochemical, thermoelectrical, and piezoelectrical effects in the contact assembly.   Equivalent d-c offsets from all these sources, as well as from signal pickup, can be made as low as a few microvolts if the chopper contacts are operated at a low impedance level (100 ohms).   Most computer choppers operate at much higher impedances (of the order of 100K) to save the expense of well-shielded transformers, so that typical long-term offsets of chopper-stabilized computer amplifiers vary between 20 and 200 μV.

Long *chopper contact life*, a very important consideration for reliable and maintenance-free computer operation, is ensured through the use of gold-alloy contacts (0 to 10 volts d-c; 0 to 1 mA) or platinum-rhodium contacts (1 to 50 volts d-c, 5 mA; at least 1 volt for low contact resistance).   Twin contacts (Fig. 4-16) permit small amounts of oxide to wear or burn off one contact without interrupting operation.   Proper circuit design will prevent excessive contact currents, especially during amplifier overloads (see Fig. 4-27 for the use of limiting diodes).   With reasonable precautions, maintenance-free chopper life between 5,000 and 14,000 hr can be expected. Faulty chopper operation due to asymmetrical contact closures, dirty contacts, etc., is sometimes corrected with the aid of a simple test socket connected to an oscilloscope to display the chopper waveforms. Some types of choppers may require vertical operation for symmetrical operation. Special chopper designs (balanced-armature choppers) can operate under conditions of shock and vibration.[23]

For economical design and maintenance-free operation, the output chopper, whose offset voltages are effectively divided by the chopper-channel gain, can be replaced by relatively crude electronic (diode) switches, so that a single high-quality chopper can serve two d-c amplifiers if adequate precautions against crosstalk are taken. Since the cost of a high-quality chopper can be a substantial fraction of the total d-c amplifier cost, such dual amplifiers are used in many computers (Fig. 4-27).

One can sometimes reduce hum-pickup effects by phasing the chopper excitation so that the pickup is in approximate quadrature with the chopped signal. In high-accuracy applications, it is advisable to employ a chopper frequency not harmonically related to the line frequency, such as 94 cps. Where the use of a separate chopper-excitation oscillator does not seem justified, one can reduce offsets due to line-frequency pickup at the expense of contact life by employing chopper reeds tuned to twice the line frequency.

(b) The A-c Amplifier. Chopper-channel a-c amplifiers are conventional resistance-coupled amplifiers with low-frequency gains between 1,000 and 15,000 (Figs. 4-15, 4-27, and 4-28 to 4-30). The gain must be positive unless separate input and output choppers are used. Even though a high-quality input capacitor (C_2 in Fig. 4-14) is used, the a-c amplifier input stage should always be cathode-biased to prevent possible drift due to leakage from the grid circuit into the chopper.[13] The input-stage grid-leak resistor should be at least as large as the sum of R_1 and R_2 in Fig. 4-14 to minimize signal attenuation.[13]

For accurate operation, choppers and chopper-amplifier cathode or cathode-bypass returns require *high-quality grounds* without d-c offsets and a-c pickup. This question is further discussed in Sec. 5-14.

With high-gain chopper amplifiers, stray capacitance in or near the chopper can cause the positive-gain amplifier to oscillate at some high frequency. This is prevented through careful circuit layout and, if necessary, by a small capacitor bypassing one of the amplifier plates, as in Fig. 4-27a.

(c) Stabilizer-channel Filters and Frequency Response. The stabilizer input and output filters (R_1, C_1 and R_3, C_3 in Figs. 4-14 and 4-15) cut off well below the chopper frequency f_C, and dominate the stabilizer-channel frequency response, so that for practical purposes

$$A_2(j\omega) = \frac{A_2(0)}{(j\omega R_1 C_1 + 1)(j\omega R_3 C_3 + 1)} \tag{4-11}$$

The *input filter* (R_1, C_1) attenuates chopper-frequency input noise and prevents stabilizer-channel errors or overloads due to the possibly relatively large high-frequency components of the summing-point error voltage E_G. C_1 and R_2 also form a filter intended to remove chopper-frequency components from the amplifier summing point. $R_1 C_1$ varies between $0.8/f_C$ and $10/f_C$, with larger values corresponding to larger stabilizer-channel gains and larger expected summing-point errors.[13]

The *ripple filter* (R_3, C_3 in Figs. 4-14 and 4-15) smoothes the stabilizer output ripple, which acts as a noise voltage (chopper noise) at the amplifier input (Secs. 3-15 and 4-10). Since the d-c output of our stabilizer must approximate the d-c offset E_{DC} of the main d-c amplifier in absolute value, the amplitude of the rectified output-chopper pulses is about $2|E_{DC}|$, assuming symmetrical chopper action. The ripple filter reduces the ripple to a roughly triangular waveform at the chopper frequency $f_{CHOPPER}$, with peak-to-peak amplitude $E_{DC}/R_3 C_3 f_C$. With a d-c offset $E_{DC} = 12$ mV, for instance, the filter time constant $R_3 C_3 = 20$ sec in Fig. 4-15 will reduce 60-cps chopper noise to 10 μV peak to peak. Note that balancing of the main d-c amplifier will reduce E_{DC}, and hence the error voltage in the chopper channel and the chopper noise.

An excessively large filter time constant $R_3 C_3$ adds to amplifier cost, restricts the benefits of the chopper-channel gain, and slows overload recovery (Sec. 4-14d). To reduce chopper noise without increasing $R_3 C_3$, one can

1. Increase the chopper frequency
2. Use a more complicated chopper (e.g., Leeds and Northrup type 3338-9), which breaks the connection to R_3 before grounding the a-c amplifier output to obtain peak detection or sample-hold action[22]
3. Add an a-c preamplifier ahead of the main d-c amplifier to divide the chopper noise by the preamplifier gain (Fig. 4-28)

In practice, however, the feedback-stability requirements outlined in Secs. 4-16 and 4-19 may require $R_3 C_3$ to be larger than needed for adequate ripple filtering, viz.,

$$R_3 C_3 > 2A_2(0)R_1 C_1 \text{ to } 4A_2(0)R_1 C_1 \tag{4-12}$$

This condition ensures that the output filter reduces the stabilizer-channel gain $|A_2(j\omega)|$ to unity before the input filter causes excessive phase shift; $|A_2(j\omega)|$ should also reduce to unity before the main-amplifier phase shift exceeds, say, 45 deg.   Where the filter time constant R_3C_3 required by Eq. (12) seems excessive, we can also "break" the stabilizer-channel gain with a rolloff network (R_4, C_4 in Fig. 4-15; see Sec. 4-17).

(d) Overload Recovery and Error Lights. Voltage overload or current limiting in the d-c or stabilizer amplifiers reduces or kills the amplifier gain; so that the summing-point error voltage E_G is no longer held near zero and can assume positive or negative values of the order of the full amplifier output.   With suitable overload indication, the operator can reset the machine and remove the cause of the overload; but unfortunately, the overload charges on the capacitances C_1, C_2, C_3, and C_B of a chopper-stabilizer circuit (Fig. 4-14) have large discharge time constants and can keep the summing point overloaded for several minutes.   To speed overload recovery, to minimize dielectric absorption errors, and to protect the chopper contacts, one shunts the summing point or the especially troublesome blocking capacitor C_B with silicon diodes which begin to conduct at ± 0.5 volt (Fig. 4-27).   It is also possible to discharge the guilty capacitors with relays.   Some amplifier designs omit the blocking capacitor C_B entirely and use a low-grid-current input stage in the main amplifier; the modified chopper-stabilizer circuit of Fig. 4-14*b* is another possibility.

The increased summing-point voltage due to even a mild overload produces a greatly increased a-c output in the stabilizer channel.   The amplifier pulses at the a-c amplifier output furnish a very useful overload indication; they can directly light neon bulbs (*error lights*), or they can be rectified for use in a central overload-warning system (Sec. 11-4).   Unlike neon or biased-diode overload indicators connected to the main amplifier output, error lights indicate not only fixed absolute voltage limits, but true voltage and/or current overloads.   An amplifier equipped with an error light may permit, for example, high-voltage operation at low current, or high-current operation at low voltage.   Error lights can also detect various types of malfunctions in amplifiers and power supplies.   Note, however, that error lights cannot indicate *momentary* overloads and will, therefore, not serve as overload lights in repetitive analog computation.

4-15. Frequency Response and Stability of Feedback Amplifiers. Computer d-c amplifiers are used in operational feedback circuits of the type shown in Fig. 4-17, where the forward gain $A(j\omega)$ and the feedback ratio $\beta(j\omega)$ are understood to include the effects of shunt impedances at the amplifier input and output (see also Sec. 3-11).   For proper operational-amplifier operation, such a feedback loop must be *stable*, i.e., the summing-point-to-output transfer function $A(s)/[1 - A(s)\beta(s)]$ must not generate undamped output modes.   This will be true if all transfer-function poles have negative real parts.

For the vast majority of operational-amplifier circuits,

1. The loop transfer function $A(s)\beta(s)$ is itself stable; i.e., the d-c amplifier contains no unstable regenerative stages.
2. The loop gain $|A(j\omega)\beta(j\omega)|$ does not increase again with increasing frequency once it has decreased to unity.

If the first condition is satisfied, the feedback loop of Fig. 4-17 will be stable if the locus of complex-plane points $z = -A(j\omega)\beta(j\omega)$ does not

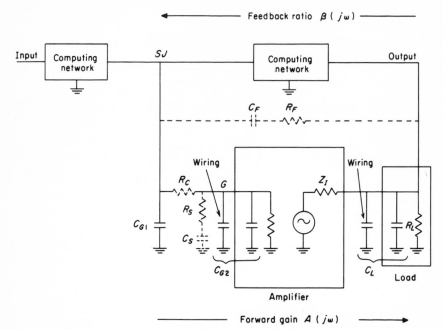

FIG. 4-17. Block diagram of a computer feedback amplifier. The forward gain $A(j\omega)$ and the feedback ratio $\beta(j\omega)$ include effects of networks and shunt impedances at the amplifier input and output. Possible external stability networks (Sec. 4-18) are indicated in dash lines.

encircle the point $z = -1$ as ω varies from $-\infty$ to ∞ (*Restricted Nyquist Stability Criterion*);[5] note that 180-deg phase reversal at unity gain would just imply critical regeneration. Reasonable design practice limits the open-loop phase lag $-\arg[-A(j\omega)]$ of the amplifier itself below 90 to 150 deg at all frequencies where the open-loop gain $|A(j\omega)|$ exceeds unity. This condition will not only ensure stability with a variety of feedback networks and capacitive loads, but will control excessive overshoot or ringing after step-function inputs and will reduce closed-loop phase shift to permit cascading of several operational amplifiers in computer applications. Realistic amplifier specifications should quote the required amplifier forward-gain response (gain and phase shift) with at least some load

capacitance to account for the effects of computer wiring. It is clear
that more precise knowledge of feedback networks and circuit capacitances (as in special-purpose computers) will permit a closer design yielding wider frequency response for given gain and phase-shift requirements.

Stability analysis based on the simplified Bode-Nyquist criterion
applies to most practical operational amplifiers. With $\beta(j\omega)$ known, all
we normally require is a plot of the amplifier forward gain $|A(j\omega)|$ and
phase shift $\arg A(j\omega) - 180$ deg against frequency. Stage-by-stage
analysis (Sec. 4-16) yields each amplifier forward-gain transfer function
for our class of amplifiers in the form

$$A(s) = (-1)^{m+n} A(0) \frac{s_1 s_2 \cdots s_n (s - s_1')(s - s_2') \cdots (s - s_m')}{s_1' s_2' \cdots s_n' (s - s_1)(s - s_2) \cdots (s - s_n)}$$

$$(n > m) \quad (4\text{-}13)$$

The *poles* s_i and the *zeros* s_k' of the loop transfer function will, moreover,
be real unless feedforward circuits (Sec. 4-19) or subsidiary feedback loops
must be considered. For real poles and zeros $s_i = -\omega_i$, $s_k' = -\omega_k'$,
graphical analysis of the resulting frequency-response function $A(j\omega)$
becomes especially convenient if we plot the amplifier gain in decibels,

$$20 \log_{10} |A(j\omega)| = 20 \log_{10} |A(0)| + 10 \log_{10} \left(\frac{\omega^2}{\omega_1'^2} + 1 \right)$$

$$+ 10 \log_{10} \left(\frac{\omega^2}{\omega_2'^2} + 1 \right) + \cdots - 10 \log_{10} \left(\frac{\omega^2}{\omega_1^2} + 1 \right)$$

$$- 10 \log_{10} \left(\frac{\omega^2}{\omega_2^2} + 1 \right) - \cdots \quad (4\text{-}13a)$$

and the amplifier (excess) phase shift

$$\varphi_A(\omega) = \arg A(j\omega) - 180 \text{ deg} = \arctan \frac{\omega}{\omega_1'}$$

$$+ \arctan \frac{\omega}{\omega_2'} + \cdots - \arctan \frac{\omega}{\omega_1} - \arctan \frac{\omega}{\omega_2} - \cdots \quad (4\text{-}13b)$$

against $\log_{10} \omega$ or $\log_{10} f$ (*Bode frequency-response plot*). Referring to
Eq. (13) and Fig. 4-18, we note that

1. The logarithmic plot permits simple addition of contributions from
   individual poles and zeros to the total gain as well as to the total
   phase shift.
2. The decibel-gain contribution $-10 \log_{10} (\omega^2/\omega_i^2 + 1)$ of a real pole
   $s_i = -\omega_i$ is neatly approximated by simple straight-line segments
   (asymptotes to the exact decibel-gain contribution curve): the gain
   is, approximately, unaffected below the *break frequency* $f_i = \omega_i/2\pi$
   and then decreases 6 db/octave (20 db/decade). The effect of a
   real zero $s_k' = -\omega_k'$ is similarly approximated by a 6 db/octave gain

increase above the break frequency $f'_k = \omega'_k/2\pi$. The *exact* gain actually has already changed by 3 db at the break frequency f_i or f'_k.

3. Each real pole contributes phase *lag* increasing from 0 deg (at $f = 0$) to 90 deg at $f = \infty$. More specifically, this lag is about 6 deg at $f = 0.1f_i$, 45 deg at $f = f_i$, and about 84 deg at $f = 10f_i$. Each real zero contributes a similar zero to 90 deg phase *lead*.

Somewhat less simple relations hold for *complex* poles and zeros $s = -\omega_i \pm j\alpha$;[5] but for $\alpha < 0.5\omega_i$ (sufficiently well-damped modes), we

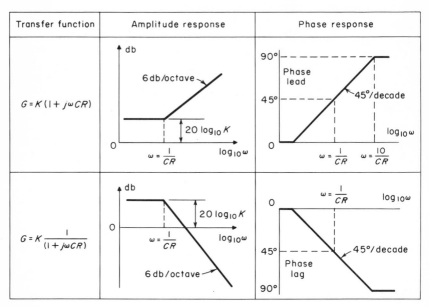

Fig. 4-18. Approximate Bode frequency-response plots for single lag and lead circuits. The error of the straight-line gain approximation is 3 db for $\omega = 1/RC$ and 1 db for $\omega = \frac{1}{2}RC$ and $\omega = 2/RC$. The error of the straight-line phase approximation is always less than 5.5 deg. Figures 4-19d and 4-20 show Bode plots for cascaded lag and lead circuits. (*From Texas Instruments, Inc., Engineering Staff, "Transistor Circuit Design," McGraw-Hill, New York, 1963.*)

can treat a pair of complex-conjugate poles or zeros like two superimposed real poles or zeros $s = -\omega_i$ (12 db/octave gain decrease or increase above $f_i = \omega_i/2\pi$; phase shift changes by 180 deg, with 90 deg shift at f_i).

The resulting Bode plot for the amplifier gain $|A(j\omega)|$ approximates the exact curve by straight-line segments sloping up or down at multiples of 6 db/octave. Since we know that each 6 db/octave slope change corresponds to added phase lag or lead increasing from 45 to 90 deg, *the Bode amplitude-response plot permits at least preliminary frequency-response analysis and design without any need to determine the phase response explicitly.* Specifically, any prolonged downward slope of 12 db/octave or more will cause amplifier phase lag in excess of our permissible margin of 90 to 150 deg, and must not be tolerated while the gain is above unity (0 db).   The most conservative amplifier designs will not tolerate *any* 12 db/octave slopes; this requires us to break the gain at a relatively low frequency in order to "submerge" all larger cascaded slopes below the 0-db line.   More frequently, one tolerates a 12 db/octave slope over an intermediate frequency range and then introduces a zero with stabilizing networks to let the gain response cross 0 db at 6 db/octave with tolerable phase shift (Sec. 4-17).   The 6 db/octave slope is usually continued for about one octave below 0 db.

4-16. High-frequency Equivalent Circuits. Miller Effect.   The small-signal frequency response of each amplifier stage in turn is readily computed with the aid of the equivalent circuits developed in Secs. 4-4 to

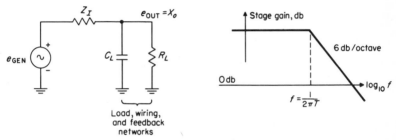

Fɪɢ. 4-19*a*. Equivalent circuit for a summer or integrator output stage, and frequency response.

4-9.   We obtain each no-load gain e_{GEN}/e_{IN} and equivalent-generator resistance Z_I from Figs. 4-2 to 4-6 and then calculate the stage frequency response including the effects of circuit, load, and vacuum-tube input and output capacitances.   Shunting due to pentode screen capacitance and cathode-to-ground capacitance in differential-amplifier stages is usually well masked by other effects and will not be considered here.

As a first example, Fig. 4-19*a* shows the equivalent circuit and frequency response of a typical vacuum-tube output stage.

Note that linear circuit analysis determines only the *small-signal* frequency response.   At larger amplitudes, one or the other amplifier stage will overload because it can no longer supply sufficient current to a load or circuit capacitance, and the resulting output voltage is *rate-limited*.

Figure 4-19*b* shows a typical voltage-amplifier stage and its small-signal equivalent circuit, including circuit and vacuum-tube capacitances. Note, in particular, that the grid-plate capacitance C_{gp} of V_2 returns a portion of the stage output voltage E_{OUT} to the potential $-a_2 E_{OUT}$, where a_2 is the grid-to-plate gain of the following stage (*Miller effect*). The current drawn by C'_i and C_{gp} is just that drawn by the equivalent

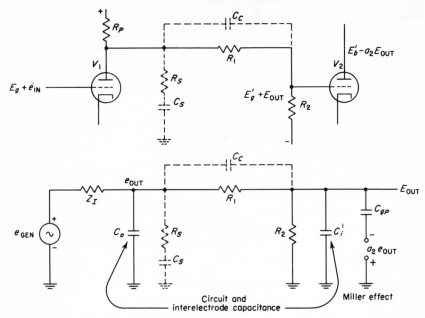

FIG. 4-19b. Typical voltage-amplifier stage with interstage network and stabilizing circuits (dash lines), and equivalent circuit.

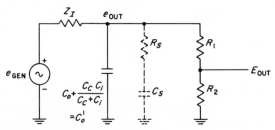

FIG. 4-19c. Equivalent circuit for the amplifier stage of Fig. 4-19b after addition of the lead capacitor $C_c \approx R_2 C_i / R_1$.

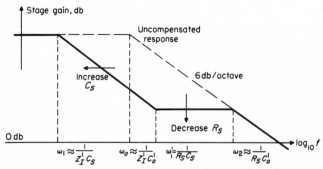

FIG. 4-19d. Effect of the rolloff network R_S, C_S on the frequency response in Fig. 4-19c. Approximate values for ω_0, ω_1, and ω_2 assume $R_S \ll Z'_I$, $C_S \gg C'_o$. The expression for ω'_1 is exact. In most practical cases, $Z_I \ll R_1 + R_2$, so that $Z'_I \approx Z_I$.

shunt capacitance

$$C_i = C_i' + (a_2 + 1)C_{gp} \qquad (4\text{-}14)$$

to ground.   Although $a_2 = a_2(j\omega)$ is actually a complex quantity, it is usually sufficient for amplifier-design purposes to consider C_i as a real capacitance with $a_2 = a_2(0)$.[12,13]   The Miller-effect shunt capacitance can be appreciable when V_2 is a triode, e.g., $C_{gp} = 2$ pF, $a_2 = 40$ yields $(a_2 + 1)C_{gp} = 82$ pF.   To avoid Miller-effect shunting of voltage-amplifier stages and amplifier input terminals, we can

1. Use pentodes rather than triodes (Fig. 4-27)
2. Insert cathode followers ahead of triodes
3. Use differential-amplifier stages with the input on the cathode-follower side (Fig. 4-26)
4. Neutralize C_{gp} by regenerative feedback, especially in push-pull stages.

4-17. Frequency-response Shaping with Stabilizing Networks. (a) Interstage Lead Capacitors.   Referring to the voltage-amplifier stage of Fig. 4-19*b*, we first cancel the lag due to the interstage resistor R_1 in connection with the shunt capacitance C_i (which includes the Miller effect).   Unless we can eliminate the interstage resistor R_1 altogether, we shunt it with a lead capacitance

$$C_c \approx \frac{R_2}{R_1} C_i \qquad (4\text{-}15)$$

to give our interstage network an approximately *real* transfer function; exact cancellation is not necessary.   Note that the capacitance $C_iC_c/(C_i + C_c)$ of C_i and C_c in series is now added to the plate-shunt capacitance C_o in Fig. 4-19*b*; sometimes C_c is made somewhat smaller than R_2C_i/R_1 to reduce this shunting effect.   If Eq. (15) holds exactly, the stage transfer function is

$$\frac{E_{\text{OUT}}}{e_{\text{IN}}} = -a_1(s) = \frac{-a_1(0)}{Z_I'C_o's + 1} \qquad (4\text{-}16)$$

with $a_1(0) = \dfrac{\mu R_2}{R_1 + R_2 + Z_I}$

$$Z_I' = \frac{(R_1 + R_2)Z_I}{R_1 + R_2 + Z_I} \qquad C_o' = C_o + \frac{C_iC_c}{C_i + C_c} \qquad (4\text{-}17)$$

Equation (16) describes a single lag with d-c gain a_1 and break (-3 db) frequency $f_0 = \omega_0/2\pi = 1/2\pi Z_I'C_o'$.

(b) "Submerging" the Effect of High-frequency Poles.   Even after each of our lead capacitors has, for practical purposes, canceled one amplifier-stage pole, the Bode frequency-response plot of a multistage amplifier still tends to exhibit the regrettable shape indicated in dash lines of Fig. 4-20. The downward slopes and phase shifts due to the individual amplifier-stage poles will add up to produce instability when a sufficiently high feedback ratio makes $|A(j\omega)\beta(j\omega)|$ greater than unity where the phase shift equals 180 deg. As a result, *it is necessary to reshape the amplifier response so as to "submerge" the highly sloped right end of the amplitude-response characteristic in Fig. 4-20 below the 0-db line.* A number of different possibilities exist:

1. We can *reduce the amplifier gain at all frequencies*, but this reduces static as well as dynamic accuracy and is rarely acceptable.

If one of the open-loop break frequencies is sufficiently far below the other break frequencies (except possibly for a single one of them), then all but one or two breaks of the amplitude characteristics will be safely "submerged" below the 0-db line. To stabilize an amplifier, we can, therefore,

2. Add *shunt or plate-to-grid capacitance* to lower the lowest break frequency at the expense of overall bandwidth (Fig. 4-20a; see also Sec. 4-18), and/or
3. Raise all but one or two of the break frequencies through resistive loading (*broadbanding*) at the expense of overall gain (see Fig. 4-29 for an example).

More sophisticated means for shaping the amplifier frequency response include

1. *Rolloff networks*
2. *Feedforward circuits* (Sec. 4-19)
3. *Regenerative circuits* (Sec. 4-20)

(c) **Rolloff Networks.** Figure 4-19b to d illustrates the addition of a *rolloff network (lag-lead network)* R_S, C_S to a d-c amplifier stage. Assuming that the lead capacitance (15) has already been added, addition of the rolloff network in Fig. 4-19c changes the stage transfer function (16) to

$$\frac{E_{OUT}}{e_{IN}} = -a_1(s)$$

$$= -a_1(0)\frac{R_S C_S s + 1}{Z_I' R_S C_o' C_S s^2 + (Z_I' C_o' + R_S C_S + Z_I' C_S)s + 1} \quad (4\text{-}18)$$

where $a_1(0)$, Z_I', and C_o' are still given by Eq. (17). In practice, we choose $R_S \ll Z_I'$, $C_S \gg C_o'$, so that Eq. (18) is approximated by

$$\frac{E_{OUT}}{e_{IN}} = -a(s) = -a(0)\frac{R_S C_S s + 1}{(Z_I' C_S s + 1)(R_S C_o' s + 1)} \quad (4\text{-}19)$$

i.e., the original pole at $s = -\omega_o = -1/Z_I' C_o'$ has been replaced with two poles $-\omega_1 \approx -1/Z_I' C_S$, $-\omega_2 \approx -1/R_S C_o'$ separated by a zero

$$-\omega_1' = -1/R_S C_S$$

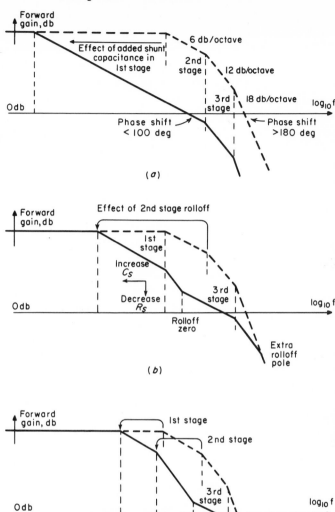

FIG. 4-20. Uncompensated multistage-amplifier forward gain (dash lines) with three stage breakpoints (poles) above 0 db, and different compensation methods used to reduce the phase shift at the unity-gain (0 db) frequency below 90 to 120 deg. (a) Crude shunt-capacitance stabilization. (b) Use of a single rolloff network (second stage). (c) Stabilization with two rolloff networks in the first and second stages. A more conservative design would *alternate* poles and zeros, so that the gain would never decrease faster than 6 db/octave above the 0-db line.

Referring to Fig. 4-19*d*, we see that the rolloff network does not affect the d-c gain but breaks the amplitude response at

$$\omega = \omega_1 \approx 1/Z_I'C_S < 1/Z_I'C_o'$$

because of the shunt effect of C_S. At frequencies above

$$\omega = \omega_1' = 1/R_S C_S$$

the resistance R_S "stops" the shunting effect of C_S, and the stage acts like an amplifier broadbanded by resistance loading with R_S, until the response finally breaks again at $\omega = \omega_2 = 1/R_S C_o'$.

Figures 4-20*b* and *c* illustrate the use of rolloff networks for "submerging" the high-frequency poles of a multistage amplifier to obtain stability. The rolloff networks extend the amplifier response farther beyond that obtained in Fig. 4-20*a* and then break it at 12 db/octave; the rolloff-network zeros restore a 6 db/octave slope as the response goes through unity gain.   The resulting frequency response is typical of that of many commercial amplifiers; note that some phase margin has been sacrificed in order to extend the useful frequency response as far as possible.

Slopes of 12 db/octave caused by rolloff networks must not continue long enough to cause over 150 deg phase shift.   The most conservative designs, intended to yield smooth transient response without ringing, employ no 12 db/octave slopes at all but *alternate* poles and zeros to cancel phase lead and lag and keep the total phase shift near 90 deg over a wide frequency range.

Equation (19) can be used to determine rolloff-network parameters if the effective shunt capacitance C_o' is adequately known.   Section 4-17*d* describes an experimental approach to rolloff-network design.

While rolloff networks are usually greatly preferable to crude bandwidth limitation with shunt capacitors, the stability networks still exact a double price:

1. Some bandwidth is still lost because of each rolloff network. Figure 4-18 shows that, even if the *amplitude*-response loss sets in at a relatively high frequency, the *phase* response is affected at much lower frequencies.
2. Rolloff networks may have to have relatively low impedances. Thus, unless voltage-amplifier stages are designed to supply substantial power, rolloff networks rather than circuit capacitances will limit the frequency range over which the amplifier can supply its full output voltage.

Rolloff-network loading can be especially serious in the high-level voltage amplifier driving a cathode-follower output stage. Rolloff in earlier stages is usually advisable in computer amplifiers; some instrumentation-type d-c amplifiers have the network in a later stage to reduce high-frequency noise generated in the earlier stages. One can also employ degenerative (plate-to-grid) feedback networks rather than shunt networks for rolloff.

As in the case of Miller-effect capacitance, a *degenerative* rolloff network comprising R'_S, C'_S in series between plate and grid of an amplifier stage with voltage gain a_2 is approximately equivalent to a series network R_S, C_S shunting the interstage-network output (not the plate) of the preceding stage to ground, where

$$R_S \approx \frac{R'_S}{a_2} \qquad C_S \approx a_2 C'_S \qquad (4\text{-}20)$$

A rolloff network consisting of R_S and C_S in series across the plates or collectors of a symmetrical differential (push-pull) amplifier has the same effect as a pair of rolloff networks $R_S/2$, $2C_S$ connected between each plate or collector and ground.

(d) Load-capacitance Effects. Figure 4-21a represents the response of most computer d-c amplifiers near the unity-gain (0-db) crossover frequency. The response has been shaped to approach 0 db at 6 db/octave and then breaks because of the output-stage pole. Increased load capacitance C_L will increase the phase lag and cause instability unless the forward gain is reduced or rolled off earlier (dash line). Since capacitive loads may be fixed by a given application, wideband amplification places a premium on low-impedance cathode-follower or emitter-follower output stages.

A different approach is illustrated in Fig. 4-21b. Here the output-stage break frequency is always lower than the break frequencies due to the broadbanded voltage-amplifier stage or stages (see also Sec. 4-17b), and capacitive loading *improves* the amplifier stability. This type of design applies to moderate-bandwidth amplifiers with amplifier-type output stages, but also to wideband amplifiers (including feedforward amplifiers, Sec. 4-19); note that it may be easier to obtain a megacycle-range voltage-amplifier stage than a wideband output stage with a given large capacitive load.

Resistive loads paralleling the load capacitance are not usually sufficient to move the output-stage pole appreciably when the output stage is a cathode follower or emitter follower. A small resistance (of the order of Z_I) *in series* with the load, however, will cause a zero following the output-stage pole in the manner of Fig. 4-19d and may improve amplifier stability without too bad an effect on static accuracy.

Our small-signal linear circuit analysis does not tell the whole story. The current drawn by a capacitive load increases with the frequency and must be included in our output-stage-power considerations if the amplifier is to supply full output voltage over a specified frequency range. In this connection, note that output stages designed in accordance with Fig. 4-21b will be driven with relatively large high-frequency voltages, which might cause overloads.

(e) **Experimental Procedure for Rolloff-network Design.** In practice, the circuit capacitances C_o, C_i', and $(1 + a_2)C_{yp}$ are not usually accurately known. The designer usually starts by obtaining a logarithmic plot of the uncompensated open-loop amplitude response (Sec. 4-21) and locates the break frequencies approximately by drawing straight-line asymptotes.

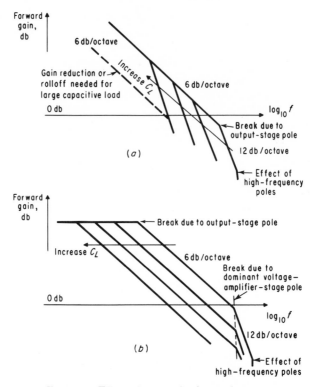

Fig. 4-21. Effect of output-load capacitance.

If it is possible to stabilize an originally unstable or underdamped operational-amplifier loop with a single rolloff network (Fig. 4-20b), the following experimental procedure may be useful.* Connect R_S and C_S in the form of decade substitution boxes to an appropriate amplifier stage. Start with an excessively large value of C_S and decrease R_S until the closed-loop step-response ringing is reduced as desired. Now decrease C_S as much as possible. One may next increase the load capacitance to deteriorate the step response again and add a second rolloff network; in general, however, multiple rolloff networks are best designed in the manner of Fig. 4-20 on the basis of the empirically determined break-frequency locations.

4-18. External Stabilizing Networks. Since it is economically desirable to use the same type of d-c amplifier with different feedback circuits

* Contributed by H. E. Koerner, Burr-Brown Research Corp., Tucson, Ariz.

and loads, it is often expedient to include *external stabilizing networks* with the various patched or switched computing feedback networks. Summer and integrator circuits, for instance, have quite different feedback ratios $\beta(j\omega)$ (Fig. 4-22). In general, an amplifier stable with $\beta = 1$ and a given capacitive output load will also be stable as an integrator with the same load. Again, the effects of summing-point and load capacitances on the amplifier stability and transient response can vary radically with different applications and installations; this is especially true when the amplifier is designed for extreme bandwidth rather than for a conservative phase margin.

As noted already in Sec. 3-19, fixed or adjustable lead capacitors shunting the input and feedback resistors of phase inverters and summers can

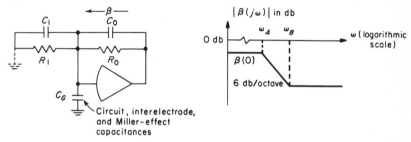

Fig. 4-22a. Feedback-network frequency response for a phase inverter or summing amplifier

$$\beta(s) = \beta(0)\frac{\omega_A(s + \omega_B)}{\omega_B(s + \omega_A)}$$

$$\beta(0) = \frac{R_1}{R_o + R_1} \qquad \omega_A = \frac{R_o + R_1}{R_o R_1(C_o + C_1 + C_G)} \qquad \omega_B = \frac{1}{R_o C_o}$$

(see also Sec. 3-19).

greatly improve their frequency response and stability by compensating phase lag due to summing-point and/or load capacitances (Fig. 4-22a). Such lead capacitors are practically essential in wideband computers working above 1 Kc and are recommended also at lower frequencies.

Where a d-c amplifier permits stable operation as a summer but not as an integrator or limiter (near-unity feedback), one frequently connects a 50K to 1M resistor R_C between summing junction and amplifier input at the patchbay (Fig. 4-22b). An existing summing or feedback resistor can often be patched in this manner (Fig. 9-1c). The resistance will combine with the existing shunt capacitance C_G at the amplifier input to break the loop-gain response and to "submerge" the high-frequency poles; in many older computers, C_G is increased artificially to make the individual amplifier responses less dependent on cable lengths. It may be preferable to employ a smaller series resistance R_C and an RC rolloff network between amplifier input and ground (dash lines in Fig. 4-22b) so

as to introduce a zero as well as a pole into the loop-gain characteristic. The correct values for R_S and C_S can usually be found by trial and error in the manner of Sec. 4-17e. This compensation technique tends to reduce the useful amplifier bandwidth (we add a new pole instead of moving existing poles) and is, in general, recommended only when it is imperative not to change the amplifier circuit proper.

The stability of implicit-computation circuits employing *high-gain amplifiers* (division loops, special diode circuits, etc.) is often improved through addition of a small capacitance (10 to 200 pF) between output

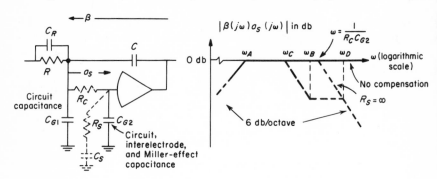

Fɪɢ. 4-22b. Feedback- and compensating-network frequency response for an integrator (see also Sec. 3-20).　Assuming $C_{G1} + C_{G2} + C_R \ll C$, we have

$$\beta(s) = \frac{s}{s + \omega_A} \qquad \text{with} \qquad \omega_A = \frac{1}{RC}$$

If the compensating network (R_C alone, or R_C, R_S, and C_S) is used, then at low frequencies, $\beta(s)a_S(s) \approx \beta(s)$, where the compensating-network response $a_S(s)$ counts as part of the amplifier forward gain $A(s)$.　At frequencies high compared with $\omega_A/2\pi$,

$$\beta(s)a_S(s) \approx a_S(s) = \frac{\omega_C\omega_D}{\omega_B} \frac{s + \omega_B}{(s + \omega_C)(s + \omega_D)}$$

with $\omega_B = 1/R_SC_S$, $\omega_C \approx 1/R_CC_S$, $\omega_D \approx 1/R_SC_{G2}$ if we can assume $R_S \ll R_C$, $C_S \gg C_{G2}$.

and summing junction so as to introduce some lead into the loop gain. If desired, we can "stop" the high-frequency feedback by including a suitably chosen resistor in series with the capacitor (C_F, R_F in Fig. 4-17).

4-19. Design of Wideband D-c Amplifiers by Feedforward Techniques.[25-31,37]　(a) With modern high-transconductance tubes, combination of a single voltage-amplifier stage with an output cathode follower (Fig. 4-31) yields a d-c amplifier of moderate d-c gain (80 to 250) but excellent frequency response and stability.　The forward-gain Bode plot has the form of Fig. 4-21 and shows only two breaks (one for each stage), both of which can be well above 2 Mc unless the load capacitance is excessively large.　When additional stages are cascaded with such an amplifier to increase the overall gain, stability will, in general, require one to compromise the high-end frequency response of the combination, and, probably, to accept the loading effects of the necessary stabilizing networks (Sec. 4-17).

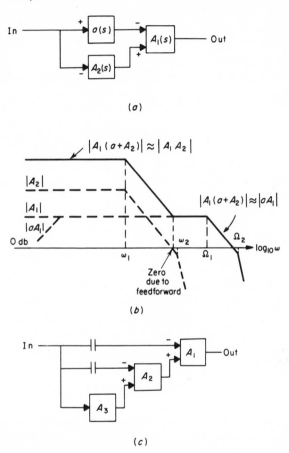

Fig. 4-23. D-c amplifier with feedforward connection (a), frequency response (b), and a multiple-feedforward circuit permitting low phase lag at 0-db crossover (c).

As an interesting alternative, the *feedforward circuit* of Fig. 4-23a passes high-frequency signal components through a high-pass filter or preamplifier directly to the wideband output amplifier, while cascading a high-gain d-c amplifier with the output amplifier for lower frequencies. Note that the chopper-stabilization scheme of Fig. 4-14 is a special case of the general feedforward scheme. Referring to Fig. 4-23a, the overall transfer function is

$$A(s) = -A_1(s)[a(s) + A_2(s)] \qquad (4\text{-}21)$$

We assume

$$A_1(s) = A_1(0) \frac{\Omega_1\Omega_2}{(s + \Omega_1)(s + \Omega_2)}$$

$$A_2(s) = A_2(0) \frac{\omega_1\omega_2 \cdots \omega_n}{(s + \omega_1)(s + \omega_2) \cdots (s + \omega_n)} \quad (4\text{-}22)$$

with positive Ω_i, ω_k. The resulting amplifier transfer function

$$A(s) = - \frac{A_1(0)\Omega_1\Omega_2}{(s + \Omega_1)(s + \Omega_2)} \\ \frac{a(s)(s + \omega_1)(s + \omega_2) \cdots (s + \omega_n) + A_2(0)\omega_1\omega_2 \cdots \omega_n}{(s + \omega_1)(s + \omega_2) \cdots (s + \omega_n)} \quad (4\text{-}23)$$

indicates the possibility of canceling all n poles $-\omega_k$ of $A_2(s)$ by suitably placed zeros, so that the high-end frequency response and stability of the amplifier will be determined solely by the wideband output amplifier. In general, we shall attempt to locate the zeros of our transfer function (23) by root-locus methods.[28] In the important special case $a(j\omega) \approx 1$ at the working frequencies, we refer to the Bode frequency-response plot of our feedforward amplifier and note

1. The phase shift arg $A_2(j\omega)$ should be kept below 90 to 150 deg at all frequencies where $|A_2(j\omega)| \geq 1$, since phase reversal would cause regeneration, or at least cancellation of the feedforward input. *We shall, therefore, let the Bode plot of $|A_2(j\omega)|$ cross 0 db at 6 db/octave and avoid any slope greater than 12 db/octave above 9 db.*

2. $|A_2(j\omega)|$ should drop to unity before phase shift due to $A_1(j\omega)$ becomes appreciable, say below one-fifth of the first break frequency of $A_1(j\omega)$.

We can readily meet these conditions by adding shunt capacitance or rolloff networks to our low-frequency amplifier in the manner of Sec. 4-17. This is preferably done at the output of the low-frequency amplifier to minimize high-frequency noise amplified by A_1. We may, instead, employ capacitance or rolloff-network feedback around A_2.[26] We can, finally, also shape the response $A_2(j\omega)$ by adding a feedforward connection around each amplifier stage to alternate poles and zeros for very low phase shift (Fig. 4-23c).[27]

(**b**) If $a(s) \approx 1$, and $A_2(s)$ has a single pole $s = -\omega_1$, i.e., $A_2(s) = A_2(0)\omega_1/(s + \omega_1)$, then

$$A(s) = - \frac{A_1(0)\Omega_1\Omega_2}{(s + \Omega_1)(s + \Omega_2)} \frac{s + (1 + \omega_1)A_2(0)}{s + \omega_1}$$

has a zero $s' = -(1 + \omega_1)A_2(0)$, and we have merely to position this zero between $-\omega_1$ and the wideband amplifier poles $-\Omega_1$, $-\Omega_2$. This type of design applies if the low-frequency amplifier is a broadband amplifier rolled off with a single fairly large shunt or feedback capacitance, which is one of the most practical ways to design a feedforward circuit. If $A_2(s)$ has more than one pole, the zeros of $A(s)$, i.e., the roots of

$$(s + \omega_1)(s + \omega_2) \cdots (s + \omega_n) + A_2(0)\omega_1\omega_2 \cdots \omega_n = 0 \qquad (4\text{-}24)$$

can be complex; they should have negative real parts and imaginary parts at most equal to the real part for good pole cancellation.[28]   We shall treat the case

$$A_2(s) = A_2(0) \frac{\omega_1\omega_2}{(s + \omega_1)(s + \omega_2)} \qquad (4\text{-}25)$$

which applies directly to the design of the chopper-stabilizer circuit in Fig. 4-14 (see also Sec. 4-14).   We have

$$A(s) = A_1(s) \frac{(s + \omega_1)(s + \omega_2) + A_2(0)\omega_1\omega_2}{(s + \omega_1)(s + \omega_2)} \qquad (4\text{-}26)$$

with zeros

$$s'_{1,2} = -\frac{\omega_1 + \omega_2}{2} \pm \frac{1}{2} \sqrt{(\omega_1 - \omega_2)^2 - 4A_2(0)\omega_1\omega_2} \qquad (4\text{-}27)$$

In practice, $A_2(0)$ is so large that these zeros are complex, and Re $s'_{1,2}$ separates the poles $-\omega_1$, $-\omega_2$; ω_1 must be much smaller than Ω_1 and Ω_2.   If we make sure that $\omega_2 > \omega_1 A_2(0)$ in order to reduce $|A_2(j\omega)|$ to unity before the break at $\omega = \omega_2$, then

$$|\arg s'_{1,2}| < \arctan \frac{\sqrt{3A_2^2(0) + 2A_2(0) - 1}}{A_2(0) + 1} \approx \arctan \sqrt{3} < 60 \deg \quad (4\text{-}28)$$

and any oscillatory response will be reasonably well damped.

Figure 4-15 illustrates the use of a rolloff network to relieve this restriction on ω_2. If we consider sampled-data effects in the chopper-stabilizer channel of Fig. 4-15 as negligible and $R_4 \ll R_3$, $C_4 \ll C_3$, then the stabilizer transfer function is approximately

$$A_2(s) = \frac{K_2}{8R_1R_4C_1C_3} \frac{s + 1/R_3C_4}{(s + 1/R_1C_1)(s + 1/R_3C_3)(s + 1/R_4C_4)} \qquad (4\text{-}29)$$

(c) The main practical difficulty in the realization of feedforward wideband amplifier circuits is the addition of two voltages in the output amplifier.   Addition by means of summing networks loses gain and can easily lead to regeneration around A_2; isolation with cathode followers[25] causes both circuit complexity and phase shift.   Addition of the two voltages in a difference amplifier, as in most chopper-stabilizer circuits, is convenient but also reduces the output-amplifier gain and bandwidth. Figures 4-31 and 5-16 show practical feedforward amplifiers.

4-20. Frequency Response of Regenerative and Degenerative D-c Amplifier Stages.   (a) A frequency-independent feedback ratio α around a single-pole amplifier stage (Fig. 4-24a) with the forward transfer function $a/(RCs + 1)$ produces the stage transfer function

$$\frac{e_{\text{OUT}}}{e_{\text{IN}}} = \frac{a}{1 - a\alpha} \frac{1}{[RC/(1 - a\alpha)]s + 1} \qquad (4\text{-}30)$$

with $a\alpha > 0$ for regeneration and $a\alpha < 0$ for degeneration.   Note that the feedback changes the d-c gain, internal impedance, and the break frequency, without much effect on the high-frequency end of the response curve.

(b) Most feedback circuits around an amplifier stage enclose *two* lags. Referring to Fig. 4-24b, we obtain the input-output transfer functions

$$\frac{e_{o1}}{e_{IN}} = \frac{a\omega_1\omega_2}{(s+\omega_1)(s+\omega_2)} \frac{1}{1 - \dfrac{a\alpha\omega_1\omega_2}{(s+\omega_1)(s+\omega_2)}}$$

$$= \frac{a}{1-a\alpha} \frac{(1-a\alpha)\omega_1\omega_2}{s^2+(\omega_1+\omega_2)s+(1-a\alpha)\omega_1\omega_2} \tag{4-31}$$

or

$$\frac{e_{o2}}{e_{IN}} = \frac{a\omega_1}{s+\omega_1} \frac{1}{1 - \dfrac{a\alpha\omega_1\omega_2}{(s+\omega_1)(s+\omega_2)}}$$

$$= \frac{a}{1-a\alpha} \frac{(1-a\alpha)\omega_1(s+\omega_2)}{s^2+(\omega_1+\omega_2)s+(1-a\alpha)\omega_1\omega_2} \tag{4-32}$$

depending on whether the lag term $\omega_2/(s+\omega_2)$ is due to the forward or return portion of the loop. As an example, the regenerative circuit of Fig. 4-9 would be described by

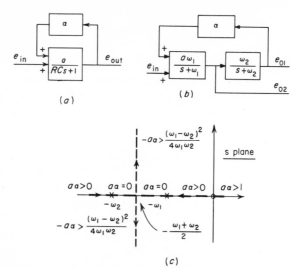

(a) (b)

(c)

FIG. 4-24. Feedback loops enclosing a single lag (a), and two lags (b); and root locus for the two-lag case (c).

Eq. (31) with $a\alpha > 0$. The poles of either transfer function are the roots of the characteristic equation

$$s^2 + (\omega_1+\omega_2)s + (1-a\alpha)\omega_1\omega_2 = 0$$

or

$$s_{1,2} = -\frac{\omega_1+\omega_2}{2} \pm \frac{1}{2}\sqrt{(\omega_1-\omega_2)^2 + 4a\alpha\omega_1\omega_2} \tag{4-33}$$

Figure 4-24c shows the resulting root locus plotted against α.

Degeneration $(a\alpha < 0)$ in excess of $|a\alpha| = (\omega_1-\omega_2)^2/4\omega_1\omega_2$ produces conjugate-complex poles without increasing the break frequency $-(1/2\pi)\,\mathrm{Re}\,s_{1,2}$ beyond $(\omega_1+\omega_2)/4\pi$. It is, generally speaking, impractical to improve amplifier high-frequency response by degenerative feedback around more than one stage.

Regeneration $(a\alpha > 0)$, on the other hand, yields real poles s_1, s_2 which separate with increasing $a\alpha$ and remain negative for $a\alpha < 1$ (subcritical regeneration). With regenerative feedback, the transfer function (32) can be used for frequency-response shaping in the manner of Sec. 4-17.

4-21. Practical Frequency-response Measurements. (a) The tremendous d-c gain of modern chopper-stabilized d-c amplifiers makes direct measurement of the zero-frequency gain practically impossible. Quoted d-c gain figures are either calculated theoretically or obtained from separate gain measurements in the d-c amplifier and chopper-stabilizer channels. Fortunately, however, the frequency-response (gain and phase) measurements most important to the design process are made at higher frequencies, say in excess of 1 Kc, where the amplifier gain has more manageable values. Two practical circuits for frequency-response measurements with simple equipment are suggested:

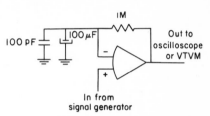

1. Connect the amplifier under test as a unity phase inverter with sinusoidal input. Vary the input to obtain a standard undistorted output amplitude, say 10 volts for ± 100-volt

Fig. 4-25. Circuit for measuring the open-loop performance of a differential-input d-c amplifier above 1 Kc. Similar connections are useful when such a d-c amplifier is to serve as an a-c amplifier.

amplifiers, and measure the amplitude at the summing point with a vacuum-tube voltmeter and/or oscilloscope. Input and output phases may be compared with the aid of a dual-trace oscilloscope.
2. Attenuate the amplifier low-frequency response with the feedback networks shown in Fig. 4-25.[31] Disconnect the chopper stabilizer and apply a known sinusoidal signal to the chopper-stabilizer (difference-amplifier) input as shown. Measure input and output.

The second method also permits one to measure open-loop output distortion at the higher frequencies, and hence the maximum output amplitude vs. frequency for specified total harmonic distortion.

While phase comparisons of two signals having a large amplitude ratio are relatively inaccurate with the simple equipment described, the amplitude response can be conveniently read directly in decibels with a suitably calibrated, well-shielded signal generator and a logarithmic voltmeter. One can then enter the amplitude response directly into a Bode plot and draw straight-line asymptotes to determine frequency breaks (Sec. 4-16). It is then often reasonable to omit explicit phase measurements altogether.

(b) If a differential-input oscilloscope (e.g., Tektronix type G) is available, one can measure the phase difference ϑ between two sinusoidal signals $a \sin \omega t$ and $b \sin (\omega t + \vartheta)$ as follows.[34] Display the difference

Table 4-2. Performance of Typical Computer D-c Amplifiers

	Output voltage (d-c), volts	Output current (d-c), mA	D-c gain	Drift (referred to input)	Peak-to-peak noise (referred to input)	Unity-gain (0-db) crossover frequency	Frequency limit of full output voltage	Power supply voltages, volts
Low-cost vacuum-tube utility amplifier; chopper stabilizer optional	±50 or ±100	1 to 5	10^4 to 10^5; 10^7 with chopper stabilizer	5 to 10 mV/8 hr; 100 μV/8 hr with chopper stabilizer	100 μV; 3 to 5 mV with chopper stabilizer	0.5 to 1 Mc	5 to 50 Kc	±300
Transistor utility amplifier	±10 to ±20	5 to 20	10^4 to 10^5	25 to 10^3 μV/deg C 1 to 100 nA/deg C	10 to 100 μV	100 Kc to 1 Mc	1 to 10 Kc	±15 or ±25
"Slow" general-purpose analog computer (vacuum-tube or transistor); chopper stabilized	±100	15 to 30	10^7 to 10^8	50 μV/8 hr	3 mV	0.3 to 2 Mc	2 Kc	±300 or ±250, −450
100-cps iterative analog computer (vacuum-tube); chopper stabilized	±50 or ±100	10 to 20	10^7	100 μV/8 hr	3 mV	3 Mc	50 Kc	±300
1-Kc iterative analog computer (transistor feedforward amplifier)	±10	30 to 50	10^5 to 10^6	25 μV/deg C 3 nA/deg C	10 μV	10 to 20 Mc	250 Kc to 1 Mc	±15

signal

$$a \sin \omega t - b \sin (\omega t + \vartheta) = r \sin (\omega t + \varphi) \qquad (4\text{-}34)$$

with
$$r = \sqrt{a^2 + b^2 - 2ab \cos \vartheta} \qquad (4\text{-}35)$$

Vary the oscilloscope gain controlling b so as to minimize the difference-signal amplitude (35); this results in

$$b = a \cos \vartheta \qquad r = a \sin \vartheta \qquad (4\text{-}36)$$

so that $|\sin \vartheta|$, $|\cos \vartheta|$, or $|\tan \vartheta|$ can be obtained as an amplitude ratio. The correct quadrant of the unknown phase difference ϑ is determined by observation of the two signals, unless it is known from the nature of the circuit being studied.

(**c**) In some applications, feedforward or rolloff networks may require a separate adjustment for smooth transient response (step response).

EXAMPLES OF VACUUM-TUBE COMPUTER-AMPLIFIER DESIGN

4-22. Representative Amplifier Specifications. Table 4-2 lists representative specifications of typical amplifiers for reference. Note that this table gives manufacturers' data, which are usually less explicit then the list of amplifier specifications given in Table 4-1.

4-23. Examples. (**a**) **Plug-in Utility D-c Amplifiers.** Figure 4-26 illustrates the design of moderate-cost plug-in vacuum-tube amplifiers widely used in many control and instrumentation applications, as well as for breadboarding and experimentation. Such amplifiers can implement accurate and sophisticated mathematical operations with a minimum of circuit-design or construction effort. They are constructed on

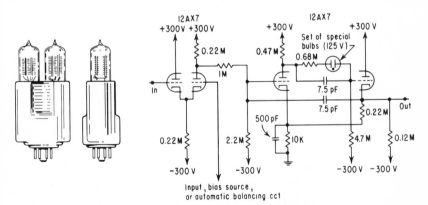

Fig. 4-26a. A low-cost plug-in d-c amplifier capable of ± 50 volts output at 1 mA up to 42 Kc. D-c gain is 15,000, 0-db frequency is 700 Kc, and 24-hr drift is 5 mV (Model K2-W, G. A. Philbrick Researches, Boston, Mass.; higher-power d-c amplifiers and a chopper stabilizer are available as similar plug-in units).

printed-circuit cards or as octal-base or ribbon-connector plug-in units. Octal-base units are cheaper but do not permit isolation of the sensitive input terminal with grounded connectors. These relatively inexpensive utility plug-in amplifiers have moderate power output (at most 5 mA

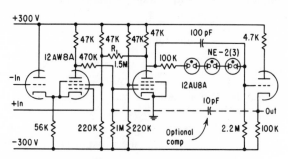

FIG. 4-26b. A plug-in d-c amplifier yielding ±100 volts output at 5 mA (with 47K booster resistor) up to 16 Kc with compensation and up to 50 Kc without compensation. D-c gain exceeds 100,000, and the 0-db frequency is 1 Mc with compensation. Unlike in Fig. 4-26a, the regeneration loop gain is independent of output loading. The optional compensating capacitor ensures stability in integrator or limiter circuits (University of Arizona Model I amplifier; see also ref. 26).

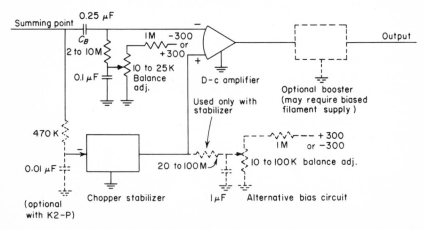

FIG. 4-26c. Practical connections for utility plug-in amplifiers such as the Philbrick K2-XA, K2-P, and K2-B. Note that the asymmetrical difference-amplifier input stages used in most operational amplifiers must be slightly biased on one side (1 to 2 volts) for minimum offset and chopper ripple. Fixed or no bias is often satisfactory. The alternative biasing circuit (dash lines) applies when no stabilizer is used, or when C_B is omitted; this type of bias circuit will, however, reduce the stabilizer gain slightly. All capacitors except C_1 are polystyrene or Mylar.

at ±100 volts), but similarly packaged plug-in booster output stages (totem-pole cathode followers, Fig. 4-6c) can increase the output current to 20 or 30 mA. All amplifiers shown permit chopper stabilization by accessory plug-in chopper-stabilizer packages (Fig. 4-26c).

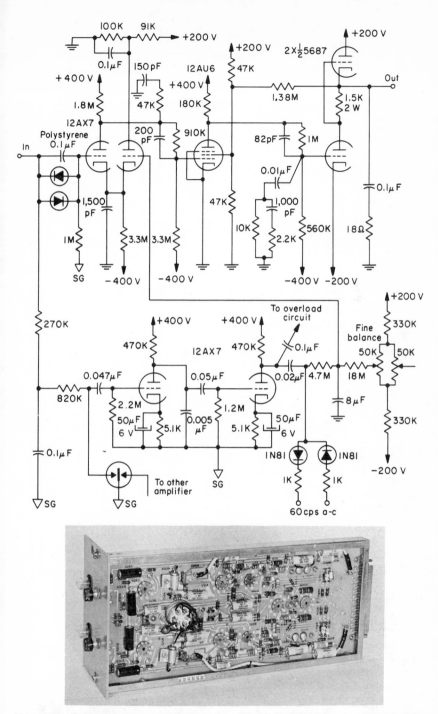

FIG. 4-27. Reeves Instrument Corporation Model A-500-1 d-c amplifier typifies economical dual-unit construction with a single chopper. The grid-blocking capacitor is bypassed with TI622C diodes for faster overload recovery.

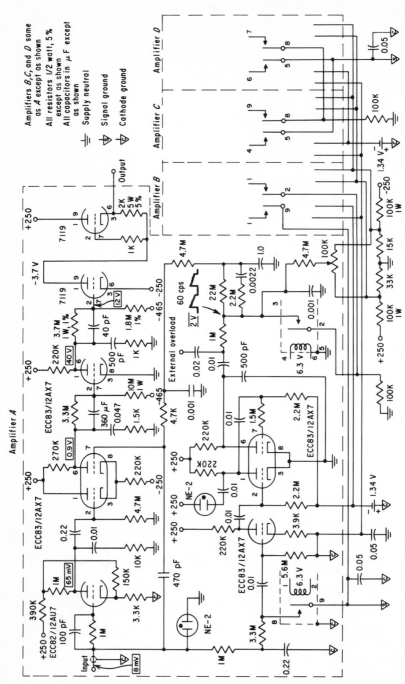

Fig. 4-28. Beckman/Berkeley Model 1148 d-c amplifier (quadruple unit). High stabilizer-channel gain produces a low long-term offset (20 μV). The preamplifier preceding the differential-amplifier stage helps to reduce chopper noise without excessive filtering; a feedforward loop (Sec. 4-19) permits very smooth gain rolloff. Boxes show peak-to-peak 100-cps voltages for 200-volt peak-to-peak output without load. Reference 29 contains very comprehensive design data and test results.

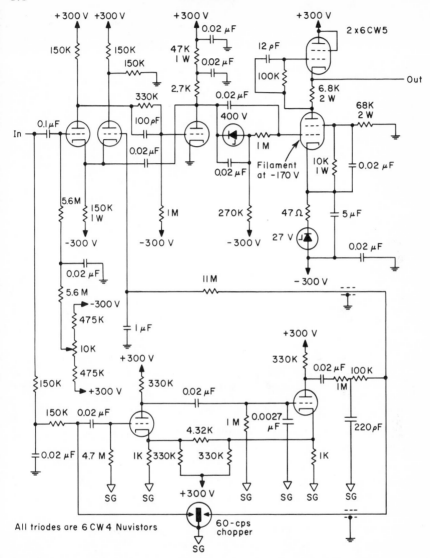

FIG. 4-29. Embree 1500-series ±100-volt, 15-mA d-c amplifier. D-c gain is greater than 10⁷. The low-gain broadband second stage rolls off long after the amplifier-type output stage, so that the response is determined by load capacitance in the manner of Fig. 5-21b. No rolloff networks are required for stability. The 0-db crossover frequency exceeds 1 Mc without load, but decreases with capacitive load. The high-transconductance Nuvistor triodes are small and reliable and dissipate less heat than larger comparable tubes. (*Embree Electronics Corp.*)

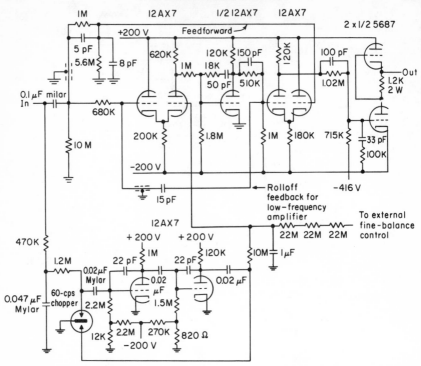

FIG. 4-30. ±100-volt, 20-mA four-stage all-triode feedforward amplifier with no-load 0-db crossover at 2 Mc. D-c gain exceeds 10^8, and 8-hr drift is less than 20 μV referred to input. Two amplifiers mount on a card. (*Systron-Donner Corp.*)

Most of the utility plug-in amplifiers employ cathode-follower output to permit operation with only two high-voltage power supplies (usually ±300 volts) and relatively low output impedance. Regeneration often supplies the required low-frequency gain with a minimum number of stages. Very respectable bandwidths permit iterative computations and fast signal processing.

(b) **High-quality D-c Amplifiers for Conventional "Slow" Electronic Analog Computers.** Figures 4-27 to 4-30 show more powerful and accurate amplifier circuits, all designed specifically for operation in conventional "slow" electronic analog computers. All have built-in chopper stabilizers, difference-amplifier input to the main d-c amplifier, efficient totem-pole output, and conservative equalization for stability in computer installations with relatively large wiring capacitances on amplifier input and output terminals. Unlike earlier designs, these amplifiers are fast enough for operation with all-electronic multipliers and function generators; their bandwidths are, however, not really sufficient for accurate iterative computation with repetition rates in excess of 5 cps.

(c) **Wideband D-c Amplifiers.** The amplifier circuit of Fig. 4-31 is a wideband design (0-db bandwidth or unity-inverter operation up to 5 Mc) intended for modern iterative analog and hybrid analog-digital computers. This circuit, like Fig. 4-28, illustrates the feedforward principle discussed in Sec. 4-19. With modern wideband amplifiers, computing speeds are

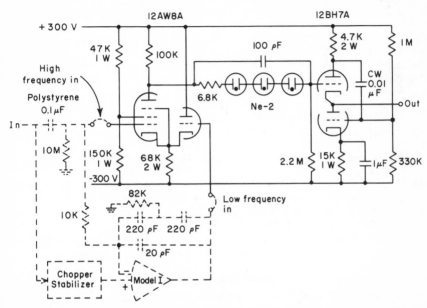

FIG. 4-31. A simple two-tube plug-in 38-db feedforward booster designed to give small ±100-volt utility d-c amplifiers ±100-volt, 10-mA output to 50 Kc, with 0-db crossover above 5 Mc. Dash lines show feedforward connections for the Model I amplifier of Fig. 4-26b or similar utility amplifiers. D-c output impedance is 550 ohms. Optional feedback through C_W (see also Fig. 4-8b) reduces the output impedance below 40 ohms between 1 Kc and 1 Mc and permits full output to 100 Kc; but reequalization may be required in some operational-amplifier circuits (University of Arizona Model II amplifier; see also ref. 26).

essentially limited by switch-timing errors and by parasitic capacitances in linear and diode networks rather than by amplifier bandwidths as such; in particular, the minimum time constant determined by the product of amplifier output impedance and capacitive load determines an upper computing-frequency limit (see also Sec. 4-17d).

REFERENCES AND BIBLIOGRAPHY

Vacuum-tube D-c Amplifiers

1. Miller, S. E.: Sensitive D-c Amplifier with A-c Operation, *Electronics*, November, 1941.
2. Artzt, Maurice: Survey of D-c Amplifiers, *Electronics*, August, 1945.
3. Ginzton, E. L.: D-c Amplifier Design Techniques, *Electronics*, March, 1944.

4. Iannone, F., et al.: Gas-tube Coupling for D-c Amplifiers, *Electronics*, October, 1946.
5. Gray, J.: Direct-coupled Amplifiers, in Valley, G. E., Jr., and H. Wallman, *Vacuum Tube Amplifiers*, MIT Radiation Laboratory Series, vol. 18, McGraw-Hill, New York, 1948.
6. Korn, G. A., and T. M. Korn: Bridge-balanced D-c Amplifier, *Radio and Television News*, Engineering Edition, January, 1950.
7. Volkers, W. K.: Direct-coupled Amplifier Starvation Circuits, *Electronics*, March, 1951.
8. Rittenhouse, J. W.: Cathode-drift Compensation in D-c Amplifiers, *Electronic Eng.*, April, 1953.
9. Revis, J. T.: High Power from Miniature Tubes, *Electronic Design*, April, 1956.
10. Wollard, S. B.: D-c Amplifiers, in Cockrell, W. D. (ed.), *Industrial Electronics Handbook*, McGraw-Hill, New York, 1958.
11. Gronner, A. D.: Direct-coupled Amplifiers, in Truxal, J. G. (ed.), *Control Engineers' Handbook*, McGraw-Hill, New York, 1958.
12. Howe, R. M.: *Design Fundamentals of Analog-computer Components*, Van Nostrand, Princeton, N.J., 1961.
13. Billinghurst, E. M.: Design of Vacuum-tube D-c Amplifiers, in Huskey, H. D., and G. A. Korn, *Computer Handbook*, McGraw-Hill, New York, 1962.
14. Gocht, R. E.: The Design of High-speed Analog Sample and Storage Gates (M.S. Thesis), Department of Electrical Engineering, MIT, Aug. 24, 1959.
15. Svechnikov, S. V., and A. I. Petrenko: Matching Stage with Low Output Resistance, *Radio Eng.*, no. 5, 1961.
16. Huskey, H. D., and B. J. Loopstra: Single-input Component Circuits, in Huskey, H. D., and G. A. Korn, *Computer Handbook*, McGraw-Hill, New York, 1962.

Automatic Balancing Circuits

17. Williams, A. J., R. E. Tarpley, and W. R. Clark: *Trans. AIEE*, **67:** 47 (1948).
18. Goldberg, E. A.: Stabilization of D-c Amplifiers, *RCA Rev.*, **11:** 206 (1950). See also U.S. Patents 2,685,000 (A. W. Vance) and 2,684,999 (E. A. Goldberg and J. Lehmann), both assigned to Radio Corporation of America.
19. McCool, W. A.: Analysis of Zero Stabilization of Wide-band D-c Amplifiers, *Rept. of NRL Progress*, Naval Research Laboratory, Anacostia, D.C., February, 1951.
20. Hamer, H.: A Stabilized Driftless Analog Integrator, *IRETEC*, June, 1954.
21. Ingerson, W. E.: Drift Compensation in D-c Amplifiers, *IRE Natl. Convention Record*, 1951.
22. Gunning, W. F., and A. S. Megel: *Report* RM 236, Rand Corporation, Santa Monica, Calif., with unpublished circuit corrections.
23. *The Contact Modulator*, series of monographs published by Airpax Products Co., Baltimore, Md., 1958–1961.
24. Fradella, R. B.: Designing Chopper-stabilized Operational Amplifiers, *Electronics*, Mar. 3, 1961.

Feedforward Techniques

25. Deering, C. S.: A Wide-band Direct-coupled Operational Amplifier, *Proc. Natl. Simulation Conf.*, Dallas, Tex., 1956, Simulation Councils, Inc., La Jolla, Calif.
26. Koerner, H.: How to Extend Operational-amplifier Response, *Electronics*, Nov. 11, 1960.
27. Polonikov, D. E.: Wide-band Operational Amplifiers, *Automatika i Telemekhanika*, December, 1960.

175   REFERENCES AND BIBLIOGRAPHY

28. Jackson, A. S.: *Analog Computation*, McGraw-Hill, New York, 1960.
29. Billinghurst, E. M.: Model 1148 Quad Operational Amplifier, *Eng. Rept. CRD* 60-21, Beckman/Berkeley Div., Richmond, Calif., December, 1960; revised August, 1961.
30. Whitman, G.: A Megacycle-range Computer D-c Amplifier (M.S. Thesis), *ACL Memo.* 57, Electrical Engineering Department, University of Arizona, 1962.
31. Ozdes, D.: Design of a Wideband Transistor D-c Amplifier (M.S. Thesis), *ACL Memo.* 79, Electrical Engineering Department, University of Arizona, 1963.

Measurements

32. Ehlers, H. L., and W. Hochwald: Design of a High-quality Transistor D-c Amplifier, in Huskey, H. D., and G. A. Korn, *Computer Handbook*, McGraw-Hill, New York, 1962.
33. Handler, H.: A Technique for Measuring the Phase Margin of an Operational Amplifier, *IRETEC*, August, 1962.
34. ————: Measurement of Phase Shift, *IEEETEC*, June, 1963.   (See also Ozdes, D., ref. 31.)

Miscellaneous

35. DiSabato, J.: Transistor Cascode and White Cathode Follower, *ACL Memo.* 68, University of Arizona, 1963.
36. Barber, D. L.: A Wide-band Computing Amplifier, *Electron. Eng.*, April, 1963.
37. Meyer-Brötz, G.: Bandbreitenvergleich von stark gegenkoppelbaren Operationsverstärkern, *Arch. d. elektr. Übertr.*, **18**: 51 (1964).

CHAPTER **5**

TRANSISTOR D-C AMPLIFIERS AND MISCELLANEOUS PRACTICAL CONSIDERATIONS

INTRODUCTION

5-1. Transistor vs. Vacuum-tube D-c Amplifiers. Compared with their vacuum-tube counterparts, solid-state amplifiers have incisive advantages with respect to size, power requirements, heat dissipation, and reliability. These properties not only are of vital interest for airborne or space-vehicle applications and high-reliability process-control computers, but also permit the design of reliable general-purpose analog-computer installations with smaller power and air-conditioning requirements. The objectionable d-c drift, low input impedance, and narrow bandwidth of early transistor d-c amplifiers have been essentially eliminated by device and circuit improvements. Solid-state d-c amplifiers can, indeed, match or surpass every specification of vacuum-tube amplifiers and permit, in many ways, greater design flexibility than the latter. Thus, only transistor amplifiers permit analog-computer operation at the low impedance levels required for true wideband computation (Sec. 3-24), and medium-accuracy transistor d-c amplifiers do not even require chopper stabilization (Sec. 5-8). The survival of vacuum-tube analog computers is mainly due to their temporarily lower cost: a transistor amplifier comparable with a five-tube ± 100-μV-offset d-c amplifier requires between 12 and 18 high-quality transistors and somewhat critical matching of circuit elements and transistors. Its 1964 price was still about twice that of its vacuum-tube counterpart, but this gap is being narrowed by the continuing trend of more economical mass production of solid-state devices and circuits.

176

SIMPLE TRANSISTOR D-C AMPLIFIER STAGES

5-2. The Common-emitter Stage. Figure 5-1 shows a common-emitter amplifier stage together with the transistor collector characteristics and an equivalent circuit,[1] where

$\alpha = \partial i_C / \partial i_E$ is the transistor *common-base current gain* at the operating point, typically 0.95 to 0.99

$\beta = \partial i_C / \partial i_B = \alpha/(1 - \alpha)$ is the *common-emitter current gain*, typically 20 to 100

I_{CBO} is the *collector-to-base leakage current* for zero emitter current i_E, typically between 0.5 nA and 2 μA for silicon transistors at 25 deg C

V_{BE} is the *base-to-emitter offset voltage*, typically between 0.2 volt (germanium) and 0.7 volt (silicon) at 25 deg C

C_C is the *collector-to-base capacitance*, typically 4 to 20 pF

In most common-emitter stages, the *base resistance* r_B is between 100 and 2,000 ohms, the (nonlinear) *emitter resistance* $r_E \approx 26 \times 10^{-3}/i_E$ is

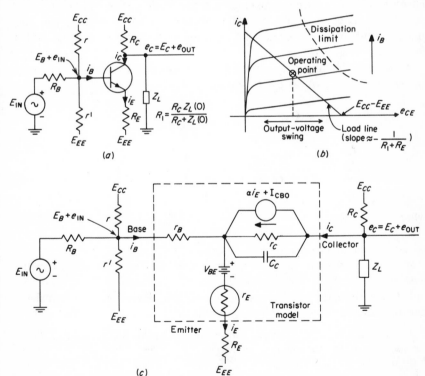

FIG. 5-1. Common-emitter *npn* amplifier stage with grounded load (*a*), transistor collector characteristics (*b*), and equivalent circuit (*c*). E_{CC} and E_{EE} are obtained from grounded low-impedance sources. Reverse all currents and d-c voltages for *pnp* stages.

below 100 ohms, and the *collector resistance* r_C is of the order of megohms. We shall, therefore, employ approximations based on

$$r_E \ll R_1 = \frac{R_C Z_L(0)}{R_C + Z_L(0)} \ll (1 - \alpha)r_C \qquad r_B \ll r_C \qquad (5\text{-}1)$$

unless the contrary is specifically stated.

Unlike the usual linear vacuum-tube models, the linear transistor model of Fig. 5-1c approximates actual operating currents and voltages as well as incremental relations, if suitable average or "large-signal" transistor-parameter values are employed.[1] The transistor *operating point* is defined by the zero-signal values I_C, E_{CE} of i_C and e_{CE} ($E_{IN} = 0$). With the approximations (1) and $\alpha \approx 1$, the operating point is given by

$$I_C \approx \frac{E_B - E_{EE} - V_{BE}}{R_E + r_E} \qquad E_{CE} \approx \frac{R_1}{R_C} E_{CC} - (R_1 + R_E + r_E)I_C \quad (5\text{-}2)$$

where E_B is the voltage at the transistor base; E_B is computed from a base-circuit node equation, usually assuming a very small quiescent base current I_B. I_C must be large enough to maintain a specified value of the (small-signal) current gain β, which peaks with increasing I_C; and E_{CE} must be sufficient to permit the required output-voltage swing for the given load (Fig. 5-1b).

Assuming the approximations (1) and $R_E \ll r_C(1 - \alpha) \approx r_C/\beta$, the *incremental stage gain* at d-c ($\alpha = $ const, $\omega C_C = 0$) is given by

$$\frac{e_{\text{OUT}}}{e_{\text{IN}}} = \frac{1}{1 + Z_I/Z_L} \frac{e_{\text{GEN}}}{e_{\text{IN}}} \qquad (5\text{-}3)$$

(see also Sec. 4-4), with

$$\left. \begin{array}{c} e_{\text{GEN}} \approx -\dfrac{\alpha R_C}{R_E + r_E + (1 - \alpha)r_B} e_{\text{IN}} = -\beta \dfrac{\alpha R_C}{Z_{\text{IN}}(0)} e_{\text{IN}} \\[2mm] Z_I(0) \approx R_C \end{array} \right\} \quad (5\text{-}4)$$

where $$Z_{\text{IN}}(0) \approx \frac{R_E + r_E}{1 - \alpha} + r_B \approx \beta(R_E + r_E) + r_B \qquad (5\text{-}5)$$

is the transistor input impedance seen at the transistor base. The *d-c stage input impedance* at the transistor base is, then, $Z_{\text{IN}}(0)$ in parallel with $rr'/(r + r')$. Degeneration due to R_E decreases the stage gain (3), but tends to make the operating point less dependent on transistor parameters and increases the stage input impedance.

Bias Stability.[2,12] To maintain the emitter current between specified values $(i_E)_{\text{MIN}}$, $(i_E)_{\text{MAX}}$, the minimum permissible R_E depends on the base-circuit resistance R_S. We require

$$R_E \geq$$

$$\frac{R_S[(1 - \alpha_{\text{MIN}})(i_E)_{\text{MIN}} - (1 - \alpha_{\text{MAX}})(i_E)_{\text{MAX}} + (I_{CBO})_{\text{MAX}}] + (V_{BE})_{\text{MAX}} - (V_{BE})_{\text{MIN}}}{(i_E)_{\text{MAX}} - (i_E)_{\text{MIN}}}$$

$$(5\text{-}6)$$

where given maximum and minimum values of α, V_{BE}, and I_{CBO} account for the design temperature range and for manufacturing tolerances. In d-c amplifiers, R_S cannot be decreased at will, and the gain-reducing resistor R_E cannot be bypassed at zero frequency; this constitutes one powerful argument for the use of differential-amplifier stages in d-c amplifiers (Sec. 5-5). Note that the overall feedback improves bias stability in some operational amplifiers but not in others (e.g., integrators). Drift effects will be studied in detail for differential-amplifier stages (Secs. 5-5 to 5-7).

5-3. Emitter-follower Stages, Current-source Loads, and Output-stage Circuits.

Low-frequency equivalent-circuit analysis of the simple *emitter-follower stage* of Fig. 5-2a, using the approximations of Sec. 5-2 and $R_E \gg r_E + (1 - \alpha)R_S$, yields

$$\left. \begin{array}{cc} \dfrac{e_{\text{GEN}}}{e_{\text{IN}}} \approx \dfrac{R_E}{R_E + r_E} \approx 1 \\[3mm] Z_I(0) \approx r_E + (1 - \alpha)R_S \qquad Z_{\text{IN}}(0) \approx \dfrac{1}{1 - \alpha} \dfrac{R_E Z_L(0)}{R_E + Z_L(0)} \end{array} \right\} \quad (5\text{-}7)$$

where R_S is given by Eq. (5). We see that the emitter follower can approximate unity gain more closely than a vacuum-tube cathode follower, but does not provide as good isolation between input and output

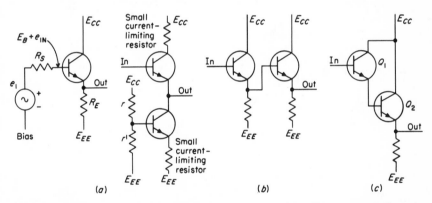

FIG. 5-2. Simple and cascaded emitter followers (a, b), and Darlington connection (c). The Darlington circuit acts approximately like a transistor with $\beta = \beta_1\beta_2$ and hence provides better isolation at low frequencies.

circuits. To obtain higher input impedance and/or lower output impedance at low frequencies, one can cascade two emitter followers (Fig. 5-2b) or use the Darlington connection of Fig. 5-2c, but such circuits can cause serious phase shift at high frequencies.

Like the analogous vacuum-tube circuits (Secs. 4-6 and 4-8), *transistor current-source loads* (Fig. 5-3) can replace amplifier or emitter-follower load resistors to combine high incremental impedance (at least equal to the collector resistance r_C) with a relatively small d-c voltage drop. The possibility of using *pnp* as well as *npn* current sources offers added design flexibility.   As in the case of vacuum-tube amplifiers, current-source loads are particularly useful in *totem-pole output stages* with and without special feedback circuits (Fig. 5-4).   Such circuits yield greater efficiency and/or lower output impedance than simple emitter followers.

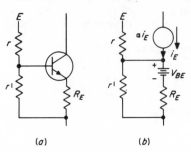

(a)   (b)

FIG. 5-3. *npn* transistor current-source load (a), and approximate equivalent circuit (b).   Reverse voltages and currents for *pnp* transistors.

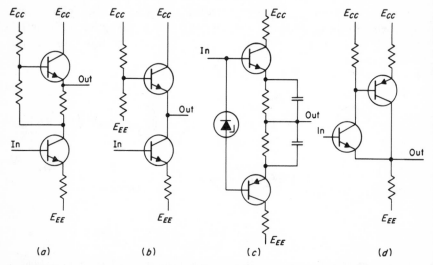

(a)   (b)   (c)   (d)

FIG. 5-4. Totem-pole output stage (a), collector follower (b), complementary-symmetry push-pull emitter follower (c), and emitter follower with bootstrap feedback (d).

TRANSISTOR DIFFERENTIAL-AMPLIFIER STAGES. LOW-DRIFT DESIGN

5-4. Low-frequency Performance.   The traditional advantages of differential-amplifier stages—drift cancellation, ease of biasing, and multiple inputs—were already introduced in Sec. 4-6.   Differential-amplifier stages are even more useful in transistor d-c amplifiers, where they permit both current- and voltage-offset cancellation, increased input impedance, and especially convenient cascading of alternate *npn* and *pnp* stages without gain-reducing interstage networks (Fig. 5-12).

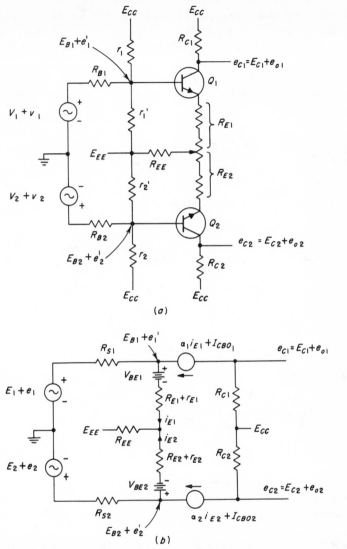

Fig. 5-5. Simple differential-amplifier stage (a), and an equivalent circuit (b).

Figure 5-5 shows a simple *npn* differential-amplifier stage and an equivalent circuit based on the approximations (1). The base-circuit resistances R_{S1}, R_{S2} in the equivalent circuit are given by

$$\left. \begin{aligned} R_{S1} &= \frac{r_1 r_1' R_{B1}}{R_{B1}r_1 + R_{B1}r_1' + r_1 r_1'} + r_{B1} \\ R_{S2} &= \frac{r_2 r_2' R_{B2}}{R_{B2}r_2 + R_{B2}r_2' + r_2 r_2'} + r_{B2} \end{aligned} \right\} \tag{5-8}$$

R_{E1} and R_{E2} are small resistances intended mainly for differential balancing, although they do improve bias stability and input impedance at the expense of some degeneration. We shall find that R_{EE} must be large for good differential action, so that it is reasonable to assume $R_{E1} + r_{E1}$, $R_{E2} + r_{E2}$, R_{S1}/β_1, $R_{S2}/\beta_2 \ll R_{EE}$. We first neglect all d-c sources (capital letters in Fig. 5-5b) to find the *incremental no-load output at zero frequency,*

$$e_{o1} \approx \frac{\alpha_1 R_{C1}}{R_{E1} + r_{E1} + R_{E2} + r_{E2} + (1 - \alpha_1)R_{S1} + (1 - \alpha_2)R_{S2}}$$
$$\cdot \left[e_2 - e_1 - \frac{R_{E2} + r_{E2} + (1 - \alpha_2)R_{S2}}{R_{EE}} e_1 \right] \quad (5\text{-}9)$$

If we consider a *symmetrical* stage, with

$$\left. \begin{array}{ccc} \alpha_2 \approx \alpha_1 = \alpha & \beta_2 \approx \beta_1 = \beta & R_{C2} = R_{C1} = R_C \\ V_{BE2} = V_{BE1} + \Delta V_{BE} \approx V_{BE1} = V_{BE} \\ R_{E2} + r_{E2} = R_{E1} + r_{E1} + \Delta R_E \approx R_{E1} + r_{E1} = R_E \end{array} \right\} \quad (5\text{-}10)$$

then
$$e_{o1} \approx \frac{1}{2} G_D(e_2 - e_1) - \frac{G_D}{2R_{EE}}\left(R_{E2} + r_{E2} + \frac{R_{S2}}{\beta_2} \right)e_1 \quad (5\text{-}11)$$

$$e_{o1} - e_{o2} \approx G_D(e_2 - e_1) + G_{CM}\frac{e_1 + e_2}{2} \quad (5\text{-}12)$$

where
$$G_D = \frac{\alpha R_C}{R_E + (1 - \alpha)(R_{S1} + R_{S2})/2}$$
$$\approx \frac{\alpha R_C}{R_E + (R_{S1} + R_{S2})/2\beta} \quad (5\text{-}13)$$

is the zero-frequency, no-load *differential gain,* and

$$G_{CM} = \frac{G_D}{2R_{EE}}\left(\frac{R_{S1}}{\beta_1} - \frac{R_{S2}}{\beta_2} - \Delta R_E \right) \quad (5\text{-}14)$$

is the *common-mode gain* of our stage. The preponderance of the desired difference term in Eq. (12) over the common-mode term is measured by the *common-mode rejection ratio* $G_D/|G_{CM}|$, which is evidently proportional to R_{EE}.

The *d-c output impedance* at the collector of Q_1 is approximately

$$Z_{I1}(0) \approx R_{C1} \quad (5\text{-}15)$$

The *d-c input impedance* at the base of Q_1 is the parallel resistance of r_1, r_1', and

$$Z_{IN}(0) \approx \beta_1\left(R_{E1} + R_{E2} + r_{E1} + r_{E2} + \frac{R_{S2}}{\beta_2} \right) \quad (5\text{-}16)$$

5-5. Operating Points and Voltage Drift. We next neglect the *signal* sources in Fig. 5-5b ($e_1 = e_2 = 0$ and hence $e_1' = e_2' = 0$) to find the quiescent (zero-signal) no-load collector voltages and currents for a symmetrical differential-amplifier stage. We use the same approximations as before and find

$$
\left.
\begin{aligned}
E_{C1} &\approx \frac{1}{2} G_D \left[E_2 - E_1 - \Delta V_{BE} + R_{S2} I_{CBO2} - R_{S1} I_{CBO1} \right. \\
&\quad - \frac{1}{R_{EE}} \left(R_{E2} + r_{E2} + \frac{R_{S2}}{\beta_2} \right) (E_1 - V_{BE1} + R_{S1} I_{CBO1} - E_{EE}) \bigg] \\
&\qquad\qquad\qquad\qquad\qquad\qquad - R_C I_{CBO1} + E_{CC}
\end{aligned}
\right\} \quad (5\text{-}17)
$$

$$
I_{C1} = \frac{1}{R_C} (E_{CC} - E_{C1})
$$

$$
\begin{aligned}
E_{C1} - E_{C2} &\approx G_D (E_2 - E_1 - \Delta V_{BE} + R_{S2} I_{CBO2} - R_{S1} I_{CBO1}) \\
&\quad + G_{CM} \left(\frac{E_1 + E_2}{2} - V_{BE} + \frac{R_{S1} I_{CBO1} + R_{S2} I_{CBO2}}{2} - E_{EE} \right) \\
&\qquad\qquad\qquad\qquad\qquad + R_C (I_{CBO2} - I_{CBO1}) \quad (5\text{-}18)
\end{aligned}
$$

These equations define the transistor operating points. The V_{BE} and I_{CBO} terms will vary with temperature and thus cause *voltage drift*. Good circuit design must minimize this effect, especially in the input stage of a d-c amplifier.

Our analysis already implies at least rough matching of β_1 and β_2, say within 10 to 20 per cent over a specified temperature and collector-current range. The strongly (exponentially) temperature-dependent I_{CBO} terms are not easily reduced by transistor matching. For suit-

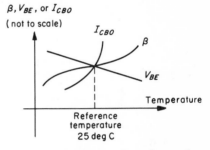

FIG. 5-6. Temperature dependence of β, V_{BE}, and I_{CBO} for a silicon transistor.

able surface-passivated silicon transistors, however, $I_{CBO} < 1$ nA at 25 deg C, and $I_{CBO} < 1$ μA at 150 deg C, so that drift due to I_{CBO} is negligible for $R_{S1}, R_{S2} < 5K$.

Temperature variation of V_{BE} and ΔV_{BE} is a more serious source of drift. The temperature coefficient of V_{BE} (see also Fig. 5-6) is about 2.5 mV/deg C. The V_{BE} terms in Eqs. (17) and (18) are common-mode terms, which can be made negligibly small by large values of R_{EE} or by special circuits improving common-mode cancellation (Sec. 5-6). The remaining voltage drift is due to ΔV_{BE}. Matching of the transistors Q_1 and Q_2 can reduce ΔV_{BE} below 10 mV between -20 and 150 deg C, with a temperature coefficient below 10 μV/deg C.[17] Note, however, that even with perfectly matched transistors, a junction-temperature *differ-ence* of only 0.01 deg C between Q_1 and Q_2 can result in an equivalent offset voltage of 20 μV referred to the input.[17] In low-drift input stages, it is, therefore, imperative to employ a good common heat sink or, preferably, a dual transistor unit for Q_1 and Q_2; and even then, differential self-heating may still be a problem.

5-6. Some Circuit Improvements. Good common-mode rejection with the circuit of Fig. 5-5 requires large values of R_{EE}. Substitution of a current-source transistor Q_3 for R_{EE} (Fig. 5-7a) introduces its large

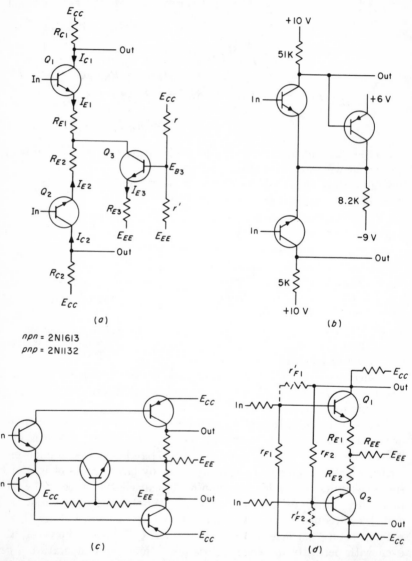

FIG. 5-7. Differential-amplifier circuits with improved input impedance and common-mode rejection (a), (b), (c), (d), and Hilbiber/Bénéteau circuit for improved ΔV_{BE} tracking (e). Such circuits can be combined. Figure 5-7f shows Hoffait and Thornton's compensation scheme (see text).

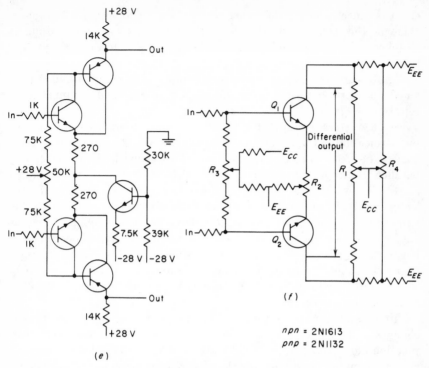

FIG. 5-7. (*Continued*).

effective incremental resistance without producing a large d-c voltage drop.   Referring to Fig. 5-7a, the current-source bias network r, r' effectively controls the base voltage E_{B3} if the current through r greatly exceeds the base current of Q_3, i.e., if $r' \ll \beta_3 R_{E3}$.*   With this assumption and $r_{E3} \ll R_{E3}$, the operating points of Q_1, Q_2, and Q_3 for a symmetrical stage are simply determined by

$$\left.\begin{array}{l} E_{B3} \approx \dfrac{r'E_{CC} + rE_{EE}}{r + r'} \\[2mm] I_C = I_{C1} = I_{C2} \approx \dfrac{1}{2} I_{C3} \approx \dfrac{1}{2} I_{E3} \approx \dfrac{1}{2R_{E3}} (E_{B3} - E_{EE} - V_{BE3}) \\[2mm] \qquad = \dfrac{1}{2R_{E3}} \left[\dfrac{r'}{r + r'} (E_{CC} - E_{EE}) - V_{BE3} \right] \\[2mm] E_C = E_{C1} = E_{C2} = E_{CC} - I_C R_C \end{array}\right\} \quad (5\text{-}19)$$

We see that changes in V_{BE3} will affect E_{C1} and E_{C2} appreciably, but this

* Note, however, that we must still observe bias-stability restrictions (Sec. 5-2) with respect to Q_3; bias stability of Q_1 and Q_2 will then be ensured by the common-mode rejection of our differential stage.   It is also possible to replace Q_3 itself by a difference-amplifier-type circuit to improve its bias stability.

effect is canceled in the difference $E_{C1} - E_{C2}$. A low-level d-c amplifier stage of this type must, therefore, be followed by a second roughly matched differential-amplifier stage, or by a stage feeding E_{C1} or E_{C2} back to Q_3.

Figures 5-7b and c show two circuits employing "common-mode feedback" proportional to E_{C1} or $E_{C1} + E_{C2}$ to improve common-mode rejection.[18,44,48]

Resistive *cross-feedback* (Fig. 5-7d) not only improves the common-mode rejection but also permits us to increase the stage d-c input resistance, if desired, up to and above 1M. The feedback circuit effectively parallels the input impedance (16) of Q_1 with the negative resistance $r_{F1}(1 - a)$, where a is the (positive) gain from the base of Q_1 to the collector of Q_2.[21,24] Since the resistances r_{F1}, r_{F2} yielding appropriately low (subcritical) regeneration may be quite large, one can combine the regeneration with near-equal degeneration through r'_{F1}, r'_{F2}. The constant-bias resistors r_1, r_2 and/or r'_1, r'_2 can often be omitted. If desired, cross-feedback makes it possible to reduce R_{EE} and hence also E_{EE}.[21] If Q_3 is used, cross-feedback also helps to regulate $I_{C1} + I_{C2}$ against the effect of temperature variations in V_{BE3}.

Circuit schemes attempting to compensate voltage drift due to V_{BE} changes with temperature-sensitive resistances or voltage sources (e.g., junction diodes)[1] are probably at least as difficult to implement as accurate V_{BE} matching of Q_1 and Q_2. To reduce matching requirements, Hilbiber[17] and Bénéteau[19,53] have suggested that the temperature coefficient of ΔV_{BE} is reduced by a factor of at least 3 when the collector currents of Q_1 and Q_2 are regulated against changes due to temperature and loading variations. This is achieved by the two-transistor blocks Q_1, Q'_1 and Q_2, Q'_2 in Fig. 5-7e, and by similar three-transistor blocks.[17] These circuits also increase the effective current gain of the stage.

The transistor base-emitter voltage V_{BE} is a function of the collector current I_C and of the absolute junction temperature T. Using well-substantiated semiconductor-junction theory, Hoffait and Thornton[25] have expressed the temperature dependence of V_{BE} in the form

$$\frac{\partial V_{BE}}{\partial T} = -a - \frac{b - V_{BE}(T, I_C) - V' - V''}{T}$$

where a and b are junction parameters independent of T and I_C; V' and V'' are external bias voltages applied between base and emitter. In Hoffait and Thornton's self-compensating amplifier (Fig. 5-7f),[25]

1. R_1 differentially adjusts I_{C1}, I_{C2} for $V_{BE1} = V_{BE2}$.
2. R_2 differentially adjusts bias terms V'_1, V'_2 respectively proportional to I_{C1}, I_{C2}, and hence to E_{C1}, E_{C2}.

3. R_3 differentially adjusts bias terms V_1'', V_2'' proportional to a weighted sum of the supply voltages E_{CC} and E_{EE}.
4. R_4 rebalances the amplifier (zero differential output for zero input).

Iterative adjustment of potentiometers R_1 to R_4 permits us to compensate temperature drift due to V_{BE1}, V_{BE2}, resistance variations, supply-voltage changes, and even current drift (for a given input circuit, see also Sec. 5-7) by introducing corresponding positive or negative changes into $\partial\Delta V_{BE}/\partial T = \partial V_{BE2}/\partial T - \partial V_{BE1}/\partial T$. Voltage drift below 0.1 $\mu V/$ deg C has been obtained with matched dual 2N2484 transistors operated at very low collector currents (7 μA) to minimize differential self-heating.[25]

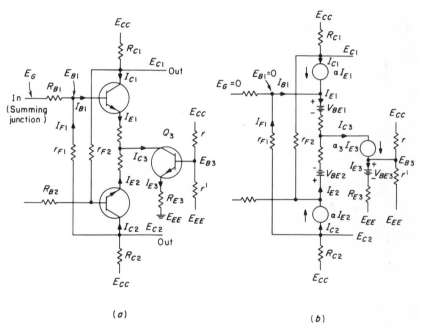

(a)   (b)

Fig. 5-8. Differential-amplifier stage (a), and equivalent circuit for current-drift analysis (b).

5-7. Current Drift and Current-drift Cancellation.

Figure 5-8 shows a practical operational-amplifier input stage incorporating a current-source transistor Q_3 and cross-feedback. With the base of Q_1 connected to the summing junction through R_{B1}, the operational amplifier will be initially balanced for zero voltage and current offset (Sec. 4-1); so that $E_{B1} = E_G = 0$, and *no current flows through R_{B1} into the summing junction*. The quiescent base current I_{B1} of Q_1 then just equals the cross-feedback current $I_{F1} = (E_{CC} - R_C i_{C2})/r_{F1}$ (plus any fixed bias currents not indicated in Fig. 5-8).

We consider a symmetrical stage with $\beta_2 \approx \beta_1 = \beta$, $I_{C2} = I_{C1} = I_C$, and negligible I_{CBO}'s (silicon transistors) and employ the approximations of Sec. 5-4. We have

$$I_{B1} = \frac{1}{\beta} I_C \qquad I_{F1} = \frac{1}{r_{F1}} (E_{CC} - I_C R_C) \Bigg\} $$

with $\qquad I_C \approx \frac{1}{2R_{E3}} \left[\frac{r'}{r + r'} (E_{CC} - E_{EE}) - V_{BE3} \right] \Bigg\}$ (5-20)

A temperature increase will upset the base-current balance by changing I_{B1} and I_{F1}; β will *increase*, and V_{BE3} will *decrease* (Fig. 5-6). Output errors due to the resulting current flow into or out of the summing junction are not usually canceled by common-mode rejection, since the two differential inputs of most operational amplifiers may be connected to entirely different circuits. The temperature-sensitive current offset can change by as much as a few microamperes per degree centigrade and constitutes a serious additional source of drift unless very low base-circuit resistances can be used.

Current drift due to V_{BE3} is substantially reduced or eliminated in the circuit of Fig. 5-7c. Current drift due to changes in β is reduced by large values of β or by compound-transistor circuits having a high effective current gain (Figs. 5-2c and 5-7d). As a more sophisticated approach to the problem, Koerner and Ozdes[24] noted that the current-drift effects of temperature-induced changes in β and V_{BE3} oppose each other and permit approximate cancellation. With a suitable choice of circuit values, they were able to reduce offset-current drift below 1 nA/deg C between -20 and $+65$ deg C, where not only dV_{BE3}/dT but also $d\beta/dT$ is reasonably constant (Fig. 5-6). To maintain current balance as the temperature changes, one requires

$$\frac{d}{dT} (I_{B1} - I_{F1}) = \left(\frac{\partial I_{B1}}{\partial \beta} - \frac{\partial I_{F1}}{\partial \beta} \right) \frac{d\beta}{dT} + \left(\frac{\partial I_{B1}}{\partial V_{BE3}} - \frac{\partial I_{F1}}{\partial V_{BE3}} \right) \frac{dV_{BE3}}{dT} = 0$$

(5-21)

Equations (20) and (21) show that approximate current-drift cancellation requires selection of I_C and/or r_{F1} so that

$$I_C = - \frac{\beta}{2R_{E3}} \left(\beta \frac{R_C}{r_{F1}} + 1 \right) \frac{dV_{BE}/dT}{d\beta/dT} \qquad (5-22)$$

In practice, I_C is matched to measured values of the temperature coefficients dV_{BE3}/dT and $d\beta/dT$ averaged over the operating-temperature range.[24]

In conclusion, voltage drift of matched differential-amplifier stages is readily kept below 50 μV/deg C over a temperature range between 0 and 120 deg C, and one-fourth this drift is claimed for carefully constructed circuits of the type shown in Fig. 5-7d. Summing-junction current offsets can be reduced below 1 nA/deg C by the cancellation scheme, and input impedances between 10 and 500K are entirely practical.

The current-drift-balance relation (22) is not affected by addition of fixed-bias resistors r_1, r_2 and/or r_1', r_2' to the circuit of Fig. 5-8 and holds also for $r_{F1} = r_{F2} = \infty$ (no cross-feedback). If degenerative-feedback resistors r_{F1}', r_{F2}' are added in the manner of Fig. 5-7c, replace $1/r_{F1}$ by $1/r_{F1} - 1/r_{F1}'$ in Eq. (22).

CHOPPER-STABILIZED TRANSISTOR AMPLIFIERS AND SOLID-STATE CHOPPERS

5-8. General Remarks. Transistor-chopper Circuits. The relatively low drift of well-designed differential-amplifier stages employing silicon transistors permits the designer to dispense with chopper stabilization in many intermediate-accuracy (0.1 to 0.3 per cent of half-scale) applications.   This is especially true since entire miniaturized transistor amplifiers or input stages can be readily mounted in controlled-temperature ovens where necessary.   Chopper stabilization can, however, reduce transistor d-c amplifier drift by another factor of 10 and has also been employed to permit the use of germanium instead of silicon transistors. At the lower computing voltages used with transistor amplifiers, choppernoise, thermoelectric-offset, and ground-current problems are somewhat more serious than with vacuum-tube circuits, but impedance levels are lower as well, and good miniature electromechanical 400-cps choppers make it possible to achieve offset and noise levels of a few microvolts. The extra cost of individual chopper-drive multivibrators in each amplifier often pays for itself by eliminating all a-c wiring and reducing a-c pickup.   Low-drift design of the main d-c amplifier is still a consideration even with chopper stabilization, since it is important to minimize chopper noise due to d-c amplifier offset (Sec. 4-14).

Besides the usual chopper-stabilization scheme of Fig. 4-14a, the alternative scheme of Fig. 4-14b has been applied to transistor amplifiers, since such circuits work well with low-impedance amplifiers and permit current-drift compensation as well as voltage stabilization.[11,20] The circuit of Fig. 4-14a with a blocking capacitor C_B to prevent current offset is, however, simpler and probably preferable.   To avoid the need for excessively large filter capacitors C_3, it is desirable to employ chopper frequencies higher than the 60-cps line frequency, and at least one circuit has used "capacitance amplification" by an electronic integrator circuit in the chopper-channel output filter.[14]

All-electronic chopper circuits may offer improved reliability and smaller size together with the possibility of higher chopper frequencies.   The most frequently used solid-state chopper is the *inverted-transistor shunt switch* discussed in detail in Sec. 6-11.   Improved inverted-transistor circuits designed especially for chopper stabilization employ matched or common-base transistors and transformer drive. It is, again, a good idea to employ individual chopper-excitation oscillators on each amplifier card instead of a central chopper-excitation supply. Figure 5-9 illustrates two transistor-chopper circuits (see also Fig. 6-20). Amplifiers of this type exhibit voltage offsets below 10 μV/deg C and 20 to 200 μV over 8 hr, all referred to the input.

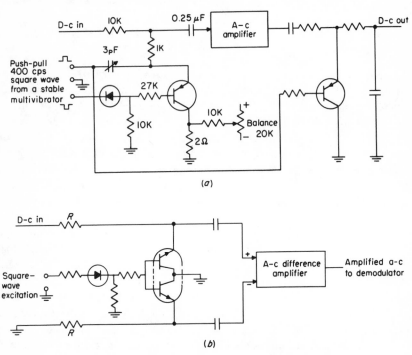

FIG. 5-9. Simple transistor-chopper stabilizer with partial spike cancellation (*a*), and matched-dual-transistor chopper with grounded excitation and differential output (*b*) (see Fig. 6-20 for additional solid-state chopper circuits).

5-9. Switching Spikes. Double-chopper Circuit. Chopper transistor base-to-emitter capacitance causes switching transients (switching spikes) due to differentiation of the switching waveform (Fig. 5-10). The shorter spike corresponds to transistor saturation; the switch-off spike is the more serious one and adds an unwanted charge of 5 to 20 $\mu\mu$coulombs per switching cycle. These transients impose an upper limit on the chopper frequency when the transient-charge current begins to mask the minimum input current of interest.[1] Figure 5-9*a* indicates a scheme for partial spike cancellation.[54]

Chopper spikes can be kept short if the chopper is followed by a wideband amplifier, and the demodulator can then sample the chopper-amplifier output after the spikes have decayed.   Since the transient charge is more or less fixed, however, short spikes will have a proportionately greater amplitude, which would overload the final amplifier stages.   We can still reduce the spike amplitude by diode clipping or by delayed resampling with a second chopper.   These operations follow initial amplification by a factor of 10 to 100 and will, therefore, not contribute excessively to the d-c error. Chaplin[1] describes a 25-Kc chopper channel which resamples the chopped waveform after initial amplification at twice the carrier frequency or 50 Kc to remove the original

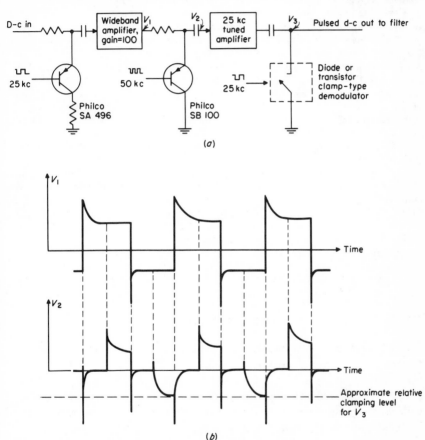

(a)

(b)

Fig. 5-10. 25-Kc double-chopper system employing 50-Kc resampling and a 25-Kc clamp-type demodulator to reduce switching-spike effects (waveforms not to scale; based on ref. 1).

short switching spikes.   The 50-Kc spikes, already effectively reduced by the preamplifier gain of about 100, are attenuated by a subsequent 25-Kc tuned amplifier and are finally made to cancel approximately in pairs in a 25-Kc clamp-type demodulator (Fig. 5-10).   Chaplin's circuit permits the use of a low-drift silicon chopper transistor with relatively high emitter-to-base capacitance as the first chopper in spite of the relatively high 25-Kc carrier frequency.   The resulting amplifier has a bandwidth of 1 Kc; its 100-μV voltage drift and 100-nA current drift between 20 and 50 deg C are comparable with thermal-noise effects in the 1-Kc bandwidth.   The wide frequency response of a double-chopper channel is rarely required for chopper-stabilizer applications but is most suitable for sampled-data-type d-c measurements and analog-to-digital conversion.

5-10. Other Electronic Choppers. Electronic choppers other than transistor choppers have been used especially in instrumentation applications and include shunt diode and diode-bridge switches (see also Sec. 6-10), variable-capacitance diodes, various magnetic modulators,[33-35] and photoelectric choppers. Photoelectric choppers[36-39] combine carrier-operated gas or incandescent light sources with CdSe or CdS photoconductors or with phototransistors. Photoelectric choppers, when carefully designed with a view to low thermoelectric offset, yield long-term offsets as low as 2 μV with negligible temperature effects between −30 and +50 deg C, low noise (2 to 5 μV rms), and long life ($\geq 10^4$ hr). Typical switching time constants, however, are of the order of milliseconds, so that the conversion efficiency (peak-to-peak a-c voltage out/d-c voltage in) decreases with frequency (85 per cent at 60 cps and 50 per cent at 400 cps for a typical unit). The switched voltage can be as large as 120 volts and can contain components up to 2 Mc. Photoelectric choppers utilizing neon lights will, unfortunately, require a high-voltage a-c supply for them.

Field-effect transistors (FET's) with sufficiently low gate-to-drain capacitances (below 20 pF)[12] are especially suitable as electronic choppers and may well replace other electronic devices in this application. FET characteristics are similar to those of vacuum pentodes, but a FET is wholly passive and hence offset-free in its ON state (zero gate voltage), with a forward resistance between 250Ω and 15K. Performance is thus limited only by temperature-dependent current leakage (gate reverse current) in the OFF condition, and by spikes due to the nonlinear gate-to-drain capacitance, which can be only partially neutralized in the manner of Fig. 5-9a. Sinusoidal rather than square-wave excitation reduces the capacitive feedthrough at the expense of switching efficiency. 100-cps operation permits amplifier offsets below 5 μV at 25 deg C and 120 μV at 100 deg C;[57] much higher switching rates are possible with low-capacitance FET's.

AMPLIFIER DESIGN

5-11. Frequency Response, Noise, and General Design Considerations. The frequency-response and stability analysis developed in Secs. 4-15 to 4-20 applies to transistor amplifiers and amplifier stages (Fig. 5-11a) as well as to vacuum-tube circuits. Transistor d-c amplifiers will rarely require resistive interstage networks to obtain suitable d-c levels at each stage, since it will be possible to employ alternate *npn* and *pnp* stages. Each common-emitter stage will, however, load the preceding stage (or the operational-amplifier summing point) very noticeably with its input impedance (5) or (16) in parallel with an effective input capacitance approximately given by

$$C_i \approx C_i' + (a_2 + 1)C_C \tag{5-23}$$

C_i' is due to the transistor base-to-emitter capacitance together with stray circuit capacitances, C_C is the base-to-collector capacitance of the following stage, and a_2 is its base-to-collector voltage gain. The second term in Eq. (23) describes the Miller effect (Sec. 4-16), a serious problem in wideband transistor d-c amplifiers. We combat the Miller effect by arranging amplifier stages in the order of gain, by using feedback-pair and cascode stages (Fig. 5-11b, c), or by separating stages with emitter followers; our experience indicates that capacitive cross-neutralization in

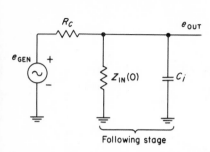

FIG. 5-11a. Approximate high-frequency equivalent circuit for a common-emitter amplifier stage operated well below the alpha-cutoff frequency.

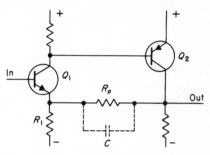

FIG. 5-11b. Feedback-pair stage for improved stage isolation. With high loop gain, the d-c gain is approximately $1 + R_o/R_1$, and the input impedance is $\beta_1 R_1$ times the loop gain. The rolloff capacitor C causes a pole at $\omega = 1/R_oC$ and a zero at $\omega = 1/R_1C$ $(R_o \gg R_1)$.[54]

differential-amplifier stages is not easily accomplished. Unfortunately, even an emitter follower reflects $1/\beta$ times its load capacitance into its input circuit (see also Sec. 5-3), an effect especially objectionable in output emitter followers driving capacitive loads.

The transistor current amplification factors α and β decrease at high frequencies; we have approximately

$$\alpha(\omega) = \frac{\alpha(0)}{j\omega/2\pi f_\alpha + 1}$$

$$\beta(\omega) = \frac{\beta(0)}{j\omega\beta(0)/2\pi f_\alpha + 1} \quad (5\text{-}24)$$

which implies additional phase shift in each transistor stage. Fortunately, at least low-voltage npn transistors with α-cutoff frequencies f_α above 400 Mc are generally and inexpensively available, so that α-cutoff effects are not too serious in

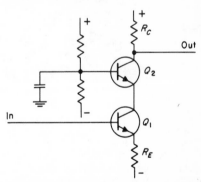

FIG. 5-11c. Transistor cascode stage. The voltage gain is approximately R_C/R_E, but the base-to-collector voltage gain of Q_1, and hence the Miller effect, is small.

± 10-volt amplifiers with unity-gain frequencies below 10 Mc. Note that transistors with high f_α will also have desirably low capacitances. α-cutoff effects will be aggravated by compound-connected transistor stages.

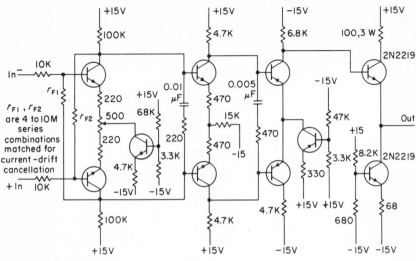

Unmarked npn transistors are 2N2222,
pnp's are 2N861

(a)

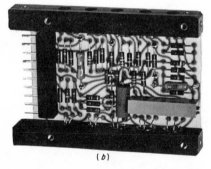

(b)

(c)

FIG. 5-12. ±10-volt, 30-mA amplifier circuit (a), plug-in version (b), and epoxy-cast printed-circuit module (c).   Matched silicon transistors and current-drift cancellation (Sec. 5-7) reduce drift below 25 μV/deg C and 1 nA/deg C.   Input and output impedances are 100K and 50 ohms.   A second version of this amplifier replaces the output stage by a feedforward high-frequency amplifier to increase the d-c gain from 3×10^4 to 10^6 and the unity-gain frequency from 1 Mc to over 10 Mc.   (Ozdes, D., M.S. Thesis, University of Arizona, 1963; Burr-Brown Research Corp., Tucson, Ariz.)

A typical transistor computer amplifier will have one or two matched differential stages to minimize drift and/or chopper noise caused by d-c offset.   The input stage is usually an npn stage (for higher β and f_α, lower noise) operated at low collector current (30 to 200 μA) to reduce current drift, self-heating, and noise.   On the debit side, low-current stages with low R_E's and R_C's tend to limit bandwidth.   The resulting compromise is especially neatly resolved by feedforward circuits with

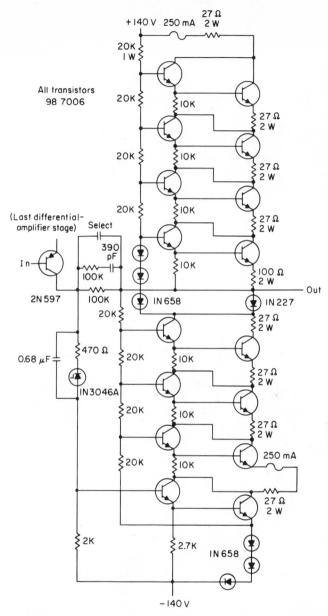

Fig. 5-13. ±100-volt, 50-mA output stage of the Astrodata/Comcor, Inc. Model CI-308 d-c amplifier. Stacked transistors avoid the need for expensive high-voltage transistors. The input stage (not shown) of this chopper-stabilized all-solid-state amplifier employs field-effect transistors for high input impedance. D-c gain $> 10^8$; 1M/1M unity-inverter gain down 3 db at 30 Kc (0.07 deg at 100 cps); d-c offset, 60 μV and 15 mV/24 hr; noise, 6 mV peak to peak. Full output is obtained up to 5 Kc.

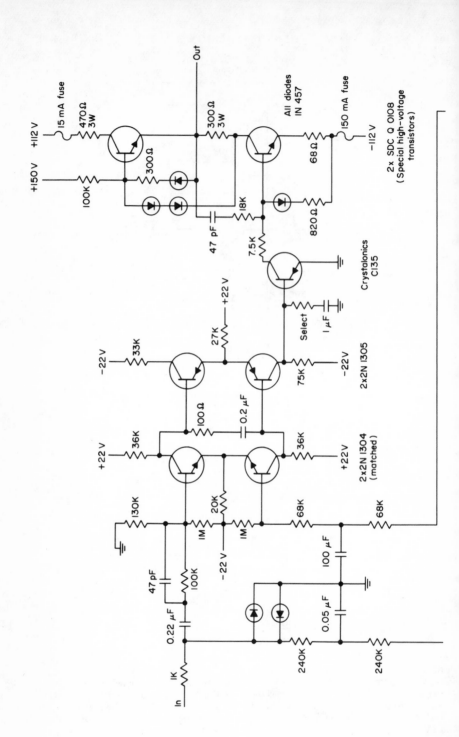

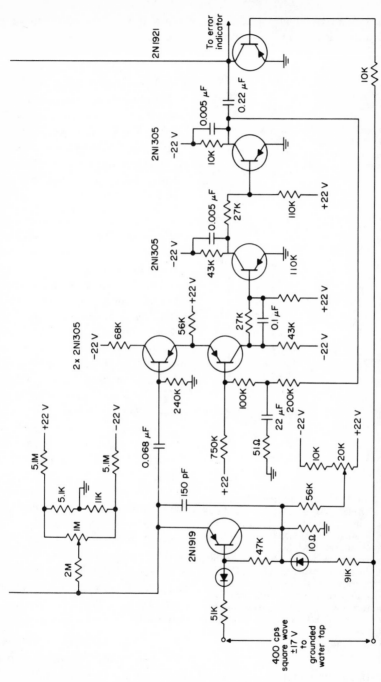

FIG. 5-14. A chopper-stabilized all-solid-state d-c amplifier with a ±100-volt, 20-mA (or 40 mA at ±60 volts) totem-pole-amplifier output stage. D-c gain > 2 × 10⁶; 100K/100K unity-inverter gain down 3 db at 50 Kc; drift, 20 μV/deg C between −55 and +55 deg C, 150 μV/8 hr; noise, 25 mV peak to peak; d-c input resistance, 500K. (*Systron-Donner Corp.*)

separate low-frequency and high-frequency inputs (Sec. 4-19 and Figs. 5-15 and 5-16). For this reason, the feedforward scheme is even more useful with transistor amplifiers than for vacuum-tube circuits.

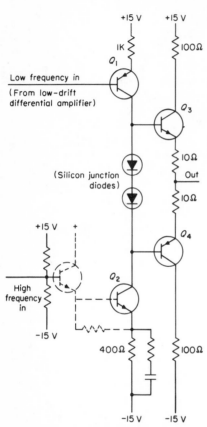

The voltage amplifier driving a transistor output stage may have to supply appreciable power, especially if a rolloff network is also used in this stage. We can often prevent current limiting by replacing the collector-load resistor R_C with an *npn* or *pnp* current-source transistor (Fig. 5-3).[24]

5-12. Typical Amplifier Specifications and Examples. Voltage and Current Balancing. Figures 5-12 to 5-16 show examples illustrating the design and specifications of transistor d-c amplifiers for computer applications (see also Table 4-2). As we have seen, medium-accuracy computers will not require chopper stabilization. The use of feedforward circuits (Figs. 5-15 and 5-16) is especially recommended. Figure 5-13 illustrates the design of a ± 100-volt output stage using series-cascaded transistors to increase the voltage rating.

Unlike most vacuum-tube amplifiers, transistor d-c amplifiers without chopper stabilization require separate balancing for offset *voltage* and offset *current*. Balancing of a differential-input d-c amplifier during manufacture may use the circuit of Fig. 5-17a and proceed as follows:[24]

FIG. 5-15. A ± 10-volt feedforward and circuit with class AB output. The Philbrick Type P45 d-c amplifier employs a similar class B stage.[24,56] Output capacitances of Q_1, Q_2 are critical. 50-mA output and 0-db bandwidth to 50 Mc are possible, depending on transistors and load. Frequency response of the type shown in Fig. 4-21b permits large capacitive loads without instability. An emitter follower ahead of the high-frequency input (dash lines) would help to prevent blocking with step inputs.

1. *Voltage balancing:* With the switch in the VOLTAGE position (symmetrical base-circuit resistances), adjust R_{E1} and/or R_{E2} for zero output.

2. *Current balancing:* With the switch in the CURRENT position (asym-

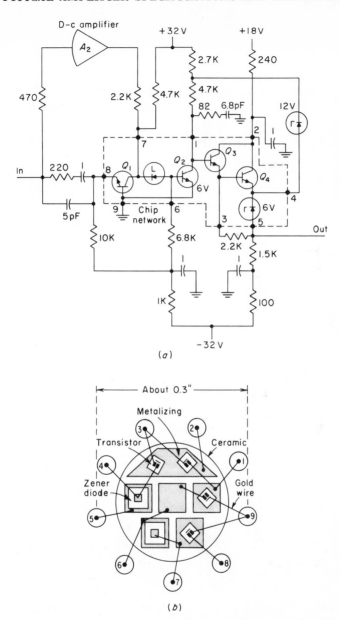

FIG. 5-16. A wideband feedforward d-c amplifier (*a*) employing 1-Gc transistors and diodes assembled on separate chips in a single T0-5 transistor header to reduce wiring capacitances. The no-load unity-gain (0-db) crossover frequency exceeds 100 Mc. Low-frequency and high-frequency inputs to the feedforward section are isolated by a grounded-base stage.[47]

metrical base circuits), adjust a bias resistor (r_1, r_1', or r_{F1}, Secs. 5-4 to 5-7) for zero output.*

3. Alternate steps 1 and 2 until no further change results.

If the amplifier is to be cast in plastic, voltage and current balance must be checked after casting. If current-drift cancellation (Sec. 5-7) is used,

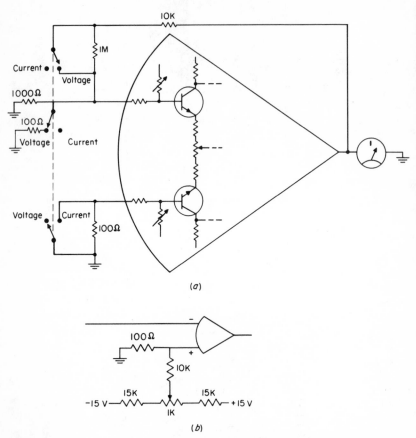

(a)

(b)

Fig. 5-17. Circuits for voltage and current balancing (a), and external voltage-balancing circuit (b).

the drift-balance condition (22) must be checked after voltage and current balancing; possibly r or r' will require readjustment. With the amplifier thus balanced by the manufacturer, the user will, in general, require only an external voltage-balance circuit like that in Fig. 5-17b for day-to-day balancing.

* If desired, r_2, r_2', or r_{F2} can be similarly adjusted with the first input grounded and the second input grounded through 100 ohms.

MISCELLANEOUS PRACTICAL CONSIDERATIONS

5-13. Construction of D-c Amplifiers. Choice of Components.
Computer d-c amplifiers are assembled and wired much like high-quality
audio-frequency electronic equipment; most commercial d-c amplifiers
are constructed on etched-circuit cards.   In general, input leads, but not
necessarily output leads, are shielded, and care is taken to avoid line-
frequency hum pickup, especially in chopper-stabilizer channels.

The following important precautions must be observed:

1. To avoid leakage over the surface of insulating materials, *summing-
   point terminations must be separated from the amplifier output and
   from all high-voltage terminations by grounded conductors* ("insulation
   with metal").   On etched-circuit cards, summing-point terminations must be separated from other terminations by grounded etched-
   circuit lands.   Circuit cards and connectors should be cleaned with
   ether or alcohol to prevent leakage through contamination due, for
   example, to soldering flux.   External connections to summing points
   are made either through coaxial connectors or, somewhat more conveniently, through ribbon-type or printed-circuit connectors with
   summing points separated from all other terminations by grounded
   terminals.

2. *No high-impedance point should ever be terminated on an etched-circuit
   card,* since this may cause both intolerable circuit capacitances to
   other printed wiring and d-c drift due to time-variable d-c leakage.
   High-impedance points are connected either directly between tube-
   socket terminals, or stand-off connectors on grounded bases can be
   installed on the etched-circuit card.   If these precautions are taken,
   amplifier cards printed on both sides can be used, although such
   cards tend to have somewhat larger circuit capacitances than cards
   printed on one side only.

In chopper-stabilized d-c amplifiers, drift due to resistance variations
with temperature is not usually a problem, but resistance and vacuum-
tube or transistor tolerances must be specified so as to keep all amplifier-
stage operating voltages within the range of linear operation.   Carbon or
metal-film resistors with 5 to 10 per cent tolerances are usually satisfactory for the resulting worst-case designs; if space permits, one may
use resistors of slightly larger power rating than necessary to reduce self-
heating.   Vacuum tubes should be well ventilated to reduce drift and
lengthen tube life. General-purpose computer amplifiers must be
designed so that they can stand routine mistreatment such as overloads,
output short circuiting, and high-frequency oscillations due to unstable
computer setups.

To minimize microphonism in vacuum-tube input stages, use nonmicrophonic tube types and/or shock-mounted tube sockets. If relays must be mounted near vacuum tubes, shock-mount the relays.

Twisted and possibly shielded vacuum-tube-filament leads will minimize hum pickup from that source. Return filament-transformer center taps (not one side of the transformer) to ground or to a well-bypassed point slightly more positive than the input-stage cathode. In some d-c

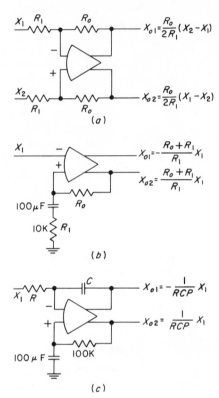

Fig. 5-18. Applications of push-pull d-c amplifiers: push-pull operational amplifier (a), a-c amplifier (b), and a-c integrator (c).[22]

amplifiers, vacuum-tube cathode-to-heater voltage ratings necessitate the use of two separate filament transformers for different stages.

D-c amplifier ground connections are quite critical and may present elusive problems in large computer installations requiring high accuracy. These problems are discussed in Secs. 5-14 and 11-9.

The design of *microminiature integrated-circuit d-c amplifier packages* is discussed in refs. 44 to 48.

5-14. D-c Amplifier Ground Connections. D-c amplifier ground connections must not be made to a metal chassis or cabinet but to special ground busses connected to the computer ground system at a single point.

High-quality ground connections free of d-c offsets and a-c pickup are especially critical in d-c amplifier input stages and in chopper-stabilizer channels operated at the line frequency (Sec. 4-14).

In accurate computers, d-c amplifier input stages are returned to high-quality *signal ground busses* separated from the *power-ground* connections of high-level and output stages with their relatively large direct return currents. Chopper ground terminals, which are also sensitive to both d-c offset and a-c pickup, are returned to signal ground or, preferably, to a

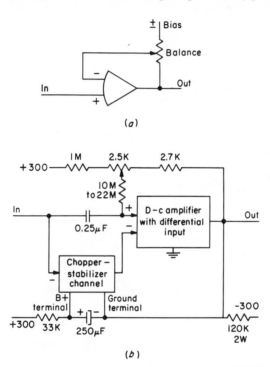

FIG. 5-19. Unity-gain followers with high-impedance input.[56]

separate *chopper ground* of similar quality. Stabilizer a-c amplifier cathodes should be heavily bypassed to the same ground, while their direct cathode currents can return through the amplifier *power-ground* connections.

Care must also be taken to follow the manufacturer's instructions for grounding chopper shields and for separating the chopper excitation circuit from signal wiring. For high-quality d-c amplifiers, the use of a chopper frequency other than the power-line frequency is highly recommended, especially since inductive ground loops encompassing line-frequency flux are almost unavoidable in large computers. The problem of grounding an entire computer system is further discussed in Sec. 11-9.

5-15. Differential Amplifiers and Unity-gain Followers. D-c amplifiers with differential-amplifier input stages (Secs. 4-6 and 5-4) produce an output proportional to the difference of two input voltages. Very accurate difference voltages (high common-mode rejection) are obtained with cascaded difference-amplifier stages and regenerative cross-feedback from later differential-amplifier stages to the input terminals. Difference amplifiers with symmetrical push-pull output stages can often save extra phase-inverting amplifiers, especially in special-purpose computers. Figure 5-18 shows a number of useful applications.[22]

Figure 5-19a illustrates the use of a typical utility d-c amplifier with differential-amplifier input stage as a *unity-gain follower* having high input impedance and low output impedance. The accuracy of the unity gain depends on the common-mode rejection. With a single difference-amplifier stage, as in most amplifiers, the gain will differ from unity by less than 1 per cent; this can be improved by common-mode feedback (Sec. 5-6). Drift voltage is equal to the equivalent offset (Sec. 3-10) of the d-c amplifier used. Figure 5-19b shows how chopper stabilization can be added to a unity-gain follower without the use of phase-inverting amplifiers. Note that the chopper ground contact is, unfortunately, isolated from ground, so that careful shielding is necessary.[54]

REFERENCES AND BIBLIOGRAPHY

Transistor D-c Amplifiers

1. Hunter, L. P.: *Handbook of Semiconductor Electronics*, 2d ed., McGraw-Hill, New York, 1962.
2. *General Electric Transistor Manual*, published periodically by General Electric Co., Syracuse, N.Y.
3. Ettinger, G. M.: Transistor Amplifiers for Analog Computers, *Electronics*, July, 1955.
4. Schenkerman, S.: Feedback Simplifies Transistor Amplifiers, *Electronics*, November, 1954.
5. Blecher, F. H.: Transistor Circuits for Analog and Digital Systems, *Bell System Tech. J.*, March, 1956.
6. Kerfoot, B. P.: Transistors in Current-analog Computing, *IRETEC*, June, 1956.
7. Stanton, J. W.: A Transistorized D-C Amplifier, *IRE Trans. PGCT*, March, 1956.
8. Chaplin, G. B.: Some Transistor Input Stages for High-gain D-C Amplifiers, *Proc. IEE*, Paper 2382, July, 1957.
9. Blecher, F.: Design Principles for Single-loop Transistor Feedback Amplifiers, *IRE Trans. PGCT*, September, 1957.
10. Goldmann, H. O., and G. Meyer-Brötz: Transistor-Operations-verstärker mit hoher Verstärkung und kleiner Drift, *Telefunken Z.*, September, 1960.
11. Okada, R. H.: Stable Transistor Wide-band Amplifiers, *Trans. AIEE (Communications and Electronics)*, **47** (March, 1960).
12. Texas Instruments, Inc., Engineering Staff: *Transistor Circuit Design*, McGraw-Hill, New York, 1963.
13. Konigsberg, R. L.: Designing Hybrid D-C Amplifiers to Withstand Missile Environments, *Electronics*, Aug. 11, 1961.

14. Hochwald, W., and H. L. Ehlers: Design of a High-quality Transistor D-C Amplifier, in Huskey, H. D., and G. A. Korn, *Computer Handbook*, McGraw-Hill, New York, 1962.

Transistor Differential-amplifier Stages

15. Slaughter, D. W.: The Emitter-coupled Differential Amplifier, *Proc. IRE*, March, 1956.
16. Depian, L., and R. E. Smith: A Stabilized D-C Difference Transistor Amplifier, *Trans. AIEE*, Paper 58-192, 1958.
17. Hilbiber, D. F.: A New Transistor Differential Amplifier, *Proc. Intern. Solid-state-circuits Conf.*, Philadelphia, February, 1961.
18. Middlebrook, R. D., and A. D. Taylor: Differential Amplifier with Regulator, *Electronics*, July 28, 1961.
19. Bénéteau, P. J.: The Design of High-stability D-C Amplifiers, *Application Data 23*, Fairchild Semiconductor, Mountain View, Calif., 1961.
20. ———, L. Blaser, and R. Q. Lane: Transistor Operational Amplifiers, *IRE Intern. Convention Record*, 1962.
21. Nambiar, K. P.: Transistor Differential Amplifiers, *Electronic Technology*, April, 1962; see also *Electronic Design*, June 7, 1963.
22. *Applications Handbook*, Burr-Brown Research Corp., Tucson, Ariz., 1964.
23. De Matteis, W. M., and J. W. Halligan: Designing Transistorized Differential Amplifiers, *Electronic Design*, Aug. 2, 16, 1962.
24. Ozdes, D.: Design of a Wideband Transistor D-C Amplifier (M.S. Thesis), *ACL Memo. 79*, Electrical Engineering Department, University of Arizona, 1963.
25. Hoffait, A. H., and R. D. Thornton: Limitations of Transistor D-c Amplifiers, *Proc. IEEE*, February, 1964.

Solid-state Chopper Circuits
(See also refs. 1 and 12 and refs. 18 to 41 in Chap. 6)

26. Bright, R. L.: Junction Transistors Used as Switches, *Trans. AIEE (Communications and Electronics)*, **74** (1): 111 (March, 1955).
27. Williams, A. J., et al.: Some Advances in Transistor Modulators for Precise Measurement, *Proc. Natl. Electronics Conf.*, **40** (1957).
28. Massey, W. S.: A Review of the Transistor Chopper, *Airpax Tech. J.*, Airpax Electronics, Inc., Ft. Lauderdale, Fla., April, 1960.
29. *Application Report 593 on Transistor Choppers*, Philco Lansdale Div., Lansdale, Pa., 1960.
30. Sommer, B.: Chopper Noise Sources and Measurement Techniques, *Automatic Control*, November, 1961.
31. Palmer, J.: Spikes on Chopper-transistor Waveforms, *Electronic Eng.*, March, 1962.
32. Berry, J. R.: Choppers—Electromechanical or Transistor?, *Electronic Design*, Aug. 16, 1962.
33. Williams, F. C., and S. W. Noble: Fundamental Limitations of the Second-harmonic Type of Magnetic Modulator, *Proc. IEE*, **97** (II): 445 (1950).
34. Rote, W. A.: Magnetic Converter D-C Amplifier, *Electronics*, December, 1953.
35. Miura, T., and C. Hirano: Reliable Magnetic Amplifier, *Electronics*, June 29, 1962.
36. Sternberg, S.: Electronic Zero Stabilization of D-c Amplifiers, *Typhoon Symposium III*, Oct. 13, 1953.
37. Schwartz, J., and R. Solomonoff: Photoelectric Chopper for Guided Missiles, *Electronics*, November, 1954.
38. *Photocom Data Sheet*, James Electronics, Inc., Chicago, Ill., 1962.
39. McDonald, R. K.: Optoelectronic Components, *Electronic Inds.*, May, 1963.

40. Fleischmann, J. S.: Total Charge Stored in Junction Transistor, *Application Note* SMA-11, Radio Corp. of America, Somerville, N.J., 1962.

41. Staff Report, *Electronic Design*, Nov. 8, 1962.

42. Staff Report, *Electronic Design*, Jan. 4, 1963.

43. Low-level Differential Chopper Amplifier, *General Engineering Memo*. 10, National Semiconductor Corp., Danbury, Conn., 1963.

Microminiature Packaging and Integrated D-c Amplifier Circuits

44. DeBoice, W. F., and J. F. Bowker: Differential Amplifier Grown in Silicon Block, *Electronics*, July 6, 1962.

45. Aarons, M. W.: Putting a Servo on a Small Silicon Wafer, *Electronics*, Dec. 28, 1962.

46. Bogert, H.: Integrated Circuits Can Be Breadboarded, *Electronic Design*, Feb. 15, 1963.

47. Waldhauer, F. D.: Latest Approach to Integrated-amplifier Design, *Electronics*, May 31, 1963.

48. *Specification Sheets* for SN 521/522 Integrated Operational Amplifiers, Texas Instruments, Inc., Dallas, Tex., 1963.

Use of Field-effect Transistors
(See also ref. 46)

49. Hilbiber, D. F.: Differential Amplifier with Field-effect Transistors, *Proc. Intern. Solid-state-circuits Conf.*, Philadelphia, 1963.

50. High-input-impedance UNIFET Amplifiers, *Application Note*, Siliconix, Inc., Sunnyvale, Calif., 1963.

Miscellaneous

51. Pettit, J. M., and M. M. McWhorter: *Electronic Amplifier Circuits*, McGraw-Hill, New York, 1961.

52. Middlebrook, R. D.: *Differential Amplifiers*, Wiley, New York, 1963.

53. Bénéteau, P. J., and E. Murari: D-c Amplifiers Using Transistors, *Electronic Eng.*, April, 1963.

54. Lucas, P.: Designing Operational Amplifiers, *Electronic Design*, Mar. 29, 1963.

55. Marimon, R. L.: Ground Rules for Low-frequency, High-gain Amplifiers, *Electronic Design*, Apr. 12, 1963.

56. *Application Notes*, G. A. Philbrick Researches, Inc., Boston, Mass., 1958.

57. Field-effect Low-level Choppers, *Application Note*, Siliconix, Inc., 1963.

CHAPTER **6**

LIMITERS, SWITCHING CIRCUITS, AND ELECTRONIC FUNCTION GENERATORS

INTRODUCTION

6-1. Function Generators and Switches. This chapter describes the basic devices required to vary a voltage X_o as a nonlinear function $F(X_1, X_2, \ldots)$ of other voltages X_1, X_2, $\ldots$. Many circuits employing nonlinear resistors, semiconductors, or vacuum tubes can produce continuous nonlinear relations $X_o = F(X_1)$ (Secs. 6-14, 6-15, and 6-19), but their characteristics are not easily reproduced with precision. For this reason, most electronic function generators employ biased diodes (rectifiers) as voltage-sensitive *switches* which select network-gain values set by accurate linear resistances. Changes in diode characteristics have, then, only a relatively small effect on the output (Secs. 6-2 to 6-6 and 6-13). Generation of functions of two or more variables is discussed in Secs. 6-16 to 6-19.

An increasing number of computer applications involve relations $X_o = F(X_1, X_2, \ldots)$ where an input X_i or the output X_o does not vary continuously but is a "digital" variable which assumes only discrete levels (e.g., $+10$ or -10 volts) corresponding to logical decisions. Timed or voltage-determined coefficient and computer-program changes are examples of such operations; their implementation requires *analog comparators* (elementary analog-to-digital converters, Sec. 6-8) and *analog switching circuits* (elementary digital-to-analog converters, Secs. 6-8 to 6-11) together with suitable digital-logic circuits (see also Secs. 9-2 to 9-4 and 10-10).

Function generators involving hybrid analog-digital computation are discussed in Sec. 11-20.

LIMITER AND SELECTOR CIRCUITS

6-2. Diode Characteristics and Diode Models. An *ideal diode* would act as a perfect voltage-sensitive switch passing current in the forward direction only; its resistance would change without delay between zero and infinity as the applied voltage reverses. Figure 6-1 shows the static (d-c) current vs. voltage characteristics of various types of physical

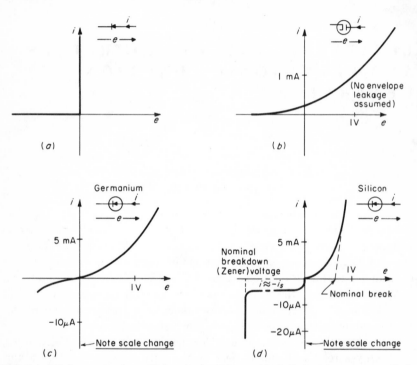

FIG. 6-1. Diode current i vs. diode voltage E for an ideal diode (a), a vacuum diode (b), a germanium point-contact diode (c), and a low-leakage silicon-junction diode (d).

diodes employed to approximate ideal-diode behavior in computer circuits. The properties of various diodes are further summarized in Table 6-1. A vacuum or semiconductor diode exhibits a finite forward resistance $R_F = \Delta e/\Delta i$ and a finite back resistance R_B in the OFF condition. In addition, a reverse-biased vacuum diode still passes a small forward current because of the finite velocities of electrons boiled off the cathode (Schottky effect). The current i through a silicon-junction diode with the voltage e applied in the forward direction is approximately given by

$$i = i_S(\exp \frac{q}{kT} e - 1) \qquad (e > -e_B) \tag{6-1}$$

where $kT/q \approx 0.026$ volt at room temperature (25 deg C).[1] As the reverse bias $-e$ increases, the diode acts essentially like a current source producing a small leakage or saturation current i_S, which doubles for a 7 to 10 deg C temperature increase.[1] The reverse current increases abruptly when the reverse voltage $-e$ reaches the *reverse-breakdown voltage* $-e_B$ (sometimes called the zener voltage) of the junction diode (Fig. 6-1d).

Piecewise-linear analysis of the nonlinear diode characteristics (Fig. 6-1) leads to various approximate equivalent circuits or *diode models* used to represent the behavior of real diodes in the ON and OFF conditions (Fig. 6-2). Suitable linear or nonlinear capacitances may be added to each diode model to approximate the dynamic (a-c) behavior of real diodes (Sec. 6-5).

Since physical diode characteristics curve strongly near zero voltage, the best piecewise-linear approximation yields a breakpoint voltage slightly different from zero (-0.2 to -0.8 volt for vacuum diodes, and $+0.1$ to $+0.8$ volt for semiconductor diodes). The piecewise-linear junction-diode model of Fig. 6-2f includes this "built-in" bias, which is, in effect, added to any external bias voltage. Unfortunately, the "built-in" bias voltage changes with cathode emission, heater current, and aging in vacuum diodes, and with ambient temperature in semiconductor diodes, so that we encounter *breakpoint drift.*

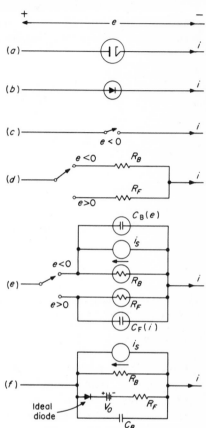

Fig. 6-2. Diode symbols and models (see also the voltage-current transfer characteristics in Fig. 6-1; these models do not include reverse breakdown). (*a*) Vacuum diode. (*b*) Solid-state diode. (*c*) Ideal-diode model. (*d*) Simple static piecewise-linear diode model. (*e*) A more realistic silicon-junction-diode model. R_F, R_B, and C_D are nonlinear circuit elements whose values depend on e, i, and also on the recent history of the junction. (*f*) Piecewise-linear junction-diode model.

Specifically, a 10 per cent increase in filament current increases vacuum-diode forward bias by about 0.1 volt, while vacuum-tube changes or tube aging can vary the bias by ± 0.25 volt.[2] The built-in reverse bias of a silicon-junction diode will decrease by approximately 2 to 3 mV/deg C of ambient-temperature increase.[3] In accurate computer circuits, break-point drift must be reduced by filament-current regulation for vacuum diodes and either by temperature control (component ovens) or by compensating temperature-sensitive bias circuits in the case of semiconductor diodes. Some two-diode circuits (e.g., Figs. 6-5, 6-23e, and 7-24)

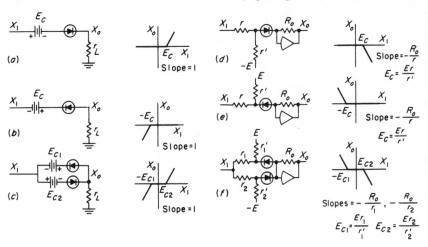

Fig. 6-3a to f. Basic series-diode limiters (a) to (c), and practical operational-amplifier circuits (d) to (f); transfer characteristics shown are for ideal diodes. E_C, E_{C1}, and $E_{C2} > -E_{C1}$ may be negative as well as positive, so that breakpoints can be positioned at will.

will reduce breakpoint-drift errors by a factor of 3 to 6 through mutual compensation. Semiconductor diodes should be physically separated from hot vacuum tubes.

If reasonable attention is given to possible temperature effects, silicon-junction diodes approximate ideal-diode behavior most closely and are also free from the noise and capacitances associated with vacuum-diode heaters. The junctions of planar silicon-junction diodes are formed by diffusion underneath an oxide layer which prevents troublesome surface-leakage effects ("surface passivation");

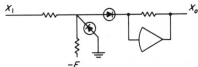

Fig. 6-3g. Addition of a grounded "catching diode" reduces interaction between the sources of X_1 and $-E$ if their source impedances are higher than a few ohms, as in operational amplifiers operated at high frequencies.[5] Catching-diode circuits combine shunt and series switching but should not be confused with the circuits of Fig. 6-5.

epitaxial-growth techniques form thin low-capacitance junctions on a semiconductor substrate sufficiently thick for good mechanical strength.[3]

6-3. The Basic Diode Limiter Circuits. (a) The basic diode limiter circuits shown in Figs. 6-3 to 6-5 use semiconductor or vacuum diodes to produce elementary nonlinear transfer characteristics. Simple limiter circuits can simulate important properties of dynamical systems (Secs. 9-7 to 9-9), and limiters can be combined to generate a large class of arbitrary functions (Sec. 6-13).

Limiter bias voltages can themselves be variables as well as constants. The series-shunt limiters of Fig. 6-5a and b, in particular, are useful as

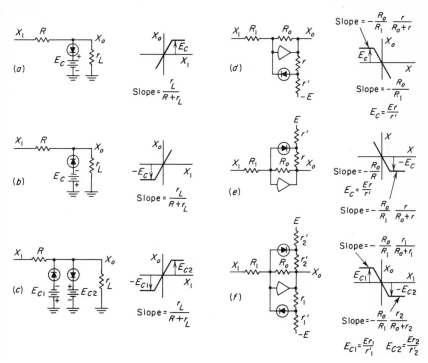

FIG. 6-4. Shunt-diode limiters (a) to (c), and feedback-diode limiters (d) to (f); transfer characteristics shown are for ideal diodes. E_c, E_{C1}, and $E_{C2} > -E_{C1}$ may be negative as well as positive, so that breakpoints can be positioned at will. The limiting accuracy of these circuits is compromised by bias-circuit impedances (see also Sec. 6-4). Excellent shunt limiting at any desired level is possible if the low-impedance output of an operational amplifier is used as the bias source.

amplitude selectors producing the respective output voltages

$$X_o = \min(X_1, E_c) \qquad X_o = \max(X_1, -E_c) \qquad (6-2)$$

where E_c as well as X can vary with time (see also Sec. 9-3).

(b) Floating diode-bias supplies (Fig. 6-3a, b, c) are not practical in most computer systems. The more realistic circuits of Figs. 6-3d to 6-5 derive the required diode-bias voltages from grounded computer reference power supplies.

The accuracy of shunt and feedback limiters (Fig. 6-4) is usually com-

promised by bias-circuit impedances in series with the diode forward
resistances, so that such circuits are more useful for easily adjustable
overvoltage protection than for accurate computation. Silicon-junction-
diode shunt limiters (Fig. 6-4a, b, c) can, however, limit more sharply if

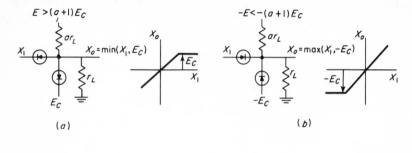

(a)   (b)

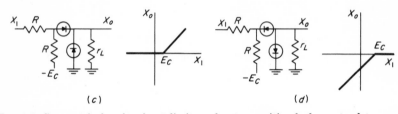

(c)   (d)

Fig. 6-5. Symmetrical series-shunt limiters shunt capacitive leakage, tend to cancel
breakpoint drift, and are recommended for computing frequencies above 0.5 to 1 Kc.
Low-capacitance germanium diodes are often used. E_C can be negative as well as
positive; r_L can be the input resistor of an operational amplifier. Circuits (a) and
(b) are supplied from low-impedance sources and have low output impedance in
either state; they are useful as amplitude selectors, gates, and logic circuits. Additional diodes can be added to yield min $(X_1, X_2, \ldots)$ or max $(X_1, X_2, \ldots)$ (see
also Sec. 9-3).

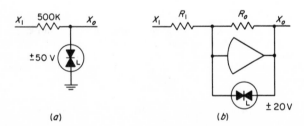

(a)   (b)

Fig. 6-6. Shunt and feedback limiters using back-to-back zener diodes.

bias is supplied from a low-impedance source such as an operational
amplifier rather than from the usual 20 to 100K potentiometer. More
accurate diode limiter circuits are discussed in Secs. 6-6 and 9-2.

(c) *Zener-diode limiters* use the reverse-breakdown characteristics (Sec. 6-2) of
specially designed diodes for limiting. Back-to-back zener diodes act like a pair of
diodes with conveniently built-in fixed bias supplies (Fig. 6-6). Zener diodes can be

obtained with a wide variety of breakdown voltages and can also be combined in series. Breakdown resistances are very low (typically between 10 and 100 ohms) and permit good shunt or feedback limiting if each diode is selected for a desired limiting voltage; the most useful application is, again, overvoltage protection (see also Secs. 6-8 and 10-9).

6-4. Low-frequency Analysis of Diode Networks. In many computer applications, diodes change the gain of a resistive network. One attempts to design these networks so that the finite forward and/or back resistances of physical diodes become negligible compared with other network resistances. With an occasional check on this condition, the simple ideal-diode model of Fig. 6-2c is very often satisfactory for analyses of "slow" analog computer circuits employing silicon-junction diodes with $R_F \leq 50$ ohms, $R_B \geq 50M$, at frequencies below 2 to 20 cps. The diode offset voltage, which could introduce errors of the order of 0.5 volt, can be disregarded when limiter breakpoints are set by empirical calibration; variations in the diode offset voltage with temperature (Sec. 6-1) will, of course, contribute to the computing error.

Figure 6-7 illustrates the static (d-c) piecewise-linear circuit analysis of the dual feedback limiter of Fig. 6-4f on the basis of our ideal-diode model. With the amplifier d-c gain between 10^4 and 10^8, it is fair to assume infinite d-c gain and zero output impedance. The circuit is drawn and analyzed for each of its three possible states:

1. D_1 and D_2 OFF (Fig. 6-7b):
$$X_o = -\frac{R_o}{R_1} X_1$$

2. D_1 ON, D_2 OFF (Fig. 6-7c):
$$X_o = -\frac{R_o r_1}{R_o + r_1}\left(\frac{X_1}{R_1} - \frac{E}{r_1'}\right) \quad \left(\approx -\frac{r_1}{R_1} X_1 + \frac{r_1}{r_1'} E \text{ for } r_1 \ll R_o\right)$$

3. D_1 OFF, D_2 ON (Fig. 6-7d):
$$X_o = -\frac{R_o r_2}{R_o + r_2}\left(\frac{X_1}{R_1} + \frac{E}{r_2'}\right) \quad \left(\approx -\frac{r_2}{R_1} X_1 - \frac{r_2}{r_2'} E \text{ for } r_2 \ll R_o\right)$$

The fourth possible combination of diode states (D_1 and D_2 ON) cannot be realized, because the diodes are back-biased. In Fig. 6-7e, the three linear transfer characteristics are combined. To pick the correct sequence of line segments, one starts with the most negative input voltage and remembers that no ideal diode can carry reverse current.

The resulting transfer characteristic accurately represents the actual circuit performance, except in the immediate vicinity of the breakpoints. Note that the output still depends on X_1 even in the limiting conditions. For sharp limiting, r_1 and r_2 should be small, but small values of r_1, r_2, r_1', r_2' also increase the amplifier load current. The circuit limits more sharply at low limiting levels and is, in general, more suitable for overvoltage protection than for accurate limiting.

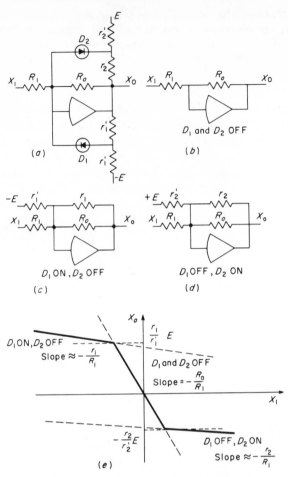

Fig. 6-7. Static piecewise-linear analysis of a typical limiter circuit (dual feedback limiter) on the basis of the ideal-diode model.

6-5. High-frequency Performance of Diode Circuits. In addition to the usual bandwidth limitations due to circuit capacitances and amplifier frequency response, the useful bandwidth of diode circuits is restricted by the effects of diode capacitances, which are highly nonlinear in junction diodes (Figs. 6-2e and 6-8a, b). The capacitance C_B of a junction diode reverse-biased by $-E$ is roughly proportional to $1/\sqrt{E}$. In addition, junction diodes exhibit nonlinear capacitance due to transit time and charge storage in the junction. The most noticeable effect is the *storage time* τ_s required to sweep minority carriers from the junction when the diode is turned OFF; this can be expressed in terms of a nonlinear capacitance C_F which increases with the forward current. While we can reduce the storage time by reducing the diode forward current, the charge-storage effect is usually masked by other capacitance effects if we employ fast-recovery diodes such as the 1N916A (Table 6-1).

Circuit and diode capacitances cause phase shift in each linear portion of a diode-circuit transfer characteristic. More seriously, circuit and diode capacitances must discharge reverse-bias voltages before each diode switches on; the resulting delays increase turn-on breakpoint voltages when the limiter-circuit input increases with time and decrease them for decreasing input. Dynamic errors, then, manifest themselves as a hysteresis-like spreading of diode-circuit transfer characteristics (Fig. 6-8a)

Table 6-1. Approximate Characteristics of Typical Diodes

	Forward resistance R_F, ohms	Leakage current i_S, or back resistance R_B (25 deg C)	Capacitance in OFF condition C_B, pF	Reverse recovery time τ_R (includes storage time τ_s)[14]	Peak inverse voltage (25 deg C), volts
Vacuum diode (½ 6AG5).......	200–1,000	50–600M	2–4	. . . .	330
Medium-speed, low-leakage silicon-junction diode (1N643A)	10 at +1 volt	0.025 μA at −10 volts, 1 μA at −100 volts	3–6	0.2–0.5 μsec (from 5 to −0.2 mA at −40 volts)	200
High-speed, low-leakage silicon-junction diode (1N916A)	50 at +1 volt	0.025 μA at −20 volts	2 at 0 volt	4 nsec (from 10 to −1 mA at −6 volts, 100-ohm load)	100
Low-leakage germanium point-contact diode (1N198A)	40–250 at +1 volt	50 μA at −50 volts	<2	0.5 nsec (to 50K)	100
Ideal diode for comparison.........	0	$R_B = \infty$	0	0	∞

which increases with frequency and with the input-voltage swing. The breakpoint shift (actually a time delay) is often roughly proportional to the rate at which the input voltage crosses the breakpoint. This effect becomes noticeable at frequencies well below those where junction-storage effects matter and is especially pronounced where the back resistances of open diodes can cause long discharge time constants. The spreading can be partially canceled by lead networks such as lead capacitors across operational-amplifier input resistors. The nonlinear nature of the circuit, however, usually permits compensation only over a portion of the working-frequency range and prevents accurate compensation near the breakpoints (Fig. 6-8b).

Aside from the use of lead networks and fast-recovery diodes, one can reduce diode-circuit capacitance effects by keeping circuit impedance levels as low as amplifier power permits; note that this also requires the

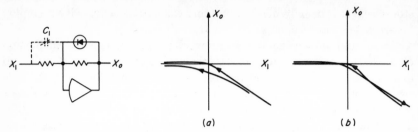

FIG. 6-8a, b. 1-Kc transfer characteristic of a feedback limiter (a), and effect of speedup capacitor C_1 (b).

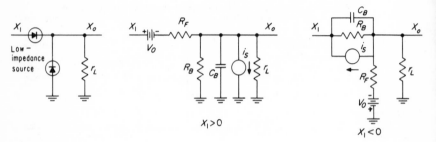

FIG. 6-8c. The equivalent circuit of a combined series-shunt limiter illustrates its beneficial effect on capacitive as well as resistive leakage. Turn-on and turn-off time constants are also low.

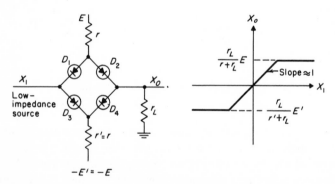

FIG. 6-9. Four-diode-bridge-limiter circuit. If desired, $r' \neq r$ and/or $-E' \neq -E$ yield asymmetrical limits, which must differ in sign. Variation of r_L (or a variable resistor shunting r_L) conveniently controls *both* limits.

use of diodes with proportionally lower forward resistances. Substitution of diodes in series for single diodes or zener diodes can also decrease capacitance effects especially in feedback branches, if the increased forward resistance can be tolerated. With such precautions, the limiter circuits of Secs. 6-3 and 6-6 can be kept accurate within 0.5 per cent of half-scale up to 200 cps; each diode circuit will require separate investigation. At higher frequencies, the designer should attempt to "short-

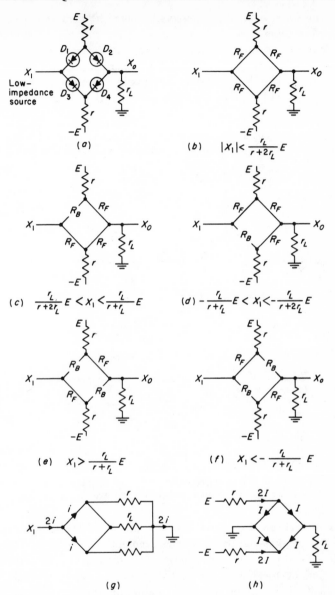

Fig. 6-10. Four-diode-bridge limiter (a), its five possible states $(b$ to $f)$, and derivation of the input-diode currents i and I when all four diodes are conducting (g, h). D_1 cuts off when $i > I$, and D_3 cuts off when $i < I$. All formulas are derived for $R_F \ll r$, $R_F \ll r_L$.

circuit" the worst capacitance effects by using *limiters and switching circuits which combine both shunt and series switching* instead of simple series, shunt, or feedback diodes (Figs. 6-5, 6-8c, and 7-24). Special circuits of this type permit accuracies within 0.3 to 1 per cent of half-scale up to at least 100 Kc. The design of such circuits is still a challenging problem, and each case will require separate consideration (see also Secs. 6-13 and 10-9).

To study diode-capacitance effects on analog-computer accuracy, we can compute at a reduced time scale and vary artificially added capacitors across each diode.

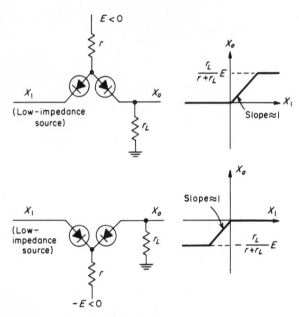

Fig. 6-11. Half-bridge limiter circuits and transfer characteristics. Each output voltage is limited between zero and a positive or negative voltage.

6-6. Diode-bridge Limiters. The four-diode-bridge limiters shown in Fig. 6-9 produce accurate and conveniently adjustable dual-limiter characteristics by series-limiter action. Referring to Fig. 6-10, all four diodes conduct for low absolute values of the input voltage. When $|X_1| = Er/(r + 2r_L)$, the absolute value of the input-diode current $i = X_1(r + 2r_L)/2rr_L$ due to X_1 exceeds the input-diode current $I = E/2r$ due to the bridge-control voltages E, $-E$, and one of the input diodes (D_1 or D_3) cuts off. Note, however, that no limiting occurs at this point, since one pair of diodes (D_1, D_2 or D_3, D_4) is still conducting. Limiter action takes place when $|X_1| \geq Er/(r + r_L)$, so that one of the output diodes D_2 or D_4 is cut off as well. Figures 6-10b to f show the resulting five possible states, and Figs. 6-10g and h illustrate the derivation of the input-diode currents i and I.[10]   The *half-bridge limiter circuits* of Fig. 6-11 will pass only input voltages of one sign.

Clipping levels are best set with the aid of a digital voltmeter or comparison potentiometer. Equivalent circuits like that of Fig. 6-10 show that, except in the immediate vicinity of the breakpoints, constant-temperature clipping levels are constant within 0.1 per cent if $1/R_B$ and any *changes* in R_F are within $10^{-3}r$; typically, $r = 100K$, $R_B = 100M$, and $R_F = 50$ to 500 ohms. The insertion loss associated with the diode-bridge limiter of Fig. 6-9 is also readily kept within 0.1 per cent. Diode-bridge limiters can still limit within 0.5 volt at 1 Kc and are widely useful in computing and instrumentation applications. No multipurpose electronic analog computer should be without patchbay-mounted or

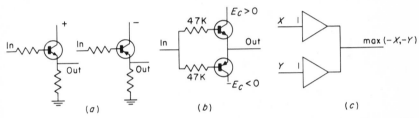

FIG. 6-12. Transistor limiters limiting at zero (a), at $E_C > 0$ and $-E_C < 0$ (b), and amplitude selector using two cathode-follower-output phase inverters without chopper stabilization (c).

plug-in bridge limiters. Refer to Sec. 6-10 for the use of diode-bridge circuits as switches.

6-7. Other Limiter Circuits (see also Sec. 9-2). Vacuum-tube amplifier stages driven into grid current or cutoff can be used as voltage limiters[6,7] but are rarely employed in analog-computer circuits. Figures 6-12a and b show a *transistor limiter* (see also Sec. 6-11).[9]

In Fig. 6-12c, the output terminals of two phase-inverting amplifiers with cathode-follower outputs have been connected together to form an interesting limiter or amplitude-selector circuit.[6,7] The amplifier with the larger input voltage drives the other one sharply into saturation; the action is somewhat similar to that of the precision amplitude-selection circuit of Fig. 9-8 but does not permit chopper stabilization

ANALOG SWITCHING CIRCUITS

6-8. Analog Switches and Comparators (see also Secs. 10-5 and 10-9). An *ideal switch* closes a desired circuit with zero forward resistance and opens it with infinite back resistance; the ideal switch has no spurious current or voltage offsets and opens and closes instantaneously. The static characteristics of ideal switches are accurately approximated by mechanical switches and relays with precious-metal contacts. When fast analog or hybrid analog-digital computation requires switching times

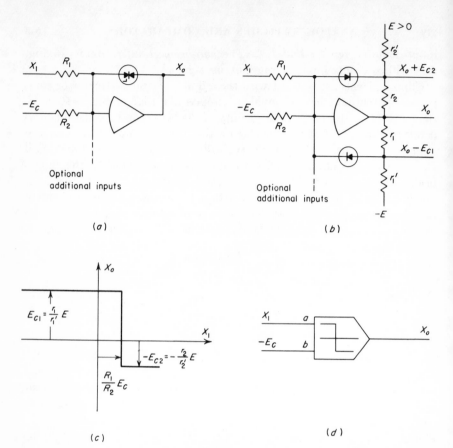

FIG. 6-13a to d. Analog-comparator circuits (a), (b), transfer characteristic (c), and block-diagram symbol (d). These circuits can drive electronic switches, relays, indicator lights, etc. Either comparator circuit may be followed by a bridge limiter (Fig. 6-9), which yields precise output levels and also removes any comparator overshoot or ringing. The circuit of Fig. 6-13b supplies extra outputs $X_o + E_{C2}$, $X_o - E_{C1}$ which vary between 0 and $E_{C1} + E_{C2}$ and $-(E_{C1} + E_{C2})$, respectively, and are especially useful for driving nonpolarized relays (see also Sec. 10-9).

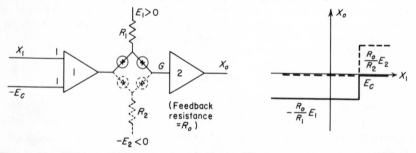

FIG. 6-13e. This comparator has precisely defined output levels and employs no diode feedback, so that there is less tendency to oscillate with capacitive loads.[93] Amplifier 1 is often available in the computer setup. The reversed diodes and bias shown in dash lines yield positive output for $X_1 > E_C$; the full bridge results in negative output for $X_1 < E_C$ and positive output for $X_1 > E_C$.

less than about 1 msec, mechanical switching devices cause intolerable time-delay errors and must be replaced by *electronic switches*.

The state of each elementary relay or switch (ON or OFF) is determined by the two possible levels of a single-ended or push-pull *control voltage;* the latter is not a continuously variable "analog" voltage, but a "digital" variable representing a *binary decision* derived from timing circuits, analog comparators, and appropriate digital-computer logic. An *analog comparator* is, essentially, an output-limited high-gain amplifier whose output changes decisively between two definite levels whenever the sum of the comparator input voltages changes sign (elementary analog-to-digital conversion). Figure 6-13 shows practical comparator circuits employing ordinary computer d-c amplifiers. Comparator design is further discussed in Sec. 10-9.

Physical electronic switches have finite forward and back resistances and produce spurious offset voltages and currents; accurate switches may require separate d-c balance controls for the ON and OFF conditions. In addition, switch-circuit capacitances and semiconductor-recovery delays produce finite switching times, which the designer must reduce as best possible.

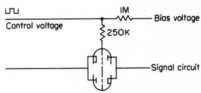

FIG. 6-14a. Simple bidirectional vacuum-triode switch. Forward resistance is less than 2K, and back resistance exceeds 50 to 500M, depending on the tube type. Grid-control pulses may feed through to the signal circuit.

Finally, proper electronic-switch design minimizes interference of the abrupt control-voltage steps with the switched signal.

The simple *bidirectional vacuum-tube switch* of Fig. 6-14a has been largely replaced by *diode switches* (Sec. 6-10) and *transistor switches* (Sec. 6-11), whose forward resistances are often negligible compared with other circuit impedances. Generally speaking, transistor switches permit lower control currents and better isolation of control and signal circuits than diode switches. On the other hand, diode switching circuits are sometimes simpler than transistor circuits, and switching diodes capable of switching voltages in excess of 20 volts are more readily available than high-voltage switching transistors. For fast switching and minimum interference between control and signal voltages, control voltages for diode and transistor switches are best obtained from low-impedance sources floating with respect to signal ground, such as pulse-transformer windings (see also Sec. 6-11c). Unfortunately, many analog switching applications require arbitrary ON and OFF periods, so that simple transformer-coupled control circuits cannot be used. Practical control-voltage sources are discussed in Secs. 10-4 and 10-9.

An electronic switch can be inserted *in series with the signal* current (Fig. 6-14b), or it can *shunt the signal to ground* (Fig. 6-14c). At higher signal frequencies, and in most critical applications, *combined shunt and series switching* is recommended to reduce capacitive as well as resistive leakage (Fig. 6-14*d*, *e*).

If three identical switches with back resistance R_B and open-circuit capacitance C_B are used in the circuit of Fig. 6-14*e*, its short-circuit transfer impedance (Sec. 1-14) in the OFF condition is

$$Z = \frac{2R_B}{j\omega R_B C_B + 1} + \frac{R_B^2}{R_F(j\omega R_B C_B + 1)^2}$$

where C_B is the leakage capacitance of each open switch. We see that capacitive as

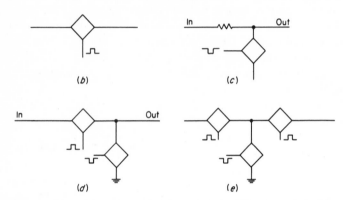

FIG. 6-14*b* to *e*. Electronic series switch (*b*), shunt switch (*c*), and combined shunt-series switches (*d*), (*e*).

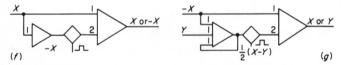

FIG. 6-14*f*, *g*. Simulation of an SPDT switch with an SPST electronic switch.

well as resistive leakage is shunted by R_F. For $R_F = 50$ ohms, $R_B = 50$M, $C_B = 5$ pF, $|Z|$ exceeds 5×10^7M at d-c, 2,000M at 100 Kc, and 20M at 1 Mc.

If it becomes desirable to suppress the (usually nonlinear) forward resistance of a given electronic switch, it may be possible to

1. *Enclose the switch in a parallel-feedback loop* (Figs. 7-17*b* and 7-19), or
2. *Feed the switch with a current source* (Figs. 7-17*a* and 7-18).

Most electronic switches are essentially single-throw (ON or OFF) switches. Figure 6-14*f* and *g* indicates how such electronic switches can, nevertheless, implement double-throw action and polarity reversal.

6-9. Operational Relays.[13] *Operational relays* (computing relays) operated by timing circuits or comparators (Secs. 6-8 and 10-9) permit convenient switching with essentially infinite back resistance and zero forward resistance (with precious-metal contacts). Relatively low operating speed (1 msec opening and closure) and possible contact bouncing limit relay switching to appropriately slow analog computations, in particular those already bandwidth-limited by computer servomechanisms.

In general-purpose computers, *reed relays* are convenient for use as operational relays, since they are sealed, relatively fast, and permit sophisticated switching interconnections with compact magnetic circuits (Sec. 10-10).   One can speed relay operation by operating the relay with the temporary overvoltage of a capacitor discharge (Sec. 10-10).   Operational relays can be *polarized* magnetically, by series diodes, or by operation with polarized comparator output voltages ($X_o - E_{c1}$ and $X_o + E_{c2}$ in Fig. 6-13*b*).   Some analog computers have special *relay comparators*, i.e., high-gain amplifiers or differential amplifiers permanently associated with operational relays.   *Relay maintenance* can be a problem especially in field environments, but this situation has been improved with the development of sealed relays and balanced relay armatures.

6-10. Diode Switches.[18-27]   The most generally useful diode switches are various types of *diode-bridge switches* (Figs. 6-15 and 6-16; Fig. 6-17 shows some other diode switches.   See also Fig. 5-27).   Four- and six-diode bridges have also been used as shunt switches (clamping circuits) and in series-shunt combinations.[19]   Diode switches work well with vacuum diodes (type 6AL5) if care is taken to minimize bulb and socket leakage, but their advantages are best realized with modern fast-recovery low-leakage silicon-junction diodes such as type 1N916A (see also Table 6-1).

To turn any diode bridge fully OFF, one requires control voltages as large or larger than the voltage to be switched.   *To turn any diode-bridge switch* ON, *the control circuit must supply a current at least as large as the signal current required to flow through the switch*, or the bridge will act as a limiter.   This is an important consideration if the switch is to supply capacitor charge or discharge current (Sec. 10-4).   Refer to Sec. 10-4 for examples of practical low-impedance control circuits used with diode switches.

The *six-diode bridge switches* of Figs. 6-15*b* and *d* combine shunt and series switching to make both resistive and capacitive leakage from the signal source essentially negligible (Sec. 6-8).   Switch forward resistance is about 50 ohms for silicon-junction diodes and 500 ohms for vacuum diodes.   Silicon-junction output-diode leakage currents can be below 0.05 μA at room temperature.   The symmetrical bridge circuits further reduce the effective leakage current by a factor of at least 3, especially if the bridge diodes are selected to match over the range of operating temperatures.   The remaining errors are caused by switching spikes due to uncanceled capacitive leakage from the control circuit and differences in the switching times of the two bridge-circuit branches and are especially

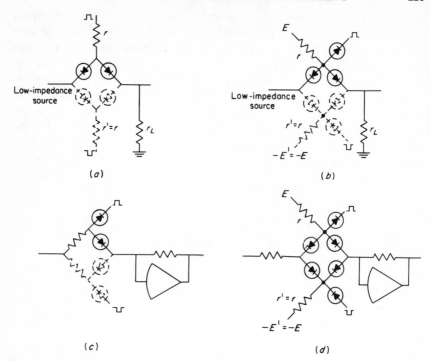

FIG. 6-15. Diode-bridge switches. r_L can be an operational-amplifier input resistor. Circuits b, c, and d combine shunt and series switching and turn off quickly. In a, b, and c, half of each circuit can be used to switch positive input voltages (solid lines) or negative input voltages (dash lines); but the leakage and spike cancellation inherent in the symmetrical circuits is desirable even with input voltages of one sign. Circuit d does not permit half-bridge operation and requires careful balancing of E/r and $-E'/r$ to minimize offset in the ON condition.

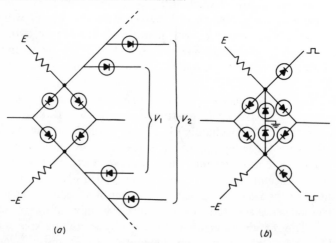

FIG. 6-16. Operation of a six-diode switch from two or more control circuits with INCLUSIVE OR logic[23] (a), and diode-bridge switch with catching diodes[25] (b). Both circuit schemes also apply to the four-diode bridge of Fig. 6-15c.

serious when the switch supplies current to a capacitor (Sec. 10-4). The switching spikes are not readily reduced by trimmer capacitors shunting the bridge diodes. Diode-capacitor compensation circuits like that in Fig. 6-17b may help, or one may use trimmer capacitors to vary the control-step rise and fall times on one side of the bridge. Above all, the use of low-capacitance fast-recovery diodes is recommended. Before diodes combining these properties with low leakage were available, series combinations of fast-recovery and low-leakage diodes were employed as output diodes, and fast diodes were used in the other branches.

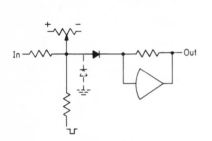

Fig. 6-17a. Series limiter used as a switch.

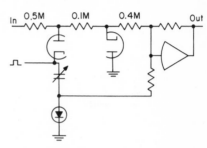

Fig. 6-17b. Double shunt switch with compensation of *average* control-pulse leakage through D_1.[26]

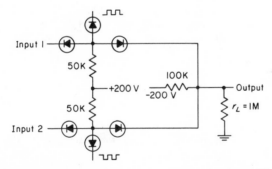

Fig. 6-17c. SPDT switch developed from the selector circuits of Fig. 6-5a and b.[27]

For a six-diode switch operated with a low-impedance control circuit, an equivalent circuit similar to that of Fig. 6-8c[18,19] indicates that the turn-off time constant is of the order of $C_B R_F$; so that six-diode switches can turn off quickly. The turn-on time will depend on the resistance in the signal circuit; turn-on times within 0.5 μsec are readily obtainable.

The reliable and inexpensive diode-bridge switches can switch voltages exceeding 100 volts and are widely useful in fast analog/hybrid computation (Secs. 10-4 to 10-6). Diode switches can also replace operational relays in many "slow" analog-computer applications where leakage and spike currents are not integrated for too long a time. Plug-in or patchbay-connected four-diode-bridge limiters are particularly convenient for use in "slow" general-purpose analog computers; their control voltages can be supplied from patched comparators and multivibrators (Secs. 6-8 and 9-5).

6-11. Transistor Switches.[28–41]   (a) **Static Characteristics.**   The collector characteristics of junction transistors (Fig. 6-18) suggest the

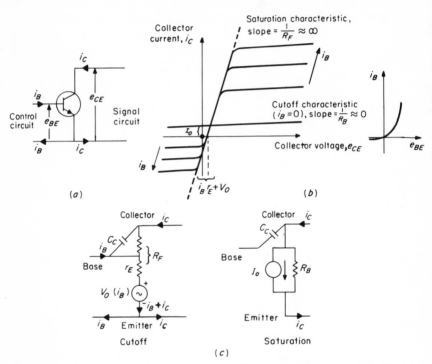

Fig. 6-18. *npn* transistor switch (*a*), transistor characteristics (*b*), and simplified equivalent circuits (*c*).

use of both *npn* and *pnp* transistors as *bidirectional* electronic switches permitting control of the emitter-collector current i_C by the—usually smaller—base current i_B.   Transistor switches can, therefore, work with smaller control currents than diode switches, and better isolation of control and signal circuits becomes possible.   Referring to Fig. 6-18*b*, a transistor switch is ON when a sufficiently positive base current i_B causes operation in the *saturation region;* for zero or negative i_B, the transistor is *cut off*, and the switch is OFF.   Since transistors, unlike vacuum tubes, are controlled by current rather than voltage, *each transistor-switch design must provide a control-current return path which will not interfere with the signal circuit.*

Actual transistor collector characteristics show that

1. The reciprocal slopes $\Delta e_{CE}/\Delta i_C = R$ of the saturation and cutoff characteristics respectively yield *forward resistances* $R = R_F$ between 10 and 100 ohms and *back resistances* $R = R_B$ between 1 and 200M, just as in the case of junction-diode switches.

2. The saturation and cutoff characteristics in Fig. 6-18b do not pass exactly through the coordinate origin, as ideal switch characteristics would. The resulting offset errors are interpreted as follows: the saturation characteristic is displaced horizontally by a positive *saturation offset voltage* $i_{B}r_E + V_0(i_B)$ of 10 to 500 mV; and the cutoff characteristic is displaced vertically by a positive *leakage current* I_0 between 0.001 and 1 μA.

This situation is summarized by the simplified equivalent circuits of Fig. 6-18c. The offset sources are often disregarded in the design of digital switches, but they are important for analog switching; I_0, in particular, varies exponentially with temperature and is a serious source of drift.

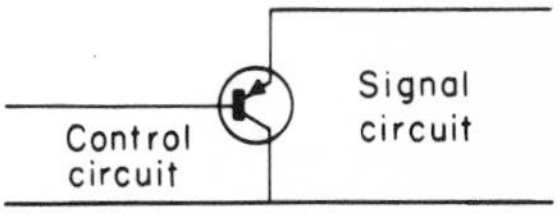

(b) The Inverted Transistor as a Switch. If an *npn* or *pnp* junction transistor is *inverted*, i.e., if one interchanges the roles of emitter and collector as in Fig. 6-19, the device still operates as a transistor whose characteristics are shaped like those in Fig. 6-18b, although they

FIG. 6-19. Inverted *pnp* transistor switch. The inverted collector characteristics are similar to those of Fig. 6-18b but are compressed vertically.

are *compressed vertically*. More specifically, experimental and theoretical investigation of the normal and inverted transistor characteristics[28-37] reveals that

1. The current amplification factor $\beta = \partial i_C/\partial i_B$ is decreased by a factor of 5 to 100 in the inverted connection, and $-\log_e \alpha = -\log_e(\partial i_C/\partial i_E)$ is decreased by about a factor of 10. The inverted connection is, therefore, not suitable for amplification or for power switching with small control currents.

2. The switch forward resistance (reciprocal slope of the saturation characteristic) is only slightly higher in the inverted connection.

3. *The offset current I_0 is decreased approximately by the factor β_I/β_N in the inverted connection, and the offset voltage V_0 is decreased approximately by the factor $\log_e \alpha_N/\log_e \alpha_I$, where the subscripts N and I refer to the normal and inverted circuit.*

The inverted transistor connection typically decreases both I_0 and $V_0 + i_{B}r_E$ by a factor of at least 10, so that the inverted connection is eminently well suited to precision switching applications.[29-38]

Transistors intended for analog switching may be alloy-junction or epitaxial-planar types combining low saturation resistance with relatively small junctions for high switching speed.[35] For typical silicon "chopper transistors" of this kind (e.g., Motorola 2N2331, Sperry 2N1918, Philco T1452) used in the inverted connection at 25 deg C, we find

Inverted-saturation offset voltage $|i_B r_E + V_0(i_B)| < 1$ mV $(i_B = 0.5$ mA).

Inverted leakage current $|I_0| < 0.1$ nA $(i_B \approx 0)$.

Inverted-saturation resistance ("dynamic resistance") $R_F < 25$ ohms $(i_B = 0.5$ mA).

Back resistance $R_B < 1$ to 100M.

Germanium-alloy transistors are also useful.[9]

Since the emitter-base and collector-base junctions of a junction transistor behave essentially like junction diodes (Sec. 6-5), a cutoff transistor switch exhibits nonlinear emitter-base and collector-base capacitances (typically 5 to 15 pF for 1 volt reverse bias) and turn-on storage time (below 0.1 μsec for switching transistors). Transistor capacitances and storage time are, approximately, inversely proportional to the quoted alpha-cutoff frequency f_α, since all these quantities depend on the junction dimensions. f_α is, therefore, a useful measure of the attainable switching speed. Since the collector-base junction is larger than the emitter-base junction, an inverted transistor has a higher input capacitance than a normal transistor, but typical switching times are still well below 1 μsec for switching transistors with $f_\alpha > 100$ Mc, and 25 nsec can be attained. *Speedup capacitors* across base-current-setting resistors will improve switching speeds by supplying fast control-current spikes when the control voltage is reversed (Figs. 6-20 and 7-20).

More specifically, the offset voltage $V_0(i_B)$ is approximately proportional to $1/i_B$;[35] so that plots of the total inverted-saturation offset $i_B r_E + V_0(i_B)$ vs. i_B, which are supplied for most switching transistors, show a shallow minimum. In the vicinity of this minimum, $i_B r_E + V_0(i_B)$ is fairly insensitive to changes in i_B, and the offset temperature coefficient is, fortunately, close to zero (typically positive and below 2 to 10 μV/deg C for practical base currents).[35] As a result, it becomes practical to balance the saturation offset partially by a d-c voltage, or by the saturation offset of a second transistor (Fig. 6-20).

The open-switch offset current I_0 is proportional to the open-emitter collector-base leakage current I_{CBO} quoted for the transistor; in the inverted connection, we have approximately[28,35]

$$I_0 \approx \frac{\alpha_I}{\alpha_N} \frac{1 - \alpha_N}{1 - \alpha_N \alpha_I} I_{CBO} \tag{6-3}$$

I_{CBO} increases exponentially with temperature, typically doubling for every 10 deg C, and decreases with the reverse base voltage used to turn the transistor off.

(c) **Practical Switching Circuits** (see also Secs. 7-12 and 10-4).[33-41] Like junction-diode switches, transistor switches can short a source of moderate impedance quite accurately but tend to compromise series switching—say, at the input of an operational amplifier—by leakage-current errors. This disadvantage is, again, partially overcome through combined series-shunt switching. *To turn a transistor switch* OFF, *the base-control circuit must supply a voltage at least large enough to reverse-bias both the emitter-base junction and the collector-base junction. To turn the transistor switch* ON, *the base current must exceed the signal current divided by β_N (normal connection) or β_I (inverted connection).*

Figure 6-20a shows an inverted *pnp* transistor operating as a low-level shunt switch or *transistor chopper* useful for low-level modulation at frequencies below 1 Kc (as in d-c amplifier stabilization, Sec. 5-8) or for

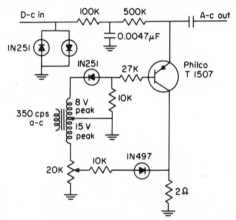

FIG. 6-20a. An accurate inverted-transistor chopper. The diode-limited input volt age cannot exceed ±0.7 volt. The OFF base voltage is approximately zero. Offset is less than 3 μV/deg C, or 50 μV/100 hr at constant temperature.[38]

digital-to-analog conversion (Sec. 11-10). A diode limiter keeps the input signal within about ±0.6 volt. Note that the transistor is cut off with zero base current to obtain a leakage current I_0 as low as 0.1 nA; the silicon-alloy transistor used still yields a back resistance between 1 and 50M.[35,38] An adjustable d-c voltage intended to balance the saturation offset is applied in the ON condition only, so that it cannot cause leakage variations in the nonconducting state of the switch. Errors due to capacitive leakage are minimized through operation at chopper frequencies below 500 cps, although the circuit works at much higher frequencies. Switching errors obtained with this switch amount to less than 100 μV d-c referred to the input over a temperature range between 10 and 50 deg C. The effects and possible neutralization of *switching spikes* in transistor choppers are discussed in Sec. 5-8.

The circuits of Fig. 6-20*b* and *c* combine *matched pairs of inverted transistor switches* for partial offset cancellation.   Two matched switching transistors can have a common collector-base structure to improve thermal matching, to reduce the number of thermoelectric junctions, and to minimize interference between control and signal currents.[40]   Unfortunately,

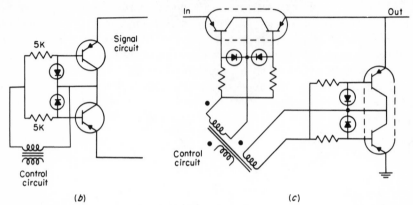

FIG. 6-20*b*, *c*. Transistor switches employing matched inverted-transistor pairs with floating control circuits.

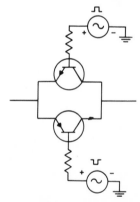

FIG. 6-20*d*. A complementary-transistor combination providing a convenient base-current return path.   Such switches can be combined in series-shunt combinations (Sec. 10-4*c*).

such dual transistor circuits require either floating-transformer control circuits or relatively complicated floating control multivibrators[41] to provide a base-current return path.   The *npn-pnp* combination of Fig. 6-20*d* provides a convenient base-return path at the expense of an additional transistor and has proved very successful in the accurate series-shunt switching circuit of Fig. 10-7*d*.   Figures 6-20*e* and *f* illustrate a different control-current return scheme;[99] such series switches are operated in a "neutral mode" (neither normal nor inverted).

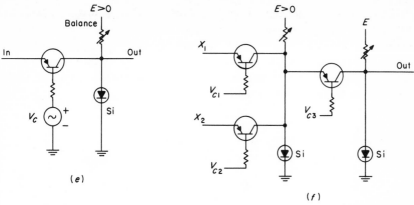

FIG. 6-20e, f. "Neutral-mode" series switch (e), and combination of switches (f).[99]

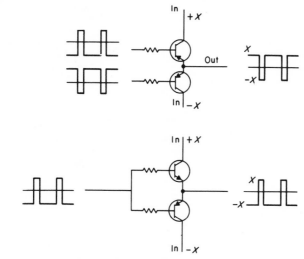

FIG. 6-20g, h. Inverted-transistor SPDT switches.

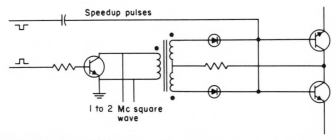

FIG. 6-20i. Section of an SPDT switch employing matched pairs of inverted transistors with floating transformer-rectifier control-current sources switched by secondary shunt switches. Only the speedup-capacitor surges can pass through the signal sources. 0.1-μsec turn-on and turn-off times are possible with Tl 2432 transistors.[100]

Figures 6-20*g* and *h* show inverted-transistor SPDT switches used, for example, for polarity changing (Sec. 7-12); both circuits combine shunt and series switching.   Unless the base control currents are supplied from floating control circuits, the base currents of the two transistors will vary with the signal voltages X_1, X_2, and the saturation-offset voltages will also change and cannot be accurately canceled.   Storage times in the two

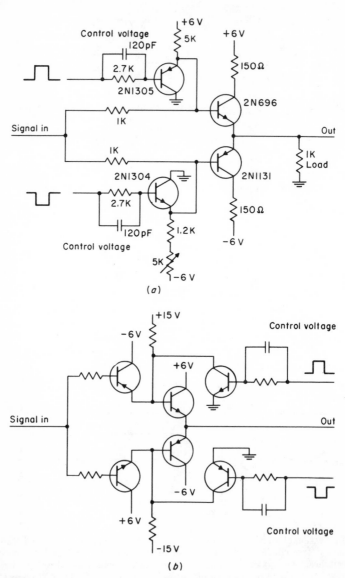

FIG. 6-21. Nonsaturating transistor switches: gated emitter follower (*a*)[94] and diamond circuit (*b*).[95]

transistors will also vary with X_1 and X_2, so that it becomes practically impossible to switch both transistors simultaneously. This results not only in switching spikes but in actual shorting of the signal sources. For this reason, and to minimize the effect of base-current leakage into the signal circuit, such switches must have low-impedance signal sources. The control-current return problem is again eliminated by a transformer-coupled control circuit (see also Fig. 7-20).[35,36] To obtain arbitrarily long OFF and ON periods with a floating-transformer control circuit, H. Schmid[100] used a transformer-rectifier source excited with an RF current turned off and on by a simple d-c-operated transistor switch (Fig. 6-20i).

The *nonsaturating transistor switches* of Fig. 6-21 switch from cutoff into the operating mode rather than into saturation. They act as single or double emitter followers in the ON condition and combine current gain and low output impedance with fast switching. Since it is difficult to match *npn-pnp* transistor pairs, drift may be objectionable in low-level circuits.[94,95]

ELECTRONIC FUNCTION GENERATORS

6-12. Introduction (see also Sec. 6-1). The simplest analytic functions of a voltage (machine variable) X are polynomials like $aX + b$, aX^2, $X^3 + bX^2 + cX$, etc.; such functions are readily produced by combinations of summers, multipliers, and coefficient-setting potentiometers. Simple differential-analyzer setups can produce analytic functions of the computer time τ (e.g., $ae^{b\tau}$, $a \sin b\tau$; Fig. 2-9) and, if we introduce generalized integration through multiplication by $dX/d\tau$, also similar functions of a voltage $X = \int_0^\tau (dX/d\tau)\, d\tau$ (see also Secs. 2-7d and 8-16).

More general types of functions must be set up on *general-purpose function generators;* most electronic analog computers employ *diode function generators* (see also Sec. 6-1). Function-generator accuracy and frequency response will depend on the nature of the function generated. We can often reduce the effects of function-generator errors substantially by using the function generator to correct a linear or analytic approximation function obtained with accurate summers, potentiometers, and multipliers. In addition, every effort should be made to utilize the full dynamic range of function-generator input and output variables by efficient scaling (Sec. 2-4c).

Figure 6-22 shows a circuit producing the *inverse function* $Y = G(X)$ of a computer-generated function $F(Y)$. The circuit continuously enforces the relation

$$X - F(Y) = 0 \qquad (6\text{-}4)$$

where the condition $\partial F/\partial Y < 0$ is necessary to ensure stability of the implicit-computation loop; high-frequency stability requires separate investigation. The initial value of Y must equal the correct initial value of $G(X)$ (see also Sec. 12-9b).

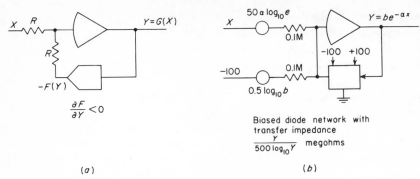

FIG. 6-22. Generation of inverse functions by implicit computation (see also Sec. 2-4b). Figure 6-21b illustrates generation of $X_o = be^{-\alpha X_1}$ ($b \geq 1$) with a commercially available logarithm-generating diode network.

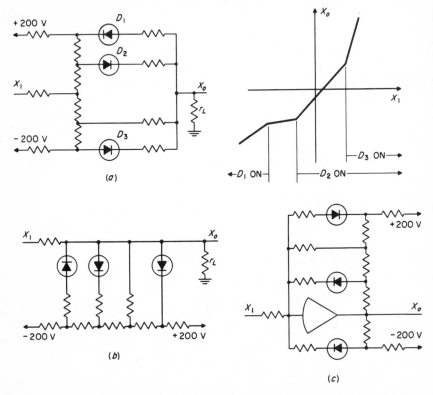

FIG. 6-23a to c. Special-purpose diode function generators for monotonic functions. Many combinations of such circuits are possible. Resistance calculations can be tedious; so that more flexible circuits similar to Figs. 6-24 and 6-25 may be preferred even for special-purpose function generation.

6-13. Diode Function Generators. (a) **Special-purpose Function Generators. Smoothing Oscillators.**[44] The broken-line transfer characteristics of resistive networks containing biased diodes can approximate a large class of functions; Fig. 6-23 shows typical arrangements.

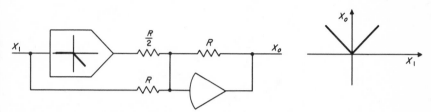

Fig. 6-23d. Diode-limiter absolute-value circuit used for instrument inputs and to generate functions symmetrical about $X_1 = 0$ (see also Secs. 7-15, 8-14, and 9-2).

Nonmonotonic functions must be obtained by addition of a nondecreasing function and a nonincreasing function. Fixed-function generators are useful in many control and instrumentation applications (Secs. 1-19 and 8-14). Diode function generators permanently set up for aX^2, $a \sin bX$, and $a \log_e X + b$ are very useful in many applications of general-purpose analog computers.

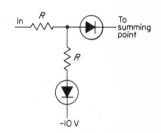

Fig. 6-23e. A junction-diode limiter with a temperature-compensating diode in the bias network.

Figure 6-24 illustrates the use of a high-frequency (5 to 500 Kc) *smoothing oscillator* for rounding diode-function-generator characteristics near the breakpoints.[44] The triangular or sinusoidal smoothing-oscillator voltage is added to the function-generator input, which is thus swept across the breakpoints. An output averaging filter yields the smoothed characteristic and, unfortunately, also introduces some low-frequency phase shift (see also Sec. 7-13).

In fixed-function generators, junction-diode breakpoint drift due to temperature changes can be partially compensated by thermistors, by

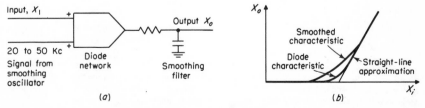

Fig. 6-24. Diode function generator with smoothing oscillator to smooth diode-network transfer characteristics (a), and smoothed limiter-channel characteristic (b).[44]

extra junction diodes in the bias networks (Fig. 6-23e), or by series-shunt diode pairs (Fig. 6-5).

(b) General-purpose Function Generators. General-purpose diode function generators sum the output currents of between 5 and 24 simple limiter channels with adjustable breakpoints and slopes to generate

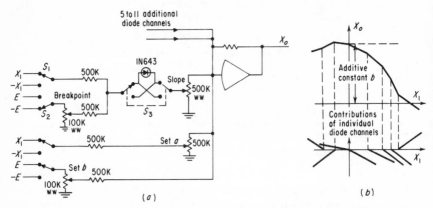

FIG. 6-25. This Reeves-type (series-limiter) diode function generator requires only a single patchbay-connected amplifier but has both X_1 and $-X_1$ inputs. The switches S_1, S_2, S_3 in each channel can be combined into a four-position "quadrant switch" yielding only the four types of segments shown in Fig. 6-25b, but this restriction is not necessary. 10-turn potentiometers set individual slopes and breakpoints with a minimum of interaction; note that the slope-adjustment scheme used loads the input much less than a set of slope-adjusting potentiometers ahead of the 500K summing resistors would.   The two lower channels add a linear function $aX_1 + b$. E is usually the computer reference voltage; if E is replaced by a second variable voltage Y, the device produces various functions of two variables (Sec. 6-18).

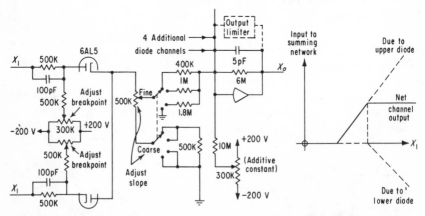

FIG. 6-26a. Each dual series-limiter channel of the Goodyear diode function generator generates line segments having equal and opposite slopes. The two breakpoints are staggered so that the channel output voltage will not contribute to the slope of any subsequent line segment. The additional circuitry facilitates slope adjustments and reduces accumulation of diode drifts. The feedback output limiter indicated in broken lines prevents calibration overloads.

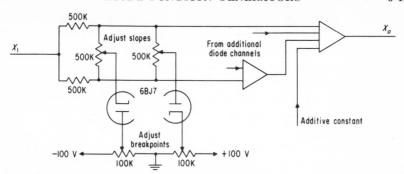

FIG. 6-26b. Shunt-limiter diode function generator (Donner Model 35). Similar circuits are used in many older electronic analog computers.

straight-line-segment approximations of different functions (Figs. 6-25 to 6-27). Natural breakpoint curvatures afford a measure of slope interpolation between line segments, and smoothing oscillators can be used if desired.

A single limiter-output-summing amplifier can yield only monotonic functions. To generate nonmonotonic functions, we can use two amplifiers to subtract two monotonic functions (Fig. 6-26b), or we can supply some of the limiter channels with $-X_1$ instead of X_1 to obtain limiter slopes of either sign (Figs. 6-25 and 6-26a). The latter method is usually preferable, since $-X_1$ is often already available in the computer setup, and because only one summing-point connection is needed. In multipurpose computers, d-c amplifiers need not be permanently committed to the diode function generators but can be patched as needed. Two diode-function-generator networks can be combined if a given function requires many breakpoints.

Diode-function-generator specifications include

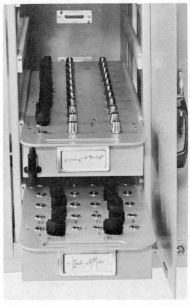

FIG. 6-27. Two storable, plug-in function-generator modules, showing breakpoint and slope potentiometers. (*Beckman/Berkeley Division.*)

1. *Maximum available slope per limiter channel,* typically 1 to 10 volts/ volt. The total absolute function slope must be limited below 30 to 100 volts/volt to keep the summing-amplifier feedback ratio β,

and thus function generator phase shift and noise, within reason (Sec. 3-19). A few of the limiter channels in each function generator can be given larger maximum slopes than others.

2. *Maximum error due to diode breakpoint drift,* referred to the *output;* this increases with the maximum available slope and with the number of segments and is typically between 0.05 and 0.3 volt.

3. *Amplitude, phase, and step response for small-signal sinusoidal input* with a specified function setup* and a specified resistance-capacitance load. Phase shift below 1 deg at 100 cps and below 8 deg at 1 Kc is typical for modern designs employing series limiters. Much faster operation is possible with series-shunt limiter channels (Figs. 6-5 and 7-24).[49]

4. *Output noise,* typically 30 to 300 μV rms for $\pm$ 100-volt machines, depending on the maximum slope set.

Both drift and frequency response deteriorate with increasing function slope. With silicon-junction diodes, which have largely replaced vacuum diodes in function generators, we can use drift-compensating diodes (Fig. 6-23e), or diodes can be placed in a small crystal oven. The function-generator circuit of Fig. 6-26a reduces the effects of accumulated breakpoint drift from several limiter channels at the expense of additional diodes and is also slightly easier to adjust. An essentially similar design has been described by Miura.[43] The series-limiter function generators of Figs. 6-25 and 6-26a tend to exhibit less phase shift than shunt-limiter types similar to Fig. 6-26b; for high-frequency operation, combined series and shunt limiting is recommended.

(c) **Multiple-function Generation.** Some computer applications (see, for example, Sec. 6-18) require generation of n functions $F_i(X)$ of the same machine variable X. If n exceeds 3 or 4, and if it is reasonable to use identical breakpoints for all n functions $F_i(X)$, then it may become practical to employ separate limiter-amplifiers (or precision limiters, Sec. 9-2) to generate precise standard-slope limiter-channel voltages like those in Fig. 6-25 or 6-26a. These standard segments are then summed into n sets of slope controls and summing-amplifier pairs generating each of the n functions $F_i(X)$ (Fig. 6-28).[89]

(d) **Function Setting and Storage.** A general-purpose diode function generator must permit convenient adjustment of breakpoints and slopes, with a minimum of interaction between adjustments. In view of the labor expended to set a function accurately, ease of *function storage* or *resetting* is also important.

Ten-turn breakpoint and slope potentiometers, or one-turn potentiometers with vernier resistors (Sec. 3-4) are required for accurate settings. The controls need not be calibrated in terms of actual breakpoints or

* A function suggested for this test is the function $X_o = X_1$ set up with evenly spaced breakpoints and alternately canceling slopes.

slopes, but they should permit precise resetting. One may save both
initial cost and setup time by supplying some limiter channels in each
function generator, or some function generators in a computer, with *fixed
breakpoints*. One can then combine fixed-breakpoint function generators
with variable-breakpoint units, as required.

To set a given function $X_o = F(X_1)$, one first determines suitable
breakpoints and slopes by fitting a graph of $F(X_1)$ (or of an appropriate
correction function, Sec. 2-4c) with the desired number of straight-line
segments. Analytical methods for optimum breakpoint selection[46,47]

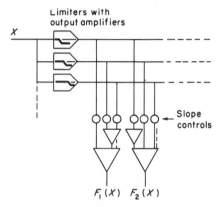

Fig. 6-28. Multiple-function generation with separate amplifier-limiters.

appear to be justified, if at all, only for special-purpose function generators. Assume now that we have a function generator of the type shown
in Fig. 6-25a and require n positive breakpoints $X_1 = e_1 < e_2 < e_3 \cdots$
and n' negative breakpoints $X_1 = e_1' > e_2' > e_3' \cdots$. We minimize
breakpoint-drift accumulation and interaction between settings by
employing *only limiter-channel segments which slope outward from zero*
(Fig. 6-25b). We read the function-generator input X_1 and the output
X_o accurately with the aid of a digital voltmeter, a comparison potentiometer, or a special decade-switch voltage divider and employ the following procedure:

1. Set n quadrant switches for slopes to the right, and set the corresponding breakpoints all the way positive. Set the remaining
   quadrant switches for slopes to the left, and set the corresponding
   breakpoints all the way negative. Set or switch all slope controls
   to about one-half maximum slope.
2. With $X_1 = 0$, set the "parallax" voltage b to obtain $X_o = F(0)$.
3. With $X_1 = e_1 > 0$, set the linear-approximation slope a to obtain
   $X_o = F(e_1)$. Now adjust the e_1 breakpoint control until X_o barely
   changes.

4. *Repeat steps* 2 *and* 3.

5. With $X_1 = e_2 > e_1$, set the e_1 slope to obtain $X_o = F(e_2)$.   Adjust the e_2 breakpoint control until X_o barely changes.

6. *Repeat steps* 3 *and* 5.

We proceed outward from zero in this manner and then repeat the procedure for the negative breakpoints, again proceeding outward from zero.   Finally, all breakpoints and slope settings are rechecked.   An alternative setup method employs an accurate xy recorder (servo table) to match a desired curve as X_1 is varied.

The function-generator adjustments can also be made with an automatic potentiometer-setting system (Sec. 11-2), so that settings can be stored on punched tape; card-controlled diode function generators are also commercially available.   In medium-priced computers, storable plug-in function-setting networks are probably the simplest means of function storage (Fig. 6-27).

To adjust a function generator precisely for simple analytic functions $F(X_1)$ like aX_1^2, $aX_1^2 + bX_1 + c$, ae^{bX_1}, and $a \sin bX_1$, we may be able to generate $F(\tau/\alpha_t)$ conveniently and precisely with a differential-analyzer setup (Fig. 2-9) and employ the error-nulling method shown in Fig. 6-29.[51,52]   This method is particularly applicable to the adjustment of diode squaring networks.

6-14. Varistor Function Generators.[50-52]   Varistor function generators (Fig. 6-30) employ current-sensitive nonlinear resistors (silicon-carbide varistors, e.g., Thyrite, Globar) to produce transfer characteristics of the general form shown in Fig. 6-30b.   The corresponding inverse functions can be generated by the method of Fig. 6-22.

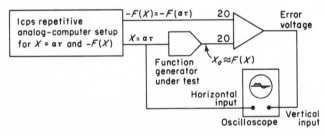

Fig. 6-29. Error-display calibration of function generators for various analytic functions such as aX^2, ae^{-bX}, and $a \sin bX$ (see also Fig. 2-9).

Schreier[51,52] discusses a wide variety of varistor circuits including sinusoid generators, calibration methods, and test results.   Factory-adjusted varistor squaring units are commercially available (Quadratron, Douglas Aircraft Co., Santa Monica, Calif.); combinations of squaring and cubing units can approximate various other functions such as truncated power series.[50]   Varistor function generators for analytic functions are best adjusted by the error-nulling method of Fig. 6-29.[51,52]

Figure 6-30a shows a fairly general varistor network; adjustment of the resistances R_1, R_2 yields different transfer characteristics. Series combination of between 2 and 10 individual varistors permits input voltages up to 100 volts and tends to average manufacturing tolerances.[50-52] Since silicon-carbide varistors exhibit a slight rectification effect (between 0 and 1 per cent), one either attempts to match series-opposed varistors, or one adds a suitably polarized diode network (Fig. 6-30c) in series with R_1 or R_2. A thermistor (Fig. 6-30a), or a small crystal oven for the entire network, will minimize the effect of varistor-resistance changes with ambient temperature.[50] Varistor self-heating is not so easily compensated and accounts for a possible drift error between 0.2 and 1 per cent

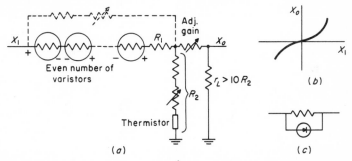

Fig. 6-30. Varistor function-generator network (a), transfer characteristic (b), and diode network used to compensate for varistor rectification (c). With 10 General Electric Type 839 6839 G1 varistors, $R_1 + R_2$ is between 5 and 20K. r_L can be an input resistor of an operational amplifier.

of half-scale added to between 0.1 and 0.8 per cent error in matching desired function characteristics.

Distributed capacitance combines with the variable varistor resistance to produce phase shift which varies with the input voltage and usually limits the use of uncompensated varistor networks to frequencies below 100 cps. This phase shift can, however, be partially compensated with a voltage-sensitive capacitor (silicon-junction diode designed for this purpose) either across R_2 or across the feedback resistor of a following operational amplifier. Another compensation scheme feeds the inverted input voltage through a trimmer capacitor around the varistors; the varistor capacitance as such does not change appreciably for currents below 1 mA.[51]

6-15. Cathode-ray-tube Function Generators. In the *photoformer* function generator of Fig. 6-31,[53-55] a feedback loop comprising the cathode-ray tube, the photocell, and the vertical deflection amplifier keeps the spot on the screen just below the edge of a prepared function mask as the input voltage X_1 (horizontal deflection voltage) varies. Hence, the output voltage X_o (vertical deflection voltage) changes as a function

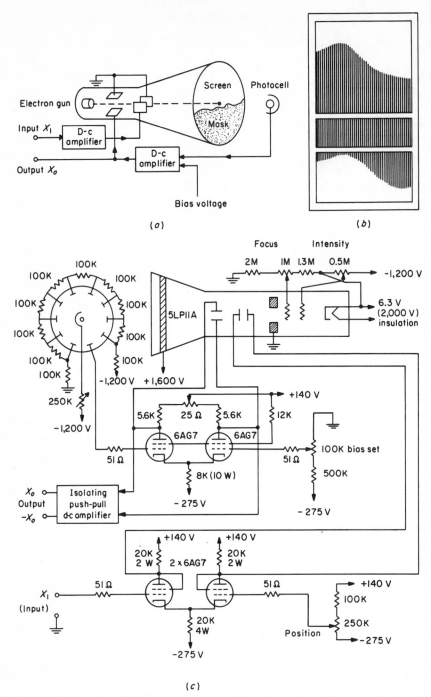

Fig. 6-31. Block diagram of a photoformer (a), adjustable photoformer mask consisting of clamped shims (b), and a practical photoformer circuit (c). Existing oscilloscopes can frequently be adapted.

242

$X_o = F(X_1)$ of X_1. For convenience, masks can be provided with calibration steps (0 and ± 50 volts) to the left or right of the function curve. A comprehensive discussion of photoformer accuracy is presented in ref. 61.

In a second type of cathode-ray-tube function generator,[57,58] the electron beam is positioned horizontally by the input voltage X_1, while a linear sawtooth sweep causes the beam to sweep vertically so as to scan an opaque or transparent function mask between 5,000 and 50,000 times per second. For each value of X_1, the photocell current is, then, pulse-width modulated in accordance with the function $F(X_1)$ shaping the mask. The resulting pulse-width-modulated square wave is filtered to yield $F(X_1)$ and can even be used to multiply other variables by $F(X_1)$, as in a time-division multiplier (Sec. 7-10).

The scanning scheme is relatively insensitive to screen and phototube persistence, changes in spot size, and variations of deflection sensitivity. Provision of an opaque or transparent reference line yields standard reference pulses for automatic calibration (see also Sec. 6-19).

Generally speaking, diode function generators are easier and less expensive to construct than cathode-ray-tube function generators, but the latter permit convenient and rapid function changes if stored function masks are available. Useful response up to 100 Kc is possible with photoformers, and up to about 1 Kc with cathode-ray scanners. With function masks prepared directly from function data, either type of cathode-ray-tube function generator can yield a static accuracy within 1 per cent of half-scale. This figure can, however, be improved if we minimize the effects of mask parallax, finite spot size, and variable deflection sensitivity

1. By employing *adjustable function masks* (Fig. 6-31b)[59] set so that the *measured* output voltage matches the desired function, or
2. By preparing function masks photographically *with the function generator itself*, using known deflection voltages.

It is, of course, again preferable to use the function generator only for correcting a linear approximation.

FUNCTIONS OF TWO OR MORE VARIABLES

6-16. Introduction. Interpolation Schemes. Although many functions $F(X, Y, \ldots)$ of several machine variables $X, Y, \ldots$ can be generated by the usual combinations of summers, multipliers, and single-variable function generators (Fig. 1-4), many simulation problems require generation of empirically tabulated or charted functions of two or more variables (e.g., vacuum-tube and transistor characteristics, drag as a function of airspeed and angle of attack), and similar requirements arise in instrumentation and control applications. Note that combinations of two-variable function generators can generate functions of *any* finite number of variables; thus, $F(X,Y,Z) = G[f(X,Y),Z]$.

Unless a convenient analytical approximation applies, the sheer amount of data involved makes the setup of most two-variable functions $F(X,Y)$ quite laborious, no matter what type of function generator is used. In applications requiring frequent changes of such functions, some sort of a hybrid analog-digital function generator (Sec. 11-20), or at least a digitally controlled setup system (Sec. 11-2) will pay for itself. As regards accuracy, the reader is reminded once again that the best way to use any

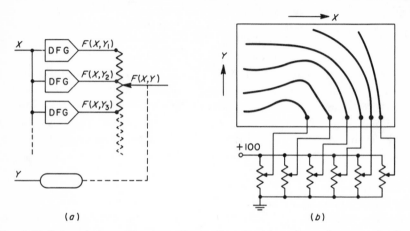

(a)   (b)

Fig. 6-32. Interpolation with a tapped potentiometer (a), and use of a servo plotting table with resistive paper for interpolation between contour lines $F(X,Y) = $ const drawn with conducting ink. In Fig. 6-32b, an ordinary xy recorder positions a probe sensing $F(X,Y)$; frequency response is limited to below 3 cps for $\frac{1}{2}$-in. excursions. Function sheets can be stored for reuse.

general-purpose function generator may be to generate only corrections to an analytical approximation of the desired function.

To generate an empirically determined function $F(X,Y)$ with conventional computing elements, $F(X,Y)$ must be fitted with an approximation function whose choice will depend on the particular application. A frequently reasonable approach is to generate $F(X,Y_i)$ accurately for a number of fixed values $Y = Y_1, Y_2, \ldots$ and to *interpolate* for other values of Y.[62-65] Since sufficiently accurate linear interpolation might require too many function generators for the $F(X,Y_i)$, one can use a nonlinear interpolation formula like[64]

$$F(X,Y) = f_1(X) + (Y - Y_1)f_2(X) + (Y - Y_1)(Y - Y_2)f_3(X) + \cdots$$
$$(6-5)$$

Three terms are often sufficient. The functions $f_1(X), f_2(X), \ldots$ are computed by successive substitution of $Y = Y_1, Y_2, \ldots$ in Eq. (5) and may be set up on tapped potentiometers (Sec. 8-8), so that each product term can be generated by servomultiplication.

Figure 6-32 shows two *mechanical interpolation schemes* adaptable for use with conventional analog computers. The Link Division of General Precision, Inc.,* has also developed a two-dimensional analog of the well-known tapped potentiometer (Sec. 8-8). A sheet of resistive material placed on a small servo table bears a grid of point contacts set to the desired voltages $F(X_i, Y_k)$ by padding-resistor networks, and a servo-positioned probe moves over the paper to provide two-dimensional interpolation.[66]

The search for convenient and practical approximation-function or interpolation methods for generating $F(X,Y)$ is by no means closed. Of interest, in particular, are simple digital or analog-computer programs which match between 5 and 100 parameters $\alpha_1, \alpha_2, \ldots$ of an analytical or diode-network approximation function to given empirical data by minimizing a suitably chosen measure of fit and thus reduce the setup of $F(X,Y)$ to a number of (manual or automatic) potentiometer settings (see also Sec. 11-20).

6-17. Diode Function Generators. (a) Simple Limiter Circuits.

Very useful piecewise-linear approximations to many functions of several

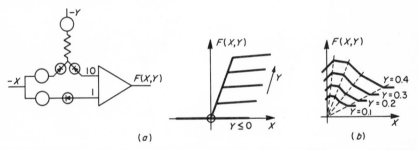

FIG. 6-33. Example of a piecewise-linear function of two variables generated with patchbay-connected diode limiters (a), and more general function $F(X,Y)$ generated by the diode function generator of Fig. 6-25 with variable bias $E = Y(b)$.

variables can be generated by simple limiter circuits (Figs. 6-3 to 6-5, 6-9, 6-11, 6-12, 9-1, 9-3, 9-4, and 9-5) with variable bias voltages. As a useful example, Fig. 6-33a shows one of many possible methods for approximating transistor characteristics with simple limiters (see also ref. 69); see Secs. 9-3 and 9-8 for other examples.

(b) Use of General-purpose Diode Function Generators. More general types of functions $F(X,Y)$ can be generated with ordinary multi-purpose diode function generators if the breakpoint-bias voltages are varied as functions of the second input variable Y. If, for instance, a variable input Y replaces the constant reference voltage E in the diode

* Binghamton, N.Y.

function generator of Fig. 6-25, the output voltage X_o will be a polygonal function of X for each value of Y (Fig. 6-33b), so that a function $F(X,Y)$ is produced.[70]

Since the breakpoint voltage of the ith limiter channel will be b_iY, where b_i is a constant, all breakpoints generated by any one limiter channel must lie on a straight line through the origin. These *breakpoint loci*

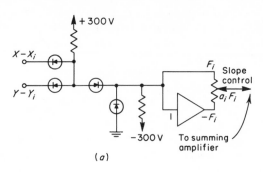

(a)

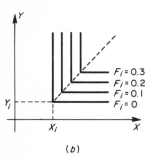

(b)

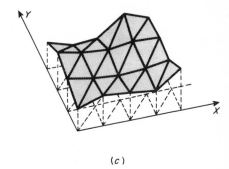

(c)

FIG. 6-34. Generation of

$$F_i(X,Y) = \max\left[\min(X - X_i,\ Y - Y_i),\ 0\right]$$

by a double selection circuit (a), contour lines of $F_i(X,Y)$ (b), and approximation of a function $F(X,Y)$ by

$$F(X,Y) \approx \sum_i a_i F_i(X,Y)$$

Note the triangular facets.

bound segments of equal slope and are indicated in broken lines in Fig. 6-33b.

One can further generalize the above procedure by adding a function of X or Y to the output voltage X_o. One obtains an even less restricted class of functions $F(X,Y)$ by introducing suitable *functions* $b_iG(Y)$ or $G_i(Y)$ of Y as bias voltages in the limiter channels of Fig. 6-25, so that the breakpoint loci are no longer straight lines. To set up a given function $F(X,Y)$, one must first locate the breakpoint loci by joining points of equal slope on a set of parametric curves like those in Fig. 6-33b.[70]

(c) **Special Diode Function Generators.** The Philbrick Model F2V function generator (G. A. Philbrick Researches, Inc., Boston, Mass.)[71] employed a set of amplitude-selector channels (Fig. 6-34a) to produce a desired function $F(X,Y)$ as a weighted sum of functions

$$F_i(X,Y) = \max [\min (X - X_i, Y - Y_i),0] \qquad (6\text{-}6)$$

The function (6) may be regarded as one two-dimensional generalization of the line segments generated in ordinary diode function generators. The contour lines of Fig. 6-34b illustrate the nature of a typical channel output $F_i(X,Y)$. To set up a desired function $F(X,Y)$, one first chooses the breakpoints (X_i,Y_i) and adjusts the slope controls to obtain the desired function values $F(X_i,Y_i)$ for successively increasing values of X_i and Y_i. Figure 6-34c shows a three-dimensional graph of a function $F(X,Y)$ generated by a Philbrick-type function generator.

A possibly simpler way to produce, say, a downward-convex function $F(X,Y)$ is to generate a set of voltages $Z_i = a_iX + b_iY + c_i$ which represent planes whose segments are to approximate the desired surface. An amplitude-selector circuit (Fig. 6-5b) is then used to obtain max $(Z_1,Z_2,$ . . .). More complicated surfaces such as hyperboloids will require two such selection processes.[102] Petternella and Ruberti[73] have developed a complete two-variable function generator operating on this principle.

6-18. Comparator/Switch-type Function Generators. The comparator/switch-type function generator or "universal nonlinear generator" was invented by Tomovič in 1952[82-87] and permits flexible approximation of a large class of functions $F(X,Y)$. Such a function generator is actually a hybrid analog-digital computing element. Referring to Fig. 6-35, n biased analog comparators set to flip at $X = X_1, X_2, \ldots,$ X_n "quantize" the input voltage X and close the kth electronic switch S_k whenever $X > X_k$. Each switch adds a function $F_k(Y)$ of the second input Y into the output summer; the resulting output voltage

$$X_o = F(X,Y)$$

varies continuously with Y and stepwise with X. If, in particular, $F_k(Y)$ is simply a potentiometer-set fixed multiple a_kY of Y, then the output X_o is a product $YG(X)$, so that we can obtain $\alpha XY, aY \sin bX, aY \cos bX$, etc.

The basic circuit can be considerably refined:

1. Addition of various types of logic circuits to the comparators (e.g., the diodes shown in dash lines in Fig. 6-35[89,90]) causes the kth electronic switch S_k to close when $X_k < X < X_{k+1}$. This simplifies the function setup and reduces accumulation of errors from the different switched inputs.

2. Various types of output filters yield rough interpolation of the stepwise output at the expense of frequency response.[87] If sufficiently

fast comparators are available, one can also add a smoothing-oscillator voltage to X in the manner of Fig. 6-24 to permit interpolation between X steps.

3. Multiple switches associated with each comparator can produce two or more functions of X and Y, and can also simultaneously generate $F(X_k, Y)$ and $F(X_{k+1}, Y)$ for linear interpolation.[89]

4. One can reduce the effects of comparator delays by adding a small voltage proportional to $\dot{X}$ or sign $\dot{X}$ to the input voltage X.[86]

Since comparator/switch-type function generators are set up by external calibration, as few as 6 to 10 relatively crude comparators and switches

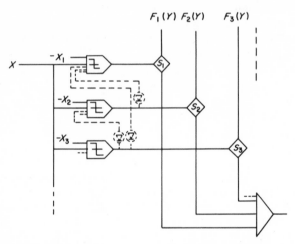

FIG. 6-35. Comparator/switch-type function generator. Without the diode logic indicated in dash lines, the kth switch S_k is closed when $X > X_k$; with the diodes in the circuit, S_k is closed when $X_k < X < X_{k+1}$.[89] For faster circuit operation, the logic diodes can, instead, feed into Schmitt triggers following each comparator.

can yield fair results at low frequencies. With modern solid-state comparators and switches, one can expect static accuracies within 0.5 per cent of half-scale and usable bandwidths up to perhaps 5 Kc; function generators of this type deserve a good deal of additional investigation (see also Sec. 11-20).

6-19. Cathode-ray-tube Function Generators. If a translucent mask of variable density is placed between the screen of a cathode-ray tube and a photocell,[78] the photocell output voltage will vary as a function $F(X, Y)$ of the horizontal and vertical deflection voltages X and Y applied to the cathode-ray tube. The accuracy of such function generators is limited to between 1 and 10 per cent by the difficulty of positioning the beam accurately. The frequency response is excellent (up to 100 Kc), and the device is suitable for use in repetitive/iterative analog computers. Mask opacity variations over a range of 200 to 1 can be produced by photographic means.

A related, more sophisticated type of cathode-ray function generator[79] employs a dual-beam cathode-ray tube. While the first beam travels over the function mask, a feedback circuit continuously positions the second beam on a calibrated comparison mask so that the light outputs from the two beams match; the deflection voltage of the comparison beam is the output voltage. A second feedback loop regulates the beam intensities.

Polimerou[80] has adapted his pulse-width modulating cathode-ray-tube function generator (Sec. 6-15) to generate functions of two variables by a switching scheme which selects one of several transparent function lines in accordance with a second voltage input (see also refs. 57 and 87).

REFERENCES AND BIBLIOGRAPHY

Diodes and Limiter Circuits

1. Pettit, J. M.: *Electronic Switching, Timing, and Pulse Circuits*, McGraw-Hill, New York, 1959.
2. Chance, B., et al.: *Waveforms*, MIT Radiation Laboratory Series, vol. 19, McGraw-Hill, New York, 1949.
3. Root, C. D.: A Look inside the Diode, *Electronic Design*, May 24, 1962.
4. Morrill, C. D., and R. V. Baum: Diode Limiters Simulate Mechanical Phenomena, *Electronics*, November, 1952.
5. Pfeiffer, P. E.: A Four-quadrant Multiplier, *IRETEC*, June, 1959.
6. Bradley, F. R., and R. P. McCoy: Voltage-limiting Circuit, *Electronics*, May, 1955.
7. Howe, R. M.: Representation of Nonlinear Functions by Means of Operational Amplifiers, *IRETEC*, December, 1956.
8. ———: The Use of Silicon-junction Diodes in Analog Simulation, *Instruments and Control Systems*, August, 1961.
9. Schmid, H.: Transistor Analog Computing Elements, in Huskey, H. D., and G. A. Korn, *Computer Handbook*, McGraw-Hill, New York, 1962.
10. Medkeff, R. J., and R. J. Parent: A Diode-bridge Limiter for Use with Electronic Analog Computers, *Proc. AIEE*, vol. 70, sec. T-1-170, 1951.
11. Tomlinson, N. P.: Fundamental Circuits and Techniques Used with Electronic Analog Computers, *Rept.* AP-77079, Goodyear Aircraft Company, Akron, Ohio, 1956.
12. Stranddorf, S. P.: High-frequency Limiter Amplifier Solves Phase-shift Problems, *Electronics*, Nov. 16, 1962.

Switching Circuits—General

13. Bennett, R. R., and A. S. Fulton: High-speed Relays in Electronic Analog Computers, *Electronic Eng.*, December, 1951.
14. Huskey, H. D., and G. A. Korn: *Computer Handbook*, McGraw-Hill, 1962.
15. Godet, S.: The Gated-amplifier Computer Technique, *Proc. Natl. Simulation Conf.*, Dallas, Tex., 1956.
16. Edwards, C. M.: Precision Electronic Switching with Feedback Amplifiers, *Proc. IRE*, **44:** 1613 (1956).
17. Koerner, H. E., and G. A. Korn: Function Generation with Operational Amplifiers, *Electronics*, Nov. 6, 1959.

Diode Switches

18. Millman, J., and T. H. Puckett: Accurate Linear Bidirectional Diode Gates, *Proc. IRE*, January, 1955.
19. Millman, J., and H. Taub: *Pulse and Digital Circuits*, McGraw-Hill, New York, 1956.

20. Diamentides, N. D.: A Multipurpose Electronic Switch for Analog Computer Simulation and Autocorrelation Applications, *IRETEC*, December, 1956.

21. Gocht, R. E.: The Design of High-speed Analog Sample and Storage Gates, M.S. Thesis, Department of Electrical Engineering, MIT, Aug. 24, 1959.

22. Strauss, L.: *Wave Generation and Shaping*, McGraw-Hill, New York, 1960.

23. Gray, H. J., M. Rubinoff, and J. Tompkins: A Diode Multiplexer for Analog Voltages, *IRETEC*, June, 1955.

24. Onstad, R. C.: Solid-state 30-channel Multiplexer, *Electronics*, Oct. 6, 1961.

25. Straehly, E. H.: A Novel Concept Applied to Airborne Communications, *Proc. Natl. Symposium on Space Electronics and Telemetry (IRE Prof. Group on Information Theory)*, San Francisco, September, 1959.

26. Lejet Lilamand, M.: A Time-division Multiplier, *IRETEC*, March, 1956.

27. Sebestyen, G.: A Design Technique for Pedestal-free Switching Circuits, *IRETEC*, September, 1957.

Transistor Switches

28. Ebers, J. J., and J. L. Moll: Large-signal Behavior of Junction Transistors, *Proc. IRE*, **42**: 1761 (1954).

29. Hunter, L. P.: *Handbook of Semiconductor Electronics*, 2d ed., McGraw-Hill, New York, 1962.

30. Bright, R. L.: Junction Transistors Used as Switches, *Communications and Electronics*, **111** (1955).

31. ———, and A. P. Kruper: Transistor Chopper for Stable D-C Amplifiers, *Electronics*, April, 1955.

32. Kruper, A. P.: Switching Transistors Used as a Substitute for Low-level Choppers, *Communications and Electronics*, March, 1955.

33. Chaplin, G. B., and A. R. Owens: Some Transistor Input Stages for High-gain D-C Amplifiers, *Proc. IEE*, **105-B**: 249 (1958).

34. ———: A Transistor High-gain Chopper-type D-C Amplifier, *Proc. IEE*, **105-B**: 258 (1958).

35. Meyer-Brötz, G.: Eigenschaften und Anwendungen von Flächentransistoren als Schalter, *Telefunken Z.*, June, 1960.

36. Schneider, W.: Der Transistor als genauer elektronischer Schalter, *Nachrichtentech. Fachberichte*, April, 1960.

37. Williams, A. J., et al.: Some Advances in Transistor Modulators for Precise Measurement, *Proc. Natl. Electronics Conf.*, 1957.

38. Hochwald, W., and H. L. Ehlers: Design of a High-quality Transistor D-C Amplifier, in Huskey, H. D., and G. A. Korn, *Computer Handbook*, McGraw-Hill, New York, 1962.

39. *Service Manual for the Dynamic-storage Analog Computer*, Computer Systems, Inc., Fort Washington, Pa., 1961.

40. Mitchell, B., and B. Bell: The INCH (Integrated Chopper), *General Engineering Memo* 7, National Semiconductor Corp., Danbury, Conn., June, 1962.

41. Transformerless Chopper Drive Circuit, *General Engineering Memo* 8, National Semiconductor Corp., Danbury, Conn., July, 1962.

Diode Function Generators
(See also data sheets on commercially available computers)

42. Meissinger, H. F.: An Electronic Circuit for the Generation of Functions of Several Variables, *IRE Natl. Convention Record*, 1955.

43. Miura, T., et al.: A New Diode Function Generator, *IRETEC*, June, 1957.

44. Smith, G. W., and R. C. Wood: *Principles of Analog Computation*, McGraw-Hill, New York, 1959.

45. Bruns, R. A.: An Improved Diode Function Generator, *Proc. Natl. Simulation Conf.*, 1956, Simulation Councils, Inc., La Jolla, Calif.
46. Hamer, H.: Optimum Linear-segment Function Generator, *Trans. AIEE*, **75-I**: 518 (1956).
47. Fitsner, L. N., and Doganovskii: On a Method for Computing the Electrical Network for Nonlinear Diode Generators, *Priborostroenie*, January, 1959; *Automation Express*, April, 1959.
48. Maslov, A. A., and Y. G. Purlov: A Universal Function Generator Based on the Principle of Quadratic Approximations, *Automatika i Telemekhanika*, **21** (February, 1960).
49. Giser, S., and R. P. Pinckney: The Sine-cosine Operator, *Rept.* R-73 (*ASTIA* 35072), Instrumentation Lab., MIT, April, 1954.

Varistor Function Generators

50. Kovach, L. D., and W. Comley: Nonlinear Transfer Functions Using Thyrite, *IRETEC*, June, 1958; see also A New Solid-state Analog Component, *IRETEC*, December, 1960.
51. Schreier, D.: Darstellung nichtlinearer Characteristiken unter Verwendung von Varistoren, *Wiss. Z. Tech. Hochsch. Ilmenau*, **7** (2) (1961).
52. Schreier, D., and H. Winkler: Design of Nonlinear Characteristics Using Varistors, *Proc. AICA 3d Intern. Conf.*, Opatija, Yugoslavia, September, 1961; Presses Académiques Européennes, Brussels, Belgium.

Cathode-ray Function Generators

53. Mynall, D. J.: Electronic Analogue Computing, *Electronic Eng.*, August, 1947.
54. Sunstein, D. E.: Photoelectric Waveform Generator, *Electronics*, February, 1949.
55. Hancock, E. J.: Photoformer Design and Performance, *Proc. Natl. Electronics Conf.*, **7**: 288 (1951).
56. Gerlach, A. A., C. N. Pederson, and R. E. Zenner: A Precise Electronic Function Generator, *Proc. Natl. Electronics Conf.*, **8** (1952).
57. Polimerou, L. G.: A New Method of Generating Functions, *IRETEC*, September, 1954.
58. Silverberg, B.: Function Generator for Radar Simulator, *Electronics*, Jan. 9, 1959.
59. MacNee, A. B.: A High-speed Product Integrator, *MIT Research Lab. Electronics Report* 136, Aug. 17, 1949.
60. Maloy, R. W.: Photoformer, *Electronics*, May 23, 1958.
61. Miura, T., and R. Abe: Error Analysis of a Photoformer, *Electronics Tech. J. Japan*, **5** (1) (1959).

Generation of Functions of Two Variables

62. Jerrard, R. P., and G. T. Jacoby: Generation of a Function of Two Variables, *ACM Conf. Paper*, Cambridge, Mass., September, 1953.
63. Kindle, W. K.: Method of Approximating Functions of Two Variables with Functions of Single Variables, *PCC Rept.* 53, July 2, 1956, Electronic Associates, Inc., Long Branch, N.J.
64. Levitt, J. R.: Bi-variable Function Generation, *AIEE Conf. Paper* CP57-311, Jan. 21, 1957.
65. Generation of a Function of Two Independent Variables, *Data Sheet*, Computer Systems, Inc., Fort Washington, Pa., 1960.
66. Analog Function Generator, *Electronic Design*, Dec. 7, 1960; see also Dual-input Computing Element, *Electronics*, March, 1959.
67. Larrowe, V., and M. Spencer: Use of Semi-conducting Surfaces in Analog Function

Generation, *Engineering Report*, Willow Run Research Lab., University of Michigan, Ypsilanti, Mich., 1959.

68. *Data Sheet on the BIVAR Function Generator Model* 1100-16a, Electronic Associates, Inc., Long Branch, N.J.

69. Rosenkranius, L.: Analog-computer Techniques for the Prediction of Transient Nuclear Radiation Effects on Transistor Circuits, *AIEE Conf. Paper* CP 62-1082, Summer General Meeting, Denver, Colo., 1962.

70. Meissinger, H. F.: An Electronic Circuit for the Generation of Functions of Several Variables, *IRE Natl. Convention Record*, 1955.

71. *Data Sheet for Model F2V Function of Two Variables Component*, G. A. Philbrick Researches, Inc., Boston, Mass., November, 1957.

72. Stern, T. E.: Piecewise-linear Network Theory, *MIT Research Lab. Electronics Report* 315, Cambridge, Mass., June 15, 1956.

73. Petternella, M., and A. Ruberti: A Diode Generator of Functions of Two Variables, *Ann. AICA*, January, 1961.

74. Smolov, V. B.: Two-input Electronic Function Generators, *Automatika i Telemekhanika*, October, 1959.

75. Peretz, R.: Calculateur I.R.S.I.A.-TABLELEC, *Proc. 2d AICA Conf.*, Strasbourg, France, 1958, Presses Académiques Européennes, Brussels, 1959.

76. ———: Opérateurs analogiques spéciaux, *Proc. 2d AICA Conf.*, Strasbourg, France, 1958, Presses Académiques Européennes, Brussels, 1959.

77. Kelley, T.: Multi-variable Function Generator, *Instruments and Control Systems*, November, 1959.

78. Wallmann, H.: An Electronic Integral-transform Computer and the Practical Solution of Integral Equations, *J. Franklin Inst.*, **250**:45 (1950).

79. Variable Density Film Yields Three Functions, *Control Eng.*, May, 1956.

80. Polimerou, L. G.: A New Method for Generating a Function of Two Independent Variables, *IRETEC*, September, 1957.

81. Wentzel, V.: Two Electronic Function Generators, *Proc. 1st AICA Intern. Conf.*, Brussels, Belgium, 1955, Presses Académiques Européennes, Brussels, 1956.

Comparator/Switch-type Function Generators

82. Tomovič, R.: A Universal Unit for the Electrical Differential Analyzer, *J. Franklin Inst.*, **254** (August, 1952).

83. ———: A Versatile Electronic Function Generator, *J. Franklin Inst.*, **257** (February, 1954).

84. ———: Sur une methode augmentante la précision d'un genérateur de fonctions, *Proc. 1st AICA Intern. Conf.*, Brussels, Belgium, 1955, Presses Académiques Européennes, Brussels, 1956.

85. ———: New Applications of an Electronic Function Generator, *IRETEC*, March, 1958.

86. ———: Hysteresis Correction of Amplitude Comparators, *Ann. AICA*, June, 1959.

87. ——— and W. J. Karplus: *High-speed Analog Computers*, Wiley, New York, 1962.

88. Mason, M. S.: Applications of the Universal Nonlinear Element (UNE), published by Thiokol Chemical Corp., Brigham City, Utah, 1962; the UNE is manufactured by Comcor, Inc., Denver, Colo.

89. Short, E.: A New Multi-variable Function Generator, Western Simulation Council paper, published by the Boeing Co., Seattle, Wash., July 1, 1962.

90. Fuchs, A.: Discussion, *Proc. 2d AICA Conf.*, Strasbourg, France, 1958, Presses Académiques Européennes, Brussels, 1959.

Miscellaneous Topics

91. Duffy, R. M., and C. P. Gilbert: A Function Generator Using Cold-cathode Selector Tubes, *IRETEC*, March, 1961.

92. Sheinin, I. S.: A Discontinuous-function Block for Analog Computers, *Priborostroenie*, March, 1961 (*Automation Express*, June 30, 1961).

93. Foote, D. D.: Pulse-width Modulator, *Instruments and Control Systems*, May, 1963.

94. Brubaker, T. A.: A Non-saturating Transistor Switch for Analog and Hybrid Computers, *ACL Memo*. 78, Electrical Engineering Department, University of Arizona, May, 1963.

95. Baker, R. H., et al.: The Diamond Circuit, *MIT Tech. Rept.* 300, Lincoln Laboratory, Lexington, Mass., January, 1963; see also *Proc. Intern. Solid-state-circuits Conference*, Philadelphia, 1963.

96. Gibbons, J. F., and H. S. Horn: A Circuit with Logarithmic Transfer Response over 6 Decades, *Proc. Intern. Solid-state-circuits Conf.*, Philadelphia, 1963.

97. Grinich, V. H., et al.: Silicon Mesa Transistors for Use as Saturating Switches, *Proc. WESCON*, 1959.

98. Mayer, R. E., et al.: Apparatus for Setting a Function Generator, U.S. Patent 2,964,709, Dec. 13, 1960 (filed Dec. 31, 1957), assigned to Reeves Instrument Corp., Garden City, N.Y.

99. Seening Yee: A High-speed Electronic Analog Switch, *IEEE Intern. Convention Record*, 1963.

100. Schmid, H.: Four-quadrant, All-electronic Pulse-time Multiplier, *Rept.* 62APJ43, General Electric Co., Johnson City, N.Y., 1962.

101. Verster, T. C., and A. R. Boothroyd: Operation of the Junction Transistor as a Fast Low-level Switch, *Proc. IEE* (Britain), February, 1963.

102. Wilkinson, R. H.: A Method of Generating Functions of Several Variables Using Analog Diode Logic, *IEEETEC*, April, 1963.

CHAPTER 7

ELECTRONIC MULTIPLIERS
AND DIVIDERS

INTRODUCTION

7-1. Survey. The earliest electronic analog computers implemented multiplication of variables and functions of variables with potentiometers positioned by computer servomechanisms in the manner described in Sec. 1-13. The use of computer servomechanisms is still economically attractive, since one single relatively simple servomechanism can position between 4 and 20 potentiometers to produce an equal number of products of the servo input variable by functions of other machine variables.[1] Although computer servomechanisms have reached a high state of development (Chap. 8), their frequency response is necessarily limited, and the installation and maintenance of electromechanical components is a nuisance in many applications. Electronic multipliers and function generators have not only replaced computer servomechanisms wherever speed of computation is essential, but high-quality electronic multipliers are also more accurate than the best servomultipliers.

The all-electrical multiplying devices most frequently employed in electronic analog computation are

1. *Time-division or pulsed-attenuator multipliers* based on simultaneous pulse-amplitude and pulse-width modulation of a pulse train (Sec. 7-9)

2. *Diode quarter-square multipliers*, which implement the relation

$$XY = \frac{1}{4}[(X + Y)^2 - (X - Y)^2] \qquad (7\text{-}1)$$

   by means of diode-function-generator squaring circuits (Secs. 7-14 and 7-15)

3. *Triangle-averaging multipliers*, which implement the relation (1) by clipping and averaging a 5-Kc to 2-Mc triangular waveform biased by the signal to be squared (Sec. 7-16)

Several other types of electronic multipliers are described in Secs. 7-17 to 7-19 and 7-22. The use of electronic multiplier circuits for *division* is discussed in Sec. 7-23.

7-2. Multiplication of Positive and Negative Quantities. Figure 7-1 shows the block-diagram representation of an electronic multiplier. The device has two input voltages X, Y corresponding to the two variables to be multiplied. The output voltage X_o will be proportional to the product of the input voltages X, Y, so that

$$X_o = \alpha XY \qquad (7\text{-}2)$$

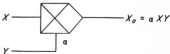

where α is a positive or negative constant.

The ideal electrical multiplier would accept both positive and negative input voltages X, Y, and its output voltage X_o would have the correct sign associated with the product XY. Such a multiplier is said to be capable of *four-quadrant operation*. Some practical multiplying

Fig. 7-1. Block-diagram representations of an (electronic) analog multiplier. α is most frequently equal to plus or minus the reciprocal of the computer reference voltage E_{REF}, so that $|X| \leq E_{REF}$, $|Y| \leq E_{REF}$ implies $|\alpha XY| \leq E_{REF}$.

devices permit only *two-quadrant operation:* one of the two inputs, say X, must remain either positive or negative for proper operation, while Y can change sign and produces the correct output-voltage polarity. A third class of multipliers can accept only voltages of one sign for both X and Y (*one-quadrant multipliers*).

Two-quadrant multipliers can readily produce four-quadrant multiplication by one of the biasing schemes of Fig. 7-2. In Fig. 7-2a, a one-quadrant multiplier multiplies Y by $\frac{1}{2}(X + E)$, where E is a positive voltage sufficiently large to keep the input voltage $\frac{1}{2}(X + E)$ positive even when X is negative. The multiplier produces the product $-(\alpha/2)$ $(XY + EY)$, and the output summing amplifier subtracts the undesired term $-(\alpha/2)(EY)$ and yields the product αXY with the correct sign in each case.

The circuit of Fig. 7-2b subtracts the outputs of two two-quadrant multipliers to yield the correct product and may cancel some errors because of the symmetrical push-pull arrangement. The biasing schemes of Fig. 7-2a and/or b can also be applied to both inputs of a one-quadrant multiplier to yield four-quadrant multiplication.

7-3. Voltage-controlled Variable-gain Devices. Modulation Schemes. Physical devices used for electrical multiplication can usually be represented by the block diagram of Fig. 7-3a. The gain $K = X_o/X$ of such a device is variable and increases or decreases monotonically with a second input voltage Y. Figures 7-3b and c illustrate two specific examples permitting only two-quadrant multiplication. Figure

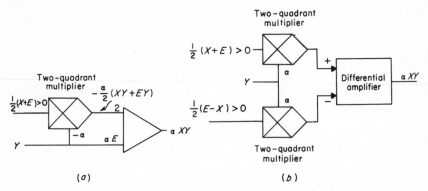

FIG. 7-2. Adaptation of two-quadrant multipliers to four-quadrant multiplication. Analogous schemes permit four-quadrant multiplication with one-quadrant multipliers.

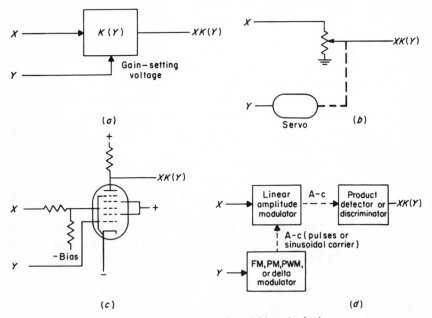

FIG. 7-3. Voltage-controlled variable-gain devices.

7-3b shows that an electromechanical multiplying device (servo-driven potentiometer) can be discussed in the same context, and Fig. 7-3c shows a simple variable-gain amplifier employing a variable-μ vacuum tube.

In general, voltage-controlled variable-gain devices depending on *con-*

tinuous nonlinear transfer characteristics of vacuum tubes or nonlinear resistances cannot be reproduced with better than about 10 per cent accuracy without frequent multiple adjustments and are, thus, useless for precise multiplication.   For this reason, many multiplication schemes employ dual modulation of a 1- to 150-Kc rectangular pulse train or a 100-Kc to 2-Mc sinusoidal carrier by the multiplier input voltages X, Y, with subsequent recovery of the low-frequency output αXY by a suitable detector circuit (Fig. 7-3c).   The nonlinearity implicit in the multiplication operation now depends on the switching (saturation and cutoff) characteristics of diodes, vacuum tubes, or transistors, which are more easily controlled than continuous transfer characteristics.   Unfortunately, the carrier-ripple filter needed in each modulation-type multiplier tends to limit the signal-frequency bandwidth (Sec. 7-13).

Referring to Fig. 7-3c, the *linear amplitude modulator* for rectangular-pulse trains is simply an electronic switch (Secs. 6-8 and 7-12) which "chops" the signal-frequency input voltage X at the carrier frequency. Phase- or frequency-modulated sinusoidal carriers can be amplitude-modulated by conventional radio circuits linearized by feedback from a linear AM detector (Fig. 7-10a).   The following dual-modulation schemes have been used for multiplication:[2]

1. *Amplitude/pulse-width modulation (AM/PWM; time-division multipliers)* of pulse trains and *amplitude/delta modulation* (a delta modulator can gate a constant-repetition-rate pulse train at a rate proportional to Y) yield the output product by simple averaging and are, thus, particularly simple (see also Secs. 7-9 to 7-13 and 11-18).

2. *Amplitude/phase modulation (AM/PM) and amplitude/frequency modulation (AM/FM)* of pulse trains or sinusoidal carriers require special detector circuits but are of interest in connection with existing PM or FM data-transmission systems and instrumentation transducers.   The use of a sinusoidal 2-Mc carrier yields good multiplication bandwidth (see also Sec. 7-7).

These modulation-type multipliers are usually employed in the feedback circuits described in Secs. 7-4 to 7-13.

Two other dual-modulation schemes have been employed for multiplication:

3. *Dual pulse-width modulation (PWM/PWM).*   Coincidence detection of two pulse-width modulated pulse trains with noncommensurable pulse-repetition rates yields a product output (*coincidence multipliers*).[3,4]

4. *Dual amplitude modulation (AM/AM).*   A sinusoidal carrier of circular frequency ω_C is amplitude-modulated with X, and the voltage $X \sin \omega_C \tau + Y$ is applied to a transducer (mixer tube or diode)

with an approximately square-law transfer characteristic. The product $\alpha XY \sin \omega_C \tau$ is the only mixer-output component at the carrier frequency and can be filtered and detected.

FEEDBACK CONTROL OF MULTIPLIER GAIN

7-4. The Basic Feedback Scheme. The output voltage $XK(Y)$ of a voltage-controlled variable-gain device or modulator/demodulator is not usually a linear function of the gain-setting voltage Y over a wide range of inputs Y, as required for multiplication. Frequently, however, the multiplier gain can be made very accurately proportional to Y with the aid of a *gain-setting feedback loop*. Referring to Fig. 7-4, Z is a constant

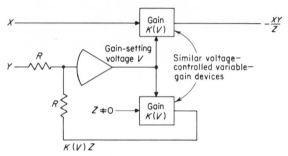

Fig. 7-4. Feedback scheme for making the gain of two or more similar voltage-controlled variable-gain devices accurately proportional to a multiplier input voltage Y.

positive or negative reference voltage (e.g., $+100$ volts or -100 volts) applied to a variable-gain device whose gain K is assumed to be independent of Z. $K = K(V)$ varies monotonically (but not necessarily linearly) with the gain-setting voltage

$$V = A(KZ + Y)$$

supplied by a summing network and d-c amplifier of combined high gain A. It follows that

$$K = K(V) = K(0) + K_1(V)V$$

where K_1 is either positive or negative. Hence

$$K = K(0) + AK_1(V)(KZ + Y) = \frac{K(0) + AK_1(V)Y}{1 - AK_1(V)Z}$$
$$= -\frac{Y}{Z} - \frac{1}{AK_1(V)Z}\left[K(0) + \frac{Y}{Z}\right] \pm \cdots \quad (7\text{-}3)$$

if the resulting feedback is stable and has a large loop gain $|AK_1(V)Z|$. A necessary (but not sufficient) condition for stability is $AK_1(V)Z < 0$

at d-c.   Additional terms in Eq. (3) are of higher order in $1/AK_1(V)Z$. It is seen that *the feedback regulates the gain K so that it is proportional to the multiplier input Y,*

$$K = -\frac{Y}{Z} \qquad (7\text{-}4)$$

with an error inversely proportional to the absolute loop gain $|AK_1(V)Z|$.

Assume now that it is possible to obtain a second variable-gain device essentially similar to the first one, i.e., with the same gain/voltage characteristic $K(V)$.   If both variable-gain blocks are controlled by the amplifier output voltage V in Fig. 7-4, the second variable-gain device will multiply its input voltage X by $K = -Y/Z$ to yield the desired multiplier output $-XY/Z$.   If additional variable-gain devices with identical gain/voltage characteristics $K(V)$ are controlled by the gain-control loop of Fig. 7-4, they can multiply additional inputs X', X'', . . . by $K = -Y/Z$ (*slave multipliers*).

The reader may find it interesting to estimate the effects of error voltages (e.g., due to d-c drift) at various points of the circuit of Fig. 7-4 on the output in the manner of Sec. 4-10.

7-5. Design Problems.   The multiplication scheme of Fig. 7-4 will require the design of a stable high-gain feedback loop to produce

$$K = -\frac{Y}{Z}$$

with the required accuracy in accordance with Eq. (3).   This is usually not difficult, but every implementation of Fig. 7-4 poses two serious problems.   One requires

1. *A type of voltage-controlled variable-gain device whose gain is accurately independent of one input (Z or X in Fig. 7-4)*
2. *Two such devices with accurately similar gain vs. gain-setting voltage characteristics $K(V)$.*

Practically all simple voltage-sensitive circuit elements, such as thyrite resistors, semiconductors, or vacuum tubes, do not satisfy either of these two requirements; their gain may be dependent on the input voltage, and their characteristics cannot be reproduced with sufficient accuracy. One can overcome these deficiencies (1) by using one and the same variable-gain device to attenuate both Z and X on a time-sharing or frequency-sharing basis (Sec. 7-8); or again, (2) by employing vacuum tubes or semiconductors only as *switches* which are either off or on (saturated). Their specific nonlinear characteristics will, then, produce only relatively small effects on the circuit output (see also Sec. 6-1).

7-6. Examples of Feedback Multipliers. **(a) Servomultipliers.**
Figure 7-5 shows that the operation of the ordinary servomultiplier (Sec.
1-13a) is based precisely on the principle of Fig. 7-4. The variable-gain
devices are now two similar potentiometers positioned by a servomotor;
the latter is actuated by the output voltage V_o of the control amplifier
(servo amplifier). Note that both positive and negative values of
$K = -Y/Z$ are obtained, so that direct four-quadrant multiplication is
possible. Accurately similar servo-driven potentiometers can satisfy
the design requirements of Sec. 7-5 very well, but the use of electromechanical components limits the multiplier bandwidth with respect to
the input Y. Servomultipliers are discussed in detail in Chap. 8.

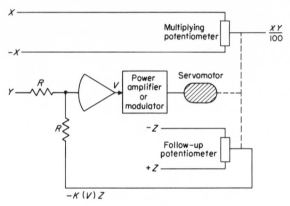

Fɪɢ. 7-5. Servomultiplier.

(b) Step Multipliers (see also Sec. 11-11).[5-7] In Fig. 7-6a, the
servomechanism of Fig. 7-5 has been replaced by a pulsed stepping
switch which steps forward and backward, as determined by a comparator-controlled relay in accordance with the sign of $Y + KZ$. The two-
gang stepping switch selects the gain-controlling input-network resistors
of the comparator and output amplifiers, so that the scheme of Fig. 7-4 is
again realized.

The stepping operation limits the multiplier bandwidth severely with
respect to the input Y. Note also that the multiplier output can follow
Y only in discrete steps; since the output would tend to oscillate about the
correct value for constant input Y, the comparator may be given a small
dead space about zero. Like servo-driven potentiometers, extra slave
sections of a stepping switch are easily added if additional products by
Y are desired.

The primitive step-multiplication scheme of Fig. 7-6a can be replaced
by the analogous *electronic step multiplier* (*analog/digital/analog converter
multiplier, binary-increment multiplier*) of Fig. 7-6b. Here, the polarized
relay of Fig. 7-6a is replaced by an electronic switch (voltage-sensitive

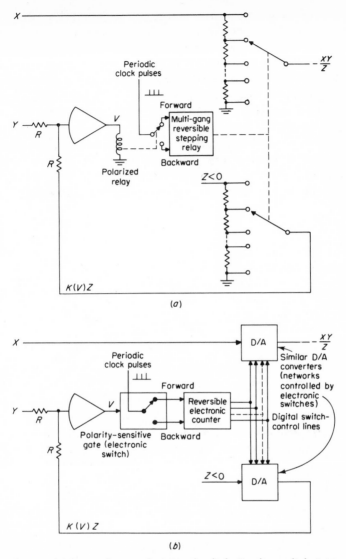

FIG. 7-6. Step multipliers using an electromechanical stepping switch (a) and electronic switches controlled by a reversible electronic counter (b). Two-quadrant multipliers are shown for the sake of simplicity; four-quadrant operation is obtained either in the manner of Fig. 7-2a or by additional switching.

gate), which gates a 10- to 200-Kc pulse train into the forward or backward inputs of a reversible binary counter, depending on the sign of the comparator input.[6] As the count proceeds, each counter stage (usually a flip-flop) opens and closes a pair of electronic switches in series with corresponding resistances in the input networks of comparator and output amplifier.　In this manner, the gain K increases and decreases with the count, and the feedback gain-control scheme is again realized.

The actual design of practical analog/digital/analog converters will be further discussed in Sec. 11-11.　Electronic step multipliers tend to be expensive, since a resolution of ϵ per cent will require at least $\log_2 (100/\epsilon)$ counter stages and $2 \log_2 (100/\epsilon)$ switches.　With accurate resistors and switches, however, step multipliers can yield the best static accuracy of all analog multipliers; static accuracies well within 0.01 per cent of half-scale are possible, and 0.1 per cent is relatively easy to get.

The multiplier frequency response with respect to the X input is essentially that of a similarly constructed summing amplifier, unless an output filter is badly needed to smooth out switching steps and spikes.　On the

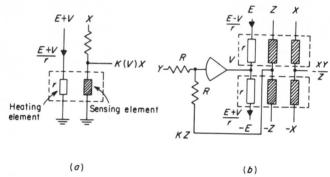

(a)　　　　　　　　　　　　　　　(b)

Fig. 7-7. Heat-transfer multiplier.

other hand, the multiplier output will follow the Y input in discrete steps of one minimum increment per clock pulse.　Existing analog switching speeds permit 10,000 to 200,000 increments or output samples per second; note that this increment rate-limits the amplitude-frequency *product aω* of sinusoids $a \sin \omega \tau$ applied to the Y output (see also Sec. 3-2c).

(c) **Heat-transfer Multipliers.**[8-11]　Remarkably small and simple feedback-stabilized multipliers employ temperature-sensitive transducers of the type shown in Fig. 7-7a.　The gain-changing voltage V_o is added to the heater voltage E; the resulting temperature change varies the resistance of the sensing element and thus the gain K.　Figure 7-7b shows a feedback-stabilized push-pull multiplier circuit based on this principle.

Each of the transducers encircled in broken lines in Fig. 7-7b comprises a bifilar heating element (No. 40 Teflon-insulated Nichrome wire) and two sensing elements (No. 40 Teflon-insulated nickel wire) wound together on a Pyrex rod.　Two or more such units may be mounted in a miniature-tube envelope; no vacuum is required.

Accuracies within 1 per cent of full scale have been obtained with carefully matched gain-setting and output-sensing elements.　The frequency response is restricted to about 10 cps by the inherent heat-transfer lag, and the output-voltage range may be limited by self-heating of the sensing elements. Such multipliers are useful mainly in special-purpose computers used as control-system components; note that Y and Z could be the amplitudes of two a-c voltages of equal phase as well as instantaneous voltage values.

(d) **Hall-effect and Magnetoresistance Multipliers.**[12-23] When suitable conducting materials carrying an excitation current i are placed

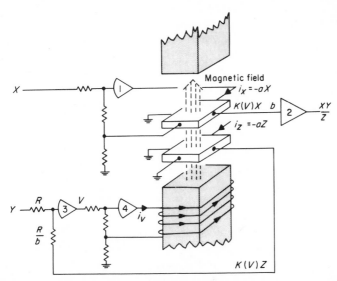

Fig. 7-8. Feedback Hall-effect multiplier using two similar Hall-effect transducers in the air gap of an electromagnet. Amplifier 1 has current feedback (Sec. 1-20) to produce an output current proportional to the multiplier input voltage X. Amplifiers 3 and 4 form a single amplifier having a current-feedback output stage preceded by voltage amplification. The reference current i_Z is obtained from a high-impedance voltage source whose sign is chosen so as to keep the gain-setting feedback loop stable.

in a magnetic field H perpendicular to i, the *Hall effect* produces a measurable voltage

$$E_H = \lambda_H i B \qquad (7\text{-}5)$$

across the conductor at right angles to both i and H, where B is the magnetic flux density due to H. Figure 7-8 shows a feedback multiplier utilizing the Hall effect. The gain-setting feedback loop controls the magnetic field for two similar thin semiconductor wafers (Hall generators) placed in the narrow air gap of a strong electromagnet. In practice, the semiconductor wafers may be sandwiched between iron or ferrite plates to reduce the air gap.[14,16]

Even for the most sensitive Hall generators, the Hall coefficient λ_H is small (50 to 100 mV/kilogauss-ampere for thin indium arsenide wafers), and the source impedance is low (of the order of 1 ohm) and therefore hard to match efficiently to a d-c amplifier.   Lofgren[14] achieved a favorable compromise of Hall coefficient and source impedance with specially doped silicon wafers, and obtained a static accuracy within 0.05 per cent of full scale (± 20 volts), using a circuit similar to that of Fig. 7-8.   His paper describes circuit details, including a simple temperature-compensation method.   It is also possible to compensate for the effects of asymmetrical contact placement.[15]

While Hall generators as such can operate at frequencies as high as at least 1 Mc, the strong electromagnet required imposes severe bandwidth restrictions.   Lofgren was able to trade flux density, and thus accuracy, for bandwidth by substituting a ferrite magnet core for the original ferromagnetic core, so that he obtained either 0.1 per cent of half-scale static accuracy with full-scale output up to 20 cps, or 0.3 per cent of half-scale static accuracy with full-scale output up to 500 cps (phase shift was not specified).[14]

Magnetoresistance, an undesirable effect in Hall-effect multipliers, causes resistance changes in suitable conductors placed in varying magnetic fields.   These resistance changes can be used for multiplication over a dynamic range of at least 10 to 1 for a magnetic-field change of between 0 and 10 kilogauss.[21]   Feedback multipliers based on the magnetoresistance effect in metallic bismuth have been built; accuracy within 0.2 per cent of half-scale is possible.[22,23]   Like Hall-effect multipliers, magnetoresistance multipliers suffer from low transducer output impedance and from frequency-response limitations due to the magnetic circuit; unlike a Hall generator, a magnetoresistance transducer requires only two connections.

(e) **Sampling Multipliers.**[24]   Figure 7-9 illustrates the operation of a *sampling multiplier*.   Referring to the simple two-quadrant multiplier circuit shown in solid lines, the output voltages E_Z and E_X of two linear RC networks are periodically reset to zero and then charged by the simultaneously applied voltages Z and X.   At the time t after the start of a charging period

$$E_Z = Z(1 - e^{-\frac{t}{RC}})   \quad   E_X = X(1 - e^{-\frac{t}{RC}})$$

A fast comparator, which here plays the part of the amplifier in the gain-setting loop, actuates the sample-hold circuit when $E_Z = -Y$ or $1 - e^{-t/RC} = -Y/Z$, so that the sample-hold output reads

$$X_o = \alpha E_X = \alpha X(1 - e^{-\frac{t}{RC}}) = -\alpha \frac{XY}{Z}$$

during each repetition period.   The dash lines in Fig. 7-9 show biasing and subtraction circuits for four-quadrant operation in the manner of Fig. 7-2a.   Various other charging or discharging circuits can be used in similar arrangements.[2,24]

The stepwise sample-hold output needs much less smoothing than the output of a modulation-type multiplier, so that sampling multipliers can produce useful results at frequencies about three octaves below their sampling repetition rate of 1 to 5 Kc.   The static accuracy depends on the three electronic switching operations, which require accurate timing and must not introduce excessive drift or switching spikes.   As usual, these requirements are more easily met for lower repetition rates (see also Sec. 7-13). For a repetition rate of 2 Kc, static accuracies within 0.2 per cent of half-scale can be obtained with the aid of high-quality sampling circuits (Secs. 6-11 and 10-4; see also Sec. 8-15).

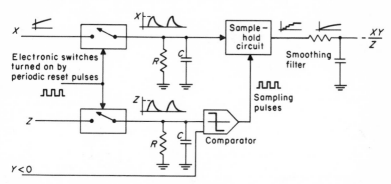

FIG. 7-9. A sampling multiplier.   A simple two-quadrant multiplier ($Y < 0$) is shown in solid lines.   Addition of the circuits indicated in dash lines permits four-quadrant multiplication.   Six-diode bridge switches (Fig. 6-15) and the sample-hold circuit of Fig. 10-7a may be used at repetition rates of several kilocycles.   With *different* RC combinations in the two channels, the circuit yields products of the form $\alpha X Y^\beta$.

7-7. AM/FM Multipliers and Other Feedback Multipliers Employing Dual Modulation.[25-28]   Dual-modulation schemes of gain control (Fig. 7-3d) are widely used with the feedback principle of Fig. 7-4, since it is, again, easier to match the switching characteristics of two similar modulators than to match continuous non-linear characteristics.

The block diagram of the feedback *AM/FM multiplier* of Fig. 7-10a follows the arrangement of Fig. 7-4; up to 12 slave products can be obtained if desired.   Use of a sinusoidal carrier permits one to employ a relatively high carrier frequency (1 to 2 Mc), to obtain wide bandwidth: phase shift is within 2 deg at 500 cps, and the multiplier still yields rough products at 15 Kc.   On the other hand, the AM/FM multiplier is a relatively complex device.   Accurate amplitude modulation of the sinusoidal carrier by Z and X requires two special feedback loops, and the multiplication accuracy depends critically on the matching of the two AM/FM detector-discriminators. Greatly improved detector-discriminators have been designed especially for analog multiplication (Fig. 7-10b),[28] and careful adjustment yields a static accuracy within 0.1 per cent of half-scale; but it is, to say the least, very difficult to maintain such accuracy for any length of time.

In modulation-type feedback multipliers employing rectangular-pulse carriers, one can obtain accurate amplitude modulation with simple switching circuits (electronic choppers) at pulse repetition rates up to several hundred kilocycles (see also Sec. 7-9). Various types of feedback multipliers combine such amplitude modulation with frequency modulation or phase modulation.[2,29,30]   Multipliers of this kind are of interest in special-purpose systems which already employ FM or PM for data transmission, range or angle tracking, navigation, etc.   The most commonly used types of dual-

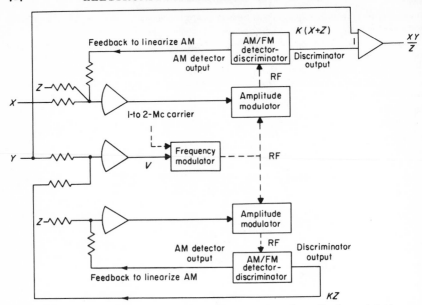

Fig. 7-10a. AM/FM multiplier with feedback-corrected amplitude modulation.

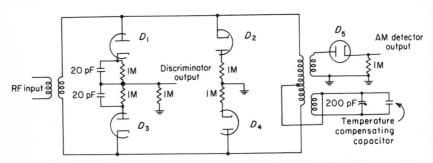

Fig. 7-10b. AM-FM detector-discriminator for analog multiplication (*Computer Systems, Inc.*). To minimize detuning of the critical tuned circuit by diode-impedance changes with signal amplitude, the discriminator diodes D_1, D_3 are placed in the primary circuit of the discriminator transformer and employ peak detection. Diodes D_2, D_4 balance the discriminator circuit. Discriminator and AM-detector outputs lead to d-c amplifier summing junctions (Fig. 7-10a). The AM-detector output is essentially independent of frequency. The main remaining error sources are temperature effects on the relative tuning and loading of the two discriminators needed for multiplication.

modulation multipliers, however, employ combined amplitude and pulse-width modulation. The reason for this popularity of AM/PWM (time-division) multiplier circuits is their relative simplicity. Simple modulator circuits are available, and product detection requires only a low-pass filter which averages the modulated pulse train, rather than nonlinear discriminators or coincidence detectors.*

---

* This last advantage is shared by feedback multipliers combining amplitude and delta modulation.[31] Relatively little work has been done in this area.

7-8. Time-sharing and Frequency-sharing Schemes. To overcome the serious problem of obtaining two accurately similar voltage-controlled variable-gain devices, one can use a single variable-gain device which is either time-shared or frequency-shared between the X and Z channels of Fig. 7-4.   As an example of a *time-shared* variable-gain device, the RCA Laboratories (TYPHOON project)[32] have tried a computer servomechanism employing a single potentiometer as both the follow-up and multiplying potentiometer (Fig. 7-11a); a triple commutator-type switch rotating at 3,600 rpm or a triple 60-cps chopper relay transfers the potentiometer inputs and output back and forth between the two channels.   The resulting sampled-data potentiometer outputs are smoothed by suitable smoothing networks in each channel.   The

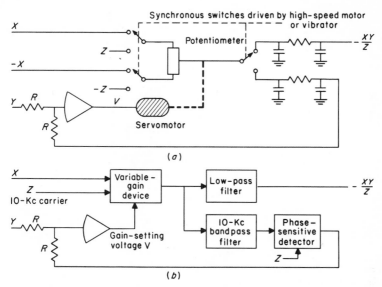

Fig. 7-11. Time-shared-potentiometer servomechanism (a), and frequency-sharing feedback multiplier (b).

use of the single potentiometer assures perfect conformity or tracking of the multiplying and follow-up sections of the circuit; but the sampled-data nature of the output severely restricts the bandwidth of the signal X which can be accepted by the servomultiplier.

In a *frequency-sharing* scheme,[33] a single voltage-controlled variable-gain device is again used in both the X and Z channels (Fig. 7-11b).   The input machine variable X and the reference voltage Z are simply added and applied to the voltage-controlled attenuator, which may be a simple variable-gain amplifier or a modulator-demodulator arrangement.   The reference voltage Z is a constant-amplitude a-c voltage whose frequency is well above the desired range of signal frequencies to be used with the multiplier.   The resulting high-frequency component of the attenuator output voltage is filtered by a bandpass filter, is rectified, and operates the gain-setting feedback loop. The product output voltage, on the other hand, is freed of high-frequency components by means of a low-pass filter.   Multipliers of this type can yield accuracies better than 0.1 per cent of full scale,[33] but such circuits require a wideband variable-gain device as well as sharp low-pass filtering; they do not seem to offer any advantage over feedback modulation schemes.

TIME-DIVISION MULTIPLIERS

7-9. Principle of Operation. *Time-division multipliers (AM/PWM multipliers, mark-space multipliers, pulsed-attenuator multipliers*) depend on combined pulse-amplitude and pulse-width modulation of a rectangular pulse train. The average (smoothed) values of the waveforms pictured in Fig. 7-12a and b are respectively given by

$$\frac{T_1}{T_1 + T_2} X = n T_1 X \qquad \frac{T_1 - T_2}{T_1 + T_2} X = (2n T_1 - 1)X \qquad (7\text{-}6)$$

where X is the pulse amplitude, and T_1 and T_2 are the widths of the positive and negative portions of the pulses; $n = 1/(T_1 + T_2)$ is the pulse

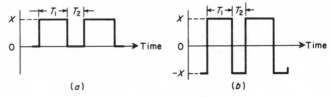

(a)   (b)

Fig. 7-12. The running-average value (d-c or low-frequency component) of the waveforms shown is $\dfrac{T_1}{T_1 + T_2} X$ in Fig. 7-12a and $\dfrac{T_1 - T_2}{T_1 + T_2} X$ in Fig. 7-12b.

repetition rate in cycles per second. These relations implement multiplication of a voltage X by a second voltage Y which controls the duty cycle $n T_1$ of the pulse train; the desired product is recovered by an averaging filter. In practice, the pulse repetition rate must be large compared with the highest signal frequency (Sec. 7-13). Repetition rates between 1 and 300 Kc are used.

Such multipliers yield high static accuracy (0.1 to 0.01 per cent of half-scale) and fair frequency response (dynamic errors within 2 per cent of half-scale for sinusoidal inputs up to $\frac{1}{25}$ of the pulse repetition rate used) at comparatively low cost. A complete four-quadrant multiplier of this type requires between 4 and 9 vacuum tubes, or 6 to 14 transistors, in addition to 3 or 4 d-c amplifiers.

7-10. Externally Excited Time-division Multipliers. In Fig. 7-13a, a phantastron or delay multivibrator is periodically triggered and produces rectangular gate pulses whose width is determined by the gain-setting input voltage V.* These gate pulses are suitably amplified and

---

* In such circuits, each trigger pulse starts a rectangular pulse which is integrated until the absolute value of the integral equals a predetermined fraction of the control voltage. At this point, the pulse is terminated by regenerative action. For a detailed discussion of phantastrons and delay multivibrators, see ref. 36, Chaps. 6 and 7.

shaped by a switch-driving amplifier and drive two electronic switches which alternately select Z, $-Z$ and X, $-X$ to be averaged by low-pass filters in the Z and X channels. The gain-control feedback loop compares the average of the pulse-width-modulated Z-switch output E_Z with the multiplier input voltage Y and sets the average of E_Z equal to $-Y/Z$. Assuming accurately synchronous switch operation, the average value of the X-switch output voltage is then proportional to XY/Z.[34]

The time-division multiplier circuit of Fig. 7-13b operates in the same manner, except for the method of pulse-width modulation.[43] Here, a

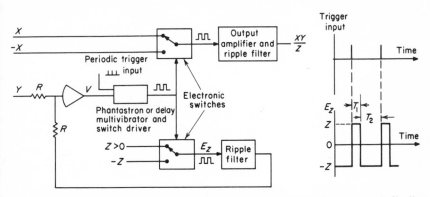

Fig. 7-13a. Externally excited AM/PWM (time-division) multiplier. A periodically triggered phantastron or delay multivibrator generates gate pulses whose width increases with the voltage V produced by the gain-setting feedback loop. The circuit is capable of four-quadrant multiplication; the waveforms shown correspond to a positive input Y.

If one desires to employ electronic switches capable of switching only between Z or X and zero rather than between positive and negative inputs, one must use a biasing scheme similar to that of Fig. 7-14b.

periodic triangular waveform is biased by the gain-controlling voltage V, so that a polarity-sensing comparator amplifier produces longer or shorter gate pulses, depending on the value of V. Both multiplier circuits shown in Fig. 7-13 are capable of four-quadrant multiplication; the electronic switches used must work with inputs of either polarity. In each case, additional switches may be driven synchronously to produce additional products by Y. The oscillators producing the triggering waveforms can be common to a number of multipliers.

7-11. Self-excited Time-division Multipliers. (a) Basic Four-quadrant Multiplier. The self-excited time-division-multiplier circuits of Fig. 7-14 oscillate of their own accord and do not require external trigger inputs.[37-42] In Fig. 7-14a, an initially positive switch output $E_Z = Z > 0$ combines with the multiplier input voltage Y to produce a positive integrator input current $Y/R_Y + Z/R_Z$ which is integrated downward. When the integrator output reaches the voltage E_{OFF}, the

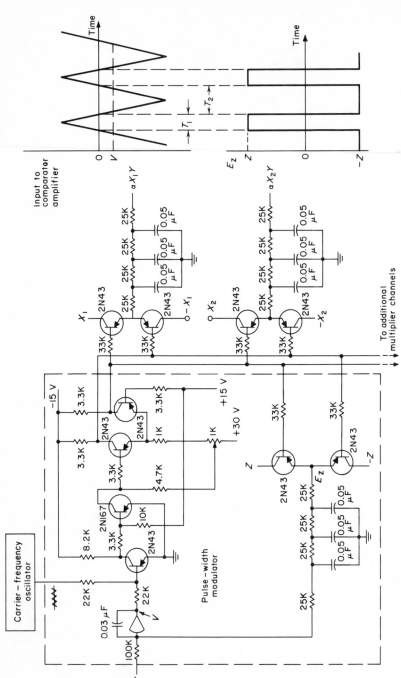

Fig. 7.13b. An externally excited all-solid-state multiplier for use at low frequencies. Instead of biasing a phantastron as in Fig. 7-13a, the gain-setting voltage V biases a periodic triangular or sinusoidal waveform at the input of a comparator amplifier. The comparator controls a set of two-transistor switches; $E_z = Z$ whenever the comparator input is positive. Static accuracy is within 0.2 per cent of half-scale (10 volts) over a 25 deg C temperature range; the pulse repetition rate is 1 Kc. [21,43]

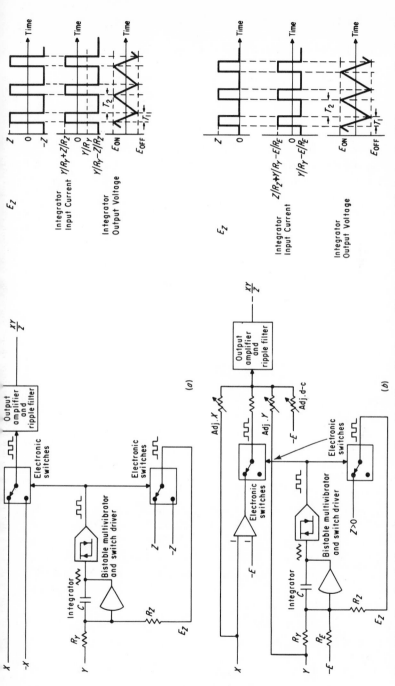

Fig. 7-14. Simplified block diagram of a self-excited time-division multiplier (a), and modified circuit (b) for use with simple single-throw electronic switches capable of passing only positive voltages. Four-quadrant multiplication is obtained through addition of a bias voltage $-E$ to both X and Y and subtraction of the unwanted product terms EX/Z, EY/Z, and E^2/Z in the output amplifier (see also Fig. 7-2a).

271

bistable multivibrator changes state and releases the electronic switches. E_Z is now equal to $-Z$, and the total integrator input current is $Y/R_Y - Z/R_Z$, which must be negative for proper operation, i.e.,

$$\frac{Z}{R_Z} - \frac{Y}{R_Y} > 0 \qquad (7\text{-}7)$$

for all values of Y. The integrator output voltage then increases until it reaches the value E_{ON} required to return the bistable multivibrator to its original state. The process then repeats in a self-oscillatory fashion. It is seen that an increase in the multiplier input voltage Y accelerates the downward integration and slows the upward integration, so that the duty cycle nT_1 decreases.

More specifically, the integrator output voltage in Fig. 7-14a decreases at the rate $-\frac{1}{C}\left(\frac{Z}{R_Z} + \frac{Y}{R_Y}\right)$ and increases at the rate $\frac{1}{C}\left(\frac{Z}{R_Z} - \frac{Y}{R_Y}\right)$, so that

$$T_1 = \frac{(E_{ON} - E_{OFF})C}{Z/R_Z + Y/R_Y} \qquad T_2 = \frac{(E_{ON} - E_{OFF})C}{Z/R_Z - Y/R_Y} \qquad (7\text{-}8)$$

Assuming perfect switching, the average value of the X-switch output equals the desired product

$$\frac{T_1 - T_2}{T_1 + T_2} X = -\frac{R_Z}{R_Y}\frac{XY}{Z} \qquad (7\text{-}9)$$

which is suitably scaled and inverted by the output amplifier to produce XY/Z. The pulse repetition rate is

$$n = \frac{1}{T_1 + T_2} = \frac{Z}{2(E_{ON} - E_{OFF})R_ZC}\left[1 - \left(\frac{R_Z}{R_Y}\frac{Y}{Z}\right)^2\right] \qquad (7\text{-}10)$$

in cycles per second. Note that n decreases in the ratio $1 - (R_Z/R_Y)^2$ to 1 as Y changes from $Y = 0$ to $Y = \pm Z$.

(b) Four-quadrant Operation with Simple Electronic Switches. Figure 7-14b illustrates the operation of a self-excited time-division multiplier designed for operation with less expensive electronic switches. Here each switch can accept only a positive input voltage and turn it on or off (see also Fig. 7-16). To permit four-quadrant multiplication, the circuit of Fig. 7-14b adds bias voltages to both multiplier inputs (see also Figs. 6-14 and 7-2a). In this case,

$$T_1 = \frac{(E_{ON} - E_{OFF})C}{Z/R_Z + Y/R_Y - E/R_E} \qquad T_2 = \frac{(E_{ON} - E_{OFF})C}{E/R_E - Y/R_Y} \qquad (7\text{-}11)$$

where, for proper operation,

$$\frac{Z}{R_Z} + \frac{Y}{R_Y} - \frac{E}{R_E} > 0 \qquad \frac{E}{R_E} - \frac{Y}{R_Y} > 0 \qquad (7\text{-}12)$$

for all values of $Y(Z > 0)$. Assuming perfect switching, the average value of the X-switch output is

$$\frac{T_1}{T_1 + T_2} (E - X) = \frac{R_Z}{Z} \left(\frac{E}{R_E} - \frac{Y}{R_Y} \right) (E - X)$$

$$= \frac{R_Z}{R_Y} \frac{XY}{Z} - \frac{R_Z}{R_E} \frac{E}{Z} X - \frac{R_Z}{R_Y} \frac{E}{Z} Y + \frac{R_Z}{R_E} \frac{E^2}{Z} \quad (7\text{-}13)$$

The unwanted terms are subtracted in the output amplifier, which also scales the output to produce $-(XY/Z)$. The pulse repetition rate is

$$n = \frac{1}{T_1 + T_2} = \frac{E/R_E - Y/R_Y}{(E_{\text{ON}} - E_{\text{OFF}})C} \left[1 - \frac{R_Z}{Z} \left(\frac{E}{R_E} - \frac{Y}{R_Y} \right) \right] \quad (7\text{-}14)$$

in cycles per second. Analogous modified switching schemes also apply to externally excited time-division multipliers.

(c) **A Modified Circuit.** The Telefunken* self-excited time-division multiplier employs an interesting modification of the circuit of Fig. 7-14a

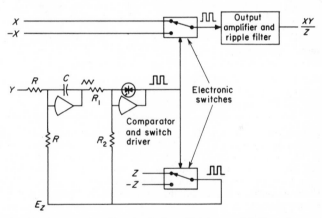

Fig. 7-15. In this improved self-excited time-division multiplier, the operate and release levels of the switch-actuating bistable circuit are proportional to the reference input Z. This reduces the dependence of the pulse repetition rate on Z, so that direct division by a variable input Z becomes practical. (*Telefunken G.m.b.H.*)

to make the pulse repetition rate less dependent on the reference input Z, so that direct division by Z becomes practical.[45,46] The modified circuit is shown in Fig. 7-15. Operation is similar to that in Fig. 7-14a, but the bistable multivibrator is replaced by a simple comparator (nominally without hysteresis), which receives positive feedback proportional to E_Z from the Z switch. The resulting regenerative loop again acts like a bistable multivibrator and changes states whenever the integrator output voltage decreases to $E_{\text{OFF}} = -(R_1/R_2)Z$ or increases to $E_{\text{ON}} = (R_1/R_2)Z$ (see also Sec. 9-5), assuming that any remaining hysteresis in the com-

* Telefunken G.m.b.H., Konstanz, West Germany.

parator circuit is negligible. The expression (9), which determines the multiplier output for ideal switching, remains unchanged. The pulse repetition rate becomes

$$n = \frac{Z}{2(E_{\text{ON}} - E_{\text{OFF}})R_Z C}\left[1 - \left(\frac{R_Z}{R_Y}\frac{Y}{Z}\right)^2\right]$$

$$= \frac{1}{4R_Z C}\frac{R_2}{R_1}\left[1 - \left(\frac{R_Z}{R_Y}\frac{Y}{Z}\right)^2\right] \quad (7\text{-}15)$$

which is seen to depend much less on the reference input Z than the repetition rate (10) for the circuit of Fig. 7-14a.

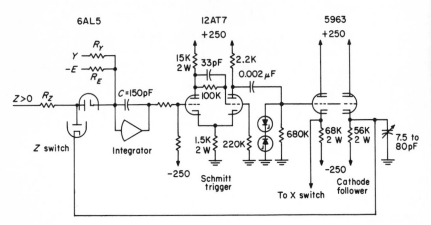

FIG. 7-16. Inexpensive Schmitt trigger/cathode follower driving two simple diode switches in the arrangement of Fig. 7-14b. R_Z is here situated between reference input and switch. $R_E = 2R_Y = 4R_Z = 400K$ yields equal repetition rates (14), about 55 Kc for $Y = -100$ volts and $Y = 100$ volts; $n \approx 40$ Kc for $Y = 0$. Static accuracy and 8-hr drift are each within 0.2 per cent of half-scale (± 100 volts), and phase shift is within 0.75 deg at 100 cps (similar to Beckman/Berkeley Type 1156 electronic multiplier).

As an example, let $R_Y = 2R_Z = 200K$, $C = 1,000\,\text{pF}$, and $Y = 10$ volts. Then in Fig. 7-14a with, say, $E_{\text{ON}} - E_{\text{OFF}} = 25$ volts, a decrease from $Z = 100$ volts to $Z = 10$ volts reduces n from about 20 Kc to 1.5 Kc. But in Fig. 7-15 with $R_2/R_1 = 8$, a similar decrease in Z reduces n from about 20 Kc to only 15 Kc. As a result, the Telefunken circuit, which provides a kind of automatic gain control for the gain-setting feedback loop, permits direct division by a variable input Z over a wide range of values, a significant advantage (see also Sec. 7-23).

7-12. Electronic Switching Circuits (see also Sec. 6-8). Figure 7-16 shows a simple one-throw electronic switch and a bistable Schmitt-trigger circuit employed in a typical inexpensive electronic multiplier using the arrangement of Fig. 7-14b. The design of Schmitt triggers is treated in detail in refs. 33 and 36. The design will be a compromise between the gate-pulse amplitude needed for good switching (about 10 volts for the switch shown), the rise and fall times of the switching waveform, and the stability of the switching voltages E_{OFF} and E_{ON}, which must be independent of the input-voltage slope.   This compromise is

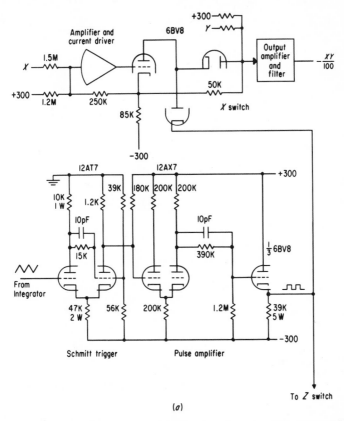

(a)

FIG. 7-17a. Current-driven X switch and Schmitt trigger/amplifier/cathode follower used in the Donner Type 3735 electronic multiplier.   The Z switch, which has a constant input voltage, is not provided with a current-driving amplifier.   Since the switches pass only *negative* inputs, the multiplier uses the arrangement of Fig. 7-14b with reversed reference and bias voltages (*Systron-Donner Corp.*; static accuracy within 0.1 per cent of half-scale, dynamic errors below 2 per cent of half-scale, and phase shift below 1 deg at 100 cps).

made easier by the addition of an amplifier stage following the Schmitt trigger (Fig. 7-17a).

The vacuum-diode switches in Figs. 7-16 and 7-17 have appreciable forward resistances (of the order of 500 ohms) which change slightly with the switch-input voltage and also with tube age; similar effects are encountered in triode switches.   To minimize the effect of the forward-resistance variation with the multiplier input X, the X switch in Fig.

7-17a is driven by a current source, while the alternative circuit of Fig. 7-17b reduces the forward resistance of a triode switch by enclosing it in a voltage-feedback loop.

Replacement of vacuum diode or triode switches by solid-state-diode or transistor switches reduces the forward resistance by an order of magnitude, but the nonlinear junction capacitances will cause small changes in switching times with the switch current, and hence with the input voltage. This effect can become noticeable at pulse repetition rates above

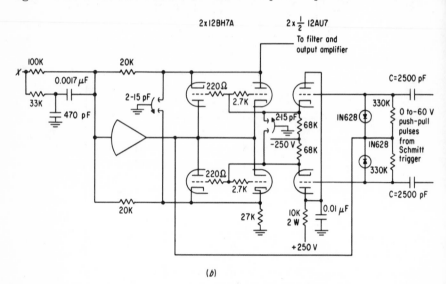

(b)

Fig. 7-17b. Voltage feedback minimizes forward-resistance effects in the X switch of the Beckman/Berkeley Type 1159 multiplier. The Z switch is, again, left uncompensated. Short-term static accuracy is within 0.04 per cent of half-scale; total dynamic error is below 0.4 per cent at 30 cps, and below 3 per cent at 100 cps. In the faster but less accurate 1159A model, substitution of a 12AU7 for the 12BH7A and $C = 220$ pF permits operation at pulse rates greater than 100 Kc. 1159A static errors are within 0.2 per cent of half-scale, dynamic errors within 0.4 per cent at 100 cps and below 6 per cent at 1 Kc.

10 Kc. Solid-state switching devices also do away with the need for filament-voltage regulation and with heater-to-cathode leakage and capacitance in vacuum-tube switches. Good circuit layout will keep solid-state diodes and transistors at reasonably constant temperatures.

The electronic switch of Fig. 7-18a employs current-driven triode switches with special provisions for balancing any effects of asymmetry in the switching tubes.[41] Since any stray capacitance between the switch-tube cathodes and ground shunts the high-impedance current generator, any difference in the switch-tube plate resistances will cause a small unbalance of the output current in spite of the current-driving scheme. To reduce this unbalance automatically, the a-c amplifier in Fig. 7-18 senses the rectangular-pulse unbalance voltage on the switch-tube cathode and controls a diode-bridge limiter to set both positive and negative gate-pulse excursions on each switch tube so as to minimize the unbalance. Note that the current-driving amplifier used in this circuit must still have some gain at the multiplier repetition-rate frequency. Figure 7-19 shows an accurate self-excited time-division multiplier employing voltage feedback to minimize forward-resistance effects in both electronic switches.[2]

Simple transistor SPDT switches of the type shown in Fig. 7-13b do not permit accurate multiplication with repetition rates much above 1Kc,

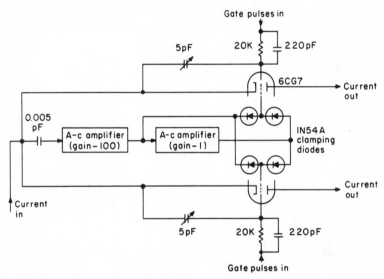

FIG. 7-18. Current-driven triode switch with dynamic compensation for tube asymmetry. (*RCA Laboratories Division.*)

because the switch timing of the transistor X switch will depend slightly on the input voltage X (see also Sec. 6-11c). References 45 and 46 describe the design of an improved transformer-driven four-transistor switch which permits compensation of this effect (Fig. 7-20); since all four transistors of the new switch are off in the absence of switching pulses, a self-excited time-division multiplier using this switch must be provided with starting pulses to initiate operation.

7-13. Static vs. Dynamic Accuracy in Multipliers Employing Ripple Filters. Ripple-filter Design. The design of every multiplier employing a high-frequency (1 Kc to 2 Mc) carrier involves an essential conflict between static multiplication accuracy, bandwidth, and carrier-ripple suppression. This problem, discussed here for time-division multipliers, is common to all modulation-type multipliers and applies also to

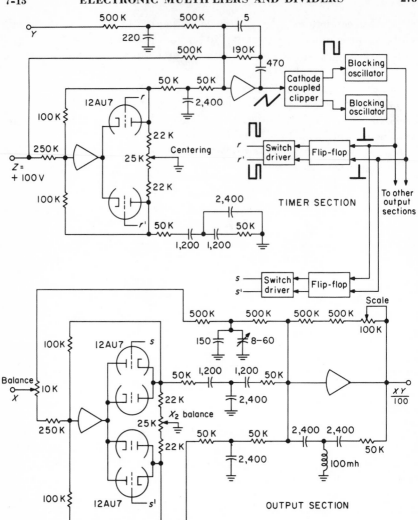

FIG. 7-19. Electronic multiplier circuit employing feedback-compensated X and Z switches and a blocking-oscillator/flip-flop bistable circuit capable of driving slave switches producing up to five additional products by Y. Inverse switch-noise injection reduces the output filtering required (Goodyear Aircraft Corporation circuit from ref. 2; static accuracy within 0.04 per cent of half-scale, phase shift within 0.5 deg. at 100 cps).

diode quarter-square multipliers with dither (Sec. 7-15) and to triangle-averaging multipliers (Sec. 7-16).

Accurate multiplication requires accurate resistance networks, possibly mounted in common oil baths to maintain resistance ratios with temperature changes; low-drift chopper-stabilized operational amplifiers with high loop gains (see also Sec. 7-21); and careful circuit layout and shield-

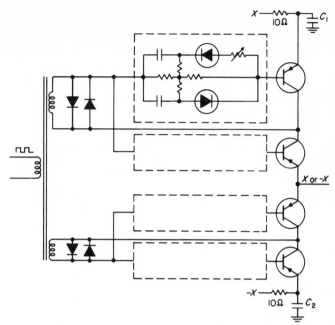

Fɪɢ. 7-20. Improved transistor switch used in the Telefunken circuit of Fig. 7-15 to yield static accuracy within 0.01 per cent of half-scale (± 10 volts). The zero error ($X = Y = 0$) is within 0.002 per cent of half-scale over a temperature variation of 20 deg C. Dynamic errors are below 0.1 per cent of half-scale at 10 cps. Note the separate turn-on-time adjustments. C_1, C_2 are small capacitors intended to bypass switching spikes around the input-voltage sources.[45,46]

ing to avoid crosstalk effects (noise and carrier beats) where several multipliers are mounted in close proximity to each other. Assuming also sufficient gain in the gain-setting loop, the remaining *static errors* in time-division multipliers will be due to

1. *Imperfect switch timing*, i.e., asynchronous operation of the Z and X switches
2. *D-c offset variations* due to changing control-voltage leakage or rectified switching spikes in electronic switches (see also Secs. 6-10 and 6-11)
3. *Variations of switch timing, forward resistance, or back resistance* with the multiplier input voltage X or with tube aging.

All these errors decrease with the ratio of the switching time to the repetition period,[40] so that lower carrier frequencies tend to yield improved static accuracy. But the frequency response of a time-division multiplier, like that of most modulation-type multipliers, is essentially that of the ripple filter needed to remove carrier-frequency components from the multiplier output, so that a compromise between static and dynamic accuracy must be made.

Phase shift and attenuation due to the ripple filter deteriorate multiplication accuracy at frequencies much lower than one-half the carrier frequency or repetition rate which, in principle, constitutes an upper frequency limit because of the sampled-data nature of the gain-setting loop. While moderate carrier-frequency noise is not usually objectionable at the input of integrators, summers, or recording devices, ripple voltages can be rectified by other multipliers or by function generators to cause low-frequency errors. Conventional low-pass ripple filters designed

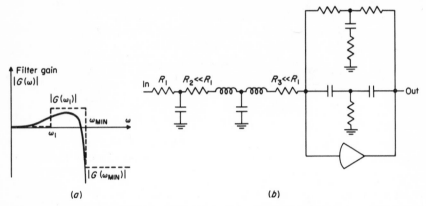

FIG. 7-21. Frequency relationships for ripple-filter design (a), and filter design for the self-excited time-division multiplier of Fig. 7-15 (b) (based on ref. 45).

to reduce rms ripple below an acceptable 0.1 per cent of full scale would cause 3 to 5 deg phase shift at least two decades below the carrier frequency.

Figure 7-21a illustrates the frequency relations determining ripplefilter design. The lowest carrier circular frequency $2\pi n$ cannot be higher than some value ω_{MIN} determined by the worst-case static errors obtained with a given switching circuit. If the amplitude response $|G(\omega)|$ of the ripple filter could have the ideal shape indicated in the dash line of Fig. 7-21a, Bode's phase/amplitude relation for minimal-phase networks[45-47] indicates that the phase shift $\varphi(\omega)$ at the computing frequency $\omega/2\pi$ cannot be less than

$$\varphi(\omega) = \frac{2\omega}{\pi} \int_0^\infty \frac{\log_e |G(\omega)|}{\omega^2} \, d\omega$$

$$= \frac{2\omega}{\pi} \left[\frac{1}{\omega_{MIN}} \log_e |G(\omega_{MIN})| - \left(\frac{1}{\omega_1} - \frac{1}{\omega_{MIN}} \right) \log_e |G(\omega_1)| \right] \quad (7\text{-}16)$$

where $|G(\omega_{MIN})|$ is the required ripple attenuation, and $|G(\omega_1)|$ is introduced to reduce the low-frequency phase shift (16) at the expense of an amplitude error at computing frequencies above $\omega_1/2\pi$. This amplitude error manifests itself, in particular, as overshoot and/or ringing in the multiplier step-input response. Real filters can only approximate the ideal filter characteristic (dash line in Fig. 7-21a) in the manner shown by the solid line, so that amplitude errors start at lower computing frequencies. Practical filter designs will compromise between low phase shift and low overshoot, using the idealized relation (16) as a rough planning guide.

Figure 7-21b shows a practical filter design.[45] The operational-amplifier circuits used simplify the design by reducing interaction between the different filter sections. Fixed-carrier-frequency multipliers, such as externally excited time-division multipliers, can use band-suppression sections sharply tuned to the carrier frequency and its harmonics. This permits somewhat better ripple filtering than is possible for self-excited time-division multipliers, whose repetition rate varies by 15 to 30 per cent as Y changes. Figure 7-21b shows a phase-compensating lead network in the output-amplifier feedback circuit, but it may be preferable to apply lead terms as a sort of high-frequency preemphasis at the multiplier inputs, so that the lead terms cannot enhance the output ripple.[2] Typical high-quality filter designs yield rms output ripple less than 0.1 per cent of half-scale, and about 0.2 deg phase shift at $\omega_{MIN}/100$; the price paid for such low phase shift is, unfortunately, a step-function overshoot as large as 20 to 30 per cent.

QUARTER-SQUARE MULTIPLIERS AND TRIANGLE-AVERAGING MULTIPLIERS

7-14. Electronic Quarter-square Multipliers. Electronic quarter-square multipliers employ electronic function generators and summing amplifiers to implement the relation

$$XY = \tfrac{1}{4}[(X + Y)^2 - (X - Y)^2] \tag{7-17}$$

Unlike modulation-type multipliers, most electronic quarter-square multipliers do not require output filters with their adverse effects on the multiplication bandwidth.

Electronic squaring circuits have been based on transfer characteristics of vacuum diodes and triodes,[2] and of special vacuum tubes. The Raytheon QK 329 electron-beam squaring tube produces a collector current proportional to the square of an input voltage X used to deflect a shaped electron beam by a parabola-shaped mask: this tube has been used for rough multiplication.[48,49] Such circuits yield static accuracies within about 2 per cent of half-scale and useful multiplication bandwidths up to at least 100 Kc, but multipliers of this type require frequent readjustments. Most practical electronic quarter-square multipliers employ either *temperature-compensated varistor-resistor networks* (Sec. 6-14)[50-54] or *special diode function generators* (Fig. 7-22).[55-60]

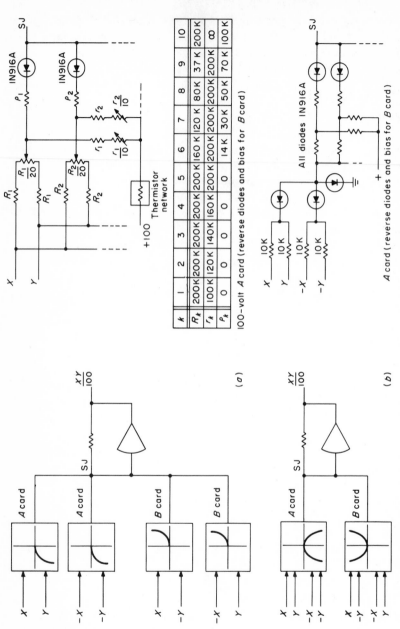

FIG. 7-22a, b. A four-card diode quarter-square multiplier (a), and a two-card multiplier incorporating absolute-value circuits (b). Such multipliers yield static accuracies within 0.1 per cent of half-scale, and phase shift below 2 deg at 1 Kc. Zero-input errors are within ±30 mV. −X and −Y are often available from the computer setup, or external phase inverters are used.

k	1	2	3	4	5	6	7	8	9	10
R_k	200K	200K	200K	200K	200K	160 K	120 K	80K	37 K	200K
r_k	100K	120K	140K	160K	200K	200K	200K	200K	200K	∞
p_k	0	0	0	0	0	14K	30K	50K	70 K	100K

100-volt A card (reverse diodes and bias for B card)

(a)

A card (reverse diodes and bias for B card)

(b)

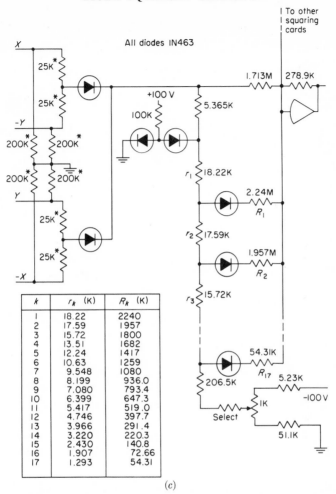

k	r_k (K)	R_k (K)
1	18.22	2240
2	17.59	1957
3	15.72	1800
4	13.51	1682
5	12.24	1417
6	10.63	1259
7	9.548	1080
8	8.199	936.0
9	7.080	793.4
10	6.399	647.3
11	5.417	519.0
12	4.746	397.7
13	3.966	291.4
14	3.220	220.3
15	2.430	140.8
16	1.907	72.66
17	1.293	54.31

(c)

FIG. 7-22c. Diode network (*B* card) with absolute-value circuit (reverse diodes and bias for *A* card). Diodes are selected for low leakage (1 nA at −36 volts); absolute-value diodes are matched within 1 mV at 0.75 mA. 0.5 per cent deposited-carbon resistors are used, and starred resistors are matched within 0.01 per cent. Multiplier short-term static accuracy is within 0.15 per cent of the 100-volt half-scale. (*Systron-Donner Corporation.*)

7-15. Diode Squaring Circuits (see also Sec. 6-13). Diode function generators approximate the desired parabolic transfer characteristic by straight-line-segment approximations slightly improved by natural rounding at the breakpoints. Since $dx^2 = 2x\,dx$, uniform breakpoint spacing conveniently permits us to use identical slope increments and, hence, identical diode-limiter channels on each side of zero. For uniform breakpoint spacing, polygonal-approximation errors can be kept within ϵ per cent of half-scale with $10/\sqrt{\epsilon}$ segments;[56,77] proper adjustment will yield equal positive and negative error peaks for all segments (Fig. 7-23). Nonuniform breakpoint spacing, discussed in refs. 56 and 77 to 79, will not reduce the required number of diode channels appreciably; it may, however, be worthwhile to add two extra breakpoints near zero in order to minimize zero-input errors.

Since an increase in the number of diodes for improved static accuracy also tends to accumulate the effects of diode capacitances and breakpoint drift, 10- to 150-Kc triangular or sinusoidal interpolation dither (Sec. 6-13a) is employed in some diode quarter-square multipliers to reduce static errors. Unfortunately, the dither voltage must be removed from the multiplier output by means of a ripple filter, which, again, tends to deteriorate the multiplication bandwidth.

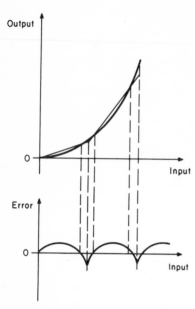

Figure 7-22 shows two diode quarter-square multipliers capable of high accuracy. Conventional series-limiter channels are used. Diode drift does not affect the zero error, since no series diodes conduct for $X = Y = 0$. Although input voltages $-X$, $-Y$ as well as X, Y are required because of the nonmonotonic nature of the square function, amplifier connections are simple; the amplifiers need not be committed permanently to the multiplier. The absolute-value circuits used in Fig. 7-22b reduce cost and simplify adjustment. The potential slight accuracy advantage of Fig. 7-22a would probably be noticeable only immediately after careful adjustment. Both circuits can yield static errors between 0.05 and 0.4 per cent of half-scale, depending on the number of diodes used. If no dither is employed, dynamic error is within 2 per cent of half-scale up to between 500 and 1,000 cps, with 10 to 20 mV peak-to-peak output noise, mostly due to line-frequency pickup. The fixed-function diode networks used in quarter-square multipliers can be temperature-compensated by temperature-sensitive resistors or diodes and show little drift with aging. If desired, one can periodically recalibrate each diode

FIG. 7-23. Polygonal approximation of the square function. We adjust the square-law diode function generator with the aid of a digital voltmeter, a comparison voltage divider, or (preferably) by the method of Fig. 6-29. Slopes and/or breakpoints are set so as to make positive and negative error peaks equal; the error peaks nearest zero input can be made somewhat smaller in order to minimize zero-input errors.

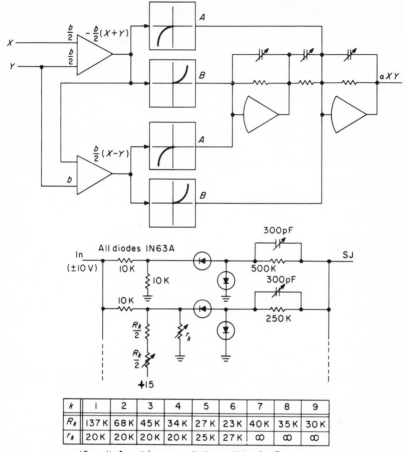

k	1	2	3	4	5	6	7	8	9
R_k	137 K	68 K	45 K	34 K	27 K	23 K	40 K	35 K	30 K
r_k	20 K	20 K	20 K	20 K	25 K	27 K	∞	∞	∞

10–volt A card (reverse diodes and bias for B card)

FIG. 7-24. This four-card multiplier drives all diode networks from low-impedance sources to obtain wideband operation. Note that the slope adjustments in the ASTRAC I card shown do not affect breakpoints. The card operates with ±10-volt input and is best suited for ±10-volt transistor computers. Since two low-impedance ±100-volt cards would, however, draw in excess of 150 mA input current, such ±10-volt multipliers have been used in several ±50-volt and ±100-volt repetitive analog computers. Static accuracy is 0.5 to 1 per cent of half-scale, and phase shift is below 1 deg at 10 Kc with suitable wideband amplifiers.

squaring card by comparing the output voltage at each breakpoint with the voltage from a precision attenuator furnished with the multiplier package.

If diode quarter-square multipliers are to work at frequencies in excess of about 2 Kc, the effects of diode capacitance make it necessary to employ limiter channels with combined shunt and series switching (Sec. 6-5) and to reduce diode-network impedances. Figure 7-24 shows a somewhat expensive four-card/four-amplifier multiplier designed for wideband operation. Such multipliers were first designed at MIT[59] and served in the GPS and ASTRAC I repetitive analog computers. Amplifiers are permanently committed to each multiplier. For low-voltage operation, one can reduce the diode-network impedances still further so as to extend the multiplier bandwidth by a factor of 10 to 80.[50,60,76]

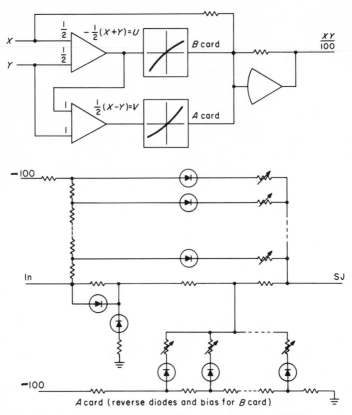

FIG. 7-25. A Reeves-type diode quarter-square multiplier.

Figure 7-25 illustrates a different diode-multiplier design developed by H. Meissinger for the Reeves Instrument Co.[75] and also used by Computer Systems, Inc., and Comcor, Inc. Only three amplifiers are required for four-quadrant multiplication. The circuit implements the relation

$$\frac{XY}{100} = F_1\left(\frac{Y-X}{2}\right) + F_2\left(-\frac{X+Y}{2}\right) - 3X \qquad (7\text{-}17a)$$

where $\qquad F_1(U) \equiv -3U - \dfrac{U^2}{100} \qquad F_2(V) \equiv -3V + \dfrac{V^2}{100} \qquad (7\text{-}17b)$

are seen to be *monotonic* functions. Note how $F_1(U)$ and $F_2(V)$ are gener-

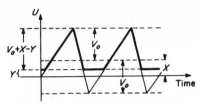

FIG. 7-26. Principle of triangle-averaging multiplication: the running average of the clipped triangular waveform shown in solid lines is $(1/4V_0)(V_0 + X - Y)^2 + Y$.

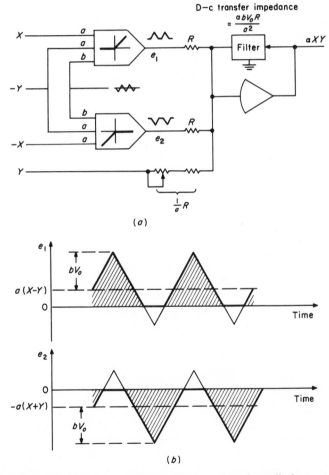

(a)

(b)

FIG. 7-27. The basic triangle-averaging multiplier (a) produces limiter-output waveforms (b) whose running averages are added together with aY to produce the desired output

$$-\frac{\alpha b V_0}{a^2} \left\{ \frac{1}{4bV_0} [bV_0 + a(X - Y)]^2 - \frac{1}{4bV_0} [bV_0 + a(X + Y)]^2 + aY \right\} = \alpha XY$$

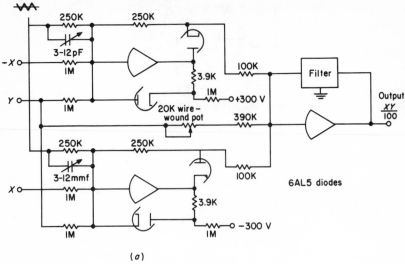

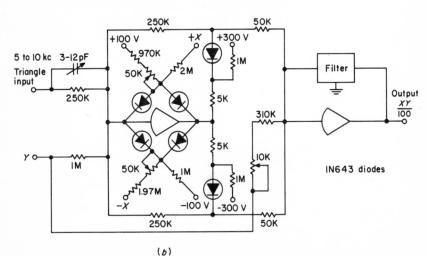

Fig. 7-28. Two triangle-averaging multipliers designed to employ the precision-limiter circuits of Figs. 9-1 and 9-5 with a carrier frequency of 5 to 10 Kc. Static accuracies better than 0.2 per cent of half-scale (± 100 volts) have been obtained. Limiter slopes and summing networks are carefully scaled so that the triangular waveform is clipped for all values of X, Y without overloading the limiter amplifiers.[65]

ated by series-limiter circuits on one side of zero, and by shunt-limiter circuits on the other side of zero, so that, again, no diode conducts for $X = 0$, $Y = 0$, and a low zero-input error is assured. Accuracy and bandwidth are comparable with those of conventional two- and four-card diode quarter-square multipliers.   The circuit has been used without and with dither, and was also implemented with varistor function-generator networks (Sec. 6-14).[50–54,77]   Meissinger's diode circuit is, unfortunately, less useful for operation much above 2 Kc, since it requires separate series and shunt limiters to obtain low zero-input error.

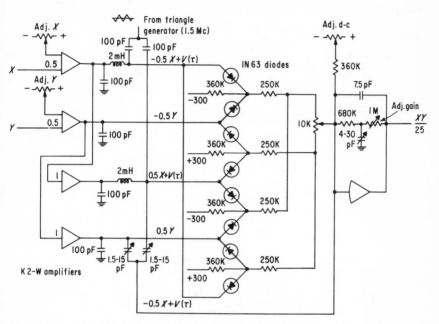

Fig. 7-29a.   The MU/DV multiplier implements the relation

$$\frac{\alpha}{4V_0}\left[\left(V_0 + \frac{X+Y}{2}\right)^2 + \left(V_0 - \frac{X+Y}{2}\right)^2 \right.$$
$$\left. - \left(V_0 + \frac{X-Y}{2}\right)^2 - \left(V_0 - \frac{X-Y}{2}\right)^2\right] = \frac{\alpha}{2V_0}XY$$

Static accuracy is within 2 per cent of half-scale (± 50 volts), with phase shift below 5 deg at 2 Kc.   An MU/DV chassis combines two multipliers with division circuits of the type illustrated in Fig. 7-36.   The G. A. Philbrick Researches Type MU/DV and K5-M triangle-averaging multipliers use relatively high carrier frequencies to yield excellent frequency response at the expense of circuit complexity.   Note that no amplifier needs to pass the carrier frequency.

Netter[74] suggests a reduction of the number of diodes required for a given polygonal square-law approximation with the aid of the relation

$$x^2 = \tfrac{1}{4}(u^2 + 2u + 1) \quad \text{with} \quad u = 2|x| - 1 \tag{7-18}$$

Suitably chosen n-breakpoint approximations to u^2 (or $n/2$-breakpoint approximations to $|u|^2$) for $-1 \le u \le 1$ will yield $2n$-breakpoint approximations to x^2 ($-1 \le x \le 1$). Note also that x^2 is a monotonic function of u.   At least in principle, the relation (18) can be applied recursively to "fold" n^2 in turn, etc.

7-16. Triangle-averaging Multipliers.[61–65]   *Triangle-averaging multipliers (triangle-integration multipliers, amplitude-selection multipliers)* are quarter-square multipliers based on the fact that a biased and clipped triangular waveform has a d-c component proportional to the square of the bias voltage (Fig. 7-26). In Fig. 7-27a, triangular waveforms $bV(t)$ respectively biased by $a(X - Y)$ and $-a(X + Y)$ are clipped at zero to

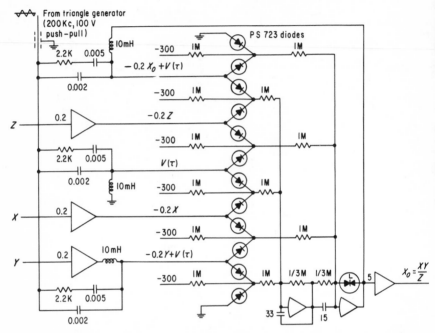

Fig. 7-29b. The K5-M multiplier-divider uses a permanently connected division circuit to produce the output XY/Z and to cancel the effect of the triangle amplitude V_0 on the output. Static accuracy is within 0.1 per cent of half-scale (± 50 volts), with phase shift below 0.5 deg at 500 cps and 10 deg at 1 Kc. SK5-M is a similar ± 100v multiplier.

produce the limiter-output voltages $e_1(\tau)$, $e_2(\tau)$ shown in Fig. 7-27b. The low-pass output-amplifier circuit averages the shaded triangle portions and adds aY to produce the desired output

$$-\frac{\alpha b V_0}{a^2}\left\{\frac{1}{4bV_0}[bV_0 + a(X - Y)]^2\right.$$
$$\left.- \frac{1}{4bV_0}[bV_0 + a(X + Y)]^2 + aY\right\} = \alpha XY \quad (7\text{-}19)$$

Note that the triangle amplitude V_0 must be accurately constant. As in the case of modulation-type multipliers, the bandwidth of a triangle-

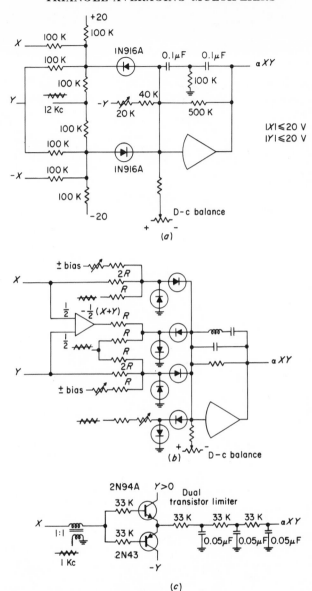

Fig. 7-30. These low-cost triangle-averaging multipliers permit static accuracies within 0.3 to 1 per cent of half-scale for 1- to 2-Kc carrier frequencies. Frequency response depends on the filter used in each case. In Fig. 7-30b (based on ref. 63), the grounded "catching diodes" are intended to minimize interaction between the input voltages while the limiter diodes are off. Figure 7-30c is adapted from ref. 6.

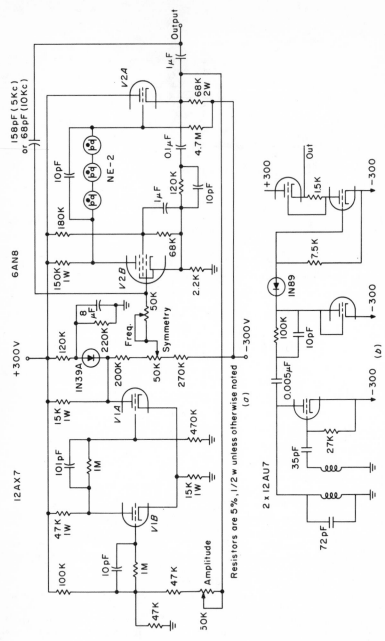

Fig. 7-31. An accurate 5- to 10-Kc triangle generator (a)[65] and a 1.5-Mc triangle generator (b). (G. A. Philbrick Researches.)

averaging multiplier is essentially that of the averaging filter; since lower carrier frequencies permit more accurate clipping, each design requires, again, a compromise between static and dynamic accuracy (Sec. 7-13).

Many different triangle-averaging multipliers have been designed. Good accuracy can be obtained at the expense of bandwidth through the use of precision limiters (Sec. 9-2) at relatively low carrier frequencies (Fig. 7-28).[65] To cancel errors due to imperfect clipping and triangle generation at higher carrier frequencies, one may average more than two clipped triangular waveforms to obtain a sort of push-pull operation (Fig. 7-29). Several triangle-integration multipliers can share a single triangle generator; but the more accurate four-quadrant multipliers of this type (Figs. 7-28 and 7-29b) tend to use more amplifiers and may also be harder to adjust than time-division multipliers of comparable performance. As a result, the most interesting triangle-averaging multipliers are, perhaps, those designed for medium to low accuracy at very low cost (Fig. 7-30); note the extraordinary simplicity of these circuits. Figure 7-31 shows practical triangle-generator circuits for low and high carrier frequencies.

OTHER ELECTRONIC MULTIPLICATION CIRCUITS

7-17. Logarithmic Multipliers.[2,6,7,66] Logarithmic multipliers implement the relation

$$\log (XY) = \log X + \log Y \qquad (7\text{-}20a)$$

for positive X, Y (one-quadrant multiplication). Logarithm and anti-logarithm functions have been generated with the aid of vacuum-diode characteristics[66] and diode function generators (Fig. 7-32). Logarithmic multipliers are employed in some special-purpose computers; note that

$$\log X^\alpha Y^\beta = \alpha \log X + \beta \log Y \qquad (7\text{-}20b)$$

is as easily implemented as (20a).

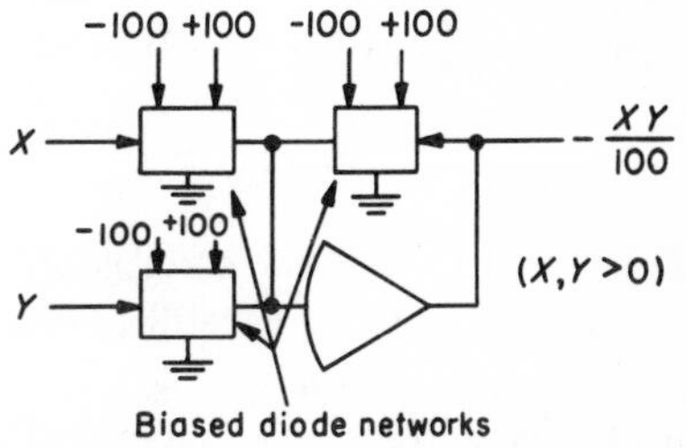

Fig. 7-32. A simple one-quadrant logarithmic multiplier using three similar shunt-diode networks.

7-18. Electron-beam Multipliers. Figure 7-33 illustrates the operation of a *crossed-fields electron-beam multiplier*.[67] An ordinary cathode-ray tube with electrostatic deflection plates and a short-persistence screen is fitted with an axial coil wound around the tube near the horizontal deflection plates. The vertical deflection plates give the beam a *vertical* velocity component proportional to the input voltage Y. As a result, the axial magnetic field due to the current $i_X = aX$ in the coil exerts a *horizontal* deflection force proportional to the product XY. Any horizontal deflection due to this force is sensed by a pair of photocells facing the cathode-ray-tube screen and is fed back to the horizontal plates so as to minimize the horizontal deflection.   If the gain of the feedback loop comprising the cathode-ray tube, the photocells, and the horizontal deflection amplifier is sufficiently large, the horizontal deflection of the electron beam will be kept very small, and the horizontal forces

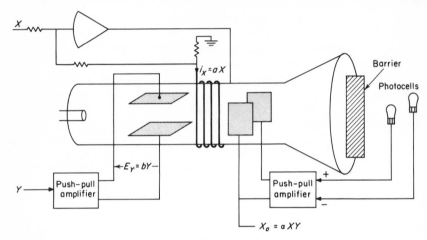

Fig. 7-33. Crossed-fields electron-beam multiplier.

acting on the beam balance; the resulting horizontal deflection voltage must then be proportional to the desired product XY.   The performance equation of a carefully adjusted unit was found to be

$$X_o = (\text{const})(i_X E_Y + 0.015 i_X + 0.009 E_Y^2 + 0.0005) \qquad (7\text{-}21)$$

It is believed that the error could be further reduced through better magnetic shielding and careful positioning of photocells and barrier.[67]

If the connections in Fig. 7-33 are changed so that the input voltage bY is applied across the *horizontal* deflection plates while the amplifier output is applied across the *vertical* plates, then the output voltage is proportional to the quotient Y/X.   The crossed-fields electron-beam multiplier is, thus, useful for division as well as multiplication.

To avoid bandwidth limitations due to the axial deflection coil in Fig. 7-33, the *hyperbolic-field electron-beam multiplier*[68,69] replaces the axial coil by four electrostatic deflection plates bent into hyperbolic-cylinder shape; alternate plates are charged with voltages kX and $-kX$ (Fig. 7-34a).   The resulting electric forces on the electron beam cancel when the beam is centered ($Y = 0$), but any vertical deflection ($Y \neq 0$) produces a corresponding horizontal deflection approximately proportional to the desired product XY. This deflection is then again nulled by the horizontal deflection plates, as in Fig. 7-33.

A third type of electron-beam multiplier[70] employs ordinary horizontal and vertical deflection plates to deflect an intentionally defocused electron beam of circular cross section. The beam center is given a horizontal displacement αX and a vertical displacement βY, and currents from the four quadrants of a special collector plate are combined algebraically to produce an output voltage proportional to the desired product XY (Fig. 7-34b).

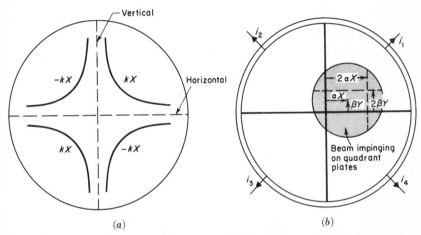

(a) (b)

FIG. 7-34a. Hyperbolic-cylinder-shaped deflection plates used for electron-beam multiplication. The horizontal force on the electron beam is proportional to the product of the vertical deflection cY and the voltage kX on the hyperbolic plates.
FIG. 7-34b. Circular electron beam and quadrant collector plates used for electron-beam multiplication. Assuming uniform beam density, the currents i_1, i_2, i_3, i_4 from the four collector quadrants are proportional to the four shaded portions of the circular beam cross section. If the horizontal and vertical beam-center displacements are respectively proportional to X and Y, then the sum $i_1 + i_3 - i_2 - i_4$ is proportional to the product XY, since all contributions outside the rectangle with sides $2\alpha X$, $2\beta Y$ cancel.

Electron-beam multipliers are not very accurate, but they excited much early interest because of their wide bandwidth, which makes them suitable for fast (repetitive) analog computers. Useful output can be obtained with frequencies as high as 100 to 200 Kc on electrostatic-deflection inputs, and with up to 5 Kc on the deflection-coil input in the case of the crossed-fields multiplier. The crossed-fields multiplier and the hyperbolic-field multiplier produce static errors of 1 to 2 per cent of half-scale. The four-quadrant multiplier can multiply only within about 4 per cent of half-scale because of beam nonuniformity. All electron-beam multipliers are sensitive to stray magnetic fields. Considering the nuisance and cost of special cathode-ray tubes and power supplies as well as accuracy, the writers prefer suitably designed quarter-square multipliers to electron-beam multipliers.

7-19. Generation of Products as Functions of Two Variables. All two-variable function generators capable of generating $F(XY) = \alpha XY$ with the correct sign can be used for analog multiplication. In particular, comparator/switch function generators and cathode-ray-type two-variable function generators (Secs. 6-18 and 6-19) can serve as multipliers.

ELECTRONIC MULTIPLIERS: GENERAL DESIGN CONSIDERATIONS, TESTING, AND DIVISION CIRCUITS

7-20. Multiplier Adjustment and Testing. The static multiplication error of an analog multiplier can be arbitrarily written in the form

$$e(X,Y) = X_o - \alpha XY = e_o + e_X X + e_Y Y + e_{XY}(X,Y)XY \quad (7\text{-}22)$$

where αXY is the desired multiplier output voltage, and e_o, e_X, e_Y are approximately constant for small X, Y. The following adjustment procedure will reduce the first three static-error terms on the right of Eq. (22):

1. With $X = Y = 0$, change e_o by adding a d-c voltage to the multiplier output until $X_o = e_o = 0$. This adjustment minimizes the *static zero error*.
2. With $Y = 0$, $X = X_{max}$ (100 volts, say), change e_X by adding a voltage proportional to X to the multiplier output until $X_o = e_X X_{max} = 0$.
3. With $X = 0$, $Y = Y_{max}$, change e_Y by adding a voltage proportional to Y to the multiplier output until $X_o = e_Y Y_{max} = 0$.
4. With $X = X_{max}$, $Y = Y_{max}$, adjust the actual multiplier gain until $e(X_{max}, Y_{max}) - \alpha XY = e_r(X_{max}, Y_{max}) = 0$.

These adjustments may interact slightly and should be repeated until no further change is noted. Since e_X and e_Y may depend somewhat on X and Y, respectively, it may be possible to reduce static errors by a compromise between the above adjustments and similar adjustments with $X = -X_{max}$ and/or $Y = -Y_{max}$. Note the readjustment of the static zero error (step 1), since errors near $X = 0$, $Y = 0$ will cause large absolute percentage errors.

Figure 7-35 shows a practical switching circuit designed to simplify the adjustment procedure. Such a calibration circuit can be shared by several multiplier channels. In most of the electronic-multiplier types discussed, the d-c, X, and Y adjustments are simply trimming resistors in the output summing network needed to obtain four-quadrant multiplication (Figs. 7-14b and 7-28b).

A possibly better, if slightly more complex, method for testing and calibrating analog multipliers is shown in Fig. 7-36. Here the input voltage Y is set to $Y = -1/\alpha$, while a triangular voltage waveform sweeps the other input X through its full range.   The error voltage

$$X_o + X = X_o - \alpha X Y$$

is slightly filtered to remove high-frequency noise and/or ripple, amplified, and continuously displayed on an oscilloscope or recording device.   With

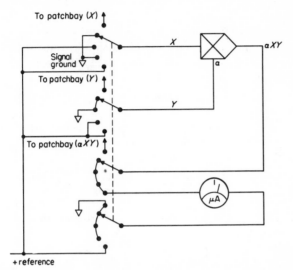

Fɪɢ. 7-35. A multiplier calibration circuit.   Such a circuit can be shared by four to eight multiplier channels.

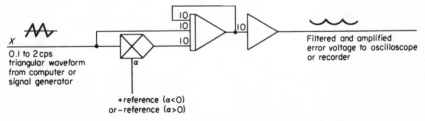

Fɪɢ. 7-36. Triangle-input circuit for multiplier testing and adjustment.

a low-frequency triangular waveform (0.1 to 2 cps), static-error adjustments are readily made by reference to the output display.   The roles of the two inputs can be interchanged.   Dynamic errors are checked with the same computer setup with higher input frequencies.   In multipurpose computers, the triangular waveform is easily generated by the computer itself (Sec. 9-5).   The entire test setup is often included in prewired test boards for electronic analog computers (Sec. 11-5).

  Small-signal amplitude and phase response of a multiplier can be measured in the manner of Sec. 4-21 with, say, $X = 10$, $Y = 10 \cos \omega\tau$.

The maximum of the *static residual multiplication error* $e_r(X,Y)XY$ remaining after careful adjustment is the static error quoted in most manufacturers' specifications. Since practical static errors are largely due to *changes* in the vacuum tubes, semiconductors, and voltage levels after calibration, honest specifications ought to state the maximum static error 8 hours and/or 1 week after adjustment as well as immediately after calibration.

7-21. Comparative Performance, Cost, and Reliability of Different Electronic Multipliers. Years of circuit improvement have made the *self-excited time-division multiplier* (Sec. 7-11) the least expensive electronic multiplier accurate within 0.1 per cent of half-scale. A single product requires only two or three vacuum-tube envelopes or four to eight transistors in addition to three d-c amplifiers. Slave multipliers are even less expensive, and the pulse-width-modulated output offers attractive possibilities in connection with tape recording and signal transmission over communications links (Sec. 11-18). Nevertheless, *diode quarter-square multipliers* are replacing time-division multipliers in general-purpose electronic analog computers because

1. Time-division-multiplier ripple filters produce an undesirable step-response overshoot as the price of reduced low-frequency phase shift (Sec 7-13).
2. Silicon-diode quarter-square multipliers require only reliable passive diode networks and standard computing amplifiers.

Although a diode multiplier requires three (more rarely four) amplifiers, they are ordinary patchbay-connected phase inverters or summers, which are available for other purposes when the multiplier is not needed. The multiplier output amplifier can readily add extra terms to the desired product and can even be an integrator. Again, the inverted input voltages required with some types of diode multipliers are frequently already available in the computer setup.

On the negative side, high static accuracy requires a relatively large number of diodes; and the piecewise-linear nature of the diode-network output is noticeable in certain applications, e.g., where a multiplier is followed by a differentiating circuit. Smoothing-oscillator interpolation (Sec. 6-13a) overcomes both these objections, but the required output filter again deteriorates frequency response.

In the class of low-cost, low-accuracy (1 per cent of half-scale) electronic multipliers of interest mainly for control purposes, the relative advantages of *diode quarter-square multipliers, varistor multipliers*, and *triangle-averaging multipliers* still deserve much investigation. The availability of packaged electromagnet/Hall-generator units has also increased interest in relatively coarse *Hall-effect multipliers*. Triangle-averaging multipliers permit fairly accurate multiplication at very low cost, especially if one-quadrant or two-quadrant operation is sufficient (Fig. 7-30). Although it is possible to build triangle-averaging multipliers accurate within 0.1 per cent of half-scale (Sec. 7-16), the writers' experience indicates that these units are difficult to keep adjusted.

The design of accurate electronic multipliers capable of operating over the extended frequency range (up to 500 Kc) of modern iterative analog computers is still an unmet challenge. Fast types of varistor quarter-square multipliers and triangle-averaging multipliers (Fig. 7-29a) are relatively inexpensive but inaccurate (1 per cent of half-scale), and electron-beam multipliers are similarly inaccurate as well as cumbersome and expensive. Diode quarter-square multipliers of the type shown in Fig. 7-25 are almost alone in the field, since they combine static accuracy within 0.5 per cent of half-scale with a usable bandwidth up to 1 Mc (see also Sec. 7-22).

Analog/digital/analog-converter multipliers (*step multipliers*, Sec. 7-6b) have the highest potential accuracy of all analog multipliers but suffer from the disadvantages of high cost, limited frequency response, and quantized output. Section 7-22 indicates how such accurate low-speed multipliers can be combined with fast and relatively coarse analog multipliers to realize the advantages of both.

Accurate carrier-type multipliers, such as time-division multipliers, require very careful shielding against cross-talk from other multipliers, especially where two or more multipliers are combined in a single chassis module. Carrier pickup in wirewound resistors can be a problem.

In judging different multiplier designs, note that the effect of a small output error can be more serious at zero output than at full-scale output; so that separate specification of this *zero error* is desirable. Finally, note that the multiplier computing bandwidth is, roughly, inversely proportional to the closed-loop d-c gain required of the output amplifier (Sec. 3-11).

7-22. Improved Electronic Multipliers Employing Coarse and Fine Channels.[71–73]

If the residual errors of an electronic multiplier are not primarily due to aging, drift, or temperature effects but stay accurately constant, one should be able to improve the accuracy by adding a *small* correction function $f(X,Y)$ generated, say, by an inexpensive two-variable function generator, to the multiplier output (see also Sec. 6-12). Although the static errors encountered with most electronic multipliers are not sufficiently constant to justify this procedure, such correction schemes offer the possibility of improving *dynamic* errors at the expense of some circuit complexity; in particular, the correction-function generator may be a relatively inaccurate wideband electronic multiplier. Proper scaling will keep the correction function sufficiently small to prevent ill effects on static errors. A sophisticated and ingenious multiplier design due to Maslov[72] (Fig. 7-37) employs a wideband varistor quarter-square multiplier to correct the output of an accurate analog/digital/analog-converter multiplier. As a feature of special interest, the operation of this multiplier is predicated on the fact that, while the analog/digital/analog-converter multiplier (Sec. 7-6b) is relatively slow with respect to its Y input, it has essentially the bandwidth of an operational amplifier

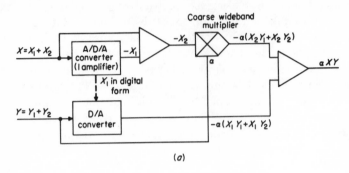

(a)

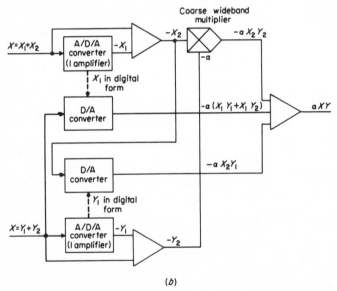

(b)

Fig. 7-37. Multiplier circuits designed to combine products from "coarse" and "fine" channels.

with respect to the X input. As a result, the coarse varistor multiplier usually has to supply only a relatively small product $-\alpha X_1 X_2$ due to high-frequency components of X and Y. The correction terms X_2, Y_2 in Fig. 7-37b are, however, automatically adjusted to compensate for errors in the A/D/A conversion. If, say, Y varies too rapidly for accurate conversion, the correction Y_2 takes up the slack, and correct multiplication continues at reduced accuracy. This is true even if the Y-channel A/D/A converter fails completely and produces an erroneous output voltage. A simple deadspace circuit (back-to-back junction diodes) following the coarse multiplier prevents the latter from contributing excessive errors when the product output is near zero.

Maslov's original multiplier used simple stepping-switch converters (Sec. 7-6b) and was able to combine static accuracy within 0.02 per cent of half-scale with 1 per cent multiplication at 10 Kc, a remarkable result. Multipliers of this sort are, of course, relatively expensive. All-electronic implementation of Fig. 7-37b would require five operational amplifiers together with a substantial number of accurate electronic switches and precision resistance networks.

7-23. Electronic Division. Electronic division is most frequently implemented through implicit solution of the equation $\alpha X_o Y + X = 0$

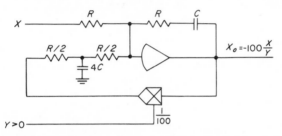

FIG. 7-38. A possible equalization scheme for high-gain division loops employing electronic multipliers with ripple filters.[2]

with a multiplier and high-gain amplifier in the manner of Figs. 1-12 and 2-4, so that $X_o = -X/Y$; Y must not change sign (see also Secs. 2-4b and 12-9b). This division technique applies to all types of multipliers; the high-gain feedback loop may require special stabilization networks for smooth loop-gain rolloff, particularly if the multiplier in question has a sharp-cutoff ripple filter (Fig. 7-38).[2] Note also that the divider accuracy, frequency response, and output noise will all vary with the input Y, since the latter affects the loop gain. Automatic gain control in the division loop can improve this situation, but the added cost is usually not justified, and a worst-case design over a suitable range of Y values suffices.

In many electronic multipliers, a switch or patchbay-controlled relay can reconnect the multiplier output amplifier as a high-gain amplifier for division (DIVIDE mode, Fig. 7-39), so that no external amplifier is required. Additional contacts on the multiply-divide switch can also change the amplifier equalization as needed.

Since in our feedback division scheme, small output voltages X_o correspond to larger products $X_o Y$, multipliers whose output error decreases with the product output perform best in division loops.   This is true for time-division multipliers, but not for diode quarter-square circuits, whose output error fluctuates more or less periodically with increasing input voltages.

In principle, every multiplier employing the feedback gain-control scheme of Fig. 7-4 can serve for division by its reference input Z, which can be variable as well as fixed.   This division scheme conveniently produces the output $\alpha XY/Z$ but usually is employed only in special-purpose computers where Z varies over a relatively small voltage range; most designers prefer a constant loop gain in the critical multiplier gain-control loop (Fig. 7-4).   Automatic gain control can, again, improve this situation.

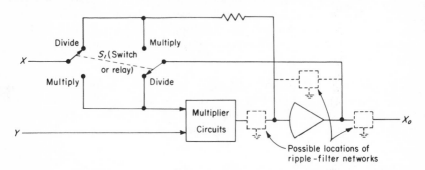

FIG. 7-39. Electronic multiplier with multiply-divide mode switch or relay. S_1 switches the input X and converts the multiplier output amplifier into a high-gain amplifier for division by Y. Additional switch or relay contacts can be used to introduce various stabilization networks into the division loop.

In particular, the Telefunken multiplier circuit of Fig. 7-15 inherently has automatic gain control in its gain-setting loop and permits direct division by Z.[45,46]

REFERENCES AND BIBLIOGRAPHY

General

1. Connelly, M. E.: Computers for Aircraft Simulation, *MIT Electronic Systems Lab., Rept.*7591-R2, Cambridge, Mass., 1959.
2. Morrill, C. D.: Electronic Multiplier and Related Topics, in Huskey, H. D., and G. A. Korn, *Computer Handbook*, McGraw-Hill, New York, 1962.

Coincidence Multipliers

3. Chance, B., et al.: *Waveforms*, vol. 19, sec. 19.5, MIT Radiation Laboratory Series, McGraw-Hill, New York, 1949.
4. Siljak, D., and R. Petrovic: Multiplication by Means of Coincidences, *Proc. 3d AICA Intern. Conf.*, Opatija, Yugoslavia, September, 1961; Presses Académiques Européennes, Brussels, Belgium.

Step Multipliers

5. Goldberg, E. A.: Step Multiplier in Guided Missile Computer, *Electronics*, **24:** 120 (1951).
6. Schmid, H.: Transistor Analog Computing Elements, in Huskey, H. D., and G. A. Korn, *Computer Handbook*, McGraw-Hill, New York, 1962.
7. Maslov, A. A.: Survey and Classification of Multiplying Devices, *Automatika i Telemekhanika*, **21** (October, 1960).

Heat-transfer Multipliers

8. Savet, P. H.: Analog Computing by Heat Transfer, *Electronic Inds. Tele-Tech,* February, 1954.
9. Davidson, G. M.: Thermal Elements Simplify Computing Circuits, *Elec. Mfg.,* 1954.
10. Davidson, G. M., W. Dijinis, and P. H. Savet: Subminiature Thermal Control Element, *Electronic Equipment,* June, 1955.
11. Savet, P. H.: Heat-transfer Computing Elements, in Huskey, H. D., and G. A. Korn, *Computer Handbook,* McGraw-Hill, New York, 1962.

Hall-effect and Magnetoresistance Multipliers

12. Chasmar, R. P., and E. Cohen: An Electrical Multiplier Utilizing the Hall Effect in Indium Arsenide, *Electronic Eng.,* December, 1958.
13. Hilsum, C.: Multiplication by Semiconductors, *Electronic Eng.,* December, 1958.
14. Lofgren, L.: Analog Multiplier Based on the Hall Effect, *J. Appl. Phys.,* **29:** 153 (February, 1958).
15. Oxeni, J.: Hall-effect Multipliers, *Nachr. tech. Z.,* May, 1958.
16. Scanga, W. A., A. R. Hilbinger, and C. M. Barrack: Hall-effect Multipliers, *Electronics,* July 15, 1960.
17. Cohen, E.: A Hall-effect Multiplier for Use at Radio Frequencies, *Electronic Eng.,* September, 1960.
18. Fuchs, H., and D. G. Flockhart: A Hall-effect Analog Multiplier, *Electronic Eng.,* November, 1960.
19. Kovatch, G., and W. E. Meserve: The Hall-effect Analog Multiplier, *IRETEC,* September, 1961.
20. Greiner, R. A.: Feedback Improves Hall-effect Multipliers, *Electronics,* Aug. 25, 1961.
21. Schmid, H.: Transistor Analog Computing Elements, in Huskey, H. D., and G. A. Korn, *Computer Handbook,* McGraw-Hill, New York, 1962.
22. Hunt, J. M.: Application of the Magnetoresistance Effect to Analog Multiplication, *Tech. Rept.* 1504-1, Stanford Electronics Laboratories, Stanford, Calif., May 25, 1960; also *Trans. Natl. Electronics Conf.,* 1960.
23. Kataoka, S.: Magnetoresistance Multiplier with Higher Gain, *Proc. IRE,* February, 1962.

Sampling Multipliers
(See also Secs. 8-15 and 10-6d)

24. Broomal, J., and L. Riebman: A Sampling Analog Computer, *Proc. IRE,* **40:** 569, May, 1952.

AM/FM Multipliers

25. Price, R.: An FM-AM Multiplier of High Accuracy and Wide Range, *MIT Research Lab. Electronics Tech. Rept.* 213, Cambridge, Mass., October, 1951.
26. Sommerville, M. J.: An Electronic Multiplier, *Electronic Eng.,* February, 1952.
27. McCool, W. A.: An AM-FM Electronic Analog Multiplier, *Proc. IRE,* **41:** 1470 (October, 1952).
28. AM-FM Demodulator Used in Multiplier System, *Electronic Design News,* July, 1959.

AM/PM Multipliers

29. Graig, L. S.: The Magnetic Amplifier as an Analog-computer Element, *Proc. IRE,* **41:** 1477 (October, 1953).

30. Keister, G. L.: Transistor Magnetic Analog Multiplier, *Electronics*, October, 1953; see also refs. 2, 7, and 21; and U.S. Patent 2,784,909 (1957), assigned to General Electric Co.

Use of Delta Modulation

31. Paul, R. J. A.: Hybrid Methods for Function Generation, *Proc. 3d AICA Intern. Conf.*, Opatija, Yugoslavia, September, 1961, Presses Académiques Européennes, Brussels, Belgium.

Frequency- and Time-sharing Feedback Multipliers

32. RCA Laboratories Division, unpublished report on Project Typhoon, 1949.
33. Chance, B., et al.: *Waveforms*, vol. 19, sec. 19.5, MIT Radiation Laboratory Series, McGraw-Hill, New York, 1949.

Time-division Multipliers

34. Sack, H. S.: *NDRC Rept.* 14-435, Cornell University, Ithaca, N.Y., 1944; see also Cornell thesis of A. C. Beer and H. W. Boehmer.
35. Greenwood, I. A., J. V. Holdam, Jr., and D. MacRae, Jr.: *Electronic Instruments*, MIT Radiation Laboratory Series, vol. 21, McGraw-Hill, New York, 1948.
36. Millman, J., and H. Taub: *Pulse and Digital Circuits*, McGraw-Hill, New York, 1956.
37. Goldberg, E. A.: A High-accuracy Time-division Multiplier, *RCA Rev.*, **23**: 265 (September, 1952).
38. Morrill, C. D., and R. V. Baum: A Stabilized Electronic Multiplier, *IRETEC*, December, 1952.
39. Walters, L. G.: A Study of the Series-motor Relay Servomechanism, Ph.D. Thesis, University of California, Los Angeles, 1951.
40. Korn, G. A., and T. M. Korn: Relay Time-division Multiplier, *Rev. Sci. Instr.*, **25**: 977 (October, 1954).
41. Sternberg, S.: An Accurate Electronic Multiplier, *RCA Rev.*, **16**: 618 (December, 1955).
42. Lilamand, M.: A Time-division Multiplier, *IRETEC*, January, 1956.
43. Schmid, H.: A Transistorized Four-quadrant Time-division Multiplier with an Accuracy of 0.1 per cent, *IRETEC*, March, 1958.
44. Gleghorn, P.: An Analog Electronic Multiplier Using Transistors as Square-wave Modulators, *Proc. IRE*, **107**(B): 94 (March, 1960).
45. Schneider, W.: Ein Transistorisierter Time-Division-Multiplikator Hoher Genauigkeit, *Telefunken Z.*, September, 1960.
46. Kettel, E., and W. Schneider: An Accurate Analog Multiplier and Divider, *IRETEC*, June, 1961.
47. Bode, H. W.: *Network Analysis and Feedback-amplifier Design*, Van Nostrand, Princeton, N.J., 1945; see also ref. 2.

Electronic Quarter-square Multipliers

48. Soltes, A. S.: Wide-band Square-law Circuit Element, *IRETEC*, April, 1955.
49. Miller, I. A., A. S. Soltes, and R. E. Scott: Wide-band Analog Function Multiplier, *Electronics*, **28** (1955).
50. Dumas, H. J.: A Pulsed Analog Multiplier-divider, MIT M.S. Thesis (Electrical Engineering), 1958.
51. Fitsner, L. N.: A Multiplication Block Using Thyrites, *Priborostroenie*, no. 4, 1956.
52. Maslov, A. A.: A Multiplier-divider Based on Thyrites, *Automatika i Telemekhanika*, **18** (April, 1957).

53. Kovach, L. D., and W. Comley: A New Solid-state Nonlinear Analog Component, *IRETEC*, December, 1960.
54. Schreier, D., and H. Winkler: Design of Nonlinear Characteristics Using Varistors, *Proc. AICA 3d Intern. Conf.*, Opatija, Yugoslavia, September, 1961, Presses Académiques Européennes, Brussels, Belgium.
55. Fisher, M. E.: A Wide-band Analog Multiplier Using Crystal Diodes, *Electronic Eng.*, **29**: 358 (1957).
56. Fisher, M. E.: The Optimum Design of Quarter-square Multipliers with Segmented Characteristics, *J. Sci. Instr.*, **34** (August, 1957).
57. Sternick, L.: Technical Data Sheet on M-400-1 REAC Diode Electronic Multiplier, *Report* TD5567, Reeves Instrument Corp., Garden City, N.Y., 1956.
58. Hannet, R. T.: A Quarter-square Multiplier, *Tech. Rept.*, May, 1959, WADC Research Laboratory, Wright-Patterson AFB, Ohio.
59. Giser, S.: All-electronic High-speed Multiplier, *MIT Instrumentation Lab. Rept.* R-67, Cambridge, Mass., November, 1953.
60. Binsack, J. H.: A Pulsed Analog and Digital Computer, *MIT Electronic Systems Lab. Sci. Rept.* 8494-R-2, Cambridge, Mass., 1960.

Triangle-averaging Multipliers

61. Mills, R. L.: A New Electronic Multiplication Method Involving Only Simple Conventional Circuits, Magnolia Petroleum Co. Field Res. Lab. *Rept.* 680 (00)-4, Dallas, Tex., Nov. 9, 1953.
62. Meyer, R. A., and H. B. Davis: Triangular-wave Analog Multiplier, *Electronics*, August, 1956.
63. Pfeiffer, P. E.: A Four-quadrant Multiplier, *IRETEC*, June, 1959.
64. G. A. Philbrick Researches, Boston, Mass., Specification Sheets for MU/DV and K5-M Multipliers.
65. Hartmann, J., G. A. Korn, and R. L. Maybach: Low-cost Triangle-integration Multipliers for Analog Computers, *Ann. AICA*, October, 1961.

Logarithmic Multipliers

66. Gray, T. S., and H. B. Frey: Acorn Diode Has Logarithmic Range of 10^9, *Rev. Sci. Instr.*, February, 1951; see also refs. 2, 6, and 7.

Electron-beam Multipliers

67. MacNee, A. B.: An Electronic Differential Analyzer, *Proc. IRE*, **37**: 1315 (1949).
68. Schmidt, W.: Die Hyperbelröhre, eine Elektronenstrahlrohre zum Multiplizieren in Analogia-rechengeraten, *Z. angew. Phys.*, no. 2, 1956.
69. Gundlach, F. W.: A New Electron-beam Multiplier with an Electrostatic Hyperbolic Field, *Proc. AICA 1st Intern. Conf.*, Brussels, 1955, Presses Académiques Européennes, Brussels, Belgium.
70. Angelo, E. I.: An Electron-beam Tube for Analog Multiplication, *Rev. Sci. Instr.*, **25** (3) (March, 1954).

Precision Multiplication Using Multiple Channels

71. Fitsner, L. M.: A Precision Multiplier, *Automatika i Telemekhanika*, **20** (January, 1959).
72. Maslov, A. A.: A Three-channel Multiplier with Frequency Division of the Signals, *Automatika i Telemekhanika*, **21** (December, 1960).
73. Schmid, H.: Combined Analog-digital Computing Elements, *Proc. Western Joint Computer Conf.*, 1961.

Miscellaneous

74. Netter, Z.: Folding Technique Extends Function-generator Range, *Electronic Design*, May 10, 1963.
75. McCoy, R. D., and H. F. Meissinger: U.S. Patent 3,031,143, assigned to Reeves Instrument Corp., Apr. 24, 1962 (filed Jan. 7, 1955).
76. Bruck, D. B.: Analog Multiplication from D-c to Mc, *Instruments and Control Systems*, August, 1962.
77. MacKay, D. M., and M. E. Fisher: *Analog Computing at Ultra-high Speed*, Wiley, New York, 1962.
78. Ream, N.: Approximation Errors in Diode Function Generators, *J. Electronics and Control*, **7**: 83 (1959).
79. Ritchie, C. C., and R. W. Young: The Design of Biased Diode Function Generators, *Electronic Eng.*, **31**: 347 (1959).

CHAPTER 8

COMPUTER SERVOMECHANISMS
AND VECTOR RESOLVERS

COMPUTER SERVOMECHANISMS

8-1. Introduction. Performance Specifications and Tests. D-c computer servomechanisms displace potentiometers, induction resolvers, dials, shaft-position encoders, etc., in proportion to the instantaneous value of an input voltage Y (*positioning servomechanisms*), or at a rate proportional to Y (*rate servomechanisms*, Sec. 8-12). In general-purpose electronic analog computers, the most frequently used servomechanisms are the d-c positioning servos already introduced in Secs. 1-13a, 2-4b, and 7-6a (Fig. 8-1a). A single computer servo can multiply between 1 and 80 (typically 3 to 5) input voltages X_1, X_2, . . . by various functions of the servo input Y; d-c servos employing a-c servomotors, moreover, do not require carefully regulated power supplies. The resulting low cost per product is still advantageous in applications where the bandwidth and maintenance problems of mechanical components can be tolerated, e.g., in special-purpose flight simulators and in large general-purpose computers used mainly for very slow real-time computation.

Referring to Fig. 8-1a, a d-c positioning servo is actuated by the difference between the servo input V and a follow-up-potentiometer voltage V_Y measuring the output-shaft position. The difference $Y - V_Y$ (*error voltage*) drives either a *d-c servomotor* through a *d-c servoamplifier*, or the control phase of a two-phase *a-c servomotor* through a *suppressed-carrier modulator* (chopper modulator) and amplifier. The servomotor usually drives the load, including the follow-up potentiometer, through a speed-reducing gear train.

The *static (d-c) accuracy* of a positioning servo is ultimately limited by

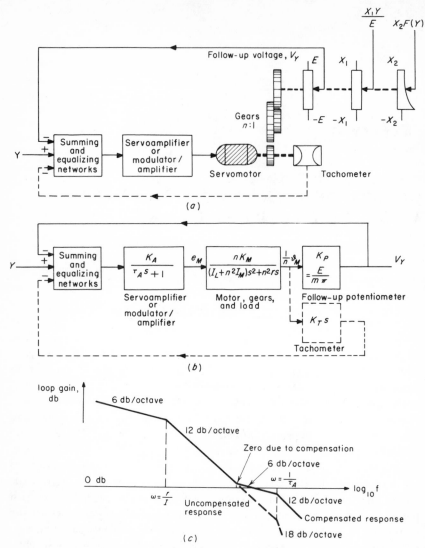

Fig. 8-1. D-c positioning servomechanism (*a*), linearized transfer-function block diagram (*b*), and Bode loop-gain-response plot (*c*). Our analysis neglects the effects of additional motor delays.

the resolution and conformity or mutual correspondence of the follow-up potentiometer and the multiplying potentiometers, function potentiometers, resolvers, etc. (Sec. 8-5) and varies between 0.15 and 0.025 per cent of the full follow-up voltage range.   Static accuracy is also affected by the *gear-backlash tolerance*, by the motor breakaway torque required to overcome *static friction*, and by the *servo loop gain*, which require matching specifications (Sec. 8-4).   The *low-speed tracking accuracy* of a positioning

servo is usually measured by its multiplication error for an input Y
changing at 10 to 25 mV/sec and should approximately equal the static
accuracy.[2]

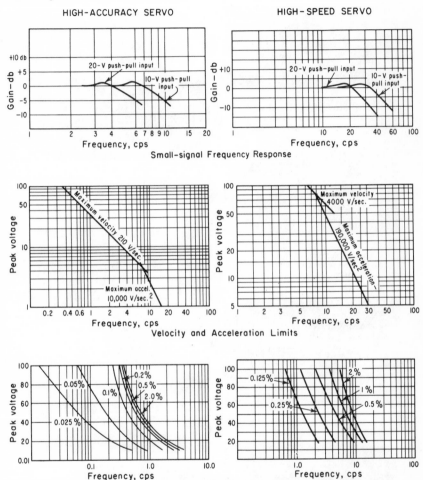

Fig. 8-2. Performance of a high-accuracy 60-cps positioning servo employing 10-turn
wirewound potentiometers, and of a high-speed 400-cps servo using single-turn film
potentiometers. (*Electronic Associates, Inc.*)

The servo *small-signal frequency response* may be specified in terms of
the amplitude and phase response for sinusoidal input of one-tenth half-
scale amplitude. For servos used with general-purpose analog computers,
the amplitude response is down 3 db at 1 to 50 cps after a slight rise corresponding to a 10 to 15 per cent overshoot in the small-signal step
response (Fig. 8-2). Small-signal phase shift reaches 5 deg between 1
and 30 cps. Unfortunately, servo bandwidth decreases radically with

signal amplitude, because the motor performance implies both speed and torque limits (Sec. 8-3a). *Large-signal frequency-response specifications*, shown graphically in Fig. 8-2 for two typical examples, must be carefully

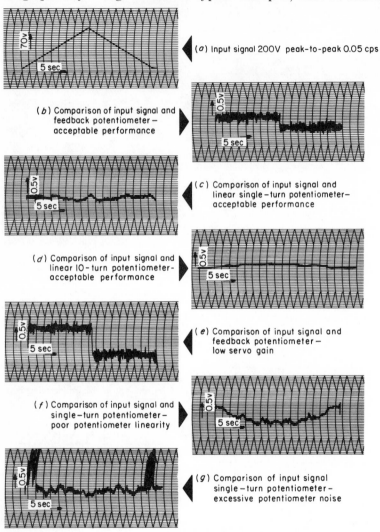

(*a*) Input signal 200V peak-to-peak 0.05 cps

(*b*) Comparison of input signal and feedback potentiometer — acceptable performance

(*c*) Comparison of input signal and linear single-turn potentiometer — acceptable performance

(*d*) Comparison of input signal and linear 10-turn potentiometer — acceptable performance

(*e*) Comparison of input signal and feedback potentiometer — low servo gain

(*f*) Comparison of input signal and single-turn potentiometer — poor potentiometer linearity

(*g*) Comparison of input signal single-turn potentiometer — excessive potentiometer noise

FIG. 8-3. Typical test records for servomultipliers checked in the test setup of Fig. 7-36. (*From H. D. Huskey and G. A. Korn, Computer Handbook, McGraw-Hill, New York, 1962.*)

stated for each computer servomechanism.   Note that servo frequency-response limitations apply only to the *servo input* (X in Fig. 8-1).   The potentiometer input voltages X_k are subject only to the potentiometer phase shift discussed in Sec. 4-6; the capacitor-compensation scheme described in that section may improve this situation substantially.

Servo output noise is mainly output-potentiometer noise[16] and varies between 20 and 100 mV peak to peak for servomultipliers. Servomultiplier static and dynamic errors are conveniently measured with a test setup similar to Fig. 7-36 and appropriately low test-signal frequencies; Fig. 8-3 shows typical test results.

Velocity limiting can be demonstrated and measured through observation of the maximum output rate for large input steps or sine waves. Acceleration limiting is shown by the distortion evident in the servo response to low-amplitude sinusoidal inputs of increasing frequency. The maximum output velocity and acceleration can also be measured by error measurements with known input ramps and parabolic inputs.[2]

Table 8-1. Representative Computer Servos for General-purpose ±100-volt Analog Computers (see also Fig. 8-2)

	High-accuracy servo	High-speed servo
Motor...............................	60 cps two-phase	400 cps two-phase
Potentiometers......................	6 wirewound 10-turn (linear) and 1-turn (sine-cosine)	4 to 6 carbon-film, 1-turn
Diameter, in......................	2 (linear) and 3–5 (sine-cosine)	2
Moment of inertia, *per section*, g-cm^2...	14	8 to 10
Starting torque, *per section*, oz-in.......	2	0.5
Resistance r......................	20–50K ± 5%	20–50K ± 10%
Terminal linearity of linear potentiometers (per cent of r).............	0.025	0.1
Conformity of sine-cosine potentiometers (per cent of r)....................	0.1	0.3
Center-tap-location accuracy (per cent of r)............................	0.025	0.2
Resolution (number of wire turns, N)...	12,000–15,000	Essentially infinite
Performance (see also Fig. 8-2):		
Static accuracy, mV.................	30–100	150–200
Low-speed tracking accuracy, mV.....	40–150	200
Velocity limit, volts/sec...............	210	4,000
Acceleration limit, volts/sec^2.........	10,000	120,000–190,000

8-2. Small-signal Performance Analysis and Servo Equalization.[1–8]

A linear transfer-function block diagram for the positioning servomechanism of Fig. 8-1a is shown in Fig. 8-1b, where

K_A is the *servoamplifier or modulator/amplifier gain* (volts/volt).

K_M is the *motor gain* (ft-lb/volt).

K_P is the *follow-up-potentiometer gain* (volts/radian); referring to Fig. 8-1a, $K_P = E/m\pi$, where m is the number of *full* potentiometer-shaft revolutions between HI and LO terminals.

$n \geq 1$ is the (speed-reducing) *gear ratio* between motor and load. $I = I_M + I_G + I_L/n^2 + I_T$, where I_M, I_G, I_L, I_T are the respective moments of inertia of the motor, gears (at motor shaft), load, and tachometer (on motor shaft), all in slug-ft^2.

r is the *motor damping coefficient* (ft-lb-sec/radian).

τ_A is the *amplifier delay time constant* (sec), which represents the amplifier-bandwidth limitation; in modulator-type servos, $1/\tau_A$ is taken to be somewhat less than the carrier frequency.[1]

We neglect motor-field and armature delays. If $\tau_A \ll I/r$, then our linearized servo reduces to a simple second-order system.

The small-signal response of our linearized system is determined by its closed-loop transfer function

$$H(s) \equiv \frac{\mathcal{L}\{V_Y\}}{\mathcal{L}\{Y\}} = \frac{A(s)}{1 - A(s)\beta(s)}$$

$$= -\frac{1}{\beta(s)} \left\{ 1 + \frac{1}{A(s)\beta(s)} + \frac{1}{A^2(s)\beta^2(s)} + \cdots \right\} \qquad (8\text{-}1)$$

and hence by the loop-gain transfer function

$$A(s)\beta(s) = -\frac{K_A}{\tau_A s + 1} \cdot \frac{K_M}{n(Is^2 + rs)} K_P$$

$$= -\frac{K_A K_P}{n} \cdot \frac{K_M}{r} \cdot \frac{1}{s(\tau_A s + 1)[(I/r)s + 1]} \qquad (8\text{-}2)$$

where $\beta(s) = -1$. At very low frequencies ($\omega \ll 1$), the servo frequency response is approximated by

$$H(j\omega) \approx 1 - \frac{j\omega}{A(0)} = 1 - j\omega \frac{n}{K_A K_P} \frac{r}{K_M} \qquad (8\text{-}3)$$

Both the dynamic errors implied by Eqs. (2) and (3) for $s = j\omega \neq 0$ and the static error

$$V_Y = \frac{1}{nK_A K_M} T_S \qquad (8\text{-}4)$$

due to a spurious torque T_S (typically due to static friction) on the output shaft are reduced by large values of the gain K_A (Sec. 8-4). The servo loop gain (2) must, however, satisfy the stability conditions of Sec. 4-15; i.e., the Bode plot for $A(j\omega)(\beta j\omega)$ (Fig. 8-1c) must cross 0 db at less than 12 db/octave to avoid excessive phase shift.

To obtain stable servo performance with a sufficiently high value of servo gain (Sec. 8-4), we modify the loop-gain transfer function (2) by one of two methods:

1. We change the feedback ratio $\beta(s)$ in Eqs. (1) and (2) from -1 to

$$\beta(s) = -(1 + K_T s) \qquad (8\text{-}5a)$$

by adding *rate feedback* from a *d-c tachometer* (permanent-magnet d-c generator) or from an a-c *induction generator*, as shown in dash lines in Fig. 8-1a and b.   Since straight proportional-plus-rate feedback (3) causes a position offset when the servo tracks a constant-rate signal, a simple high-pass filter is added to the tachometer to produce

$$\beta(s) = -\left(1 + K_T \frac{\tau_T s}{\tau_T s + 1} s\right) \qquad (8\text{-}5b)$$

which essentially reduces to (5a) at frequencies much above $1/2\pi\tau_T$ cps.

2. We leave $\beta(s) = -1$ but add an equalization network (simple or multiple *lead network*) in the forward part of the servo loop to introduce poles and zeros into $A(s)$ (*error-rate equalization*, see also Sec. 4-17).   Our original loop transfer function (2) is, then, multiplied by the transfer function of an equalization network, say,

$$a\frac{(s - s_1')}{(s - s_1)} \qquad \text{or} \qquad a\frac{(s - s_1')(s - s_2')(s - s_3')}{(s - s_1)(s - s_2)(s - s_3)} \qquad (8\text{-}6)$$

with appropriately placed poles s_i and zeros s_k' (Fig. 8-4).

The effects of such equalization on the loop-gain frequency response are indicated in Fig. 8-1c.   Reference 1 discusses optimum servo equalization for various relative magnitudes of τ_A and I/r in detail; consideration of the Bode plot indicates that the largest possible amplifier gain K_A which yields a stable linear system is approximately given by

$$K_A \leq \begin{cases} \dfrac{3}{25}\dfrac{nI}{K_M K_P \tau_A^2} & \left(\tau_A < \dfrac{1}{25}\dfrac{I}{r}\right) \\ \dfrac{1}{5}\dfrac{nI}{K_M K_P \tau_A^2} & \left(\tau_A \approx \dfrac{1}{5}\dfrac{I}{r}\right) \\ \dfrac{nr}{K_M K_P \tau_A} & \left(\dfrac{1}{5}\dfrac{I}{r} < \tau_A < \dfrac{I}{r}\right) \end{cases} \qquad (8\text{-}7)$$

Many computer servomechanisms have external gain and/or rate-feedback adjustments, which are set for stable operation with 10 to 20 per cent step-response overshoot.   Rate feedback and network equalization may be combined; one can also introduce nonlinear diode networks to compensate for amplifier or motor saturation or to increase the servo gain for large errors.   Figure 8-4 shows practical equalization circuits used with modulator-type d-c computer servomechanisms.   D-c motor servos usually employ an operational amplifier to provide both voltage amplification and equalization ahead of the d-c power amplifier (Fig. 8-6a), so that the equalization networks are easily designed with the aid of Table A-1.

In practice, error-rate-network equalization tends to amplify follow-up potentiometer noise and is, therefore, most effective with film-type fol-low-up potentiometers (Sec. 8-5). Feedback tachometers, which are best connected directly to the motor shaft to avoid amplification of gear chatter, permit high servo gain,[1] yield a very smooth rate-feedback signal,

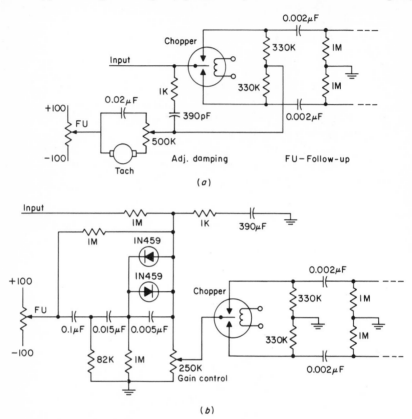

FIG. 8-4. Modulator-equalizer circuits used to supply push-pull input for an a-c servoamplifier. The circuit of Fig. 8-4a incorporates d-c tachometer feedback and an 0.02-μF speedup capacitor. Note also that the static (d-c) impedance presented to the follow-up potentiometer is infinite, although transients can cause up to 600 μA current flow. Figure 8-4b illustrates network equalization; diodes modify the network for large error signals to allow for the reduced servo gain at saturation. The static impedance presented to the follow-up potentiometer is 1M, but transient currents are less than 100 μA. The 1K, 390-pF network in each circuit reduces chopper-switching transients. (*Reeves Instrument Corp.; adapted from ref. 2.*)

and permit accurate low-speed operation, but they add cost as well as inertia and friction to the mechanical system. Specific types of tachome-ters are discussed in refs. 4, 5, and 8.

One can improve the small-signal frequency response of some computer servo-mechanisms by inserting a suitable equalization circuit ahead of the servo input (open-cycle equalization).[60]

8-3. Motors, Amplifiers, and Gear Trains. (a) **Motors and Amplifiers.** Besides power and environmental ratings, the motor manufacturer will supply

1. The motor-armature moment of inertia I_M which, together with the inertia of gears and load, determines the time constant I/r, and hence the small-signal bandwidth of the servomechanism (Fig. 8-1).

2. A set of motor torque/speed characteristics (Fig. 8-5) relating the motor torque T_M and the (constant) motor angular velocity $\dot\vartheta_M$ for various values of the control voltage e_M up to its rated maximum max $|e_M|$.

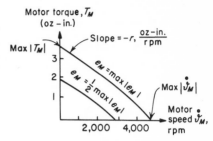

FIG. 8-5. Torque/speed characteristics for a 400-cps two-phase servomotor.

We use the curve for $e_M = \text{max } |e_M|$ to find the *servo velocity and acceleration limits*

$$\left.\begin{aligned} \max\left|\frac{dV_Y}{d\tau}\right| &= \frac{K_P}{n}\max|\dot\vartheta_M| = \frac{E}{30mn}\max|\dot\vartheta_M|_{\text{in rpm}} \\ \max\left|\frac{d^2V_Y}{d\tau^2}\right| &= \frac{K_P}{nI}\max|T_M| \end{aligned}\right\} \qquad (8\text{-}8)$$

(which determine the large-signal frequency response, Fig. 8-2), and to approximate the linear-system parameters

$$K_M = \frac{\max|T_M|}{\max|e_M|} \qquad \frac{1}{r} = \left|\frac{\Delta\dot\vartheta_M}{\Delta T_M}\right|_{\dot\vartheta_M=0} \qquad (8\text{-}9)$$

It is desirable to have large velocity and acceleration limits and a small *motor time constant* I_M/r; motor gain and efficiency are not usually important in small computer servomechanisms. Table 8-2 shows parameter values for some typical servomotors. All other things being equal, 60-cps motors require more iron and thus have somewhat more inertia than 400-cps motors. Perhaps more significantly, $\tau_A > \frac{1}{60}$ sec for 60-cps modulation, so that the bandwidth of 60-cps computer servos is severely restricted. D-c-motor servos have no amplifier-bandwidth restriction other than the delay required for the amplifier to produce motor-armature current ($\tau_A \ll I/r$), and special d-c motors can yield torques so high that no gear train may be needed. Unlike two-phase a-c motors, d-c motors require brush maintenance.

Figure 8-6b shows the circuit of a *vacuum-tube servo amplifier* designed to drive the split control field of a two-phase induction motor. The field is tuned to improve output-stage efficiency. To obtain 90 deg phase shift

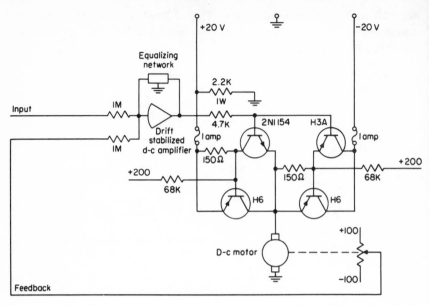

Fig. 8-6a. In this all-d-c computer servo, an operational amplifier with suitably limited output voltage drives a transistor d-c power amplifier. (*Goodyear Aircraft Corp.*)

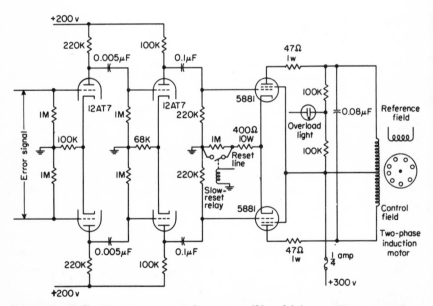

Fig. 8-6b. 66-db 10-watt vacuum-tube a-c amplifier driving a 400-cps two-phase induction motor. Push-pull 400-cps input is obtained from one of the chopper-modulator input circuits of Fig. 8-4. (*Reeves Instrument Corp.*)

between the motor control and fixed fields, we can adjust either the fixed-field phase or the chopper-excitation phase; note that a phase-shift network in the motor field tends to reduce motor damping.[2] *Transistor servo amplifiers*[63] are smaller, cooler, and more reliable than vacuum-tube amplifiers; in vacuum-tube general-purpose computers, however, they require separate power supplies and protection from excessive input voltages. *Magnetic amplifiers* for a-c servos are, generally speaking, too slow for most computer-servo applications.[1,5]

Table 8-2. Representative Servomotor Characteristics (Ref. 2)

Characteristics	No. 1	No. 2	No. 3
Frequency, cps	d-c	60	400
Max control power, watts	20	8	9
Rotor inertia, g-cm^2	4.5	4.0	4.0
Torque at stall, oz-in	1.7	3.5	2.5
No-load speed, rpm	12,000	3,400	4,800
Time constant, msec	46	6	12
Theoretical acceleration at stall, radians/sec^2	27,000	62,000	40,000
Weight, oz	4	12	12

To prevent rapid potentiometer slewing when a general-purpose electronic analog computer is reset to initial conditions, a relay connected to the computer RESET bus (Sec. 10-3) may restrict the motor-control voltage in RESET and thus extend potentiometer life (Fig. 8-6b).[2] Where computer servos operate only during relatively short computer runs, similar relay circuits are sometimes employed to effect motor operation at higher than rated control voltages and reference-field voltages to increase max $|T_M|$ and max $|\dot\vartheta_M|$ during the COMPUTE interval.

(b) Gear Trains and Limit Stops. High-performance computer servomechanisms usually have gear trains mounted in special castings and running in oil. If it is desirable to fit and interchange special transducers, mechanical components can be mounted on slotted or drilled plates. The choice of the gear ratio n is discussed as part of the overall servo-design problem in Sec. 8-4. Accurate servo operation requires precision-matched gears with low friction and specified low backlash (Sec. 8-4). The number of gear-train steps is usually a compromise between low inertia and a minimum number of steps to reduce friction and backlash. Motor-shaft pinions are used with gear-ratio steps up to 1:20, while other gear ratios are usually at most 1:6 per step. Reference 4 discusses the design of multigear trains for minimum effective inertia.

The relatively high static and dynamic torque developed by the servomotor and gear train at the potentiometer shaft can easily destroy the usual built-in potentiometer limit stops without additional precautions. *Electrical limit stops* employ conductors beyond the end of each potentiometer winding to reverse the servo follow-up voltage. Such stops are ineffective if the follow-up voltage fails. Typical *mechanical limit stops* used with 10-turn potentiometers[2] have a torque capacity of 500 oz-in.

8-4. Servo-design Considerations. (a) A specified *static four-quadrant multiplication error* of ϵ per cent *of full scale* requires potentiometer conformity and resolution (Sec. 8-5) within ϵ per cent together with a *static follow-up voltage error* less than $2\epsilon E/100$ volts. This error voltage must cause sufficient motor torque to overcome the static-friction torque T_{SL}/n due to the load and gears, so that we shall require

$$nK_A \geq \frac{50T_{SL}}{\epsilon E K_M} \tag{8-10}$$

Equation (10) constitutes a constraint on the smallest usable gear ratio n, since we cannot increase the amplifier gain K_A indefinitely without causing instability in accordance with Eq. (7).

The product nK_A is further constrained by nonlinear considerations. Referring again to Fig. 8-1, δ deg of *gear backlash* measured at the follow-up-potentiometer shaft corresponds to an error voltage $\pm 2E\delta/360m$ which will cause gear chatter if it generates sufficient motor torque to overcome the static-friction torque T_{SL}/n due to load and gears. This will be true unless

$$nK_A \leq \frac{180mT_{SL}}{EK_M\delta} \tag{8-11a}$$

Similarly, if we use a wirewound follow-up potentiometer having N wire turns between HI and LO, the servo will chatter or "hunt" between potentiometer wire turns if the error voltage $2E/N$ corresponding to one wire turn can overcome static friction, i.e., unless

$$nK_A \leq \frac{NT_{SL}}{2EK_M} \tag{8-11b}$$

Either gear chatter or wire-turn hunting will cause undue potentiometer wear and must be prevented. In high-accuracy computer servos, the backlash corresponds to less than one-half of a potentiometer wire turn, and nK_A can be over 10 times as large as required by Eq. (10); so that the static error is essentially determined by the potentiometer conformity.

(b) For specified servo velocity and acceleration limits (8), the servo-motor maximum speed and torque max $|\dot{\vartheta}_M|_{\text{in rpm}}$, max $|T_M|$ and the gear ratio n must satisfy

$$\left. \begin{array}{l} \max |\dot{\vartheta}_M|_{\text{in rpm}} \geq \dfrac{30mn}{E} \max \left| \dfrac{dV_Y}{d\tau} \right| \\[3mm] \max |T_M| \geq \dfrac{nI}{K_P} \max \left| \dfrac{d^2V_Y}{d\tau^2} \right| \end{array} \right\} \tag{8-12}$$

In addition, smooth tracking requires that the maximum motor torque (stall torque) max $|T_M|$ be at least five (preferably ten) times as large as the maximum static-friction torque T_{LOAD}/n due to load and gears:

$$\max |T_M| \geq \frac{10}{n} T_{\text{LOAD}} \tag{8-13}$$

The conditions (12) and (13) will be satisfied by various combinations of motors and gear ratios, with larger motors corresponding to smaller gear ratios. *It remains, then, to choose a motor having a low time constant I_M/r and low power requirements while still satisfying the conditions (12) and (13)*

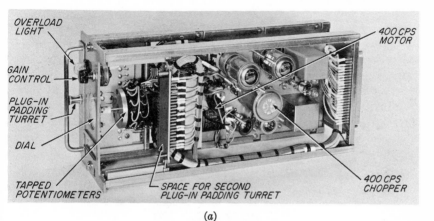

(a)

(b)

Fig. 8-7. A high-performance computer servomechanism. A 400-cps servomotor drives four linear two-tap potentiometers and two nine-tap potentiometers. The upper plug-in tap-voltage-setting turret (Sec. 8-8) has been removed; two such turrets are shown in Fig. 8-7b. Note the taper-pin connections. (*Reeves Instrument Corporation.*)

subject to the constraint (10) on the gear ratio n. The actual choice of motor and gear ratio will usually require several successive preliminary-design estimates involving rough calculations of the largest permissible amplifier gain K_A for linear-system stability from Eq. (7), until the desired compromise is obtained.

High static accuracy implies accurate wirewound multiturn potentiometers ($m \geq 10$, $N > 100/\epsilon$), small backlash ($\delta < 180m/N$ deg), and relatively large values of n, I, and T_{SL}, so that bandwidth is reduced. Fast servos employ single-turn film potentiometers and relatively low values of K_A and n at the expense of static accuracy. A detailed design example will be found in ref. 1; Table 8-2 illustrates typical computer-servo specifications. Figure 8-7 illustrates the construction of computer-servo units.

SERVO-DRIVEN POTENTIOMETERS

8-5. Potentiometer Specifications. The fractional resistance tapped off by the wiper of a servo-driven computing potentiometer (Fig. 8-8) must equal a given function of the potentiometer shaft displacement within a maximum *conformity error* specified as a percentage of the largest resistance measured between the potentiometer LO and ARM terminals (Sec. 3-4). Potentiometers can be designed, and conformity errors specified, either for

(*a*)

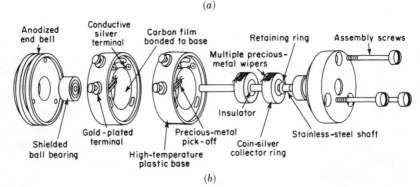

(*b*)

FIG. 8-8. Single-turn wirewound servo potentiometer (*a*), and dual carbon-film potentiometer (*b*). (*Figure 8-8a copyright 1954, HELIPOT Corporation; Fig. 8-8b copyright 1960, Computer Instruments Corporation. Reprinted by permission.*)

an infinite-impedance load or for a specified load, such as 1M (preloading, Sec. 8-7). The conformity of a *linear* follow-up or multiplying potentiometer is given by its *terminal linearity* (Fig. 8-9); note that finite potentiometer end resistances produce terminal-linearity errors even for 0 and 100 per cent shaft displacement. The static multiplication error in per cent of full scale due to nonconformity of follow-up and multiplying or function potentiometers can reach twice the potentiometer conformity error, plus any errors due to inaccurate alignment (phasing) of the ganged potentiometers. Typical potentiometer conformity errors vary between 0.02

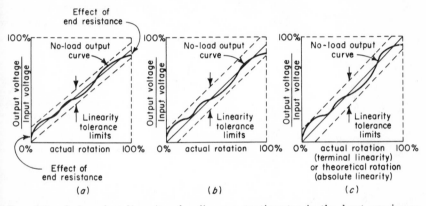

FIG. 8-9a. *Independent linearity* of a linear potentiometer is the least maximum deviation of the actual output curve from a straight line.
FIG. 8-9b. *Zero-based linearity* is the least maximum deviation from a straight line through the origin.
FIG. 8-9c. *Terminal linearity* is the maximum deviation from a straight line through the origin and a point corresponding to 100 per cent input voltage and the *actual* potentiometer rotation between end taps. *Absolute linearity* is the maximum deviation from a straight line through the origin and a point corresponding to 100 per cent input voltage and the *theoretical* rotation (between the theoretical end-tap locations).

FIG. 8-9. Specification of potentiometer linearity (errors are exaggerated).

and 0.5 per cent (Table 8-1). Some computer servomechanisms use trimmer resistors at the end of each potentiometer to adjust a set of potentiometers for optimum mutual conformity.[2]

Follow-up and multiplying potentiometers with accurately positioned *grounded center taps* will reduce the multiplier zero error (for $Y = 0$), but unless the conformity error at the ungrounded center tap is zero, grounding the tap can double conformity errors away from the tap.[2]

In addition to requirements for resolution, stability, and mechanical ruggedness similar to those for coefficient-setting potentiometers (Sec. 3-4), servo-driven potentiometers should exhibit

1. A low *starting torque*
2. Low *inertia*

3. Low *noise* due to wiper motion (typically below the servo static error for ± 100-volt computers)

4. A long useful *life* at the rated potentiometer-shaft speed, typically above 10^6 revolutions at 4 to 15 rps (see also Table 8-1)

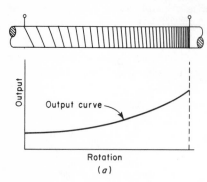

(a)

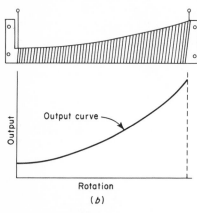

(b)

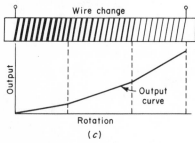

(c)

Fig. 8-10. Wirewound function potentiometers produced by variable wire spacing *(a)*, a tapered potentiometer card *(b)*, and changes in wire size and/or composition *(c)*. Combinations of these techniques may be used. (*Copyright 1954, HELIPOT Corporation—reprinted by permission.*)

The construction of both wirewound and film-type potentiometers with those desirable properties is a highly developed art described extensively in the literature.[4,11–18] Figure 8-10 illustrates the construction of two representative types of servo-driven potentiometers (see also Sec. 3-4).

A wirewound potentiometer will either fail due to a broken potentiometer-card winding, or the potentiometer noise increases intolerably (Fig. 8-3). In the latter case, it may be possible to salvage the potentiometer by a cleaning process.

It is recommended that potentiometer tap and slider terminations be fused to prevent burnouts due to faulty connections.

8-6. Function Potentiometers. Potentiometers used to multiply an input voltage by a function $F(Y)$ of the servo input variable Y are constructed so that the fraction of the total resistance tapped off by the wiper is a nonlinear function of the shaft displacement. Special-purpose servomechanisms may also employ a nonlinear follow-up potentiometer. Linear potentiometers with cam-displaced wipers[8] and servo plotting tables with curve-follower attachments (Sec. 11-3c) are used less frequently.

Wirewound function-potentiometer resistance elements are given the proper "taper" by suitable changes in card shape, winding pitch, and/or wire diameter (Fig. 8-10); in addition, fixed resistors connected between potentiometer taps can be used to change the taper (Sec. 8-8).   Generation of *nonmonotonic* functions of the wiper displacement necessarily requires taps in the potentiometer winding (Fig. 8-14).   *Film-type function potentiometers* have flat carbon-film resistance elements of varying width, or they incorporate special electrode shapes to vary the current-flow pattern in the resistance element.[17]   Tapered function potentiometers for various frequently used functions are commercially available (see also Sec. 8-10).   A large variety of nonlinear functions of the servo shaft displacement can also be obtained by combining *linear* servo-driven potentiometers with external resistance networks.[23-29]   A number of practical circuits of this type are listed in the Appendix; such techniques should not be overlooked, especially in the design of special-purpose computers.

8-7. Potentiometer-loading Errors.[19-22]   The output voltage X_o of a potentiometer loaded by a finite resistance r_L is no longer proportional

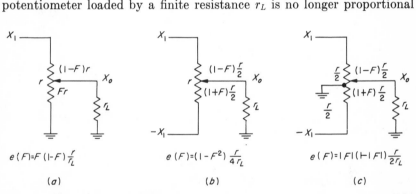

FIG. 8-11. Effects of potentiometer loading.   For each of the circuits shown, $F \equiv F(\vartheta)$ is a function of the fractional shaft displacement ϑ; $F \equiv \vartheta$ for simple multiplication (linear potentiometer).   In each case

$$\frac{X_o}{X_1} = \frac{F}{1 + e(F)} = F\left[1 - \frac{e(F)}{1 + e(F)}\right] \approx F[1 - e(F)]$$

The approximate expression is useful if $r/r_L \leq 0.1$.

to the resistance tapped off between the zero-voltage point on the potentiometer and the potentiometer wiper (see also Sec. 3-5).   Figure 8-11 specifies the resulting *loading errors* for the three most important potentiometer circuits.   Again, if the linear servo follow-up potentiometer in Fig. 8-1a is loaded by a finite resistance r_L, the fractional servo shaft displacement ϑ is no longer accurately proportional to the servo input Y; we have

$$\vartheta = \frac{Y}{E}[1 + e(\vartheta)] \qquad (8\text{-}14)$$

where the function $e(\vartheta)$ is given in Fig. 8-11.   This effect is of interest where a servomechanism is to drive indicating dials (servo voltmeter) or function potentiometers (see also Sec. 8-10).   Note that the servo input circuit of Fig. 8-4a does not load the follow-up potentiometer.

The loading errors can be neglected in low-accuracy computations. In a typical application $r = 20K$, $r_L = 1M$; so that the loading errors will be less than 0.6 (true) per cent in Fig. 8-11a and b, and less than 0.3 per cent in Fig. 8-11c.   If such errors are to be tolerated, the accuracy (linearity, resolution, etc.) of the potentiometer used usually need not exceed 0.1 per cent.

If necessary, potentiometer-loading errors can be eliminated with the aid of special follower amplifiers (Sec. 5-15), or with the bootstrap circuit

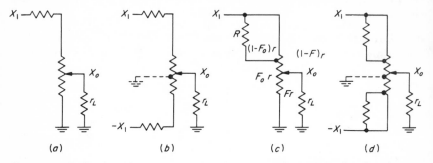

FIG. 8-12. Reduction of potentiometer-loading errors by means of end resistances (a, b) and by preloading (c, d).   The two methods may be combined.

of Fig. 1-23.   In servomultipliers employing linear potentiometers, one can theoretically eliminate loading errors by loading the linear follow-up and multiplying potentiometers with equal resistances (Sec. 2-4).   Exact error cancellation, however, requires equal ratios r/r_L for all potentiometers, and potentiometer resistances r are rarely controlled within less than 5 per cent.   Reference to Fig. 8-11 shows that a 5 per cent discrepancy in the ratios r/r_L for follow-up and multiplying potentiometers causes a maximum residual loading error of about 0.03 (true) per cent for $r/r_L = 0.1$ so that this effect must be watched in accurate computations.[2]

The following methods may be used singly or in combination to reduce loading errors:

1. *End resistances* (Fig. 8-12a and b) restrict the effective range of the quantity F in Fig. 8-11 and reduce the fractional errors due to loading.   The resulting unfavorable scale change may increase the effects of other errors.

2. Multiplying or function-generating potentiometers may be given a taper which corrects the loading errors associated with a fixed load (*preloading*).

3. *Tapped potentiometers* (Sec. 8-8) permit convenient corrections for loading errors and winding imperfections. Figure 8-12c and d illustrates a simple preloading method. In the circuit of Fig. 8-12c, $R = 0.31 r_L$ and $F_0 = 0.74$ are useful design values.[21]

4. The function actually generated by the potentiometer may fit $kF(Y)$ better than $F(Y)$, where k is a suitable constant. Once k is chosen for best fit (least maximum error), one obtains

$$X_o = X_1 F(Y_2) = \frac{X_1}{k} [kF(Y_2)]$$

by a simple coefficient change.

8-8. Tapped-potentiometer Function Generators.[30−37] A widely useful type of function potentiometer is easily constructed as follows.* A linear potentiometer having the required resolution is tapped 7 to 99 times. A set of *padding networks* establishs conveniently adjustable resistance ratios at the various taps, so that the tap voltages can be set to approximate values of a desired function corresponding to the angular displacement of each tap. The potentiometer output will then approximate linear interpolation between successive tap voltages (Fig. 8-13). Figure 8-14 shows padding networks commonly used to obtain a wide variety of functions; it is possible to use storable plug-in padding networks to obtain different functions with the same padded potentiometer (Fig. 8-7b).

To set a given function on a tapped potentiometer, one begins by plotting the desired graph of output voltage vs. servo input voltage. The input voltages corresponding to the tap locations must be marked on the graph; servo input voltages corresponding to equally spaced taps will not be exactly equally spaced if the servo follow-up potentiometer is loaded (Sec. 8-7). The desired tap voltages are determined to fit the given function in the manner of Fig. 8-13. Once the desired tap voltages are known, suitable resistance values for the adjustment networks can be computed from Kirchhoff's laws; each tap must have the correct voltage with the load connected.[31,34,35] The padding-network design is constrained by the current rating of the source driving the potentiometers, and the maximum function slope obtainable is limited by the power rating of one potentiometer segment.

Since padding-resistor computations tend to be cumbersome, it is often preferable to set the desired tap voltages empirically, but the various resistance settings tend to interact badly. When a monotonic function is set up with simple padding resistors in the manner of Fig. 8-14a without

---

* According to P. G. Redgemont of the British Admiralty Signal and Radar Establishment, tapped-potentiometer function generators were used in England as early as 1933.

intermediate connections to the HI and LO terminals, we can, however, ground the LO terminal and drive the HI terminal with a *constant-current generator* (Fig. 1-21 or 1-22).[2]   It is then possible to set the tap voltages with a minimum of interaction; we always move the potentiometer slider to the tap whose voltage we want to adjust.

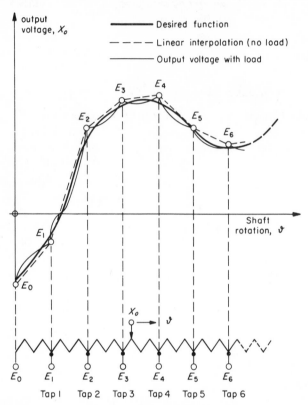

Fig. 8-13. Approximation of a desired function by means of a tapped potentiometer. For best results, the tap voltages may have to be set slightly above or below the function values corresponding to the tap locations.   The effects of loading have been exaggerated in the diagram to show the method of curve fitting used for best accuracy. One can obtain even better interpolation by averaging the voltages from two or three close-spaced potentiometer wipers.

The more elaborate calibration scheme of Fig. 8-15 avoids most of the interaction between tap adjustments.   The adjustment networks (not shown) associated with the first, second, . . . tap are adjusted *in numerical order*.   In the diagram, tap 1 has already been adjusted.   Switch section S_1 permits one to apply suitably spaced positioning voltages to the servomechanism driving the tapped potentiometer.   To adjust tap 2, the potentiometer wiper is positioned near tap 2 to approximate correct loading.   While tap 2 is being adjusted, the d-c amplifiers shown tem-

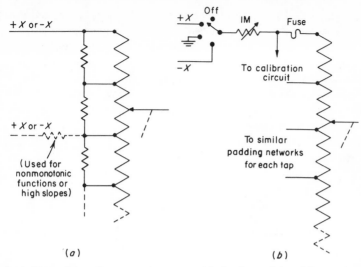

Fig. 8-14. Tapped function potentiometers with fixed parallel padding resistors (a), and with adjustable series padding networks (b).

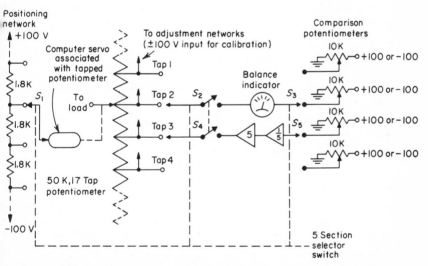

Fig. 8-15. Calibration of tapped-potentiometer function generators in the PACE computer (Electronic Associates, Inc.). The adjustment networks (not shown) are similar to those of Fig. 8-14b. The balance meter is protected by limiting rectifiers. The 5-megohm input impedance of the d-c amplifier shown does not load the comparison potentiometer appreciably.

porarily approximate the correct voltage at tap 3. The selector switch is next advanced to adjust taps 3, 4, . . . ; it is seen that each tap is adjusted *with the load connected and with the two adjacent taps near their final correct voltages.* A single set of comparison potentiometers, two amplifiers, and a balance meter serve all tapped potentiometers of a computer installation by means of plug-in connections.   Individual position-ing networks and selector switches are packaged together with the adjust-ment networks for each tapped potentiometer.   To reduce the cost of such a calibration unit, one can replace the 10 to 20 high-resolution comparison potentiometers with a single pair of potentiometers which are alternately adjusted and switched to successive pairs of taps; the resulting calibration procedure is not essentially more complicated.[37] Each function calibration should be rechecked after all taps are set.

The accuracy (conformity) of the output function will depend on the slope and curvature of the desired function, on the number of taps, and on the potentiometer load.   The interpolation characteristic will be

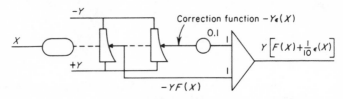

Fig. 8-16. Use of a correction function generator to improve the accuracy of a servo-multiplier or function generator.   The correction function generator may be a tapped potentiometer, so that the additive correction function can be set empirically.   Note that the effects of small imperfections in the correction function generator will be very small.   Analogous correction methods may apply to electronic function generators; such devices cannot, of course, correct errors due to drift or parameter changes.[9]

linear between taps for an infinite load, but the output will "droop" between taps if the load resistance is appreciably smaller than the resist-ance R_S of the potentiometer segment between taps.   It is possible to show with the aid of Thévenin's theorem that *the largest absolute deviation e from linear interpolation between taps is given by*

$$e \leq \frac{2R_S}{r_L} |X| \tag{8-15}$$

where r_L is the load resistance, and X is the larger of the two voltages at the adjacent taps; more accurate bounds can be calculated for specific padding networks and functions.[30]   Conformities within 0.25 per cent of full scale for many useful functions are possible with 10 to 20 taps; *much better accuracy may be obtained when the tapped potentiometer is used to produce a correction to an analytical approximation of the desired function* (Fig. 8-16; see also Sec. 2-4c).

VECTOR RESOLUTION AND COMPOSITION.   RESOLVER SERVOS

8-9. Vector Resolution and Composition.   Important computer applications, such as navigation, range instrumentation, trajectory com-putation, and flight simulation require one to implement relations of the form

$$x = r \cos \vartheta \qquad y = r \sin \vartheta \qquad (8\text{-}16)$$

Equation (16) represents, in particular, the *resolution of a vector of magnitude r along rectangular cartesian axes*, or the *transformation* from polar point coordinates r, ϑ to rectangular *cartesian coordinates* x, y (Fig. 8-17a). Such relations are also combined in the transformation

$$u = x \cos \vartheta + y \sin \vartheta \qquad v = -x \sin \vartheta + y \cos \vartheta \qquad (8\text{-}17)$$

which represents either (1) the new components (coordinates) u, v of a given vector in a u, v coordinate system rotated through the positive angle ϑ with respect to the x, y system, or (2) the components u, v of a vector rotated through the angle $-\vartheta$ (Fig. 8-17b). Three-dimensional

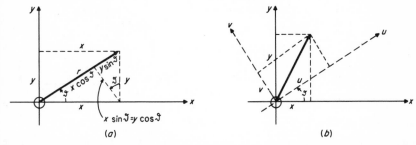

FIG. 8-17. Resolution of a vector in polar coordinates (a), and transformation of vector components or coordinates (b).

rotations are described by similar somewhat more complicated formulas.[45] The great practical importance of such relationships has led to the development of multiplier/function generators known as *resolvers*, which are specifically designed to produce products of the form (16).

Vector composition (*inverse resolution*, rectangular-to-polar coordinate conversion) requires computer setups which produce outputs corresponding to

$$r = \sqrt{x^2 + y^2} \qquad (8\text{-}18a)$$

$$\vartheta = \arctan \frac{y}{x} \qquad (x^2 + y^2 \neq 0) \qquad (8\text{-}18b)$$

for pairs of inputs proportional to x and y. Although Eq. (18a) can be implemented directly, one more frequently obtains ϑ through implicit solution of the equation

$$-x \sin \vartheta + y \cos \vartheta = 0 \qquad (8\text{-}19a)$$

so that r can be produced in the form

$$r = x \cos \vartheta + y \sin \vartheta \qquad (8\text{-}19b)$$

(Fig. 8-17a; see also Sec. 8-13).   Commercially available resolvers usually yield two pairs of products ($\pm X \sin \vartheta, \pm X \cos \vartheta, \pm Y \sin \vartheta, \pm Y \cos \vartheta$) and can be set up to implement Eq. (19) (*inverse-resolver* or POLAR mode of operation) as well as Eqs. (16) and (17) (*resolver* or RECTANGULAR mode).

8-10. Resolver Servos Using Sine-Cosine Potentiometers.   Figure 8-18 shows a *resolver servomechanism* positioning precision continuous-rotation sine-cosine potentiometers in accordance with the input voltage $a_\vartheta\vartheta$.   Such servo resolvers can have static accuracies within 0.05 per

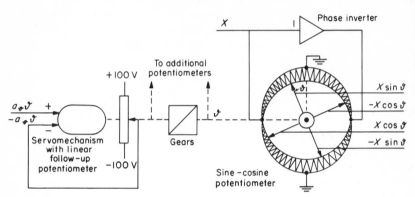

FIG. 8-18. Basic resolver servo employing wirewound continuous-rotation sine-cosine potentiometers.   The sine-cosine potentiometer is geared to the (1-turn or 10-turn) linear follow-up potentiometer, so that the resolver-potentiometer shaft turns through ϑ deg corresponding to $a_\vartheta\vartheta$ volts follow-up voltage.   In ±100-volt computers, the scale factor a_ϑ is usually $\frac{1}{2}$ volt/deg (-200 deg $\leq \vartheta \leq 200$ deg) or $\frac{1}{4}$ volt/deg (-400 deg $\leq \vartheta \leq 400$ deg).   It is possible to use end resistances on the follow-up potentiometer to obtain, instead, a ±180-deg or ±360-deg range with slightly improved accuracy.

cent of full scale (200 volt) for 2 volts/deg scaling.   Film-type sine-cosine potentiometers permit greater servo bandwidth with 0.3 per cent static accuracy (see also Table 8-1).   Different gear ratios permit 4 volts/deg scaling with -360 deg $\leq \vartheta \leq 360$ deg at reduced accuracy; the range of ϑ can, instead, be extended with relay or diode quadrant-switching circuits (Sec. 8-12).   Servo resolvers used in general-purpose analog computers usually have two sine-cosine potentiometers and two or more linear potentiometers for follow-up and multiplication.   Their sine-cosine potentiometers are usually connected (preloaded, Sec. 8-7) for 1M load resistances.

Figure 8-19 illustrates different ways of using the smaller commercially available -90- to $+90$-deg and 0- to 180-deg sine-function potentiometers.   *Square-card sine-cosine potentiometers* (Fig. 8-20) employ a relatively simple square card to produce sine and cosine outputs; precision-cam correction of the contact positions permits static accuracies within

0.5 per cent of full scale.[8] It is also possible to wind square-card potentiometers with specially shaped holes to permit ganging of several such potentiometers on a single shaft.

Table A-2 shows a number of circuits yielding trigonometric functions of a servo input voltage through special connections of *linear* servo-driven potentiometers.

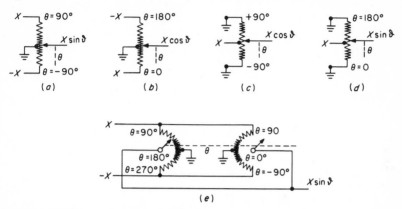

FIG. 8-19. Different connections for small 180-deg-range sine-cosine potentiometers (*a*) to (*d*), and combination of two such potentiometers to permit continuous rotation (*e*).

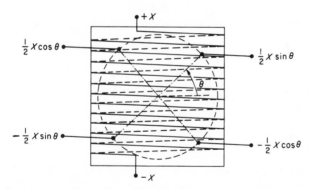

FIG. 8-20. Square-card sine-cosine potentiometer. It is possible to wind similar potentiometer cards with a center hole to permit ganging of potentiometers.

8-11. Induction Resolvers. Modulation and Demodulation. *Induction resolvers* may be regarded as special a-c transformers with two mutually perpendicular *stator windings* and two mutually perpendicular *rotor windings* rotated by a servo shaft. If modulated a-c voltages $X \sin \omega \tau$, $Y \sin \omega \tau$ are applied to the resolver stator windings, the two rotor output voltages are $U \sin \omega \tau$, $V \sin \omega \tau$, with

$$U = X \cos \vartheta + Y \sin \vartheta \qquad V = -X \sin \vartheta + Y \cos \vartheta \qquad (8\text{-}20)$$

where ϑ is the servo-shaft displacement, so that Eq. (16) or Eq. (17) can be implemented with aid of phase-sensitive modulators and demodulators (Fig. 8-21). Note that carrier phase reversal corresponds to a sign change in the modulating waveform. The most frequently employed carrier frequency $\omega/2\pi$ is 400 cps, which permits the modulation waveforms $X(\tau)$, $Y(\tau)$, $U(\tau)$, $V(\tau)$ a useful bandwidth between 0 and 5 to 15 cps. As a rule, a square-wave carrier rather than a sinusoidal carrier is used in order to simplify modulation and demodulation.

The design of accurate induction resolvers is described in refs. 4 and 5. High-quality induction resolvers have at least as good conformity as

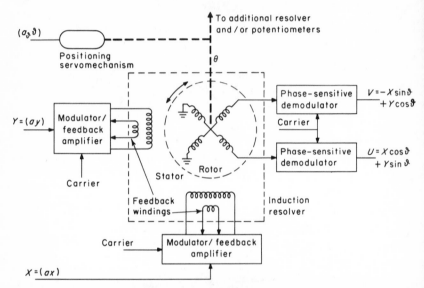

FIG. 8-21. Servo resolver employing an a-c induction resolver with precision modulators and demodulators to implement the coordinate-rotation transformation (20). For $X = 0$, one obtains the simpler outputs $Y \cos \vartheta$, $Y \sin \vartheta$. Many induction resolvers have push-pull rotor outputs instead of the single-ended outputs indicated here.

sine-cosine potentiometers. Induction resolvers have infinite resolution and, since their only rotating contacts are sliprings, there is no wear on precision parts; for the same reason, one obtains lower output noise, reduced friction, and a longer maintenance-free life. The main disadvantage of a-c resolvers is the requirement for very accurate modulation and demodulation; in addition, the carrier phase must be carefully controlled throughout each resolver system to avoid errors in addition and/or demodulation.

Conventional 400-cps-chopper modulation with accurate electromechanical or electronic chopper circuits can be used (see also Secs. 4-14 and 5-8). A very successful resolver modulator described in refs. 2 and 39 employs a pair of four-diode bridges (Sec. 6-10) in the feedback circuit of Fig. 7-18*b* to minimize errors due to the nonlinear forward resistance of the switch.   Accurate demodulation is complicated by the fact that the resolver output is no longer a square wave but contains transients caused by the winding inductance.   Special peak-to-peak demodulators have been designed to sample the resolver output waveform, once per carrier cycle, after the inductive transient has decayed.   Such relatively complex modulators and demodulators yield excellent output static accuracy (within 0.05 per cent of half-scale), but they add substantially to the resolver cost.

In special-purpose computers, several operations on trigonometric functions can be combined without intermediate demodulation and modulation.

8-12. Quadrant Switching and Rate Resolvers.   (a) Although many sine-cosine potentiometers (Figs. 8-18 and 8-20) permit continuous rotation and hence do not limit the range of the resolver angle ϑ, the resolver-servo follow-up potentiometer limits the range of ϑ within fixed limits, usually ± 90 deg, ± 180 deg, or ± 360 deg.   In applications requiring a wider range of angles (e.g., tumbling aircraft motion, special maneuvering turns), one can implement relations like

$$\left. \begin{aligned} \sin\left(\pm\frac{\pi}{2}+\varphi\right) &= \sin\left(\pm\frac{\pi}{2}-\varphi\right) \\ \sin\left(\pm\frac{3\pi}{2}+\varphi\right) &= \sin\left(\pm\frac{3\pi}{2}-\varphi\right) \cdots \end{aligned} \right\} \tag{8-21a}$$

$$\cos\left(-\varphi\right)=\cos\varphi \qquad \cos\left(\pm\pi+\varphi\right)=\cos\left(\pm\pi-\varphi\right) \tag{8-21b}$$

with *quadrant-switching circuits* actuated whenever ϑ reaches predetermined limits.   A quadrant switch intended to extend the range of a ± 90-deg sine potentiometer to $+180$ deg would, for instance, replace the servo input $a_\vartheta \vartheta$ by $a_\vartheta(\pi - \vartheta)$ whenever ϑ exceeds $\pi/2$.   Quadrant switches can be comparator-actuated latching relays or latching switches operated by the potentiometer shaft, or the all-electronic quadrant-switching circuits described in Sec. 8-14 can be used.

(b) In many applications, a voltage proportional to the time derivative $d\vartheta/d\tau$ of the desired resolver angle ϑ is available in the computer setup.   In this case, we can, if desired, obtain unlimited resolver rotation by driving the resolver with a *rate servo* whose output-shaft displacement ϑ changes at a rate proportional to the input voltage $d\vartheta/d\tau$, so that

$$\vartheta = \int_0^\tau \frac{d\vartheta}{d\tau}\, d\tau + \vartheta(0) \tag{8-22}$$

In such a *rate resolver*, the follow-up potentiometer feedback is replaced by d-c tachometer feedback.   Since the resolver now acts as an integrator as well, we shall require control relays for resetting to initial conditions $[\vartheta = \vartheta(0)$, see also Sec. 10-2]; the servo feedback must be switched from a rate signal to a position follow-up in RESET.[2] The follow-up potentiometer used with a resolver having a rate-resolver mode must be a single-turn potentiometer bridged to permit continuous rotation; either solenoid-retractable limit stops or switched electrical limit stops may have to be provided (see also Sec. 8-3b).[2] The design and equalization of computer servomechanisms with rate feedback are discussed in some detail in refs. 1, 2, and 40.

Rate feedback can be obtained with d-c tachometers or with a-c induction generators; the latter permit somewhat better integration accuracy.[40] Operational-amplifier integration is, generally speaking, more accurate than servo integration, especially at low rates $d\vartheta/d\tau$. On the other hand, a rate servo can have better high-frequency response than an operational-amplifier/positioning-servo combination.[40] As an interesting alternative, it is possible to obtain accurate rate-resolver operation with the implicit-computation scheme of Fig. 8-30b, which lends itself well to implementation with multigang servomultipliers. Although this computer setup requires four operational amplifiers and two servomultipliers to produce $X \sin \vartheta$, $X \cos \vartheta$, $Y \sin \vartheta$, and $Y \cos \vartheta$, these computing elements need not be permanently committed, and no special resolver components are used.

8-13. Inverse Resolvers. Automatic Gain Control. Figure 8-22 shows a resolver-servo connection implementing Eq. (19) to yield voltages

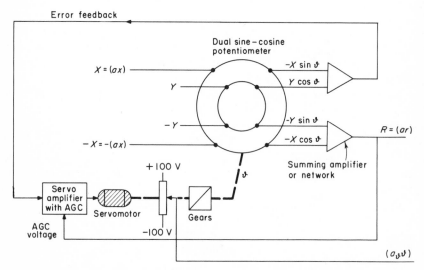

FIG. 8-22. Rectangular-to-polar coordinate transformation (POLAR mode of resolver operation, inverse resolver). A voltage proportional to the angle ϑ is obtained from the servo follow-up potentiometer, which is not used in the feedback loop.

proportional to r and ϑ when the rectangular coordinates or vector components x, y are given.   The servomechanism seeks a position which will null an error signal proportional to $x \sin \vartheta - y \cos \vartheta$.   The resulting feedback ratio is proportional to $r = \sqrt{x^2 + y^2}$, and $\vartheta = \arctan (y/x)$

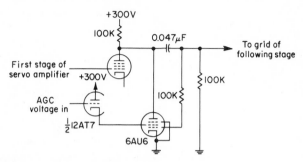

Fig. 8-23a. Simple AGC circuit inserted between two single-ended a-c servo-amplifier stages.   A (positive) AGC voltage applied to the screen of the AGC tube will increase its transconductance.   The resulting increased degeneration reduces the amplifier gain.   The circuit is useful for AGC voltages between 1 and 100 volts.   (*Electronic Associates, Inc.*)

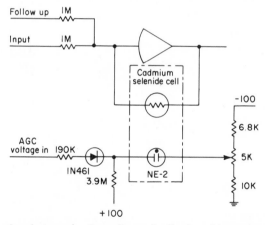

Fig. 8-23b. Use of a photoconductive cell as a feedback resistance to provide AGC in all-d-c servos.   The AGC input controls the neon-bulb light intensity; the 100-volt sources keep the neon bulb on.[41]

is necessarily indeterminate for $x = y = 0$.   To improve the servo performance, we employ automatic gain control (AGC) to increase the servo-amplifier gain for small r.   Figure 8-23 shows two different AGC circuits; additional AGC circuits, including a diode-function-generator gain-control network, will be found in refs. 2, 61, and 62.   Typical resolver-servo AGC circuits keep the loop gain constant within about 6 db as r varies over a 50:1 to 100:1 range.

ELECTRONIC RESOLVERS

8-14. Introduction.   Combination of Function Generators and Multipliers.   Accurate sine-cosine potentiometers are both expensive and relatively large, so that accurate resolver servos are not only costly but also slow (see Table 8-1 under high-accuracy servo).   All-electronic implementation of the multiple products by trigonometric functions required especially in aircraft and space-vehicle simulation still represents a challenging and somewhat difficult problem because of the possible error accumulation in differences of products.   Conventional analog-computer setups for three-dimensional coordinate transformations are all cumbersome and expensive; it is to be hoped that more elegant and more easily serviced hybrid analog-digital techniques will be developed in the future (see also Sec. 11-20).

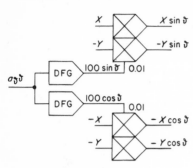

FIG. 8-24. Electronic resolver using diode function generators and electronic multipliers.

The most straightforward electronic resolver circuits simply combine the best available diode function generators with electronic multipliers

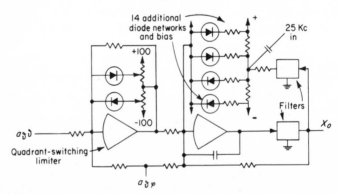

FIG. 8-25. 18-segment diode function generator employing a 25-Kc smoothing oscillator (Sec. 6-13a) and −270- to +270-deg quadrant switching.   The φ input is zero for $X_o = 100 \sin \vartheta$, and adds 90 deg to ϑ for $X_o = 100 \cos \vartheta$.   (*Beckman/Berkeley Division.*)

(Figs. 8-24 and 8-25).   A suitable patchbay layout permits different connections such as POLAR and RECTANGULAR modes, complete Euler-angle transformations, and individual use of the electronic multipliers and function generators.[42–46,58]   To obtain voltages proportional to $\sin \vartheta$ and $\cos \vartheta$ over several quadrants with diode function generators, it is best to use the latter to generate sin ϑ between $\vartheta = -90$ and $+90$ deg, where the function is monotonic.   We can then employ simple *quadrant-switching function generators* (Fig. 8-26) to obtain, say, sin ϑ between -270 and $+270$ deg.   The precision-limiter circuits of Figs. 9-4 to 9-6 permit static accuracies well within 0.1 per cent of half-scale in quadrant-switching applications and, if desired, can also operate quadrant-indicating lights

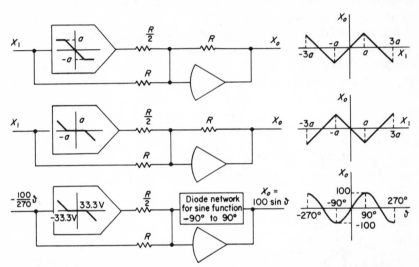

Fig. 8-26. Electronic quadrant-switching circuits used to extend the range of trigonometric-function generators.   The precision-limiter circuits of Sec. 9-2 are particularly useful in this application.

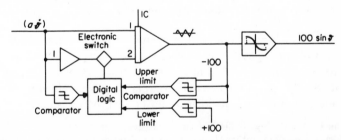

Fig. 8-27. Quadrant-switching scheme for an electronic rate resolver.   Comparator-actuated digital logic reverses the integrator input whenever $|\vartheta|$ exceeds 90 deg.

with their built-in comparator outputs (Sec. 9-2).   Figure 8-27 shows an all-electronic circuit capable of generating sin ϑ or cos ϑ without scale-factor restrictions if a voltage proportional to $\dot\vartheta$ is available in the computer (electronic rate resolver, see also Sec. 8-12).[56,57]

8-15. Use of Sampling and Comparator Circuits.   (a) The *sample-hold resolver* shown in Fig. 8-28 is based on the principle of the sampling

multiplier of Fig. 7-9. A carefully adjusted repetitive-analog-computer setup (shaded integrators in Fig. 8-28) generates the voltages $-R \sin \omega\tau$, $-R \cos \omega\tau$, and $(b/\pi)(\omega\tau - \pi)$ 20 to 1,000 times per second. A fast comparator samples $-R \sin \omega\tau$ and $-R \cos \omega\tau$ whenever the periodic ramp voltage $(b/\pi)(\omega\tau - \pi)$ reaches the value of the input voltage $(a\vartheta)$. The filtered sample-hold output voltages are, then, $R \sin (a\pi/b)\vartheta$ and $R \cos (a\pi/b)\vartheta$, where both $(a\vartheta)$ and the initial-condition input R can be slowly varying machine variables.[52,55]

A sample-hold resolver performs both sine-cosine generation and multiplication in one operation but is subject to a severe compromise between computing bandwidth (about $\frac{1}{20}$ of the repetition rate for, say, 1 per cent of dynamic error) and accuracy. For an accuracy within ϵ per cent

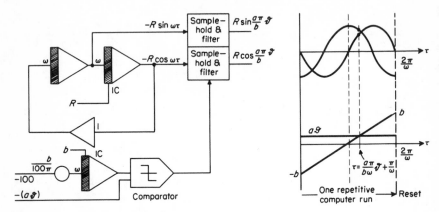

FIG. 8-28. A sample-hold resolver using repetitive-analog-computer circuitry. Shaded integrators are under rep-op control. (See also Sec. 10-6d.)

of half-scale, the worst comparator/switch timing error must be below $\epsilon/2$ per cent of one repetitive-computer-run period $2\pi/\omega$ so that, for example, a 10-μsec timing error limits the repetition rate to 450ϵ runs per second if we allow for a 10 per cent reset period after each run. The corresponding computing bandwidth would be less than 25ϵ cps.

(b) The circuit of Fig. 8-29a[48-50] employs the linear pulse-width modulator of Fig. 7-19 with sinusoidal rather than triangular excitation to generate periodic pulses of width $(\pi - 2X)/\omega$ symmetrical with respect to the sine-wave peaks, where X is measured in radians ($|X| < \pi/2$). These pulses gate the same sine-wave carrier to produce a chopped sinusoidal waveform whose running average is proportional to

$$\omega \int_{-\frac{\pi - 2X}{2\omega}}^{\frac{\pi - 2X}{2\omega}} \cos \omega\tau \, d\tau = 2 \cos X \tag{8-23}$$

Static accuracy within 0.2 per cent of half-scale (± 10 volts) is possible if we combine push-pull chopped sinusoids.[48] In the arcsine-function generator of Fig. 8-29b,[50,51] the input voltage X is added to $a \sin \omega \tau$ to produce a biased sinusoid positive and negative for alternate periods $T_1 = (2/\omega) \arccos (X/a)$ and $T_2 = (2/\omega) [\pi - \arccos (X/a)]$; so that the running average of the comparator output is

$$b \frac{T_1 - T_2}{T_1 + T_2} = -\frac{2b}{\pi} \left(\frac{\pi}{2} - \arccos \frac{X}{a} \right) = -\frac{2b}{\pi} \arcsin \frac{X}{a} \qquad (8\text{-}24)$$

where X is measured in radians. Such arcsine generators can have static accuracies within 0.2 per cent of half-scale and may be used in the inverse-function loop of Fig. 6-22 to yield $\sin cX$.

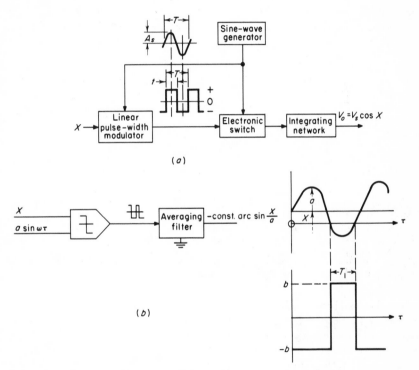

(a)

(b)

Fig. 8-29. Generation of $\cos X$ (a) and $\arcsin X/a$ (b) by operations on a periodic sine-wave voltage.

Each of the circuits of Fig. 8-29 requires an accurate sine-wave oscillator, which can serve several function generators. If some type of phase-shift oscillator is used, we must minimize oscillator amplitude jitter even at the expense of increased distortion (Sec. 9-7), since distortion effects can be corrected with the aid of crude diode correction-function generators in the manner of Fig. 2-5.[51]

8-16. Implicit-computation Schemes. If, as is often the case, a voltage proportional to ϑ is available in the computer, then we can employ the generalized-integrator circuit of Fig. 2-10 to generate $X = 50 \cos \vartheta$ and $Y = 50 \sin \vartheta$ without scale-factor restrictions (Sec. 8-12) as solutions of the differential equations

$$\frac{dX}{d\vartheta} = -Y \qquad \frac{dY}{d\vartheta} = X \qquad\qquad (8\text{-}25)$$

where ϑ is measured in radians (Fig. 8-30a). To prevent exponential sine-wave-amplitude changes due to integrator and multiplier phase shift

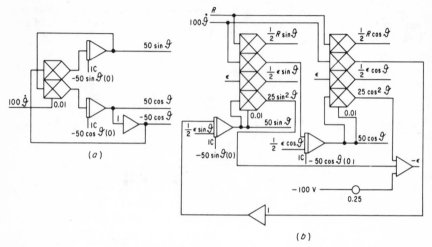

(a)

(b)

FIG. 8-30. Generation of sin ϑ and cos ϑ by implicit computation (a), and electronic rate resolver with steepest-descent-type correction of the amplitude error cos² ϑ + sin² ϑ − 1 (b). (*From H. D. Huskey and G. A. Korn, Computer Handbook, McGraw-Hill, New York, 1962.*) If the 25-volt input to the ϵ amplifier is replaced by a (slowly) variable input $r^2(\tau)/100$, the two integrators will produce the products $r(\tau)$ cos ϑ, $r(\tau)$ sin ϑ with suitable initial conditions, although the response to $r(\tau)$ may be somewhat sluggish (see also Sec. 12-9).

(Sec. 3-24), Howe and Gilbert[53] have devised an ingenious amplitude-correction circuit. Referring to Fig. 8-30b, we continuously compute the amplitude-error voltage

$$\epsilon = A(\cos^2 \vartheta + \sin^2 \vartheta - 1) = A(X^2 + Y^2 - 1) \qquad (A > 0) \quad (8\text{-}26)$$

and minimize ϵ^2 by feeding voltages proportional to

$$\frac{1}{4}\frac{\partial \epsilon^2}{\partial X} = \epsilon X \qquad \frac{1}{4}\frac{\partial \epsilon^2}{\partial Y} = \epsilon Y \qquad\qquad (8\text{-}27)$$

as respective corrections to $-dX/d\tau$ and $-dY/d\tau$ into the integrators producing $X = 50 \cos \vartheta$ and $Y = 50 \sin \vartheta$. Note that the correction voltages are zero whenever the output amplitude is correct. This computer circuit, a special instance of the steepest-descent method discussed in Sec. 12-9, employs only multipliers and linear computing elements to generate sin ϑ and cos ϑ with about the component accuracy of the multipliers used. Brunner[54] has reduced the relatively large number of electronic multipliers required by minimizing $|\epsilon|$ rather than ϵ^2. Section 12-9b describes a modified circuit, which also substitutes simple electronic switches for two of the multipliers required in Fig. 8-30b.

An analogous correction scheme also permits computation of three direction cosines $\cos \alpha$, $\cos \beta$, $\cos \gamma$ for three-dimensional coordinate transformations; our correction feedback must, in this case, enforce the relation[59]

$$\cos^2 \alpha + \cos^2 \beta + \cos^2 \gamma - 1 = 0 \qquad (8\text{-}28)$$

Such implicit-computation methods are economical only if the relatively large number of accurate products required can be obtained at reasonable cost. Solid-state time-division multipliers with multiple transistor-switch slave channels (Sec. 7-11) may be suitable for this purpose. Figure 8-30b can, of course, also be implemented with two multiproduct servomultipliers.

REFERENCES AND BIBLIOGRAPHY

Computer-servomechanism Design

1. Gilbert, E. O.: The Design of Position and Velocity Servos for Multiplying and Function Generation, *IRETEC*, September, 1959.
2. Loveman, B. D.: Computer Servomechanisms and Servo Resolvers, in Huskey, H. D., and G. A. Korn, *Computer Handbook*, McGraw-Hill, New York, 1962.
3. Harris, M.: Servomultiplier Performance, *Berkeley Engineering*, no. 1, April, 1957, Beckman/Berkeley Div., Richmond, Calif.
4. Gibson, J. E., and F. B. Tuteur: *Control System Components*, McGraw-Hill, New York, 1958.
5. Truxal, J. G.: *Control Engineers' Handbook*, McGraw-Hill, New York, 1958.
6. Biernson, G. A.: Comparison of Lead-network, Tachometer, and Damper Stabilization for Electric Servos, *IRE Trans. PGAC*, May, 1959.
7. Adise, H.: One Solution to Servomechanism Hunting, *Electronic Inds.*, January, 1961.
8. Greenwood, I. A., Jr., J. V. Holdam, Jr., and D. MacRae, Jr.: *Electronic Instruments*, MIT Radiation Laboratory Series, vol. 21, McGraw-Hill, New York, 1948.
9. Gunning, W. F., and A. S. Mengel: *Rept.* RM 236, Rand Corporation, Santa Monica, Calif.
10. Ehlers, H. L., and W. Hochwald: Maintenance Procedures and Test Circuits, in Huskey, H. D., and G. A. Korn, *Computer Handbook*, McGraw-Hill, New York, 1962.

Multiplying and Function-generating Potentiometers

11. Blackburn, J. F.: *Components Handbook*, chap. 8, by F. E. Dole, MIT Radiation Laboratory Series, vol. 17, McGraw-Hill, New York, 1948.
12. Duncan, D. C.: Characteristics of Precision Servo Computer Potentiometers, *Trans. AIEE Conf. Feedback Systems*, Atlantic City, N.J., 1951.
13. Schmidt, H. A.: The Precision Potentiometer as a Voltage Divider, *Product Engineering—Annual Handbook of Product Design*, 1954.
14. Bradley, F. R., and R. D. McCoy: Computing with Servo-driven Potentiometers, *Electronic Inds.*, September, 1952.
15. Frost, J.: Compact Analog Computer, *Electronics*, July, 1948.

16. Hogan, I. J.: Electrical Noise in Wirewound Potentiometers, *WESCON Record*, 1952.

17. Adise, H. H.: Precision Film Potentiometers, *WESCON Record*, 1960.

18. Nettleton, L. A., and F. E. Dole: Potentiometers, *Rev. Sci. Instr.*, **17**: 356 (1946).

19. ———: Reducing Potentiometer Loading Error, *Rev. Sci. Instr.*, **18**: 332 (1947).

20. Cahn, L.: Automatic Compensation of Potentiometer Loading Errors, *Helinews*, Helipot Corporation, South Pasadena, Calif., June, 1953.

21. Gilbert, J.: Here's a Shortcut in Compensating Potentiometer Loading Errors, *Control Eng.*, February, 1955.

22. ———: Compensating Function Potentiometers for Loading Errors, *Control Eng.*, March, 1955.

23. Hofstadter, R.: A Simple Potentiometer Circuit for Production of the Tangent Function, *Rev. Sci. Instr.*, **17**: 298 (1946).

24. Chance, B., F. C. Williams, V. Hughes, D. Sayre, and E. F. MacNichol, Jr.: *Waveforms*, MIT Radiation Laboratory Series, vol. 19, McGraw-Hill, New York, 1949.

25. *Project Typhoon Summary Progress Rept. 4*, vol. 2, RCA Research Laboratories, Princeton, N.J. (unclassified).

26. Levenstein, H.: Generating Non-linear Functions with Linear Potentiometers, *Electronic Inds.*, October, 1953.

27. Seay, P. A.: An Accurate Tangent Computing Circuit, *REAC Newsletter*, August, 1954 (Reeves Instrument Corp., New York).

28. Bolie, V. W.: Synthesis of Function Generators by Continued-fraction Theory, *Electronic Inds.*, March, 1956.

29. Lazarus, H.: Cosine Computing Circuit, U.S. Patent 2,864,924, September, 1958 (assigned to Reeves Instrument Corp.).

Tapped-potentiometer Function Generators

30. Korn, G. A.: Design and Construction of Universal Function Generating Potentiometers, *Rev. Sci. Instr.*, **21**: 77 (1950). Equation (15) corrects an error in this reference.

31. Harris, H. E., and R. D. McCoy: Simplified Calculations for Servo Function Generators, *Electronic Design*, March, 1957.

32. Williams, R. W., and H. Marchant: Resistance Potentiometers as Function Generators, *Electronic Eng.*, October, 1958.

33. Garner, K. C.: Linear Multi-tapped Potentiometers with Loaded Outputs, *Electronic Eng.*, April, 1959.

34. Kislitsyn, S. G., and F. L. Litvin: On Calculating Function-generating Shunted Potentiometers for Chebyshev Approximations, *Automatika i Telemekhanika*, November, 1959.

35. Sherchaut, I.: The Correction of Errors in Potentiometer Function Generators, *Electronic Eng.*, August, 1960.

36. Parezanovic, N., and M. Dujmovic: Accuracy Improvements of the Tapped-potentiometer Function Generators, *IRETEC*, February, 1962.

37. Korn, G. A.: Calibration of Padded-potentiometer Function Generators, *Instruments and Control Systems*, October, 1959.

Servo Resolvers and Rate Resolvers
(See also refs. 1 to 8)

38. Electrical Resolvers: Staff Report, *Electromechanical Design*, February, 1960.

39. Godet, S.: The Gated-amplifier Computer Technique, *Proc. Natl. Simulation Conf.*, Dallas, Tex., 1956; Simulation Councils, Inc., La Jolla, Calif.

40. Connelly, M. E.: Computers for Aircraft Simulation, *Report* 7591-R-2, MIT Electronic Systems Laboratory, Cambridge, Mass., Dec. 15, 1959.
41. Morrill, C. D., and R. C. Weyrick: Unique AGC System for D-c Servos, *Control Eng.*, July, 1958.

Electronic Resolvers and Inverse Resolvers

42. Morrill, C. D.: Electronic Multipliers and Related Topics, in Huskey, H. D., and G. A. Korn, *Computer Handbook*, McGraw-Hill, New York, 1962.
43. Thaulow, P.: Electronic Resolver System, *Memo. Rept.*, Beckman/Berkeley Division, Richmond, Calif., Dec. 4, 1959; see also Beckman/Berkeley specification sheets for Models 1154 sine/cosine generator.
44. Sine-cos Generator Model 8.054: *Product Information Release* 6079, Electronic Associates, Inc., Long Branch, N.J., 1960.
45. Grado, G. R.: A Solution to the Euler-angle Transformations, *IRETEC*, September, 1960.
46. Kindle, W. K.: High-accuracy, High-speed Electronic Resolver, *Engineering Application Release* 4-1, Electronic Associates, Inc., Long Branch, N.J., 1961.
47. Hartmann, J., G. A. Korn, and R. L. Maybach: Low-cost Triangle-integration Multipliers for Analog Computers, *Ann. AICA*, October, 1961.
48. Schmid, H.: A Transistorized, All-electronic Cosine/sine Function Generator, *WESCON Record*, 1958.
49. ————: Function Generator for Sines and Cosines, *Electronics*, Jan. 23, 1959.
50. ————: Transistor Analog Computing Elements, in Huskey, H. D., and G. A. Korn, *Computer Handbook*, McGraw-Hill, New York, 1962.
51. Maybach, R. L.: A Sine-cosine Generator for Use in Analog Computers, M.S. Thesis, Electrical Engineering Department, University of Arizona, 1961.
52. Andrews, J.: The Operational Amplifier with DYSTAC as a General-purpose Nonlinear Element, *Application Data Sheet* 0005, Computer Systems, Inc., Fort Washington, Pa., 1960.
53. Howe, R. M., and E. G. Gilbert: Trigonometric Resolution in Analog Computers by Means of Multiplier Elements, *IRETEC*, June, 1957.
54. Brunner, W.: Steepest Ascent, *PCC Rept.* 151, Electronic Associates, Inc., Princeton, N.J., 1959.
55. Miura, T.: Japanese patent issued in 1958.
56. Korn, G. A.: The Impact of Hybrid Analog-digital Techniques on the Analog-computer Art, *Proc. IRE*, May, 1962.
57. Raymond, F. H.: Methode d'intégration fractionnée, *Ann. AICA*, July, 1960.
58. Pinckney, R. P., and S. Giser: The Sine-cosine Operator, *Rept.* R-73, MIT Instrumentation Laboratory, Cambridge, Mass., 1954.
59. Stability of Electronic Analog Computers, *WADC Rept.* 57-425, Wright Air Development Center, Ohio, 1957.
60. Moore, J. R.: Lectures given in the UCLA Extension Division, University of California, Los Angeles, 1952/3.

Miscellaneous

61. Susi, F.: Solving the AGC Dilemma, *Electronics*, July 19, 1963.
62. Koeblitz, W.: Photocell in Feedback Circuit Regulates Output, *Electronic Design*, June 21, 1963.
63. Texas Instruments Staff: *Transistor Circuit Design*, McGraw-Hill, New York, 1963.

CHAPTER 9

SPECIAL ANALOG-DIGITAL CIRCUITS FOR INSTRUMENTATION, CONTROL, AND SIMULATION

INTRODUCTION

9-1. Introductory Remarks. This chapter draws on the experience and know-how of many laboratories to present a useful collection of special circuits. The *precision-limiter circuits* described in Secs. 9-2 to 9-4 employ special feedback connections to implement limiter characteristics essentially as accurate as linear operational amplifiers at least at low computing frequencies. Accurate and inexpensive *selectors, timers,* and *maximum-excursion indicators* with both analog and digital outputs are obtained in this manner.

Sections 9-5 and 9-6 deal with *bistable operational-amplifier circuits* and *special signal generators* employing analog computing elements. These techniques yield a wide variety of modulated and unmodulated test signals for use in accurate *test oscillators* and in communication-system simulation. Sections 9-7 to 9-9 describe special computer circuits simulating *common nonlinearities in control systems and other dynamic systems,* including limit stops, friction, backlash, granularity, and hysteresis.

PRECISION LIMITERS, SELECTORS, AND TIMERS

9-2. Precision Limiters, and Some Related Circuits. (a) The basic diode-limiter circuits described in Sec. 6-3 yield static accuracies between 0.2 and 1 volt, depending on the particular application. By comparison, the *precision-limiter circuits* of Fig. 9-1 approximate ideal static limiter characteristics within 0.05 volt with the aid of high-gain low-drift d-c amplifiers.[1,2]   When each diode D_1 in Fig. 9-1 conducts, it is inside a high-gain degenerative feedback loop, so that the nonlinear diode forward resistance and the "built-in bias voltage" (Fig. 6-2) are effectively divided by the loop gain.   As D_1 ceases to conduct, the degenerative

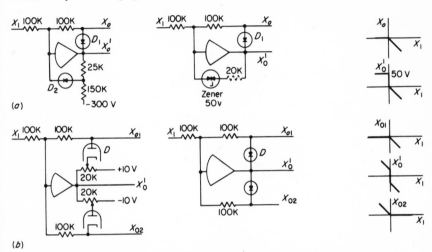

(a)

(b)

Fig. 9-1. Precision-limiter circuits.   The circuits of Fig. 9-1b each produce two precision-limiter outputs.   The second circuit of Fig. 9-1b utilizes the built-in bias of a silicon-junction diode to produce an 0.4- to 0.8-volt comparator step and cannot be used with vacuum diodes; external bias does, however, yield slightly better accuracy.

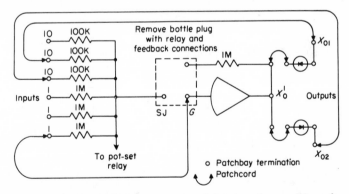

Fig. 9-1c. Patchbay connections converting one of the summing amplifiers of a general-purpose analog computer into the silicon-junction-diode precision limiter of Fig. 9-1b. One of the existing summing resistors serves as a feedback stabilizing resistor between summing junction (SJ) and amplifier input (G) (Sec. 5-18); this resistor can be replaced by a short circuit in modern computers.

feedback decreases; the open-loop gain of the amplifier produces a decisive step in the voltage X'_o and cuts D_1 off with a very sharp break.   Figure 9-2a compares a precision-limiter characteristic with ordinary series-limiter characteristics produced with silicon-junction and vacuum diodes.

Such accurate nonlinear characteristics have a wide variety of applications in computation, instrumentation, and control.

At higher frequencies, precision-limiter operation is modified by the combined effects of circuit and diode capacitances and amplifier rise time (Fig. 9-2b; see also Sec. 6-5). The phase-shift and comparator-step-delay errors illustrated in Fig. 9-2b increase with the input-voltage swing.

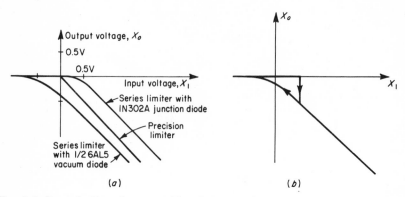

Fig. 9-2. Reproduction of an actual low-frequency (0.02-cps sweep) servo-table plot comparing a precision-limiter characteristic and series-limiter characteristics obtained with the circuit of Fig. 6-3d using silicon-junction and vacuum diodes (a), and a precision-limiter characteristic taken at 5 Kc (b).

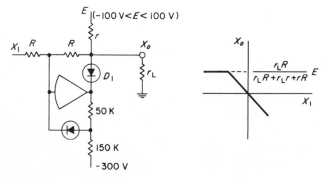

Fig. 9-3. A precision-limiter circuit producing a nonzero limiting level. Reversal of diodes and bias yields a reversed (bottom-limited) characteristic.

High-frequency errors are minimized by fast amplifiers, low circuit impedances, and careful attention to low-capacitance layout. One further reduces the comparator-step delay by reducing the precision-limiter bias; the bias can be reduced to about 1 volt without affecting the static limiting accuracy. As with other diode circuits, speedup capacitors across the input resistor or resistors will improve the frequency response at least over a limited frequency range (Sec. 6-5). With low computing resistances (2K), suitable amplifiers and fast diodes (1N916A), precision limiters can still yield 0.2 per cent accuracy at 10 Kc.

(**b**) Figure 9-3 shows a precision limiter capable of limiting at a precisely adjustable positive or negative level other than zero (see also Sec. 9-3).[2]   As in the precision-limiter circuits of Fig. 9-1a, reversal of diodes and bias yields a reversed limiter characteristic (bottom limit instead of top limit).   The *dual precision limiter* of Fig. 9-4[2] again produces comparator steps to drive a diode bridge (Sec. 6-6) decisively into its positive and negative limits.   Because of the relatively large circuit capacitances involved, this circuit works best at frequencies below 50 cps.   As in Fig. 9-3, the limit levels depend on the load resistance.

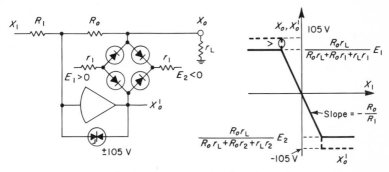

FIG. 9-4. A dual precision limiter.   The output X'_o again produces comparator steps to cut the diode bridge off decisively.

Figures 9-5a and b illustrate the use of diode-bridge feedback to produce useful *deadspace characteristics*.   Figure 9-5c combines such a deadspace circuit with precision-limiter feedback to produce two precision-limiter outputs and comparator steps separated by a precisely adjustable deadspace.   This *precision-deadspace circuit*[3,4] combines 0.05 volt static accuracy with useful operation up to at least 10 Kc.   The circuits of Figs. 9-5b and c are not only useful for control-system simulation; they can perform automatic switching operations whenever the input voltage X_1 exceeds set limits, as required, for example, for

Go/no-go testing
Circuit protection
Automatic scale changes
Carry generation in hybrid computers (Sec. 11-19)
Counting control-transient cycles
Amplitude-distribution analysis
Resolver quadrant switching (Sec. 8-12)

Figure 9-6 shows the use of a precision limiter in a *precision absolute-value circuit*.

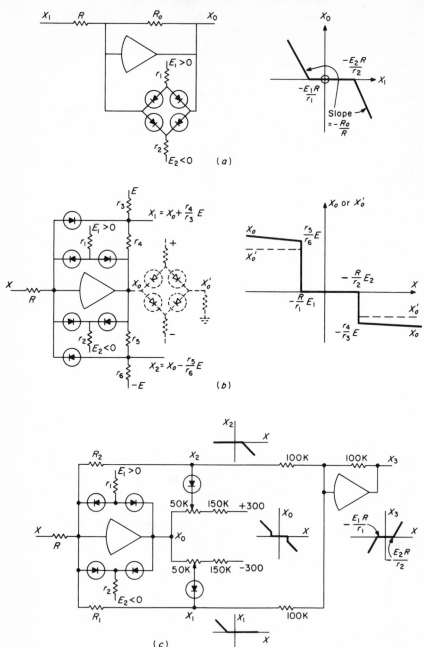

Fig. 9-5. Deadspace circuit using a diode bridge (a), deadspace comparator (b), and precision deadspace circuit (c).

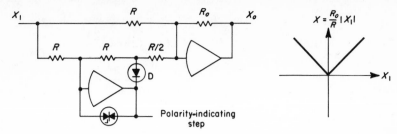

Fig. 9-6. Precision absolute-value circuit. Reversal of the limiter diode D yields $-(R_o/R)|X_1|$.

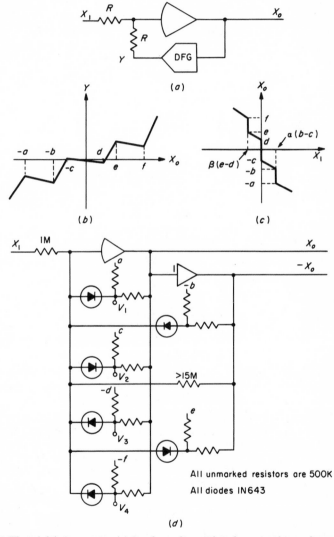

(a)

(b)

(c)

All unmarked resistors are 500K

All diodes IN643

(d)

Fig. 9-7. The multicomparator (a) employs alternating degenerative and very slightly regenerative feedback (b) to produce a transfer characteristic with multiple comparator steps (c). Figure 9-7d shows a practical circuit which, in addition to its multicomparator outputs X_o, $-X_o$, produces individual comparator steps V_1, V_2, V_3, V_4.

349

(c) Precision limiters (and related selector circuits, Sec. 9-3) can be regarded as basic "analog-to-hybrid-code converters." *Precision limiters produce not only very accurate analog limiter characteristics but also "digital" step outputs indicating the precise time when the input voltage crosses predetermined limits.* These step outputs are widely useful for actuating limit-indicating lights, relays, and/or digital-computer circuits (Secs. 8-12 and 11-19).

While the precision limiters of Figs. 9-1 and 9-4 or 9-5 respectively produce step outputs marking a single limiting level and two limiting levels, the "multicomparator" or quantizing circuit of Fig. 9-7[5] is a generalized precision limiter capable of marking 10 to 15 discrete voltage levels. Such a circuit can be useful for hybrid analog-digital computation, statistical sorting, or step-function generation. Figure 9-7*a* shows a high-gain d-c amplifier with nonlinear feedback through a diode function

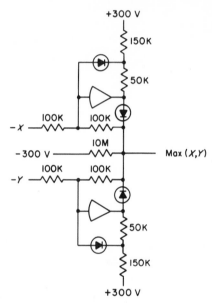

Fig. 9-8. A precision-selector circuit producing the larger of two voltages X, Y. Reversal of diodes and bias would yield min (X,Y) instead of max (X,Y).

generator having the transfer characteristic (Y vs. X_o) defined by Fig. 9-7*b*. The resulting feedback is alternately degenerative and zero (or very slightly regenerative) as the input voltage X_1 changes. It follows that the forward transfer characteristic (output X_o vs. input X_1, Fig. 9-7*c*) exhibits sharp comparator steps at accurately defined input-voltage values; the regenerative action will tend to make the breakpoint values of X_1 independent of diode characteristics and temperature.

Figure 9-7*d* illustrates a practical circuit. *Note that the output terminals marked* V_1, V_2, V_3, V_4 *yield positive or negative comparator steps starting at zero*, which is particularly useful for operation of associated digital circuitry. Addition of extra diode channels yields up to 15 comparator steps ($16 = 2^4$ states); $2n$ diodes yield $n + 1$ states, and only two amplifiers are used. Unity slopes and equal breakpoint intervals are shown for simplicity, although other values may be preferable for various applications. Too much regeneration will cause comparator steps with hysteresis.

The multicomparator circuit works up to at least 20 cps with Philbrick K2XA/K2P

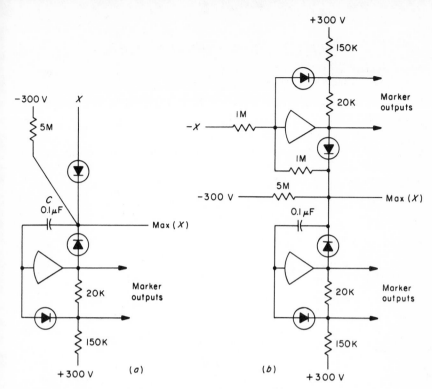

FIG. 9-9a, b. These maximum-holding circuits accurately store the largest past value of a voltage $X = X(\tau)$ and produce sharp comparator steps marking successive relative maxima.

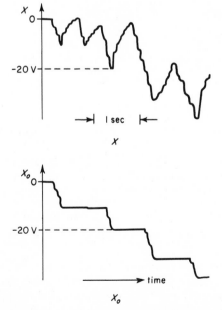

FIG. 9-9c. Record produced by a *minimum-holding* circuit obtained from Fig. 9-9a or b by reversal of diodes and bias.   A 0.1-μF holding capacitor was used.

amplifiers and short wiring; for operation at low frequencies, the circuit can be patched with ordinary computer amplifiers and diode function generators.

9-3. Accurate Selectors, Extreme-value Holding Circuits, and Peak Detectors.

The precision-limiter circuit of Fig. 9-8 functions as a *precision selector*[2] which produces the larger of two constant or variable voltages X, Y. Reversal of diodes and bias would yield min (X,Y)

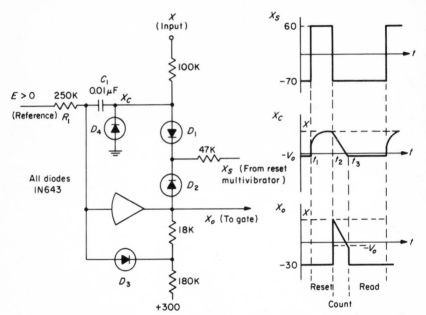

FIG. 9-10a. Precision voltage-to-time converter using a single operational amplifier switched by a control multivibrator, comparator, or manual switch. Diodes D_1, D_2 form a half-bridge switch, which opens when the control waveform X_S is positive. X_o is then negative, D_3 is ON, D_4 is OFF, and the capacitor charges to the voltage X to be measured. When X_S becomes negative, D_1, D_2 are ON, D_3 is OFF, and X_C is the low-impedance output of an integrator. X_C decreases at the rate $-E/R_1C_1$ until it reaches the small negative value $-V_0$ (about -0.6 volt) necessary to turn D_4 ON. The current into D_4 turns the bridge diode D_2 OFF with decisive precision-limiter action; X_o decreases sharply, and D_3 turns ON. X_o marks the time interval $t_3 - t_2 = (R_1C_1/E)(X + V_0)$ and can gate 100-Kc pulses into a counter; the slightly temperature-sensitive offset voltage V_0 can be compensated by an extra diode in series with the input X. 0.1-volt accuracy is possible.

instead of max (X,Y). Unlike most precision-limiter circuits, this two-amplifier selector has a low source impedance in *both* of its two switching states.

Each of the *maximum-holding circuits*[6,7] of Fig. 9-9 combines a precision selector with an integrator. These circuits mark successive relative maxima with precisely timed digital steps and hold the largest past value of the input X. These circuits were originally developed for spacecraft applications (rocket-thrust measurements) and are also useful in many simulation problems. If the storage capacitors are shunted with suitably large resistances, the same circuits become accurate *peak detectors* for a-c waveforms.

9-4. Simple Voltage-to-time Converters and Digital Voltmeters.

The *voltage-to-time* converter of Fig. 9-10a combines a ramp-producing integrator with a precision limiter to generate a precisely timed waveform suitable, for example, for accurate analog-to-digital conversion by means of a gated oscillator and counter.[2,8,9] Conversion accuracy is within 0.1 volt between 3 and 100 volts. Improved low-voltage accuracy can be obtained by rescaling; a better method adds, say, a 50-volt bias to the input voltage X and subtracts this bias by resetting the indicating counters to -50.0 instead of to zero at the start of each count. With suitable counter logic, one can, in fact, add, say, a 120-volt bias to X and reset to -120.0, so that it becomes possible to read negative as well as positive values of X.

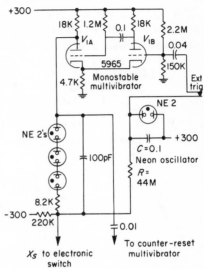

Fig. 9-10b. This simple oscillator circuit generates 5- to 20-cps reset pulses for the voltage-to-time converter of Fig. 9-10a. A second output actuates the reset multivibrator of the pulse counter used with the converter. R and C set the repetition rate.

Figure 9-10b shows a simple multivibrator circuit suitable for periodic resetting of the voltage-to-time converter and counters.[8] If the converter is to operate with a positive input voltage X, the converter input can be obtained from a precision absolute-value cir-

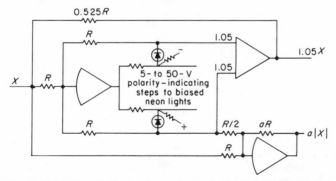

Fig. 9-11. A combination absolute-value, polarity-indication, and bootstrap unloading circuit for a digital voltmeter.

cuit (Fig. 9-6), which can also yield a polarity-indicating step for automatic polarity indication.   Figure 9-11 shows a combination absolute-value, polarity-indication, and bootstrap unloading circuit (see Fig. 1-23) which uses only two amplifiers.[10]   The circuits of Figs. 9-10 and 9-11 may be combined into inexpensive *digital voltmeters* with 0.1 volt accuracy, automatic polarity indication, and 500M input impedance.

**BISTABLE OPERATIONAL-AMPLIFIER CIRCUITS,
SPECIAL SIGNAL GENERATORS, AND
COMMUNICATION-SYSTEM SIMULATION**

9-5. Bistable Operational-amplifier Circuits.   Figure 9-12a shows a simple analog bistable circuit.[1,2]   The comparator biases itself through

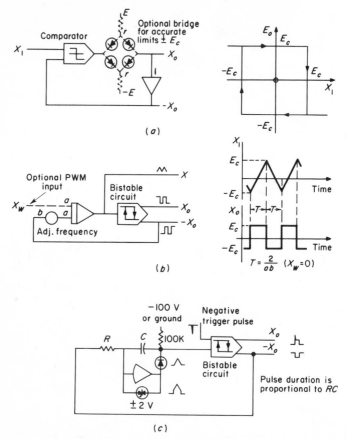

Fig. 9-12. Analog bistable element with push-pull output (*a*), astable (free-running) multivibrator (*b*), and monostable multivibrator (*c*).   If only one accurate analog output $-X_o$ is needed, we can interchange the positions of bridge limiter and inverter in Fig. 9-12a and substitute an inexpensive one-stage inverter for the precision feedback inverter without any loss in accuracy.   We can also vary the amount of hysteresis by changing the regenerative loop gain.

a phase-inverting amplifier, so that an input voltage equal to or larger than $+E_C$ is needed to change the output state. The input voltage then loses control until it reaches the negative value $-E_C$.

The addition of an integrator to the basic multivibrator circuit of Fig. 9-12a yields a *free-running (bistable) multivibrator* (Fig. 9-12b). Figure 9-12c shows a *monostable multivibrator circuit* capable of delivering precisely timed pulses after triggering (see also Sec. 9-4).

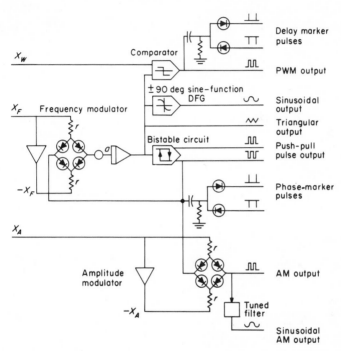

Fig. 9-13a. Generation of different modulated waveforms with the simple free-running multivibrator of Fig. 9-12b. All outputs permit electrical frequency modulation completely independent from their amplitude or pulse-width modulation. Depending on the components used, the frequency range between 0.0001 and 10 cps can be covered with timing and amplitude accuracies within 0.1 per cent of half-scale; accuracies within 1 per cent of half-scale can be obtained up to 50 Kc. Clearly, only the portion of the circuit specifically needed for a given application need be built or patched.

The astable multivibrator of Fig. 9-12b is widely useful as an accurate and versatile signal generator producing various periodic waveforms with analog-computer accuracy. With the addition of a simple −90 to +90 deg sine-generating diode network, one obtains an accurately timed sine wave as well as triangular-wave and push-pull square-wave or pulse outputs (Fig. 9-13).[1,2,11,12] The triangular waveform is invaluable for measuring transfer characteristics of function generators, transistors, etc., at different frequencies, and for testing multipliers (Sec. 7-20). The pulse outputs can operate electronic switches, relays, lights, or digital computing elements, and pulse differentiation yields useful phase-reference markers.   Figure 9-13 also shows how easily various accurately modulated signals are produced by multivibrator-type signal generators. Frequencies all the way between 0.005 cps and 200 Kc can be obtained with suitable amplifiers.

Low-frequency signal generators of this type are easily patched on general-purpose analog computers; the resulting signals will be more accurate than those produced by most commercially available test instruments.   Permanently connected analog-computer bistable circuits used

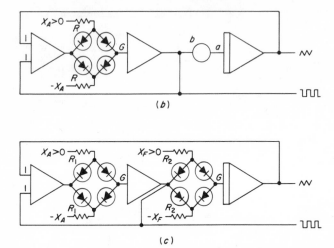

Fig. 9-13b, c. Two accurate astable multivibrators using the fast comparator circuit of Fig. 6-13e.   Figure 9-13b permits amplitude modulation of both triangle-wave and pulse output at constant frequency.   Figure 9-13c provides for frequency modulation at constant amplitude, or for amplitude modulation at constant triangle slope (see also refs. 52 and 53).

in special-purpose equipment need not always employ expensive chopper-stabilized d-c amplifiers.   Depending on the particular application, only one or two amplifiers may require drift stabilization, or a-c coupling may be possible (Fig. 7-31a).

Figure 9-14a and b shows two computer-patched bistable circuits which permit symmetrical triggering, e.g., for scale-of-2 applications.[13,14] Referring to Fig. 9-14a, with $X_{01} > 0$, $X_{02} < 0$ (D_1 ON, D_2 OFF), diode D_2 will pass only positive trigger pulses exceeding $-X_{02}$.   Such a trigger pulse will flip X_{02} and therefore also X_{01}.   The roles of the two comparators will be reversed for alternate trigger pulses.   The circuit is insensitive to negative input pulses.

Figure 9-14c shows a simplified two-amplifier astable multivibrator.

9-6. Accurate Sine-wave Oscillators. Multivibrator/function-gen-erator-type oscillators are probably the most widely useful general-purpose signal generators. Direct generation of sinusoidal waveforms is, however, preferred if segmented sinusoidal output cannot be tolerated, if the square-wave and triangular multivibrator waveforms are not needed, and/or where both quadrature outputs $\pm a \sin \omega t$ and $\pm a \cos \omega t$ are required, as in servomechanism testers and for plotting circles or ellipses.

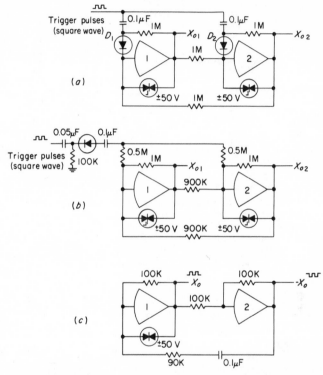

FIG. 9-14. Two bistable circuits which permit symmetrical triggering (a), (b), and a simplified astable multivibrator (c). Regenerative circuits similar to Fig. 9-14b also yield various interesting d-c transfer characteristics for different combinations of coupling and feedback resistors.

An *induction resolver rotated by a simple rate servomechanism* at a manu-ally adjustable angular velocity ω (Sec. 8-11) yields 60 cps to 10 Kc output modulated by $\pm a \sin \omega t$ and $\pm a \cos \omega t$. A second induction resolver manually rotated through a desired phase angle ϑ can be used to produce "variable phase output" modulated by $a \cos (\omega t + \vartheta)$ for null-type phase measurements (see also Sec. 8-12).[15]   The resulting modulated test signals serve as inputs to 60- or 400-cps control-system components, or a phase-sensitive demodulator is used to yield low-frequency sinusoidal output.

By contrast, *all-electronic sine-cosine generators* produce voltages $\pm a \sin \omega t$, $\pm a \cos \omega t$, and $a \cos (\omega t + \vartheta)$ which can still, if desired, modulate 60- or 400-cps control-system voltages with the aid of simple bridge modulators in the manner of Fig. 9-13. Electronic signal generators are smaller and lighter, require less maintenance, and have a vastly wider frequency range than servo-type signal generators. Since LC oscillators do not easily yield low distortion, and heterodyne signal generators tend

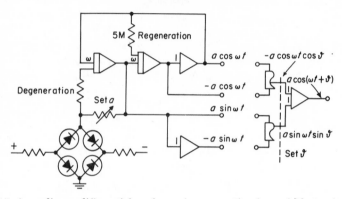

FIG. 9-15. An ordinary differential-analyzer sine-generating loop yields $\pm a \sin \omega t$, $\pm a \cos \omega t$, and with a manually adjusted dual sine-cosine potentiometer, $a \cos (\omega t + \vartheta)$. A diode-bridge limiter controls the oscillation amplitude; better accuracy is possible with an AGC circuit like that in Fig. 9-17*b*.

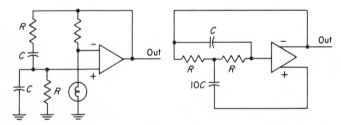

FIG. 9-16. Simple Wien-bridge and bridged-T phase-shift oscillators.

to have poor frequency stability, practically all sine-wave oscillators operating in the frequency range between 0.001 cps and 50 Kc are RC *phase-shift oscillators.*

Figures 9-15 to 9-17 show different types of RC phase-shift oscillators employing inexpensive computer-type d-c amplifiers to permit accurate operation at frequencies all the way between 0.01 cps and 1 Mc.[16-23] If output below, say, 10 cps is not required, d-c coupling and chopper stabilization are, of course, unnecessary, but utility-type plug-in d-c amplifiers are still convenient and yield high gain to reduce distortion and output impedance. Each phase-shift oscillator comprises a regenerative linear feedback loop with phase shift slightly in excess of 180 deg at the oscil-

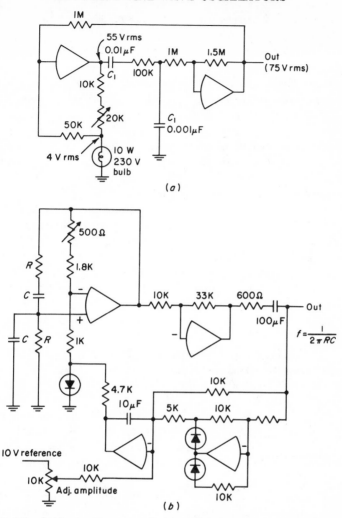

Fig. 9-17. Wien-bridge oscillators employing utility-type vacuum-tube d-c amplifiers (a), and transistor d-c amplifiers (b). A practical frequency-range switching scheme might employ the same capacitor as C_1 and as $C_2 = 0.1\ C_1$ in different frequency ranges. Arrows indicate where quadrature voltages 90 deg out of phase with the main oscillator output could be taken off with the aid of additional amplifiers. Very accurate amplitude-control circuits require a-c coupling, chopper stabilization, or low-drift differential-input transistor amplifiers. The circuit of Fig. 9-17b yields amplitude stability within ±0.02 db, frequency stability within ±1 per cent, and less than 0.5 per cent distortion between 100 cps and 6 Kc. (*Burr-Brown Research Corporation, Tucson, Ariz.*)

lator frequency.   The resulting oscillation must be limited to a stable amplitude with a *nonlinear amplitude-control circuit*.   The simplest circuit of this type is a simple feedback limiter or bridge limiter in the sine-generating loop (Fig. 9-15); the resulting distortion can be kept as low as 1 per cent of the amplitude if the sine-generating loop is adjusted to be only very slightly regenerative.   Reference 19 describes a similar *three-phase oscillator* with three sinusoidal outputs.

Improved sine-wave accuracy requires automatic gain control throughout the cycle instead of simple clipping.   Medium-accuracy oscillators operating above 20 cps have long employed the nonlinear resistance of a tungsten-filament lamp or other temperature-sensitive resistor to control the oscillation amplitude (Fig. 9-16).   Such simple amplitude-control circuits involve a compromise between distortion and amplitude stability, especially if the oscillator is to operate over a wide frequency range.[17,18] At the lower frequencies, temperature-sensitive resistors tend to follow the instantaneous oscillator output instead of its rms value, and nonlinear distortion results; at higher frequencies, increasingly linear operation may permit amplitude jitter due to hum and line or load transients. Temperature-sensitive resistors should also be operated at temperatures high enough to render the effects of ambient-temperature variations negligible.

More recent types of low-voltage transistor phase-shift oscillators replace the tungsten-lamp amplitude control by the nonlinear resistance of a silicon-junction diode or diodes biased by an AGC voltage.   The diode is operated in the knee of its characteristic.   Figure 9-17 shows an amplified-AGC or integral-control scheme.   The AGC voltage is obtained through precision full-wave rectification of the sinusoidal oscillator output (Sec. 9-2);[20] peak detection could be used instead.[17]   Such circuits permit amplitude control within 0.1 per cent with 0.25 per cent distortion down to at least 20 cps.

Without question, the most accurate low-frequency sine-cosine oscillator is a two-integrator sine-generating loop with continuous minimization of the amplitude error $|\epsilon| = |\sin^2 \omega t + \cos^2 \omega t - 1|$ through feedback into one or both integrators, as in Fig. 8-30b.[21]   Such circuits can yield amplitude accuracy and distortion within 0.05 per cent but are relatively expensive (see also Sec. 12-9b).

SIMULATION OF SPECIAL CONTROL-SYSTEM NONLINEARITIES

9-7. Saturation, Limit Stops, and Backlash.   A simple saturation characteristic (Fig. 9-18a) approximating the behavior of various amplifiers, valves, motors, etc., is readily obtained with simple shunt, feedback, or bridge-limiter circuits (Secs. 6-3 and 6-6).   Some care is, however, necessary if the simulated saturation characteristic is to be preceded by an integrator or time-lag circuit.   Figures 9-18b and c illustrate two different possibilities; the behavior of such circuits must be carefully compared with the properties of the devices to be simulated in each particular case.

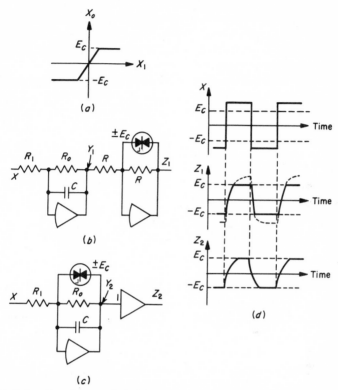

FIG. 9-18. Saturation characteristic (a), two types of saturation limiters preceded by a simple lag (b, c) and square-wave responses (d).   The case $R_o = \infty$ corresponds to an integration preceding the simple lag.

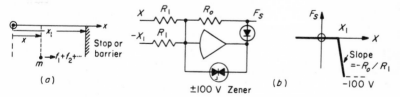

FIG. 9-19. Linear motion of a body restrained by a (fixed or movable) limit stop (a), and precision-limiter representation of an elastic stop with moderate stiffness (b).

The action of a fixed *limit stop* on a moving particle body (Fig. 9-19) is *not* correctly represented by simple limiting of the particle displacement x. Direct simulation requires one to generate voltages proportional to the actual forces exerted by the limit stop as the moving particle penetrates the stop slightly.

These forces may be elastic in nature (*elastic stop*, energy is conserved); i.e., the force f_S exerted by the stop is given by

$$f_S = \begin{cases} -k_S(x - x_1) & (x > x_1) \\ 0 & (x \le x_1) \end{cases} \qquad (9\text{-}1)$$

where $x - x_1$ is the penetration distance (Fig. 9-21), or the force f_S may be approximated by a viscous force

$$f_S = \begin{cases} -C_S \dfrac{d}{dt}(x - x_1) & \left[x > x_1, \dfrac{d}{dt}(x - x_1) > 0 \right] \\ 0 \text{ otherwise} \end{cases} \qquad (9\text{-}2)$$

(viscous-type *inelastic stop*). If the force (2) were not zero for $(d/dt)(x - x_1) > 0$, the moving body would stick to the stop.[34] Combinations of such forces, or nonlinear forces depending on both $x - x_1$ and $\dot{x}$, result in *semielastic stops* with different coefficients of restitution, i.e., with partial dissipation of the initial kinetic energy. Figure 9-20 shows fabricated diode circuits for the simulation of inelastic stops.[34,38] If the

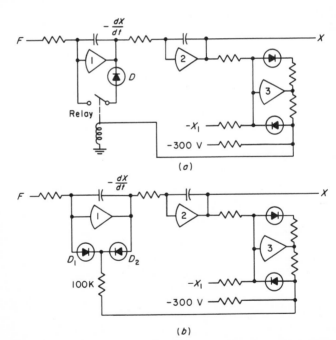

FIG. 9-20. Simulation of an *inelastic* stop with a relay (*a*) and with a diode switch (*b*). Diode *D* prevents "sticking." Note that the diode-bridge switch will limit the rate of discharge of integrator 1 (Sec. 6-10). In both circuits, finite diode forward resistances (50 to 100 ohms) permit the output of integrator 1 to differ slightly from zero for $F > 0$, so that some applications may require a second switch ahead of integrator 2 to prevent *X* from creeping.

moving body is limited to an interval between *two stops* ($x_1 \geq x \geq x_2$), the circuits of Figs. 9-19 and 9-20 may be duplicated with appropriately reversed diodes and bias voltages, or a deadspace circuit can be used. Many other variations and generalizations are possible. In particular,

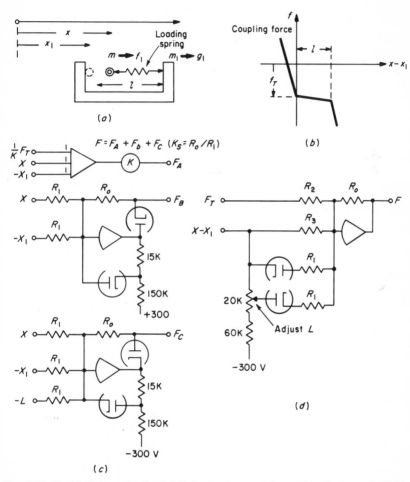

FIG. 9-21. Backlash in spring-loaded linkages or gears (*a*), coupling force on the driven member (*b*), and two diode circuits generating voltages proportional to the coupling force (*c, d*). The loading spring (anti-backlash device) can be omitted. Note that an equal and opposite force acts on the driving member.

the stops themselves may be moving bodies, so that x_1 becomes a variable. The impact force on the stop will be equal and opposite to the force f_S; the computer can deal with motions involving impacts for two or more moving rigid bodies. In this manner, one can simulate *elastic backlash* (Fig. 9-21).

By contrast, the "pseudo-backlash" circuit of Fig. 9-22[4] represents neither elastic impact nor a reaction force on the driving (input) member. This circuit is, however, useful for the simulation of backlash in potentiometers, process-control sensors, and other instruments which measure a process variable but do not affect the measured variable appreciably.

To simulate *oblique impacts* on smooth barriers, one must separately consider components of the impact forces in the coordinate directions (see also Sec. 12-10). It is, for instance, readily possible to simulate the rebound of a billiard ball from a barrier.

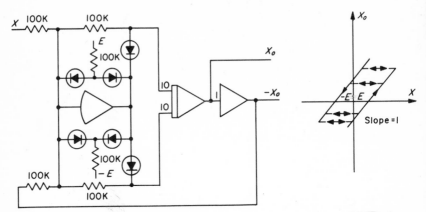

FIG. 9-22. An accurate "pseudo-backlash" circuit employing the precision deadspace limiter of Fig. 9-5c. Other deadspace circuits can be substituted.

Simulation of hard elastic impact (e.g., steel on steel) requires caution, because the true impact forces can be so very large compared with all other forces in question that accurate scaling becomes quite impossible. In such cases, simulation circuits like those of Figs. 9-19 to 9-21 are necessarily inaccurate. Correct simulation of hard elastic, semielastic, or inelastic impacts requires *comparator-switched sample-hold-integrator circuits* which can store, reverse, and attenuate voltages proportional to each preimpact velocity component. A simulation circuit of this type is described in Sec. 10-12.

9-8. Simulation of Static and Coulomb Friction. Dry friction acting, say, on a body capable of sliding in the x direction is commonly represented as a force

$$F_{\text{FRICTION}} = \begin{cases} -F_{\text{APPLIED}} & (|v| < \epsilon, |F_{\text{APPLIED}}| < F_S) \\ -F_S \text{ sign } (F_{\text{APPLIED}}) & (|v| < \epsilon, |F_{\text{APPLIED}}| \geq F_S) \\ -F_C \text{ sign } (v) & (|v| \geq \epsilon) \end{cases} \quad (9\text{-}3)$$

where F_{APPLIED} is any external force applied in the x direction and $v = \dot{x}$ is the velocity of the sliding body. With the body at rest ($v = 0$), we have *static friction* equal and opposite to F_{APPLIED} until $|F_{\text{APPLIED}}|$ exceeds the breakaway force F_S.   As the body begins to slide ($v > \epsilon$, where ϵ is a small velocity, say $\frac{1}{500}$ of the total velocity range), we have *Coulomb friction*, i.e., a constant force of value $F_C < F_S$ opposing the velocity.

It will be noted that analog-computer simulation of dry friction requires generation of a function of *two* variables, since F_{FRICTION} depends on F_{APPLIED} as well as on v.   McLeod[36] has implemented Eq. (3) with operational relays for slow real-time simulation; Fig. 9-23 shows an all-electronic circuit[45] believed to be substantially simpler as well as faster and more accurate than other diode circuits proposed for dry-friction simulation.[39-44]   The circuit of Fig. 9-23 requires only two amplifiers in addition to three diode-bridge limiters (Sec. 6-6), which are available in many analog-computer patchbays.   Phase inverter and diode-bridge limiter 1 cancel the applied-force voltage by adding $-F_{\text{APPLIED}}$ from the input of integrator 2 as long as $|v| < \epsilon$ and $F_{\text{APPLIED}} < F_S$.   When F_{APPLIED} exceeds F_S, the bridge output is limited to F_S or $-F_S$, and the resulting net integrator input can produce a velocity output in accordance with

$$\ddot{x} = \dot{v} = F_{\text{APPLIED}} - F_S \operatorname{sign}(F_{\text{APPLIED}}) \tag{9-4}$$

where a body of unit mass is assumed for simplicity.

Amplifier 3 serves as a deadspace comparator (Sec. 9-2), whose output equals zero when feedback diode bridge 2 conducts for $|v| < \epsilon$, but equals $a \operatorname{sign}(v)$ for $|v| \geq \epsilon$.   The diode-bridge limiter 3 at the comparator output sets accurate limits $\pm a$ and also clips any comparator ringing. The comparator output is applied to amplifier 1 and drives the output of bridge 1 decisively into its limit $-F_S \operatorname{sign}(v)$ whenever $|v| > \epsilon$.   Since the required Coulomb-friction force is $-F_C \operatorname{sign}(v)$, a portion $(F_C - F_S) \operatorname{sign}(v)$ of the comparator output is added to the integrator input.   Amplifier 4 is not part of the computer setup proper but was added to display and record the total friction force.

Figure 9-23*b* shows results obtained using a 1-μF integrating capacitor; the transition between static and Coulomb friction is clearly visible as the simulated body starts to move.   Essentially similar results were obtained with a repetitive analog computer operating on a 1:1,000 time scale (0.001-μF integrating capacitor and Philbrick K2XA/K2P amplifiers).[45]

9-9. Other Common Nonlinearities.   Figure 9-24 illustrates simple representations of *relays* and *dry-friction clutches*.   Figure 9-25 shows a circuit simulating *granularity* in wirewound potentiometers or other instruments.

A variety of *hysteresis-type transfer characteristics* can be obtained through combination of diode function generators with the bistable circuit of Fig. 9-12*a* or the "pseudo-backlash" circuit of Fig. 9-22.   Although such computer setups do exhibit hysteresis, they do not usually simulate

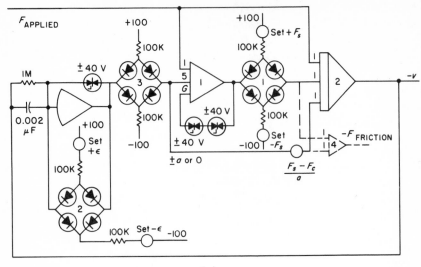

(a)

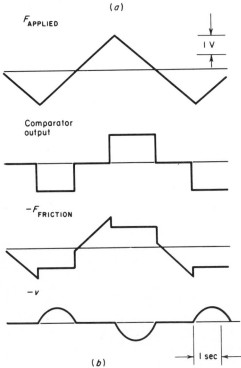

(b)

Fig. 9-23. Simulation of static and Coulomb friction.

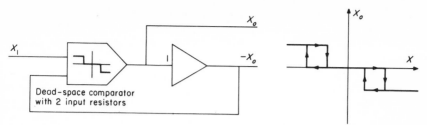

FIG. 9-24a. Deadspace/hysteresis circuit useful for simulation of relays, solenoids, clutches, and valves. The deadspace comparator of Fig. 9-5b is used.

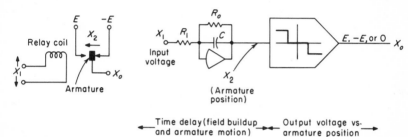

FIG. 9-24b. Another simplified representation of a polarized double-throw relay. The delays involved in field-current buildup and armature motion are approximated by the transfer function $\dfrac{X_2}{X_1} = -\dfrac{R_o}{R_1}\dfrac{1}{R_oCP + 1}$, which is not unreasonable for well-designed relay circuits and sufficient armature damping. A more detailed simulation of the spring-restrained armature with damping and stops would be used for investigations of contact bouncing, effects of static friction, etc.

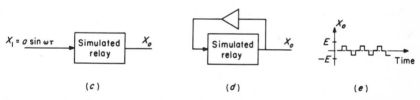

FIG. 9-24c, d, e. Generation of relay-chopper waveform with the circuit of Fig. 9-24b: externally driven relay (a), self-excited relay (buzzer) (b), and waveform (c).

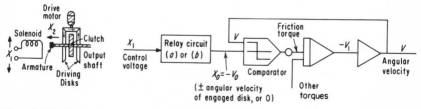

FIG. 9-24f. Simulation of a solenoid-operated dry-disk clutch. The dry-friction torque (see also Sec. 9-11) is developed from the difference between the output speed and speed of the driving disk engaged.

the hysteresis characteristics of plastic and magnetic materials, steam-engine and compressor cycles, etc., correctly. Phenomena of this kind should not be simulated by trick diode circuits; correct hysteresis behavior must, instead, be reproduced by a computer setup implementing the differential equations governing the system dynamics.[48,49]

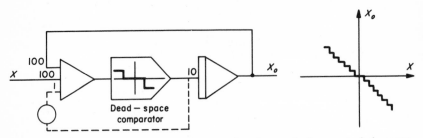

FIG. 9-25. Simulation of granularity in potentiometers and other control elements.

REFERENCES AND BIBLIOGRAPHY

Precision Limiters and Related Circuits

1. Morrill, C. D., and R. V. Baum: Diode Limiters Simulate Mechanical Phenomena, *Electronics*, November, 1952.
2. Koerner, H., and G. A. Korn: Function Generation with Operational Amplifiers, *Electronics*, Nov. 6, 1959.
3. Hartmann, J., G. A. Korn, and R. L. Maybach: Low-cost Triangle-integration Multipliers for Analog Computers, *Ann. AICA*, October, 1961.
4. Korn, G. A.: Control Applications for New Deadspace Limiter, *Control Eng.*, March, 1962.
5. ————: A Multi-comparator Circuit, *Instruments and Control Systems*, January, 1963; see also *Ann. AICA*, April, 1963.
6. ————: Electronic Function Generators, Switching Circuits, and Random-noise Generators, in Huskey, H. D., and G. A. Korn, *Computer Handbook*, McGraw-Hill, New York, 1962.
7. ————: Maxima and Minima, in Anderson, T. C., Analog Techniques, *Instruments and Control Systems*, March, 1962.
8. Barker, B., and M. McMahan: Digital Voltmeter Employs Voltage-to-time Converter, *Electronics*, May 5, 1961.
9. Becker, C. L., and J. Wait: Two-level Correlation on the Analog Computer, *IRETEC*, December, 1961.
10. Rubin, A. I.: A Combination "Bang-bang," Absolute-value, Unloading Circuit Using Only Two Amplifiers, *PCC Rept.* 143, Electronic Associates, Inc., Computing Center, Princeton, N.J., June 25, 1959.

Bistable Operational-amplifier Circuits and Special Signal Generators
(See also refs. 1 and 2)

11. Cockrell, W. D.: *Industrial Electronics Handbook*, McGraw-Hill, New York, 1958.
12. Morrison, J.: A Versatile Forcing-function Generator, *Electronic Eng.*, March, 1961.
13. Berbert, A. G., and C. R. Kelley: Piloting Nuclear Submarines, *Electronics*, June 8, 1962.

14. Eckes, H. R.: A New Analog-simulated Bistable Element Permitting Symmetrical Triggering, *IRETEC*, October, 1962.
15. Korn, G. A., and T. M. Korn: Modern Servomechanism Testers, *Electronic Eng.*, September, 1950.
16. Howe, R. M., and C. Leite: Low-frequency Oscillator, *Rev. Sci. Instr.*, **24**: 901 (1953).
17. Cochran, D. S.: The Transistorized RC Oscillator, *Hewlett-Packard J.*, Hewlett-Packard Co., Palo Alto, Calif., January, 1962.
18. Oliver, B. M.: The Effect of μ-circuit Nonlinearity on the Amplitude Stability of RC Oscillators, *Hewlett-Packard J.*, Hewlett-Packard Co., Palo Alto, Calif., April, 1960.
19. Witsenhausen, H.: Three-phase Oscillator, *Ann. AICA*, April, 1962.
20. *Application Notes*, Burr-Brown Research Corp., Tucson, Ariz., 1962.
21. Meyer-Brötz, G.: Anwendungen Analoger Rechenelemente in der Tiefstfrequenz-Messtechnik, *Frequenz*, **16**: 1 (1962).
22. Good E. F.: A Two-phase Low-frequency Oscillator, *Electronic Eng.*, May, 1957.
23. Klein, G., and J. M. Hertog: A Sine-wave Generator with Periods of Hours, *Electronic Eng.*, June, 1959.

Simulation of Communication and Detection Systems

24. Palumbo, O. J., and E. A. Sevian: Analog Study of FM Discriminator, *Memorandum*, Radio Corporation of America, Moorestown, N.J., 1959.
25. Lambert, J. M., and A. J. Heidrich: Radar System Simulation Techniques, *IRE Natl. Convention Record*, part 4, 1959.
26. Frazier, J. P., and J. M. Lambert: Analog Simulation of Radio Guidance and Space Communication Systems, *Rept.* R60D SD15, General Electric Co., Syracuse, N.Y., Oct. 31, 1960.
27. Frazier, J. P., and J. Page: Phase-lock Loop Frequency Acquisition Study, *Rept.* R61 DSD25, General Electric Co., Syracuse, N.Y., 1961.
28. Berger, E. L., and R. M. Taylor: Optimization of Radar in Its Environment by GEESE Techniques, *Proc. Western Joint Computer Conf.*, 1961.
29. Fischer, L. G., and G. Frenkel: Search-radar Analog Simulator Reproduces Jamming, Scintillation, *Electronics*, Aug. 25, 1961.
30. Kettel, E.: Die Anwendungsmöglichkeiten der Analogrechentechnik in Messtechnik and Nachrichtenverarbeitung, *Telefunken Z.*, **33** (September, 1960).
31. Korn, G. A.: Electronic Analog/Hybrid Computers and Their Use in Systems Engineering, in Machol, R. E., S. N. Alexander, and W. P. Tanner, *System Engineering Handbook*, McGraw-Hill, New York, 1965.
32. Diamantides, N. D.: Nonlinear Filter Detects Envelope or Backbone, *Electronics*, June 19, 1960.
33. ————: Artificial Neurons through Simulation, *Proc. 3d AICA Conf.*, Opatija, Yugoslavia, September, 1961, Presses Académiques Européennes, Brussels, Belgium.
See also Simulation Council Newsletter, *Instruments and Control Systems*, November, 1962, for an additional bibliography.

Simulation of Control-system Nonlinearities
(See also refs. 1 to 4)

34. Johnson, C. L.: *Analog Computer Techniques*, 2d ed., McGraw-Hill, New York, 1963.
35. Smith, G. W., and R. C. Wood: *Principles of Analog Computation*, McGraw-Hill, New York, 1959.

36. McLeod, J.: Electronic-analog-computer Techniques for the Design of Servo Systems, in Huskey, H. D., and G. A. Korn, *Computer Handbook*, McGraw-Hill, New York, 1962.

37. Korn, G. A., and T. M. Korn: Special Circuits for Dynamical-system Studies, in Huskey, H. D., and G. A. Korn, *Computer Handbook*, McGraw-Hill, New York, 1962.

38. Korn, G. A.: Simulation of Inelastic Stops, *IRETEC*, March, 1960.

39. Monastyrshin, G. I.: Mathematical Simulation of Dry Friction, *Automatika i Telemekhanika*, December, 1958.

40. Wang, H., and C. N. Shen: Simulating True Dry Friction, *Control Eng.*, October, 1962.

41. Dunsmore, C. L.: Computer Analogs for Common Nonlinearities, *Control Eng.*, October, 1959.

42. Langill A. W.: Accurate Simulation of Nine Common Nonlinearities, *Electronic Design*, June 21, 1961.

43. Zampino, J.: Southeastern Simulation Council Meeting, Oct. 20, 1961, reported in *Instruments and Control Systems*, March, 1962.

44. Terrazas, C., and B. B. Fannin: Simulating Discontinuous Nonlinear Functions, *Electronic Inds.*, August, 1962.

45. Korn, G. A.: A New Analog-computer Setup for Simulation of Static and Coulomb Friction, *Instruments and Control Systems*, September, 1962.

46. Wong, Ming S.: Refraction Anomalies in Airborne Propagation, *Proc. IRE*, September, 1958.

47. Howe, R. M.: Analog Techniques, *Instruments and Control Systems*, August, 1961.

48. Steingroewer, H.: Circuit for Hysteresis Loop, *PCC Rept.* 142, Electronic Associates, Inc., Princeton Computation Center, Princeton, N.J., 1959.

49. Simulation of a Reciprocating Compressor, *Application Bull.*, Electronic Associates, Inc., Long Branch, N.J.

Miscellaneous Circuits

50. Paynter, H. M.: Ordering and Selection Processes and Ultrareliable Systems, AAAS paper, December, 1958; reprinted by G. A. Philbrick Researches, Inc., Boston, Mass.

51. Conant, B. K.: Analog-computer Setup for an Accurate Monostable Multivibrator, *Instruments and Control Systems*, June, 1963.

52. Hausner, A.: Multiple Integrals on a Non-repetitive Analog Computer, *Proc. Spring Joint Computer Conference*, Detroit, Mich., 1963.

53. Foote, D. D.: Pulse-width Modulator, *Instruments and Control Systems*, May, 1963.

PART III

ANALOG MEMORY, HYBRID ANALOG-DIGITAL COMPUTATION, AND COMPUTER-SYSTEM DESIGN

CHAPTER 10

INTEGRATOR-MODE CONTROL, ANALOG MEMORY, AND ITERATIVE COMPUTATION

INTRODUCTION

10-1. Survey. Sections 10-2 to 10-5 describe relay and electronic circuits for switching analog-computer integrators into their RESET, COMPUTE, and HOLD modes (see also Sec. 1-6) and for storing analog voltages on capacitors (track-hold circuits). Clock-controlled automation of these switching operations permits repetitive computer operation (see also Sec. 1-7) and use of stored results in later computer runs. We add decision-making comparators and digital logic set up to switch analog circuits; the resulting *iterative differential analyzer* is a hybrid computer combining high-speed analog computation with memory and control (Secs. 10-6 to 10-16).

Sections 10-17 to 10-20 discuss function storage and transport-delay simulation.

INTEGRATOR-MODE CONTROL AND TRACK-HOLD MEMORY

10-2. Integrator-control Relays. Figure 10-1 illustrates a practical integrator-control circuit for a "slow" electronic differential analyzer. Like the simple integrator-resetting relay of Fig. 1-10, the two mode-control relays in Fig. 10-1a are deenergized in the COMPUTE (OPERATE) *mode* to permit integration (Fig. 10-1b). When the *hold relay* K_H alone is energized (HOLD *mode*, Fig. 10-1b), it removes and grounds the integrator input network, so that the integrator "holds" the last-computed output voltage. In the RESET *mode*, both K_H and the *reset relay* K_R are energized. K_H still disconnects the integrator input, while the reset relay K_R connects the initial-condition (IC) input to the amplifier. The circuit then acts as a phase-inverting operational amplifier with transfer function $-1/(rCs+1)$ (Sec. 1-14); the integrating capacitor charges

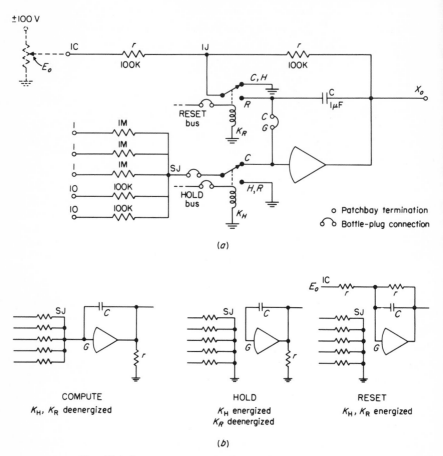

(a)

(b)

FIG. 10-1. Integrator-control relays and integrator modes.

to the desired initial output voltage $X_o = -E_0$ with a charging time constant equal to rC.

Ordinarily, the reset and hold relays for all the integrators of a computer are connected to common RESET and HOLD busses, so that the integrators can be switched simultaneously by the computer COMPUTE/HOLD/RESET switch or pushbuttons (Sec. 10-3). The HOLD mode is useful for slow readout into digital voltmeters, printers, etc., and for manual or automatic program changes. Modern analog-computer patchbays also let us disconnect selected integrators from the main control busses for separate control-circuit patching. We can, for instance, use integrators to provide analog storage for slow iterative computation (Sec. 10-8). In any case, the control relays K_H and K_R must release, and K_H must close within 1 to 2 msec without prolonged bouncing; integrator switching times must not differ by over a fraction of a millisecond if we are to avoid serious timing errors (Sec. 3-2c). It is usually easier to synchronize two single-pole relays than to synchronize the contacts on one relatively heavy double-pole-relay armature. We shall also require a careful choice of precious-metal relay contacts to keep contact resistances below 10 ohms.

With sufficiently fast relays (reed relays, chopper relays, Sec. 10-10), it becomes practical to reset the computer periodically for slow (1 to 10 cps) *repetitive operation* (Sec. 1-7); for higher repetition rates, we prefer electronic switching (Secs. 10-4 and 10-5). Figure 10-2 shows a simplified initial-condition-setting circuit which has been especially useful for inexpensive repetitive computation (see also Sec. 11-6).

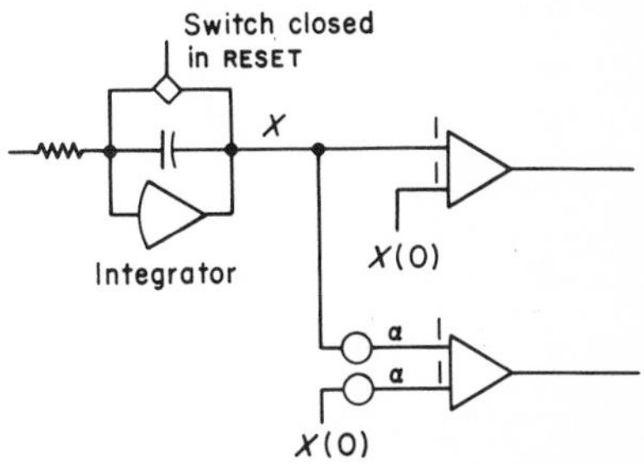

Fig. 10-2. This simplest of all initial-condition-setting schemes requires initial-value voltages to be added into each separate computing element following an integrator; as an alternative, an initial-condition-adding summing amplifier can follow each integrator whose initial output differs from zero.

10-3. Control Systems for "Slow" Electronic Differential Analyzers.
(a) Requirements. The POT SET Mode. An *analog-computer control system* comprises the switches and relays required to turn the machine on and off and to select operating modes (COMPUTE, HOLD, RESET) and auxiliary modes such as STANDBY (high voltage off) and REFERENCE OFF (patchbay deenergized, see also Sec. 11-1a). Most computer systems add a POT SET *mode*, which resets all integrators and grounds all summing-amplifier summing junctions to prevent overloads while coefficients are set (Fig. 10-3). The POT SET mode may also deenergize the computer patchbay for patching (REFERENCE OFF *mode*) and ground amplifier input terminals through small resistors, so that a slight unbalance will cause the overload indicator to light until the amplifier is rebalanced (BALANCE CHECK *mode*). We can, incidentally, eliminate the need for pot-set-relay circuitry by adding suitable zener-diode limiters to each d-c amplifier.

(b) A Simple Control System. Figure 10-4a shows a simple rotary-switch control system. In practice, there is little need for manual switching into the HOLD mode, which is more commonly actuated automatically by timers or comparators. For small computers, one may prefer a simple RESET/COMPUTE lever switch with RESET in the center and fixed and momentary COMPUTE positions up and down. The switch may be paralleled with a jack for a pushbutton cord permitting the operator to control the machine while standing up to set potentiometers, adjust recorders, etc. Repeated pushbutton operation also permits a

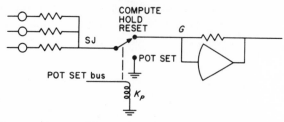

FIG. 10-3. The summing-amplifier *pot-set relays* K_P (and, similarly, the integrator hold relays K_H, Fig. 10-1a) prevent amplifier overloads due to potentiometer setting (see also Fig. 4-7a). Each potentiometer still "sees" the same load as in the COMPUTE mode.

primitive repetitive-computer display on an oscilloscope with driven sweep; note that the control circuit of Fig. 10-4a provides for an oscilloscope trigger step to start the sweep.

(c) **A Practical Pushbutton Control System.** Analog-computer operating controls are used so much that they deserve very careful design to minimize operator errors and fatigue. The simple lighted-pushbutton

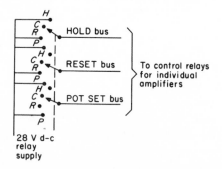

FIG. 10-4a. A simple operating-control system.

control system shown in Fig. 10-4b does not merely offer pushbutton convenience; the built-in relay logic automatically prevents operating-mode sequences other than those diagrammed as follows:

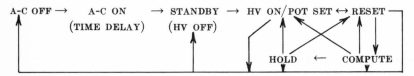

We cannot, for instance, place the machine into COMPUTE without high voltage, or directly from the POT SET condition.

The main circuit breaker energizes filaments and relay power supply, and hence also the HOLD, RESET, and POT SET busses. The machine is, then, in the POT SET/REFERENCE OFF/BALANCE CHECK mode, and returns automatically to this condition whenever the high voltage has been off and a-c is on. The *mode relays HV, R* (RESET), *C* (COMPUTE), *H* (HOLD),

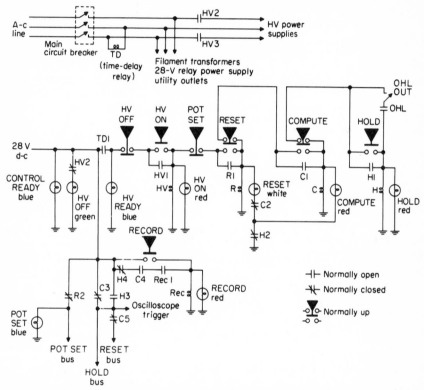

FIG. 10-4b. A pushbutton control system. The relay spark-suppression circuits are not shown.

and *Rec* (RECORDER MOTOR ON) perform the actual switching operations if the corresponding pushbuttons are momentarily depressed in an admissible sequence. Each mode relay will latch itself electrically, except for *Rec*, which latches only in COMPUTE. The strip-chart-recorder motor will, however, run in any other mode as long as the RECORD button is depressed, so as to permit paper advance and recorder calibration. The RECORD button is immediately adjacent to the COMPUTE button; the operator uses his index finger to start the motor and, a fraction of a second later, presses the COMPUTE button with his third finger and thus also latches the recorder-motor relay until the end of the COMPUTE period.

This system permits the recorder to come up to speed before each computer run and is vastly simpler than systems involving recorder time-delay relays.   It is, of course, also possible to make computer runs without the recorder.

The control system of Fig. 10-4b also provides for an oscilloscope trigger and for an *overload-hold circuit*.   A contact of the main overload relay (Sec. 11-4b) switches the

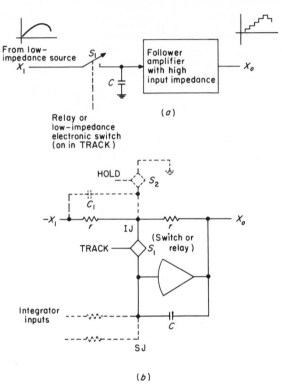

FIG. 10-5. Basic switched-capacitor sample-hold circuit (*a*), and simple operational-amplifier sample-hold (*b*).   The speedup capacitor $C_1 = C$ improves small-signal phase shift once tracking is achieved, but will *not* improve the charging time constant unless the shunt switch S_2 is employed.

computer into HOLD after every overload in the COMPUTE mode, unless the OHL switch is opened.

Computer control relays (especially the mode-control relays) may switch very appreciable currents and/or inductive loads.   Relay contacts should be protected with arc-suppression circuits employing diodes, capacitors, and/or varistors, as recommended by the relay manufacturer.[2]

10-4. Track-hold Circuits.   (a) Basic Track-hold Circuits.   The
output X_o of the basic capacitor-storage *track-hold circuit* (*sample-hold circuit*) of Fig. 10-5a tracks the input signal X_1 while the switch is ON

(TRACK *mode*).   A HOLD command opens the switch, so that the capacitor stores the last input value, and the output ideally remains constant (HOLD *mode*).   The operational-amplifier track-hold of Fig. 10-5b similarly tracks its inverted input X_1 with the switch ON (TRACK *mode*), like any integrator in RESET.   The HOLD command turns the switch off, and the output again holds its last value, since we now have an integrator without input.   Both storage circuits can drive external loads without discharging their holding capacitors.

   (b) Track-hold Performance.   An ideal track-hold circuit would follow its input instantaneously and exactly in TRACK, and would hold

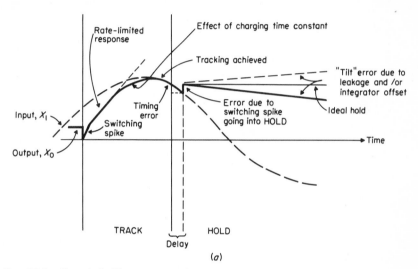

FIG. 10-6a. Sample-hold response and error effects.   Rate limits are determined by current capacities of switches and/or amplifiers and may differ for positive and negative rates.   Switching spikes (for electronic switches only) can be positive or negative. Timing error and switching spike going into TRACK will not affect HOLD output. Errors due to d-c offset and phase shift in TRACK are not shown.

instantaneously and exactly for an indefinite time after receiving a HOLD command.   Figure 10-6a illustrates the response of an actual track-hold circuit.   The *current capacity of amplifiers and switches* not only limits the maximum tracking rate, but also places a lower limit on the TRACK period required to catch up with specified input-signal excursions (Fig. 10-6b).   For accurate tracking of high-frequency signal components too small to cause rate limiting, we require low phase shift in TRACK, i.e., sufficient bandwidth in the capacitor-charging input circuit or amplifier. The effect of the capacitor-charging time constant on small-signal phase shift can be compensated with suitable equalizing networks (speedup capacitor C_1 in Fig. 10-5b).   The charging time constant must, in any case, be less than one-seventh of the shortest contemplated TRACK period for 0.1 per cent accuracy (about one-tenth for 0.01 per cent) to allow for exponential step response.

The ideally constant HOLD output *drifts* because of capacitor leakage and dielectric absorption (Sec. 3-9), switch and amplifier-input leakage, and amplifier voltage offset. A total error current i_E contributes the absolute drift error

$$e_H = \frac{|i_E|}{C}\tau_H \qquad (10\text{-}1a)$$

where C is the holding capacitance, and τ_H is the elapsed time in HOLD. An amplifier offset of e_D volts referred to the input contributes an output

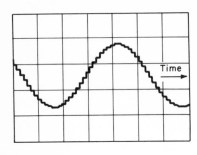 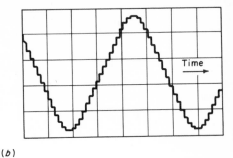

(b)

FIG. 10-6b. Response of a sample-hold circuit to sine waves at two different amplitudes. The rate limiting is due to a TRACK period too short in relation to the maximum tracking rate.

error e_D in Fig. 10-5a, and an absolute output drift

$$e'_H = \frac{|e_D|}{RC}\tau_H \qquad (10\text{-}1b)$$

in Fig. 10-5b, where R is the resistance from summing point to ground in the HOLD mode (see also Sec. 3-21).

With electronic switching, the *switching spike* caused by differentiation of the HOLD control step in the switch capacitances charges the holding capacitor and contributes a spurious voltage step (Fig. 10-6a). Its amplitude is approximately

$$e_S = a_S E_C \frac{C_S}{C} \qquad (10\text{-}2)$$

where E_C is the control-step amplitude, and C_S is the effective switch capacitance. a_S is a proportionality factor, which we attempt to reduce through push-pull spike cancellation in symmetrical switching circuits (Fig. 10-7c, d), and/or by adding inverted spikes through a trimmer capacitor (Fig. 10-7c). Nonlinearity of electronic-switch capacitances makes accurate spike cancellation for all input-voltage values imprac-

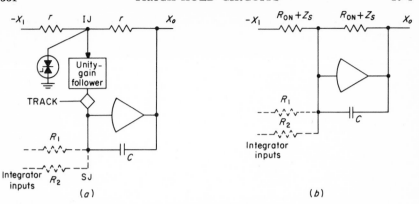

FIG. 10-7a, b. Operational-amplifier track-hold or integrator using a follower amplifier to reduce the charging time constant (a), and approximate equivalent circuit (b). Z_S is the follower-amplifier source impedance, and R_{ON} is the resistance of the closed switch. The zener-diode limiter permits low-voltage switching even in ± 100-volt computers.

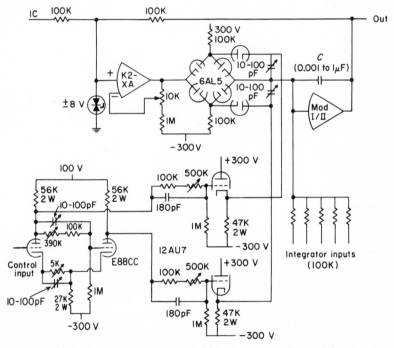

FIG. 10-7c. ASTRAC I ± 100-volt track-hold or integrator designed for simple and inexpensive construction without temperature-sensitive switching diodes. With a chopper-stabilized integrator amplifier, the circuit holds within 0.1 volt for 25C (μF) sec. The 3.3-mA current capacity of follower amplifier and switch permits a tracking rate of 3,300/C(μF) volts/sec; this is increased to 10,000/C(μF) volts/sec if we substitute the Model 2 amplifier of Fig. 5-26b for the K2XA and make $r = 30$K. Switching times are of the order of 1 μsec followed by 0.5 to 5 μsec transients, depending on amplifier bandwidth and stability. Switching-spike charges are of the order of picocoulombs with careful adjustment. (*University of Arizona*; see also ref. 11.)

tical, but considerable improvement is possible. With well-designed circuits, switching-spike errors are not serious in ordinary track-hold operation, but they may accumulate in certain computations (Secs. 10-8*d* and 10-19).

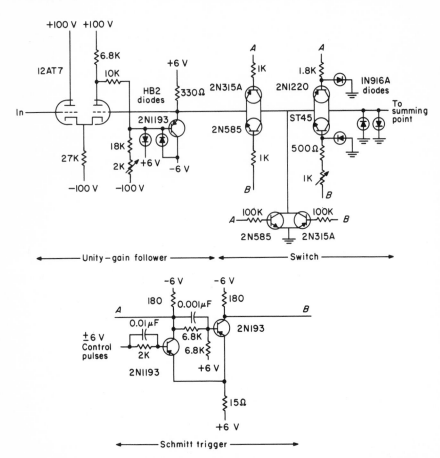

FIG. 10-7*d*. A Computer Systems, Inc., DYSTAC ±100-volt track-hold or integrator switching circuit modified at the University of Arizona to yield 20 mA current capacity. Holding performance is about the same as that in Fig. 10-7*c*.

Finally, switch- or relay-response delays in executing the HOLD command result in possibly serious *timing errors*, i.e., the sample-hold circuit actually holds a later input voltage value than desired (see also Sec. 3-2*c*).

The holding errors (1) and (2) are seen to improve with increasing holding capacitance C, while low values of C require less current and favor fast tracking. *The required compromise is best resolved with high-current solid-state amplifiers and switches, which permit the use of relatively large holding capacitances.* In practice, i_D and e_D can be kept below 25 to

250 nA and 50 to 500 μV, respectively.   Figures 10-7 and 10-8 show typical circuit specifications.

(c) **Improved Track-hold Circuits.**   The track-hold circuit of Fig. 10-7a decreases the capacitor-charging time constant without excessively low resistances r.   A ± 5-volt zener-diode limiter permits the use of a low-voltage/high-current follower amplifier and switch even for ± 100-volt track-hold circuits.   The follower amplifier, main amplifier,

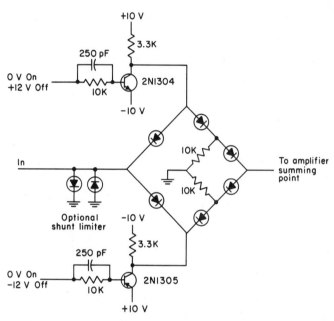

Fɪɢ. 10-7e. A combined diode-bridge/transistor switch for track-hold or integrator switching in ± 10-volt computers.   Two-diode networks in the output legs of the bridge reduce leakage and capacitance.   (*University of Arizona, based on ref. 102.*)

and switch must all be capable of supplying the full capacitor-charging current for a specified tracking rate.   The follower amplifier is in the feedback loop in Tʀᴀᴄᴋ and, in view of its capacitive load, requires low output impedance and sufficient bandwidth to avoid instability or ringing.   Low switch leakage minimizes holding errors; we also require a low-drift follower amplifier to limit d-c offset in Tʀᴀᴄᴋ.   Figures 10-7b and c show practical ± 100-volt circuits and specifications; Fig. 10-7d shows a combined diode-bridge/transistor switch for medium-speed ± 10-volt transistor machines.   For low-impedance ± 10-volt computers, a current-amplifying transistor switch (Fig. 6-21) can serve as both amplifier and switch.[12]   The diamond switch of Fig. 6-21b, in particular, can yield an output impedance well below 10 ohms, currents up to 50 mA, and switching times below 0.1 μsec.   Such switches do, however, require

close V_{BE} tracking of dissimilar (*npn* and *pnp*) transistors with temperature changes for low d-c offset in TRACK.   Drift below 2 mV/deg C is
possible with matched transistors; compensation with temperature-
sensitive diodes or thermistors, or a constant-temperature Peltier oven,
may help beyond this point.   Figure 10-7e shows a suitable switch driver.

The multiple-switch track-hold circuits of Fig. 10-8 do not require a
high-current follower amplifier, since the integrating amplifier alone

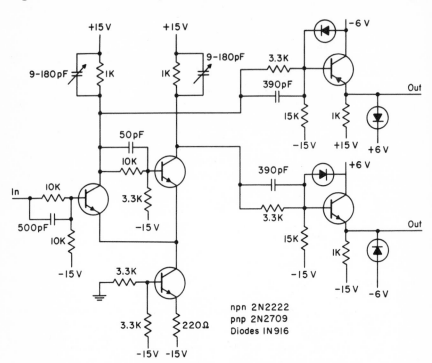

FIG. 10-7*f*. A fast Schmitt trigger with level-changing networks and clamped output
suitable for driving electronic switches or digital logic.   Output rise times and delay
are less than 100 nsec and are matched by trimmer capacitors to reduce switching
spikes.

supplies the capacitor-charging current.   The symmetrical arrangement
of Fig. 10-8*b* is very appealing from the point of view of switching spikes.
The shunt switches also enable this circuit to be switched with low-
voltage pulses from commercially available digital modules.   The circuit
of Fig. 10-8*b* makes a good integrator for ±100-volt computers employing
100K to 1M computing resistances and operating at real-time or low
repetitive frequencies.   At higher frequencies, say above 10 Kc, and
with low-impedance circuitry, the forward resistance R_F of the shunt
transistor or transistor pair S_2 (10 to 100 ohms) causes a serious phase
lag (equal to arctan $\omega R_F C$) in the capacitor voltage; this can be partially

canceled with a lead capacitor C_1.   Figure 10-8b has also been implemented with relays.[39]

The "tail-switching" amplifier pair of Fig. 10-8c permits excellent track-hold performance, since its switches are enclosed in feedback loops (see also Sec. 7-12); but the two-amplifier circuit is somewhat expensive.

(a) (b)

FIG. 10-8a, b. Multiple-switch track-hold or integrator circuits.   In (a), the resistance r_1 (100 ohms to 10K) saves a switch but reduces loop gain and bandwidth in TRACK. The symmetrical circuit (b) permits low-voltage switching.   In either circuit, the frequency-dependent signal-voltage drop across S_2 in TRACK may cause serious tracking errors at high frequencies.

Electronic switches suitable for track-hold circuits are further discussed in Secs. 6-10 and 6-11.   Since switch-control-waveform amplitudes, rise times, and/or push-pull balance can be critical, it is best to associate each track-hold circuit permanently with a switch-driving Schmitt trigger or flip-flop which can be actuated by single-ended control voltages (Fig. 10-7c, d, e).

Note that *all the track-hold circuits of Figs. 10-7 and* 10-8 *can add several* TRACK *inputs* if the single TRACK-input resistor is replaced by a summing network.

FIG. 10-8c. A "tail-switching" track-hold or integrator circuit.

10-5. Electronically Switched Integrators and Other Operational Amplifiers.   (a) Integrator Circuits.   Each of the track-hold circuits in Figs. 10-7 and 10-8 becomes an electronically switched integrator if we add the integrator input resistors indicated in dash lines.

The HOLD mode becomes a COMPUTE mode, and TRACK becomes RESET. Note that the circuits of Fig. 10-7 do not make the integrator inputs truly inoperative in RESET but merely divide them by a factor $(R_{ON} + Z_S)/R$. With $R_{ON} + Z_S$ typically between 1 and 500 ohms, this is not too objectionable in high-impedance computers (R of the order of 1M) if initial conditions are set with a digital voltmeter at the integrator output. The integrator-input gain in RESET is too low to cause computing-loop instability, but initial-condition settings of different integrators will

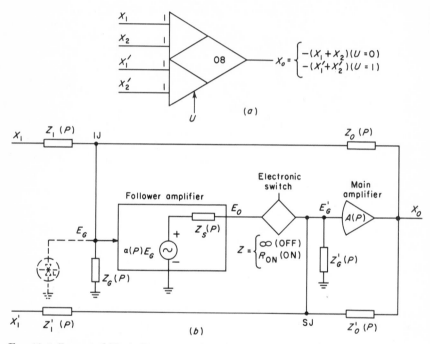

FIG. 10-9. Suggested block-diagram symbol for a switched phase inverter/summer (a), and a more general switched operational amplifier (b).

interact slightly. The situation becomes more serious in fast low-impedance transistor computers (R between 1 and 10K). If desired, additional electronic switches can ground integrator-resistor taps in RESET, or disconnect and ground the integrator summing junction in the manner of Fig. 10-1. In the latter case, we can even provide for a separate HOLD mode.

(b) Switched Operational Amplifiers. Substitution of a resistance r for the integrator/hold capacitance C in any of the operational-amplifier sample-hold circuits of Figs. 10-7 and 10-8 yields an electronic two-input SPDT switch with sign-inverted low-impedance output (switched phase inverter or summer, Fig. 10-9a). Figure 10-9b shows a more general type of switched operational amplifier implementing

$$X_o = -\frac{Z_o(P)}{Z_1(P)} X_1 \quad \text{or} \quad X_o = -\frac{Z_o'(P)}{Z_1'(P)} X_1' \quad \left(P \equiv \frac{d}{d\tau}\right) \quad (10\text{-}3)$$

In addition to switching-spike and switch-leakage errors, switched operational amplifiers will have transfer-function errors due to finite amplifier gain and follower and/or switch impedances. Such errors are readily calculated by the methods of Secs. 3-11 to 3-14.[14] The circuit of Fig. 10-9b, for example, is an ordinary operational amplifier with the switch OFF; with the switch ON, $X_o = -(Z_o/Z_1)X_1 + e$. The error $e = e(\tau)$ is given by

$$\left.\begin{array}{l} e \approx -\left(\dfrac{1}{A_{ON}\beta_{ON}}\dfrac{Z_o}{Z_1}X_1 + \dfrac{\beta_1}{\alpha\beta_{ON}}\dfrac{Z_o'}{Z_1'}X_1'\right) \\[2ex] A_{ON} = \dfrac{\alpha A}{1 - A\beta_1} \qquad \beta_{ON} = \left(1 + \dfrac{Z_o}{Z_1} + \dfrac{Z_o}{Z_G}\right)^{-1} \qquad \beta_1 \approx \dfrac{Z_S + R_{ON}}{Z_o'} \end{array}\right\} \quad (10\text{-}4)$$

at frequencies where $|A_{ON}\beta_{ON}| \gg 1$ and $|Z_S + R_{ON}| \ll |Z_o'|, |Z_1'|, |Z_G'|$.[14] Note that the second error term makes this one-switch circuit less practical than multiswitch circuits if low computing impedances are to be used. Stability considerations usually will not permit follower-amplifier gains α much above unity.

ITERATIVE DIFFERENTIAL ANALYZERS: OPERATION AND CONTROL

10-6. Introduction. Subroutines and Flow Charts. (a) Iterative Differential Analyzers.[44] An analog computer with integrator-mode and program switches operable by sequence-controlling timers, analog comparators, and/or digital logic will be called an *iterative differential analyzer*.* Such machines can automatically perform successive analog-computer runs utilizing stored results of earlier runs and can, therefore, implement iterative computations[16] converging to a desired solution. The automatic programming features have many other applications as well (Sec. 10-6d).

(b) Subroutines and Control Variables. Iterative differential analyzers, like digital computers, are programmed through a series of *subroutines*. A subroutine is a sequence of operations, such as an analog-computer run or a number of repetitive-analog-computer runs. We associate each subroutine with a digital (binary) *control variable* U_i representing the state of a control relay or flip-flop. The subroutine proceeds when $U_i = 1$; $U_i = 0$ "resets" the computing elements involved in the subroutine (e.g., integrators, counters) for renewed use. Note that the complementary control variable $\tilde{U}_i$ (0 for $U_i = 1$, 1 for $U_i = 0$)

---

* This term was, to the best of our knowledge, first suggested by Dr. M. Gilliland in ref. 39 and appears to be in general use. The corresponding initials IDA, however, are a registered trademark of Beckman Instruments, Inc., and refer to their specific product.

may also define a subroutine. Subroutines can be "nested," i.e., they may involve component subroutines.

EXAMPLES: An ordinary differential-analyzer run and the subsequent RESET period are subroutines controlled by the states $\tilde{R} = 0$, $\tilde{R} = 1$ of the COMPUTE relay or switch in a "slow" analog computer and by a RESET flip-flop in a fast repetitive computer. A preset sequence of, say, 1,000 repetitive-computer runs is a subroutine controlled by the output state of a preset run-counter coincidence circuit (Sec. 10-11).

Typical *analog-subroutine changes* are combinations of the following operations:

1. *Switching a group of integrators* from RESET or COMPUTE, or from RESET (TRACK) to HOLD, and vice versa (complementary subroutines)
2. *Switching to new values of parameter or initial-value settings* (e.g., parameter optimization, automatic scale-factor changes)
3. *Switching interconnections* to produce computer-setup changes

Subroutines start and terminate when the corresponding binary control variables change state as logical functions of

1. External control (manual switching, commands from associated equipment)
2. States of preset timers and run counters
3. Analog-comparator decisions

Appropriate Boolean functions and sequences of these inputs will be implemented by patched electronic or relay logic (Sec. 10-10).

Figure 10-10a illustrates the special *hybrid-analog-digital structure* of an iterative differential analyzer. Relays or electronic switches implement analog-subroutine changes under control of digital (binary) control variables U_i and constitute the digital-to-analog interface of our hybrid computer. Analog solutions, in turn, can modify digital control variables, and hence the computer program, by way of analog comparators actuating digital logic (analog-to-digital interface). Finally, track-hold circuits (or other analog-memory elements, Secs. 10-17 to 10-20) make computed analog data available for use in later subroutines, while digital variables can be stored as flip-flop states.

Comparator decisions can be made in the course of analog-computer runs and may, for instance, terminate a run, command sampling, etc. If there is any choice, however, both comparator decisions and subroutine changes should be made in RESET or HOLD states for improved accuracy.

(c) Flow Charts. The operation of iterative differential analyzers, like that of digital computers, is conveniently represented by *flow charts*. The flow chart (Fig. 10-10b) indicates a sequence of switch-controlled subroutines (rectangular *operation boxes*) and program-stepping decisions (oval and diamond-shaped *decision boxes*). We shall employ oval decision boxes for *preset* decisions determined beforehand by digital timers and/or run counters, and diamond-shaped decision boxes for "computed" decisions involving analog comparators or comparator-actuated digital logic. The flow-chart structure is implemented by the interplay of analog and digital components in the machine (Fig. 10-10a). Flow-chart loops will represent cycles of repetitive or iterative computations.

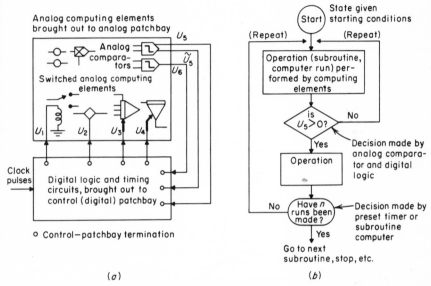

(a)   (b)

FIG. 10-10a. Iterative-differential analyzer operation. Operations (operation boxes in Fig. 10-10b) are mainly analog-computer runs "ordered" by electronic switches or relays while corresponding digital control variables U_i are equal to 1. Control-variable changes are preset by timers and counter choices and/or "computed" by analog comparators and digital logic. Switches and comparators form the digital-analog and analog-digital interfaces. It is reasonable to provide separate patchbays for programming analog and digital (logic) operations.

FIG. 10-10b. Iterative-differential-analyzer flow chart. Rectangular boxes specify operations. Oval decision boxes refer to preset digital-timer and/or counter decisions, while diamond-shaped decision boxes involve analog comparators and/or comparator-actuated digital logic. Boxes may be numbered for reference.

(d) Applications (see referenced sections for examples). Iterative differential analyzers can implement vastly more sophisticated models than ordinary analog computers and still retain some of their intuitive appeal. We start our list of applications with those most peculiarly suited to iterative analog computation.

1. *Iterative parameter optimization.* The machine varies parameters of a simulated or real engineering system so as to improve a performance measure in successive computer runs (Secs. 12-7 to

    12-16). Many more general problems can be recast as parameter optimization problems.

2. *Monte-Carlo studies of random processes.* The computer measures statistics over many fast-time computer runs simulating control systems, communication, detection, queuing problems with random inputs.[111]

3. *Real-time and fast-time simulation of sampled-data systems,* including digital computers (Secs. 10-13 to 10-16).

Repetitive analog computation at the highest possible speed is practically indispensable for Monte-Carlo studies of dynamical systems. Parameter optimization benefits most from high computing speed if we are required to *track* optimum-parameter combinations under changing conditions, as in cross-plotting studies or real-time control applications (Secs. 12-13 to 12-16). In applications requiring more accurate arithmetic or more extensive storage capability, the iterative differential analyzer is nicely equipped to communicate with a digital computer (Sec. 11-13).

A large volume of work, especially in connection with chemical-process-control and nuclear-power problems, requires

4. *Approximate solution of partial differential equations,* frequently in the course of real-time control-system simulation (Secs. 12-17 to 12-22).

Here, iterative analog computation, while in our opinion less than brilliantly successful, has at times been the only way out (see also Sec. 12-22).

Other applications do not involve true iteration, but exploit the programming flexibility of fast automatic switching and sampling circuits:

5. *Automatic sequencing* of routine computations, automatic parameter changes for plotting families of curves, special displays, crossplotting, etc. (see also Sec. 10-12).

6. *Introduction of artificial errors* (offset, phase shift, parameter and function changes, etc.) into alternate computer runs. This can be a very powerful method for gauging the reliability of computer results.[105]

7. *Automatic scale-factor changes.*[54]

8. *Multiplexing expensive computing elements* or blocks of computing elements (e.g., coordinate-transformation circuits) for multiple use in slow computations.[3,4,6] The sampled-data precautions of Sec. 10-15 apply.

9. *Special simulation and data-processing circuits,* e.g., patchbay-assembled time-division and sampling multipliers, special function generators, modulators, and demodulators (see also Secs. 6-12, 7-6e, 7-11, 8-15, and 9-2 to 9-9), transport delays (Sec. 10-19), and simulation of special dynamical and control systems (Sec. 10-12; see also refs. 70 and 71).

Iterative differential analyzers may, again, communicate with digital computers for increased accuracy and memory capacity (Sec. 11-13).

10-7. Block-diagram Notation. Figure 10-11 introduces our block-diagram notation for hybrid analog-digital computer setups. Digital (binary) variables can take the *symbolic* values 0 and 1 respectively represented by deenergized and energized relays or digital-module outputs (typically 0 and -3 to -12 volts). Binary variables can be stored,

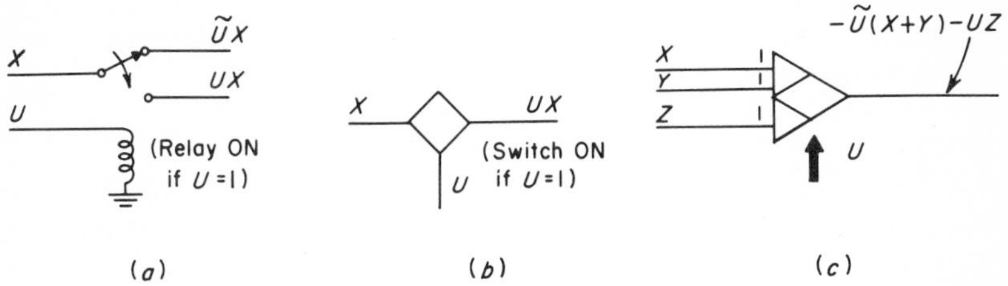

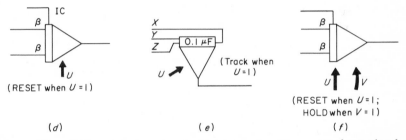

FIG. 10-11a, b, c. Relays, electronic switches, and a switched operational amplifier.

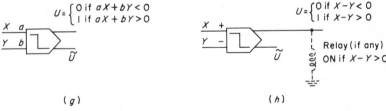

FIG. 10-11d, e, f. Two-state (COMPUTE/RESET) integrator (d), suggested notation for integrators used primarily for analog storage (e), and three-state (COMPUTE/HOLD/RESET) integrator (f).

$$U = \begin{cases} 0 \text{ if } aX + bY < 0 \\ 1 \text{ if } aX + bY > 0 \end{cases}$$

$$U = \begin{cases} 0 \text{ if } X - Y < 0 \\ 1 \text{ if } X - Y > 0 \end{cases}$$

Relay (if any) ON if $X - Y > 0$

(g) (h)

FIG. 10-11g, h. Analog comparator (g), and differential-input analog comparator (h) with complementary outputs. The sign convention is arbitrary but should be consistent. In the case of relay-driving comparators, the relay may be indicated as shown in (h). See Fig. 10-15 for digital-module notation.

FIG. 10-11. Suggested block-diagram notation for hybrid analog-digital computer setups.

complemented, and logically combined by digital modules (Sec. 10-10). Note, in particular, that

1. Each SPST relay or electronic switch has a binary control input equal to 1 if and only if the relay or switch is *closed*. SPDT relays have an arrow to indicate the "closed" state (Fig. 10-11a, b, c).

2. Each integrator or track-hold circuit has a binary control input (RESET input) equal to 1 if and only if the circuit is in RESET or TRACK (Fig. 10-11d, e). Reset pulses or levels controlling groups of integrators will usually be labeled R, R', R'', . . . ; R is the only control variable in simple "slow" or repetitive analog computation.

3. Three-state (COMPUTE/HOLD/RESET) integrators, if used, have a HOLD control input V as well as a RESET input U (Fig. 10-11f) defined so that we have*

COMPUTE if and only if $U = 0$, $V = 0$
HOLD   if and only if $U = 0$, $V = 1$
RESET   if and only if $U = 1$

10-8. Analog Point Storage and Memory-pair Operation. (a) **Point-storage Requirements.** To store the computed value $X(\tau_1)$ of an analog-computer voltage $X(\tau)$ (*point storage*), we track $X(\tau)$ or $-X(\tau)$ with a track-hold circuit and switch into HOLD at the computer time $\tau = \tau_1 = \alpha_t t_1$. If the time derivative $PX = dX/d\tau$ is available in our computer setup, we can also store $X(\tau_1)$ by switching an integrator with input $-PX$ into HOLD. The stored voltage $X(\tau_1)$ may be used

1. *As a (constant) input or parameter value during the same computer run.* The storage circuit then becomes again available for tracking at the start of the next RESET period.
2. *To set an initial condition for the following computer run.* The storage circuit will be available for renewed tracking at the start of the next COMPUTE period.
3. *As a (constant) input or parameter value during the following computer run.* In this case, the storage circuit will not be free to track again until the end of the next COMPUTE period.
4. During a later RESET or COMPUTE period.

Since a single storage capacitor cannot track and hold simultaneously, we shall require at least *two* storage circuits to transfer information between successive COMPUTE periods.

(b) Memory Pairs. Figure 10-12 illustrates various applications of *memory pairs* comprising two cascaded phase-inverting track-hold circuits.

In Fig. 10-12a, the control pulses S' for track-hold 2 are delayed so that amplifier 2 tracks the HOLD output of amplifier 1 and stores or "presents" it while amplifier 1 is free to track again. The memory-pair output is a delayed sequence of clean sampled-data steps. Suitably

---

* The definition of a separate HOLD variable V will be found convenient. Note, however, that the respective inputs to the relays K_R and K_H in Fig. 10-1 are U and $U + V$, *not* U and V.

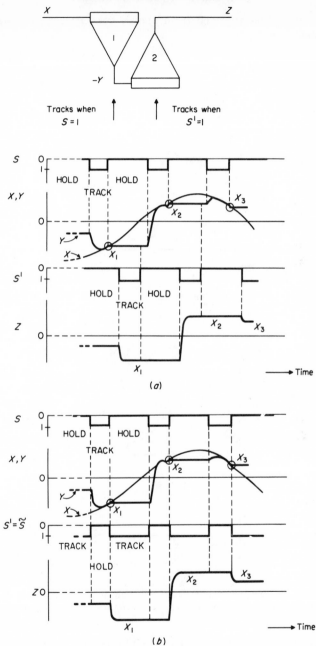

Fig. 10-12a, b. Memory-pair operation with delayed pulses S' (a), and with complementary control pulses S_1, $S' = \tilde{S}$ (b). No initial-reset circuits are shown.

timed pulses can be obtained from one-shot multivibrators[24] or from a digital clock (Sec. 10-11).

The *complementary memory pair* of Fig. 10-12b employs complementary control pulses, i.e., $S' = \tilde{S}$; amplifier 2 is in TRACK while amplifier 1 holds,

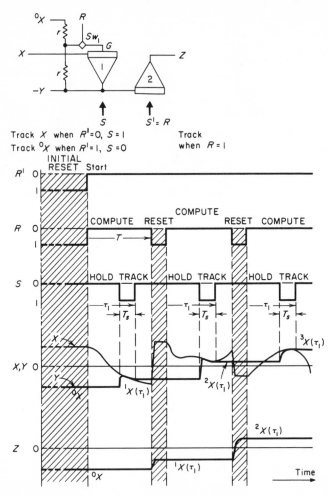

FIG. 10-12c. A simple memory pair can present a solution sample $^{k}X(\tau_1)$ during the entire following iterative-differential-analyzer run if $\tau_1 > T_S$. Note the initial-reset-circuit operation; integrator 1 tracks the initial-reset input when $S = 0$, $R' = 1$.

and vice versa. This circuit is often used for comparator-timed sampling (Sec. 10-12);[19] actually, amplifier 2 should begin to hold slightly before amplifier 1 tracks.

Figures 10-12c to e illustrate *memory-pair operation for information transfer between successive analog-computer runs*. In Fig. 10-12c, the

TRACK pulses $S' = R$ for track-hold 2 are delayed so that amplifier 2 tracks the HOLD output of amplifier 1 during the computer RESET period and then holds or "presents" the stored voltage during the entire subsequent COMPUTE period. Amplifier 1, in the meantime, is free to

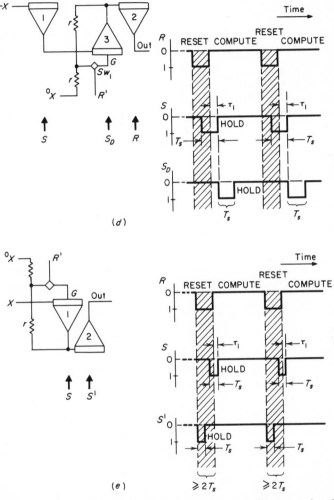

FIG. 10-12d, e. For $\tau_1 < T_S$, the simple memory scheme of Fig. 10-12c breaks down, since the S and R pulses overlap. To present $X(\tau_1)$ during the following computer run, we can either use an extra track-hold circuit with delayed sampling (d), or employ three-period control (e).

track again. Unfortunately, this scheme breaks down whenever the sampling time τ_1 is shorter than the period T_S required for tracking, for now amplifier 1 is already in TRACK during the RESET period (Fig. 10-12d). There are two ways out:

1. We can interpose a third track-hold circuit between track-holds 1 and 2 to resample the voltage Y at a more convenient time $\tau_2 > T_S$ (Fig. 10-12d).
2. We can use a longer computer RESET period (at least equal to $2T_S$) and switch amplifier 2 into HOLD T_S seconds after the start of the RESET period ("three-period control," Fig. 10-12e).

Both techniques complicate our control circuits (Sec. 10-11). Three-period control permits flexible operation of three-state integrators but tends to waste possibly valuable computing time.

Frequently, a stored voltage $X(\tau_1)$ is required only during the subsequent RESET period, e.g., for setting initial values, or for performing an intermediate subroutine. In this case, a single track-hold circuit suffices for storage if $\tau_1 > T_S$ (Fig. 10-12c).

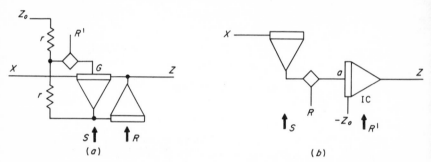

(a)   (b)

FIG. 10-13. Accumulator circuits for summing sample values. With electronic switching, such circuits require careful adjustment to minimize switching-spike addition. Accumulators with constant input are useful for automatic parameter stepping.

(c) **The INITIAL RESET Mode.** In many applications (see, e.g., Sec. 10-13), the memory-pair output Z in Fig. 10-12c must assume a specified initial value ^0X during the first COMPUTE period. This is achieved by the *initial-reset circuit* shown in Fig. 10-12c. The INITIAL RESET mode established by $R' = 1$ implies $R = 1$, $S = 0$; Sw_1 closes, and the memory output Z assumes the correct initial value $Z = {}^0X$. To start the computation, we switch to $R' = R = 0$ and let R and S cycle normally (see also Sec. 10-11e).

(d) **Accumulator Circuits.** *The delayed output of a memory pair can be combined with its input for many useful and interesting sampled-data operations* (Secs. 10-13 to 10-15). As a first example, the *accumulator circuit* of Fig. 10-13a implements summation of successive sample values. Figure 10-13b shows an alternative accumulator circuit (see also Sec. 10-12).

10-9. Fast Analog Comparators.[25-27] Iterative differential analyzers require fast analog comparators whose digital output indicates the sign of the analog input sum or difference (basic analog-to-digital conversion, decision making).   The most frequently employed comparator circuits are

1. *Operational-amplifier comparators* with diode or zener-diode feedback and low input-resistor values (Sec. 6-8).
2. *Transistor differential amplifiers* with or without regeneration.
3. *Schmitt or Eccles-Jordan trigger circuits preceded by a d-c amplifier* which divides the trigger hysteresis by the amplifier gain (Fig. 10-14).   If the d-c amplifier is chopper-stabilized, it must have a feedback-limiter circuit to prevent blocking.

The trigger circuits yield fast rise times (within 0.2 μsec) independent of the input-voltage rate and are needed if the comparator must trigger

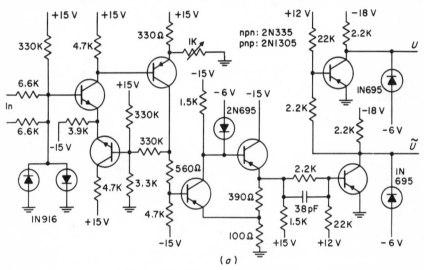

FIG. 10-14a. Differential-amplifier/Schmitt-trigger comparator.   D-c drift and static hysteresis within 10 mV between 20 and 30 deg C; dynamic error within 100 mV for input rates up to 10,000 volt/sec.   (*University of Arizona.*[27])

flip-flops (Sec. 10-10).   The comparator circuits of Fig. 10-14a and b are inexpensive and especially suitable for existing $\pm$ 100-volt and $\pm$ 10-volt computers operating at moderate repetition rates (at most 100 runs/sec). Faster computers can still employ these circuits to operate on track-hold outputs *only;* comparator operation in the course of, say, a 1-msec computer run requires a high-quality feedforward amplifier or preamplifier, unless static accuracy is sacrificed to fast response (Sec. 5-12).

Comparator *static errors* are determined by d-c amplifier drift, which is minimized by chopper stabilization and by matched differential-amplifier circuits (Chap. 5).   In some comparators, diode-breakpoint drift (Sec. 6-2) contributes to the static error.   Comparators involving regeneration or regenerative trigger circuits also exhibit some static hysteresis. Static accuracies within $\pm 100\ \mu V$, or $\pm 20\ nA$ input current, are readily obtained; the problem is to get fast response without compromising the static accuracy.

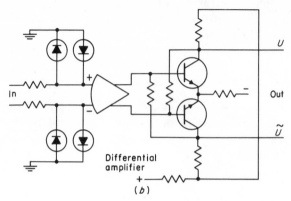

FIG. 10-14*b*. A completely symmetrical differential-amplifier/Eccles-Jordan-trigger comparator. Preamplifier design will be a compromise between low drift/low noise and bandwidth.[109]

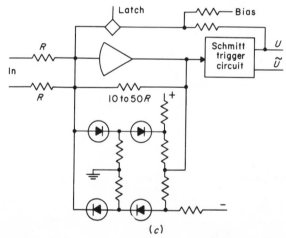

FIG. 10-14*c*. Fast low-drift comparator employing a high-quality feedforward d-c amplifier for preamplification. The feedback limiter employs diodes in series and shunt resistors to reduce leakage and capacitance effects. Note the latching circuit.

Figure 10-15 shows the shape of a typical *dynamic transfer characteristic*, taken, say, at 25 Kc. Most or all of the hysteresis-like spreading is not true hysteresis, but a *time-delay effect* due to linear and nonlinear circuit capacitances, as in the case of diode-limiter circuits (Sec. 6-5). The spread is, again, roughly proportional to the rate at which the input voltage X_1 crosses the breakpoint. Typical comparator delay errors vary between fractions of a microsecond and 100 μsec.

The comparator of Fig. 10-14c has a "latching" connection which permits only a single state change while the digital latching input is equal to 1. In this way, we can, for instance, prevent a comparator from responding more than once per computer run. Many types of *pulsed-oscillator comparators* have been designed, chiefly for applications requiring comparator steps in one direction only. *Pulse comparators* employ clamps or choppers to sample an input voltage at clock-selected times (Sec. 5-8), and are frequently used in analog-to-digital converters (Sec. 11-11). Neither type has found wide application in iterative differential analyzers.

10-10. Digital Operations. (a) Digital-module Logic. Electronic logic circuits used to combine binary control variables in iterative differential analyzers employ d-c logic; i.e., control variables are represented by instantaneous voltage levels. Most frequently, digital 0 and 1 are respectively represented by 0 and -3 to -12 volts. These logic levels should be securely clamped (Fig. 10-15), even if this requires special power supplies, to avoid analog noise due to stray-capacitance differentiation of ringing and "tilted" logic levels.

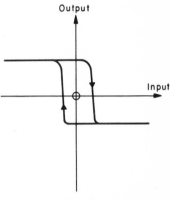

Fig. 10-15. High-frequency input-output transfer characteristic of a typical analog comparator. The spreading (time-delay error) is roughly proportional to the input rate of change.

Vacuum-tube logic for iterative differential analyzers, described in refs. 38 and 43, is obsolete but can save addition of low-voltage power supplies to vacuum-tube analog computers requiring only a few logic operations. Note that low-voltage logic can readily switch ± 100-volt analog-computer circuits (Sec. 10-4). The design of solid-state logic circuits is treated in detail in refs. 28 to 33; in general, it pays to purchase manufactured plug-in modules, just as one buys vacuum tubes or relays.

Combinatorial-logic functions (Boolean functions of binary control variables) are implemented with a variety of diode-transistor *gates* together with clamped inverting amplifiers and emitter followers serving as buffer amplifiers (Fig. 10-16). We must observe manufacturers' directions with respect to the allowable number of input and output connections (fan-in and fan-out) for each module.

Subroutine-sequence control also requires storage of control-variable states affecting future operations (sequential logic). Control-variable storage is implemented with bistable *flip-flops* together with gates and inverting amplifiers. Figure 10-17a illustrates the operation of a clamped general-purpose flip-flop; digital 0 and 1 correspond to 0 and -3 to -12 volts, respectively.

In the normal or *reset* state of the flip-flop, transistor Q_1 is ON, and Q_2 is OFF, so that $V = 0$, $\tilde{V} = 1$. The flip-flop is set or reset

1. By a 1 on the *d-c set* or *d-c reset* input. In practice, the d-c set and reset variables U_S, U_R are most frequently mutually exclusive $(U_S U_R = 0)$; in any case, one d-c reset input is usually biased so that it overrules any other d-c or a-c input ("common reset").

2. By differentiation of a positive step (or the trailing edge of a negative

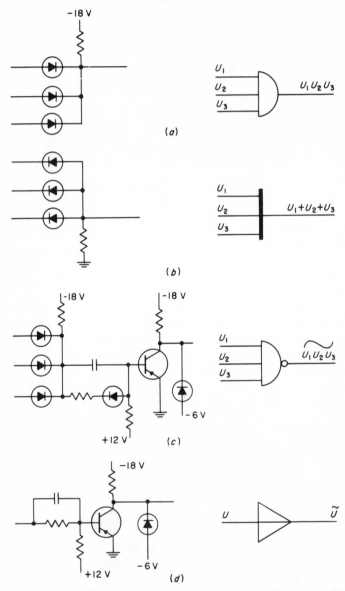

Fig. 10-16. Typical combinatorial-logic modules and block-diagram symbols: AND gate (*a*), OR gate (*b*), NAND gate (*c*), and inverter (*d*).

pulse) into any *a-c set* input or *a-c reset* input which is not inhibited by a 1 (negative voltage) on an associated *threshold-gate* input.

The *trigger input* (*count input*) is an a-c input connected to *both* transistors of a flip-flop, with or without a threshold gate. Each positive step or trailing edge of a negative pulse into the trigger input reverses the flip-flop state.

In Fig. 10-17*a*, multiple a-c and d-c inputs can implement logical OR operations, while threshold gates implement logical AND. A flip-flop

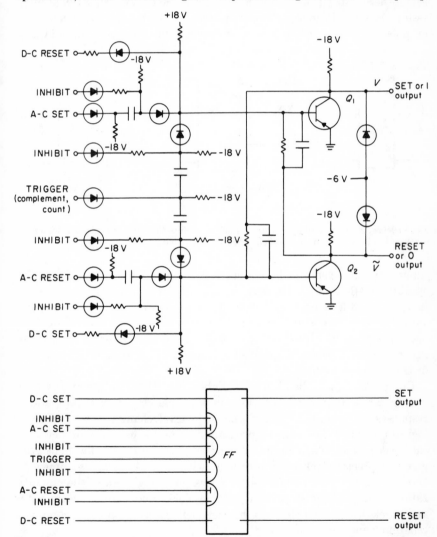

Fig. 10-17*a*. A clamped general-purpose flip-flop with 0-, −6-volt logic levels, and block-diagram symbol.

with a binary variable U on a threshold-gate input and sampling pulses on the corresponding a-c input acts like a binary-variable track-hold circuit (binary memory cell).   General-purpose flip-flops combine neatly into many different counters, shift registers, and other sequential-logic circuits.   Figure 10-18 shows a number of useful examples; refs. 28 to 33 should be consulted for more details.

(b) Timing Problems and Clock-gated Logic.   Flip-flops and other logic circuits are designed to resolve suitable voltage steps following each other at specified maximum rates, with inversely proportional processing delays.   Proper a-c-input differentiation requires specified step or pulse rise times as well as amplitudes; and d-c and threshold-gate

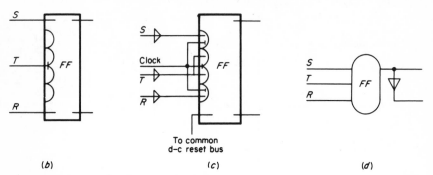

Fig. 10-17b, c, d. Patchbay terminations for a flip-flop with simple d-c logic (b) clock-gated logic (c), and simplified block-diagram symbol (d).

inputs must have specified settling times to operate properly.   Generally speaking, 100-Kc to 1-Mc logic is sufficient for subroutine sequencing in iterative differential analyzers, but *accurate timing during 50-cps to 1-Kc computer runs requires 5- to 10-Mc logic.*   Some sequential-logic circuits are simplified by *one-shot (monostable) multivibrators*[30] designed to generate square pulses of specified or adjustable duration after each step or trigger-pulse input.

Comparator-controlled binary variables may change state at any time during an analog-computer run, so that closely spaced comparator responses can result in "races" between level changes with equivocal logical results.   The resulting programming problems are simplified with *clock-gated logic,* which produces logic-level changes with flip-flops triggered at precise clock-pulse intervals, with control variables applied to threshold gates (Fig. 10-17b, c, d).   Clock-gated logic causes time quantization (e.g., 0.5-μsec steps with a 2-Mc clock) and requires extra gates and clock wiring, which must be weighed against improved computer reliability and programming.[23]

(c) Relay Logic.   *Dry-reed relays* sealed in an inert atmosphere (Fig. 10-19a) combine operating times below 1 msec and long life (10^7 to

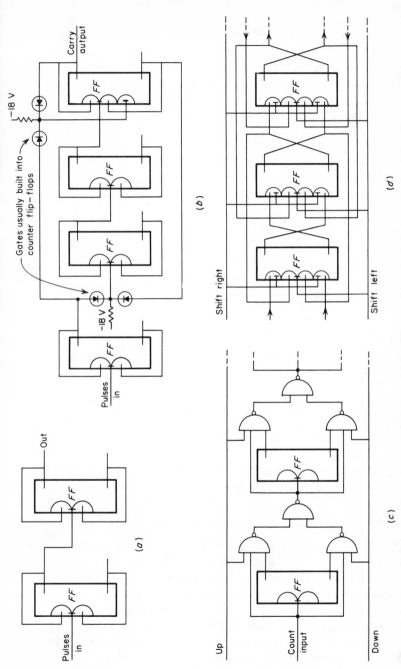

Fig. 10-18. A simple binary counter (*a*), a binary-coded decimal (BCD) counter (*b*), a reversible binary counter (*c*), and a reversible shift register (*d*). D-c reset connections are not shown.

403

10^9 operations). Spike-free switching and low bounce make them especially suitable for sampled-data-system simulation (Secs. 10-13 to 10-15) at moderate computing speeds.[34-36] Relays used in conjunction with electronic comparators or logic circuits are best driven by transistor relay drivers (Fig. 10-19b). We can sometimes speed up relay pickup (but not relay release) by driving relays with high-voltage capacitor discharges (Fig. 10-19c). Reed relays can be polarized with small permanent magnets (Fig. 10-19e), and multiple coils permit a variety of multi-input

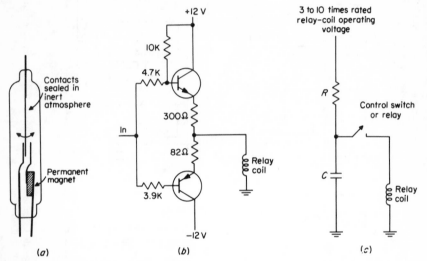

Fig. 10-19. Dry-reed-relay contact structure (a), transistor relay driver (b), and capacitor-discharge driving circuit (c).

gating operations. Such relays can be combined into counters, flip-flops, shift registers, and complex selection matrices for analog programming, memory, and readout (see also Secs. 6-9, 10-2, and 10-3).[36]

Where logic-type relays control high currents, it is desirable to switch the relay-coil circuit only while the contact circuit is deenergized, but this is not always possible.

10-11. Design of a Digital Control Unit.[44] **Oscilloscope Displays. (a) Introduction.** The simplest type of iterative-differential-analyzer control involves merely a source of RESET pulses for repetitive operation, which can be a simple astable multivibrator. All other subroutine control operations can, in principle, be relegated to patched digital logic.

We feel, however, that oversimplified control circuits constitute quite false economy. First, accurate repetitive-computer operation requires stable timing to prevent synchronization of the repetition rate with the power-line frequency or its harmonics. Such synchronization tends to cause systematic errors, even though it makes oscilloscope displays in low-cost computers look "clean," i.e., free from line-frequency jitter. Timing pulses are best obtained from a simple crystal-controlled digital clock, which will also pay for itself as a source of reliable timing pulses for memory control, digital logic, oscilloscope and digital displays, noise generators,[111] etc. *The addition of simple logic circuits to the basic digital clock can, next, produce the most frequently useful subroutine sequences with little or no digital-circuit patching.* This opens the iterative technique to a much wider class of operators, for detailed iterative-subroutine design is far from easy for most analog-computer users. With a neat compromise between control-unit sophistication and complexity, important "packaged" subroutines can be selected by switching. Less frequently employed subroutine sequences can, of course, still be patched on a digital patchbay or pinboard adjacent to our digital control unit (Sec. 11-1b).

Figure 10-20a illustrates the design of a very flexible iterative-differential-analyzer control unit[44] built from commercially available logic cards. Control functions are divided among a *master timer* and an *auxiliary timer* built with 5-Mc logic modules to minimize timing errors and a *subroutine counter* or counters using 200-Kc logic. Modular design permits us to start with the master timer and to add other functions as needed.

(b) Basic Digital Clock and Sample Timer. Referring to Fig. 10-20a, we begin with a 4-Mc crystal clock and count down to obtain *timing pulses* for various control and display purposes. Clock pulses at 4 Mc, 2 Mc, 1 Mc, and 500 Kc are always available, and the repetition-rate selector Sw_1 selects clock pulses Cl at exactly 1,000 times the desired computer repetition rate $f_R = 1/T_R = 1,000, 500, 250, 100, 50, 25$, or 10 computer runs per second. All further timing is performed in terms of these Cl pulses (1,000 per computer run), so that the repetition-rate selector automatically changes the time scale of all timing and counting operations. If desired, the repetition-rate selector can also change integrator capacitors through relays to provide completely automatic time-scale changes.

The *master timing counter* C_1 fed by Sw_1 is a three-decade dual-preset decimal counter designed to perform the following timing functions:

1. It counts down by 1,000 to mark the start of periodic COMPUTE periods ($\tau = 0$, Fig. 10-20b).
2. It produces timing markers at 10 times and 100 times the computer repetition rate (e.g., for oscilloscope displays).
3. Thumbwheel decade switches select preset-counter outputs $\tau = T$ and $\tau = \tau_1$ sec after the start of each COMPUTE period in steps of $T_R/1,000$ sec.

In normal repetitive operation (Fig. 10-20b), flip-flop $FF1$ is reset at $\tau = 0$ and set at $\tau = T$ to produce periodic computer RESET pulses R, so

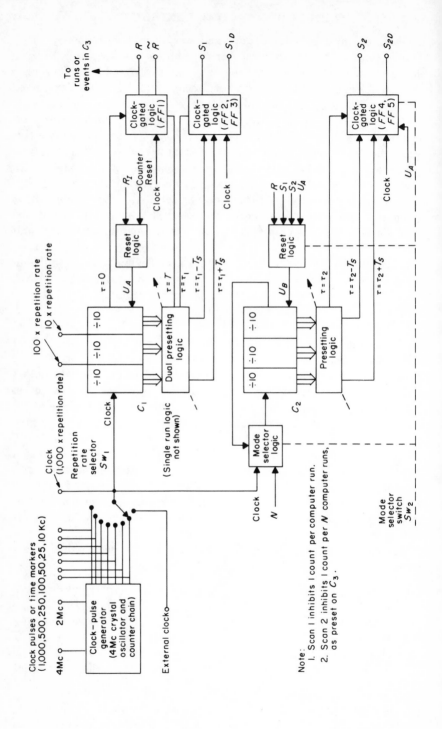

Note:
1. Scan 1 inhibits 1 count per computer run.
2. Scan 2 inhibits 1 count per N computer runs, as preset on C_3.

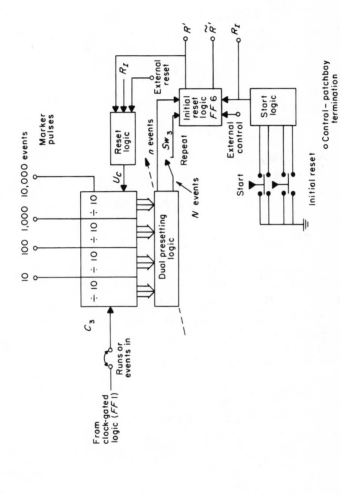

FIG. 10-20a. Simplified block diagram of a digital iterative-differential-analyzer control unit (ASTRAC II, University of Arizona; see also Sec. 11-7).

that COMPUTE periods of length T alternate with RESET periods of length $T_R - T$. Note that we can independently select $T_R = 1/f_R$ and T. The preset output at τ_1 feeds a two-flip-flop timing-logic block to produce periodic track-hold control pulses S_1 and delayed pulses S_{1D} of length

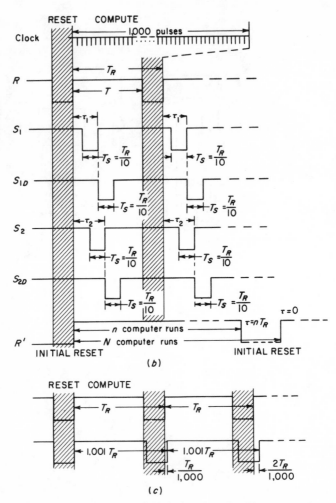

Fig. 10-20b, c. ASTRAC II timing (see also Fig. 10-12c, d).

$T_S = T_R/10$ (Fig. 10-20b). A track-hold circuit controlled by S_1 (Sec. 10-8) will periodically track for T_S sec and switch into HOLD at $\tau = \tau_1$. S_{1D} switches T_S sec later than S_1 for memory-triplet operation (Fig. 10-12d).

All timing pulses, reset pulses, and track-hold control pulses are available in a small *control-variable patchbay* for flexible control of individual integrators and switches (Fig. 10-21; see also Sec. 11-1b). In normal repetitive-computer operation, integrators are controlled by R, and a track-hold circuit is controlled by S_1 for digital readout of solution values $X(\tau_1)$ at the accurately preset computer time τ_1. Different patching connections can employ R, S_1, and S_{1D} to produce flexible memory control, including three-period control (Sec. 10-8).

The patchable COUNTER RESET input to C_1 resets the counter to zero and permits finer control of the computer-run period than is possible by repetition-rate selection. We can, for instance, use S_1 to reset the counter at $\tau = \tau_1$ and to reset integrators at

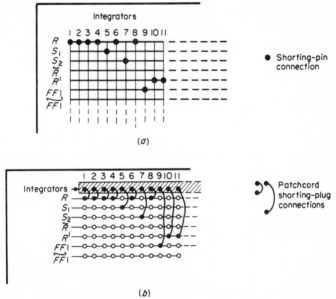

(a)

● Shorting-pin connection

(b)

⟩ Patchcord shorting-plug connections

FIG. 10-21. Integrator connections on a control pinboard (a), and on a control patchboard (b). Integrators 1, 2, 3, 4 are normal repetitive integrators; 5, 6 and 7, 8 are track-hold pairs; 9 is switched by flip-flop $FF1$, and 10, 11 are "slow" integrators controlled by R'.

$\tau = \tau_1 - T_R/10$. Many other possibilities exist; it is, in particular, possible to control the lengths of individual computer runs with patched comparator logic to conserve time in long computations.

(c) Auxiliary Timer and Scanning Readout. The *auxiliary timing counter* C_2 in Fig. 10-20a is another three-decade preset counter. With its associated logic circuits, C_2 adds the following functions to the basic clock:

1. With switch Sw_2 in the "τ_2" position, C_2 produces a preset output τ_2 sec after the start of each COMPUTE period. Logic circuits yield track-hold control pulses S_2 and S_{2D} analogous to S_1 and S_{1D}.

2. With Sw_2 in the "τ_D" position, C_2 is reset periodically at $\tau = \tau_1$. The timing pulses switching S_2 to 0 (HOLD) occur at $\tau = \tau_1 + \tau_D$,

with τ_1 and τ_D thumbwheel-preset on C_1 and C_2. This produces, in particular, sample pairs $X(\tau_1)$, $Y(\tau_1 + \tau_D)$ for correlation and prediction studies (ref. 111).

3. With Sw_2 in the "T" position, C_2 is reset at $\tau = T$, and S_2, S_{2D} serve for readout during the RESET period just as S_1, S_{1D} serve during the COMPUTE period. This is useful for "alternating" differential-analyzer runs using integrator groups controlled by R and $\bar{R}$ and also permits flexible three-period control (Sec. 10-8).

4. With Sw_2 in the "SCAN 1" position, C_2 recycles after 1,001 input pulses. With C_1 and C_2 initially reset to $0.9T_R$ and zero (Sec. 10-11d) and C_2 preset to $T_R/1,000$ sec, S_2 will read out at $\tau_2 = T_R/1,000$ sec during the first computer run, at $\tau_2 = 2T_R/1,000$ sec during the second computer run, etc. *Track-hold circuits controlled by S_2 and S_{2D} will then "scan" periodic repetitive-computer solutions once every 1,000 computer runs for readout into slow recorders, printers, or digital computers.* With $f_R = 100$ cps, for instance, a complete scan requires 10 sec (Fig. 10-20c).

5. With Sw_2 in the "SCAN 2" position, the subroutine counter (Sec. 10-11d) permits the scan to step forward only after a preset number N of computer runs or other events.

6. With Sw_2 in the "REVERSE SCAN" position, C_2 resets after $m < 1,000$ input pulses. With C_1 and C_2 initially reset to zero and C_2 preset to $mT_R/1,000$ sec, τ_2 starts at that time and scans *backward* in steps of $(1 - m/1,000)T_R$ sec per computer run.

The SCAN modes are useful for slow recording of repetitive solutions (X vs. τ or Y vs. X), and also for automatic parameter changing [new values of a repetitive solution $X(\tau)$ are used in successive computer runs], for multiple-solution oscilloscope displays, and for solution checks with slow computers. The "REVERSE SCAN" mode, with its wide choice of scanning rates, is useful for computing convolution integrals, for backward integration (e.g., in boundary-value problems, ref. 23), for modified-adjoint-system techniques (ref. 111), and for controlling delay-line-memory read/write cycles (Sec. 10-20). The "SCAN 2" mode is intended for automatic computation of statistics over N computer runs (ref. 111).

(d) Subroutine Counter and REPEAT Switch. Referring again to Fig. 10-20a, the *subroutine counter C_3*, another dual-preset four-decade counter, is patched to count computer runs, comparator-output steps, or other events. C_3 produces output pulses every 10, 100, 1,000, and 10,000 events, as well as preset-counter outputs after n and N events (n, $N < 20,000$). These counter outputs are used to terminate and/or start subroutine sequences. In particular, the REPEAT switch Sw_3 permits us to reset C_3 to zero after N events and to recycle the sequence.

(e) Starting, Two-time-scale Operation, and External Control. Before computation, we depress the INITIAL RESET *button* (Fig. 10-20a) momentarily to produce the following conditions:

1. The subroutine counter C_3 is reset to zero and establishes the INITIAL RESET mode ($R' = 1$, Sec. 10-8c).
2. The main timing counter C_1 is reset to $T_R - T_S = 0.9T_R$; and flip-flops $FF1$ to $FF5$ are set or reset to produce $R = 1$ and correct initial values of S_1, S_{1D}, S_2, and S_{2D}. C_2 is reset to zero, except in the "τ_D" mode, where it is reset to $T_R/1,000$.
3. In any SCAN mode, counter C_2 is reset to zero.

It follows that all integrators, memory pairs, and/or statistical averaging devices controlled by R and R' are now reset to suitable initial conditions, ready for computation.

This state is maintained until we release (or depress and release) the START button momentarily. Then C_1 runs through 100 Cl pulses (T_S sec) and then starts the first COMPUTE period (see also Fig. 10-12c). To produce "nested" iterative subroutines, the REPEAT switch Sw_3 reestablishes the INITIAL RESET mode ($R' = 1$) after a preset number n of subroutine-counter input pulses, and resets the subroutine counter after $N > n$ pulses to repeat the cycle (Fig. 10-20b). In particular, we can reset fast integrators with R and slow integrators with R' (*two-time-scale operation*).

If the SINGLE-RUN *switch* Sw_4 is closed, then the START button produces a single computer run ($R = 0$) without resetting C_1, C_2, or C_3, so that we can check the progress of iterative subroutines computer run by computer run. The various resetting, sampling, and starting operations can also be ordered electronically by external command pulses into appropriate lines.

(f) Multitrace Oscilloscope Displays.[46-49] Repetitive analog-computer solutions are readily displayed on oscilloscopes synchronized with the computer RESET pulses R. For real insight into an iterative computation, it is, however, practically essential to display 4 to 10 analog and binary variables simultaneously as functions of time.

At high iteration rates (100 to 1,000 cps), truly simultaneous multitrace displays require multiple or multigun cathode-ray tubes with electrostatic deflection, although electronic commutation of several oscilloscope inputs can still display a few inputs at 100 sweeps per second. Normally, we shall be able to see 1-Kc computer solutions only if they repeat periodically; in this case, we can switch to different variables during successive computer runs, so that eye persistence creates a multitrace effect. *Run-to-run changes of iterative solutions* can be conveniently observed only at low repetition rates.

At repetition rates below 60 cps, the best multitrace displays are B-scan (television-type) displays on large (17- to 24-in.) electromagnetic-deflection cathode-ray tubes (Fig. 10-22a). Figure 10-22b illustrates the operation of such a display with, say, a 25-cps repetition rate. The horizontal (slow) sweep is driven at the computer repetition rate or at an integral fraction of this rate. Each horizontal sweep corresponds to one

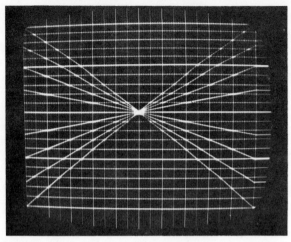

Fig. 10-22a. Portion of a multitrace television-type display with time and voltage reference lines ("electronic graph paper," G. A. Philbrick Researches, Inc.).

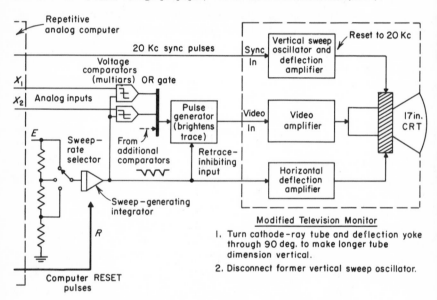

Fig. 10-22b. A multitrace television-type display system.

computer run, two runs, or several runs. The vertical (fast) sweep is driven by time markers (Sec. 10-11b) 100 to 500 times per computer run. A set of comparators (e.g., multiar circuits, refs. 28 and 49) compares each vertical-sweep ramp with the input voltages $X_1(\tau)$, $X_2(\tau)$, . . . and unblank the oscilloscope at each comparator step to produce the desired multitrace display. In addition, we unblank, say, every tenth vertical sweep to create very accurate time markers. Fixed voltage inputs also

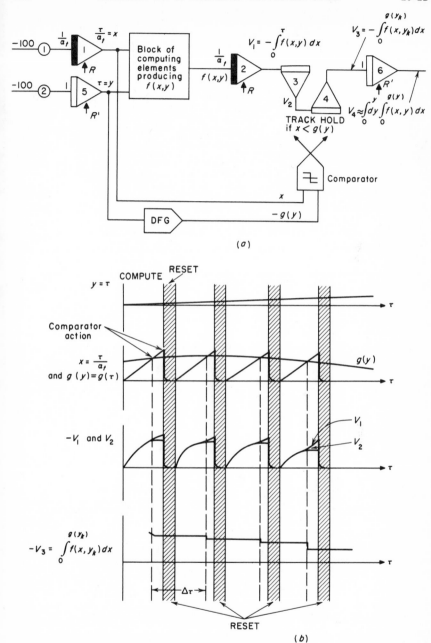

Fig. 10-23. Computation of a double integral[19] illustrates two-time-scale operation and comparator control of a track-hold pair. The primitive output accumulator (Euler integration rule) could be replaced by the trapezoidal-integration circuit of Table 10-1 for improved stepwise integration with respect to y.

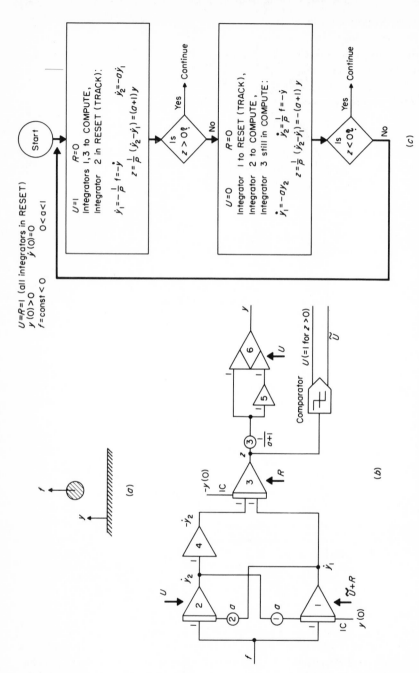

Fig. 10-24. Semielastic impact (a), computer setup (b), and flow diagram (c).

produce voltage-reference lines ("electronic graph paper" in G. A. Philbrick Researches, Inc., displays). Instead of providing very accurate
comparators and voltage-reference lines, we prefer digital readout through
a track-hold circuit operated at the thumbwheel-selected time $\tau = \tau_1$
during each computer run (Sec. 10-11b). The S_1 pulses can be used to
unblank a vertical sweep serving as a variable τ_1 marker.

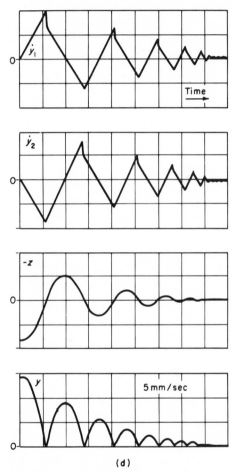

(d)

FIG. 10-24d. Solution records.

Many useful display variations can be obtained with various unblank-
ing circuits. To display solutions and/or binary control variables against
a dependent variable $X(\tau)$, the linear horizontal sweep voltage is replaced
by $X(\tau)$ on a suitable scale. Existing television monitors convert readily
into computer display units, and Polaroid Land cameras permit convenient oscilloscope recording. Unfortunately, magnetic-deflection frequency response will not permit good displays at much over 60 frames/sec.

10-12. Two Simple Applications. We present two simple computer setups as examples of iterative-differential-analyzer programming; more significant applications will be described in Chap. 12.

(a) **Double Integration.**[19] While other analog-computer techniques for computing double integrals exist,[100,101] the setup of Fig. 10-23 is an especially simple example of a two-time-scale computation employing repetitive-computer subroutines to feed data into a real-time computer run. The crude sampled-data integration with respect to x (Euler approximation, Sec. 11-14) employs an accumulator circuit similar to Fig. 10-13b for readout of $\int_0^\tau f(x,y)\,dx$ and $-\int_0^{a(y_k)} f(x,y)\,dx$. Section 10-14 shows how to implement better integration formulas (e.g., the open trapezoidal rule).

(b) **Simulation of Semielastic Impact.**[43] In Fig. 10-24a, a steel ball impinges on a steel plate with velocity $-\dot{y}$ and rebounds practically instantaneously with velocity $a\dot{y}$; the coefficient of restitution a is between 0 and 1. The impact force is usually too large for satisfactory analog scaling (Sec. 9-7). Our iterative-differential-analyzer setup treats the period after each impact as a new subroutine; the new initial velocity $a\dot{y}$ is obtained through analog storage (Fig. 10-24b, c). Figure 10-24d is a record of the real-time solution; the circuit also works nicely for 10-cps repetitive operation.

TRACK-HOLD OPERATIONS WITH SAMPLED DATA AND SIMULATION OF DIGITAL COMPUTERS

10-13. Sampled-data Sequences and Solution of Difference Equations (see also Sec. 10-8). Let τ represent real time, and let

$$X(\tau) = X(\tau_i) = X_i \qquad (\tau_i < \tau < \tau_{i+1}; \ k = 0,1,2, \ \ldots) \qquad (10\text{-}5)$$

be the stepwise output of a track-hold circuit, memory pair, or digital-to-analog converter. The step-function voltage $X(\tau)$ represents a *sampled-data sequence* $X_0, X_1, X_2, \ldots$; X_i may be regarded as a function of its integral-valued subscript $i = 0, 1, 2, \ldots$. Such data sequences are often encountered in iterative-differential-analyzer work; in particular, they simulate the stepwise operation of digital computers, e.g., in studies of sampled-data control systems. Unlike true digital data, data sequences represented by step-function voltages can be neatly added, multiplied, etc., with analog computing elements; and important *difference operations* can be implemented with the aid of memory pairs.

Reference to Fig. 10-25 shows that *the stepwise output $Y(\tau)$ of a suitably timed memory pair with input* (5) *will represent the input sampled-data sequence delayed by one step*, i.e.,

$$Y_i = Y(\tau_i) = X(\tau_{i-1}) = X_{i-1} = \mathbf{E}^{-1}X_i \qquad (i = 0,1,2, \ \ldots \ ; X_{-1} = 0)$$
$$(10\text{-}6)$$

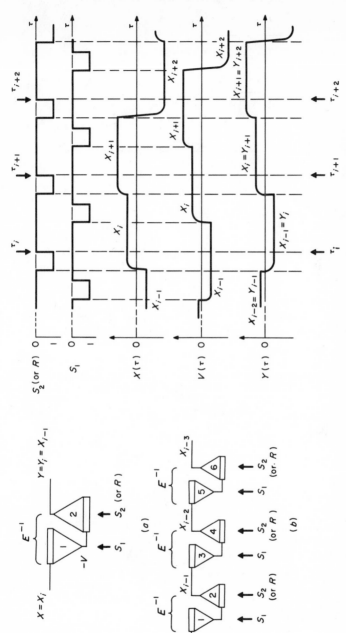

Fig. 10-25a, b. Memory pair with sampled-data input (a), and cascaded memory pairs (b).

417

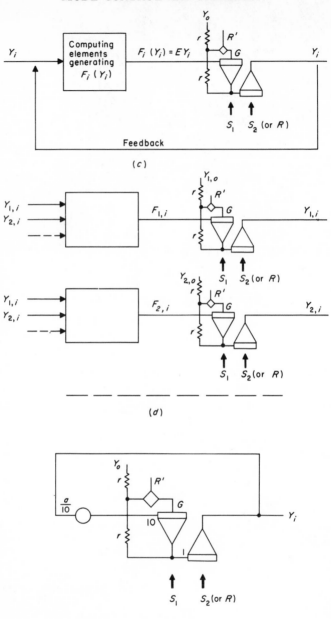

Fig. 10-25c, d, e. Implementation of recursion formulas (solution of difference equations). The "exponential accumulator" setup in Fig. 10-25e implements $EY_i = aY_i$, so that $Y_i = Y_0 a^i$ $(i = 0, 1, 2, \ldots)$. This circuit can step parameters for logarithmic-scale plotting.

The track-hold pair of Fig. 10-25a implements the linear *discrete-delay operator* $\mathbf{E}^{-1}$ defined by Eq. (6)* exactly like an analog integrator implements the linear reciprocal-derivative operator $-P^{-1} \equiv -(d/d\tau)^{-1}$. A cascade of memory pairs synchronized in the manner of Fig. 10-25b will, then, produce successively delayed data sequences

$$\left.\begin{aligned}\mathbf{E}^{-1}X_i &= X_{i-1} \\ \mathbf{E}^{-1}X_{i-1} &= E^{-2}X_i = X_{i-2} \\ &\dots\dots\dots\dots\dots\end{aligned}\right\} \quad (i = 0,1,2, \ . \ . \ . \ ; X_i = 0 \text{ for } k < 0)$$

$$(10\text{-}7)$$

and the input data sequence $X_0,\ X_1,\ X_2\ \dots$ will proceed, step by step, through the memory chain (analog shift register, "bucket-brigade" time delay,[75] see also Sec. 10-19).

We next employ a track-hold pair to solve a *first-order difference equation* or recurrence relation

$$\mathbf{E}Y_i = Y_{i+1} = F_i(Y_i) \qquad (i = 0,1,2, \ . \ . \ .) \qquad (10\text{-}8)$$

for the unknown data sequence Y_i, given Y_0 *(initial value)* and $F_i(Y_i)$ as a function of Y_i and i. We implement Eq. (8) with a feedback loop (Fig. 10-25c) quite analogous to those customarily employed for analog-computer solution of *differential* equations. The important accumulator circuit of Fig. 10-13a, for example, implements the simple difference equation $\mathbf{E}Y_i = Y_i + X_i$. The correct initial memory-pair output Y_0 must be established with an initial-reset circuit (Fig. 10-12).

Figure 10-25d similarly solves a *system of first-order difference equations*

$$\mathbf{E}Y_{j,i} = Y_{j,i+1} = F_{j,i}(Y_{1,i};Y_{2,i}; \ \cdot \ \cdot \ \cdot \ ;Y_{r,i}) \qquad \begin{aligned}(i &= 0,1,2, \ . \ . \ .; \\ j &= 1,2, \ . \ . \ .,r)\end{aligned} \quad (10\text{-}9)$$

for the r unknown sequences $Y_{j,i}(j = 1,2, \ . \ . \ .,r)$. An *rth-order difference equation*

$$\mathbf{E}^rY_i = Y_{i+r} = F_i(Y_i,Y_{i+1}, \ \cdot \ \cdot \ \cdot \ ,Y_{i+r-1}) \qquad (i = 0,1,2, \ . \ . \ .) \quad (10\text{-}10)$$

reduces to the form (9) if we introduce $Y_{i+1},\ Y_{i+2},\ \dots$ as new variables related by the first-order difference equations

$$\mathbf{E}Y_i = Y_{i+1} \qquad \mathbf{E}Y_{i+1} = Y_{i+2} \qquad \cdot \ \cdot \ \cdot \qquad (10\text{-}11)$$

in exact analogy with Sec. 2-7b. Note that the number of initial values given with Eq. (9) or Eq. (10) must again equal the order r of our system; each memory pair requires an initial-reset circuit.

Note that these procedures apply to nonlinear as well as to linear dif-

---

* In the Laplace-transform domain, the operator P^{-1} corresponds to multiplication by s^{-1}. Similarly, if we introduce z transforms[55] $\mathsf{z}[X(s)] = \sum\limits_{k=0}^{\infty} X_k z^{-k}$ of our data sequences X_i, then the operator $\mathbf{E}^{-1}$ corresponds to multiplication by z^{-1}.

ference equations, and that they do *not* necessarily require periodic sampling, as long as all track-hold pairs are synchronized in the manner of Fig. 10-25b. This technique permits analog-computer simulation of relatively complex digital-computer and digital-differential-analyzer operations.

10-14. Linear Operations on Sampled Data.[55-64] The output sequences Y_i (responses) of many sampled-data processors are related to their input sequences X_i (stimuli) by linear difference equations of the form

$$Y_i + a_{n-1}Y_{i-1} + \cdots + a_0Y_{i-n} = b_mX_i + b_{m-1}X_{i-1} + \cdots + b_0X_{i-m}$$
(10-12a)

with given constant coefficients a_i, b_k; current-data processing implies $n > m$. Just as in Sec. 2-12, we rewrite the input-output relation $(12a)$ in terms of a linear operator $O(\mathbf{E})$ operating on X_i to produce Y_i:

$$Y_i = O(\mathbf{E})X_i = \frac{b_{n-1}\mathbf{E}^{n-1} + b_{n-2}\mathbf{E}^{n-2} + \cdots + b_0}{\mathbf{E}^n + a_{n-1}\mathbf{E}^{n-1} + \cdots + a_0} X_i \quad (10\text{-}12b)$$

Such operators commute and may be cascaded and added in the manner of Fig. 2-16.

Computer setups implementing the difference equation (12) *are exactly analogous to the computer circuits implementing the differential equation* (2-46); *it is merely necessary to replace every integrator operation* $-P^{-1}$ *in Figs.* 2-17 *and* 2-18 *by the memory-pair operation* $-\mathbf{E}^{-1}$. Note, however, that memory pairs, unlike integrators, do not usually invert the output-voltage sign. Table 10-1 shows some useful examples.

By analogy with Sec. 2-15, the difference operator $O(\mathbf{E})$ can also be factored or expressed as a sum of *partial fractions* of the form $\dfrac{1}{A_1\mathbf{E} + A_2}$, $\dfrac{A_3\mathbf{E} + 1}{\alpha_0\mathbf{E}^2 + \alpha_1\mathbf{E} + \alpha_3}$. Partial-fraction representations may reduce switching-spike accumulation, and each partial-fraction term can be implemented and checked separately.[64]

Difference-equation setups conveniently implement relatively complicated sampled-data operations and are especially useful for simulation of digital controllers. Systems with finite-time sampling, quantization (Sec. 9-9), and pulse-width modulation are also readily simulated with combinations of track-hold circuits, analog computing elements, and digital modules.[64,1,103]

Unfortunately, the requirement of two switched integrators per memory pair makes difference-operator setups somewhat expensive. Figure 10-26 shows a simplified relay-switched memory-pair circuit useful in slow computations.

All computer setups should be checked for switching-spike accumulation in memory-pair chains and feedback loops. Reed relays, while slower than electronic switches, are more satisfactory in this respect; a chain of 12 relay track-hold circuits (6 memory pairs) can reproduce its input within 25 mV.[59]

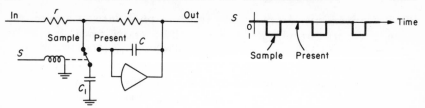

Fig. 10-26. Simplified one-amplifier memory-pair circuit.

Table 10-1. Examples of Linear Difference Operators

Operator	Formula	Computer setup (add initial-reset circuits as needed)
1. Backward-difference operator	$Y_i = X_i - X_{i-1} = (1 - E^{-1})X_i$ $= \dfrac{E - 1}{E} X_i = \nabla X_i = E^{-1} \Delta X_i$	
2. An approximate-differentiation formula	$Y_i = \dfrac{1}{2\Delta t}(3X_i - 4X_{i-1} + X_{i-2})$ $= \dfrac{1}{2\Delta t} \dfrac{3E^2 - 4E + 1}{E^2} X_i$	
3. Euler rule for approximate integration, simple accumulator (see also Fig. 10-13)	$Y_i = Y_{i-1} + X_{i-1}\,\Delta t$ $= \dfrac{1}{E - 1} X_i\,\Delta t = \Delta^{-1}X_i\,\Delta t$ $= \displaystyle\sum_{k=0}^{i-1} X_k\,\Delta t + Y_0$	
4. Trapezoidal rule for approximate integration	$Y_i = Y_{i-1} + \frac{1}{2}(X_i + X_{i-1})\,\Delta t$ $= \dfrac{\Delta t}{2}\dfrac{E + 1}{E - 1} X_i$	
5. Open trapezoidal rule	$Y_i = Y_{i-1} + \frac{1}{2}(3X_{i-1} - X_{i-2})\,\Delta t$ $= \dfrac{\Delta t}{2}\dfrac{3E - 1}{E(E - 1)} X_i$ $= \dfrac{\Delta t}{2}\left(\dfrac{1}{E} + \dfrac{2}{E - 1}\right) X_i$	

10-15. Conversion from and to Sampled-data Representations.[55-64]   **(a) Sampling.**   A periodically operated track-hold circuit with continuous input $X(\tau)$ will produce an output sequence $X(\tau_0)$, $X(\tau_1)$, $X(\tau_2)$, . . . ($\tau_k = k \Delta t$, $k = 0,1,2, . . .$), which represents a portion of the input information.   The fundamental sampling theorem[55] states that an

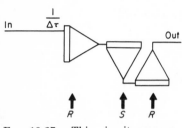

FIG. 10-27a. This circuit averages its analog input and presents the average during the following interval.

analog signal $X(\tau)$ without Fourier or spectral components beyond B cps can be reconstructed exactly from $2B$ periodic samples $X(\tau_k)$ per second.   Actual practice usually requires at least five times this minimum sampling rate.   *Unequivocal data reconstruction requires careful removal of any signal and/or noise components beyond B cps* by low-pass filters or averaging circuits (Fig. 10-27a) preceding the sampler.   Sampler inputs beyond B cps can result in spurious low-frequency components (*folding or aliasing errors*, Fig. 10-27b).   This precaution applies, in particular, to analog-to-digital converters (Sec. 11-11).

(b) Data Reconstruction.   The stepwise sample-hold (zero-order-hold) analog output $Y(\tau_k)$ of a real or simulated sampled-data system represents the reconstructed analog variable correctly only at the beginning of each HOLD period; even then, it usually represents a *delayed* output.

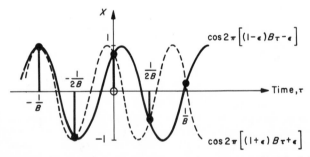

FIG. 10-27b. Folding-error demonstration.   Sample values are identical for the two functions shown.

Simple smoothing with low-pass filters may help; for more accurate data reconstruction, we employ computer circuits to generate *extrapolation polynomials* matching successive data points $Y(\tau_k)$ (Fig. 10-28).[55]

The simplest example is the *first-order hold*, which implements linear extrapolation between data points.   It may be followed by a smoothing filter. rth-degree polynomial interpolation will yield exact reconstruction if the desired output is itself a polynomial of degree $\leq r$.

The especially simple first-order hold of Fig. 10-28c, d is an improved version of an earlier circuit developed by L. Lofgren.[3]   Referring to Fig. 10-28c, the circuit equation in HOLD (switch OFF) is

$$R_1 C_1 \frac{di}{d\tau} + i = aC_1 \frac{dX_o}{d\tau} \qquad \text{with } i = C \frac{dX_o}{d\tau}$$

For first-order-hold action, $dX_o/d\tau$ must be constant in HOLD, so that $di/d\tau = 0$, and

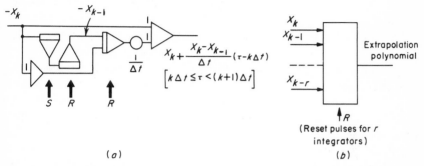

FIG. 10-28a, b. First-order-hold circuit (a), and more general hold circuit (b), for periodic sampling at the rate $1/\Delta t$.

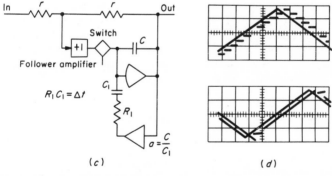

FIG. 10-28c, d. Simple modification of a zero-order hold circuit for first-order-hold operation.   The a-c coupled d-c amplifier need not be a low-drift amplifier, so that this circuit is an economical choice for data reconstruction after real or simulated digital operations, multiplexing, time delays, etc.   Figure 10-28d shows zero-order-hold and first-order-hold input and output with $C = 0.01$ μF, $C = 1$ μF, $\Delta t = 0.5$ sec.

$a = C/C_1$.   With C and C_1 initially discharged, let C be charged quickly to ΔX_o during the first TRACK interval.   First-order-hold action requires that the initial current $-a \, \Delta X_o/R_1$ into C_1 be equal to $-C \, dX_o/d\tau = -C \, \Delta X_o/\Delta t$, where Δt is the time between periodic samples.   It follows that we must have $R_1 C_1 = \Delta t$.

10-16. Application to Iterative Computation.   Difference equations of the form (9) and (12) represent many useful differencing and approximate-integration formulas (Table 10-1) and iterative recurrence relations.   Many iterative-differential-analyzer setups can be regarded as memory-pair difference-equation solvers which exchange sampled-data information with repetitively operated analog-computing elements (Chap. 12).

TIME-DELAY SIMULATION AND FUNCTION STORAGE

10-17. Problem Statement and General Remarks. A variety of control-system and data-processing applications require *time-delay elements,* i.e., computing elements whose output $Y(\tau)$ is a delayed version of the input $X(\tau)$:

$$Y(\tau) = X(\tau - \tau_D) \tag{10-13}$$

The *time delay* τ_D, which can be as large as one computer-run time, may be constant or a function $\tau_D(\tau)$ of time. In a typical application, X and Y are fluid temperatures at the input and output of a pipe, and the resulting *transport delay* τ_D can vary with time because of a variable flow rate.

Ideal time-delay implementation implies *function storage:* we must store a segment of $X(\tau)$ τ_D sec long and provide for continuous read-in and readout. A more general requirement for analog-function storage (as contrasted with *point storage* of discrete voltage values only) exists in various iteration techniques for solving differential and integral equations, and for solution checks (Secs. 12-5 and 12-21).

Sections 10-18 and 10-19 describe the more promising function-storage methods. Other techniques, such as storage-tube memories,[21,65,69] have had only indifferent success in the past, but may merit periodic reappraisal.

10-18. Operational-amplifier and Network Approximations. (a) **Introduction.** For *constant* delay τ_D and suitably differentiable input $X(\tau)$, Taylor expansion of Eq. (13) yields the operator relation

$$Y(\tau) = X(\tau - \tau_D) = \left[1 - \tau_D P + \frac{1}{2!}(\tau_D P)^2 \mp \cdots \right] X(\tau)$$
$$= e^{-\tau_D P} X(\tau) \quad \left(P \equiv \frac{d}{d\tau} \right) \tag{10-14}$$

For steady-state sinusoidal input and output, the *constant-time-delay operator* $e^{-\tau_D P}$ corresponds to constant unity gain and negative phase shift (lag) proportional to the frequency f:

$$|e^{-j\omega\tau_D}| = 1 \qquad \arg e^{-j\omega\tau_D} = -\omega\tau_D = -2\pi f\tau_D \tag{10-15}$$

At reasonably low frequencies, we can approximate $e^{-\tau_D s}$ by a rational transfer function $H(s)$ implemented with operational amplifiers and/or passive linear networks. In view of Eq. (15), correct phase shift at the frequency f will require at least $2f\tau_D$ energy-storing network elements (capacitors or inductors), since the phase shift contributed by each can increase (from zero at d-c) to at most 180 deg even in active networks.[68]

Table 10-2 shows differential-analyzer setups for constant-delay

Table 10-2. Time-delay Approximations

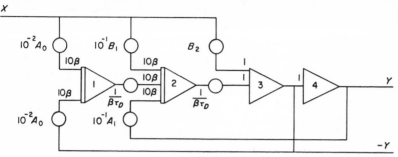

1. Second-order and Cascaded Second-order All-pass Delay Approximations
   (Primed quantities refer to the second network of a cascade circuit)

	A_0	$A_1 = B_1$	A_0'	$A_1' = B_1'$	$\omega\tau_D$ limit for $\delta(\omega) < 0.1$ radian
All-pass Padé,[66] $P_{2,2}$......	12	6	.....	....	2.9
Smith and Wood,[82] $W_{2,2}$...	10	4.7	.....	....	3.4
Cunningham,[87] $C_{4,4}$.......	30.88	10.56	45.64	7.48	6.9
Stubbs and Single,[86] $S_{4,4}$..	19.4	7.63	54.9	5.94	7.6

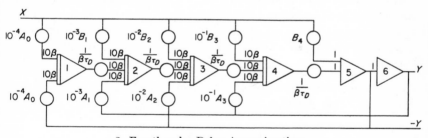

2. Fourth-order Delay Approximations

	A_0	A_1	A_2	A_3	B_1	B_2	B_3	B_4
All-pass Padé,[87] $P_{4,4}$.............	1,680	840	180	20	840	180	20	1
All-pass Single-type,[84] $S_{4,4}'$.......	1,074	537	120	13.59	536	120	13.55	1
Low-pass Padé,[87] $P_{3,4}$...........	840	480	120	16	360	60	4	0
King and Rideout,[87] $K_{3,4}$........	537	361.2	101.9	12.98	175.8	22.45	1.51	0
King and Rideout,[87] $R_{3,4}$........	476	309	91.8	12.1	160.5	22.8	1.48	0

approximations of the form

$$H(P) = \frac{A_0 - B_1(\tau_D P) + B_2(\tau_D P)^2 \mp \cdots + (-1)^n B_n(\tau_D P)^n}{A_0 + A_1(\tau_D P) + A_2(\tau_D P)^2 + \cdots + A_n(\tau_D P)^n}$$

$$\left(P \equiv \frac{d}{d\tau}\right) \quad (10\text{-}16)$$

with positive coefficients (see also Sec. 2-13). Several different synthesis techniques[87] yield suitable coefficients A_i, B_k; the choice will depend on the nature of our signals and on the objective of the simulation.

(b) All-pass Approximations. With input signals $X(\tau)$ limited in frequency below about $1/\tau_D$ cps (e.g., filtered signals and noise in control-system simulation), we can use *all-pass (zero-attenuation) approximations*. For $B_k = A_k$ ($k = 1, 2, \ldots, n$), Eq. (16) yields the desired unity gain $|H(j\omega)| = 1$. The A_k are then chosen to produce low phase error

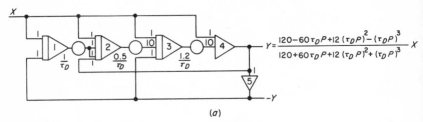

$$Y = \frac{120 - 60\tau_D P + 12\,(\tau_D P)^2 - (\tau_D P)^3}{120 + 60\tau_D P + 12\,(\tau_D P)^2 + (\tau_D P)^3}\, X$$

(a)

FIG. 10-29a. This simplified setup for the third-order all-pass Padé approximant $P_{3,3}$ saves potentiometers at the expense of setting convenience.

$\delta(\omega) = \arg H(j\omega) + \omega\tau_D$. Referring to Table 10-2 and Fig. 10-30a, all-pass *Padé approximations*[87] $P_{n,n}$ yield a monotonically increasing phase error which is very small at low frequencies. A number of other all-pass approximations[82-89,110] alternate positive and negative phase errors to reduce the error near $f = 1/\tau_D$ at the expense of low-frequency phase errors; this is usually preferable.

In practice, advanced synthesis is often replaced by simple curve fitting.[86] All-pass approximants of even order $n = 2m$ are written in the form

$$H(P) = \prod_{k=1}^{m} \frac{(T_k P)^2 - 2\zeta_k T_k P + 1}{(T_k P)^2 + 2\zeta_k T_k P + 1} \qquad \left(P \equiv \frac{d}{d\tau}\right)$$

with

$$\tau_D = 4\sum_{k=1}^{m} \zeta_k T_k$$

$\left.\begin{array}{c}\\ \\ \\ \\ \\ \\ \\ \end{array}\right\}$ (10-17)

The phase error is given by

$$\delta(\omega) = \sum_{k=1}^{m} \delta_k(\omega) \qquad \delta_k(\omega) = 4\zeta_k T_k \omega - 2\arctan \frac{2\zeta_k T_k \omega}{1 - \omega^2 T_k^2} \qquad (10\text{-}18)$$

Carefully plotted graphs[66,85,86] of $2\arctan 2\zeta T\omega/(1 - \omega^2 T^2)$ vs. $4\zeta T\omega$ are used to match the individual terms $\delta_k(\omega)$ for a small overall error $\delta(\omega)$. $\delta_k(\omega)$ will be positive for low ω if and only if $\zeta_k < \sqrt{3}/2$. For $m = 1$ ($n = 2$), $\zeta_1 = \sqrt{3}/2$ yields the all-pass Padé approximant $P_{2,2}$, and $\zeta = 0.8165$ results in a useful approximation with initially negative phase error. A good fourth-order approximant ($m = 2$, $n = 4$) is

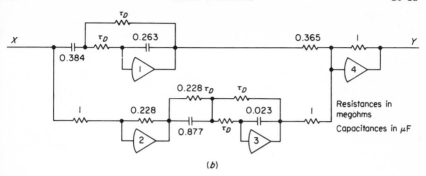

(b)

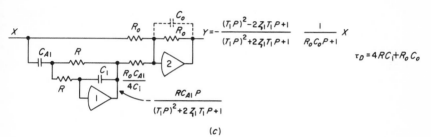

(c)

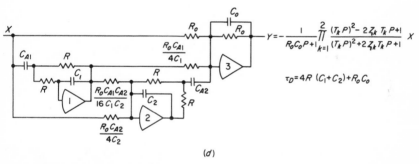

(d)

FIG. 10-29b, c, d. A four-amplifier circuit for $K_{3,4}$ (Table 10-1)(b), and Single-type operational-amplifier circuits (c), (d). A-c coupling can save chopper stabilization in some amplifiers. With chopper stabilization, circuit (d) tends to be noisy for low delays τ_D, so that two cascaded circuits (c) are preferable. We have

$$T_1 = R \sqrt{C_1 C_{A1}} \qquad T_2 = R \sqrt{C_2 C_{A2}} \qquad \zeta_1 = \sqrt{\frac{C_1}{C_{A1}}} \qquad \zeta_2 = \sqrt{\frac{C_2}{C_{A2}}}$$

and preferred values are given by

$$\zeta_1 = \sqrt{3}/2 \qquad \zeta_2 = 0.4 \qquad T_1/T_2 = 1.68 \qquad R_0 C_0 \leq \tau_D/100$$

(Based on refs. 86 and 87.)

obtained with

$$\zeta_1 = \frac{\sqrt{3}}{2} \qquad \zeta_2 = 0.4 \qquad \frac{T_1}{T_2} = 1.68 \qquad (10\text{-}19)$$

(Table 10-1 and Fig. 10-29).[86]   Reference 82 also gives sixth-order and eighth-order approximations.

(c) **Low-pass Approximations.** If our signals are not band-limited (e.g., step inputs), then we require *low-pass delay approximations*, since we must attenuate high-frequency components which cannot be

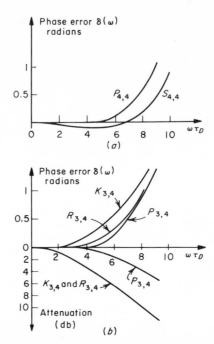

Fig. 10-30*a*, *b*. Frequency response of all-pass delay networks (*a*), and low-pass delay networks (*b*).   (*Data based on ref. 87.*)

correctly delayed.   Such high-frequency components will, in particular, cause unpleasant transient oscillations in the step response (Fig. 10-30*c*, *d*). Delay-approximation synthesis methods are based on different compromises between good approximations to the ideal frequency response (15) and clean step response (e.g., minimum mean-square step-response error).[86,87]   Several synthesis techniques simply combine an all-pass delay network with a low-pass filter (Fig. 10-29*d*).

Table 10-2 gives several low-pass approximations of the form (16) with $B_n = 0$, and Fig. 10-30 illustrates typical frequency and step responses.

(d) Practical Considerations. Treatment of Variable Time Delays. Several similar delay networks can be cascaded for higher-order approximations to longer delays, although this will not yield the best high-order approximants. Approximations of order $n > 4$ are, in any case, best implemented as combinations of (in general, different) lower-order networks to avoid computer-setup instability (see also Sec. 2-15). The general differential-analyzer setups of Table 10-2 can be simplified if we do not need to vary the delay τ_D frequently (Fig. 10-29a).

For permanently assembled time-delay elements or simulation-board setups (Sec. 11-1c), we can save amplifiers as well as potentiometers with

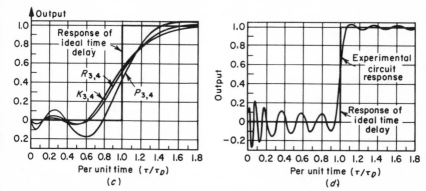

FIG. 10-30c, d. Unit-step response of fourth-order low-pass delay networks (c), and of three cascaded identical low-pass networks of the type shown in Fig. 10-29a (9 amplifiers, $n = 15$), (d). The step response of all-pass delay networks is practically unusable, since "precursor" oscillations start with the full step amplitude. (*Datd based on refs. 86 and 87.*)

special operational-amplifier setups.[86,87] Commercially available units of this type employ low-pass circuits similar to those of Fig. 10-29 to obtain adjustable constant delays between 0.005 and 10 sec with switched 20:1 ranges. Two or three channels can be cascaded for longer delays.

If the delay time τ_D is variable, representation of $Y(\tau) = X[\tau - \tau_D(\tau)]$ in the form (14) requires caution.[88] Since now $\tau_D P + P\tau_D$, the $1/\beta\tau_D$ potentiometers in Table 10-2 must be replaced by Summers and multipliers (or dividers) *preceding* each integrator.[112]

In many variable-flow transport-delay situations, the delay $\tau_D(\tau)$ varies as a nondecreasing or nonincreasing differentiable function of the time τ. In such cases, it may be practical to introduce a new independent variable $q(\tau)$ such that

$$X(\tau) = \xi(q) \qquad Y(\tau) = X[\tau - \tau_D(\tau)] = \xi(q - Q) \qquad (10\text{-}20)$$

where Q is now a constant delay.[89]

(e) **Passive-network Delay Lines.** Repetitive analog computers work over a frequency range (50 cps to 1 Mc), where passive capacitance-inductance constant-delay networks can be used for $\omega\tau_D$ products up to perhaps 10, and transistor amplifiers can drive delay networks with practical circuit values. A substantial volume of literature[90]–[98] describes sophisticated methods for delay-line synthesis, and such devices deserve further investigation. Construction will require shielding to prevent inductance coupling, and transistor buffer amplifiers to compensate for line attenuation.

10-19. Switched-capacitor Memories. A second type of analog function storage employs multiple point storage to store an input function in sampled-data form. The sampling theorem[55] shows that we shall again require at least $2f\tau_D$ capacitors (track-hold circuits) to store signal components of frequency f for τ_D sec.

The track-hold chain of Fig. 10-25 readily yields delayed output $X(\tau - \tau_D)$ ("bucket-brigade" delay,[75] analog shift register). We can even vary the delay τ_D by controlling the sequence and timing of sampling pulses along the chain. But the circuit tends to accumulate leakage errors, offset, and switching noise and is, therefore, not practical for any but the shortest delays, especially with electronic switching.

The switched-capacitor schemes of Fig. 10-31 will not accumulate errors and have been implemented with motor-driven switches,[76,77,79] stepping relays,[17] reed-relay arrays driven by a ring counter,[78,80] and with counter-driven electronic switches.[81] Variable time delays are obtained through control of the stepping speed. The stepwise output waveform can be improved by low-pass filters, by linear interpolation with a tapped potentiometer rotating in synchronism with the motor-driven switch (see also Fig. 6-32a),[79] and, perhaps most conveniently, with a zero-order-hold or first-order-hold output circuit (Fig. 10-28).[67] Switched-capacitor memories permit relatively longer storage than operational-amplifier delays, although permanent storage is not possible. Capacitors switched with individual reed relays or electronic switches permit random access to stored data. Circuit complexity limits switched-capacitor memories to about 300 capacitors[77] or $f\tau_D < 150$. Even a 16-capacitor memory can be useful with low-frequency signals and moderate delays,[80] if we remain aware of its limitations.

Wierville[107,108] has approximated the delayed function $X(\tau - \tau_D)$ by generating a set of sinusoidal Fourier components of the input $X(\tau)$ by the ringing-filter method of Sec. 2-16. The filters (each a three-amplifier sine-generating loop, Fig. 2-19) are placed into HOLD for τ_D sec, and the filter outputs are added to reconstitute $X(\tau - \tau_D)$. This technique, which is at least academically interesting, may be regarded as a combination of network and switched-capacitor storage. Note that storage of a signal of bandwidth f for τ_D sec again requires at least $2f\tau_D$ integrators.

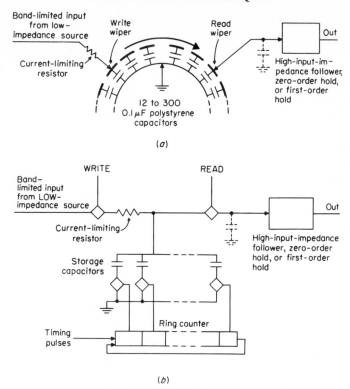

(a)

(b)

FIG. 10-31. Switched-capacitor memory circuits: capacitor-wheel or stepping-switch memory (a), and ring-counter-controlled capacitor memory with electronic or reed-relay switching (b). Many alternate circuits are possible.[75-81]

10-20. Other Storage Techniques. (a) Magnetic Storage of Analog Data. *Analog storage* on *magnetic tape, drums,* or *disks* by direct amplitude modulation of the magnetic field will not readily preserve d-c levels, so that such magnetic storage usually implies other types of modulation. *Frequency modulation* requires a reference track, which provides a frequency reference to make d-c output levels independent of tape, drum, or disk speed. We prefer the mixed pulse-width/pulse-frequency modulation (*pulse-ratio modulation*) generated by the modulator of a self-excited time-division multiplier (Sec. 7-11),[66] which needs no reference track and requires only simple averaging for demodulation. Such recording schemes are useful up to a few kilocycles, with static accuracies within 0.1 per cent of half-scale. Variable delays can be obtained with servo-positioned playback heads or by rate-servo control of the recording speed.

Multiaperture magnetic cores permit nondestructive storage of analog as well as digital data. The ingenious feedback scheme of Fig. 10-32 permits storage of d-c levels and was suggested by W. Karplus[24] for inexpensive multipoint analog memories. Acquisition time is about 1 msec, and circuit complexity is about the same as that of capacitor track-hold circuits of similar accuracy, but storage is nondestructive, and switching might be simpler.

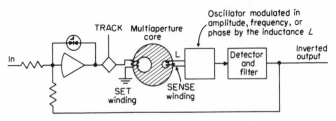

FIG. 10-32. Feedback circuit for analog storage on a multiaperture magnetic core. (*Based on ref.* 24.)

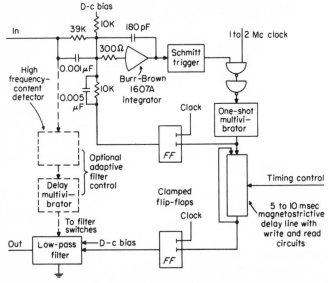

FIG. 10-33. A delta-sigma modulation scheme for function storage on a magneto-strictive delay line.[71]

(b) Digital Storage.   *Digital storage* on magnetic tape,[66,73] drums,[66,72] disks, cores,[74] and magnetostrictive delay lines[23] permits efficient bandwidth utilization in these media, but requires expensive converters and is subject to the usual sampled-data limitations. The use of digital storage is indicated where a conversion linkage already exists.

Magnetostrictive sonic delay lines are relatively rugged and inexpensive.[67,70]   A 5-msec torsion delay line allows reliable non-return-to-zero (NRZ) pulse transmission at bit rates up to 2 Mc, so that the line will hold, for instance, 500 20-bit samples or 1,000 10-bit samples. This permits serial recording of fast analog data (e.g., a 200-cps sine wave), but without random access or variable delay.   With slow analog data (e.g., a 0.1-cps sine wave), we record successive function samples during later delay-line recirculation cycles, so that suitable D/A conversion-time selection affords random access to, say, any one of 500 20-bit samples during each 5-msec cycle.   Suitable read and write timing can, then, yield variable delays.[23]

(c) **Delay-line Storage and Pulse Modulation.**   Digital-delay-line storage of analog data is greatly simplified if we replace true A/D conversion by *delta-sigma modulation* (d-c sensitive modified delta modulation) of 1- to 2-Mc digital-clock pulses.[70,71]   A delta-sigma modulator (Fig. 10-33) passes clock pulses at an average rate linearly related to the analog input signal.   The feedback circuit operates somewhat like the pulse-width-control feedback loop of a self-excited time-division multiplier.   Unlike *pulse-frequency modulation*, which has also been suggested for delay-line storage,[67] delta-sigma modulation permits true digital-computer-type pulse regeneration and timing with clock-gated logic. Demodulation, moreover, requires only simple averaging of a clamped-flip-flop output, and the averaging-filter time constant can be switched so as to trade accuracy for bandwidth and vice versa, even during computation (Fig. 10-33).   While the useful bandwidth obtainable with delta-sigma modulation is necessarily less than that obtainable with true digital (i.e., pulse-code modulated) data, conversion is much simpler.   With a 2-Mc bit rate, a 5-msec delay line can reproduce 1-Kc sinusoids within 0.2 per cent of half-scale, and 8 Kc sinusoids within 5 per cent of half-scale.

REFERENCES AND BIBLIOGRAPHY

Analog-computer Control Circuits

1. Loveman, B. D.: Control Circuits, in Huskey, H. D., and G. A. Korn, *Computer Handbook*, McGraw-Hill, New York, 1962.
2. How to Suppress the Arc, Staff Report, *Electronic Inds.*, June, 1962.

Track-hold Circuits and Multiplexing

3. Lofgren, L.: Predictors in Time-shared Analog Computer, *Proc. 1st AICA Conf.*, Brussels, 1955; Presses Académiques Européennes, Brussels, 1956.
4. Analog-computer Multiplexer, *Final Rept.* F/123, Columbia University Engineering Center, August, 1955.
5. Close, R. N., and G. O. Thogersen: Using an Electronic Analog Memory, *Electronic Design*, December, 1955.
6. Rawdin, E.: Time Multiplexing as Applied to Analog Computation, *IRETEC*, March, 1959.
7. Andeen, R. E.: A Wide-range Sampler with Zero-order Hold, *Control Eng.*, May, 1959.
8. Turner, W. W.: A Transistorized Sampler for Analog Computers, *Control Eng.*, August, 1959.

9. Bickart, T. A., and R. P. Dooley: Level Holding, *Rept.* TR AF-86, Johns Hopkins University, February, 1961; see also *Electronics*, Dec. 9, 1960.
10. Brubaker, T. A.: Precision Analog Memory Has Extended Frequency Response, *Electronics*, Sept. 29, 1961.
11. ———: A Study of High-speed Analog-computer Performance (ASTRAC I), *ACL Memo* 72, Electrical Engineering Department, University of Arizona, 1963.
12. ———: A Nonsaturating Transistor Switch for Analog/Hybrid Instrumentation and Computers, *ACL Memo* 78, Electrical Engineering Department, University of Arizona, 1963.
13. Wagner, J. H.: A Short-term Analogue Data-storage Unit, *Electronic Eng.*, April, 1963.
14. Korn, G. A.: Performance of Operational Amplifiers with Electronic Mode Switching, *IEEETEC*, June, 1963.

Iterative Analog Computation—General

15. Wadel, L. B.: An Electronic Differential Analyzer as a Difference Analyzer, *J. ACM*, July, 1954.
16. Wadel, L. B.: Automatic Iteration on an Electronic Analog Computer, *Proc. WESCON*, 1954.
17. Stubbs, G. S.: SADSAC: A Sampled-data Simulator and Computer Using Stepping Relays, *Automatic Control*, April, 1958.
18. Blanyer, C. G.: Sampled-data Techniques in Complex Simulation, Eastern Simulation Council Paper, Hydel, Inc., Waltham, Mass., January, 1959.
19. Andrews, J. M.: Mathematical Applications of the Dynamic Storage Analog Computer, *Proc. Western Joint Computer Conf.*, 1960.
20. Jury, S. H.: High-speed Memory Analog Computer, *Ind. Chem. Eng.*, **53:** 173, 177, 883 (1961).
21. McKay, D. M., and M. E. Fisher: *Analogue Computing at Ultra-high Speed*, Wiley, New York, 1962.
22. Tomovič, R., and W. J. Karplus: *High-speed Analog Computers*, Wiley, New York, 1962.
23. *Hybrid Computation Course Notes*, published by Electronic Associates, Inc., Princeton, N.J., 1962–1964.
24. Karplus, W. J.: in *Lecture Notes on Hybrid Computing Techniques*, University of California, Los Angeles, 1963.

Comparator Circuits

25. Strassberg, D. D.: High-speed Voltage Comparators, MIT M.S. Thesis, 1958.
26. Hoehn, G. L.: Semiconductor Comparator Circuits, *Tech. Rept.* 43, Stanford Electronics Laboratories, Stanford University, 1958.
27. Wait, J. V., and R. L. Hampton: A Solid-state Analog Comparator for Hybrid Analog-digital Computers, *ACL Memo* 63, Electrical Engineering Department, University of Arizona, 1963; *Electronic Design*, Aug. 30, 1963.

Digital Circuits
(See also ref. 23)

28. Millman, J., and H. Taub: *Pulse and Digital Circuits*, McGraw-Hill, New York, 1956.
29. Pettit, J. M.: *Electronic Switching, Timing, and Pulse Circuits*, McGraw-Hill, New York, 1959.
30. Strauss, L.: *Wave Generation and Shaping*, McGraw-Hill, New York, 1960.

31. Schwartz, S.: *Selected Semiconductor Circuits Handbook,* Wiley, 1960 (originally a U.S. Navy publication).
32. Texas Instruments, Inc., Engineering Staff: *Transistor Circuit Design,* McGraw-Hill, New York, 1963.
33. Nothman, M. H.: Digital Methods in Measurement and Control, *Electronic Mfg.,* September, 1959.

See also application handbooks of digital-module manufacturers, in particular manuals issued by Computer Control Corp., Framingham, Mass., Digital Equipment Corp., Maynard, Mass., General Applied Science Laboratories, Inc., Westbury, L.I., N.Y.

Reed Relays

34. Cullin, A.: Taking Bounce out of Reed Relays, *Electronics,* July 6, 1962.
35. Fasal, J.: Magnetic Reed Switches and Relays, *Electronic Design,* July 5, 1963.
36. Counting, Selection, and Logic, *Application Manuals* 401–403, C. P. Clare and Co., Chicago, Ill., 1962.

Iterative Differential Analyzers—Design

37. Korn, G. A.: Repetitive Analog Computers at the University of Arizona, *Instruments and Control Systems,* September, 1960.
38. Brubaker, T., and H. R. Eckes: Digital Control Unit for a Repetitive Analog Computer, *Proc. Western Joint Computer Conf.,* 1961.
39. Gilliland, M. C.: Iterative Differential Analyzer Function and Control, *Instruments and Control Systems,* April, 1961.
40. Korn, G. A.: New High-speed Analog and Analog-digital Computing Techniques: The ASTRAC System, *Proc. 3d AICA Conf.,* Opatija, Yugoslavia, 1961, Presses Académiques Européennes, Brussels, 1962.
41. ————: ASTRAC Offers New Computing Methods, *Electronic Inds.,* July, 1962.
42. Brubaker, T. A.: ASTRAC I Design Performance and Accuracy Studies, Ph.D. Thesis, University of Arizona, May, 1962; *Ann. AICA,* April, 1964.
43. Eckes, H. R.: Digital Expansion System for ASTRAC I, M.S. Thesis, *ACL Memo* 75, University of Arizona, May, 1963; *Ann. AICA,* January, 1964.
44. ———— and G. A. Korn: Digital Program Control for Iterative Differential Analyzers, *ACL Memo* 86, Electrical Engineering Department, University of Arizona, 1963; *SIMULATION,* February, 1964.
45. Korn, G. A.: The ASTRAC II Project, *ACL Memo* 89, Electrical Engineering Department, University of Arizona, 1964; *Proc. 4th AICA Conf.,* Brighton, England, 1964.

Oscilloscope-display Generators

46. Carlson, R., et al.: Sampling Oscillography, *Application Note* 36, Hewlett-Packard Co., Palo Alto, Calif., 1959.
47. Miura, T.: Low-speed Recording of High-speed Repetitive Waveforms, *Electronic Tech. J. Japan,* **5** (314) (1960).
48. Fitzgibbon, T. P.: ADEPT, an Automatic Data Extractor and Plotting Table, *Rept.* R-297, MIT Instrumentation Laboratory, 1961.
49. Markle, R.: A Low-cost Multitrace Display for Analog and Hybrid Computers, *ACL Memo* 77, Electrical Engineering Department, University of Arizona, 1963.

Miscellaneous Iterative-differential-analyzer Applications
(See also Chap. 12)

50. Bekey, G. A.: Generalized Integration on the Analog Computer, *IRETEC,* June, 1959.

51. *DYSTAC Applications* (Eastern Simulation Council Presentations, Dec. 12, 1960), Computer Systems, Inc., Fort Washington, Pa., 1960.
52. Olsen, R.: Multiplier Scale Changer, *Instruments and Control Systems*, November, 1961.
53. *Application Notes*, GPS Instrument Co., Inc., Newton, Mass., 1962.
54. Hara, H.: *Special Techniques for Two-dimensional Missile Simulation*, Beckman/Berkeley Div., Richmond, Calif., November, 1962.

Simulation of Sampled-data Systems and Digital Computers

55. Ragazzini, J. R., and G. F. Franklin: *Sampled-data Control Systems*, McGraw-Hill, New York, 1958.
56. Chestnut, H., et al.: Analog-computer Study of Sampled-data Systems, AIEE Paper 58-1324, Fall General Meeting, Pittsburgh, Pa., 1958.
57. Elgerd, O. I.: Analog-computer Study of Serial-type Digital Data Systems, *Trans. AIEE (Communications and Electronics)*, July, 1958.
58. Shumate, M. S.: Simulation of Sampled-data Systems Using Analog-to-digital Converters, *Proc. Western Joint Computer Conf.*, 1959.
59. Reich, J. E., and J. J. Perez: Design and Development of a Sampled-data Simulator, *Proc. Western Joint Computer Conf.*, 1961.
60. Bourbeau, A.: Theory and Error Analysis of an Analog Sampled-data Simulator, *Proc. 3d AICA Conf.*, Opatija, Yugoslavia, 1961, Presses Académiques Européennes, Brussels, 1962.
61. Brulé, J. D.: Polynomial Extrapolation of Sampled Data with an Analog Computer, *IRE Trans. PGAC*, January, 1962.
62. Saucedo, R., and T. W. Sze: Analog Simulation of Digital-computer Programs, *Trans. AIEE (Communications and Electronics)*, January, 1962.
63. Fluegel, D. A., and L. R. Freeman: Simulating Sampled-data Control, *Control Eng.*, June, 1962.
64. Bekey, G.: *Hybrid Computation Course Notes*, UCLA Extension Division, Los Angeles, Calif., 1963.

Function Storage—General

65. Bergman, G. D.: A New Electronic Analog Storage Device, *Proc. 1st AICA Conf.*, Brussels, Belgium, 1955, Presses Académiques Européennes, Brussels, 1957.
66. Kennedy, J. D.: Representation of Time Delays, in Huskey, H. D., and G. A. Korn, *Computer Handbook*, McGraw-Hill, New York, 1962.
67. Jury, S. H.: Memory and Function Generation in Analog Computers, *Military Systems Design*, January/February, 1962.
68. Vichnevetsky, R.: An Extension of a Theorem of Linear Circuit Theory to Discontinuous Delay Simulators, *Ann. AICA*, October, 1962.
69. Tomovič, R., and W. J. Karplus: *High-speed Analog Computers*, Wiley, New York, 1962 (note bibliography).
70. Korn, G. A.: Analog/Hybrid Storage and Pulse Modulation, *IEEETEC*, August, 1963.
71. Mangels, R.: 2 Mc Bit-rate Delta-Sigma Modulation, M.S. Thesis, University of Arizona, 1964; see also *Proc. SJCC*, 1964.

Magnetic Storage
(See also ref. 66)

72. Donce, J. L., and J. C. West: Magnetic-drum Storage for Analogue Computing, *Proc. IEE*, November, 1958.
73. Hofman, C. D., and H. L. Pike: Analog Time-delay System, *Proc. Western Joint Computer Conf.*, 1960.

74. Eide, M. A., and J. H. Forrester: A Hybrid Transport-delay Simulator, *Report* 2-5323-4/77, The Boeing Co., Seattle, Wash., 1963.

Capacitor-storage Memory

75. *A Palimpsest on the Electronic Analog Art,* G. A. Philbrick Researches, Boston, Mass., 1955.
76. Stone, R. S., and R. A. Dandl: A Variable Function Delay for Analog Computers, *IRETEC*, September, 1957.
77. Kozak, W. S.: An Analog Memory, *Proc. WESCON*, 1958.
78. Landauer, P. J.: Automatic Storage, *PCC Rept.* 130, Electronic Associates, Inc., Princeton, N.J., 1958.
79. McCoy, R., Variable-time-delay Apparatus, U.S. Patent 2,966,641, assigned to Reeves Instrument Corp., Dec. 27, 1960.
80. Transport-delay Simulator Type 2-448, *Product Information Release*, Electronic Associates, Inc., Long Branch, N.J., 1962.
81. Anderson, W. W.: Magnetic Contour Display System, *Electronics*, Aug. 9, 1963.

Operational-amplifier Time-delay Approximations

82. Smith, G. W., and R. C. Wood: *Principles of Analog Computation*, McGraw-Hill, New York, 1959.
83. Warfield, J. N.: *Electronic Analog Computers*, Prentice-Hall, Englewood Cliffs, N.J., 1959.
84. Rogers, A. E., and T. W. Connolly: *Analog Computers in Engineering Design*, McGraw-Hill, New York, 1960.
85. Jackson, A. S.: *Analog Computation*, McGraw-Hill, New York, 1960.
86. Single, C. H.: Time-delay Circuits for Analog Computers, *Tech. Bull.* 5059-1, Beckmann/Berkeley Div., Richmond, Calif., 1956; see also *Control Eng.*, October, 1956.
87. King, W. J., and V. C. Rideout: Improved Transport-delay Circuits for Analog-computer Use, *Proc. 3d AICA Conf.*, Opatija, Yugoslavia, 1961, Presses Académiques Européennes, Brussels, 1962 (note bibliography).
88. Korn, G. A.: Network Approximations of Variable Time Delays Require Caution, *IRETEC*, February, 1962.
89. Margolis, S. G., and J. J. O'Donnell: Rigorous Treatment of Variable Time Delays, *IEEETEC*, December, 1963.

Passive Delay Networks

90. Storch, L.: Synthesis of Constant-time-delay Ladder Networks Using Bessel Polynomials, *Proc. IRE*, November, 1954.
91. Kuh, E. S.: Synthesis of Lumped-parameter Precision Delay Lines, *Proc. IRE*, December, 1957.
92. Benedict, J., et al.: Design of a Delay Line for an Analog Correlator, *Proc. Natl. Electronics Conf.*, 1958.
93. Weinberg, L.: Constant-resistance All-pass Networks with Maximally Flat Time Delay, *J. Instr. Appl. Math.*, January, 1959.
94. Ulbrich, E., and H. Piloty: Über den Entwurf von Allpässen, Tiefpässen und Bandpässen mit einer im Tschebyscheffschen Sinne approximierten Konstanten Gruppenlaufzeit, *A.E.U.*, October, 1960.
95. Zackon, D. L.: Variable Time Delay by Padé Approximation, *IRETEC*, December, 1961.
96. Geffe, P. R.: On the Approximation Problem for Band-pass Delay Lines, *Proc. IRE*, September, 1962.

97. Liu, B.: A Time-domain Approximation Method and Its Application to Lumped Delay Lines, *IRE Trans. PGCT*, September, 1962.

98. Time-domain Synthesis Based on a Passive Tardigrade Delay Line, *The Lightning Empiricist*, G. A. Philbrick Researches, Inc., Boston, Mass., July 1, 1963.

Miscellaneous

99. Mitrovic, D. M.: Organes á Fonctionnement Discontinu, *Bull. Inst. "Boris Kidric,"* Belgrade, Yugoslavia, June, 1954.

100. Bayly, J. G., and A. C. Soudack: Use of the Berkeley EASE Computer in Evaluating Double Integrals, *Ann. AICA*, April, 1963.

101. Hausner, A.: Multiple Integrals on a Non-repetitive Analog Computer, *Proc. Southern Joint Computer Conf.*, 1963.

102. Maybach, R.: A Hybrid Analog-digital Sample-averaging Computer, *ACL Memo* 85, Electrical Engineering Department, University of Arizona, 1964.

103. Landauer, J. P.: Simulation of Space Vehicle with Reaction-jet Control System, *Application Study* 3.4.1h, Electronic Associates, Inc., Princeton, N.J., 1963.

104. HYDAC Simulation of a Terrain-avoidance Flight-control System, *Application Study* 3.4.2h, Electronic Associates, Inc., Princeton, N.J., 1963.

105. Korn, G. A.: Parameter-perturbation Generator for Analog-computer Error and Optimization Studies, *Ann. AICA*, April, 1963.

106. Halbert, P.: Analog-computer Logic Building Blocks, *PCC Rept.* 181, Electronic Associates, Inc., Princeton, N.J., 1963.

107. Wierville, W. W.: Delay of Time Functions by Means of Frequency-domain Sampling, *Trans. AIEE (Communications and Electronics)*, March, 1962.

108. ————: A New Method for Obtaining Continuous Delays on the Analog Computer, *IEEETEC*, January, 1963.

109. Frank, R. W.: Zero to 300 KC with Five-digit Accuracy, *General Radio Experimenter*, June, 1963; General Radio Co., Cambridge, Mass.

110. Kiseda, J. R., and D. J. Ford: Ripple-type Delay Networks Using Elliptic Functions, *Trans. AIEE (Communications and Electronics)*, January, 1960.

111. Korn, G. A.: *Random-process Simulation and Measurements*, McGraw-Hill, New York (in press).

112. Vichnevetsky, R.: Analog-computer Simulation of a Time-dependent Delay Using the Concept of Generalized Transfer Function, *Ann. AICA*, April, 1964.

CHAPTER 11

ANALOG AND HYBRID ANALOG-DIGITAL COMPUTER SYSTEMS

THE MAN-MACHINE INTERFACES: PROGRAMMING, READOUT, AND CHECKING SYSTEMS

11-1. Patchbays and Other Programming Systems. (a) **Patchbay Construction and Layout.** General-purpose analog computers are set up through plug-in interconnections with *patchcords*. Direct patchcord connections between jacks on computing-element panels permit a minimum of wiring and shunt capacitance; incomparably better computer utilization, however, is obtained when setups are patched on *removable problem boards* (*patchboards, prepatch panels*), which can be plugged into a central *patchbay*. This system permits patching away from the computer, which is, then, free for other work; and patched programs can be stored for later reuse. The plug-in simulation boards described in Sec. 11-1c can serve as prepatch panels in small (5- to 20-amplifier) computers; most larger machines have *contact-spring patchbay systems* like those shown in Fig. 11-1.

D-c leakage and crosstalk considerations (Fig. 11-2) make it mandatory to employ *shielded patching systems* with coaxial patchcords in all but the most inexpensive computers, in spite of the added shunt capacitances. Grounded printed-silver grids on plastic patchboards will, however, at least eliminate surface leakage. Shielded systems use either all-metal patchboards (Fig. 11-1a) or the short-circuit-proof but more expensive cellular construction shown in Fig. 11-1c. Another short-proof technique employs metal boards with *female* shielded-patchcord connectors. Metal patchboards can have pressure-sensitive overlays printed in bright

colors to identify terminations.   This makes it possible to change terminations, add new components, etc.   Large patchboards have to be quite
rigid; they must not deform appreciably under the substantial forces
required for positive contact of 1,000 to 3,000 patchcord tips.

Good system design minimizes wiring between computing elements
and patchbay (see also Fig. 11-12), for signal wiring and connectors cause

Fig. 11-1a. This solid-metal problem board grounds the shields of coaxial patchcords.
The patchbay locking lever raises the protruding patchcord tips against corresponding
contact springs with a self-cleaning wiping action.   To avoid accidental shorting of
"hot" patchcord tips against the grounded patchboard, the operator must deenergize
the patchbay before making any patching connections.   (*Electronic Associates, Inc.*)

capacitive loading, noise, and crosstalk, as well as added initial and maintenance expenses.   Computing networks, mode-control relays, electronic
switches, diode networks, and solid-state amplifiers are best constructed
as separately shielded modules plugged directly into the rear of the patchbay (Figs. 11-1d and 11-15b).   *Patchbay ovens* complicate access to components and are really needed only for high-precision capacitors.   Note
that such capacitors may require recalibration each time the oven is

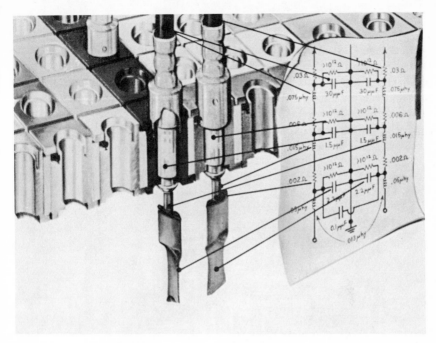

FIG. 11-1b. Unshielded patchbay system with patchbay springs installed directly on the amplifier-module front panels. (TR-48 ±10-volt transistor computer, *Electronic Associates, Inc.*)

FIG. 11-1c. Construction and equivalent circuit of an AM-P shielded patchbay system. This construction grounds patchcord shields but will not permit accidental grounding of patchcord tips. (*Aircraft-Marine Products.*)

opened (Sec. 3-8) and are, therefore, best off in an oven by themselves. Ovens can employ blanket-type heating elements to reduce temperature gradients without recirculating fans. An even better scheme employs refrigeration for both cooling and heating and is recommended especially where semiconductor temperatures are to be stabilized. Such oven/refrigerators can be operated near room temperature to reduce semiconductor and capacitor leakage as well as oven insulation requirements.

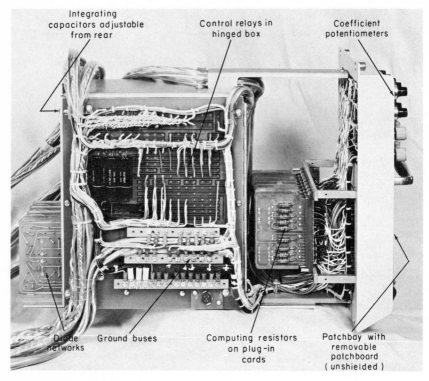

Fig. 11-1d. Rear view of a small (unshielded) patchbay module with plug-in networks, relays, and diode function generators. (*Applied Dynamics, Inc.*)

Clever *patchbay layout*, with a view to short patching connections, improves operating convenience and reduces errors due to patchcord clutter (Fig. 11-3; see also Sec. 11-1b). In larger computations, though, patchcord clutter is practically unavoidable, and one can no longer "see" the block-diagram structure on the patchbay. For this reason, some large computers simply collect all integrators, all potentiometers, etc., in specific parts of the patchbay to simplify computer setup from setup sheets rather than block diagrams (Sec. 2-17).

(b) Relay-circuit Patching. Control-variable Patchbays and Pinboards. Conventional analog computers require a substantial number of patchbay terminations for integrator-relay connections to the computer RESET and HOLD busses.   POT SET relay connections are usually also terminated in the patchbay.   Other relay terminations should provide for *patchbay switching* of multipliers into DIVIDE modes, resolvers into POLAR and RECTANGULAR modes, and similar control functions, since front-panel mode switches are apt to be forgotten during problem changes. The various control-relay connections are conveniently made with single or multiple shorting links (bottle plugs, Fig. 11-3).   Although the relay connections do not require shielding, they still use our relatively expensive shielded patchbay terminations (at least $1 each).   With a separate

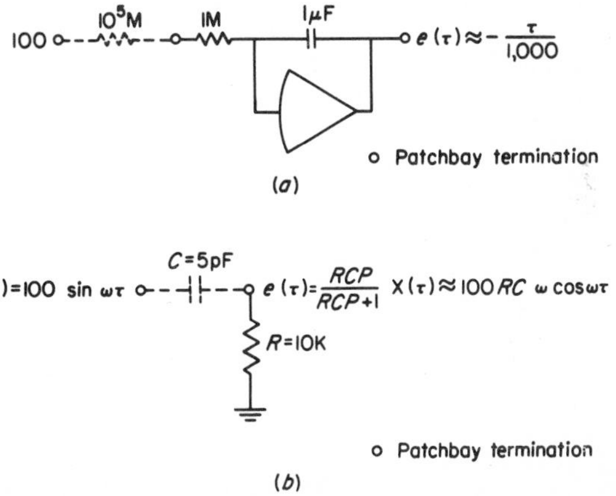

(a)

(b)

FIG. 11-2. Effects of leakage and crosstalk in unshielded patchbays and connectors. (a) During a 100-sec computer run, patchboard-surface or patchcord-leakage resistances as high as 10^5 *megohms* can cause integrator errors exceeding 0.1 per cent of half-scale.   (b) 5 pF between terminations can produce crosstalk exceeding 0.3 per cent of half-scale at points 10K away from ground at 100 cps.   Crosstalk is alleviated by (otherwise objectionable) shunt capacitances to ground, but is especially serious with step and pulse voltages.

copper-bar signal ground behind the patchbay (Sec. 11-9), we can use the patchbay shielding as a relay ground and return each relay-coil connection through a single patchplug grounded to its shield.[7]   This procedure saves one-half of the relay terminations, and is surely justified for pot-set and multiplier or resolver mode-control relays; compute- and hold-relay connections should be separately investigated for possible ground-noise effects.

Iterative differential analyzers, which require frequent patching of integrator and memory control circuits, will usually provide small separate control patchbays or pinboards for all control patching (Figs. 1-1, 10-21, 11-4, and 11-13 to 11-15).   Control-patching systems need not be shielded.   They may or may not be combined with digital-module patchbays.

(c) **Simulation Boards.** Computing circuits involving special networks, complex operational amplifiers, special signal generators and diode
circuits, etc. (Chap. 9), are often most conveniently set up on *simulation
boards.* These are simply panels or

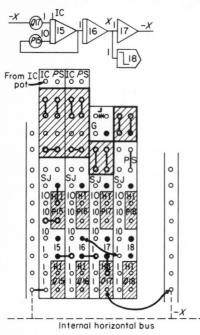

From IC
pot

Internal horizontal bus

chassis units (preferably metal) with
banana-jack or combined jack/bind-
ing-post terminations for two to six
d-c amplifiers, potentiometers, reference and power-supply voltages, and
trunks to the main computer patchbay. Simulation boards are best
plugged, directly or through a cable,
into a computer-front-panel connector, so that simulation-board setups
can be stored.

Figure 11-5 shows a very convenient board layout. Colored-
nylon-jack terminations on ¾-in.
centers work with plug-in circuit
components mounted on dual banana plugs, and with banana-plug
mounted solid-state-circuit panels
made of standard perforated plastic
circuit board. Special bottle-plug
positions on the main computer
patchbay commit five amplifiers to
the simulation-board connector, a
simple 32-point ribbon connector
with grounded guard terminations to
protect summing points. The simulation board shown also serves as an
inexpensive plug-in patch board for
small educational analog computers.

Simulation boards are also convenient for connections to external
equipment, especially if signal-condi-
tioning filters, limiters, etc., are to
be used. Finally, the simulation-
board connector can commit com-

Fig. 11-3. A simple problem patched on
an Electronic Associates patchbay, with
amplifier and potentiometer terminations grouped to facilitate shorting-
link (bottle-plug) connections. Amplifier output terminations are shown
blacked in. Large bottle plugs (heavy
shading) conveniently connect integrator and summer feedback and control
relays and can be moved to change
integrators into summers. This patchbay was modified to effect all right-to-
left connections with internal busses, so
that all patching is from left to right.
A bottle-plug connection makes amplifier 18 into a comparator with
zener-diode feedback. (*University of
Arizona.*)

puter amplifiers to various permanently packaged external apparatus,
such as special operational-amplifier filters, signal generators, etc.

11-2. Potentiometer and Function-generator Setting (see also
Secs. 3-5 and 6-13d).[8] Coefficient potentiometers and diode function

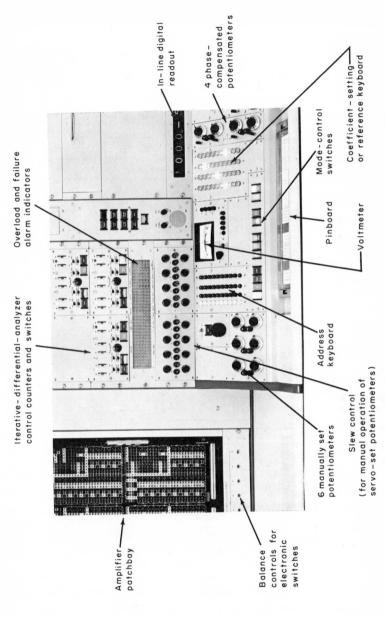

Iterative-differential-analyzer control counters and switches

Overload and failure alarm indicators

In-line digital readout

4 phase-compensated potentiometers

Mode-control switches

Coefficient-setting or reference keyboard

Pinboard

Voltmeter

Address keyboard

Slew control (for manual operation of servo-set potentiometers)

6 manually set potentiometers

Amplifier patchbay

Balance controls for electronic switches

Fig. 11-4. Control area of a Beckman/Berkeley EASE iterative differential analyzer with servo-set potentiometers and digital iteration control permitting three-period operation (Sec. 10-8). A removable pinboard controls integrators, multiplier modes, alarm circuits, etc. The four phase-compensated potentiometers (Sec. 4-6) are useful in fast computations.

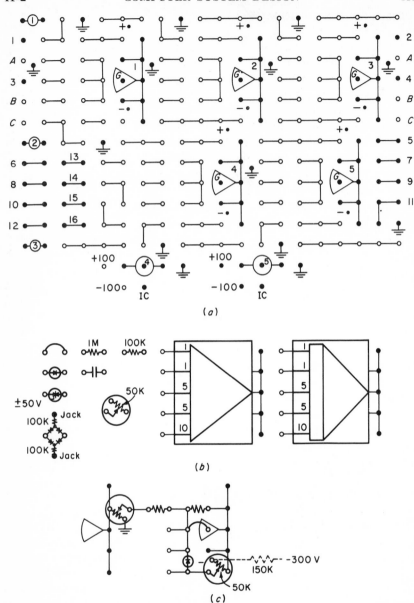

FIG. 11-5. An especially flexible simulation-board layout (*a*), plug-in components (*b*), and utilization of three-legged plug-in potentiometers as attenuators and bias sources (*c*). Many special operational amplifiers (including, for instance, T-network input and/or feedback), function generators, and switching circuits are easy to set up. Points *AA*, *BB*, etc., are connected together; points 1, 2, . . . are external busses. A 32-point ribbon-type connector joins simulation board and computer. (*University of Arizona.*)

generators are conveniently set with the aid of a digital voltmeter, which can also read amplifier output voltages in RESET and HOLD. For manual potentiometer setting, simple calibration pushbuttons immediately adjacent to each potentiometer (Fig. 3-7) are greatly preferable to relay-selector switching, which requires the operator to check the potentiometer number against the selector keyboard.

Most large analog computers have *servo-set potentiometers and function generators* controlled individually from a central control panel or, in any preselected sequence, by storable punched tape to permit rapid problem changes. Tape-controlled potentiometer-setting systems can also control integrator modes and may, for instance, produce a sequence of computer runs with preprogrammed coefficient changes.

Potentiometers can have individual servomotors, or a motor serves 10 to 40 solenoid-engaged rubber-idler friction drives associated with each potentiometer. Relays operated by a *selector keyboard* place the computer into POT SET, apply a reference voltage to a potentiometer, and connect it into the servosystem. The potentiometer is set when its output equals that of an accurate comparison voltage divider set by a *coefficient-setting keyboard* or by reed relays controlled with a punched-tape reader. The potentiometer setting can be checked visually and independently by the computer digital voltmeter. In addition to the coefficient-setting keyboard, the control panel may have a comparison potentiometer permitting *continuous* adjustment of servo-set potentiometers (Fig. 11-4).

Ten-turn potentiometers can be servo-set within 0.02 per cent of full scale (20 mV for ± 100-volt computers, since the LO terminal is grounded). A typical servo-setting operation takes 1 to 3 sec. A punched-tape system (or, alternatively, a digital computer, Sec. 11-4c) can servo-set 100 potentiometers in less than 12 minutes.

11-3. Readout Systems. (a) **Analog-computer Readout.** The most accurate way to extract numerical data from analog-computer solutions is by sampled-data digital readout (Sec. 10-11). In practice, however, we require insight into an entire solution rather than discrete numerical data; and immediately available, storable graphical computer-solution records are an indispensable machine-man link. This is true even though the accuracy, speed, cost, and maintainability of electromechanical recorders leave much to be desired. Direct-writing *strip-chart recorders* (Fig. 1-20) capable of recording two, four, six, or eight variables against time are still the principal means for recording computer solutions; simultaneous presentation of multiple records can provide very valuable insight into the operation of a simulated system. Strip-chart recorders are inaccurate, slow, and expensive. *Servo plotting boards*, while more accurate, are even slower and still more expensive. Light-beam galvanometer recorders, with or without direct-writing features, are faster (useful up to several kilocycles), but are also inaccurate and expensive. Multistylus and facsimile recorders are too slow.

Even in "slow" analog computers, *oscilloscope displays* are useful for preliminary checking and scaling runs as well as for servicing; they also produce permanent Land-camera records. Oscilloscope voltage and time scales should duplicate those of the recorders used with the computer. Sampling and multitrace oscilloscope displays for fast iterative differential analyzers are discussed in Sec. 10-11.

(b) **Strip-chart Recorders.** Strip-chart-recorder penmotors are either galvanometer movements or miniature a-c servo actuators. Permanent records are

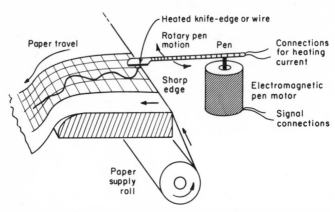

Fig. 11-6. Heated-pen strip-chart recorder. The heated edge of each pen contacts the heat-sensitive recorder paper along a sharp edge perpendicular to the direction of paper travel and produces rectilinear-coordinate records.

produced either with ink fed through tubular recorder pens by gravity or pressure (aerosol can), or on heat-sensitive paper contacted by heated ridges on each pen along a sharp edge perpendicular to the paper feed (Fig. 11-6). The latter method inherently converts the angular pen motion into a rectilinear displacement along the contact edge; in ink recorders, a special pen linkage is required to produce rectilinear-displacement records. Although not more accurate, records with rectilinear coordinate lines are much more pleasing.

A recorder penmotor is, essentially, a second-order dynamical system with mechanical inertia, spring stiffness supplied either by a spring or by the penmotor-servo stiffness, and damping through friction together with equalization in the penmotor drive or amplifier circuit. Damping is usually adjusted for a slight overshoot. The best strip-chart recorders claim accuracies between 0.5 and 1 per cent of half-scale up to a few cps, with useful output at reduced accuracy up to between 100 and 150 cps. Ink recordings are crisper, use more durable paper (heat-sensitive paper is pressure-sensitive as well), and their trace width does not change with pen-displacement rate and paper speed; they also tend to be somewhat faster than heat-writing recorders. Heated-pen recorders, however, do away altogether with the recurring nuisance of filling and maintaining ink-supply systems.

Gear-shift levers or remotely controllable solenoid systems permit a range of paper speeds between 0.05 and 200 mm/sec. The paper feed is driven by a line-frequency synchronous motor or, preferably, by a tuning-fork-oscillator-controlled motor. A chart-speed accuracy within 0.25 per cent is reasonable. In many analog-computer installations, recorders can be controlled from the main console, which may provide for starting and stopping (Sec. 10-3c), paper-speed changes, and remotely controlled calibration inputs (zero, ± 10 volts, and/or ± 100 volts). It is also possible to print computer-run numbers on the recorder track. It is very convenient to have all recorder voltage and speed scales duplicated on a checkout oscilloscope, since preliminary oscilloscope runs to check scales and presentation can save a great deal of chart paper.

Modern computer d-c amplifiers can drive recorder penmotors directly, but most recorders contain their own d-c amplifiers complete with output-current limiters and equalizing networks producing a desired pen-displacement step response.

(c) Servo Plotting Boards and Curve Followers. *Servo plotting boards (xy recorders)* produce inked plots of a computer variable $y(t)$ against another variable $x(t)$ or against the time with the aid of a servo-positioned pen (Fig. 11-7). The larger plotting boards may have two pens with separate y-servo drives on the same x carriage to record two functions $y_1(x)$ and $y_2(x)$; a relay comparator interchanges the roles of the pens whenever the two curves intersect. Servo plotting boards can have static accuracies within 0.1 per cent of half-scale, but they are quite slow, with typical output rates and accelerations respectively below 20 in./sec and 750 in./sec², and 5 deg phase shift for 3-cps 8-in.-peak-to-peak sine waves. In some recorders, the y displacement (pen) can respond more quickly than the x displacement (pen carriage). As with strip-chart recorders, preliminary oscilloscope runs can save scaling troubles.

Fig. 11-7a. A large servo plotting board permitting vertical, horizontal, or tilted operation. (*Computer Systems, Inc.*)

Most xy recorders can be fitted with photoelectric* *curve-follower heads* which are connected to the y servo to follow an inked curve $y = f(x)$ as the pen carriage is driven in the x direction, so that the y-follow-up potentiometer produces an output voltage $y = f(x)$. Curve followers will not be misled by suitably colored coordinate lines and are a very convenient means for entering low-frequency data into computations.

Most servo tables can be obtained with internal time-base circuits or time motors to record y against the time with a variety of time scales. Servo tables fitted with multiple pen carriages and a paper-feed drive can record $f(t)$ and read $f(t - \tau_D)$ to produce fixed or variable *transport delays* (Fig. 11-7b; see also Sec. 10-17).

(d) Amplifier-readout Switching. Recorder connections are usually patched, but a system of switches or relays connecting a selected amplifier output to a readout voltmeter and/or oscilloscope is convenient for quick checks of computer setups, solutions, and amplifier balance. Stepping relay, reed-relay matrix, or crossbar switching systems require maintenance and are justified only with automatic or semiautomatic checking and setup systems (Sec. 11-4b, c). The simplest readout selectors are

---

* Earlier inductive, capacitive, and resistive curve followers[16] could only follow special conducting-ink traces and may be considered obsolete.

inexpensive rotary switches. They are inconvenient to use with more than a few amplifiers; interlocking pushbuttons are more convenient, but a system of n parallel-connected switches loads the readout circuit with $n - 1$ switch capacitances (Fig. 11-8a, b). *We can, however, practically eliminate readout-circuit capacitance effects on amplifier bandwidth and stability by inserting an accurately known 100-ohm to 5K*

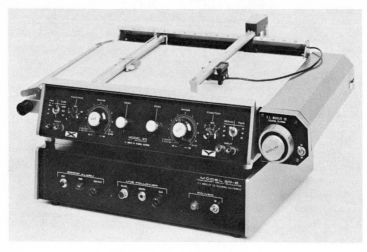

Fig. 11-7b. Table-top xy recorder with chart-drive and photoelectric curve-follower accessories set up as a transport-delay simulator. In this application, the x servo is not used, but a chart drive feeds paper at 2, 4, 8, 16, 24, or 32 in./sec. The servo-positioned pen records $f(t)$, and the curve follower reads $f(t - \tau_D)$, with delays τ_D between 4 sec and 7 min determined by the adjustable distance between pen carriage and curve follower and by the paper speed. With the pen replaced by a second curve-follower head, the device also reads $f(t)$ and $f(t - \tau_D)$ from a given curve for correlation measurements. With the time-delay accessory removed, the recorder functions as a normal xy recorder or curve follower. (*F. L. Moseley Co., Pasadena, Calif.*)

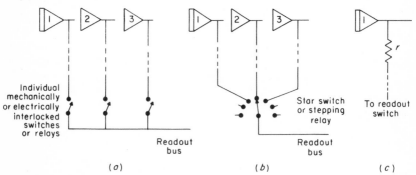

Fig. 11-8. Readout scanning circuits. Circuit (a) employs separate switches or relays and loads amplifier 2 with nC_{SWITCH} plus wiring capacitance. Circuit (b) produces the smaller load C_{SWITCH} plus wiring capacitance. Resistance r (10 ohms to 1K) in (c) "stops" amplifier phase shift due to readout-circuit capacitances at the expense of a simple calibration change in d-c readout instruments; the high-frequency response of oscilloscope and sampling readout circuits will be impaired, although equalization-network correction may be possible.

resistance between each amplifier output and its readout connection (Fig. 11-8c). Readout voltmeters are readily recalibrated to allow for the added resistances. In "slow" analog computers, even oscilloscopes and recorders can be suitably recalibrated and reequalized.

11-4. Calibration and Program Checks. Programming Automation. (a) Calibration and Amplifier-balance Checks. Since most chopper-stabilized d-c amplifiers will overload briefly when high voltage is switched off and on, the POT SET/BALANCE CHECK mode (see also Sec. 10-3a) of most analog computers removes only the computer reference voltages from patchbay and diode function generators to permit safe patching; in this condition, outputs of all properly functioning computing elements read zero. A *balance-check relay or pushbutton* in each d-c amplifier can decrease the feedback ratio, so that amplifier offset above a few millivolts will light the overload light without causing too serious an overload. The amplifier is then balanced so as to extinguish the overload light, by reference to a balance meter, or for minimum chopper noise.

A conveniently located set of *calibration pushbuttons* operative in POT SET or RESET makes it easy to check the positive and negative reference voltages and the recorder calibration and null against the digital voltmeter.

(b) Overload-alarm Systems and Minimum-excursion Indicators. *Overload alarm systems* inform the operator that an amplifier overload due to scaling or malfunction has made the current computer solution meaningless. The simplest *overload indicators* for ± 100-volt computers are simply 60- to 80-volt neon lights connected across each amplifier output through voltage-divider networks. *Error lights* at the outputs of d-c amplifier chopper-stabilizer channels (Sec. 4-14d) indicate excessive d-c amplifier summing-point voltages, and therefore detect not only voltage overloads but also current overloads and a variety of amplifier malfunctions. Error lights are usually preferred in "slow" analog computers. Error lights will, however, miss overload peaks too short for the low-pass chopper-stabilizer channels and are, therefore, not appropriate for overload detection in repetitive analog computers, where our main interest is in transient voltage overloads.

Since the operator might overlook a momentary overload in one of a large number of amplifiers, the individual overload indicators are often connected to a common *master overload-alarm circuit* (Fig. 11-9a). We can also design overload indicators so that they will remain on until reset by the operator (stored overload); finally, the overload-alarm circuit may place the computer into the HOLD mode so as to "freeze" conditions at the time of the overload for investigation (Fig. 10-4b).

Appropriately biased neon lights can still be used for overload indication in ± 50-volt computers, but overload indication in ± 10-volt computers is more difficult and requires biased-transistor lamp drivers.

A *minimum-excursion indicator* (MEI)[9] indicates that a corresponding amplifier output voltage has exceeded, say, 10 per cent of its total dynamic range in the course of a computer run.   MEI's show up excessively low scale factors; with proper scaling, all MEI lights must be extinguished at the end of each computer run.   Figure 11-9b shows a practical MEI circuit;[9] similar diode-transistor circuits are also useful as overload indicators in ± 10-volt computers.

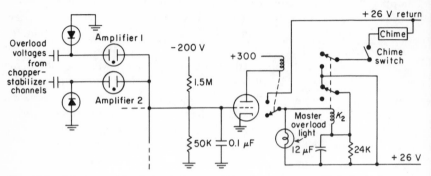

Fig. 11-9a. Master overload circuit for a ± 100-volt computer.   If desired, the overload relay could place the machine in HOLD.

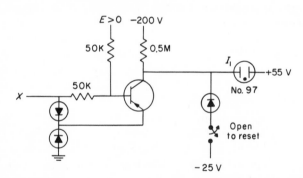

Fig. 11-9b. Reeves Instrument Corp. minimum-excursion indicator (MEI, ref. 27). The input diodes form a floating absolute-value circuit, so that transistor Q_1 conducts and extinguishes neon light I_1 as soon as $|X| > E$. I_1 (Ne 97) fires at 130 volts and sustains at 70 volts; the indicator is reset (turned on) before each computer run. Similar circuits are even more useful for overload indication in ± 10-volt computers.

(c) Static Checks, Rate Tests, and Time-scale Check.[2,9]   In the RESET mode, the output voltages of potentiometers, summers, multipliers, etc., must be specified functions of the integrator initial-condition settings. *Static checks* of analog-computer programs check these output voltages to detect programming errors or malfunctions.   Improved static checking systems also permit one to switch each integrator summing junction into a summing-amplifier circuit whose output is read out to indicate the *initial rate of change* of the integrated variable.   Furthermore, since ordinary static checks cannot properly check points whose initial voltage is zero, one may introduce *artificial initial conditions* during a preliminary static check with the true initial conditions. Similar tests can also be applied in mid-problem with the computer in the HOLD condition.

In an alternative static-checking scheme (PROBLEM CHECK STATIC mode in Reeves Instrument Corp. computers), a relay disconnects each integrator output from the computer setup and substitutes a test voltage. The same relay shunts a feedback resistor across each integrating capacitor, so that the integrator output can be used to read the input sum.[2,9]

To check integrator and control-relay operation, a variety of *rate-test* relay circuits permit each integrator to integrate a known input for a known time interval. The computer is then switched into HOLD, and integrator outputs are read.

A rapid check for effects of insufficient computing bandwidth, especially in computer servos, is to repeat the solution at one-half the original time scale. Large analog computers may provide a *time-scale-check* switch which doubles all integrating capacitors and halves the recorder speed through appropriate relays.

The static checks described in this section help to check out new computer setups, but they must not be regarded as substitutes for the numerical checks of analog-computer solutions (Sec. 4-1).

(d) Checkout, Scaling, and Setup Automation. In general-purpose analog-computer laboratories handling large problems, the time required for problem preparation, setup, and checking is substantially larger than the time spent on actual computation. To simplify setup and checking tasks, all large analog computers provide automatic punched-tape control of servo-set potentiometers (Sec. 11-2), amplifier readout switching (Sec. 11-3d), and computer modes including checkout modes (Sec. 11-4c). Typical systems of this type can

1. Set potentiometers and function generators and tabulate actual settings with a printer operated by the computer digital voltmeter.
2. Read and tabulate static-check and rate-test outputs of all amplifiers.
3. Perform a series of computer runs with specified parameter settings.
4. Warn the operator of overloads or malfunctions.

Punched tape and tabulated data provide a permanent, reusable record of static checks and computation. If a general-purpose digital computer is available, the logical next step is to let the digital computer check static-test results. An increasing number of computer laboratories go further. It is possible to write digital-computer programs which accept a FORTRAN or ALGOL problem statement and prepare complete analog-computer setup sheets (Sec. 2-17) and scale factors, set potentiometers, and perform all static checks.[28-30] Digital and analog computers may communicate by way of punched tape or by direct interconnections (Secs. 11-12 and 11-13).

Automatic analog-computer patching, which would be the final step to complete programming automation, is possible in principle; high-quality crossbar relays can handle most real-time simulation bandwidths quite readily. The number of connections required for a large analog computer is, however, formidable, and there has been little economic justification to develop a completely automatic system. References 3 and 4 describe efforts in the direction of card-programmed analog computers.

11-5. Analog-computer Accuracy Checks and Maintenance Procedures.[21-27] Effective computer utilization requires a preventive-maintenance program to minimize operating failures and computer down

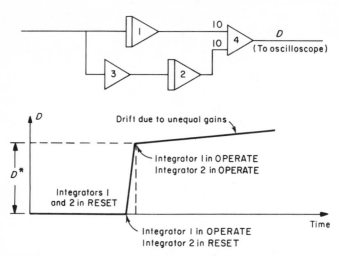

FIG. 11-10. Relay timing and integrator-gain comparison test. D^* is proportional to the relay-timing difference, with 1 volt representing 1 msec. (*Contributed by B. D. Loveman, Reeves Instrument Corp., Garden City, N.Y.*)

time; it is also desirable to check component accuracies periodically. Depending on the size and work load of the computer installation, one performs daily, weekly, and/or monthly checks on

Power-supply and reference voltages
Resistor and potentiometer continuity
Calibration of readout devices
Amplifier gain, noise, and offset
Amplifier input gains
Integrating-capacitor calibration (rate test, Sec. 11-4c) and integrator-relay timing (Fig. 11-10)
Operation of servo and electronic multipliers (triangle test, Secs. 7-20 and 8-1)
Operation of function generators, diodes, and relays

Digital-module operation
Spikes and offset in electronic switches
Recorder ink and paper supplies

Suitable test circuits are wired permanently on special test patchboards substituted for the computer problem boards; references 21 to 27 list many such circuits (see also Chaps. 4 to 8 and Sec. 11-4). Defective or inaccurate components are unplugged and replaced. It is desirable to have about one spare amplifier in 20, and one spare computer servo-mechanism in 10, for this purpose.[26]

Annual maintenance cost in high-quality analog-computer installations with two-shift operation may run between 10 and 20 per cent of capital expenditures.[26] Clearly, open-shop operation of computers by customer personnel, which may be desirable, tends to increase the maintenance load. Maintenance and repair of defective components is best done on carefully designed test benches supplied with suitable power supplies, readout equipment, chopper-test sockets, etc.[26]

Proper maintenance procedure must include a filing system for *failure reports* and *service reports* designed to locate sources of frequent failures for eventual circuit modification, to ensure a proper supply of spare parts, and to establish responsibilities.

DESIGN OF COMPLETE ELECTRONIC DIFFERENTIAL ANALYZERS

11-6. Analog-computer Systems. (a) **Introduction.** Computing elements for new general-purpose analog computers are increasingly restricted to operational amplifiers, coefficient potentiometers and passive diode networks for multiplication and function generation, plus a complement of electronic switches, comparators, and digital modules. With continuing improvements in 100-volt transistor-amplifier bandwidths and costs, there will be less and less justification for using vacuum-tube amplifiers in new equipment. The 200-Kc to 2-Mc 0-db bandwidths of the d-c amplifiers used with modern "slow" analog computers permit optional 10- to 20-cps repetitive operation at reduced accuracy.

With low-drift d-c amplifiers available at reasonable cost, one is no longer justified in building analog computers designed exclusively for fast-time repetitive operation, since we can have both repetitive and "slow" operation at little extra cost. Figure 11-11 shows two circuits employed to minimize d-c drift effects in early repetitive analog computers.[114,116] Such circuits may still be useful for low-cost special-purpose equipment.

(b) **Small Analog Computers. Educational-computer Systems.** Small (5 to 20 amplifier) table-top analog computers may use low-output vacuum-tube amplifiers (± 100 volts, 5 mA) or transistor amplifiers (± 10 to ± 20 volts, 10 mA); 1-Mc 0-db bandwidth will permit optional 20-cps repetitive operation. Small portable analog computers (Fig. 1-2) are most useful as stand-ins for signal generators, filters, controllers, aircraft, etc., in various partial-system tests (Chaps. 1 and 9) and may serve individual engineers for small problems.

Even the smallest analog computers should have removable, storable patchboards (preferably simulation boards, Sec. 11-1c) with plug-in ribbon-type connectors. Plug-in resistors and capacitors are satisfactory with 5 to 10 amplifiers; with more amplifiers, programming convenience demands committed integrators and summers, or at least committed summing networks. In small machines, inexpensive coefficient potentiometers and summing networks can be built or plugged into each patchboard

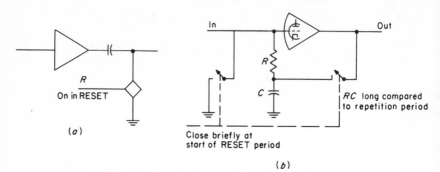

(a)

(b)

Fig. 11-11. Circuits used to reduce d-c drift effects in early repetitive analog computers. In Fig. 11-11a, a d-c amplifier is replaced by an a-c coupled amplifier clamped to zero during the first part of each RESET period (d-c restoration[116]). The circuit of Fig. 11-11b accumulates a d-c drift voltage on a capacitor and returns it to the amplifier input once per computer run.[114]

(Fig. 11-5) to save connector terminations. Two 32-point ribbon connectors can then connect 20 amplifiers with 24 terminations left for ground, reference voltages, multipliers, etc.

In our judgment, analog-computer setups for undergraduate instruction require *at most* 10 amplifiers, but ought to be designed with a measure of showmanship to impress students strongly with the power and pushbutton convenience of modern computer methods. An alternative to table-top analog computers is a normal 60-amplifier machine usable for research outside of class hours. Suitably wired patchboards on the main computer commit groups of computing elements (usually five amplifiers and two multipliers) plus test signals to each of 10 attractive bench-top student stations. A "red box" in the connecting conduit protects amplifiers with fuses and zener diodes. Normally, students do not use the relatively expensive coefficient potentiometers and control relays of the main computer; lighted lever or tablet switches are used to reset two to four integrators at each student position. Plug-in student boards can be simulation boards, replicas of typical patchbay layouts, or permanently wired setups for special experiments.

(c) **General-purpose Analog Computers.** System design begins with selection of the voltage scale, current output, and bandwidth required of the computer d-c amplifiers.   Experience shows that computers will be expanded as users begin to realize their possibilities, so that *ease of expansion is a very important design consideration*.   Increasing installation size does increase current demand on individual amplifiers, but only moderately so.   Hence an initial 30-amplifier installation intended for later expansion to 200 amplifiers might as well use the same d-c amplifiers as a 500-amplifier machine, say ± 100-volt 30-mA transistor amplifiers. This approach reduces manufacturers' inventories and permits small computer installations to expand with yearly appropriations.

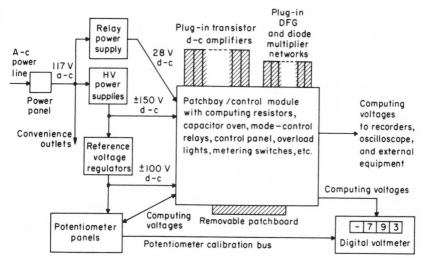

Fɪɢ. 11-12. A solid-state analog-computer system, showing the principal interconnections.   Smaller machines can begin with a small patchbay/control module (possibly mounting 0.1 per cent rather than 0.02 per cent computing networks).   This small patchbay/control module need not be discarded when the installation is expanded, for dual patchbays are very convenient for independent solution of two smaller problems.

High-quality ± 10-volt analog computers can match the accuracy of ± 100-volt machines,[11] although the smaller dynamic range tends to make nonlinear operations either less accurate or more expensive.   We recommend ± 10-volt operation only for very fast computation (Sec. 11-7).

Figure 11-12 illustrates the design of a typical solid-state analog computer around a central *patchbay/control module*, with a minimum of interunit wiring.   If vacuum tubes are used, they should be physically separated from critical networks and semiconductors; power transistors can be located in heat sinks at the well-ventilated far end of a circuit card mounting other semiconductors.   Forced-draft ventilation is advisable in all-solid-state machines.   Amplifier input leads should have coaxial connectors or ribbon-type connectors with grounded guard terminations (Sec. 5-13).

Figures 1-1, 1-2, and 11-13 to 11-15 show examples of complete computers. All employ rather similar computing elements, and most offer semiautomatic potentiometer setting, program checks, and digital readout as optional features. Optional solid-state integrator switching is also available. Different manufacturers do differ in their implementation of iterative-differential-analyzer techniques with patchable relay and/or digital logic (Fig. 11-4, Sec. 11-7).

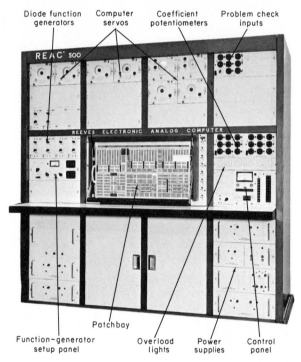

Fig. 11-13a. Like its many predecessors, this 500-series REAC is designed mainly for conventional simulation. It includes servomultipliers with plug-in tap-loading networks and servo resolvers as well as diode multipliers and function generators. The unshielded patchbay has a grounded silver grid to prevent surface leakage. (*Reeves Instrument Corporation.*)

The relative numbers of integrators, summers, potentiometers, multipliers, etc., desirable for each computer installation will depend on its principal applications.[10] The best way to solve this problem is to provide for simple expansion with plug-in computing elements. One typical second-order equation of motion (Sec. 2-7) will require two integrators, one summer, and one to three phase inverters; one of the integrators usually has only a single input. Some general-purpose analog computers have independent summing networks which can be added to any integrator or summer when needed. Diode function generators and diode quarter-square multipliers, like servomultipliers and servo resolvers in older computers, require extra phase inverters to produce inputs of both signs ($X, -X; Y, -Y; \ldots$). A few manufacturers per-

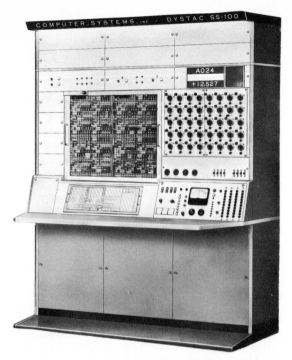

FIG. 11-13b. This all-solid-state machine permits iterative operation with electronic mode switching; the small patchboard controls integrators and memory operation. ±100-volt transistor amplifiers mount behind the shielded patchbay to shorten lead lengths. Electronic digital attenuators and fast ±10-volt computing elements are optional accessories. (*Computer Systems, Inc.*)

FIG. 11-13c. The Comcor, Inc., analog-computer control module, shown here in the company's ±100-volt all-solid-state computer, is also available separately for addition of flexible mode control, digital readout, and servo-set potentiometers to existing machines. Serial-entry keyboards simplify readout selection and coefficient setting. (*Comcor, Inc.*)

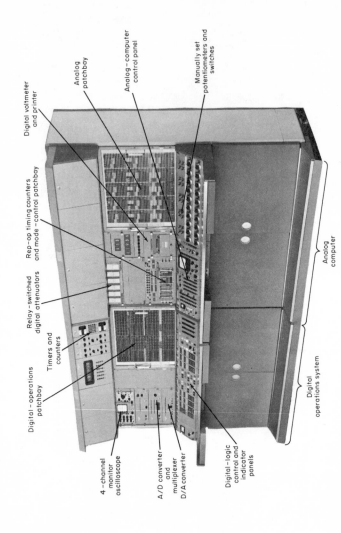

Digital-operations patchbay

Timers and counters

Rep-op timing counters and mode-control patchbay

Relay-switched digital attenuators

Digital voltmeter and printer

Analog patchbay

Analog-computer control panel

Manually set potentiometers and switches

4-channel monitor oscilloscope

A/D converter and multiplexer

D/A converter

Digital-logic control and indicator panels

Analog computer

Digital operations system

FIG. 11-14. The Electronic Associates HYDAC system comprises an analog computer with servo-set potentiometers (right-hand console) and a digital operations system (left-hand console) with mode-control and digital-logic patchbays, D/A/D converters, and optional digital adders and delay-line memory units. A general-purpose digital

460

manently commit phase inverters to all integrators and summers. This simplifies programming and permits very convenient patching of diode multipliers and function generators with double patchcords. This convenience is, however, bought at a relatively high price, and a clever patchbay layout with bottle-plug connections to phase inverters appears preferable. Possibly a better case could be made for committing phase inverters permanently to integrators only.

11-7. A Fast Iterative Differential Analyzer (see also Secs. 10-6 to 10-11).   In fast iterative analog computers (over 50 computer runs per second), low-impedance ± 10-volt or ± 20-volt transistor circuits are almost mandatory for low phase-shift errors (Sec. 3-24).   If desired, one can, however, employ ± 10-volt components for fast subroutines and more accurate ± 100-volt computing elements for slow computations in the same computer setup.   Translation from ± 100 volts to ± 10 volts requires only a ± 10-volt amplifier, while ± 10-volt to ± 100-volt conversion is achieved with track-hold pairs (Sec. 10-8) comprising one fast ± 10-volt amplifier and one slow ± 100-volt amplifier.

While many iterative differential analyzers are expanded "slow" analog computers, Fig. 11-15 shows a computer system designed specifically for iterative techniques.   The ASTRAC II system (Arizona STatistical Repetitive Analog Computer, University of Arizona)[99-103] employs ± 10-volt computing elements in shielded boxes plugged directly into the rear of an Electronic Associates shielded patchbay; ± 10-volt transistor amplifiers with 50-mA class AB output and 20-Mc 0-db bandwidth work with low-impedance networks (5 and 1K resistors, 0.01-, 0.1-, and 1-μF capacitors) to permit iteration rates as high as 1,000 computer runs per second; larger resistors are added for real-time operation.   John Fluke single-turn wirewound 2K coefficient potentiometers with concentric vernier resistances and special dials combine low phase shift with high resolution.   Design static accuracy of operational amplifiers, electronic switches, and diode quarter-square multipliers is only 0.25 per cent of half-scale, but a few ± 100-volt computing elements are available for accurate slow routines.   ASTRAC II plug-in modules can also be plugged into existing "slow" analog computers to provide them with fast-iteration capability.

A flexible digital clock/control unit designed to minimize control-variable patching furnishes reset and sampling pulses, subroutine-sequence markers, and timing markers for multitrace oscilloscope displays (Sec. 10-11).[99]   Integrator-switch lines, comparator outputs, and a set of digital-logic modules are also available in a simple unshielded control patchbay with removable, storable patchboards.   Special hybrid analog-digital accessories, intended for statistical and optimization studies, include

1. A dual shift-register-type *pseudo-random-noise generator*[102] with several digital and analog (binary and Gaussian noise) outputs.

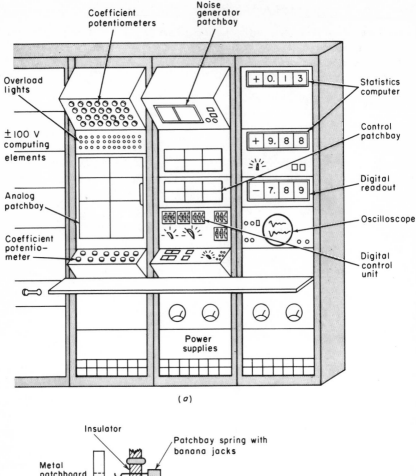

Coefficient
potentiometers

Noise
generator
patchbay

Overload
lights

±100 V
computing
elements

Analog
patchbay

Coefficient
potentio-
meter

Statistics
computer

Control
patchbay

Digital
readout

Oscilloscope

Digital
control
unit

Power
supplies

(a)

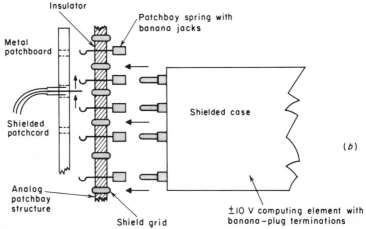

Insulator

Patchbay spring with
banana jacks

Metal
patchboard

Shielded
patchcord

Shielded case

(b)

Analog
patchbay
structure

Shield grid

±10 V computing element with
banana-plug terminations

FIG. 11-15. The University of Arizona's ASTRAC II, designed around an elaborate
digital control system, permits iterative operation at up to 1,000 computer runs per
second as well as real-time simulation.   Subprograms for mode control, optimizer,
and noise generator are patched on separate digital patchboards.   Fast solid-state
±10-volt analog circuits plug directly into the rear of the shielded analog patchbay
without any signal wiring (Fig. 11-15b)

2. A *statistical averaging unit,* which adds 100 to 10,000 solution samples on digital counters.[103]

3. An *amplitude-distribution analyzer,* which counts the number of solution samples in a manually or electronically adjustable class interval.

4. A packaged *parameter optimizer*[101] employing simple counter-driven D/A converters for parameter setting with various digitally controlled optimization strategies (Sec. 12-14). The D/A converters are also available in the control patchbay.

5. An experimental delay-line *function memory* employing 2-Mc delta-sigma modulation (Sec. 10-20c).

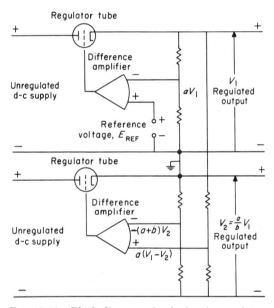

Fig. 11-16a. Block diagram of a dual series regulator.

11-8. Computer Power Supplies.[17-20,124] Regulated power supplies produce *operating and bias voltages* for vacuum tubes and transistors and *computer reference voltages* (usually ± 100 or ± 10 volts). *Relay control systems* and *digital modules* should have power supplies separate from analog circuits. *Filament voltages* for chopper-stabilized vacuum-tube d-c amplifiers do not, in general, require regulation. Saturable-reactor filament-voltage regulators are used but may contribute to objectionable high-frequency harmonic pickup in the computer system.

Vacuum-tube and transistor power supplies in the examples of Fig. 11-16 employ *series regulation,* since shunt regulators would waste current in most analog-computer applications. Referring to the block diagram of Fig. 11-16a, the circuit functions as a feedback amplifier attempting to match a fraction of the supply voltage to a fixed reference voltage. The

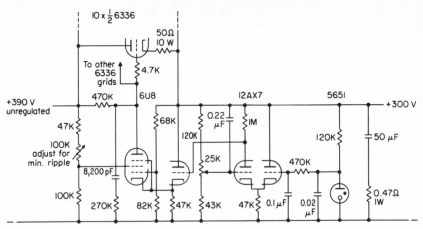

FIG. 11-16*b*. A typical 300-volt 2-amp regulator. Feedforward of the unregulated input improves line-voltage regulation and internal impedance; this so-called "compensation" is adjusted for minimum output ripple. The regulator-tube cathode-lead resistors help to distribute the load current among the regulator tubes and suppress high-frequency parasitic oscillations. (*Electronic Associates, Inc.*)

series-regulator tubes or transistors may be regarded as cathode-follower or emitter-follower output stages, and the entire d-c amplifier theory of Chap. 4 applies. As a matter of fact, ordinary computer d-c amplifiers make excellent regulators, especially for reference power supplies (Figs. 1-21*a* and 11-16*d*);[20] chopper stabilization is rarely needed. Two or more power-supply regulators for positive and/or negative voltages can be slaved to the same voltage reference (Fig. 11-16*a, c*).

Table 11-1 shows the range of available power-supply specifications. Unstabilized d-c amplifiers will require more accurately maintained power-supply voltages than chopper-stabilized amplifiers. Computer reference voltages must be maintained within the computer accuracy specifications. The positive and negative reference voltages should match even more closely, and it is wise to provide for digital-voltmeter checks. The most important requirement is *low power-supply source impedance* to prevent interaction of computing elements. Power-supply output impedance is

Table 11-1. Specifications for Typical Analog-computer Power Supplies
Note that actual requirements vary widely

Voltage change for a 5 per cent line-voltage change............................	0.5 to 0.005 per cent
Voltage change for a load-current change of 50 per cent of rated load, and recovery time to 99.9 per cent of steady state....................................	0.5 to 0.005 per cent; 250 to 2 μsec
24-hr drift, hum, and noise....................	0.5 to 10 mV
Source impedance............................	0.1 to 0.01 ohm (1 to 10 Kc); shunt capacitance at higher frequencies

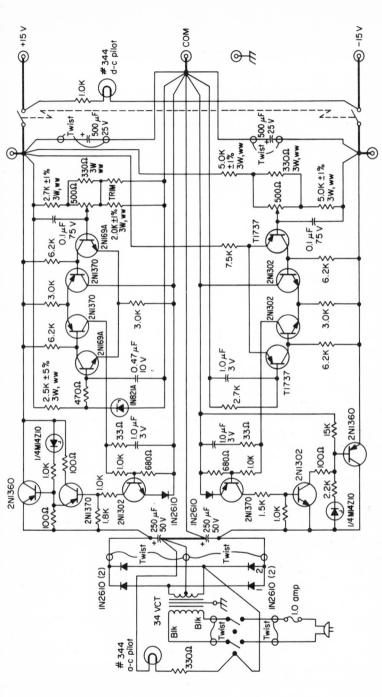

Fig. 11-16c. A small high-quality ±15-volt 150-mA supply. 24-hr drift, ±2 mV; hum and noise <150 μV rms; load and line regulation within 1 mV (105 to 125 volts a-c, no load to full load); source impedance within 0.01 ohm (500 μF at high frequencies); positive and negative supplies track within 0.01 per cent over a 10 deg C range. Preregulators supply base current for the series-regulator transistors; additional series transistors could be used to supply more current. Note ground-lead wiring. (*G. A. Philbrick Researches, Inc.*)

465

inversely proportional to the regulator loop gain, as for any feedback amplifier (Sec. 3-13). Since computing elements may have greater bandwidths than their power-supply regulators, most computer power supplies ensure low output impedance at high frequencies by shunt capacitors across the power-supply output, even though this decreases the operating bandwidth of the regulator as such. In addition, decoupling capacitors across the power-supply terminals on each individual chassis unit may be useful. Large filter or decoupling capacitors should be shunted with small noninductive capacitors.

Commonly used *power-supply reference elements* are zener diodes, strings of zener diodes and/or constant-current diodes[19] selected for mutual temperature compensation, gas-filled regulator tubes, and, for the most accurate reference power supplies,

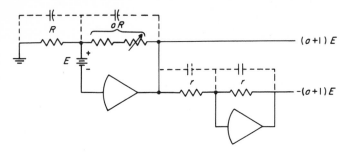

FIG. 11-16d. A simple reference-power-supply circuit using a mercury cell.

mercury batteries or standard cells. Batteries and temperature-compensated zener-diode strings fed from the regulated side of the supply can keep voltage fluctuations as low as 0.01 per cent, and preaged high-quality gas-tube regulators (e.g., RCA type 5651A), also fed from the regulated side of the supply, can stay within 0.05 per cent of a nominal voltage; a drop of radioactive jeweler's paint ensures good ionization.

References 17, 18, and 124 are recommended for detailed discussion and additional examples of power-supply design.

11-9. Noise and Ground Systems (see also Sec. 5-13). Noise in analog-computer signal circuits and ground systems is due to line-frequency components and harmonics, chopper noise, and/or high-frequency pickup from digital circuits and radio-frequency disturbances. A few millivolts rms of noise are usually tolerable. Fluctuations of millivolt amplitude will not affect solutions appreciably, but noise rectified in multipliers or function generators might be integrated to cause more serious errors. Chopper-frequency-noise pickup can cause chopper-channel offsets (Sec. 5-13).

Ground-system noise and common-ground impedances can cause serious problems, especially in low-voltage, high-frequency computers. A good earth ground is not always easy to come by, and the power-line "industrial" ground should be used for a-c return only. To minimize common-ground impedances, we select a single *common-ground point*, usually near a patchbay.   We employ *separate* copper-bar, No. 10 wire, or heavy braid returns from amplifier signal ground and/or chopper ground (Sec. 5-13), power ground, coefficient-potentiometer ground points for (small) groups of computing elements, and a single chassis-ground connection to the computer cabinet (Fig. 11-17a).[1,122,123]

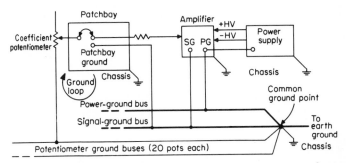

Fig. 11-17a. Analog-computer ground system, showing separate ground returns and an unavoidable ground loop.   Low-impedance transistor computers may require individual potentiometer returns.

Even with a properly designed ground system, we still have electro-magnetic noise pickup from ground loops, which are unavoidable at least in general-purpose analog computers (Fig. 11-17a).   Circulating currents can cause ground-return voltage drops of the order of millivolts rms.   Aside from high-frequency pickup, ground noise is mostly induced by magnetic fields at the line fre-quency and its harmonics.   Third-harmonic pickup can be especially troublesome but may be reduced by the symmetrical input-transformer connection of Fig. 11-17b, and possi-bly by power-line filters and balanc-ing.   Harmonic fields may also be generated by saturable-reactor fila-ment-voltage regulators and by ordi-nary transformers operated near their maximum ratings.   If practicable, the entire power-supply system can be housed away from the main com-

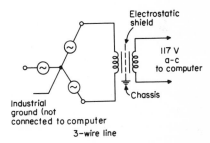

Fig. 11-17b. Use of an isolation trans-former to cancel third-harmonic line-voltage components.   (*Contributed by H. Stewart, University of Arizona.*)

puter cabinet; but most vacuum-tube computers still employ individual filament transformers on the computing-element modules to avoid high-current a-c wiring.   All a-c filament leads must be twisted.

Electrostatic shielding of signal wiring, modules, and power-supply transformers reduces high-frequency pickup but increases shunt capaci-tances.   In stubborn cases, even ground returns and filament leads have been shielded, while "slow" analog computers may omit shielding of low-impedance amplifier-output connections. Cable shields should never carry ground-return currents, but tests may show that it pays to ground both ends of some ground-cable shields.[123]

In hybrid-computer systems, digital and analog circuits should be physically separated wherever possible. *Digital-voltage levels should be securely clamped* to prevent noise due to voltage-change differentiation and circuit ringing.

CONVERSION CIRCUITS AND COMBINED ANALOG-DIGITAL COMPUTATION

11-10. D/A Converters and D/A Multipliers. A *digital-to-analog converter* (*D/A converter, decoder*) designed to produce a voltage

$$X_A = \alpha E X_D$$

proportional to a given positive binary number

$$X_D = a_0 2^0 + a_1 2^1 + a_2 2^2 + \cdots + a_{n-1} 2^{n-1} \qquad (a_k = 0 \text{ or } 1,$$
$$k = 0, 1, 2, \ldots, n-1) \quad (11\text{-}1)$$

usually starts with X_D loaded into an n-bit flip-flop register (parallel representation). The flip-flop levels then switch branches of a resistive attenuator network with constant reference-voltage input. In particular, we can switch summing-amplifier input resistances (Fig. 11-18a); we use consecutively larger resistances (or T-network transfer impedances to avoid excessively large resistance values) for $a_{n-1}, a_{n-2}, \ldots, a_0$. Note that the summing-network branches corresponding to the less significant bits will not require as accurate resistances and switches as the branches switched by a_{n-1}, which is the most critical one. Figure 11-18b shows an example of a switched ladder network for D/A conversion.

D/A converters employ reed relays, diode switches, or transistor switches in many different shunt, series, and series-shunt switching circuits (Secs. 6-10 and 6-11). Careful design must keep the effects of finite electronic-switch forward and back resistances, offset voltages, and offset currents within given accuracy specifications. Output errors below 0.01 per cent of half-scale (10-bit accuracy) can be obtained, with conversion times between 100 msec and 100 nsec.[124] Conversion switching must be synchronized with the arrival of data in the input register; with suitable logic, the network switches can "hold" the analog output until the register is reloaded. The resulting sampled-data output may require filtering and/or extrapolation (Sec. 10-15b).

Conversion of negative as well as positive inputs requires consideration of the digital code used to represent negative numbers. If X_D appears in the form (1) plus a *sign bit* (*signed-magnitude code*, Table 11-1), the

Short-circuit transfer in impedance $= 8R$

(a)

(b)

(c)

FIG. 11-18a to c. Digital-to-analog converters or D/A multipliers: switched summing network (a), ladder network for reed-relay switching (b), and bipolar complemented-code converter (c).

sign bit can simply switch an inverter into the analog output, or switch the sign of the reference input.   The latter method may require more complex (bipolar) switches.   Figure 11-18c shows a converter circuit for positive or negative binary numbers (1) given in a *complemented code* (Table 11-2), which is often convenient.

Table 11-2. Simple Digital Codes Used in Hybrid Computation

Decimal representation	Signed-magnitude code (last bit is sign bit)	A complemented code
0	0000	0000
1, −1	0010, 0011	0001, 1111
2, −2	0100, 0101	0010, 1110
3, −3	0110, 0111	0011, 1101
4, −4	1000, 1001	0100, 1100
5, −5	1010, 1011	0101, 1011

If the reference input E of a D/A converter is replaced by a variable analog input Y_A (note that $-Y_A$ may also be required), then we have a *D/A multiplier:* the analog output X_A is proportional to the product

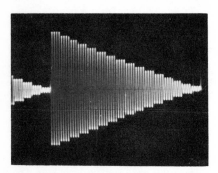

FIG. 11-18d. Multiplication of a ±10-volt 200-Kc sine wave by digital words (3 bits plus sign) at 50,000 samples/sec with the circuit of Fig. 11-18c. (*University of Arizona; see also ref.* 40.)

$X_D Y_A$ of digital and analog inputs. With high-frequency input Y_A, we must ensure low phase shift in the converter network by using phase-compensating capacitors and sufficiently low resistance values, always remembering the effects of nonlinear switch capacitances and finite switch resistances (Secs. 6-10 and 6-11).   In spite of these design problems, *every D/A converter used with a general-purpose analog computer should be designed to permit multiplication, for D/A multiplication can be extraordinarily useful.*

Applications include digital filter control (e.g., for speech synthesis),[73] parameter switching and optimization (Sec. 12-14), and various hybrid analog-digital computing schemes (Secs. 11-16 and 11-19; see also Sec. 7-22).   Figure 11-18e shows typical results obtained with the simple D/A multiplier circuit of Fig. 11-18c.

The *switched-capacitance decoder*[36,38] shown in Fig. 11-18d decodes a serial digital input directly with moderate accuracy and speed.

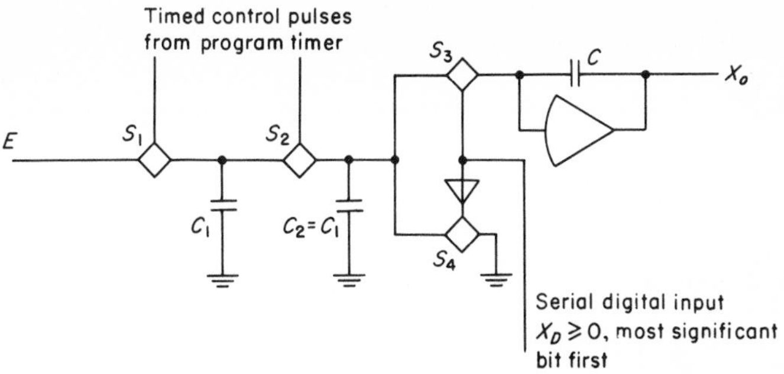

Timed control pulses
from program timer

S_3

C

X_o

E S_1 S_2

C_1 $C_2 = C_1$

S_4

Serial digital input
$X_D \geqslant 0$, most significant
bit first

FIG. 11-18e. This simplified switched-capacitor decoder accepts unipolar serial input. Switches close *momentarily* to transfer charges in the following sequence:

1. At the start of each sample period, S_1, S_2 open to charge C_1 and $C_2 = C_1$ to E volts.
2. If first (most significant) bit is 1, S_3 discharges C_2 into integrator, and $X_o = -(C_1/C)E$.
   If first bit is 0, S_4 discharges C_2 to ground.
3. S_2 opens; C_1 and C_2 are each charged to $E/2$ volts.
4. If second bit is 1, S_3 adds $-(C_1/2C)E$ to X_o.
   If second bit is 0, S_4 discharges C_2 to ground.
5. S_2 opens; C_1 and C_2 are each charged to $E/4$ volts, etc.

10-bit accuracy is possible.

11-11. A/D Converters. (a) **Introduction.** The basic ingredients of all *analog-to-digital converters* (*A/D converters, encoders*) are analog comparators (Secs. 6-8 and 10-9), whose binary output indicates the sign of an analog input sum or difference. Like D/A converters, A/D converters necessarily produce sampled data, either periodically or in response to command pulses. Figure 11-19 illustrates A/D conversion schemes of particular interest for hybrid analog-digital computation. Code wheels and code masks for encoding mechanical displacements and cathode-ray deflections are described in ref. 36.

(b) **Ramp/comparator Converters.** *Ramp/comparator converters* (*analog-to-time-to-digital converters*) gate clock pulses into a counter (output register) while an accurate ramp voltage varies between zero and the analog input $X_A > 0$ (Fig. 11-19a). Simple one-amplifier circuits permit very inexpensive 7-bit conversion (Sec. 9-4). More accurate conversion requires a separate ramp generator and comparator to make the ramp amplitude independent of X_A; this can reduce errors due to capacitor dielectric absorption (Sec. 3-9) to about 0.02 per cent of half-scale. Sampling rates up to several kilocycles are feasible.

(c) **A/D Converters with D/A Converter Feedback.**[31-40] To obtain high accuracy (to within 0.001 per cent of half-scale) with a single comparator, we reconvert our digital output X_D to a voltage $\alpha E X_D$, which is compared with the analog input X_A (Fig. 11-19b). Assuming $|X_A| \leq E$ and $|\alpha X_D| \leq 1$, we vary X_D during each conversion cycle until

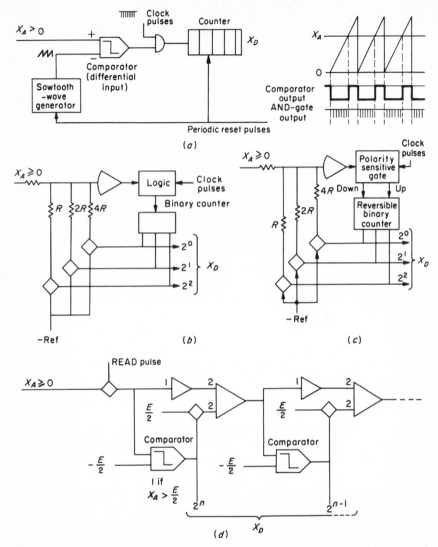

FIG. 11-19. Analog-to-digital converters: ramp/comparator converter (a), use of D/A converter feedback (b), incremental converter (c), and cascade encoder (d).

the magnitude of the analog error $e_A = \alpha E X_D - X_A$ is sufficiently small, i.e.,

$$X_D = \frac{X_A + e_A}{\alpha E} \qquad |e_A| < \frac{2E}{2^n} \qquad (11\text{-}2)$$

where n is the required number of bits, *including the sign bit*. Different schemes for varying X_D yield various compromises between circuit simplicity and maximum n-bit conversion time. We shall measure conversion time in *clock periods*, where each clock period must be sufficiently long to permit comparator, logic, and D/A converter switches to settle. Typical clock periods will be between 0.5 and 100 μsec for all-electronic circuits, and of the order of milliseconds with relay D/A converters.

In the simplest scheme, the D/A converter register is a clock-driven 2^n-step counter which starts at the most negative value once per conversion cycle and counts up to produce a staircase D/A output analogous to the sawtooth voltage in Fig. 11-19a. X_D is read when the staircase voltage reaches X_A. The maximum conversion time is 2^n clock periods, since each staircase step will be just $2E/2^n$ volts.

To reduce the average conversion time, the D/A converter register can be a reversible counter; we count up or down as required by the sign of the error $e_A = \alpha E X_D - X_A$ (*incremental converter, digital servo*, Fig. 11-19c). A small comparator deadspace about $e_A = 0$ will prevent oscillation about the correct output. Incremental converters save appreciable time if X_A is not a random input (like a multiplexer output), but a time-variable analog voltage known to increase and decrease no faster than $R < 2E/2^n$ volts per clock period. In this case, each conversion requires at most $2^n R/2E$ clock periods. We can speed the conversion at the expense of circuit complexity if we add comparators which sense large analog errors and transfer the counter input to a higher digit position (variable-increment counter).[31]

For faster conversion without restriction to rate-limited analog input, we program the D/A converter register with digital logic to "weigh" X_A by successive binary-digit approximations. We start with $X_D = 0$ to find the sign of X_A. If $X_A > 0$, we next try $\alpha E X_D = E/2$ to see if the most significant binary digit is 0 or 1, and continue on to the last binary digit (*successive-approximation converter*).[35,37] The required conversion time will be n clock periods, one for each bit in X_D.

(d) A/D Converters with Multiple Comparators.[33,39] Converters employing parallel comparators for each quantization level (Fig. 6-35) permit the highest possible conversion speed, since all digits are produced simultaneously. The *cascade encoder* (Fig. 11-19d) reduces the required number of comparators, but produces binary digits in succession. Referring to Fig. 11-19d ($X_A > 0$), comparator 1 decides whether $X_A > E/2$. If $X_A > E/2$, comparator 2 decides whether $X_A > E/2 + E/4$; if $X_A < E/2$, comparator 2 decides whether $X_A > E/4$, etc. Cascade encoders can be very fast. The converter shown in Fig. 11-19d requires one clock period per bit, but improved circuits (e.g., Raytheon Co. Model A/D-50A) separate the converter stages with analog delay lines one clock period (0.2 μsec) long, so that the earlier stages can begin to work on the next analog sample before each conversion is completed.

11-12. Combined Simulation. (a) Introduction. Real-time simulation problems requiring high computing accuracy (e.g., trajectory computations with three-dimensional coordinate transformations) and/or simulation of digital system components have led naturally to combination of existing analog computers with general-purpose digital computers through suitable conversion linkages.   In the examples of Fig. 11-20,[46,95] the digital computer performs that part of the real-time computation for which it is most suited, namely, accurate coordinate conversions, trajectory computations, and the simulation of digital control equipment.   The analog computer simulates dynamics and control functions requiring greater bandwidth and less accuracy.   Other striking applications of combined multipurpose computers include postflight analysis of tape-recorded aircraft maneuver flight-load histories,[42] real-time space-vehicle simulation with human operators in the loop, trajectory optimization

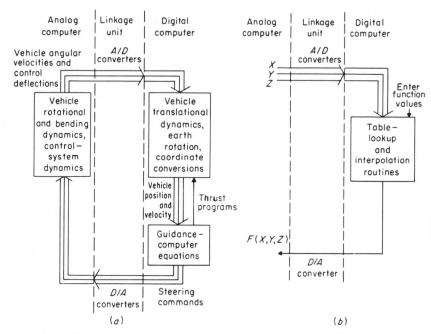

FIG. 11-20. Combined analog-digital simulation of a space vehicle (*a*), and digital function generation in combined simulation (*b*).   (*Based on refs.* 46 and 95.)

(Chap. 12), and statistical analyses.[43-50]   In some combined simulations requiring greater digital-computer speed for specific operations such as coordinate conversion, operational digital computing devices such as digital differential analyzers (Sec. 11-17*b*) supplement or replace the conventional digital computer.[48,50]

Errors due to finite conversion sampling rates or digital-computer execution time in combined simulation are the subject of continuing studies, because they bear strongly on the optimal assignment of computing tasks between analog and digital computing elements.[51,52]   Such error effects can be alleviated by more sophisticated data reconstruction involving first-order and possibly higher-order interpolation with track-hold circuits or additional digital-to-analog converter channels (Sec. 10-12*b*).   Another interesting technique commits additional analog computing equipment to duplicate the digital computations coarsely for correction of high-frequency errors.[51] Errors due to roundoff or quantization in the digital computer also have received attention.[49,50]

(b) Complete Conversion Linkages. The block diagram of Fig. 11-21 illustrates the requirements for a complete analog/digital/analog linkage unit forming the interface between an electronic analog computer and a general-purpose digital computer. Linkage units are commercially available or may be built up from packaged solid-state modules.

Four to thirty A/D *channels* and a similar but not necessarily equal number of D/A *channels* each permit 5,000 to 30,000 11- to 14-bit (0.1

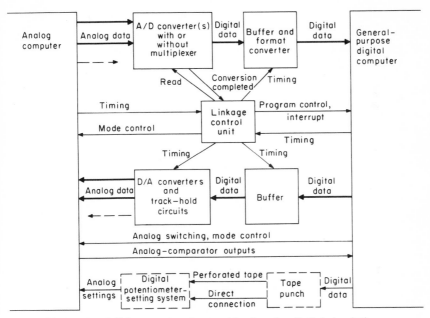

Fig. 11-21. A linkage system for combined analog-digital simulation.

to 0.01 per cent of half-scale, plus sign) conversions per second. The required conversion rate is, in general, determined by the data-handling capability of the digital computer rather than by analog requirements. Since the digital computer can address only one data channel at a time, a common arrangement employs analog multiplexing of a single fast successive-approximation A/D converter (Sec. 11-11). The stepwise D/A converter outputs feed through smoothing filters or track-hold circuits permitting first-order interpolation (Sec. 10-15). Multiplexing is again possible, although multiple D/A converter channels are not excessively expensive and may save track-hold circuits.

Especially in "open-loop" combined operation involving, say, analog processing or display of digital-computer output data, unused A/D channels can be employed to reconvert analog to digital data to check the D/A conversion during the computation.[49]   Unused converter channels are also used for implementing more sophisticated interpolation between digital-computer output samples.

The conversion channels are linked to the digital computer with *input and output buffer modules.*   These serve, first, for intermediate storage of data, since the linkage conversion rates are not necessarily synchronized with the digital-computer program.   Secondly, the buffer modules provide for format changes relating the parallel number representations in converter input and output registers to the digital-computer code.   Many small digital computers, in particular, will require shift-register input and output for conversion to and from serial number representation.[50]

The buffering operations, as well as sampling, conversion, and multiplexing, are timed in suitable relationship to one another by a *linkage control unit* comprising timing and logic circuits capable of communicating with the digital-computer program control.   The control unit alternates digital-computer program cycles with the presentation of appropriate converter output and input samples and also controls analog-computer integrators and track-hold circuits.   Master timing pulses may originate in the digital computer or in the linkage control unit itself.   Some iterative-differential-analyzer control units (Sec. 10-11) with added patched logic are suitable for linkage control.

Aside from numerical-data links, Fig. 11-21 also shows *logical* interconnections ("sense lines") linking the digital computer with the analog computer and linkage-control unit.   Commands from the digital-computer program control unit may be fed to the analog computer to control RESET/COMPUTE and TRACK/HOLD cycles, analog-program switches, and/or parameter changes.   Similarly, overload indications, comparator decisions, and patched-digital-logic outputs can interrupt and/or modify the digital-computer program.

In addition to the "dynamic" conversion linkages just described, a digital computer can set analog-computer coefficient potentiometers and provide checking and setup automation (Sec. 11-4*d*).   The digital computer can prepare storable potentiometer-setting tape for the analog computer; it seems reasonable, however, to provide also for direct interconnection of the digital-computer output register and the potentiometer-setting converter.

(c) **Choice of Digital Computer.**[48,50,53]   With large general-purpose digital computers, such as the IBM 7094, high digital computing speeds and parallel input-output permit flexible real-time hybrid computation at high conversion rates.   A program-interrupt feature makes it possible to time-share the expensive large digital computer between hybrid simulation and other tasks.   But the question of computer availability vs. idle time may lead to unhappy administrative problems.   The writers would prefer a smaller general-purpose digital computer associated permanently with the analog-computer facility; this also eliminates technical difficulties associated with long cables between analog and digital computers. It is desirable, though, to obtain a small digital computer with fairly fast arithmetic and parallel input and output, in spite of the added expense. Serial/parallel/serial conversion, in particular, not only increases linkage complexity but may use so much computer time that digital-computer programming flexibility is affected. We may, in other words, have to do without certain useful but time-consuming digital subroutines to maintain satisfactory analog/digital/analog conversion rates. We can, of course, simplify digital-computer requirements at the expense of flexibility if our installation is to be used for a limited class of problems only. The choice of digital computers is further discussed in refs. 48, 50, and 53.

11-13. A Complete Hybrid System. The Electronic Associates, Inc., HYDAC system illustrated in Fig. 11-14 combines a large analog computer, or several analog computers, with a general-purpose digital computer (Computer Control Corp. DDP-24) through a digital-operations system (DOS) console.[48,53] The latter combines the functions of the usual linkage unit (conversion, buffers, and control, Sec. 11-12) with an elaborate system of patchable digital logic for iterative-differential-analyzer control (Sec. 10-11) and an optional digital memory system. A large patchbay, similar to an analog-computer patchbay, includes terminations for

1. D/A converters and multiplexed A/D converters.
2. Buffer shift registers (see also Sec. 11-12b).
3. Digital-computer input and output sense lines, for communication with the digital-computer program.
4. A field of thumbwheel-preset digital counters for iterative-differential-analyzer sequence control and similar applications. Counters, like shift registers, can be cascaded.
5. 20-Mc logic modules (clock-gated flip-flops, gates, inverters, and delay multivibrators).
6. A 2-Mc clock.
7. (Optional) dual digital adder/subtractors, which also permit serial multiplication with additional patched logic.
8. An (optional) assortment of digital serial-memory units (magnetostrictive delay lines and control circuits) used in connection with A/D/A converters for time-delay simulation and function storage (Sec. 10-20b).
9. Connections to the analog-computer readout switching system, digital voltmeter, and potentiometer-setting systems which can, then, communicate with the digital computer.

A small separate patchbay in each analog-computer console controls integrator and track-hold-circuit modes, multiplier functions, etc., in the manner of the EASE pinboard or transfers control to the digital-operations system. Elaborate recording and display systems are available.

The HYDAC system provides an extraordinarily flexible combination of analog and digital computing elements. HYDAC systems are suitable mainly for very large computer laboratories, not only because of their price but also because of their very flexibility: each new HYDAC setup is not unlike the design of a new hybrid computer, and many analog-computer users simply lack the necessary skill. As with any large iterative differential analyzer, there is a real need for packaged software in the form of tried standard control programs for optimization, statistics, etc. A library of programs might be implemented with small permanently wired patchboards, or by card- or tape-controlled switching. Electronic Associates, in any case, also markets smaller assemblies of electronically controlled integrators, track-hold circuits, and digital logic for smaller installations.

The Electronic Associates analog computers used with the HYDAC system include the usual low-speed, high-accuracy computing elements, and also medium-speed equipment suitable for repetitive operation. For optimum utilization of the high-speed iterative subroutines made possible by HYDAC's fast digital control, the machine could benefit substantially from fast low-impedance transistor coupling elements plugged directly into the Electronic Associates analog patchbay (Sec. 11-7).

DIGITAL-COMPUTER SOLUTION OF DIFFERENTIAL EQUATIONS, AND MISCELLANEOUS HYBRID COMPUTING TECHNIQUES

11-14. Truncation Errors and Frequency Response of Digital Integrators. Digital computers necessarily approximate true (continuous) integration,

$$x(t) = \int_0^t \dot{x}(t) \, dt + x(0) \tag{11-3}$$

by *stepwise-integration formulas* relating the sampled-data sequences

$$\dot{x}_k = \dot{x}(k \, \Delta t) \qquad x_k = x(k \, \Delta t) \qquad (k = 0,1,2, \ldots) \tag{11-4}$$

We shall consider integration with respect to real time t and assume periodic sampling (constant increments Δt). We must refer the reader to ref. 115 for the theory of numerical integration; we shall merely quote three of the simplest integration formulas (Table 11-3) as examples of interest for digital-differential-analyzer design (Sec. 11-17). General-purpose digital computers commonly employ more sophisticated integration routines, which utilize additional past values of $\dot{x}$ for improved accuracy.[58,64,115]

Most integration formulas other than predictor-corrector formulas[115] represent linear operations on the sampled-data input sequence $\dot{x}_0$, $\dot{x}_1$, $\dot{x}_2$, . . . (see also Secs. 10-13 to 10-15). If the $\dot{x}_k$, x_k are periodic samples, we can study the *frequency-response effects of stepwise integration and processing delays* by substituting

$$\dot{x}_k = \dot{x}(k \, \Delta t) = e^{j\omega k \Delta t} \qquad x_k = x(k \, \Delta t)$$
$$= H(j\omega \, \Delta t)e^{j\omega k \Delta t} \qquad (k = 0,1,2, \ldots) \tag{11-5}$$

into each integration formula. The amplitude and phase of the complex frequency-response function $(Hj\omega \, \Delta t)$ represent the gain and phase shift produced by our "digital integrator" for steady-state sinusoidal input and output sequences, just as in the more familiar case of continuous net-

Table 11-3. Frequency-response Data for Simple Integration Formulas

$$x_k = H(j\omega\,\Delta t)x_k \text{ if } \dot{x}_k = e^{j\omega k\,\Delta t} \qquad (k = 0,1,2, \ldots)$$

Integration formula	$H(j\omega\,\Delta t)$	$|H(j\omega\,\Delta t)|$	arg $H(j\omega\,\Delta t)$
$x_k = x_{k-1} + \dot{x}_{k-1}\,\Delta t$ (EULER'S RULE)	$\dfrac{\Delta t}{2}e^{-j\omega\,\Delta t}\left(1 - j\cot\dfrac{\omega\,\Delta t}{2}\right)$	$\dfrac{\Delta t}{2}\left|\dfrac{1}{\sin\dfrac{\omega\,\Delta t}{2}}\right|$	$-\dfrac{\pi}{2} - \dfrac{\omega\,\Delta t}{2}$
$x_k = x_{k-1} + \frac{1}{2}(\dot{x}_k + \dot{x}_{k-1})\,\Delta t$ (TRAPEZOIDAL RULE)	$-j\dfrac{\Delta t}{2}\cot\dfrac{\omega\,\Delta t}{2}$	$\dfrac{\Delta t}{2}\left|\cot\dfrac{\omega\,\Delta t}{2}\right|$	$-\dfrac{\pi}{2}$
$x_k = x_{k-1} + \frac{1}{2}(3\dot{x}_{k-1} - \dot{x}_{k-2})\,\Delta t$ (OPEN TRAPEZOIDAL RULE)	$\dfrac{\Delta t}{2}e^{-j\omega\,\Delta t}\left(2 - j\cot\dfrac{\omega\,\Delta t}{2}\right)$	$\dfrac{\Delta t}{2}\left|4 + \cot^2\dfrac{\omega\,\Delta t}{2}\right|^{1/2}$	$-\omega\,\Delta t - \arctan\frac{1}{2}\cot\dfrac{\omega\,\Delta t}{2}$

works.[65,115] For an ideal integrator with unity gain, we should have

$$H(j\omega\,\Delta t) = \frac{1}{j\omega}$$

for all circular frequencies ω. Substitution of Eq. (5) into each approximate-integration formula yields the frequency-response data of Table 11-3 and Fig. 11-22. Each integrator is seen to approximate ideal integration at very low frequencies; at higher frequencies, each approximation begins to cause amplitude and phase errors. The trapezoidal rule,

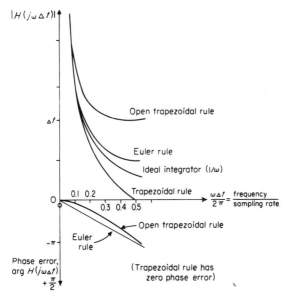

FIG. 11-22. Frequency response of simple digital integrators. (*Data based on ref.* 65.)

curiously enough, causes only amplitude errors, but most real-time digital computers cannot supply $\dot{x}_k$ in time to be used in the computation of x_k. In such cases, the open trapezoidal rule, which requires only $\dot{x}_{k-1}$ and $\dot{x}_{k-2}$, is substituted. Note that frequency response can be improved either by a more complicated integration formula or simply by a higher iteration rate (smaller Δt). Our simple linear analysis cannot be applied directly to predictor-corrector integration.[115]

In addition to the *truncation errors* resulting from stepwise integration, digital integration is subject to *roundoff errors* due to amplitude quantization. In this connection, we prefer digital integrators whose truncation errors represent excessive high-frequency *attenuation* so that high-frequency "quantization noise" is reduced in the integration process. This is true, for instance, for the trapezoidal rule, but not for the Euler (rectangular) rule (Fig. 11-22).[115]

If all integrators of a digital equation solver acquire their input data at the same time $k\,\Delta t$, we can employ the frequency-response data of Table 11-3 to estimate errors in linear-differential equation solutions (e.g., circle-test errors) by the method of Secs. 3-23 and 3-24.[62-65,96] The analysis becomes somewhat more complicated if integrators operate successively.

11-15. Digital Computers with Special Assembler Programs and Digital Simulation. Representation of differential equations by analog-computer-type block diagrams has, as we have noted, an important intuitive appeal, especially in engineering applications. We can combine such block-diagram programming with precise digital computation by writing *special assembler programs* for general-purpose digital computers. Such programs, known by names such as MIDAS, DYSAC, and DAS,[54-57] automatically assemble differential-equation-solving routines from punched-card or tape instructions based directly on analog-computer-type block diagrams or, more correctly, on analog-computer-type setup sheets (Sec. 2-17). Typical instructions might take the form

$$A08A17 + A09P21 = I18 \tag{11-6}$$

which means CONNECT PRODUCT OF OUTPUT OF ADDER 08 AND ADDER 17 PLUS PRODUCT OF ADDER 09 AND COEFFICIENT ("POTENTIOMETER") SETTING 21 TO INPUT OF INTEGRATOR 18. A variety of accurate integration routines can be used, and routines for frequently needed functions (e.g., sin x, cos x) can be called for by special instructions. Even though such assembler programs may sacrifice some computer time as compared with optimum direct programming, they can be highly useful, especially to engineering personnel more familiar with analog computation than with digital programming. The technique may also facilitate digital checks on existing analog-computer setups. The better assembler programs provide *automatic scaling* through the use of digital-floating-point arithmetic.

With suitable programming, fast general-purpose digital computers with large high-speed memories, such as the IBM 7094A, permit real-time digital simulation of respectable engineering problems, such as three-dimensional aircraft flight;[71] such all-digital computation could, in particular, often replace combined simulation with analog and digital computers.   Simulator-type system parameter optimization, with frequent reruns of solutions and manual parameter or setup changes is, however, a time-consuming and hence expensive application for a multi-million-dollar digital-computer system, nor are such machines designed for spur-of-the-moment program changes in the manner of analog computers.   The logical result of this situation has been the development of new relatively small, fast, general-purpose digital computers with accessory features facilitating real-time solution of differential equations. These facilities include special program structures to shorten the time and memory capacity required for frequently used subroutines such as function lookup; a command structure related to setup with block-diagram assembler programs; and accessory arithmetic elements for performing such time-consuming operations as coordinate transformations.

Reference 58 describes an early computer of this type, essentially a modified small but fast general-purpose digital computer in the $300,000 class, a price comparable with that of a large analog-computer installation. The machine (Scientific Data Systems DES-1) permits selection of five different integration routines (open trapezoidal rule, Runge-Kutta, higher-order-predictor and predictor-corrector types[115]) by a simple switch, is programmed with a special assembler program, and has facilities for solution plotting and interconnection with real-time analog computers.   During one typical 11-msec integration cycle, the DES-1 can perform operations corresponding to those of 30 7-input summer-integrators (with four-point predictor routine), 45 summers, 150 coefficient potentiometers, 100 multipliers or servos, 5 resolvers, 10 relay comparators, and 20 10-segment function generators.   Depending on the type of problem, an 11-msec integration cycle permits representation of full-scale sinusoids at perhaps 6 cps with 0.001 per cent resolution (see also Sec. 11-17*b*).   The machine still also functions as a general-purpose digital computer and can, for instance, perform iterative optimization routines.

In our judgment, improved machines of this type will eventually replace many large analog computers, particularly those working on large routine problems at the very limit of their accuracy, so that frequent checking and maintenance are required.   The advance of digital simulation will depend not just on improved computing speed, but on improved displays and programming convenience.   We believe that radical advances in the art of man/machine intercourse are possible, and that digital differential-

equation solvers will tie in neatly with very fast digitally controlled iterative analog computation.   Such a development would return analog computation to the role for which it is best suited, namely, high-speed,
moderate-accuracy computation at modest cost.

11-16. Digital Computers with Fast Analog Subroutines.   Where
moderate computing accuracy is sufficient, the use of *analog subroutines
in general-purpose digital-computer programs* can produce remarkable
savings in computing time and memory requirements.   As a case in
point, several special-purpose digital computers have substituted multiplication by digital-to-analog-to-digital converters (Sec. 11-10) for slower

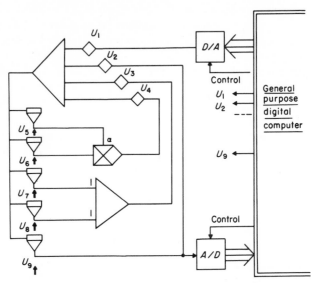

Fig. 11-23. A pulsed-analog arithmetic element.   Binary control variables U_1, U_2,
. . . , U_9 from the digital computer control analog switching and storage to produce
expressions like $x + y$, $ax + y$, xy within 0.5 to 1 per cent of half-scale in a single
1- to 5-μsec instruction time.

true digital-multiplication routines.[117,119,120]   More significant time savings can be realized with small digitally controlled "analog arithmetic
elements" (Fig. 11-23) combining analog multiplication and addition.
Going still further, analog subroutines for generating special functions or
for solving algebraic or differential equations produce results in a single
digital instruction time, where purely digital computation would require
many instructions and additional fast-access digital memory.   Such
accessory "analog arithmetic elements" ("pulsed analog computers"[66])
were originally developed at MIT to improve the program structure of
digital flight simulators.[66-71]   While most flight simulation does not
really require extraordinary computing speeds, the analog-subroutine

technique offers great promise for the much more time-consuming iterative computations required to solve partial differential equations (see also
Sec. 12-22).[72,73]   Analog subroutines can also simplify many real-time
digital data-processing systems, especially those with analog inputs
and/or outputs (digital controllers, digital-analog display generation[73]).

11-17. Operational Digital Computers.   (a) Introduction.   *Operational digital computers* represent variables by digital words but, unlike
most general-purpose digital computers, provide digital adders, multipliers, integrators, etc., for each operation; these digital computing elements are interconnected in the manner of analog-computer setups.   Such
parallel operation reduces intermediate-storage requirements and permits
relatively fast computation with digital-computer precision and ease of
maintenance.   The nuisance of transferring complete n-digit words
between computing elements is often avoided through *incremental-
transfer computation*.   With incremental transfer, we transmit only *increments* ΔX of variables X between computing elements once per clock
period Δt. ΔX equals $+1$, 0, or -1, so that at most two lines are needed
to transfer ΔX and its sign.   An incremental computer, then, represents
the rate of change of each variable X by the repetition rate of the ΔX
pulse train; reversible counters can generate X itself wherever needed.
Figure 11-24 shows block diagrams of some operational digital computing
elements with total transfer and with incremental transfer.[59-60,95]   Special
operational digital computing elements are often useful in hybrid analog-
digital computers as well as in all-digital machines (Fig. 11-24a, b, c; see
also (Fig. 12-13c).
   (b) Parallel Digital Differential Analyzers.   The best known
operational digital computers are *parallel digital differential analyzers
(parallel DDA's)*, which employ incremental integration and multiplication together with digital function generators based on table-lookup and
interpolation routines.[59-65]   Unlike analog computers, they can integrate
directly with respect to dependent variables.   General-purpose machines
of this type (e.g., Packard-Bell TRICE, Hazeltine Electronics SPEDAC)
can be patched just like analog computers, operate at 10^5 to 10^6 incre-
ments/sec, and implement open-trapezoidal integration rather than the
simple Euler integration (Table 11-3) obtained in Fig. 11-24d.   Each
integrator requires hundreds of semiconductors and costs several thousand
dollars.   Scaling, resetting, and program changes in the course of computation can be conveniently controlled by an auxiliary digital computer.
   Such machines permit real-time simulation of, say, aircraft.   But,
although 30-bit or better resolution is available, incremental computation
exacts a price in accuracy, for computer variables can change by at most
n (10^5 to 10^6) increments (bits) per second.   Note, in particular, that this
rate limit forces us to scale a real-time sine wave $x(t) = a \sin 2\pi f t$ so that

x is represented by at most $n/2\pi f$ bits out of the available 2^{30}, since

$$\left|\frac{dx}{dt}\right|_{\text{MAX}} = 2\pi fa \qquad (11\text{-}7)$$

must not correspond to more than n bits/sec.   As an example, TRICE, with $n = 10^5$ increments/sec, cannot represent a 16-cps sine wave more accurately than within about 0.1 per cent.   The resulting roundoff errors, combined with truncation errors due to the relatively primitive integration formula used, can have serious effects in some fast calculations.[60-64] For this reason, incremental digital differential analyzers are most successful as *special-purpose* computers for fire control, process control, coordinate transformation in combined simulation, etc., where errors can be estimated, and possibly corrected, before computation.   Some special-purpose DDA's (General Electric Co.) have facilities for automatic rescaling (change of increment-step size) to trade accuracy for speed when following fast signals.

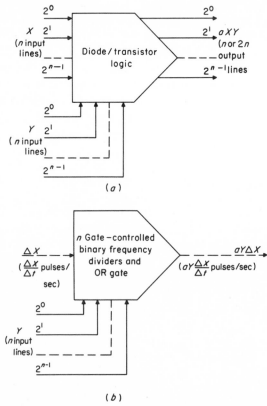

FIG. 11-24a, b. Total-transfer parallel multiplier (a), and pulse-rate multiplier (b). Another incremental-transfer multiplication scheme employs DDA integrators to produce $\Delta XY \approx X\,\Delta Y + Y\,\Delta X$.

$$_k\Sigma\, a_k\, Y_k\, \Delta t + Z_0 \approx \int_0^t Y dt + Z_0 = Z$$

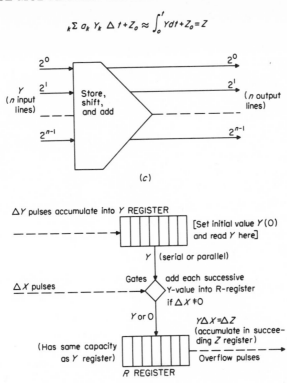

(c)

(d)

FIG. 11-24c, d. Total-transfer digital integrator (c), and incremental-transfer DDA integrator (d).

11-18. Pulse-modulation Representation of Variables.[104–113]   For many instrumentation and control applications, operational digital computation offers the significant advantage of practically error-free data switching, data storage, and data transmission over possibly noisy channels; but the relative cost of A/D/A conversion equipment is usually highest for the smallest systems.   For this reason, we consider operations with pulse-modulation data representations other than true digital coding (PCM).   Suitably modulated pulse trains can still be switched, stored on tape or drums, and transmitted over communication links by largely digital techniques, and relatively simple modulators and demodulators take the place of expensive A/D/A converters (Fig. 11-25).   The price of this convenience is reduced coding efficiency: to double the resolution (number of distinguishable increments, code size) of any continuous-modulation scheme, we must *double* computing time or logic speed, while a true digital representation would merely add *one bit* per word.

Table 11-4 summarizes essential properties of various pulse-modulation

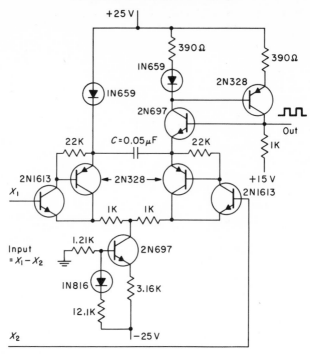

FIG. 11-25a. A compact self-excited pulse-ratio modulator. Pulse-output average is proportional to the input difference within 0.1 per cent. Minimum pulse ON and OFF times are 700 C sec. The differential input circuit and current source are carefully temperature-stabilized (see also Sec. 5-26; refs. 106 and 107).

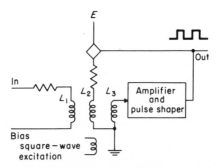

FIG. 11-25b. Compact externally excited saturable-reactor modulator. The feedback loop switches the reference voltage E on and off so that the average ampere-turns per excitation cycle in L_2 equal those in the input winding L_1; hence the input can be either a low-frequency signal or itself a pulse train. Multiple input windings can sum several input signals. Pulse frequency is of the order of 1 Kc, and accuracy is within 0.2 per cent of half-scale. (*General Electric HYDAPT modulator;* see ref. 109 for circuit, core, and winding details.)

Table 11-4. Pulse-modulation Representation of Data

Type of modulation and references	Modulator	Demodulator	Conversion to digital code	Remarks
Pulse-width modulation (PWM). Some pulse-position modulation (PPM) systems are similar[104,108,109-113]	Figs. 7-13a and 11-25b	Integration once per cycle, or simple averaging	Each pulse gates counter	Usually synchronous total transfer of one sample per pulse, as in HYDAPT system (see text)
Pulse-ratio modulation (PRM). Both pulse width and rate are modulated, as in self-excited time-division multipliers (Sec. 7-11)[106,107]	Figs. 7-14 to 7-19 and 11-25a	Simple averaging	Count pulses for a fixed averaging period	Asynchronous, incremental data transfer. Simple system for data transmission, tape storage
Continuous pulse-frequency modulation (PFM)	Many electro-mechanical transducers (telemetering); voltage-controlled oscillators with and without feedback; Fig. 9-13	Discriminator, phase-lock loop, or step counter		Asynchronous, incremental data transfer. Widely used for telemetering and tape storage; tape needs reference track
Pulse-phase modulation (PPM)	Some electro-mechanical transducers; voltage-controlled oscillator and frequency-dividing counter	Phase detector, phase-lock loop	Phase detector gates counter for a fixed averaging period	Asynchronous, incremental data transfer. Rarely used
Pulse-count modulation[111]	Pulse-width modulator gates counter, or step counter	Step counter, i.e., integration of pulse train for one sampling period	Digital code	Synchronous, total transfer of one sample per sampling period, analogous to PWM. Used in HYDAPT system; permits clock-gated logic
Delta-sigma modulation (d-c sensitive delta modulation, see also Sec. 10-20c)[105]	Integrator/comparator loop (Fig. 10-33)	Simple averaging of flip-flop output (Fig. 10-33)	Count pulses for a fixed averaging period	Synchronous, incremental data transfer, permits clock-gated logic. Useful for function storage

systems used for data processing and refers the reader to relevant circuit diagrams. Recalling our discussion of electronic multipliers in Sec. 7-3, we note that each pulse-modulation detector multiplies its output by a reference voltage (pulse amplitude) and can, therefore, multiply its output by an analog voltage, just like a D/A converter. At high repetition rates, such multiplication is subject to errors due to nonlinear switch capacitances, just as in the case of time-division multipliers (Sec. 7-12). We

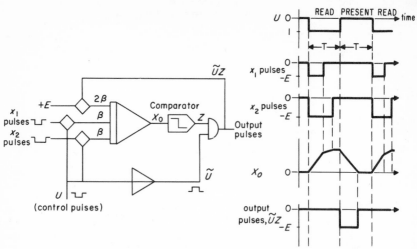

FIG. 11-26a. Pulse-width addition. A number x between, say, -100 and 100 is represented by a pulse of length $a(x + 100)$ with $a \leq T/200$, where T is the control-pulse repetition period. Control pulses mark alternate READ and PRESENT periods of lengths T. Two input pulses of widths $a(x_1 + 100)$, $a(x_2 + 100)$ are added and integrated for T sec (READ period), so that $X_o = +abE(x_1 + x_2 + 200)$ at the start of the PRESENT period. Now we integrate $+E$ with double gain, and the output pulse lasts until the comparator indicates $X_o = 0$; hence the output pulse width is $a\left(\dfrac{x_1 + x_2}{2} + 100\right)$. The processing delay is T.

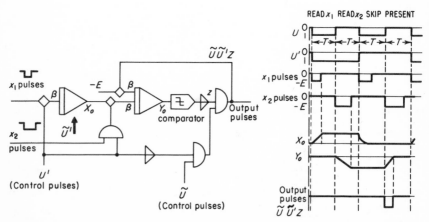

FIG. 11-26b. Pulse-width multiplication of two positive numbers. A pulse of width ax_1 is integrated during the first READ period, so that $X_o = +abx_1E$. A pulse of width ax_2 is entered during the second READ period and gates X_o into integrator 2 until $Y_o = -(abE)^2 x_1 x_2$, which is converted to the output pulse width $abEx_1x_2$ during the following PRESENT period. We skip one period before starting another READ cycle to obtain periodic operation with a processing delay $2T$.

note also that operations with pulse-modulation data imply *processing delays* and/or *rate limiting*, just like digital operations.

While pulse-to-pulse modulation changes in output-averaging modulation schemes represent *incremental data transfer*, the General Electric HYDAPT (Hybrid Analog Pulse Time) system[109-113] transfers complete data samples as widths of successive periodic pulses (*total transfer*). HYDAPT computing elements must use alternating control-pulse repetition periods (Fig. 11-26a) or even alternating pairs of periods (Fig. 11-26b) to read input pulses and to construct output pulses, unless dual elements are used. Hence interconnections require careful attention to timing, and computing elements cause processing delays.

An advanced version of the HYDAPT system replaces the pulse-width representation by a similarly timed pulse-count representation.[111] With pulse width corresponding to the *duration of a pulse group* once per computer repetition period, analog integrators in Fig. 11-26 are replaced by digital counters, and voltage corresponds to a pulse count. The resulting system is an operational *digital* computer with a relatively inefficient digital code (pulse count), but extremely simple A/D/A conversion through ordinary HYDAPT modulators and demodulators. The system permits reliable digital data handling, multiplexing, use of majority logic,[110] etc. Computation is slow: for a resolution of 0.01 per cent of half-scale, we must be able to count at least 20,000 pulses per computer repetition period; so that 2-Mc logic yields at best only a 100-cps sampling rate. If integration is required, the total-transfer Euler-rule integration scheme used with HYDAPT[110,111] slows the computation still further (Sec. 11-14); but the system offers remarkable circuit simplicity and reliability for airborne and process-control applications with low bandwidth requirements.

11-19. Hybrid-code Computing Elements and Differential Analyzers. (a) Hybrid-code Representation of Variables. In principle, a *pair* of analog variables, each specified only within, say, 1 per cent, can represent a number to within 0.01 per cent. This fact is used in the familiar vernier scales. On closer inspection, though, we realize that such two-variable codes require *quantization of at least one variable* to prevent spurious readings, no matter how the code is defined. It makes, then, more sense to define a *hybrid-code representation* of variables in the form

$$X = X_D + X_A \tag{11-8}$$

where X_D is an *integer* between -2^n and $+2^n$ (n-bit digital word plus sign), while X_A is an *analog interpolating voltage* between $-E$ and $+E$ volts, representing the fractional part of X. Either one digital unit or E volts (typically 10 volts) represents one *machine unit* (Fig. 11-27). With X_A accurate to within p per cent of its half-scale E, our hybrid code represents $100(2^n/p)$ distinguishable increments between 0 and 2^n, so that its half-scale accuracy is within $2^{-n}p$ per cent.

Computation with such hybrid-code variables requires *carry generation* whenever an analog variable X_A exceeds E volts or one machine unit in absolute value. This will be sensed by analog comparators in each computing element; to produce a carry, we then increase or decrease X_D by one unit and simultaneously decrease or increase X_A by E volts.

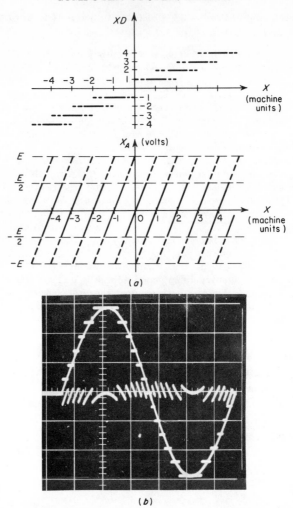

Fig. 11-27. Recommended hybrid-code representation of dependent variables (a), and oscilloscope display of X_D, X_A, and $X = X_D + X_A$ for an 8-cps sine wave (b). The analog range accommodates ± 2 machine units rather than just ± 1 machine unit, so that, for example, $X = 2.9$ machine units may be represented either by $X_D = 2$, $X_A = 0.9E$ volts, or by $X_D = 3$, $X_A = -0.1E$ volts. While this redundancy sacrifices analog accuracy, it permits the use of very inexpensive comparators for carry generation (hybrid-differential-analyzer data taken at the University of Arizona; ordinarily, X_D would be read out digitally).

In the hybrid code of Fig. 11-27a, X_A ranges over $2E$ volts or *two* machine units, so that our code is intentionally redundant: for $0 < e < E/2$ volts, $X_D + e/E$ and $(X_D + 1) + (e - E)/E$ represent the same value of X. This redundancy halves our analog resolution (doubles p), but is well worth this price, for

1. It permits us to employ inexpensive comparators (accurate only to within, say, $\pm E/20$ volts) for carry generation.

2. It permits us, if we wish, to perform carry operations only at clock-synchronized periodic times $\tau = kT$ ($k = 1,2, \ldots$), provided only that

$$T < \frac{1}{2|dX/d\tau|_{\text{MAX}}} \tag{11-9}$$

so that we have at most one carry per time interval T.

Figure 11-27b illustrates the hybrid-code representation of a sine wave with periodic testing for carries; note that the various carries are produced at distinctly different voltages.

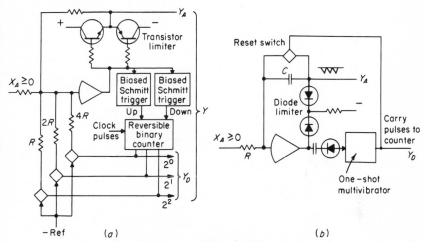

FIG. 11-28. An analog-to-hybrid-code converter for positive input (a), and integrator scale extension with a counter-reset circuit (b) (see also Fig. 8-28).

(b) Analog-to-hybrid-code Converters and Extended-scale Integrators.[87-92]   Interest in hybrid-code representations stems from the possibility of combining relatively inexpensive low-accuracy analog and digital computing or measuring devices to obtain respectable accuracies (0.1 to 0.01 per cent of half-scale).   The availability of a continuous interpolating voltage instead of a purely digital representation is also useful in certain control applications, notably those involving human operators.   Figure 11-28a shows an *analog-to-hybrid-code converter* which permits us to read X_D on a counter and X_A on a voltmeter or servo dial. Figure 11-28b shows a simple *hybrid-code integrator* for instrumentation purposes.

With suitable scaling, the hybrid-code instruments of Fig. 11-28 can accept input voltages larger than their rated analog outputs.   Note, however, that hybrid-code scale extension in analog-input instruments does *not* improve instrument accuracy.

(c) **Hybrid-code Differential Analyzers.** A complete hybrid-code differential-equation solver was originally suggested by H. Skramstad;[93] his concept was further elaborated by H. Schmid[94] and by J. Wait,[96] who built the first working model. Figure 11-29a, based on Wait's work at the University of Arizona, shows a hybrid-code integrator. Figure 11-29b illustrates hybrid-code multiplication. As in the DDA, hybrid-code

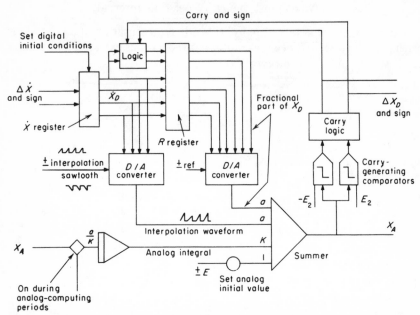

FIG. 11-29a. A hybrid-code integrator (see text). For hybrid codes permitting analog errors above 8 per cent, the analog integrator can be replaced by a passive RC network, so that each integrator requires only one amplifier.[96,97]

multiplication by constant coefficients requires almost as much equipment as multiplication of variables.[93–98]

To minimize interference between digital and analog operations, the Arizona hybrid-code differential analyzer employs periodic carry testing (Sec. 11-19a), and all carries and digital operations are performed with the analog integrators in HOLD. For this purpose, a brief updating period of length $0.05T$ to $0.1T$ follows each analog-computing period T. In practice, T is between 100 and 1,000 μsec; suitable time scaling and first-order-hold readout (Sec. 10-15b) still permits real-time simulation and partial-system tests in spite of the stepwise analog computation.

Tests of a hybrid-code differential analyzer combining fast ± 10-volt analog computation ($p = 1$ per cent) with $n = 3$ digital bits plus sign have vindicated Skramstad's prediction of 0.125 per cent half-scale accu-

racy (Fig. 11-27b).[96]   The machine may be regarded as a digital differential analyzer whose truncation errors are eliminated by continuous
analog interpolation.   A modified form of Wait's machine[97] combines
even cruder analog computation ($p = 8$ per cent) with $n = 5$ bits plus
sign to permit replacement of the analog integrator in Fig. 11-29a by a
passive RC network, so that each integrator requires only one relatively
inexpensive d-c amplifier.   Tests with artificial analog errors indicate
that their effects are as small as predicted.[96,97]

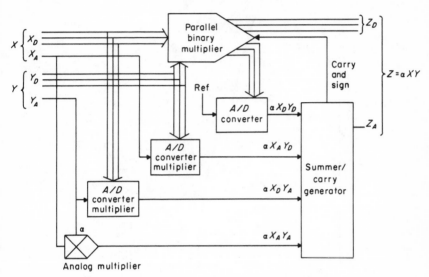

FIG. 11-29b. A hybrid-code multiplier.   The circuit implements

$$\alpha XY = \alpha(X_D + X_A)(Y_D + Y_A) = \alpha X_D Y_D + \alpha X_D Y_A + \alpha X_A Y_D + \alpha X_A Y_A$$

with $\alpha = 2^{-n}$, where X_D, X_A, Y_D, Y_A are measured in machine units.   Hybrid-code
multiplication is an especially attractive application of the hybrid-code technique.
Since $|\alpha X_A Y_A| \leq 2^{-n}$, the analog-multiplier accuracy need only be within $2^n p$ per cent
of analog half-scale; it may, then, be possible to omit the analog multiplier entirely.

Digital data transfer between computing elements can be total or incremental.
Each increment $\Delta \dot{X}_D$, like ΔX_D, is simply represented by a carry pulse plus a d-c
carry-sign signal.   With the complemented code of Table 11-1, a simple reversible
counter then produces $\dot{X}_D$ from $\Delta \dot{X}_D$.   The digital integrator adds $\dot{X}_D$ into an R
register, like a DDA integrator (Sec. 11-17b); the less significant R-register bits contribute to the analog output X_A and/or its carries.   Referring to Fig. 11-29a, X_A
appears at the output of a summer, which sums three contributions:

1. The fractional part of the R-register output, obtained through a D/A converter.
2. An interpolating voltage, which increases linearly from zero to $a\dot{X}_D T$ during
   each analog computing period and then returns to zero; this is obtained through
   multiplication of $\dot{X}_D$ by a constant sawtooth waveform in a second D/A
   converter.[94,96]
3. The integrated analog voltage $a \int_0^\tau \dot{X}_A \, d\tau$.

It will be wise to avoid programs producing digital integrator outputs due solely to analog inputs. The reader is referred to Wait's paper for further details.

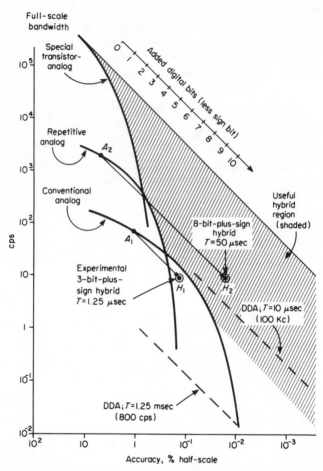

FIG. 11-30. Accuracy/bandwidth relations for analog, incremental-transfer DDA, and hybrid-code representations of dynamical variables. Accuracy is represented by the smallest correctly resolved increment expressed in per cent of half-scale. Full-scale bandwidth is the frequency B of the fastest full-scale sine wave $a \sin 2\pi Bt$ reproducible without rate limiting. Points for each hybrid-code representation are obtained by adding digital-bit "vectors" to points representing analog-component performance, as shown by two examples (based on refs. 95 and 96).

(d) Accuracy/Bandwidth Limitations.[95] The computing speed of any hybrid-code integrator is ultimately limited by the maximum possible analog-voltage rate of change, for

$$E \left| \frac{dX}{d\tau} \right|_{\text{MAX}} = \left| \frac{dX_A}{d\tau} \right|_{\text{MAX}} = 2\pi EB_{\text{ANALOG}} \qquad (11\text{-}10)$$

where B_{ANALOG} is the *full-scale analog bandwidth*, i.e., the frequency of the fastest full-scale sinusoidal voltage $E \sin 2\pi B_{\text{ANALOG}}\tau$ reproducible with the specified accuracy. It follows that the *full-scale hybrid-code bandwidth* B_{HYBRID}, i.e., the frequency of the fastest full-scale sinusoid $2^n \sin 2\pi B_{\text{HYBRID}}\tau$ (machine units) is

$$B_{\text{HYBRID}} = \frac{1}{2\pi}\frac{1}{2^n}\left.\frac{dX}{d\tau}\right|_{\text{MAX}} = \frac{B_{\text{ANALOG}}}{2^n} \qquad (11\text{-}11)$$

Hence, *every digital bit added to double the computing accuracy will halve the computing bandwidth*. This accuracy/bandwidth relationship limits the spectrum of possible hybrid-code differential analyzers with true continuous integration (Fig. 11-30).

11-20. Hybrid Analog-digital Function Generators.[74–86]   Hybrid analog-digital function generators may be designed to work with analog or hybrid-code computing systems, or even with digital computers (Sec. 11-16). Existing designs are largely experimental, fairly complex, and not much more accurate than combinations of high-quality diode function generators and electronic multipliers. Nevertheless, the convenience of digital function storage and fast function setting is of interest, especially in connection with functions of two variables.

Most hybrid function generators designed to generate a given analog function of an analog input X actually produce a suitably fitted polygonal approximation $F(X)$ defined by

$$\left.\begin{aligned}F(X) &= F(X_i) + a_i(X - X_i)\\ a_i &= \frac{F(X_{i+1}) - F(X_i)}{X_{i+1} - X_i}\end{aligned}\right\} \quad (X_i \le X < X_{i+1}; i = 1,2,\ldots) \quad (11\text{-}12)$$

with breakpoints X_i and slopes a_i, just like a diode function generator. Referring to Fig. 11-31a, the X_i, $F(X_i)$, and a_i are stored in digital form. We convert X with a coarse (4- to 6-bit) A/D converter to identify the nearest breakpoint $X_i \le X$ and use a digital table, typically a diode matrix,[83] to find $F(X_i)$ and a_i. The desired polygonal approximation (12) is now generated with D/A multipliers and summing amplifiers. With uniformly spaced breakpoints, $X_i = X_D$ and $(X - X_i) = X_A$ constitute a hybrid-code representation (Sec. 11-19) of X, so that our function generator is also suitable for hybrid-code input.[83] Several different versions of this basic design have been suggested.[83,84] To produce functions of two analog inputs X, Y, one can similarly generate approximations of the form

$$F(X,Y) = F(X_i,Y_k) + a_{ik}(X - X_i) + b_{ik}(Y - Y_k) \quad (11\text{-}13)$$

over triangular or square regions of the XY plane.[84]

The Comcor, Inc., Universal Nonlinear Element (UNE, Fig. 11-31b)[86] is a hybrid function generator designed to produce analog products $\beta Y F(X)$, where X, Y are analog

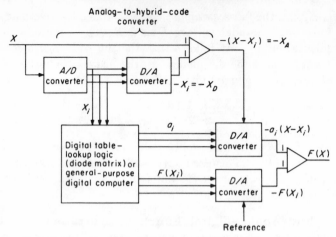

FIG. 11-31a. A hybrid analog-digital function generator using linear interpolation.

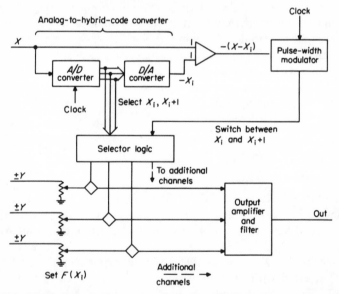

FIG. 11-31b. Block diagram illustrating the principle of the Comcor, Inc., Universal Nonlinear Element (see text). Accuracy (not including polygonal-approximation errors) specified to be within 0.05 per cent of the 100-volt half-scale at d-c, and within 1 per cent at 100 cps. Output ripple and noise are within 100 mV peak to peak.

inputs. Starting again with an analog-to-hybrid-code converter, the digital output X_i in Fig. 11-31b operates digital logic to select two analog switches connected to voltages $YF(X_i)$ and $YF(X_{i+1})$. The X_i are uniformly spaced breakpoint voltages, and the $F(X_i)$ are set on potentiometers. The residual analog output $X - X_i$ of the converter modulates the pulsewidth of a switching waveform S, just as in a triggered time-division multiplier. Scaling is such that the ON period of S is proportional to $X - X_i$, while that of its complement $\tilde{S}$ is proportional to $X_{i+1} - X$. Now S and $\tilde{S}$ alternately gate $YF(X_{i+1})$ and $YF(X_i)$ into the output filter to produce the filtered output

$$\alpha Y[F(X_i)(X_{i+1} - X) + F(X_{i+1})(X - X_i)]$$
$$= \beta Y\left[F(X_i) + \frac{(FX_{i+1}) - F(X_i)}{X_{i+1} - X_i}(X - X_i)\right] \qquad (X_i \le X < X_{i+1}; i = 1,2, \ldots)$$
$$(11\text{-}14)$$

so that we again have linear interpolation between the $F(X_i)$. More complicated functions of X and Y may be obtained through substitution of a function $G_i(Y)$ for each potentiometer input Y in Fig. 11-31b.

REFERENCES AND BIBLIOGRAPHY

Analog-computer System Design

See also *Proc. 1st to 4th AICA Conf.*, Presses Académiques Européennes, Brussels; and refs. 37 to 45 in Chap. 10.

1. Edwards, C. M.: A New Approach to Grounding in D-c Analog Computers, *Proc. Western Joint Computer Conf.*, 1955.
2. McCoy, R. D., and B. D. Loveman: Problem Checker Checks Computer, Too, *Control Eng.*, July, 1955.
3. Kamm, L. J.: Analog-computer Problem Connector Employs Punched Card and Crossbar, *Electronics*, Aug. 18, 1961.
4. ———: Contact Pattern Aligns Printed-circuit Matrix, *Electronics*, Aug. 25, 1961.
5. Korn, G. A.: Analog Computers in the Electrical Engineering Department, *Instrument and Control Systems*, September, 1959.
6. ———: Complete Electronic Analog Computers; Small and Medium-sized Computers, in Huskey, H. D., and G. A. Korn, *Computer Handbook*, McGraw-Hill, New York, 1962.
7. Kusto, T. J.: Patchbays, Interconnections, and Enclosures, in Huskey, H. D., and G. A. Korn, *Computer Handbook*, McGraw-Hill, New York, 1962.
8. Loveman, B. D.: Semiautomatic Programming, in Huskey, H. D., and G. A. Korn, *Computer Handbook*, McGraw-Hill, New York, 1962.
9. ———: Problem-checking Circuits and Procedures, in Huskey, H. D., and G. A. Korn, *Computer Handbook*, McGraw-Hill, New York, 1962.
10. Rogers, S.: Complete Electronic Analog Computers: Large Installations, in Huskey, H. D., and G. A. Korn, *Computer Handbook*, McGraw-Hill, New York, 1962.
11. Meyer-Brötz, G.: Ein transistorisierter Präzisions-Analogrechner, *Telefunken Z.*, September, 1960.

Direct-writing Recorders

12. Pierce, D. E.: Pressurized-ink Recording, *Instruments and Control Systems*, March, 1962.
13. Zusi, F. C.: Nomenclature for Direct-writing Recorders, *Instruments and Control Systems*, July, 1961.
14. Miller, A.: Factors Affecting Accuracy of Oscillographic Records, *The Right Angle*, Sanborn Co., Waltham, Mass., August and November, 1953.
15. ———: Design Considerations of d'Arsonval-Galvanometer/Power-amplifier Systems, *The Right Angle*, Sanborn Co., Waltham, Mass., August and November, 1958.
16. Vance, P. R., and D. L. Haas: An Input-output Unit for Analog Computers, *Proc. IRE*, October, 1953.

Power Supplies

17. Hunter, L. P. (Ed.): *Handbook of Semiconductor Electronics,* 2d ed., McGraw-Hill, New York, 1962.
18. Texas Instruments, Inc., Engineering Staff: *Transistor Circuit Design,* McGraw-Hill, New York, 1963.
19. Currector Current Regulators: *Application Notes* A-500, Circuitdyne Corp., Laguna Beach, Calif., 1962.
20. Foiles, C., J. Hartmann, and H. Koerner: Reference Power Supply, *Electronic Design,* May 10, 1959.

Analog-computer Test Circuits and Maintenance Procedures
(See also bibliographies for Chaps. 4 to 8)

21. Hamer, H., and J. D. Kennedy: Testing Operational Amplifiers, *J. Assoc. Computing Machinery,* April, 1955.
22. Horwitz, R. D.: Maintaining an Analog Computing System, *Electronic Inds.,* December, 1958.
23. Sykes, R. P.: A Preventive-maintenance Program for Large General-purpose Electronic Analog Computers, *Memorandum,* Space Technology Laboratories (then Ramo-Wooldridge Corp.), Los Angeles, Calif., 1958.
24. ———: Calibration of High-resistance Padded Resistors, *Instruments and Control Systems,* October, 1959.
25. ———: Calibrating Analog-computer Integrators, *Instruments and Control Systems,* September, 1960.
26. Ehlers, H. L., and W. Hochwald: Maintenance Procedures and Test Circuits, in Huskey, H. D., and G. A. Korn, *Computer Handbook,* McGraw-Hill, New York, 1962.
27. Loveman, B. D.: Problem-checking Circuits and Procedures, in Huskey, H. D., and G. A. Korn, *Computer Handbook,* McGraw-Hill, New York, 1962.

Computer-aided Analog Programming

28. Green, C., et al.: The Code APACHE for the Programming of an Analog Problem by Means of a Digital Computer, *Proc. 3d AICA Conf.,* Opatija, Yugoslavia, 1961; Presses Académiques Européennes, Brussels, 1962; reprinted in *Ann. AICA,* April, 1963.
29. ———: APACHE—A Breakthrough in Analog Computing, *IRETEC,* October, 1962.
30. Stein, M. L.: Automatic Digital Programming of Analog Computers, *IEEETEC,* April, 1963.

Digital/Analog/Digital Converters

31. Truitt, T.: A High-speed Analog-digital Converter, *PCC Rept.* 134, Electronic Associates, Inc., Princeton, N.J., 1958.
32. Susskind, A. K.: *Notes on Analog-digital Conversion Techniques,* Wiley, New York, 1958.
33. Savitt, A.: A High-speed Analog-to-digital Converter, *IRETEC,* March, 1959.
34. Platzek, R. C., et al.: A High-speed Electronic Analog-to-digital Encoder, *Publ.* 516B, Autonetics Division, North American Aviation, Inc., Downey, Calif., 1959.
35. Rall, B.: Ein Digitalvoltmeter hoher Genauigkeit mit Transistoren, *Telefunken Z.,* September, 1960.

36. Farrand, W. A.: A/D Converters and D/A Converters, in Huskey, H. D., and G. A. Korn, *Computer Handbook*, McGraw-Hill, New York, 1962.
37. *Analog/Digital Conversion Handbook*, Digital Equipment Corp., Maynard, Mass., 1962.
38. Barbour, C. W.: Capcoder A/D Converter, *Instruments and Control Systems*, August, 1962.
39. Kiyono, T., et al.: Analog-to-digital Converter Utilizing an Esaki-diode Stack, *IRETEC*, December, 1962.
40. Wait, J. V., and B. A. Mitchell: A Simple Solid-state Digital-to-analog Converter for Hybrid Computing Systems, *ACL Memo* 61, Electrical Engineering Department, University of Arizona, 1963.

Combined Analog-digital Simulation

41. Paskman, M.: Operation and Application of the GE-MSVD combined Analog-digital Computer System, *Flight Mechanics Fundamentals Memo* 11, General Electric Co./MSVD, Philadelphia, Pa., 1960.
42. Levy, H.: New NASA/AF/Navy Joint Computing Facility Combines Analog and Digital Techniques, *Datamation*, 1960.
43. Burns, A. J., and R. E. Kopp: Combined Analog-digital Simulation, *Proc. Eastern Joint Computer Conf.*, 1961.
44. Wilson, A.: Use of a Combined Analog-digital System for Re-entry Vehicle Flight Simulation, *Proc. Eastern Joint Computer Conf.*, 1961.
45. *Proc. Combined Analog-digital Systems Symposium*, Philadelphia, 1960, Simulation Councils, Inc., La Jolla, Calif., 1961.
46. Greenstein, J. L., and R. M. Leger: Combined Use of Analog and Digital Computers, in Huskey, H. D., and G. A. Korn, *Computer Handbook*, McGraw-Hill, New York, 1962.
47. Miura, T., et al.: The Design and Application of a Hybrid Computer, *Proc. 3d AICA Conf.*, Opatija, Yugoslavia, 1961, Presses Académiques Européennes, Brussels, 1962.
48. *Hybrid Computation Course Notes*, Electronic Associates, Inc., Princeton, N.J., 1962, 1963, 1964.
49. King, C. M., and R. Gelman: Experience with Hybrid Computations, *Proc. Fall Joint Computer Conf.*, 1962.
50. Karplus, W., and G. Bekey: Hybrid Computing Techniques, *Course Notes*, UCLA Extension Division, Los Angeles, Calif., 1963.
51. Gelman, R.: Corrected Inputs, A Method for Improving Hybrid Simulation, *Proc. Fall Joint Computer Conf.*, 1963.
52. Miura, T., and J. Iwata: Effects of Digital Execution Time in a Hybrid Computer, *Proc. Fall Joint Computer Conf.*, 1963.
53. Truitt, T. J.: HYDAC 2400, *ASG Rept.* 11-63, Electronic Associates, Inc., Princeton, N.J., 1963.

Digital-computer Programming for Simulation

54. Hurley, J. R.: DEPI (Differential Equations Pseudo-code Interpreter), An Analog-computer Simulator, *Allis-Chalmers Mfg. Co. Memo.*, January, 1960.
55. Ohlinger, L. A.: "Anatran"—First Step in Breeding the "Diganalog," *Proc. Western Joint Computer Conf.*, 1960.
56. Gaskill, R. A., et al.: DAS—A Digital Analog Simulator, *Proc. Spring Joint Computer Conf.*, 1963.
57. Hurley, J. R., and J. J. Skiles: DYSAC, a Digitally Simulated Analog Computer, *Proc. Spring Joint Computer Conf.*, 1963.

58. Palevsky, M., and J. V. Howell: The DES-1, a Real-time Simulation Computer, *Proc. Fall Joint Computer Conf.*, 1963.

59. Grabbe, E. M., S. Ramo, and D. E. Wooldridge: *Handbook of Automation, Computation, and Control*, vol. 2, Wiley, New York, 1958.

60. Palevsky, M.: Digital Differential Analyzers, in Huskey, H. D., and G. A. Korn, *Computer Handbook*, McGraw-Hill, New York, 1962.

61. Bradley, R. E., and J. F. Genna: Design of a One-megacycle Iteration Rate DDA, *Proc. Spring Joint Computer Conf.*, 1962.

62. Nelson, D. J.: DDA Error Analysis Using Sampled-data Techniques, *Proc. Spring Joint Computer Conf.*, 1962; see also *Comm. ACM*, **5:** 143 (1962).

63. Hills, F.: Application Studies of Combined Analog-digital Computation Techniques, *Rept.* E SL-FR-165, MIT Electronic Systems Laboratory, 1963.

64. ————: Characteristics and Limitations of Digital-computer Solutions to Differential Equations, MIT Ph.D. Thesis, Cambridge, Mass., 1963.

65. Burt, R. W.: Optimum Design and Error Analysis of Digital Integrators, M.S. Thesis, University of Arizona, 1963.

MIT Pulsed-analog-computer Project
(Electronic Systems Laboratory, MIT)

66. Herzog, A. W.: Pulsed Analog Computer for Simulation of Aircraft, *Proc. IRE*, May, 1959.

67. Lee, R. C., and F. B. Cox: A High-speed Analog-digital Computer for Simulation, *IRETEC*, June, 1959.

68. Bell, C. G.: The Pulsed Analog System for Evaluating Correlation Functions for Radar, *Rept.* 8494-R-1, Aug. 9, 1960.

69. Binsack, J. H.: A Pulsed Analog and Digital Computer for Function Generation, *Rept.* 8494-R-2, October, 1960.

70. Krasny, L. M.: The Functional Design of a Special-purpose Digital Computer for Real-time Flight Simulation, *Rept.* ESL-R-118, August, 1961.

71. Connelly, M. E.: Analog-digital Computers for Real-time Simulation, *Rept.* ESL-FR-110, June, 1961; see also *IRETEC*, February, 1962.

72. Decanini, J.: Dynamic Simulation of a Distillation Column with a Combined Analog-digital Computer, *Rept.* ESL-R-102, no. 4, 1962.

73. Hills, F. B.: Application Studies of Combined Analog-digital Computation Techniques, *Rept.* ESL-FR-165, 1963.

Hybrid Function Generators

74. Harris, J. N.: A Programmed Variable-rate Counter for Generating the Sine Function, *IRETEC*, March, 1956.

75. Hofheimer, R. N., and K. E. Perry: Digital-analog Function Generators, *IRETEC*, March, 1958.

76. Alexander, M. A.: Generate Better Curves with Digital-analog Techniques, *Electronic Design*, Mar. 4, 1959.

77. Smolov, V. B.: One Method of Designing Two-input Electronic Function Generators, *Automatika i Telemekhanika*, October, 1959.

78. ————: Electronic Decoding and Coding Function Generators, *Automatika i Telemekhanika*, February, 1961.

79. Eggers, C. W., and T. W. Sze: A New Function Generator, *Trans. AIEE (Communications and Electronics)*, January, 1961.

80. *A Digital-controlled Function Generator*, Navigation Computer Corp., Philadelphia, Pa., 1961.

81. Beck, R. M., and J. M. Mitchell: DAFT—A Digital/Analog Function Table,

Proc. *Western Joint Computer Conf.*, 1960; see also *Automatic Control*, February, 1960.

82. Schmid, H.: *Proc. Combined Analog-digital Computer Systems Symposium*, Philadelphia, Pa., Dec. 16–17, 1960; published by Simulation Councils, Inc., 8484 La Jolla Shores Dr., La Jolla, Calif.

83. ———: Linear-segment Function Generator, *IRETEC*, December, 1962.

84. Chapelle, W. E.: Hybrid Techniques for Analog Function Generation, *Proc. Spring Joint Computer Conf.*, 1963.

85. Heid, J. P.: *A Hybrid Polar/Cartesian Coordinate Converter*, Drexel Dynamics Corp., Horsham, Pa., 1963.

86. Universal Nonlinear Element Model CI-230, *Instruction Manual*, Comcor, Inc., Denver, Colo., 1963.

Computers with Hybrid-code Representation of Variables

87. Myers, G. H.: Extending the Operational Time of Integrators, *IRETEC*, March, 1957.

88. Jarrett, R. J.: An Analog RC Integrator with Digital Output, *Proc. Natl. Electronics Conf.*, 1960.

89. Systron-Donner Corp.: Advertisement, *Instruments and Control Systems*, July, 1962.

90. An Electronic Two-variable Function Generator, *WADC Tech. Rept. 59-546*, Wright Aeronautical Development Center, Ohio, 1959.

91. Schmid, H.: A High-accuracy Partial Analog-to-digital Converter, *Rept. DRL 557*, Link Aviation, Inc., Binghamton, N.Y., 1960.

92. Haddican, P. J., and G. B. Whitman: An Analog-to-hybrid Converter, *ACL Memo 53*, Electrical Engineering Department, University of Arizona, 1962.

93. Skramstad, H. K.: A Combined Analog-digital Differential Analyzer, *Proc. Eastern Joint Computer Conf.*, 1959.

94. Schmid, H.: Combined Analog-digital Computing Elements, *Proc. Western Joint Computer Conf.*, 1961.

95. Korn, G. A.: The Impact Hybrid Analog-digital Techniques on the Analog-computer Art, *Proc. IRE*, May, 1962 (anniversary issue).

96. Wait, J. V.: A Hybrid Analog-digital Differential-analyzer System, Ph.D. Thesis, University of Arizona, 1963; see also *Proc. Fall Joint Computer Conf.*, 1963.

97. O'Grady, P.: A Simplified Hybrid Differential Analyzer, M.S. Thesis, University of Arizona, 1964.

98. Whigham, R.: A Hybrid-computer Multiplier, M.S. Thesis, University of Arizona, 1964.

ASTRAC II Project

99. Eckes, H. R., and G. A. Korn: Digital Program Control for Iterative Differential Analyzers, *ACL Memo 86*, Electrical Engineering Department, University of Arizona, 1963; *SIMULATION*, February, 1964.

100. Korn, G. A.: High-speed Iterative Analog-digital Computation: The ASTRAC II Project, *Proc. 4th AICA Conf.*, Brighton, England, 1964; Presses Académiques Européennes, Brussels, 1965.

101. Mitchell, B. A.: Hybrid Analog-digital Parameter Optimizer for ASTRAC II, M.S. Thesis, University of Arizona, 1964; *Proc. Spring Joint Computer Conf.*, 1964.

102. Hampton, R.: A Hybrid Analog-digital Pseudo-random-noise Generator, M.S. Thesis, University of Arizona, 1964; *Proc. Spring Joint Computer Conf.*, 1964.

103. Maybach, R.: A Hybrid Analog-digital Sample-averaging Computer, *ACL Memo 85*, Electrical Engineering Department, University of Arizona, 1963.

Pulse-modulation Representation of Data

104. Bohn, E. V.: A Pulse-position-modulation Analog Computer, *IRETEC*, June, 1960.

105. Paul, R. J. A.: Hybrid Methods for Function Generation, *Proc. 3d AICA Conf.*, Opatija, Yugoslavia, 1961, Presses Académiques Européennes, Brussels, 1962. See also *Control Eng.*, 1962.

106. Schaefer, R. A.: Pulse Modulator for Accurate D-c Amplification, *IRE Trans. PGI*, September, 1962.

107. ———: New Pulse Modulation Method, *Electronics*, Oct. 12, 1962.

108. Crayford, R. M.: APD Coding and Logic, *Instruments and Control Systems*, January, 1962.

109. Seegmiller, W. R.: Accurate Analog Computation with Pulse-time Modulation, *Electronics*, Mar. 30, 1962.

110. Digital-analog Pulse-time Circuits, Staff Report, *Computer Design*, June, 1963.

111. Schmid, H.: A Hybrid Operational Computing System, M.S. Thesis, Syracuse University, 1963; see also *IEEETEC*, October, 1963.

112. ———: A Repetitive Analog Computing Technique with a Digital Integrator, *Proc. Intern. Aerospace Conference*, Phoenix, Ariz., 1964.

113. ——— and B. Grindle: A Precision Pulse-width Modulator, *Electronics*, May 12, 1964.

Miscellaneous Techniques

114. MacKay, D. M., and M. E. Fisher: *Analogue Computing at Ultra-high Speed*, Wiley, New York, 1962.

115. Hamming, R. W.: *Numerical Methods for Scientists and Engineers*, McGraw-Hill, New York, 1962.

116. MacNee, A. B.: An Electronic Differential Analyzer, *Proc. IRE*, **37**: 1315 (1949).

117. Palevsky, M.: Hybrid Analog-digital Computing Systems, *Instruments and Automation*, October, 1957.

118. Truitt, T. D.: An Analog-digital Real-time Computer, *IRETEC*, February, 1962.

119. Hagan, T. G.: Ambilog Computers: Hybrid Machines for Measurement-system Calculation Tasks, *Proc. 17th Annual ISA Conf.*, New York, October, 1962.

120. ———: Hybrid Logic for Special-purpose Computers, *Control Eng.*, October, 1962.

121. Baker, R. H., et al.: The Diamond Circuit, *Tech. Rept.* 300, Lincoln Laboratory, MIT, Lexington, Mass., 1963.

122. Stewart, E. L.: Grounds, Grounds, and More Grounds, *Analog Rept.* 9, The Martin Co., Baltimore, Md., 1963.

123. Sargent, R. S., and T. R. Kuchlewski: The Reduction of Noise in Low-impedance (Ground) Lines, *Analog Rept.* 16, The Martin Co., Baltimore, Md., 1963.

124. Transistorized Voltage Regulators, *Application Guide*, Radio Corp. of America, Camden, N.J., 1961.

125. Pearman, C. R., and A. E. Popodi: How to Design High-speed D/A Converters, *Electronics*, Feb. 21, 1964.

ADVANCED COMPUTER
UTILIZATION

CHAPTER **12**

MORE ADVANCED
COMPUTING TECHNIQUES

INTRODUCTION AND SURVEY

12-1. Requirement for Advanced Computing Techniques. Analog computers, and especially fast analog computers, are, essentially, relatively inaccurate. Although static component accuracies within 0.1 per cent of half-scale are not uncommon, dynamic errors measured at the 100-cps to 100-Kc signal frequencies of modern iterative differential analyzers are rarely below 0.5 per cent of half-scale. Errors in this range would be perfectly acceptable in most engineering applications, if we could only be sure that component errors will not accumulate into intolerable solution errors.

A very powerful computing technique employs the analog computer to produce *corrections* to an accurate analytically or digitally precomputed approximate solution (Secs. 12-2 to 12-4). Such a *perturbation method* may reduce solution errors well below the level of analog-component errors, which will now affect only a small correction to our solution. Where applicable, such techniques are greatly preferable to expensive and probably futile schemes for increasing analog component accuracies. New combinations of analog and digital computing elements often make it possible to let the accurate but slow digital computer produce a precisely known drift- and noise-free approximate solution, which can then be corrected by fast analog computing elements.

We are, next, vitally interested in *methods for estimating component-error effects on computer solutions.* Sections 12-4 and 12-5 discuss techniques employing the computer itself to perform such estimates.

The development of new fast iterative differential analyzers with

505

memory and sophisticated sequential logic (Chap. 10) offers computing possibilities way beyond ordinary direct simulation, but only if mathematical development of convergent iteration techniques and error control keeps pace with circuit and system design.   The most urgent requirement is for methods utilizing the extraordinary speed of iterative analog computation directly to make up for its poor accuracy.   Aside from random-process studies,[107] the most promising application of iterative differential analyzers is *automatic parameter optimization* (Secs. 12-7 to 12-16); many important problems can be reduced to the computation of maxima or minima.   Even more badly needed, but in a less satisfactory state of development, are computer techniques for *iterative solution of partial differential equations*, especially in connection with process-control and nuclear-power applications (Secs. 12-17 to 12-22).

**GAUGING AND IMPROVING COMPUTER ACCURACY:
PERTURBATIONS, PARAMETER SENSITIVITY,
RESUBSTITUTION, AND AUTOMATIC SCALING**

12-2. Perturbations and Linearization.[3]   Our problem is to solve the first-order differential equation

$$\frac{d}{dt}\, x(t) = f(t,x;\alpha) \tag{12-1}$$

for the state variable $x = x(t)$, where α is a given parameter, initial value, or forcing function; note that α can be a function $\alpha(t)$ of the independent variable t.   We assume that $\alpha(t) = \alpha_0(t) + \delta\alpha(t)$ does not change greatly from its nominal or unperturbed value $\alpha_0(t)$, and that we know the *nominal or unperturbed solution* $x_0(t)$ defined by

$$\frac{d}{dt}\, x_0(t) = f(t,x_0;\alpha_0) \tag{12-2}$$

accurately from analysis or from another computation.   Granting suitable differentiability, we introduce $\delta x = x - x_0 = \delta x(t)$ and use the Taylor-series approximation

$$\frac{dx}{dt} = \frac{dx_0}{dt} + \frac{d}{dt}\, \delta x = f(t,x;\alpha) \approx f(t,x_0;\alpha_0) + f_x(t,x_0;\alpha_0)\, \delta x + f_\alpha(t,x_0;\alpha_0)\, \delta\alpha \tag{12-3}$$

We subtract Eq. (2), so that, *for sufficiently small* $\delta\alpha$, δx,

$$\frac{d}{dt}\, \delta x = f_x(t,x_0;\alpha_0)\, \delta x + f_\alpha(t,x_0;\alpha_0)\, \delta\alpha \tag{12-4}$$

This *perturbation equation** is a *linear* differential equation relating the

---

* See footnote to Sec. 12-4.

unknown small *perturbation* δx of our nominal solution to the given input $\delta\alpha$.   Computer solution of Eq. (4) for δx is simple *if* we can produce the derivatives $f_x(t,x_0;\alpha_0)$, $f_\alpha(t,x_0;\alpha_0)$ which will, in general, depend on the nominal solution $x_0(t)$.   *If $x_0(t)$ is accurately precomputed analytically, digitally, or by accurate "slow" analog computation, then errors in the solution $\delta x(t)$ of Eq. (4) will have a relatively small effect on the total solution* $x(t) = x_0(t) + \delta x(t)$.

Our linear perturbation analysis is easily extended to cases involving n state variables $x_1, x_2, \ldots, x_n$ and r parameters $\alpha_1, \alpha_2, \ldots, \alpha_r$. Given

$$\left.\frac{dx_i}{dt} = f_i(t;x_1,x_2, \ldots ,x_n;\alpha_1,\alpha_2, \ldots ,\alpha_r) \atop \text{with} \quad x_i = x_{0i} + \delta x_i \quad\quad \alpha_k = \alpha_{0k} + \delta\alpha_k \right\} \begin{array}{l}(i = 1,2, \ldots ,n; \\ \quad k = 1,2, \ldots ,r)\end{array} \quad (12\text{-}5)$$

we find, assuming differentiability and valid linearization,

$$\frac{d}{dt}\delta x_i = \sum_{k=1}^{n} \frac{\partial f_i}{\partial x_k}\delta x_k + \sum_{k=1}^{r} \frac{\partial f_i}{\partial \alpha_k}\delta\alpha_k \quad\quad (i = 1,2, \ldots ,n) \quad (12\text{-}6)$$

This is, again, a linear system with (in general) variable coefficients. Equations (1) and (4) are equivalent to Eqs. (5) and (6) if we regard x, x_0, δx, f as $n \times 1$ matrices, α, α_0, $\delta\alpha$ as $r \times 1$ matrices, f_x as an $n \times n$ matrix, and f_α as an $n \times r$ matrix.

The linear nature of the perturbation equations (4) or (6) can be of the greatest value even where increased accuracy is not needed.   In an important class of applications (e.g., space-vehicle trajectory computation), $\delta\alpha$ represents a small random forcing function or random initial-condition perturbation with known statistics. It is then relatively simple to obtain the resulting mean-square perturbation of x or x_i.[6,107]

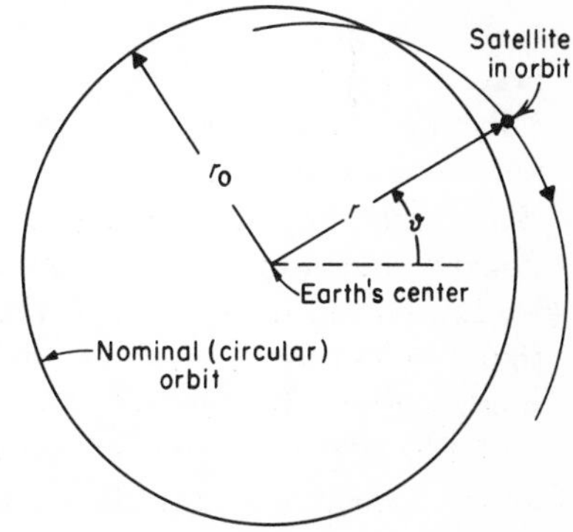

FIG. 12-1. Satellite-orbit geometry.

12-3. Example: Earth-satellite Orbit and Reentry Computation.[8-10]

Figure 12-1 illustrates a plane earth-satellite trajectory.   In terms of the inertial-reference coordinates r, ϑ, the equations of motion are

$$m\frac{d\dot{r}}{dt} = mr\dot{\vartheta}^2 - \frac{mg_0r_0^2}{r^2} + F_r \quad\quad m\frac{d}{dt}(r^2\dot{\vartheta}) = rF_\vartheta \quad\quad (12\text{-}7)$$

if we regard the vehicle as a constant point mass. $mr\dot{\vartheta}^2$ is a kinetic reaction (centrifugal "force"), $mg_0r_0^2/r^2$ is the idealized inverse-square-law gravity force, and F_r, F_ϑ are forces due to aerodynamic effects and gravity changes.

For an ideal circular orbit with $F_r = F_\vartheta = 0$, $r = r_0$ implies

$$\vartheta = \vartheta_0(t) = \vartheta(0) + t\sqrt{\frac{g_0}{r_0}} \tag{12-8}$$

Since the subtraction of the two large first terms on the right of the first Eq. (7) tends to make direct computer solutions inaccurate, we write

$$r = r_0(1 + \delta\rho) \qquad r\dot\vartheta = \sqrt{g_0 r_0}\,(1 + \delta u) \tag{12-9}$$

$\delta\rho$ and δu are new dimensionless variables describing the relative perturbation of a nominal circular orbit due to nonzero values of F_r, F_ϑ, $\dot r(0)$, and $\dot\vartheta(0) - \sqrt{g_0/r_0}$. $\delta\rho$ measures the relative altitude increase, and δu is the fractional change in the horizontal velocity component. We introduce Eqs. (8) and (9) into Eq. (7) to find new equations of motion in terms of $\delta\rho$ and δu:

$$\left.\begin{aligned}
\frac{d^2}{dt^2}\delta\rho &= \frac{g_0}{r_0}\left[\frac{2\delta u + \delta u^2}{1 + \delta\rho} + \frac{\delta\rho}{(1 + \delta\rho)^2} + \frac{F_r}{mg_0}\right] \\
\delta u &= \frac{1}{1 + \delta\rho}\left\{\sqrt{\frac{g_0}{r_0}}\int_0^t (1 + \delta\rho)\frac{F_\vartheta}{mg_0}\,dt - \delta\rho \right. \\
&\qquad\qquad\left. + (\delta\rho + \delta u + \delta\rho\,\delta u)_{t=0}\right\}
\end{aligned}\right\} \tag{12-10}$$

Note carefully that the differential equations (10) are *not* linearized; their exact solution would yield the perturbations $\delta\rho$, δu *exactly*. In practice, computer errors affect only perturbations of a precisely (analytically) known nominal orbit, so that remarkably accurate trajectory computations result. For $r_0 = 4{,}000$ miles, $r_0|\delta\rho| < 80$ miles, we have $|\delta\rho| < 0.02$, so that $(5{,}000\delta\rho)$ is a suitably scaled computer voltage. Fogarty and Howe[8-10] have implemented the divisions by $1 + \delta\rho$ required for Eq. (10) in the manner of Fig. 2-4d with $a\alpha = 1$ and $b/100 = 0.02$, so that the effects of multiplication errors on the quotient were relatively small. Errors in many computed earth orbits were within 200 ft.

If the relative perturbations $\delta\rho$ and δu remain small compared with unity, one can linearize the equations of motion (10) by neglecting nonlinear terms. In particular, for the classical case of a low-eccentricity elliptical inverse-square-law orbit in air-free space, Eq. (10) reduces approximately to

$$\frac{d^2}{dt^2}\delta\rho = \frac{g_0}{r_0}(2\delta u + \delta\rho) \qquad \delta u = -\delta\rho + [\delta\rho + \delta u]_{t=0} \tag{12-11}$$

which correctly describes sinusoidal perturbation of a nominal circular orbit by given initial velocities.

12-4. Parameter-influence Coefficients and Parameter-sensitivity Studies.[1,2,5,6] If the parameter α in the given differential equation (1) is independent of t (e.g., a constant coefficient or an initial value), we can define the *parameter-influence coefficient*

$$\lim_{\delta\alpha \to 0} \frac{\delta x(t)}{\delta\alpha} = \frac{\partial x}{\partial\alpha} = x_\alpha(t) \tag{12-12}$$

Again, assuming suitable differentiability, $x(t)$ *measures the sensitivity of our solution* $x(t)$ *to small changes* $\delta\alpha$ *in the parameter* α. For each nominal parameter value $\alpha = \alpha_0$,

$$x(t) = x_0(t) + \delta x \approx x_0(t) + x_\alpha(t)\,\delta\alpha \tag{12-13}$$

The parameter-influence coefficient $x_\alpha(t)$ satisfies the linear *sensitivity equation**

$$\frac{d}{dt}\,x_\alpha(t) = f_x(t,x_0;\alpha_0)x_\alpha(t) + f_\alpha(t,x_0;\alpha_0) \tag{12-14}$$

obtained by partial differentiation of the given differential equation (1) with respect to α. We can obtain $x_\alpha(t)$ as a solution of Eq. (14) with the suitably assigned initial value $x_\alpha(0)$.

In the multidimensional case, we have an $n \times r$ matrix of parameter-influence coefficients $x_{ik}(t) = \partial x_i/\partial\alpha_k$ ($i = 1,2, \ldots ,n; k = 1,2, \ldots ,r$), with

$$x_i(t) = x_{0i}(t) + \delta x_i \approx x_{0i}(t) + \sum_{k=1}^{r} x_{ik}(t)\delta\alpha_k \quad (i = 1,2, \ldots ,n) \tag{12-15}$$

and $n \times r$ linear sensitivity equations

$$\frac{d}{dt}\,x_{ik}(t) = \sum_{j=1}^{n} \frac{\partial f_i}{\partial x_j}\,x_{jk}(t) + \frac{\partial f_i}{\partial\alpha_k} \quad (i = 1,2, \ldots ,n; k = 1,2, \ldots ,r)$$

$$\tag{12-16}$$

Analytical or computer studies of parameter sensitivity can yield valuable information on the effects of various computer errors[1,2,11] and on the variation of solutions over reasonable parameter ranges.[5] With modern iterative differential analyzers, however, there is less need for actual computer solution of sensitivity equations. The true effects of parameter changes switched in and out during alternate repetitive-computer runs are conveniently observed on an oscilloscope without any need for linearization.[11] If function memory is available, we can also compute true perturbations $\delta x(t)$ by subtracting the stored nominal solution $x_0(t)$ from the perturbed solution $x(t)$.

---

* While $\delta x(t)$ satisfies Eq. (4) only approximately for small $\delta\alpha$, $x_\alpha(t)$ satisfies Eq. (14) *exactly*. $x_\alpha(t)\,\delta\alpha = \delta^1 x(t)$, which satisfies the linear perturbation equation exactly, is a *first-order perturbation* approximating $\delta x(t)$ for small $\delta\alpha$, δx.

12-5. Resubstitution Checks. Exact solutions $x_i = x_i(t)$ of a given system of differential equations

$$\frac{dx_i}{dt} = f_i(t;x_1,x_2, \ldots ,x_n) \qquad (i = 1,2, \ldots ,n) \tag{12-17}$$

must satisfy

$$x_i(t) = \int_0^t f_i(t;x_1,x_2, \ldots ,x_n)\, dt + x_i(0) \qquad (i = 1,2, \ldots ,n) \tag{12-18}$$

If now the $x_i(t)$ are replaced by necessarily nonideal computer solutions $x_i'(t)$, then the functions

$$\Delta x_i(t) = \int_0^t f_i(t;x_1',x_2', \ldots ,x_n')\, dt + x_i'(0) - x_i'(t) \qquad (i = 1,2, \ldots ,n) \tag{12-19}$$

are measures of the solution errors. Each $\Delta x_i(t)$ is, in fact, a useful correction whose addition to $x_i'(t)$ tends to improve our computed solution.[12,13] This fact becomes interesting when we can implement the checking operation (19) economically and more accurately than our original differential-equation-solving operations. In particular, a repetitive analog computer with scanning readout (Sec. 10-11c) can read solutions into accurate "slow" analog computing elements or into a digital computer to check selected solutions. Correction of fast solutions would require function memory, although partial correction may be simpler. The validity of corrections (19) computed with *imperfect* computing equipment is an interesting topic for further investigation.[12]

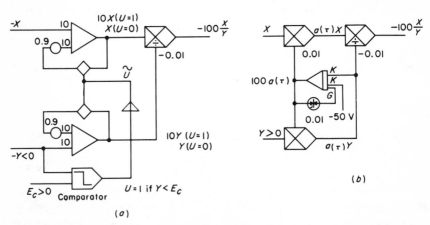

Fig. 12-2. Automatic scaling for a divider circuit. The comparator in (a) need not be accurate.

12-6. Special Scaling Problems and Automatic Scaling.[97,100] When the magnitude of a machine problem variable varies over a wide range in the course of a problem solution, automatic rescaling at appropriate points of the computer setup may yield significantly increased solution accuracy. Examples are found in nuclear-reactor simulation and in control problems where an initially large error is nulled by the control-system action, as in homing-missile simulation.

Figure 12-2a illustrates the use of comparator/switch circuits for automatic rescaling of the divisor Y in an electronic divider. In some problems, we shall require dual comparators for testing $|Y|$ rather than simply Y as in Fig. 12-2a, but relatively inaccurate comparators, such as the inexpensive circuit of Fig. 11-9b, are perfectly sufficient for automatic scaling. Figure 12-2a shows a circuit for *continuous* automatic rescaling.[100] True automatic rescaling can sometimes be replaced by scale-factor changes programmed as functions of time.

In many control problems, an error measure $v(t)$ is always small but appears as the difference of two large quantities. We can sometimes avoid the resulting large percentage errors by computing $v(t)$ as $\int_0^\tau \dot{v}(t)\,dt + v(0)$ at the expense of additional equipment. In beam-rider missile control systems, for instance, a problem variable

$$v = -x \sin \vartheta + y \cos \vartheta \qquad (12\text{-}20)$$

is a small difference, while

$$\dot{v} = -\dot{x} \sin \vartheta + \dot{y} \cos \vartheta - (x \cos \vartheta + y \sin \vartheta)\dot{\vartheta} \qquad (12\text{-}21)$$

has a magnitude comparable with those of the various terms on the right.[100]

CONTINUOUS OPTIMIZATION, EQUATION SOLVERS, CONSTRAINTS, AND MODEL MATCHING

12-7. Maxima and Minima. **(a) Introduction.** Many practical and theoretical problems require determination of parameter combinations $(x_1, x_2, \ldots, x_n)$ which will maximize or minimize a suitably given function

$$F = F(x_1, x_2, \ldots, x_n) \qquad (12\text{-}22)$$

(*criterion function, objective function, measure of effectiveness*), possibly subject to constraints of the form

$$\varphi_k(x_1, x_2, \ldots, x_n) = 0 \qquad (k = 1, 2, \ldots, m) \qquad (12\text{-}23)$$

and/or

$$\Psi_k(x_1, x_2, \ldots, x_n) \geq 0 \qquad (k = 1, 2, \ldots, r) \qquad (12\text{-}24)$$

Practically all engineering problems involve parameter optimization (maximum performance, minimum cost), and a much larger class of problems can be reduced to optimization by way of minimum-error requirements. Error minimization through stable feedback-loop setups is a natural application for conventional and iterative analog computers, but also for digital and hybrid machines. In the following, we shall assume the existence of meaningful criterion functions and constraints, all differentiable as needed; and we assume the actual existence of maxima or minima, each with a finite neighborhood without other maxima or minima.

The simplest optimizer setup on an analog computer is merely a computing-element block generating $F(x_1, x_2, \ldots, x_n)$, with each parameter x_i adjusted manually to maximize or minimize the output (optimization

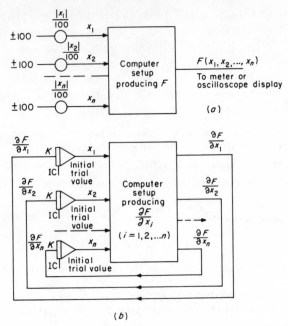

Fig. 12-3. Optimizer with manual parameter adjustments (a), and steepest-descent minimizing scheme (b).

by trial and error, Fig. 12-3a. To account for constraints (23) on the variables x_i, we simply optimize the modified criterion function

$$\Phi(x_1, x_2, \ldots, x_n) \equiv F(x_1, x_2, \ldots, x_n) + \frac{1}{2} \sum_{k=1}^{m} c_k \varphi_k^2(x_1, x_2, \ldots, x_n)$$

$$(12\text{-}25)$$

$$\text{or} \quad \Phi(x_1, x_2, \ldots, x_n) \equiv F(x_1, x_2, \ldots, x_n) + \sum_{k=1}^{m} c_k |\varphi_k(x_1, x_2, \ldots, x_n)|$$

$$(12\text{-}26)$$

where the c_k are arbitrary but large positive constants for minimization (negative for maximization). Inequality constraints (24) are reduced to ordinary constraints of the form (23), viz.,

$$\varphi_k'(x_1, x_2, \ldots, x_n) \equiv \Psi_k(x_1, x_2, \ldots, x_n) U(\Psi_k) = 0 \left.\right\}$$

$$\text{with} \qquad U(\Psi_k) = \begin{cases} 0 \text{ if } \Psi_k \leq 0 \\ 1 \text{ if } \Psi_k > 0 \end{cases} \left.\right\} \qquad (12\text{-}27)$$

We see that a computer can deal with analytically rather involved questions in a relatively simple-minded way. We also note that any nondecreasing function of F or Φ will be optimized by the same parameter combination $(x_1, x_2, \ldots, x_n)$. This is often convenient; the criterion function (26), for instance, is usually easier to handle with computers, while (25) is simpler analytically.

(b) Automatic Optimization: Continuous Steepest Descent. For continuous automation of our optimization procedure, we replace the parameter-adjusting potentiometers of Fig. 12-3*a* with integrators (Fig. 12-3*b*). Positive or negative integrator inputs will respectively decrease or increase parameter values; for zero input, each integrator will hold the last parameter value. We note that the *i*th integrator input will tend to

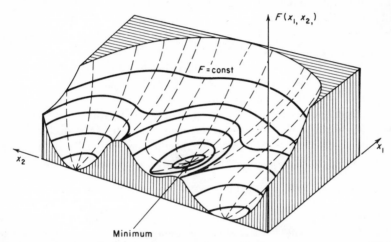

Fig. 12-4. Criterion-function surface for a two-parameter minimum problem, showing three minima, level lines, and gradient lines. In this example, all three minima of $F(x,y)$ have the same value zero. (*Based on ref. 28.*)

decrease F if and only if it has the same sign as $\partial F/\partial x_i$; in the two-parameter example of Fig. 12-4, this drives the parameter-space point (x_1,x_2) "downhill." If all n integrators in Fig. 12-3*b* are driven so that

$$\frac{dx_i}{d\tau} = -K \frac{\partial F}{\partial x_i} \qquad (K > 0; i = 1,2, \ldots ,n) \qquad (12\text{-}28)$$

the parameter-space "point" $(x_1,x_2, \ldots ,x_n)$ will move so as to decrease the criterion function $F(x_1,x_2, \ldots ,x_n)$ along a *line of steepest descent* (*gradient line*) in parameter space, as shown in Fig. 12-4 for the two-dimensional case. $F(x_1,x_2, \ldots ,x_n)$ will thus decrease until we either reach a minimum of F on a boundary of admissible values for the x_i (*boundary minimum*), or until we reach an *interior minimum* with

$$\frac{\partial F}{\partial x_1} = \frac{\partial F}{\partial x_2} = \cdots = \frac{\partial F}{\partial x_n} = 0 \qquad (12\text{-}29)$$

With multiple minima, each additional minimum must be found by a renewed search starting with a different parameter combination. Note that there is no guarantee of convergence toward the smallest of a set of minima; different minima must be compared after all have been located. Frequently, however, we are looking only for a single minimum, whose location may be approximately known. Maxima of $F(x_1, x_2, \ldots , x_n)$ are similarly found with $K < 0$, or as minima of $-F$.

Large values of the integrator gain $|K|$ in the optimizing feedback loops (i.e., fast integration) will speed convergence. In practice, computer-system time lags may cause the parameter values to "overshoot" the desired optimum point, so that excessively large values of $|K|$ can cause oscillations. We can prevent this by reducing $|K|$, by replacing the criterion function with one having smaller derivatives near the minimum, or by making K a function of the $\partial F/\partial x_i$ and their time derivatives. In the important special cases where the value of the desired minimum of $F(x_1, x_2, \ldots , x_n)$ is known to be *zero* (e.g., in equation solvers, Sec. 12-8), we can simply switch all integrators into HOLD when F goes through zero.

Important applications of the steepest-descent technique are described in Secs. 12-8 and 12-9. Another interesting example is the analog computation of eigenvectors $(x_1, x_2, \ldots , x_n)$ and eigenvalues[106] of a matrix $[a_{ik}]$ through minimization or maximization of the quadratic form $\sum_{i=1}^{n} \sum_{k=1}^{n} a_{ik} x_i x_k$ subject to suitable constraints.[23]

Note that continuous steepest descent requires *explicit generation* of the derivatives $\partial F/\partial x_i$. If these are not known or cannot be readily generated, we must resort to the slower but more generally applicable optimization methods of Secs. 12-11, 12-14, and 12-15. In some applications, optimization setups based on

$$\frac{dx_i}{d\tau} = -K \operatorname{sign} \left(\frac{\partial F}{\partial x_i} \right) \qquad (i = 1, 2, \ldots , n) \qquad (12\text{-}30)$$

will also be convenient.

12-8. Solution of Equations.   **(a) Algebraic and Transcendental Equations.**   Analog-computer solution of equations

$$\varphi(x) = 0 \qquad (12\text{-}31)$$

or systems of equations makes sense mainly when we require quick information on the effect of parameter changes on the roots x, or when a voltage proportional to a root is required in simulation work. The inverse-function technique of Fig. 6-22 can yield real roots of suitable equations (31); another perfectly feasible solution method[28] sweeps x rapidly through its range and samples x whenever a computer-generated voltage $\varphi(x)$ goes through zero. In general, we prefer to solve Eq. (31) for real roots by minimizing $\frac{1}{2}\varphi^2(x)$ or $|\varphi(x)|$; we implement

$$\frac{dx}{d\tau} = -K\varphi(x)\frac{\partial \varphi}{\partial x} \qquad \text{or} \qquad \frac{dx}{d\tau} = -K\frac{\partial \varphi}{\partial x}\operatorname{sign}\varphi(x) \qquad (K > 0) \quad (12\text{-}32)$$

Figure 12-5 illustrates the behavior of $\varphi^2(x)$ near real roots and indicates that our search must start in a suitable neighborhood of each root.

To find complex as well as real roots of an algebraic equation

$$\left.\begin{array}{l} \varphi(z) \equiv a_n z^n + a_{n-1} z^{n-1} + \cdots + a_0 = 0 \\ z = x + jy = r(\cos \vartheta + j \sin \vartheta) = re^{j\vartheta} \end{array}\right\} \quad (12\text{-}33)$$

with

we minimize

$$F \equiv [\operatorname{Re} \varphi(z)]^2 + [\operatorname{Im} \varphi(z)]^2 \quad \text{or} \quad F \equiv |\operatorname{Re} \varphi(z)| + |\operatorname{Im} \varphi(z)| \quad (12\text{-}34)$$

as a function of the real variables x, y or r, ϑ. Further details will be found in refs. 14 to 28, which also discuss a number of special-purpose equation solvers.

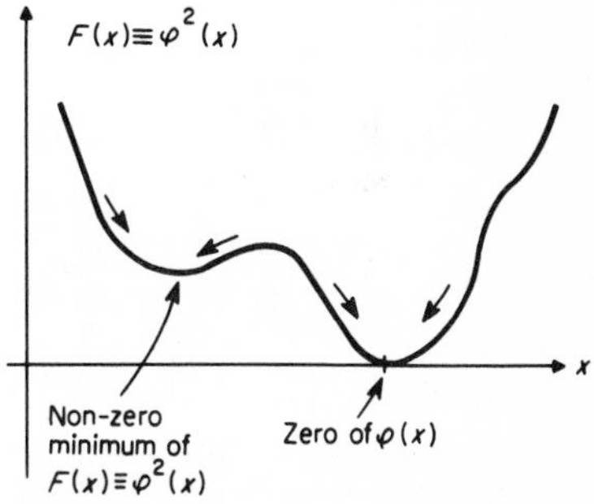

(b) Simultaneous Linear Equations.[14-18,28] The important problem of solving a set of simultaneous linear equations

$$\sum_{k=1}^{n} a_{ik} x_k + b_i = 0$$

$$(i = 1, 2, \ldots, n) \quad (12\text{-}35)$$

is suitable for analog computation if n is not too large; $n = 10$ is reasonable, and $n = 20$ is feasible. We introduce the *residuals* (errors)

FIG. 12-5. Solution of an equation $\varphi(x) = 0$ by minimization of $F(x) = \varphi^2(x)$, showing a false minimum.

$$f_i = \sum_{k=1}^{n} a_{ik} x_k + b_i \qquad (i = 1, 2, \ldots, n) \quad (12\text{-}36)$$

Several solution methods exist.

1. *Steepest-descent minimization* of $F(x_1, x_2, \ldots, x_n) \equiv \frac{1}{2} \sum_{i=1}^{n} f_i^2$ calls for a computer setup for the n differential equations

$$\frac{dx_j}{d\tau} = -K \frac{\partial F}{\partial x_j} \equiv -K \sum_{i=1}^{n} a_{ij} \left(\sum_{k=1}^{n} a_{ik} x_k + b_i \right)$$

$$(K > 0; j = 1, 2, \ldots, n) \quad (12\text{-}37)$$

This requires n summing integrators, up to n phase inverters, and up to $2n^2 + n$ coefficient potentiometers (2 for each a_{ik} different from 0 or 1).

2. *Manual trial-and-error minimization* or *iterative optimization* of

$$F(x_1,x_2, \ldots ,x_n) \equiv \tfrac{1}{2} \sum_{i=1}^{n} f_i^2 \text{ or } F(x_1,x_2, \ldots ,x_n) \equiv \sum_{i=1}^{n} |f_i| \text{ is often}$$

preferable. This requires only up to $n^2 + n$ potentiometers; we shall need n squarers or absolute-value circuits and an output amplifier to produce F.

These methods converge, in principle, whenever a solution exists, since the normal-mode poles of the linear system (37) correspond to the necessarily nonpositive eigenvalues of the symmetrical matrix $-[a_{ji}][a_{ik}]$.[14] Solution accuracies depend on the nature of the coefficients a_{ik}, with errors below 0.1 to 0.5 per cent of half-scale typical for 0.01 per cent resistance networks. Some steepest-descent setups may exhibit high-frequency instability.

If the matrix $[a_{ik}]$ is positive-definite,[106] computer setups for

$$\frac{dx_i}{d\tau} = -Kf_i = -K \sum_{k=1}^{n} a_{ik}x_k + b_i \qquad (K > 0, i = 1,2, \ldots ,n) \quad (12\text{-}38)$$

will produce integrator outputs converging to the desired solution with only $n^2 + n$ potentiometers, again subject to possible high-frequency instability.[16] We can, instead, manually or automatically null e_1 by varying x_1, then null e_2 by varying x_2, etc. (*Gauss-Seidel iteration*).[18,28] We may be able to improve convergence by reordering and/or rewriting the given equations (35) so as to obtain as large positive diagonal terms a_{ii} as possible.

(c) **Hybrid Iteration.** Given an analog-computer approximation ${}^1x_k = x_k - e_k$ to the correct solution x_k ($k = 1,2, \ldots ,n$) of a suitable linear system (35), then the unknown corrections e_k must satisfy the linear system

$$\left. \begin{array}{c} \displaystyle\sum_{k=1}^{n} a_{ik}({}^1x_k + e_k) + b_i = 0 \quad \text{or} \quad \sum_{k=1}^{n} a_{ik}e_k + {}^1f_i = 0 \\[4mm] \text{where} \qquad {}^1f_i = \displaystyle\sum_{k=1}^{n} a_{ik}{}^1x_k + b_i \end{array} \right\} \quad (i = 1,2, \ldots ,n) \quad (12\text{-}39)$$

It may be convenient to compute the residuals ${}^1f_i$ accurately with a digital computer (even a desk calculator). We can then use the analog computer, with unchanged coefficients a_{ik}, to approximate the corrections e_k, using as large scale factors for the ${}^1f_i$ and e_k as possible. We thus obtain a new approximation ${}^2x_k$; we digitally compute new residuals ${}^2f_i = \displaystyle\sum_{k=1}^{n} a_{ik}{}^2x_k + b_i$ and repeat, until all ${}^rf_i$ are as small as required.

12-9. Steepest Descent and Dynamical Constraints.[29-39] (a) **Dynamical Constraints.** A steepest-descent setup can "track" a parameter combination $x_1, x_2, \ldots , x_n$ satisfying a compatible system of equations even when these equations depend on the time t, i.e.,

$$\varphi_k(x_1,x_2, \ldots ,x_n;t) = 0 \qquad (k = 1,2, \ldots ,m) \qquad (12\text{-}40)$$

provided that the optimization-loop responses are sufficiently fast.   More generally, let $x_1, x_2, \ldots, x_n$ be dynamical variables (state variables) known to satisfy given differential equations

$$\frac{dx_i}{dt} = f_i(t;x_1,x_2, \ldots ,x_n) + u_i \qquad (i = 1,2, \ldots ,n) \qquad (12\text{-}41)$$

and let the $u_i = u_i(t)$ be forcing terms to be chosen so as to enforce a compatible set of constraints (40) at all times t, given that the constraints hold for $t = 0$.   Assuming that a solution with the desired properties exists, a computer setup implementing

$$u_i = -K \frac{\partial F}{\partial x_i} \qquad (K > 0; i = 1,2, \ldots ,n) \qquad (12\text{-}42)$$

with sufficiently large K and

$$F(x_1,x_2, \ldots ,x_n;t) = \tfrac{1}{2} \sum_{k=1}^{m} c_k \varphi_k^2$$

or $\qquad F(x_1,x_2, \ldots ,x_n;t) \equiv \sum_{k=1}^{m} c_k|\varphi_k| \qquad (c_k > 0; k = 1,2, \ldots ,m)$

$$(12\text{-}43)$$

will enforce the given relations (40) between the system variables x_i; *we must adjust the initial values $x_i(0)$ so that they satisfy the constraints for* $t = 0$.   The stability of such computer setups is discussed in ref. 39.

In most conventional simulations, constraints are applied directly to eliminate variables, or new constraint-free coordinates are introduced. *The steepest-descent technique, however, is especially useful for adding constraints to dynamical systems already set up on an analog computer.*

In mechanics, fixed constraints

$$\varphi_k(x_1,x_2, \ldots ,x_n) = 0 \qquad (k = 1,2, \ldots ,m) \qquad (12\text{-}44)$$

to the generalized coordinates x_i of a dynamical system lead to equations of motion of the form

$$\frac{d\dot{x}_i}{dt} = f_i(t;x_1,x_2, \ldots ,x_n;\dot{x}_1,\dot{x}_2, \ldots ,\dot{x}_n) + u_i \qquad \frac{dx_i}{dt} = \dot{x}_i \qquad (i = 1,2, \ldots ,n)$$

$$(12\text{-}45)$$

where the $u_i = u_i(t)$ are again forcing terms required to enforce the given constraints (44).   Since forces due to fixed constraints cannot do work, they must be perpendicular to all displacements permitted by the constraints; it follows that

$$u_i = \sum_{k=1}^{m} \lambda_k(t) \frac{\partial \varphi_k}{\partial x_i} \qquad (i = 1,2, \ldots ,n) \qquad (12\text{-}46)$$

where the $\lambda_k(t)$ are uniquely determined by Eqs. (44) and (45).[106]   Each term in Eq.

(46) can be interpreted in terms of physical generalized-force components due to the constraints.

In analog-computer simulation, the $\lambda_k(t)$ are rarely known explicitly. We approximate the correct expressions (46) by heuristic steepest-descent methods, which often admit physical interpretation. We may, for instance, attempt to minimize

$$F(x_1, x_2, \ldots, x_n) = \sum_{k=1}^{m} c_k \varphi_k^2 \quad (c_k > 0, k = 1, 2, \ldots, m) \quad (12\text{-}47)$$

by taking

$$u_i = -K \frac{\partial F}{\partial x_i} = -2K \sum_{k=1}^{m} c_k \varphi_k \frac{\partial \varphi_k}{\partial x_i} \quad (K > 0; i = 1, 2, \ldots, n) \quad (12\text{-}48)$$

which can be interpreted as a sort of elastic reaction resisting any violation of our constraints. We can, instead, try to minimize

$$F(x_1, x_2, \ldots, x_n; \dot{x}_1, \dot{x}_2, \ldots, \dot{x}_n) = \sum_{k=1}^{m} c_k' \dot{\varphi}_k^2 \quad (c_k' > 0, k = 1, 2, \ldots, m)$$

by

$$u_i = -K' \frac{\partial F}{\partial \dot{x}_i} = -2K' \sum_{k=1}^{m} c_k' \dot{\varphi}_k \frac{\partial \varphi_k}{\partial x_i} \quad (K' > 0; i = 1, 2, \ldots, n) \quad (12\text{-}49)$$

which corresponds roughly to viscous reactions against constraint violation and has less tendency to "elastic" oscillations. We can also combine constraint "forces" of the forms (48) and (49). The reader should note carefully that such steepest-descent methods are *necessarily approximate*. The correct forcing terms (46) do *not* in general vanish when all constraints are satisfied, while our approximations (48) and (49) require small violations of the constraints to generate the desired forcing terms. In a sense, this is a realistic simulation of forces resisting deformations of actual constraining rods, strings, tracks, etc. Assuming true *equality* constraints satisfied initially by all x_i, and a stable computer setup with large K or K', the exact form of F will not matter too much. The case of *inequality constraints* (e.g., limit stops, barriers, loose strings) is more complicated, and F must be carefully chosen to fit the energy considerations of the problem. As in the case of limit stops (Sec. 9-10), the method of Sec. 10-12b may yield more accurate results.

(b) Steepest-descent Methods for Improving Differential-analyzer Accuracy.[34–37] Steepest-descent implementation of suitable constraints often produces *quotients* and *inverse functions* more accurately and stably than the high-gain-amplifier circuits of Figs. 2-4 and 6-22, although slightly more equipment is required. In particular, the *four-quadrant division circuit* of Fig. 12-6 produces $Z = 100X/Y$ by continuously minimizing

$$F(X, Y, Z) \equiv \frac{1}{2} \varphi^2(X, Y, Z) = \frac{1}{2} \left(\frac{YZ}{100} - X \right)^2 \quad (12\text{-}50)$$

The circuit implements

$$\frac{dZ}{d\tau} = -K \frac{\partial F}{\partial Z} \equiv -K \frac{Y}{100} \left(\frac{YZ}{100} - X \right) \quad (12\text{-}51)$$

and works with divisors Y of either polarity; X and Y can even go through zero together.   Figure 12-7 shows a steepest-descent *square-root circuit*, which continuously minimizes $\frac{1}{2}\varphi^2(X,Z) = \frac{1}{2}(Z^2/100 - X)^2$.   *Note that all such circuits must be supplied with correct initial conditions.*

The extra analog multipliers required for the steepest-descent circuits in Figs. 12-6 and 12-7 can be replaced by simple analog switches if we

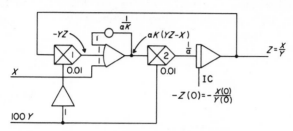

FIG. 12-6. This four-quadrant division circuit produces $Z = X/Y$ by continuously minimizing $F = \frac{1}{2}(YZ - X)^2$.   For constant Y, Z follows X with a lag time constant equal to the reciprocal loop gain $1/KY^2$, which is ordinarily quite small. The circuit permits computation of $\lim_{\tau \to t_1} [X(\tau)/Y(\tau)]$ with $X(\tau_1) = Y(\tau_1) = 0$, if the limit exists.   Note that the initial output $Z(0) = X(0)/Y(0)$ must be supplied.

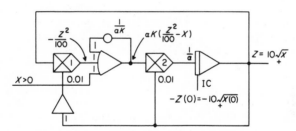

FIG. 12-7. Steepest-descent square-root circuit.

minimize the absolute value of $|\varphi|$ instead of $\frac{1}{2}\varphi^2$.   The corresponding steepest-descent equations are

$$\frac{dZ}{d\tau} = -K \frac{Y}{100} \text{sign}\left(\frac{YZ}{100} - X\right) \qquad \frac{dZ}{d\tau} = -K \frac{Z}{100} \text{sign}\left(\frac{Z^2}{100} - X\right)$$

$$(12\text{-}52)$$

Multiplication by sign φ, less expensive than true analog multiplication, can be implemented by a simple comparator-driven switch in the manner of Fig. 6-14*f*, or by the bridge circuit of Fig. 12-8*a*.[37]   Such steepest-descent loops have a tendency toward small limit-cycle oscillations, since their loop gains do not decrease proportionally with φ; a small deadspace in the error-detecting comparator may be helpful.

Another potentially highly useful application of the steepest-descent technique is the *enforcement of known properties of a computer solution as redundant constraints implemented just as in Sec. 12-9a.* The best-known application is the amplitude stabilization of rate resolvers and sine-wave oscillators by continuous minimization of $(X^2 + Y^2 - R^2)^2$, where X and Y are differential-analyzer solutions $X = R \cos \vartheta$, $Y = R \sin \vartheta$ (Secs. 8-16 and 9-6).[30] Exact computer solutions X, Y would satisfy the constraint in any case (redundant constraint), but the steepest-descent feedback continuously corrects the effects of small phase-shift errors and thus improves the solution accuracy very significantly.

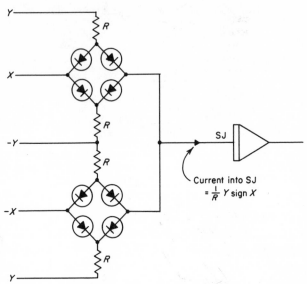

FIG. 12-8a. Sign-multiplier circuit.

The main objection to the resolver circuit of Fig. 8-30b is the relatively large number of multipliers required. The simplified stabilized resolver of Fig. 12-8b replaces the two multipliers required to generate EX, EY by sign multipliers producing $E \operatorname{sign} X$, $E \operatorname{sign} Y$. Since these simplified corrections are monotonic functions of EX, EY, they will minimize $(X^2 + Y^2 - 2,500)^2$. Since EX, EY do not switch abruptly when E goes through zero, there is less tendency toward limit-cycle oscillations than in earlier circuits employing sign-multiplier outputs $X \operatorname{sign} E$, $Y \operatorname{sign} E$ to minimize $|X^2 + Y^2 - 2,500|$.[32,37]

12-10. Linear Programming and Related Problems.[18-20,22,23,26,27,28] *Linear-programming problems* in operations analysis, game theory, and economics require the determination of *a set of n numbers $x_1, x_2, \ldots, x_n$ which minimizes (or maximizes) a linear expression*

$$v(x_1, x_2, \ldots, x_n) = c_1 x_1 + c_2 x_2 + \cdots + c_n x_n \qquad (12\text{-}53)$$

while satisfying $m \geq n$ *linear inequalities*

$$y_i \equiv a_{i1}x_1 + a_{i2}x_2 + \cdots + a_{in}x_n - y_{i0} \geq 0$$
$$(i = 1, 2, \ldots, m) \quad (12\text{-}54)$$

In a typical application, the problem is to buy necessarily positive quantities x_k of n types of raw materials ("inputs") so as to minimize the cost (53) while keeping the respective quantities y_i of $m - n$ output products at or above $m - n$ specified levels $y_{i0}(i = n + 1, n + 2, \ldots, m)$.

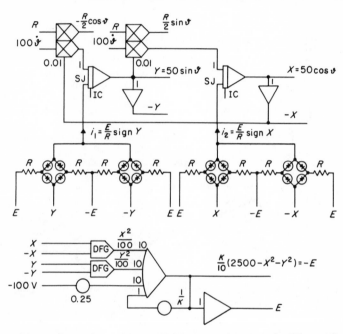

FIG. 12-8*b*. Electronic resolver with amplitude correction (see also Sec. 8-16). The feedback currents EX, EY are monotonic functions of EX, EY, so that the circuit continuously minimizes $(X^2 + Y^2 - 2,500)^2$.

Note that, since $x_i \geq 0$ $(i = 1, 2, \ldots, n)$, we actually have m inequalities of the form (54).

The linear-programming problem defined by Eqs. (53) and (54) is equivalent to the minimization (or maximization) of the function

$$F(x_1, x_2, \ldots, x_n) \equiv v + \lambda_1|y_1| + \lambda_2|y_2| + \cdots + \lambda_m|y_m| \left.\vphantom{\begin{cases}0\\B\end{cases}}\right\}$$
$$\text{with} \qquad \lambda_i = \begin{cases} 0 \ (y_i \geq 0) \\ B \ (y_i < 0) \end{cases} \qquad (i = 1, 2, \ldots, m) \qquad\left.\vphantom{\begin{cases}0\\B\end{cases}}\right\} \quad (12\text{-}55)$$

where B is a large positive constant. Assuming the existence of a solution, the analog computer minimizes $F(x_1, x_2, \ldots, x_n)$ by implementing the n differential equations

$$\frac{dx_k}{d\tau} = -\alpha\frac{\partial F}{\partial x_k} = -\alpha(c_k + a_{1k}\lambda_1 + a_{2k}\lambda_2 + \cdots a_{mk}\lambda_m)$$

$$(k = 1, 2, \ldots, n) \quad (12\text{-}56)$$

where α is a positive constant, and τ is the computer time (real time). The resulting steepest-descent feedback will decrease $F(x_1, x_2, \ldots, x_n)$ and hence minimize v subject to the given constraints (12-54).

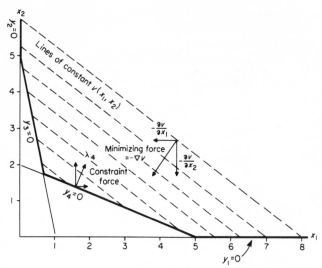

FIG. 12-9a. Dynamical-analogy interpretation of a linear programming problem: steepest-descent minimization of

$$v(x_1, x_2) = \tfrac{1}{4}x_1 + \tfrac{1}{3}x_2$$

subject to the constraints

$$y_1 \equiv x_1 \geq 0 \qquad\qquad y_2 \equiv x_2 \geq 0$$
$$y_3 \equiv 10x_1 + 2x_2 - 10 \geq 0 \qquad y_4 \equiv 2x_1 + 5x_2 - 10 \geq 0$$

Constraint "forces" prevent penetration of "barriers" corresponding to each constraint inequality.

In the example of Fig. 12-9a, x_1 and x_2 may be regarded as the rectangular cartesian coordinates of a particle moving in a viscous medium. The constraints are satisfied for all points (x_1, x_2) above and to the right of the convex polyhedron of smooth straight-line barriers indicated in heavy lines. The broken lines are lines of equal potential energy $v(x_1, x_2)$. The particle will move in the negative-gradient direction until it strikes a barrier, say by violating the inequality $y_4 \geq 0$. The particle then experiences an additional force perpendicular to the barrier. As a result, the particle will move along the heavy lines to the barrier vertex with the lowest potential energy $v(x_1,x_2)$. The problem is degenerate if ∇v is perpendicular to a barrier; in this case, the solution may not be unique.

Maximization problems would be solved similarly, with the minus sign in Eq. (56) replaced by a plus sign.

Figure 12-9b shows the analog-computer setup for the steepest-descent equations (56). The problem variables x_k, y_i, and v are represented by

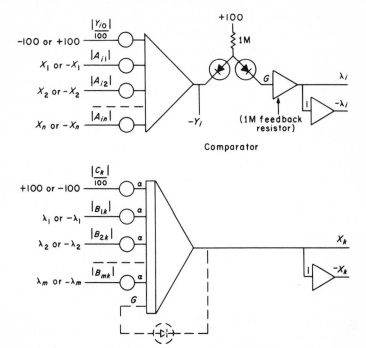

Comparator

FIG. 12-9b. Analog-computer setup for the solution of linear-programming problems. The inverted input voltages $-X_k$, $-\lambda_i$, or -1 are used with negative coefficients A_{ik} or C_k. If, as in many practical problems, an inequality $Y_i \geq 0$ takes the simple form $X_j \geq 0$, then the entire block of computing elements generating the corresponding voltage λ_i is simply replaced by a feedback diode connected across the jth integrator so as to limit its output to nonnegative values (dash lines).

corresponding voltages $X_k = a_k x_k$, $Y_i = b_i y_i$, so that Eqs. (54) and (56) take the form of machine equations

$$
\left.
\begin{aligned}
Y_i &= A_{i1}X_1 + A_{i2}X_2 + \cdots + A_{in}X_n - Y_{i0} \\
PX_k &= -\alpha(C_k + B_{1k}\lambda_1 + B_{2k}\lambda_2 + \cdots + B_{mk}\lambda_m)
\end{aligned}
\right\}
\tag{12-57}
$$

$$
\text{with} \quad C_k = a_k c_k \qquad A_{ik} = \frac{b_i}{a_k}a_{ik} \qquad B_{ik} = a_k a_{ik}
$$

$$
Y_{i0} = b_i y_{i0} \qquad (i = 1,2, \ldots ,m;\ k = 1,2, \ldots ,n)
$$

m voltages $-Y_i$ are produced by summing amplifiers and applied to analog comparators generating the constraint-free voltages λ_i. Each X_k is obtained at the output of a summing integrator. Phase inverters also produce the voltages $-\lambda_i$ and $-X_k$ as needed for multiplication by negative coefficients. Coefficients exceeding unity in absolute value are obtained with the aid of amplifier input gains in the usual manner. Solutions converge within fractions of a second, depending on the integrator gain α used. A voltage proportional to v, if required, could be readily generated with an additional summing amplifier.

The analog-computer method is practical for linear-programming problems with $m, n \le 20$; the practically instantaneous solution makes it particularly convenient to study effects of coefficient changes on the values of v and of the "slack variables" y_i. The n variables y_i closest to zero correspond to those of the m inequalities (54) which actually determine the solution vertex (see also Fig. 12-9a). One can, then, obtain solutions of essentially unlimited accuracy by solving the corresponding n simultaneous *equations* $y_i = 0$ by the hybrid iteration method of Sec. 12-8c. Our analog-computer technique is easily extended to suitable, more general programming involving *nonlinear* objective functions and constraints.[21]

12-11. Optimization by Parameter Perturbation. Although direct implementation of the steepest-descent relations (28) is successful in suitable applications, one must remember that computer generation of the required derivatives $\partial F/\partial x_k$ may well be impractically complicated or, indeed, impossible. In particular, the function $F(x_1, x_2, \ldots, x_n)$ might be known only as the result of measurements or partial system tests, rather than as an explicit differentiable relationship. In such situations, we may replace the derivatives $\partial F/\partial x_k$ with measured ratios $\delta F/\delta x_k$ corresponding to small changes δx_k produced either by normal system operation or by test-signal injection (*parameter perturbation*).

Referring to Fig. 12-10, a sinusoidal perturbation $\delta x_1 = a \cos \omega\tau$ causes a sinusoidal variation $\delta F \approx \dfrac{\partial F}{\partial x_1} \delta x_1 = \dfrac{\partial F}{\partial x_1} a \cos \omega\tau$. This is multiplied by δx_1 to produce

$$\delta F\, \delta x_1 \approx \frac{\partial F}{\partial x_1} a^2 \cos^2 \omega\tau = \frac{a^2}{2} \frac{\partial F}{\partial x_1} + \frac{a^2}{2} \frac{\partial F}{\partial x_1} \cos 2\omega\tau$$

which is averaged and inverted to yield the desired steepest-descent feedback proportional to $-(\partial F/\partial x_1)$. It is convenient to replace the sinusoidal perturbation by a square-wave signal, so that the multiplication reduces to simple switching. Depending on the nature of our system, it is usually possible to optimize two or more parameters x_k simultaneously with noninterfering (orthogonal) perturbation signals (typically square waves or sine waves of different frequencies), at the price of slower convergence.

If $F(x_1,x_2, \ldots ,x_n)$ is a dynamical-system output rather than just a "static" function of the x_k, then the periodic variation δF will lag the periodic input δx_1. For this reason, Fig. 12-10 includes a phase-shifting circuit (not shown) to be adjusted for optimum feedback. From a more sophisticated point of view, our parameter-perturbation-optimizer feedback approximates a value of the time-cross-correlation function of δx_1 and F, which must vanish for $\partial F/\partial x_1 = 0$.[69] The artificial parameter perturbation is felt as noise in the system output, and the normal system input similarly causes interference in the optimizer loop. The choice of the perturbation frequency involves a compromise between optimizer-loop response and minimum interference.[68-70] It is also possible to replace periodic parameter perturbation with a noiselike signal.

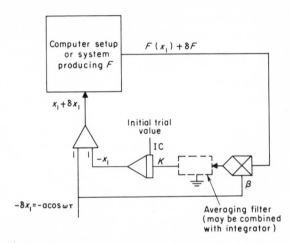

Fig. 12-10. A simple parameter-perturbation optimizer.

12-12. Continuous Optimization and Model Matching.

Our technique for enforcing dynamical constraints (40) on time-varying dynamical variables $x_1, x_2, \ldots , x_n$ by steepest descent was interpreted as continuous minimization of a criterion function (error measure) (43). The question naturally arises whether similar steepest-descent techniques can continuously minimize more general criterion functions. In actual fact, such problems are only rarely meaningful. In the case of our compatible constraints, an actual minimum corresponding to $F = 0$ *can* be realized at all times, since we were careful to assume all constraints to be satisfied at $t = 0$. In general, the situation is not so simple; the best we can usually do is to find control functions $u_i(t)$ which will minimize a time average, weighted time average, or running average of F. This, however, is a problem in *functional* optimization (Secs. 12-13 and 12-16); the technique of Sec. 12-9a may or may not yield a useful approximation.

A very important application *apparently* calling for continuous minimization is the problem of *model matching*. Referring to Fig. 12-11, we should like to match the parameters $\alpha_1, \alpha_2, \ldots , \alpha_n$ of a computer-represented mathematical model to its prototype (real system or computer setup) by continuously minimizing an error measure, say,

$$F(\alpha_1, \alpha_2, \ldots, \alpha_n)$$
$$= \frac{1}{2} \sum_{k=1}^{m} c_k[y_k(t;\alpha_1,\alpha_2, \ldots, \alpha_n) - \eta_k(t)]^2 \qquad (c_k > 0; \ k = 1, 2, \ldots, n)$$

$$(12\text{-}58)$$

as both model and prototype are subjected to the same test input or inputs.

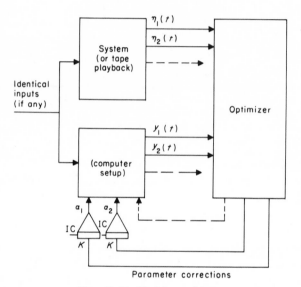

Fig. 12-11. Model matching.

Model matching is of the greatest practical importance

1. For deriving *simplified models* of complicated systems, including biological systems and human operators.[65,66,71]
2. For *system identification (parameter estimation)*, especially for adaptive control of systems with time-varying parameters.

Conversely, certain adaptive control systems attempt to match parameters of an actual physical system to those of a model with desirable properties.[67,72,73]

Referring again to Fig. 12-11, let the model be described by the differential equations

$$\frac{dy_i}{dt} = f_i(t;y_1,y_2, \ldots, y_m;\alpha_1,\alpha_2, \ldots, \alpha_n) \qquad (i = 1, 2, \ldots, m) \quad (12\text{-}59)$$

where the $\alpha_k = \alpha_k(t)$ are time-variable parameters to be determined so as to minimize the criterion function (58). In actual fact, continuous minimization of (58) makes sense only in rare cases, as in parameter *tracking*, where system and model satisfy similar differential equations (59) with initially identical parameters.

Purely formally, steepest-descent minimization of (58) would require

$$\frac{d\alpha_k}{dt} = -K\frac{\partial F}{\partial \alpha_k} = -K\sum_{i=1}^{m} c_i(y_i - \eta_i)\frac{\partial y_i}{\partial \alpha_k} \qquad (K > 0;\ k = 1,2,\ldots,n) \quad (12\text{-}60)$$

Several investigators[64-66] have implemented these relations with parameter-influence coefficients $\partial y_i/\partial \alpha_k$ obtained through continuous solution of sensitivity equations

$$\frac{d}{dt}\left(\frac{\partial y_i}{\partial \alpha_k}\right) = \sum_{j=1}^{m}\frac{\partial f_i}{\partial y_j}\frac{\partial y_j}{\partial \alpha_k} + \frac{\partial f_i}{\partial \alpha_k} \qquad (i = 1,2,\ldots,m) \quad (12\text{-}61)$$

in the manner of Sec. 12-4. The varying success[71] of these methods depends on the extent to which they approximate a really meaningful functional minimization; parameter-influence coefficients, in fact, were originally defined for *constant* parameters α_k only.[71]

Model matching through *parameter perturbation* (Sec. 12-11) is more easily made consistent with valid theory, for the computer setup of Fig. 12-10 approximates true functional optimization as soon as we insert any kind of short-term averaging filter at the output of the function generator producing the criterion function F. The success of parameter-perturbation model matching, although necessarily subject to compromises between averaging time and accuracy, is thus more easily predictable.[68-70]

ITERATIVE OPTIMIZATION

12-13. Parameter Optimization of Functionals: Examples. We turn next to the optimization of *functionals* or numerical functions of the entire time history of a function $y(t)$ (or of several such functions) obtained in the course of a computer run. True functional optimization requires us to select an optimal *function* $y(t)$ (Sec. 12-16), but we start with the important problem of *parameter optimization*. $y(t) = y(t;\alpha_1,\alpha_2,\ldots,\alpha_n)$ is to be completely determined by n constant parameters $\alpha_1,\alpha_2,\ldots,\alpha_n$, and we want to determine $\alpha_1,\alpha_2,\ldots,\alpha_n$ so as to maximize or minimize a functional dependent on $y(t)$. Simple examples of functionals are $\int_0^T \Phi[y(t)]\,dt$, where $\Phi(y)$ is a given function, or simply $\Phi[y(T)]$; note that *each such functional is simply a numerical function $F(\alpha_1,\alpha_2,\ldots,\alpha_n)$ of the parameters $\alpha_1,\alpha_2,\ldots,\alpha_n$.* In most applications,

$$y(t) = y(t;\alpha_1,\alpha_2,\ldots,\alpha_n)$$

is not explicitly given as a function of the parameters, but as the solution of a differential equation containing the parameters,

$$\frac{d^r y}{dt^r} = f(t;y,\dot{y},\ddot{y},\ldots;\alpha_1,\alpha_2,\ldots,\alpha_n) \quad (12\text{-}62)$$

The unknowns $\alpha_1,\alpha_2,\ldots,\alpha_n$ are, typically, design parameters for a dynamical system described by Eq. (62), and our functional is a performance measure; unknown initial values $y(0)$, $\dot{y}(0)$, . . . , too, can play the role of unknown parameters. The following examples, simple as they are, illustrate the most significant applications:

1. *A Boundary-value Problem* (Fig. 12-12a, b). The two-point boundary-value problem

$$\frac{d^2y}{dt^2} = -\omega^2 y \quad y(0) = 0 \quad y(T) = y_T \quad \left(T \neq \frac{k\pi}{\omega}, k = 0,1,2, \ldots\right)$$

(12-63)

is conveniently solved by minimization of the functional (error measure)

$$[y(T) - y_T]^2 = F[\dot{y}(0)]$$

(12-64)

as a function of the unknown parameter $\alpha_1 = \dot{y}(0)$.

2. *An Eigenvalue Problem* (Fig. 12-12c). Eigenfunctions $y(t)$ and eigenvalues[106] α_1^2 satisfying

$$\frac{d^2y}{dt^2} = -\alpha_1^2 y \quad y(0) = 0 \quad \dot{y}(0) = \dot{y}_0 \quad y(T) = 0 \quad (12\text{-}65)$$

are found by minimization of the functional

$$|y(T)| = F(\alpha_1)$$

(12-66)

as a function of the unknown parameter α_1.

3. *Constant-parameter Model Matching* (Fig. 12-12d); see also Sec. 12-12). Two unknown constant parameters α_1, α_2 of a mathematical model defined by

$$\frac{d^2y}{dt^2} + \alpha_1 \frac{dy}{dt} + \alpha_2 y = x(t) \quad y(0) = \dot{y}(0) = 0 \quad (12\text{-}67)$$

are matched to a physical prototype system ("black box") with input $x(t)$ and output $\eta(t)$ through minimization of the error measure

$$\int_0^{t_1} [y(t) - \eta(t)]^2 \, dt = F(\alpha_1, \alpha_2)$$

(12-68)

4. *Control-system Optimization* (Fig. 12-12e). Optimal constant parameters α_1, α_2 for a simple servomechanism described by

$$\frac{d^2y}{dt^2} + \alpha_1 \frac{dy}{dt} + \alpha_2 y = x(t) \quad y(0) = \dot{y} = 0 \quad (12\text{-}69)$$

for a given input $x(t)$ are determined through minimization of an error measure such as

$$\int_0^{t_1} [y(t) - x(t)]^2 \, dt = F(\alpha_1, \alpha_2)$$

(12-70)

As a natural generalization, the functional to be optimized can depend on m functions $y_i(t)$ given by m first-order differential equations like Eq. (59), with n unknown constant parameters α_1, α_2, . . . , α_n.

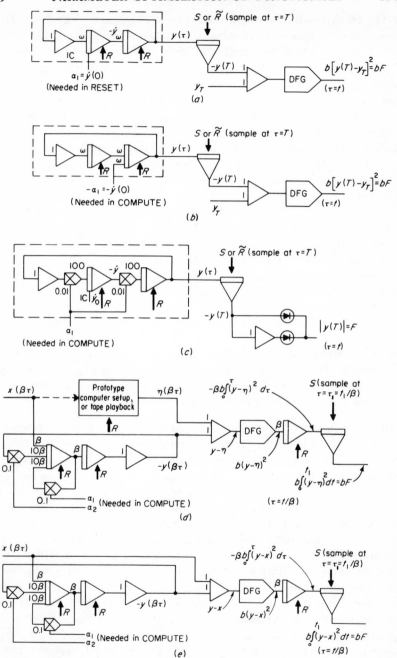

FIG. 12-12. Parameter optimization of functionals. Four typical problems are illustrated: a simple boundary-value problem (a, b), an eigenvalue problem (c), a constant-parameter model-matching problem (d), and two-parameter control-system optimization (e).

12-14. Iterative-differential Analyzer Techniques. (a) **Introduction.** Many parameter-optimization problems are conveniently solved with iterative differential analyzers (Sec. 10-6). In each example of Fig. 12-12, successive differential-analyzer runs with new parameter values α_1, α_2, . . . , α_n will produce new solutions $y(t)$, and hence new values of the given criterion functional $F(\alpha_1,\alpha_2, . . . ,\alpha_n)$; the machine acts as a function generator for $F(\alpha_1,\alpha_2, . . . ,\alpha_n)$, with sampled-data output once per computer run. With sufficiently fast iteration (5 to 1,000 computer runs/sec), a track-hold output representing $F(\alpha_1,\alpha_2, . . . ,\alpha_n)$ can be displayed on an oscilloscope or meter and will appear to change more or less continuously with parameter settings. Such a display permits *optimization by successive manual parameter adjustments*. With a favorable ("convex") criterion function $F(\alpha_1,\alpha_2, . . . ,\alpha_n)$ and a fast computer, such trial-and-error iteration can converge rapidly and is simple, practical, and useful. *Automatic iterative optimization* replaces the human operator with suitable optimization logic, i.e., with a sampled-data control system designed to set optimal parameter values. Automatic optimization is needed especially

1. For rapid plotting of optimal values of F and/or α_1, α_2, . . . , α_n against other system parameters.
2. If the optimal values of F and/or α_1, α_2, . . . , α_n are to be used as inputs to other computing elements, or to actual physical systems.[73]
3. If we want to use a (possibly more accurate) differential analyzer too slow for repetitive-display optimization.

Our assumption of a "meaningful" criterion function presupposes the *existence* of an optimal parameter combination, but we may have to deal with more than a single maximum or minimum. As in our example of Fig. 12-4, an iteration scheme attempting to decrease F, say, might lead us to a different minimum depending on our initial trial values for α_1, α_2, . . . , α_n ("starting point" in parameter space). Our simple eigenvalue problem defined by Eq. (65) is a case in point. Unless all but one of the "optimal" parameter combinations can be eliminated by other considerations, we may have to find two or more maxima or minima and select the best one. With one, two, or even three or four unknown parameters, we may get an impression of the nature of $F(\alpha_1,\alpha_2, . . .)$ through preliminary computations over a coarse net of parameter values. For a larger number of parameters, however, some analytical or physical *a priori* knowledge about the location of the desired optimum is virtually indispensable. It is also usually a good idea to recheck each maximum or minimum located through iteration by renewed iteration with a different starting point.

(b) **Automatic Iteration.** To automate our sampled-data optimization, we can, as in Sec. 12-7, replace each manual parameter adjustment with an integrator (Fig. 12-13a). For functional optimization, we

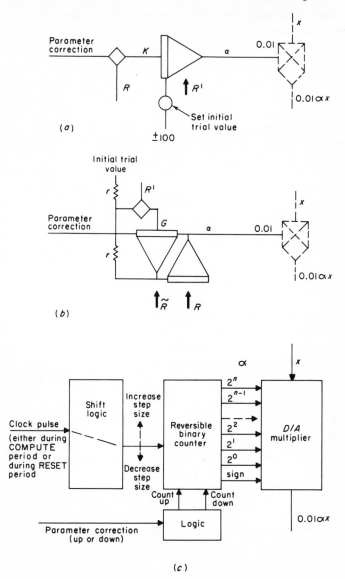

FIG. 12-13. Parameter-setting devices.   In Fig. 12-13c, the analog integrator/accumulator and multiplier are replaced by a simple reversible counter driving a D/A multiplier.   Optional logic shifts the counter input to higher or lower digits for digitally controlled step-size changes.   A shorter control pulse just after the start of each RESET period may replace R if the parameter is an initial value needed during the RESET period.

place these integrators into HOLD during differential-analyzer COMPUTE periods; the parameter-setting integrators integrate only during computer RESET periods. We denote parameter values during the first, second, . . . computer run by $^0\alpha_k, ^1\alpha_k, \ldots$, so that Fig. 12-12a implements

$$\left.\begin{array}{l} ^rF = F(^r\alpha_1, ^r\alpha_2, \ldots, ^r\alpha_n) \\ ^r\alpha_i = ^{r-1}\alpha_i + ^r\Delta\alpha_i \end{array}\right\} \quad (r = 1,2, \ldots ; i = 1,2, \ldots, n) \quad (12\text{-}71)$$

The memory-pair-accumulator circuit of Fig. 10-13a can be similarly employed to hold and correct parameters (Fig. 12-13b); Fig. 12-13c shows

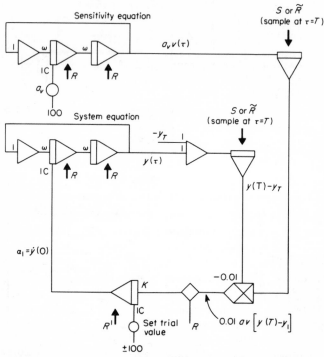

FIG. 12-14. Parameter optimization using a parameter-influence coefficient. In this example, α_1 is needed during the RESET period.

a hybrid analog-digital parameter adjuster.[62] It remains to determine suitable corrections $^r\Delta\alpha_i$ for automatic optimization.

(c) Use of Parameter-influence Coefficients.[65] By analogy with Eq. (28), iteration on the basis of

$$^r\alpha_i = ^{r-1}\alpha_i - h \left.\frac{\partial F}{\partial \alpha_i}\right]_{^{r-1}\alpha_1, ^{r-1}\alpha_2, \ldots, ^{r-1}\alpha_n}$$

$$(h > 0; r = 1,2, \ldots ; i = 1,2, \ldots, n) \quad (12\text{-}72)$$

would approximate steepest-descent minimization of $F(\alpha_1, \alpha_2, \ldots, \alpha_n)$

for a reasonably small *step-size factor h*.   Since F is a functional, we cannot usually express $\partial F/\partial \alpha_i$ as an explicit function of the α_k.   We may, however, be able to generate the $\partial F/\partial \alpha_i$ as functions of parameter-influence coefficients $\partial y_k/\partial \alpha_i$ found through solution of sensitivity equations (Sec. 12-4).

As an example, consider the boundary-value problem of Eq. (63).   Here $\dot{y}(0)$ is the only unknown parameter, and

$$\frac{\partial F}{\partial \dot{y}(0)} = \frac{\partial}{\partial \dot{y}(0)} [y(T) - y_T]^2$$

$$= 2[y(T) - y_T] \frac{\partial y}{\partial \dot{y}(0)}\bigg]_{t=T} \quad (12\text{-}73)$$

where the parameter-influence coefficient $\partial y/\partial \dot{y}(0) = v(t)$ satisfies the sensitivity equation

$$\frac{d^2 v}{dt^2} = -\omega^2 v$$

with   (12-74)

$$v(0) = 0$$
$$\dot{v}(0) = 1$$

obtained by differentiation of Eq. (63) with respect to $\dot{y}(0)$.   We can, then, solve the sensitivity equation (74), along with Eq. (63), once per computer run; we sample $v(t)$ at $t = T$ to obtain $v(T)$, and implement Eq. (73) to produce $\partial F/\partial \dot{y}(0)$ (Fig. 12-14).   Analogous procedures apply to our other examples. With multiparameter problems involving nonlinear differential equations, though, the sensitivity equations tend to be impractically cumbersome (or we may not even

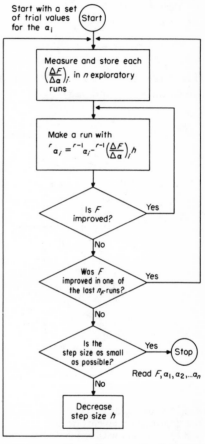

FIG. 12-15. Flow diagram for iterative parameter optimization by the "optimum gradient method."

be able to write them in explicit form, Sec. 12-4).   This technique applies, mainly, to linear boundary-value problems.

(d) **Gradient Methods** (Figs. 12-15 and 12-16).   A more generally useful approach to steepest-descent minimization employs iteration based on

$$^r\alpha_i = {^{r-1}\alpha_i} - {^{r-1}}\!\left(\frac{\Delta F}{\Delta \alpha}\right)_i h \qquad (h > 0; r = 1, 2, \ldots ; i = 1, 2, \ldots, n)$$

$$(12\text{-}75)$$

where the $^{r-1}(\Delta F/\Delta \alpha)_i$ are approximate gradient components *measured* and stored during n exploratory computer runs preceding each actual iteration step or "working step":

$$
\begin{aligned}
^{r-1}\left(\frac{\Delta F}{\Delta \alpha}\right)_i &= \frac{1}{\Delta \alpha}\, [F(^{r-1}\alpha_1, {}^{r-1}\alpha_2, \ldots, {}^{r-1}\alpha_i + \Delta \alpha, \ldots, {}^{r-1}\alpha_n) \\
&\quad - F(^{r-1}\alpha_1, {}^{r-1}\alpha_2, \ldots, {}^{r-1}\alpha_n)] \qquad (r = 1,2, \ldots; i = 1,2, \ldots, n)
\end{aligned}
$$

$$(12\text{-}76)$$

The basic gradient method requires $n + 1$ differential-analyzer runs per iteration step, and n track-hold memory circuits or storage capacitors

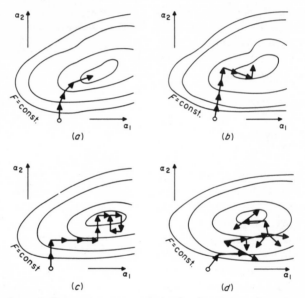

Fig. 12-16a, b, c, d. Two-parameter optimization by the gradient method (a), by the "optimum gradient method" (b), by successive one-parameter optimizations (c), and by iteration with sequential random perturbations (d).

switched by suitable subroutine counters will be needed to store the $^{r-1}(\Delta F/\Delta \alpha)_i$ during each cycle. Two important modifications of the gradient methods are available:

1. *"Optimum Gradient Method"* (Figs. 12-15 and 12-16b).[40–44,71] After finding a set of approximate gradient components (76), we do not remeasure the gradient at each step but continue with additional "working steps" based on the $^{r-1}(\Delta F/\Delta \alpha)_i$ *until F no longer decreases.* Only then we perform n exploratory runs to measure new gradient components. This saves steps, but requires extra logic.

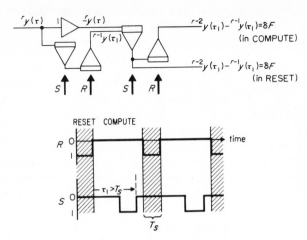

FIG. 12-16e. A circuit for presenting successive differences

$$\delta F = F(^{r-2}\alpha_1, {}^{r-2}\alpha_2, \ldots, {}^{r-2}\alpha_n) - F(^{r-1}\alpha_1, {}^{r-1}\alpha_2, \ldots, {}^{r-1}\alpha_n) = {}^{r-2}f(\tau_1) - {}^{r-1}f(\tau_1)$$

during the following COMPUTE period, or during the following RESET period.

2. *Quantized-gradient Method.*[51]   To avoid working with continuously variable values of the $^{r-1}(\Delta F/\Delta\alpha)_i$, we replace each of them

By 1 if $^{r-1}\!\left(\dfrac{\Delta F}{\Delta\alpha}\right)_i > e$

By 0 if $e > {}^{r-1}\!\left(\dfrac{\Delta F}{\Delta\alpha}\right)_i > -e$

By -1 if $^{r-1}\!\left(\dfrac{\Delta F}{\Delta\alpha}\right)_i < -e$

where e is a suitably chosen positive threshold. *This replaces analog storage by less critical and costly digital shift-register storage* at some expense in the rate of convergence.

Both methods are usually combined.[51]

Gradient-method optimizers for as many as 12 parameters were pioneered by Soviet investigators,[40-45] who employed digital subroutine counters controlling simple capacitor memories through relays or electronic switches. Their later reports[44] also suggest supplementary search routines for identification of saddle points and/or multiple maxima and minima. The "quantized-gradient" method is due to H. Witsenhausen.[51]

(e) Termination of the Iteration. Step-size Determination.
When an optimization routine no longer yields any improvement, we may

1. Continue to let the parameter point oscillate about the optimum parameter combination, as in most optimizing control systems.

2. Terminate the iteration and read the optimum parameter values, say as averages over the last few iteration steps.
3. Terminate the iteration and change to a new optimization routine capable of producing more accurate results.

The iteration may simply be terminated by an operator observing the process by reading F and/or $\alpha_1, \alpha_2, \ldots, \alpha_n$. For automatic termination and readout, we must add special circuits to detect, say, that all $\partial F/\partial \alpha_i$ have equal signs, or that recent iterations have not improved F. In particular, the maximum/minimum-reading circuit of Fig. 9-9 will not only store the highest or lowest value of F, but also produces a voltage step each time an improvement takes place. We terminate the iteration when a counter indicates that a preset number n_F of iteration steps have failed to improve F.

In general, a small step-size factor h in Eqs. (72) and (75) will produce more accurate results, but slower convergence to the desired optimum. Large steps may speed the iteration, but might produce incorrect gradient measurements and large oscillations about optimal points. To combine speed and accuracy, it appears desirable to decrease the step size as we approach the desired optimum. With fast iterative differential analyzers, logic requirements will be simplified if we compromise on a reasonably small initial step size (say, 1 to 5 per cent of half-scale) and reduce the step size once or twice as the search terminates. The hybrid parameter-setting circuit of Fig. 12-13c permits especially simple digital control of step size.

In certain optimization problems, we know *a priori* that the value of a minimum must be zero (as in the case of boundary-value problems, Fig. 12-12a and b) or near zero (as in many model-matching problems, Fig. 12-12d). In such cases, we may know that we are close to a minimum when F becomes small; we can then make the step size proportional to F, or to a monotonic function of F (see also Fig. 12-17a).

Even more rapid convergence to minima equal to or near zero may be obtained by a step-size factor h such that each new trial point $(^r\alpha_1, {}^r\alpha_2, \ldots, {}^r\alpha_n)$ causes the linear approximation

$$F \approx F(^{r-1}\alpha_1, {}^{r-1}\alpha_2, \ldots, {}^{r-1}\alpha_n) + \sum_{i=1}^{n} \frac{\partial F}{\partial \alpha_i} (^r\alpha_i - {}^{r-1}\alpha_i)$$

to vanish, where the derivatives are computed for $^{r-1}\alpha_1, {}^{r-1}\alpha_2, \ldots, {}^{r-1}\alpha_n$. We substitute $^r\alpha_i - {}^{r-1}\alpha_i$ from Eq. (72) to find[65]

$$h = h(r) = \frac{F(^{r-1}\alpha_1, {}^{r-1}\alpha_2, \ldots, {}^{r-1}\alpha_n)}{\sum_{i=1}^{n} (\partial F/\partial \alpha_i)^2} \qquad (r = 1, 2, \ldots) \qquad (12\text{-}77)$$

and employ $^{r-1}(\Delta F/\Delta \alpha)_i$ instead of $\partial F/\partial \alpha_i$ when measured gradient components are

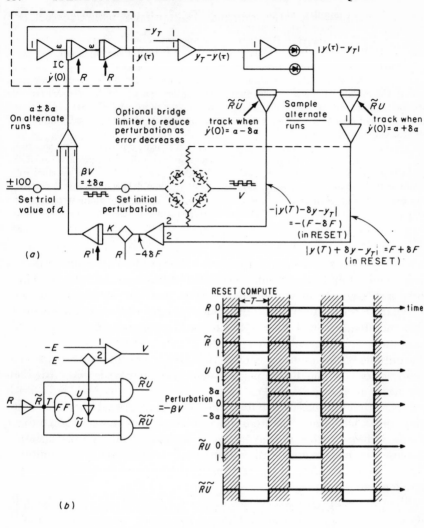

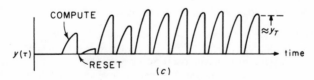

FIG. 12-17. A simple one-parameter parameter-perturbation optimizer (a), digital logic (b), and 10-cps iterative solution of a simple boundary-value problem (c). For the boundary-value problem, the parameter $\alpha = y(0)$ is used only in RESET.

used.   Analog-computer implementation of Eq. (77) is rather complicated for our taste, but convergence may be rapid.

(f) **Other Optimization Routines.**   One-parameter optimization is a relatively simple computing task (Fig. 12-17), while multiparameter optimization, say by a gradient method, requires a rather substantial amount of analog or digital memory and logic.   With fast analog computers, we might like to trade computing speed for simplified logic.   Slow analog computers controlled by general-purpose digital computers, on the other hand, can employ more complicated optimization schemes involving higher-order extrapolation-prediction of maxima and minima and controlled step-size variation.[71]

A relatively simple multiparameter optimization routine optimizes F first as a function of a single parameter, say α_1.   When the maximum or minimum is reached, we switch to the second parameter, optimize F again, and proceed until we start once more with the first parameter α_1 (Fig. 12-16c).   Although this method will converge for reasonably smooth convex functions $F(\alpha_1,\alpha_2, \ldots ,\alpha_n)$ and small step sizes, the iteration can "hang up" on two-dimensional ridges which maximize F in all parameter directions.   Although such obstacles can be removed by supplementary search routines, this again detracts from the simplicity of the method.

12-15. Optimization by Sequential Random Perturbations.   A completely different iteration method[56-62] permits multiparameter optimization with a minimum of control logic, again at the expense of convergence speed.   Referring, for simplicity, to the two-parameter example of Fig. 2-16d, we start with a trial point $(^0\alpha_1,{}^0\alpha_2)$ and vary α_1, α_2 simultaneously by independent *random* positive or negative increments $\delta\alpha_1$, $\delta\alpha_2$ obtained from a noise generator.   If $F(\alpha_1,\alpha_2)$ is not improved, we try new random increments $\delta\alpha_1$, $\delta\alpha_2$ until an improvement is obtained; then we use $(^0\alpha_1 + \delta\alpha_1, \ {}^0\alpha_2 + \delta\alpha_2)$ as the next trial point $(^1\alpha_1,{}^1\alpha_2)$.   With random perturbations distributed about zero with a small standard deviation (small step sizes), the iteration will converge whenever the gradient method does.   Although convergence is slower, our random-perturbation scheme involves no exploration steps, varies all parameters simultaneously, and is not affected by ugly parameter-space terrain features, such as ridges and canyons.

Since unused perturbations $\delta\alpha_1$, $\delta\alpha_2$ must be stored and subtracted out, it appears best to restrict perturbation values to h, $-h$ or to h, $-h$, and 0, where h is a suitably chosen step size; increment values can then be stored digitally, say in flip-flops.[62]   A shift-register noise generator is an especially convenient source of binary random perturbations.[62]

Random-perturbation optimization is especially suitable for very fast iterative differential analyzers like ASTRAC II (Sec. 11-7), where it is conveniently implemented with hybrid analog-digital coefficient-setting circuits (Fig. 12-13c).   The following improvements can speed convergence at the expense of relatively little added digital logic:[62]

1. The parameter-setting circuit of Fig. 12-13c makes it easy to change the step size h as a function of past failures or successes, or as a function of F (Sec. 12-14e).
2. We can make, say, every tenth or twentieth step a large one to detect secondary maxima or minima, or saddle points.[61]

3. We can *correlate* successive random perturbations; i.e., we can make perturbations in the direction of the last success more likely than perturbations in the directions of past failures.

12-16. True Functional Optimization. The problems of Sec. 12-13 required determination of optimal constant *parameters* α_1, α_2, ... By contrast, true *functional optimization* requires us to find an unknown *function* or functions which will optimize a given functional. Consider, as an example, a simple control system with a control input $u(t)$ controlling a state variable $q(t)$ so that

$$\dot{q} \equiv \frac{dq}{dt} = f(q,u,t) \tag{12-78}$$

Given $q(0) = q_0$, we want to determine $u(t)$ so as to minimize the integral

$$S(T) \equiv \int_0^T F(q,u,t)\,dt \tag{12-79}$$

subject to the dynamic constraint (78). We shall employ the classical calculus of variations.[106] Although we might be able to use Eq. (78) for eliminating q in Eq. (79), a more general approach is to write Euler-Lagrange equations[106] with respect to both q and u for the "augmented" integrand

$$\Phi(q,\dot{q},u,t) \equiv F(q,u,t) + p(t)[\dot{q} - f(q,u,t)] \tag{12-80}$$

where $p(t)$ is a variable Lagrange multiplier.[106] The resulting necessary conditions for a minimum are two Euler-Lagrange equations

$$\frac{d}{dt}\left(\frac{\partial \Phi}{\partial \dot{q}}\right) - \frac{\partial \Phi}{\partial q} \equiv \frac{dp}{dt} - \frac{\partial F}{\partial q} + p\,\frac{\partial f}{\partial q} = 0 \tag{12-81}$$

$$\frac{d}{dt}\left(\frac{\partial \Phi}{\partial \dot{u}}\right) - \frac{\partial \Phi}{\partial u} \equiv p\,\frac{\partial f}{\partial u} - \frac{\partial F}{\partial u} = 0 \tag{12-82}$$

and a natural boundary condition[106]

$$\frac{\partial \Phi}{\partial \dot{q}}\bigg]_{t=T} = p(T) = 0 \tag{12-83}$$

The differential equations (78) and (81) are conveniently rewritten as

$$\frac{dq}{dt} = \frac{\partial H}{\partial p} \qquad \frac{dp}{dt} = -\frac{\partial H}{\partial q} \quad \text{(CANONICAL EQUATIONS)} \left.\right\} \tag{12-84}$$

with $\qquad\qquad H = pf(q,u,t) - F(q,u,t)$

Equation (82) implies that the *Hamiltonian function* H satisfies $\partial H/\partial u = 0$ for optimal $q(t)$, $p(t)$, and $u(t)$. Assuming that an optimizing control exists, we may thus be able to express $u(t)$ in terms of $q(t)$ and $p(t)$, which are then found *through solution of a two-point boundary-value problem.* We must solve the differential equations (84) subject to the boundary conditions

$$q(0) = q_0 \qquad p(T) = 0 \tag{12-85}$$

The far-end boundary condition $p(T) = 0$ can be matched by iteration in the manner of Sec. 12-15.

As a simple example, let q represent an error in a control system described by

$$\frac{dq}{dt} = -q + u \equiv f(q,u,t) \tag{12-86}$$

We want to minimize a combination of error costs and control costs, say

$$S(T) \equiv \tfrac{1}{2} \int_0^T (q^2 + u^2)\, dt \equiv \int_0^T F(q,u,t)\, dt \tag{12-87}$$

Equation (82) implies $u = p$, and our boundary-value problem becomes

$$\left. \begin{array}{cc} \dfrac{dq}{dt} = -q + p & \dfrac{dp}{dt} = q + p \\[2mm] q(0) = q_0 & p(T) = 0 \end{array} \right\} \tag{12-88}$$

with

This is easy to solve with an iterative differential analyzer.

If we cannot solve $\partial H/\partial u = 0$ explicitly for u, it may still be possible to find u through continuous steepest-descent maximization of $H(q,p,u)$ in the manner of Sec. 12-9 (Pontryagin's maximum principle).[108] Our theory is readily generalized to the case of n state variables $q_1, q_2, \ldots , q_n$ and r control variables $u_1, u_2, \ldots , u_r$ if Eqs. (78) to (85) are interpreted as analogous matrix relations (see also Sec. 12-2). Functional optimization is the subject of much current research, especially in connection with predictive optimization of space-vehicle trajectories and chemical processes.[46,50,52,55]

SOLUTION OF PARTIAL DIFFERENTIAL EQUATIONS AND INTEGRAL EQUATIONS

12-17. Introduction. Electronic-analog-computer solution of partial differential equations requires us to reduce the latter to sets of ordinary differential equations or, possibly, to a multivariable equation-solving problem. It appears best to continue our discussion in terms of a simple specific example, say, that of heat conduction in a homogeneous slab of infinite extent (Fig. 12-18a). The temperature $u(x,t)$ at the depth x and time t satisfies the heat-conduction or diffusion equation

$$\frac{\partial^2 u(x,t)}{\partial x^2} = \frac{1}{a} \frac{\partial u(x,t)}{\partial t} \tag{12-89}$$

a homogeneous second-order linear partial differential equation with two independent variables x, t. We are also given *boundary conditions*

$$u(0,t) = u_0(t) \qquad u(L,t) = u_L(t) \tag{12-90}$$

and *initial conditions* $u(x,0) = u_I(x)$.   Several different approaches are possible.

12-18. Separation of Variables and Integral-transform Methods.   The classical method of *separation of variables* substitutes trial solutions of the form

$$u(x,t) = f(x)g(t) \tag{12-91}$$

into a given partial differential equation (89), so that we are led to ordinary differential equations for $f(x)$ and $g(t)$.   For linear equations (like our example), more general solutions can be found as sums or integrals over elementary solutions of the form (91). In this case, a more convenient way to obtain an ordinary differential equation may be

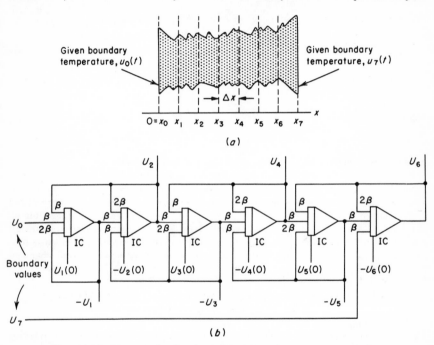

FIG. 12-18. Heat conduction in a slab (a), and computer setup (b).

to subject Eq. (89) to an *integral transformation* with respect to one of the independent variables.

These well-known methods of classical analysis apply only to a restricted class of problems.   Their analog-computer implementation,[81,86] equally restricted in application, is occasionally useful, especially if we require only, say, oscillation frequencies rather than actual solutions.

12-19. Space-variable Differencing.   The most generally accepted analog-computer approach to a partial differential equation like Eq. (89) considers the solution $u(x,t)$ only for a discrete set of values $x = 0$, Δx, $2\Delta x$, . . . , $n\,\Delta x = L$ of the space variable x; for convenience, we shall here consider only fixed increments Δx.   Derivatives with respect to x are replaced by suitably chosen *difference approximations* (Table 12-1).

In particular, a first-order central-difference approximation to $\partial^2 u/\partial x^2$ in Eq. (89) yields

$$\frac{du_i}{dt} = \frac{a}{(\Delta x)^2}(u_{i+1} - 2u_i + u_{i-1}) \qquad (i = 1, 2, \ldots, 6) \qquad (12\text{-}92)$$

if we take $\Delta x = L/7$ (Fig. 12-18a). This is a set of ordinary differential equations (*differential difference equations*) to be solved for the variables

Table 12-1. First-order Difference Approximations for Constant Δx

	$\left(\dfrac{\partial u}{\partial x}\right)_k$	Magnitude of first error term
Central difference.........	$\dfrac{1}{2\Delta x}(u_{k+1} - u_{k-1})$	$\dfrac{(\Delta x)^2}{6}\left\|\dfrac{\partial^3 u}{\partial x^3}\right\|_k$
Backward difference......	$\dfrac{1}{2\Delta x}(u_{k-2} - 4u_{k-1} + 3u_k)$	$\dfrac{(\Delta x)^2}{3}\left\|\dfrac{\partial^3 u}{\partial x^3}\right\|_k$
Forward difference........	$\dfrac{1}{2\Delta x}(-u_{k+2} + 4u_{k+1} - 3u_k)$	

	$\left(\dfrac{\partial^2 u}{\partial x^2}\right)_k$	Magnitude of first error term
Central difference.........	$\dfrac{1}{(\Delta x)^2}(u_{k+1} - 2u_k + u_{k-1})$	$\dfrac{(\Delta x)^2}{12}\left\|\dfrac{\partial^4 u}{\partial x^4}\right\|_k$
Backward difference......	$\dfrac{1}{(\Delta x)^2}(-u_{k-3} + 4u_{k-2} - 5u_{k-1} + 2u_k)$	$\dfrac{11}{12}(\Delta x)^2\left\|\dfrac{\partial^4 u}{\partial x^4}\right\|_k$
Forward difference........	$\dfrac{1}{(\Delta x)^2}(2u_k - 5u_{k+1} + 4u_{k+2} - u_{k+3})$	

$u_i = u_i(t) = u(i\,\Delta x, t)$; we are given $u_0(t)$, $u_7(t) = u_L(t)$ and the initial values $u_1(0)$, $u_2(0)$, . . . , $u_6(0)$.

Figure 12-18b shows a suitable computer setup, with the following typical features:

1. The variables $U_i = a_u u_i(t)$ permit direct physical interpretation and can represent process outputs (or inputs, like U_0 and U_7 in Fig. 12-18) in simulation setups.
2. Both boundary conditions and initial conditions are directly and conveniently implemented.

3. The method is, in principle, easily generalized for the case of two or more space variables x, y, ...   All we require is additional variables $u(x_i, y_k, \ldots ; t)$.

We have, in fact, replaced the continuous system represented by the original differential equation with a *lumped-parameter model* made up of partial discrete "zones."   The possibility of such physical interpretation is also useful for solution checks and system changes.   The simple computer setup of Fig. 12-18b is readily modified to account for variable conductivity, various types of boundary heat transfer (see below), and even melting or ablation at a boundary.[74,77,86]   Successful applications also include simulation of heat exchangers, chemical and nuclear reactors, and elastic structures, including bending and torsion of beams and aircraft flutter.[75,76,86]   But the difference-approximation technique also presents serious difficulties:

1. A sufficiently large set of differential difference equations may require a formidable number of computing elements.
2. Truncation-error effects resulting from finite-difference approximations require careful investigation.   In particular, it is by no means always obvious or even necessary that difference-approximation solutions converge to the correct solution of our partial differential equation as Δx, Δy, . . . decrease.[106]
3. Computer setups can be unstable or conditionally stable, so that noise and component-error effects are intolerably exaggerated.[87,88]

The computer setup for our simple example is stable, as are many similar diffusion-type setups in process-control simulation.   In general, however, analog-computer setups based on difference approximations may well turn out to be unstable or conditionally stable, with instability due to amplifier phase shift and/or to the very nature of the difference approximation.   This is especially true in simulations of elastic structures.   Even a marginally stable computer setup can be uncomfortably sensitive to small component errors and noise.[87]   Computer-setup stability can often be improved through a change of difference approximations; in particular, higher-order difference approximations may help.[82,84,87]   A more recently suggested remedy is the imposition of redundant constraints (Sec. 12-9b) prescribing, for instance, energy conservation.[78,83]   A simple time-sharing scheme may pay if the differential difference equations are highly nonlinear.

To illustrate a computer-setup stability problem, we return to Eq. (89) and replace our boundary conditions (90) with the homogeneous conditions

$$\frac{\partial u}{\partial x} = 0 \qquad (x = 0, x = L) \tag{12-93}$$

We are, then, investigating the temperature transient generated by a given initial temperature distribution $u_I(x)$ in a slab sandwiched between perfect insulators. To introduce the boundary conditions (93), we add two more stations corresponding to $i = -1$, $i = 8$ and represent Eq. (93) by the central-difference approximation

$$u_1 - u_{-1} = 0 \qquad u_8 - u_6 = 0 \qquad \text{(12-94)}$$

Equations (92) and (94) are easily implemented in the manner of Fig. 12-18b. The resulting computer setup, however, is only conditionally stable because of amplifier phase shift.[88]

12-20. Time-variable Differencing. We can also replace *time derivatives* with suitable difference approximations and represent x by the computer time τ. For our example (89), we introduce

$$u(x, i\,\Delta t) = v_i(x) \qquad (i = 0,1,2, \ldots) \qquad \text{(12-95)}$$

and try a first-order backward-difference approximation to $\partial/\partial t$. We obtain

$$\frac{d^2 v_i}{dx^2} = \frac{1}{2a\,\Delta t}\,(v_{i-2} - 4v_{i-1} + 3v_i) \qquad (i = 1,2, \ldots) \qquad \text{(12-96)}$$

with
$$v_i(0) = u_0(i\,\Delta t) \qquad v_i(L) = u_L(i\,\Delta t) \qquad \text{(12-97)}$$
$$v_0(x) = u_I(x) \qquad \text{(12-98)}$$

To find v_{-1}, we draw on the central-difference approximation

$$\frac{d^2 v_0}{dx^2} \approx \frac{1}{2a\,\Delta t}\,(v_1 - v_{-1}) \qquad \text{(12-99)}$$

where $d^2 v_0/dx^2$ is known.

Unfortunately, each equation (96) involves a regenerative two-integrator loop (Fig. 12-19a) whose loop gain increases with $1/\Delta t$. If we decrease Δt to reduce truncation errors, we also increase sensitivity to component errors and noise.[87]

Generally speaking, the time-differencing approach shares the disadvantages and lacks the advantages listed for space-variable differencing; in particular, we need an iteration routine (Sec. 12-14) to enforce the two-point boundary conditions (97). Time-differencing is, nevertheless, of interest because of its application to iteration methods.

12-21. Iteration Methods. With a realistic number of stations, parallel setup of many differential difference equations commonly requires an uncomfortably expensive amount of analog-computing equipment, especially for nonlinear problems. Much current research, therefore, attempts to multiplex a block of computing elements so as to solve many more or less similar differential equations like Eq. (92) *serially;* the (usually relatively few) coupling terms relating different equations must be supplied through function storage (Secs. 10-17 to 10-20). In general, iteration through successive-approximation cycles is needed until all conditions of a given problem are met. With reasonably fast iteration, solutions can, however, still adapt rather quickly to account for slowly changing input functions, boundary conditions, or problem parameters.

If stable computer setups are possible, then differential difference equations based on *backward-difference approximations to time derivatives* appear especially well suited to serial computation. For our example (89), for instance, the computer setup of Fig. 12-19a implements Eq. (96). We first compute $v_1(x)$ from $v_0(x)$ and $d^2 v_0/dx^2$, and store $v_1(x)$. We next compute $v_2(x)$ from $v_0(x)$ and $v_1(x)$ (stored), etc. Unfortunately, each stage of the computation requires iteration to meet the far-end boundary condition of Eq. (97).

By contrast, the computer setup of Fig. 12-19b implements the central-difference equation (92) to produce $u_i(t)$ if $u_{i-1}(t)$ and $u_{i+1}(t)$ are available as inputs. We start with a set of trial functions $^0u_i(t)$ satisfying the given initial conditions; these $^0u_i(t)$ might, simply, be constants. The iteration proceeds as follows:[89]

1. Compute $^1u_1(t)$ from $u_0(t)$ (given) and $^0u_2(t)$. Store $^1u_1(t)$, say on tape.[89]
2. Compute $^1u_2(t)$ from $^1u_1(t)$ (stored) and $^0u_3(t)$; store $^1u_2(t)$, and proceed in this manner until $^1u_6(t)$ is computed from $^1u_5(t)$ (stored) and $u_7(t)$ (given). Store $^1u_6(t)$, and erase $^1u_1(t)$.

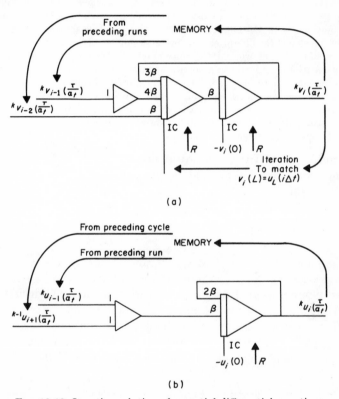

(a)

(b)

Fig. 12-19. Iterative solution of a partial differential equation.

3. Now compute the next approximation $^2u_1(t)$ from $u_0(t)$ (given) and $^1u_2(t)$ (stored). Erase $^1u_2(t)$. Compute $^2u_2(t)$ from $^2u_1(t)$ and $^1u_3(t)$ (both stored). Erase $^1u_3(t)$, and proceed.

The process can be shown to converge, although accumulated errors do not permit very accurate results.[89] Note that we must provide for storage of *all* functions $^ku_i(t)$ for a complete cycle.

As a third possibility, we could approximate $\partial^2/\partial x^2$ by a backward-difference operator, but would, then, require iteration to meet the far-end boundary condition for $x = L$.

In actual practice, differential-difference-equation iteration is beset with serious error-accumulation and conversion problems in addition to the already troublesome truncation errors and setup-stability questions. The reader is referred to M. E. Fisher's account of many error sources;[87] references 78, 79, 83, and 84 summarize later developments. Each problem requires a separate error study. The relatively simple cases already treated theoretically may give only a glimpse of the difficulties associated with complicated nonlinear problems (e.g., magnetohydrodynamics) where ultimate success is quite problematical.

12-22. Transformation to a System of Equations. If both time *and* space variables are differenced (DSDT or discrete-space/discrete-time method), our problem reduces to that of solving a large number of *simultaneous equations* for solution values $u_{ik} = u(i\,\Delta x,\, k\,\Delta t)$. Frequently, most of the equations are of similar form, and each involves only a few of the unknowns u_{ik}. Many iterative-approximation methods have been developed for digital computers, and simpler problems have been solved with the aid of resistor networks.[74,80] Since purely digital iterative solution of a large number of equations requires large amounts of machine time, W. Karplus has suggested a hybrid-computer approach which involves calculation of successive approximations with a few analog computing elements under control of a general-purpose digital computer.[80] This approach requires a large analog or digital memory, but does not involve the computer-setup stability and error-accumulation problems so often associated with differential difference equations.

12-23. Solution of Integral Equations.[90,91] Figure 12-20 illustrates a two-time-scale iteration method designed to solve a linear *integral equation* of the form

$$y(x) = f(x) + \lambda \int_0^b K(x,\xi)y(\xi)\,d\xi \qquad (0 \le x \le b) \qquad (12\text{-}100)$$

for the unknown function $y(x)$; λ, $f(x)$, and the *kernel* $K(x,\xi)$ are given. The integration variable ξ is represented by "fast" time $\tau = \alpha_t \xi$ in an iterative differential analyzer, while x varies in, say, 200 discrete steps Δx between 0 and b, stepping once per computer run. A recirculating function memory (capacitor wheel, delay line, drum, etc., Secs. 10-17 to 10-20) supplies a complete trial approximation $^k y(\tau/\alpha_t)$ once per computer run, and one function value is erased and corrected at the end of each run.

We start with a trial function $^0 y(\tau/\alpha_t)$ (usually simply $^0 y \equiv 0$) loaded into the function store. The first run computes

$$^1 y(0) = f(0) + \lambda \int_0^b K(0,\xi)\,^0 y(\xi)\,d\xi$$

We also replace $^0 y(0)$ by $^1 y(0)$ in the memory. The second run computes

$$^1 y(\Delta x) = f(\Delta x) + \lambda \int_0^{\Delta x} K(\Delta x,\xi)\,^1 y(\xi)\,d\xi + \lambda \int_{\Delta x}^b K(\Delta x,\xi)\,^0 y(\xi)\,d\xi$$

and replaces $^0 y(\Delta x)$ by $^1 y(\Delta x)$ in the memory. The third run yields

$$^1 y(2\Delta x) = f(2\Delta x) + \lambda \int_0^{2\Delta x} K(2\Delta x,\xi)\,^1 y(\xi)\,d\xi + \lambda \int_{2\Delta x}^b K(2\Delta x,\xi)\,^0 y(\xi)\,d\xi$$

and we proceed until $^1y(199\Delta x) = {}^1y(b - \Delta x)$ is stored.   The cycle then repeats to store $^2y(\tau/\alpha_i)$, and so on, until no further change is noted.   The process will converge, at least, whenever the classical Neumann-series iteration does, and generally at a faster rate.   Reference 90 presents a more detailed analysis of convergence and errors.

One reason for our interest in automatic integral-equation solution is the possibility of reducing suitable boundary-value problems and differential difference equations to the form of integral equations of known convergence.[78]

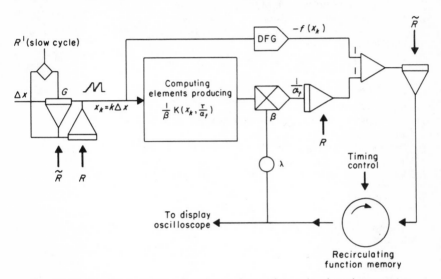

FIG. 12-20. Iterative solution of an integral equation, using function memory.

REFERENCES AND BIBLIOGRAPHY

Perturbation Methods, Parameter Sensitivity, and Resubstitution Checks

1. Miller, K. S., and F. J. Murray: The Mathematical Basis for the Error Analysis of Differential Analyzers, *MIT J. Math. Phys.*, nos. 2, 3, 1953.
2. Bihovski, J. L.: Foundations of Mathematical Error Analysis of Electrical and Mechanical Circuits, *Akad. Nauk*, Moscow, 1958.
3. Bush, L., and P. Orlando: A Perturbation Technique for Analog Computers, *IRETEC*, June, 1958.
4. Rademaker, J. R., and A. S. Lange: Vector Perturbation Method for Instrumenting Miss Distance, *Memos 7/25-SA-101 and 102*, Bendix Corp., Ann Arbor, Mich., 1960.
5. Meissinger, H. F.: The Use of Parameter-influence Coefficients in Computer Analysis of Dynamic Systems, *Proc. Western Joint Computer Conf.*, 1960.
6. ———: Parameter-influence Coefficients and Weighting Functions Applied to Perturbation Analysis of Dynamic Systems, *Proc. 3d AICA Conf.*, Opatija, Yugoslavia, 1961, Presses Académiques Européennes, Brussels, 1962; see also *IEEETEC*, 1964.

7. Favreau, R. R., and W. Brunner: Application of the Parameter-influence-coefficient Technique to Boundary-value Problems, *PCC Rept.* 156, Electronic Associates, Inc., Princeton, N.J., 1960.
8. Fogarty, L. E., and R. M. Howe: Analog-computer Solution of the Orbital Flight Equations, *IRETEC*, August, 1962.
9. ———: Analog Simulation of the Re-entry of a Ballistic-missile Warhead and Multiple Decoys, *Proc. Spring Joint Computer Conf.*, 1962.
10. Howe, R. M.: High-speed Analog Simulation of Re-entry Trajectories in Three Dimensions, *Memo*, Applied Dynamics Corp., Ann Arbor, Mich., 1962.
11. Korn, G. A.: Parameter-perturbation Generator for Analog-computer Error and Optimization Studies, *Ann. AICA*, April, 1963.
12. Meissinger, H. F.: Substitution Methods for the Verification of Analog Solutions, *Proc. Natl. Simulation Conf.*, Dallas, Tex., 1956; Simulation Councils, Inc., La Jolla, Calif.
13. Tomovič, R.: Picard's Method and Analog Computation, *IRETEC*, March, 1957.

Solution of Algebraic Equations, Linear Programming, and Related Problems

14. Adcock, W. A.: An Automatic Simultaneous-equation Computer, *Rev. Sci. Instr.*, **19:** 181 (1948).
15. Goldberg, E. A., and G. W. Brown: An Electronic Simultaneous-equation Solver, *J. Appl. Phys.*, **19:** 339 (1948).
16. Korn, G. A.: Stabilization of Simultaneous-equation Solvers, *Proc. IRE*, **37:** 1000 (1949).
17. Marshall, B. O.: The Electronic Isograph for Roots of Polynomials, *J. Appl. Phys.*, **21:** 307 (1950).
18. Murray, F. J.: *The Theory of Mathematical Machines*, 2d ed., King's Crown, New York, 1958.
19. Pyne, I. B.: Linear Programming on an Analog Computer, *Communications and Electronics*, May, 1956.
20. DeLand, E. C.: Continuous Programming Methods on an Analog Computer, *Rand Rept.* P-1815, The Rand Corp., Santa Monica, Calif., 1959.
21. Rogers, A. E., and T. W. Connolly: *Analog Computation in Engineering Design*, McGraw-Hill, New York, 1960.
22. Levine, L., and H. F. Meissinger: An Automatic Analog-computer Method for Solving Polynomials and Finding Root Loci, *IRE Natl. Convention Record*, part 4, 1957.
23. Neustadt, L. W.: A Method of Computing Eigenvectors and Eigenvalues on an Analog Computer, *Mathematical Tables and Other Aids to Computation*, **13:** 194 (1959).
24. ———: Applications of Linear and Nonlinear Programming Techniques, *Proc. 3d AICA Conf.*, Opatija, Yugoslavia, 1961, Presses Académiques Européennes, Brussels, Belgium, 1962.
25. Karplus, W. J., and W. W. Soroka: *Analog Methods*, 2d ed., McGraw-Hill, New York, 1959.
26. Rybashov, M. V.: Analog Solution of Algebraic and Transcendental Equations by the Gradient Method, *Automatika i Telemekhanika*, January, 1961.
27. Brunner, W.: Solution of Linear Algebraic Problems, *PCC Rept.* 176, Electronic Associates, Inc., Princeton, N.J., 1962.
28. Kovach, L. D., and H. F. Meissinger: Solution of Algebraic Equations, Linear Programming, and Parameter Optimization, in Huskey, H. D., and G. A. Korn, *Computer Handbook*, McGraw-Hill, New York, 1962 (note bibliography).

Representation of Constraints and Related Steepest-descent Techniques

29. Greenwood, D. T.: The Representation of Constraints, *IRETEC*, September, 1956.
30. Howe, R. M., and E. Gilbert: Trigonometric Resolution in Analog Computers by Means of Multiplier Elements, *IRETEC*, June, 1957.
31. Corbett, J., et al.: Stabilization of Computer Circuits, *WADC Tech. Rept.* 57-425, Wright Air Development Center, November, 1957.
32. Brunner, W.: Steepest Ascent, *PCC Rept.* 151, Electronic Associates, Inc., Princeton, N.J., 1959.
33. Skramstad, H. K.: Contour Tracing with an Analog Computer, AIEE Paper 59-461, Winter General Meeting, February, 1959.
34. Turner, R. M.: On the Reduction of Error in Certain Analog-computer Calculations by the Use of Constraint Equations, *Proc. Western Joint Computer Conf.*, 1960.
35. Rubin, A.: Analog-computer Programming, Scaling, and Problem Preparation, in Huskey, H. D., and G. A. Korn, *Computer Handbook*, McGraw-Hill, New York, 1962.
36. Anderson, T. C.: Four-quadrant Division Circuits, *Instruments and Control Systems*, April, 1962.
37. Brunner, W., and R. Beadle: Amplitude Stabilization of Harmonic Oscillator with Diode Gates, *PCC Rept.* 173, Electronic Associates, Inc., Princeton, N.J., 1962.
38. Keller, R. E.: An Analog-computer Realization of the Euclidean Tools, *IRETEC*, August, 1962; see also Ph.D. Thesis, Stanford University, 1962.
39. Talkin, A. I.: A Systematic Approach to Programming an Analog Computer to Generate a Large Class of Trajectories, *Memorandum*, Harry Diamond Laboratories, U.S. Army Material Command, Washington, D.C., 1963.

Optimization with Iterative Differential Analyzers
(See also refs. 56 to 73)

40. Stakhovskii, R. I.: Development and Investigation of an Automatic Optimizer, *Automatika i Telemekhanika*, August, 1958.
41. ———: A Multi-channel Automatic Optimizer for Solving Variational Problems, *Automatika i Telemekhanika*, November, 1959.
42. Feldbaum, A. A.: An Automatic Optimizer, *Automatika i Telemekhanika*, August, 1958.
43. ———: Statistical Theory of the Gradient Method, *Automatika i Telemekhanika*, February, 1960.
44. ——— and I. N. Bocharov: An Automatic Optimizer Which Searches for the Minimum of Several Minima (Global Optimizer), *Automatika i Telemekhanika*, March, 1962.
45. Shubin, A. B.: 10-channel Automatic-electronic Relay Optimizer, *Automatika i Telemekhanika*, May, 1960.
46. Neustadt, L. W.: Synthesizing Time-optimal Control Systems, *J. Math. Analysis Appl.*, December, 1960.
47. Moser, J. H., C. O. Reed, and H. L. Sellars: A Nonlinear Programming Technique for Analog Computation, Eastern Simulation Council Paper, December, 1960, Shell Oil Co., Houston Research Lab., Deer Park, Tex.; see also *Instruments and Control Systems*, March, 1961.
48. Vichnevetsky, R.: One-dimension Iteration on the Analog Computer, *ECC Rept.* 43, Electronic Associates, Inc., European Computation Center, Brussels, Belgium, 1961.
49. ———: Application of the Digital Expansion System to an Automatic-iteration

Problem: Eigenvalues Search, *PCC Rept.* 178, Electronic Associates, Inc., Princeton, N.J., 1962.

50. —— and J. P. Waha: Dynamic Programming and Hybrid Computation, *Ann. AICA*, April, 1963.

51. Witsenhausen, H.: Hybrid Techniques Applied to Optimization Problems, *Proc. Spring Joint Computer Conf.*, 1962.

52. Halbert, P., J. P. Landauer, and H. Witsenhausen: *Hybrid-computation Demonstration Using Pontryagin's Maximum Principle*, Princeton Computation Center, Electronic Associates, Inc., Princeton, N.J., 1963.

53. Eckes, H. R.: Digital Expansion System for ASTRAC I, M.S. Thesis, University of Arizona, 1963; *Ann. AICA*, January, 1964.

54. Mitchell, B.A.: A Hybrid Analog-digital One-parameter Optimizer, *ACL Memo* 69, University of Arizona, 1963.

55. Gilbert, E. G.: Hybrid-computer Solution of Time-optimal Problems, *Proc. Spring Joint Computer Conf.*, 1963.

Optimization by Random Perturbations

56. Brooks, S. H.: A Discussion of Random Methods for Seeking Maxima, *Operations Research*, March–April, 1958.

57. ——: A Comparison of Maximum-seeking Methods, *Operations Research*, July–August, 1959.

58. —— and M. Ray Mickey: Optimum Estimation of Gradient Directions in Steepest-ascent Experiments, *Biometrics*, March, 1961.

59. Favreau, R. R., and R. Franks: Random Optimization by Analog Techniques, *Proc. 2d AICA Conf.*, Strasbourg, France, 1958, Presses Académiques Européennes, Brussels, 1959.

60. Munson, J. K., and A. I. Rubin: Optimization by Random Search on the Analog Computer, *IRETEC*, June, 1959.

61. Karnopp, D. C.: Search Theory Applied to Parameter-scan Optimization, Ph.D. Thesis, MIT, 1961.

62. Mitchell, B. A.: Hybrid Analog-digital Parameter Optimizer for ASTRAC II, M.S. Thesis, University of Arizona, 1964; *Proc. Spring Joint Computer Conf.*, 1964.

Model-matching Applications

63. Corbin, R. M., and E. Mishkin: On the Measurement Problem in Adaptive Systems Utilizing Analog-computer Techniques, *Research Rept.* R-699-58, P1B-627, Microwave Research Laboratory, Brooklyn Polytechnic Institute, 1958.

64. Margolis, M., and C. T. Leondes: A Parameter-tracking Servo for Adaptive Control Systems, *WESCON Record*, 1959.

65. Brunner, W.: An Iteration Procedure for Parametric Model Building and Boundary-value Problems, *Proc. Western Joint Computer Conf.*, 1961.

66. Potts, T. F., G. N. Ornstein, and A. B. Clymer: The Automatic Determination of Human and Other System Parameters, *Proc. Western Joint Computer Conf.*, 1961.

67. Osburn, P. V., H. P. Whitaker, and A. Kezer: New Developments in the Design of Model-reference Adaptive Control Systems, *Paper* 61-39, Institute of Aerospace Sciences, 29th Annual Meeting, New York, 1961.

68. McGrath, R. J., and V. C. Rideout: A Simulator Study of a Two-parameter Adaptive System, *IRE Trans. PGAC*, February, 1961.

69. McGrath, R. J., et al.: A Parameter-perturbation Adaptive Control System, *IRE Trans. PGAC*, May, 1961.

70. Rajaraman, V.: Theory of a Two-parameter Adaptive Control System, *IRE Trans. PGAC*, July, 1962.

71. Bekey, G.: Hybrid Computer Techniques, *Course Notes*, UCLA Extension Division, 1963.
72. Howell, M.: Automatic Parameter Optimization as Applied to Transducer Design, *Proc. Spring Joint Computer Conf.*, 1963.
73. Halbert, P. W.: Hybrid Simulation of an Aircraft Adaptive Control System, *Proc. Fall Joint Computer Conf.*, 1963.

Solution of Partial Differential Equations
(See also ref. 21)

74. Karplus, W. J.: *Analog Simulation: Solution of Field Problems*, McGraw-Hill, New York, 1958.
75. Clymer, A. B.: Operational-analog Simulation of the Vibration of Beams, *IRETEC*, September, 1959.
76. ———: *Handbook of Equations and Operational-analog Circuits for the Solution of Structural Problems*, North American Aviation, Inc., Columbus, Ohio, 1959.
77. Gilliland, M. G., and H. H. Hara: Use of Analog Memory for Simulation of a Melting Slab, *Instruments and Control Systems*, September, 1960.
78. Witsenhausen, H.: Survey of Non-standard Techniques for Analog Solution of Partial Differential Equation, *Memo.*, Electronic Associates, Inc., Princeton, N.J., 1961.
79. Brunner, W.: Serial Solution of Partial Differential Equations on an Electronic Analog Computer, *PCC Rept.* 180, Electronic Associates, Inc., Princeton, N.J., 1961.
80. Karplus, W. J.: A New Active-passive Network Simulator for Transient Field Problems, *Proc. IRE*, January, 1961.
81. Liban, E.: The Application of Finite Fourier Transforms to Analog-computer Simulations, *Proc. Spring Joint Computer Conf.*, 1962.
82. Vichnevetsky, R.: A Spectral Method of Analyzing the Truncation Error in the Finite-difference Technique, *Memo.*, Electronic Associates, Inc., Brussels, Belgium, 1962.
83. Stubbs, G. S.: Application of Time-sharing Techniques, in *Hybrid Computation Course Notes*, Electronic Associates, Inc., Princeton, N.J., 1962.
84. Greenwood, D. T.: A Comparison of Higher-order Difference Methods in the Solution of Beam-vibration Problems, *IRETEC*, February, 1962.
85. ———: Network Analogies of Dynamical Systems, in Huskey, H. D., and G. A. Korn, *Computer Handbook*, McGraw-Hill, New York, 1962 (note bibliography).
86. Howe, R. M.: Solution of Partial Differential Equations, in Huskey, H. D., and G. A. Korn, *Computer Handbook*, McGraw-Hill, New York, 1962.
87. MacKay, D. M., and M. E. Fisher: *Analogue Computing at Ultra-high Speed*, Wiley, New York, 1962 (summarizes Fisher's earlier papers; note bibliography).
88. Giloi, W.: Über Stabilitätsschwierigkeiten bei der Lösung gewisser Fälle der Diffusionsgleichung, *Ann. AICA*, April, 1963.
89. Miura, T., and J. Iwata: Time-sharing Computation Utilizing Analog Memory, *Ann. AICA*, July, 1963.

Solution of Integral Equations

90. MacKay, D. M., and M. E. Fisher: *Analogue Computing at Ultra-high Speed*, Wiley, New York, 1962 (summarizes Fisher's earlier papers; note bibliography).
91. Tomovič, R., and W. J. Karplus: *High-speed Analog Computers*, Wiley, New York (also summarizes Tomovič's earlier work reported in *IRETEC*, December, 1960).

Biological and Medical Applications of Analog Computers

92. DeLand, E. C.: Simulation of a Biological System on an Analog Computer, *IRETEC*, February, 1962.
93. Warner, H. R.: The Use of an Analog Computer for Analysis of Control Mechanisms in the Circulation, *Proc. IRE*, November, 1959.
94. Clynes, M.: Respiratory Control of Heart Rate: Laws Derived from Analog-computer Simulation, *IRE Trans. PGME*, January, 1960.
95. Bekey, G., et al.: An Analog-computer Study of Fetal Circulation, *Proc. San Diego Biomedical Eng. Symposium*, Simulation Councils, Inc., La Jolla, Calif., 1963.
96. *Human Simulations Résumé*, Electronic Associates, Inc., El Segundo, Calif., 1962 (note bibliography).

Miscellaneous Computing Techniques

97. Matsuno, S.: Techniques for Obtaining Terminal Readout Accuracy in Homing-missile Simulations, *Memo.*, Hughes Aircraft Co., Culver City, Calif., 1959.
98. Bekey, G.: Generalized Integration on the Analog Computer, *IRETEC*, June, 1959.
99. Glinski, G. S.: Simulation of Economic Systems, *Instruments and Control Systems*, December, 1960.
100. Bauer, L.: Aircraft, Autopilot, and Missile Problems, in Huskey, H. D., and G. A. Korn, *Computer Handbook*, McGraw-Hill, New York, 1962.
101. Kovach, L. D.: Miscellaneous Techniques, in Huskey, H. D., and G. A. Korn, *Computer Handbook*, McGraw-Hill, New York, 1962.
102. Berbert, A. G., and C. R. Kelley: Piloting Nuclear Submarines with Controls That Look into the Future, *Electronics*, June 8, 1962.
103. A Dual-time-scale Simulation Technique for Prediction Guidance Systems, *Application Note AN-13*, GPS Instrument Co., Inc., Newton, Mass., 1963.
104. Witsenhausen, H.: Hybrid Solution of Boundary-value Problems by Backward and Forward Integration, *PCC Rept.* 175, Electronic Associates, Inc., Princeton, N.J., 1961.
105. Terasaki, R. M.: Analog Computation of Green's Function for Integrating Two-point Boundary-value Problems, *IRETEC*, February, 1962.
106. Korn, G. A., and T. M. Korn: *Mathematical Handbook for Scientists and Engineers*, McGraw-Hill, New York, 1961.
107. Korn, G. A.: *Random-process Simulation and Measurements*, McGraw-Hill, N.Y. (in print).
108. ———: Steepest-descent Optimization by Pontryagin's Maximum Principle, *ACL Memo* 998, Electrical Engineering Department, University of Arizona, 1964.

APPENDIX

Table A-1. Short-circuit Transfer Impedances for Operational Amplifiers*
(Sec. 1-14; see Secs. 3-10 to 3-17 for error analysis)

This table is used to find networks whose transfer impedances $Z_o(P)$, $Z_1(P)$, $Z_2(P)$, . . . , match the desired performance equation

$$X_o = -\frac{Z_o(P)}{Z_1(P)} X_1 \quad \text{or} \quad X_o = -Z_o(P) \left[\frac{X_1}{Z_1(P)} + \frac{X_2}{Z_2(P)} + \cdots \right]$$

for an operational amplifier of one of the types shown in Figs. 1-15a, b, c, d. See Fig. 1-16a for an example illustrating the use of the table.

Short-circuit transfer impedances for many additional networks can be derived with the aid of the following theorems:

1. *Two or more networks may be paralleled to yield a new transfer impedance*

$$Z(P) = \left[\frac{1}{Z_1(P)} + \frac{1}{Z_2(P)} + \cdots \right]^{-1}$$

2. *For every (asymmetrical as well as symmetrical) T network, the output-input transfer impedance is identical with the input-output transfer impedance given in the table.*

Table A-1. Short-circuit Transfer Impedances for Operational Amplifiers* (*Continued*)

Transfer-impedance function	Network	Relations	Inverse relations
A		$A = R$	$R = A$
$\dfrac{A}{1 + PT}$		$A = R$ $T = RC$	$R = A$ $C = \dfrac{T}{A}$
$A(1 + PT)$		$A = 2R$ $T = \dfrac{RC}{2}$	$R = \dfrac{A}{2}$ $C = \dfrac{4T}{A}$
$A\left(\dfrac{1 + P\theta T}{1 + PT}\right)$ $\theta < 1$		$A = R_1 + R_2$ $T = R_2C$ $\theta = \dfrac{R_1}{R_1 + R_2}$	$R_1 = A\theta$ $R_2 = A(1 - \theta)$ $C = \dfrac{T}{A(1 - \theta)}$
		$A = R_1$ $T = (R_1 + R_2)C$ $\theta = \dfrac{R_2}{R_1 + R_2}$	$R_1 = A$ $R_2 = \dfrac{A\theta}{1 - \theta}$ $C = \dfrac{T(1 - \theta)}{A}$
$A\left(\dfrac{1 + PT}{1 + P\theta T}\right)$ $\theta < 1$		$A = \dfrac{2R_1R_2}{2R_1 + R_2}$ $T = \dfrac{R_1C}{2}$ $\theta = \dfrac{2R_1}{2R_1 + R_2}$	$R_1 = \dfrac{A}{2(1 - \theta)}$ $R_2 = \dfrac{A}{\theta}$ $C = \dfrac{4T(1 - \theta)}{A}$
		$A = 2R_1$ $T = \left(R_2 + \dfrac{R_1}{2}\right)C$ $\theta = \dfrac{2R_2}{2R_2 + R_1}$	$R_1 = \dfrac{A}{2}$ $R_2 = \dfrac{A\theta}{4(1 - \theta)}$ $C = \dfrac{4T(1 - \theta)}{A}$
		$A = 2R$ $T = \dfrac{R}{2}(C_1 + C_2)$ $\theta = \dfrac{2C_2}{C_1 + C_2}$	$R = \dfrac{A}{2}$ $C_1 = \dfrac{2T(2 - \theta)}{A}$ $C_2 = \dfrac{2T\theta}{A}$

Table A-1. Short-circuit Transfer Impedances for Operational Amplifiers* (Continued)

Transfer-impedance function	Network	Relations	Inverse relations
		$B = C_1$ $T_2 = (R_1 + R_2)C_2$ $T_1T_3 = R_1R_2C_1C_2$ $T_1 + T_3 = R_1C_1 + R_2C_2 + R_1C_2$	$R_1 = \dfrac{T_1 + T_3 - T_2}{B}$ $R_2 = \dfrac{T_1T_3(T_1 + T_3 - T_2)}{B(T_3 - T_2)(T_2 - T_1)}$ $C_1 = B$ $C_2 = \dfrac{B(T_3 - T_2)(T_2 - T_1)}{(T_1 + T_3 - T_2)^2}$
$\dfrac{1}{PB}\left[\dfrac{(1 + PT_1)(1 + PT_3)}{1 + PT_2}\right]$ $T_1 < T_2 < T_3$		$B = C_1 + C_2$ $T_2 = R_2\left(\dfrac{C_1C_2}{C_1 + C_2}\right)$ $T_1T_3 = R_1R_2C_1C_2$ $T_1 + T_3 = R_1C_1 + R_2C_2 + R_1C_2$	$R_1 = \dfrac{T_1T_3}{BT_2}$ $R_2 = \dfrac{(T_1T_2 + T_2T_3 - T_1T_3)^2}{BT_2(T_3 - T_2)(T_2 - T_1)}$ $C_1 = \dfrac{BT_2^2}{T_1T_2 + T_2T_3 - T_1T_3}$ $C_2 = \dfrac{B(T_3 - T_2)(T_2 - T_1)}{T_1T_2 + T_2T_3 - T_1T_3}$
		$B = C_1$ $T_2 = R_2C_2$ $T_1T_3 = R_1R_2C_1C_2$ $T_1 + T_3 = R_1C_1 + R_2C_2 + R_2C_1$	$R_1 = \dfrac{T_1T_3}{BT_2}$ $R_2 = \dfrac{(T_3 - T_2)(T_2 - T_1)}{BT_2}$ $C_1 = B$ $C_2 = \dfrac{BT_2^2}{(T_3 - T_2)(T_2 - T_1)}$
		$B = C_1$ $T_2 = R_2C_2$ $T_1T_3 = R_1R_2C_1C_2$ $T_1 + T_3 = R_1C_1 + R_2C_2 + R_1C_2$	$R_1 = \dfrac{T_1T_3}{BT_2}$ $R_2 = \dfrac{T_1T_2T_3}{B(T_3 - T_2)(T_2 - T_1)}$ $C_1 = B$ $C_2 = \dfrac{B(T_3 - T_2)(T_2 - T_1)}{T_1T_3}$
$\dfrac{1}{PB}(1 + PT_1)(1 + PT_2)$ $T_1 \neq T_2$		$B = C_2$ $T_1T_2 = R_1R_2C_1C_2$ $T_1 + T_2 = R_1C_1 + R_2C_2 + R_1C_2$	$R_1 = \dfrac{(\sqrt{T_1} - \sqrt{T_2})^2}{B}$ $R_2 = \dfrac{\sqrt{T_1T_2}}{B}$ $C_1 = \dfrac{B\sqrt{T_1T_2}}{(\sqrt{T_1} - \sqrt{T_2})^2}$ $C_2 = B$
$\dfrac{1}{PB}\left[\dfrac{(1 + PT_1)(1 + PT_2)}{P\sqrt{T_1T_2}}\right]$ $T_1 \neq T_2$		$B = C_2$ $T_1T_2 = R_1R_2C_1C_2$ $T_1 + T_2 = R_1C_1 + R_2C_2 + R_1C_2$	$R = \dfrac{(\sqrt{T_1} - \sqrt{T_2})^2}{B}$ $R_2 = \dfrac{\sqrt{T_1T_2}}{B}$ $C_1 = \dfrac{B\sqrt{T_1T_2}}{(\sqrt{T_1} - \sqrt{T_2})^2}$ $C_2 = B$
$\dfrac{1}{PB}\left[\dfrac{(1 + PT_1)(1 + PT_2)}{P^2T_1T_2}\right]$ $T_1 < T_2$		$B = \dfrac{C_1C_2}{C_1 + 2C_2}$ $T_1 = RC_1$ $T_2 = R(C_1 + 2C_2)$	$R = \dfrac{T_1(T_2 - T_1)}{2BT_2}$ $C_1 = \dfrac{2BT_2}{T_2 - T_1}$ $C_2 = \dfrac{BT_2}{T_1}$

Table A-1. Short-circuit Transfer Impedances for Operational Amplifiers* (*Continued*)

Transfer-impedance function	Network	Relations	Inverse relations
$A\left(\dfrac{1 + PT_1}{1 + P^2T_1T_2}\right)$	$R_1C_1 = 4R_2C_2$	$A = 2R_1$ $T_1 = \dfrac{R_1C_1}{2} = 2R_2C_2$ $T_2 = R_1C_2$	$R_1 = \dfrac{A}{2}$ $R_2 = \dfrac{AT_1}{4T_2}$ $C_1 = \dfrac{4T_1}{A}$ $C_2 = \dfrac{2T_2}{A}$
$\dfrac{1}{PB}$		$B = C$	$C = B$
$\dfrac{1}{PB}(1 + PT)$		$B = C$ $T = RC$	$R = \dfrac{T}{B}$ $C = B$
$\dfrac{1}{PB}\left(\dfrac{1 + PT}{PT}\right)$		$B = \dfrac{C}{2}$ $T = 2RC$	$R = \dfrac{T}{4B}$ $C = 2B$
$\dfrac{1}{PB}\left(\dfrac{1 + PT}{1 + P\theta T}\right)$ $\theta < 1$		$B = C_1$ $T = R(C_1 + C_2)$ $\theta = \dfrac{C_2}{C_1 + C_2}$	$R = \dfrac{T(1 - \theta)}{B}$ $C_1 = B$ $C_2 = \dfrac{B\theta}{1 - \theta}$
		$B = C_1 + C_2$ $T = RC_2$ $\theta = \dfrac{C_1}{C_1 + C_2}$	$R = \dfrac{T}{B(1 - \theta)}$ $C_1 = B\theta$ $C_2 = B(1 - \theta)$
$\dfrac{1}{PB}\left[\dfrac{(1 + PT_1)(1 + PT_3)}{1 + PT_2}\right]$ $T_1 < T_2 < T_3$		$B = C_1 + C_2$ $T_1 = R_1C_1$ $T_2 = (R_1 + R_2)\left(\dfrac{C_1C_2}{C_1 + C_2}\right)$ $T_3 = R_2C_2$	$R_1 = \dfrac{T_1(T_3 - T_1)}{B(T_2 - T_1)}$ $R_2 = \dfrac{T_3(T_3 - T_1)}{B(T_3 - T_2)}$ $C_1 = \dfrac{B(T_2 - T_1)}{T_3 - T_1}$ $C_2 = \dfrac{B(T_3 - T_2)}{T_3 - T_1}$
$A\left(\dfrac{1 + PT_1}{1 + PT_1 + P^2T_1T_2}\right)$		$A = R_2$ $T_1 = 2R_1C$ $T_2 = \dfrac{R_2C}{2}$	$R_1 = \dfrac{AT_1}{4T_2}$ $R_2 = A$ $C = \dfrac{2T_2}{A}$
$A\left(\dfrac{1 + PT_2}{1 + PT_1 + P^2T_1T_2}\right)$		$A = 2R$ $T_1 = 2RC_2$ $T_2 = \dfrac{RC_1}{2}$	$R = \dfrac{A}{2}$ $C_1 = \dfrac{4T_2}{A}$ $C_2 = \dfrac{T_1}{A}$

Table A-1. Short-circuit Transfer Impedances for Operational Amplifiers* (Continued)

Transfer-impedance function	Network	Relations	Inverse relations
		$A = \dfrac{2R_1R_2}{(2R_1+R_2)}$ $T_1 = \dfrac{R_1(R_1C_1+2R_2C_2)}{2R_1+R_2}$ $T_2 = \dfrac{R_1R_2C_1C_2}{R_1C_1+2R_2C_2}$ $T_3 = \dfrac{R_1C_1}{2}$	$R_1 = \dfrac{AT_3^2}{2[T_3^2 - T_1(T_3 - T_2)]}$ $R_2 = \dfrac{AT_3^2}{T_1(T_3 - T_2)}$ $C_1 = \dfrac{4[T_3^2 - T_1(T_3 - T_2)]}{AT_3}$ $C_2 = \dfrac{T_1T_2}{AT_3}$
$A\left[\dfrac{1+PT_3}{1+PT_1+P^2T_1T_2}\right]$ $T_3 > \dfrac{T_1}{4}$ (complex roots) $T_3 > T_2$		$A = 2R_1$ $T_1 = R_2C_1 + 2R_1C_2$ $T_2 = \dfrac{R_1(R_1 + 2R_2)C_1C_2}{R_2C_1 + 2R_1C_2}$ $T_3 = \left(R_2 + \dfrac{R_1}{2}\right)C_1$	$R_1 = \dfrac{A}{2}$ $R_2 = \dfrac{AT_1(T_3 - T_2)}{4[T_3^2 - T_1(T_3 - T_2)]}$ $C_1 = \dfrac{4[T_3^2 - T_1(T_3 - T_2)]}{AT_3}$ $C_2 = \dfrac{T_1T_2}{AT_3}$
		$A = 2R$ $T_1 = R(C_2 + 2C_3)$ $T_2 = \dfrac{RC_3(C_1 + C_2)}{C_2 + 2C_3}$ $T_3 = \dfrac{R}{2}(C_1 + C_2)$	$R = \dfrac{A}{2}$ $C_1 = \dfrac{2[2T_3^2 - T_1(T_3 - T_2)]}{AT_3}$ $C_2 = \dfrac{2T_1(T_3 - T_2)}{AT_3}$ $C_3 = \dfrac{T_1T_2}{AT_3}$
		$A = R_2$ $T_1 = 2R_1C_1 + R_2C_2$ $T_2 = \dfrac{R_1R_2C_1(C_1 + 2C_2)}{2R_1C_1 + R_2C_2}$ $T_3 = 2R_1C_1$	$R_1 = \dfrac{AT_3^2}{4[T_1T_2 - T_3(T_1 - T_3)]}$ $R_2 = A$ $C_1 = \dfrac{2[T_1T_2 - T_3(T_1 - T_3)]}{AT_3}$ $C_2 = \dfrac{(T_1 - T_3)}{A}$
$A'\left[\dfrac{1+PT_3}{1+PT_1+P^2T_1T_2}\right]$ $T_3 > \dfrac{T_1}{4}$ (complex roots) $T_3 < T_1$		$A = R_2$ $T_1 = \dfrac{C_1(2R_1C_2 + R_2C_1)}{2C_1 + C_2}$ $T_2 = \dfrac{R_1R_2C_1C_2}{2R_1C_2 + R_2C_1}$ $T_3 = \dfrac{2R_1C_1C_2}{(2C_1 + C_2)}$	$R_1 = \dfrac{AT_3^2}{4[T_1T_2 - T_3(T_1 - T_3)]}$ $R_2 = A$ $C_1 = \dfrac{2T_1T_2}{AT_3}$ $C_2 = \dfrac{4T_1T_2[T_1T_2 - T_3(T_1 - T_3)]}{AT_3^2(T_1 - T_3)}$
		$A = R_3$ $T_1 = \dfrac{R_1(2R_2 + R_3)C}{R_1 + R_2}$ $T_2 = \dfrac{R_2R_3C}{(2R_2 + R_3)}$ $T_3 = \dfrac{2R_1R_2C}{(R_1 + R_2)}$	$R_1 = \dfrac{AT_3^2}{2[2T_1T_2 - T_3(T_1 - T_3)]}$ $R_2 = \dfrac{AT_3}{2(T_1 - T_3)}$ $R_3 = A$ $C = \dfrac{2T_1T_2}{AT_3}$
$A(1+PT_1)(1+PT_2)$ $T_1 < T_2$		$A = 2R_1 + R_2$ $T_1 = \left(\dfrac{R_1R_2}{2R_1 + R_2}\right)C$ $T_2 = R_1C$	$R_1 = A\left(\dfrac{T_2 - T_1}{2T_2}\right)$ $R_2 = A\dfrac{T_1}{T_2}$ $C = \dfrac{2T_2^2}{A(T_2 - T_1)}$

Table A-1. Short-circuit Transfer Impedances for Operational Amplifiers* (Continued)

Transfer-impedance function	Network	Relations	Inverse relations
$\dfrac{1}{PB}\left(\dfrac{1+P\theta T}{1+PT}\right)$ $\theta < 1$	(circuit)	$B = C_2$ $T = RC_1\left(\dfrac{2C_2+C_1}{C_2}\right)$ $\theta = \dfrac{2C_2}{2C_2+C_1}$	$R = \dfrac{T\theta^2}{4B(1-\theta)}$ $C_1 = \dfrac{2B(1-\theta)}{\theta}$ $C_2 = B$
	(circuit)	$B = \dfrac{C_1^2}{2C_1+C_2}$ $T = RC_2$ $\theta = \dfrac{2C_1}{2C_1+C_2}$	$R = \dfrac{T\theta^2}{4B(1-\theta)}$ $C_1 = \dfrac{2B}{\theta}$ $C_2 = \dfrac{4B(1-\theta)}{\theta^2}$
	(circuit)	$B = \left(\dfrac{R_1}{R_1+R_2}\right)C$ $T = R_2C$ $\theta = \dfrac{2R_1}{R_1+R_2}$	$R_1 = \dfrac{T\theta^2}{2B(2-\theta)}$ $R_2 = \dfrac{T\theta}{2B}$ $C = \dfrac{2B}{\theta}$
$A\left[\dfrac{1+PT_2}{(1+PT_1)(1+PT_3)}\right]$ $T_1 < T_2 < T_3$	(circuit)	$A = R_1 + R_2$ $T_1 = R_1C_1$ $T_2 = \left(\dfrac{R_1R_2}{R_1+R_2}\right)(C_1+C_2)$ $T_3 = R_2C_2$	$R_1 = \dfrac{A(T_2-T_1)}{T_3-T_1}$ $R_2 = \dfrac{A(T_3-T_2)}{T_3-T_1}$ $C_1 = \dfrac{T_1(T_3-T_1)}{A(T_2-T_1)}$ $C_2 = \dfrac{T_3(T_3-T_1)}{A(T_3-T_2)}$
	(circuit)	$A = R_2$ $T_2 = R_1C_1$ $T_1T_3 = R_1R_2C_1C_2$ $T_1 + T_3 = R_1C_1 + R_2C_2 + R_2C_1$	$R_1 = \dfrac{AT_2^2}{(T_3-T_2)(T_2-T_1)}$ $R_2 = A$ $C_1 = \dfrac{(T_3-T_2)(T_2-T_1)}{AT_2}$ $C_2 = \dfrac{T_1T_3}{AT_2}$
	(circuit)	$A = R_1 + R_2$ $T_2 = \left(\dfrac{R_1R_2}{R_1+R_2}\right)C_2$ $T_1T_3 = R_1R_2C_1C_2$ $T_1 + T_3 = R_1C_1 + R_2C_2 + R_2C_1$	$R_1 = \dfrac{AT_2^2}{T_1T_2+T_2T_3-T_1T_3}$ $R_2 = \dfrac{A(T_3-T_2)(T_2-T_1)}{T_1T_2+T_2T_3-T_1T_3}$ $C_1 = \dfrac{T_1T_3}{AT_2}$ $C_2 = \dfrac{(T_1T_2+T_2T_3-T_1T_3)^2}{AT_2(T_3-T_2)(T_2-T_1)}$
	(circuit)	$A = R_1$ $T_2 = R_2(C_1+C_2)$ $T_1T_3 = R_1R_2C_1C_2$ $T_1 + T_3 = R_1C_1 + R_2C_2 + R_2C_1$	$R_1 = A$ $R_2 = \dfrac{A(T_3-T_2)(T_2-T_1)}{(T_1+T_3-T_2)^2}$ $C_1 = \dfrac{T_1+T_3-T_2}{A}$ $C_2 = \dfrac{T_1T_3(T_1+T_3-T_2)}{A(T_3-T_2)(T_2-T_1)}$

Table A-1. Short-circuit Transfer Impedances for Operational Amplifiers* (Continued)

Transfer-impedance function	Network	Relations	Inverse relations
$A\left[\dfrac{1+PT_2}{(1+PT_1)(1+PT_3)}\right]$ $T_2 \leq T_1 \leq T_3$		$A = 2R_1 + \dfrac{R_1^2}{R_2}$ $T_1 = R_1C_1$ $T_2 = \left(\dfrac{R_1R_2}{R_1+2R_2}\right)(C_1+C_2)$ $T_3 = R_1C_2$	$R_1 = \dfrac{AT_2}{(T_1+T_3)}$ $R_2 = \dfrac{AT_2^2}{(T_1+T_3)(T_1+T_3-2T_2)}$ $C_1 = \dfrac{T_1(T_1+T_3)}{AT_2}$ $C_2 = \dfrac{T_3(T_1+T_3)}{AT_2}$
$A\left[\dfrac{1+PT_2}{(1+PT_1)(1+PT_3)}\right]$ $T_1 \leq T_3 \leq T_2$		$A = R_1 + R_2$ $T_1 = R_1C_1$ $T_2 = \dfrac{R_1R_2}{R_1+R_2}(2C_1+C_2)$ $T_3 = R_2C_1$	$R_1 = \dfrac{AT_1}{(T_1+T_3)}$ $R_2 = \dfrac{AT_3}{(T_1+T_3)}$ $C_1 = \dfrac{(T_1+T_3)}{A}$ $C_2 = \dfrac{(T_1+T_3)}{A}\left(\dfrac{T_2}{T_3}+\dfrac{T_2}{T_1}-2\right)$

* Reproduced by permission of the McGraw-Hill Publishing Company from F. R. Bradley and R. McCoy, Driftless D-c Amplifier, *Electronics*, April, 1952. This table was developed by S. Godet of the Reeves Instrument Corporation, New York City.

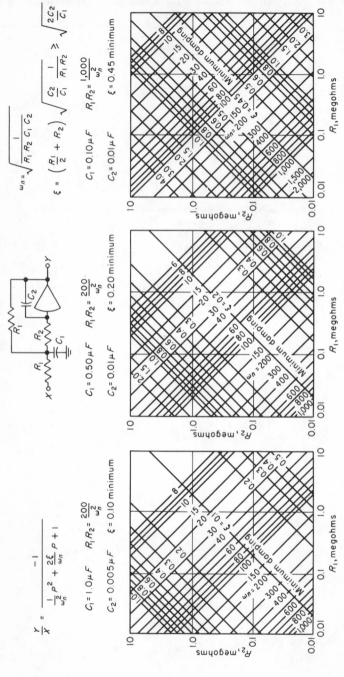

$$\frac{Y}{X} = \frac{-1}{\frac{1}{\omega_n^2}P^2 + \frac{2\xi}{\omega_n}P + 1}$$

$C_1 = 1.0\mu F \quad R_1 R_2 = \frac{200}{\omega_n^2} \quad \xi = 0.10 \text{ minimum}$

$C_2 = 0.005\mu F$

$$\omega_n = \sqrt{\frac{1}{R_1 R_2 C_1 C_2}}$$

$$\xi = \left(\frac{R_1}{2} + R_2\right)\sqrt{\frac{C_2}{C_1}}\sqrt{\frac{1}{R_1 R_2}} \geq \sqrt{\frac{2C_2}{C_1}}$$

$C_1 = 0.10\mu F \quad R_1 R_2 = \frac{1,000}{\omega_n^2}$

$C_2 = 0.01\mu F \quad \xi = 0.45 \text{ minimum}$

$C_1 = 0.50\mu F \quad R_1 R_2 = \frac{200}{\omega_n^2} \quad \xi = 0.20 \text{ minimum}$

$C_2 = 0.01\mu F$

FIG. A-1. Design nomographs for a simple circuit permitting economical computer representation of many mass-spring-dashpot or equivalent systems (valves, pressure pickups, rate gyros, accelerometers, etc.). (Nomographs prepared by H. J. Shear, Ryan Aeronautical Co., San Diego, Calif., for G. W. Smith and R. C. Wood, Principles of Analog Computation, McGraw-Hill Book Co., N.Y., 1959; reproduced by permission of the publishers.)

Table A-2. Generation of Functions with Linear Potentiometers

r_L may be a load resistance.   *Errors are computed for perfect resistors and potentiometers, negligible source impedances, and infinite-gain amplifiers.*

No.	Machine equation	Circuit or block diagram	Remarks
1	$X_o = X|Y|$		Subject to loading error, which may be corrected by loading the servo follow-up potentiometer
2	$X_o = X \dfrac{1}{2 - Y^2} \approx \dfrac{X}{2} \sec Y$		Error $\approx \frac{1}{24} Y^4$
3a	$X_o = X \dfrac{2Y}{3 - Y^2} \approx \dfrac{2}{3} X \tan Y$ for $r_L = 0.5r$		Angular error within $\pm 0.04°$ for $|Y| \leq \frac{1}{2}$*
3b	$X_o = X \dfrac{1.792Y}{2.792 - Y^2} \approx \dfrac{1.792}{2.792} X \tan Y$ for $r_L = 0.448r$		Angular error within $\pm 0.1°$ for $|Y| \leq 1$*
4	$X_o = -X \dfrac{(2.8 - Y)Y}{(1.8 + Y)(1 - Y)}$ $\approx -X \tan \dfrac{\pi}{2} Y$		Angular error within $0.034°$ for $0 \leq Y < 1$†

Table A-2. Generation of Functions with Linear Potentiometers (*Continued*)

No.	Machine equation	Circuit or block diagram	Remarks
5	$X_o \approx -\sqrt{\dfrac{R_o}{R_1}}\,X \quad X > 0$		$r \ll R_o$
6a	$X_o = 0.2X \sin \dfrac{\pi}{2} Y$		Error less than 1% for $0 \leq Y \leq 1$‡
6b	$X_o = X \sin \dfrac{\pi}{2} Y$		Error less than 0.4% for $0 \leq Y \leq 1$‡
7	$X_o = X \sin \dfrac{\pi}{2} Y$		Error less than 0.4% for $0 \leq Y \leq 1$‡

* Hofstadter, R., A Simple Potentiometer Circuit for Production of the Tangent Function, *Rev. Sci. Instr.*, **17**: 298, 1946.

† Seay, P. A., An Accurate Tangent Computing Circuit, *REAC Newsletter*, August, 1954 (Reeves Instrument Corporation, New York City).

‡ *Project TYPHOON Summary Progress Report No. 4*, Vol. 2, RCA Research Laboratories, Princeton, N.J. (unclassified).

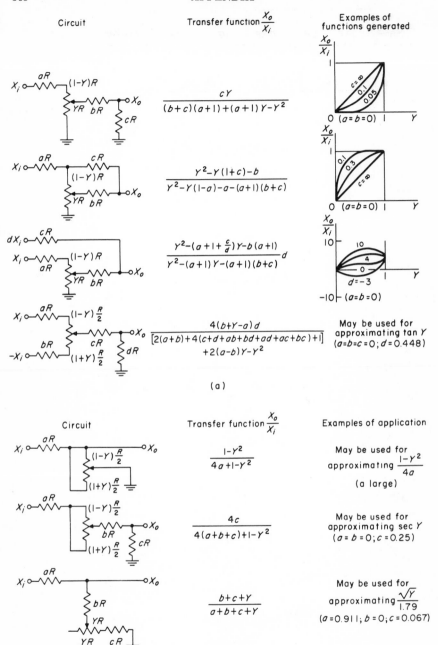

FIG. A-2. Generation of various nonlinear functions of a servo-shaft displacement Y with the aid of linear potentiometers (Refs. 8 and 24, Chap. 8).

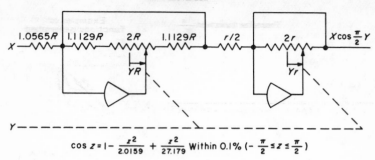

$$\cos z = 1 - \frac{z^2}{2.0159} + \frac{z^2}{27.179} \text{ Within 0.1\% } \left(-\frac{\pi}{2} \leq z \leq \frac{\pi}{2}\right)$$

FIG. A-3. Cosine computing circuit (*Lazarus, H., Cosine Computing Circuit, U.S. Patent No.* 2,864,924, *December,* 1958).

AUTHOR INDEX

The author index refers by page number to the entries in the *References and Bibliography* sections arranged by subject matter at the end of each individual chapter. To obtain references by subject matter, consult the subject index and refer to the *References and Bibliography* sections for the appropriate chapters.

Aarons, M. W., 206
Abe, R., 251
Abrahanian, V. V., 74
Adcock, W. A., 548
Adise, H., 341, 342
Airpax, 174
Alexander, M. A., 500
Andeen, R. E., 433
Anderson, T. C., 549
Anderson, W. W., 437
Andrews, J. M., 343, 434
Angelo, E. L., 305
Artzt, M., 173
Aseltine, J. A., 73

Baker, R. H., 253, 502
Barber, D. L., 175
Barbour, C. W., 499
Barker, B., 368
Barrack, C. M., 303
Bauer, L., 552
Baum, R. V., 249, 304, 368
Bayly, J. G., 438
Beck, C., 73
Beck, R. M., 34, 500
Beer, A. C., 304
Bekey, C., 435, 436, 499, 551, 552
Bell, B., 250
Bell, C. G., 500
Benedict, J., 437
Bénéteau, P. J., 205, 206
Bennett, R. R., 249
Berbert, A. G., 368, 552
Berger, E. L., 369
Bergman, G. D., 436
Berry, J. R., 205

Bickart, T. A., 35, 434
Biernson, G. A., 341
Bihovski, J. L., 547
Billinghurst, E. M., 174, 175
Binsack, J. H., 305, 500
Blackburn, J. F., 120, 341
Blanyer, C. G., 434
Blaser, L., 205
Blecher, F. H., 204
Blum, N. A., 35
Bocharov, I. N., 549
Bode, H. W., 304
Boehmer, H. W., 304
Bogert, H., 206
Bohn, E. V., 502
Bolie, V. W., 342
Boothroyd, A. R., 253
Bourbeau, A., 436
Bowker, J. F., 206
Bradley, F. R., 341
Bradley, R. E., 500
Bright, R. L., 205, 250
Brog, K. C., 35
Brooks, S. H., 550
Broomal, J., 303
Brown, G. W., 548
Brubaker, T. A., 120, 253, 434, 435
Bruck, D. B., 306
Brulé, J. D., 436
Brunner, W., 343, 548–551
Bruns, R. A., 251
Brussolo, J. A., 120
Burns, A. J., 499
Burns, L. F., 35
Burr-Brown Research Corp., 205, 369
Burt, R. W., 500
Bush, L., 547

Cahn, L., 342
Carlson, R., 435
Chance, B., 249, 302, 304, 342
Chapelle, W. E., 501
Chaplin, G. B., 204, 250
Chasmar, R. P., 303
Chestnut, H., 436
Circuitdyne Corp., 498
Clare, C. P., and Co., 435
Clark, W. R., 174
Close, R. N., 433
Clymer, A. B., 550, 551
Clynes, M., 552
Cochran, D. S., 369
Cockrell, W. D., 368
Cohen, E., 303
Columbia University, 433
Comcor, Inc., 501
Comley, W., 251, 305
Computer Control Corp., 435
Computer Systems, Inc., 250, 251, 436
Conant, B. K., 370
Connelly, N. E., 302, 343, 500
Connolly, T. W., 17, 36, 437, 548
Corbett, J., 549
Corbin, R. M., 550
Cox, F. B., 500
Crayford, R. M., 502
Cullin, A., 435

Dandl, R. A., 437
Davidson, G. M., 303
Davis, H. B., 305
DeBoice, W. F., 206
Decanini, J., 500
Deering, C. S., 174
DeLand, E. C., 548, 552
DeMatteis, W. M., 205
Depian, L., 205
Diamantides, N. D., 35, 250, 369
Digital Equipment Corp., 435, 499
Dijinis, W., 303
DiSabato, J., 175
Doganovskii, I., 251
Dole, F. E., 120, 342
Donce, J. L., 436
Dooley, R. P., 434
Dow, P. C., 120
Duffy, R. M., 253
Dujmovic, M., 342
Dumas, H. J., 304
Duncan, D. C., 341
Dunsmore, C. L., 370

Ebers, J. J., 250
Eckes, H. R., 369, 435, 501, 550
Edwards, C. M., 249, 497

Eggers, C. W., 500
Ehlers, H. L., 175, 205, 250, 341, 498
Eide, M. A., 437
Eklund, K., 34
Electronic Associates, Inc., 252, 343, 370, 434, 437, 438, 499, 552
Electronic Design Staff, 206
Elgerd, O. I., 436
Ernst, D., 35
Eterman, I. I., 35
Ettinger, G. M., 204

Fannin, B. B., 370
Farrand, W. A., 499
Favreau, R. R., 73, 548, 550
Feldbaum, A. A., 35, 549
Fifer, S., 35, 73, 120
Fischer, L. G., 369
Fisher, M. E., 36, 73, 305, 306, 434, 502, 551
Fitsner, L. M., 251, 304, 305
Fitzgibbon, T. P., 435
Fleischmann, J. S., 206
Flockhart, D. G., 303
Fluegel, D. A., 436
Fogarty, L. E., 548
Foiles, C., 498
Foote, D. D., 253, 370
Ford, D. J., 438
Forrester, J. H., 437
Fradella, R. B., 174
Frank, R. W., 438
Franklin, G. F., 436
Franks, R. 550
Frazier, J. P., 369
Freeman, L. R., 436
Frenkel, G., 369
Frey, H. B., 305
Frost, J., 341
Fuchs, A., 252
Fuchs, H., 303
Fulton, A. S., 249

Garner, K. C., 342
Gaskill, R. A., 499
Geffe, P. R., 437
Gelman, R., 499
General Applied Science Laboratories, 435
General Electric Co., 204
Genna, J. F., 500
Gerlach, A. A., 251
Gibbons, J. F., 253
Gibson, J. E., 341
Gilbert, C. P., 253
Gilbert, E. G., 343, 549, 550
Gilbert, E. O., 341

Gilbert, J., 120, 342
Gilliland, M. G., 435, 551
Giloi, W., 34, 551
Ginzton, E. L., 173
Giser, D., 251, 305, 343
Gleghorn, P., 304
Glinski, G. S., 552
Gocht, R. E., 174, 250
Godet, S., 249, 342
Goldberg, E. A., 174, 302, 304, 548
Goldmann, H. O., 204
Good, E. F., 369
Goode, H. H., 35
GPS Instrument Co., 436, 552
Grabbe, E. M., 35, 500
Grado, G. R., 343
Graig, L. S., 303
Gray, H. J., 250
Gray, J., 174
Gray, T. S., 305
Green, C., 498
Greenstein, J. L., 499
Greenwood, D. T., 549, 551
Greenwood, I. A., 304, 341
Greiner, R. A., 303
Grindle, B., 502
Grinich, V. H., 253
Gronner, A. D., 174
Gundlach, F. W., 305
Gunning, I. A., 341
Gunning, W. F., 174

Haas, D. L., 497
Haddican, P. J., 501
Hagan, T. G., 502
Halbert, P. W., 438, 550, 551
Halligan, J. W., 205
Hamer, H., 174, 251, 498
Hamming, R. W., 502
Hampton, R. L., 434, 501
Hancock, E. J., 251
Handler, H., 175
Hannet, R. T., 305
Hara, H. H., 436, 551
Harbert, F. C., 73
Harris, H. E., 342
Harris, J. N., 500
Harris, M., 341
Hartmann, J., 305, 343, 368, 498
Hausner, A., 73, 370, 438
Heid, J. P., 501
Heidrich, A. J., 369
Hertog, J. M., 369
Herzog, A. W., 500
Hilbiber, D. F., 205, 206
Hilbinger, A. R., 303
Hills, F., 500
Hilsum, C., 303

Hirano, C., 205
Hochwald, W., 175, 205, 250, 341, 498
Hoehn, G. L., 434
Hoffait, A. H., 205
Hofheimer, R. N., 500
Hofman, C. D., 436
Hofstadter, R., 342
Hogan, I. J., 342
Holdam, J. V., 304, 341
Honnell, P. M., 73
Horn, H. S., 253
Horn, R. E., 73
Horwitz, R. D., 498
Howe, R. M., 35, 120, 174, 249, 343, 369, 370, 548, 549, 551
Howell, J. V., 500
Howell, M., 551
Hubaut, E. E., 120
Hughes, V., 342
Hunt, J. M., 303
Hunter, L. P., 204, 250, 498
Hurley, J. R., 499
Huskey, H. D., 35

Iannone, F., 174
Ingerson, W. E., 174
Iwata, J., 499, 551

Jackson, A. S., 35, 73, 175, 437
Jacoby, G. T., 251
James Electronics, Inc., 205
Jarrett, R. J., 501
Jerrard, R. P., 251
Johnson, C. L., 35, 369
Jury, S. H., 434, 436

Kamm, L. J., 497
Karnopp, D. C., 550
Karplus, W. J., 35, 121, 252, 434, 436, 499, 548, 551
Kataoka, S., 303
Katell, E., 35
Keister, G. L., 304
Keller, R. E., 549
Kelley, C. R., 368, 552
Kelley, T., 252
Kennedy, J. D., 436, 498
Kerfoot, B. P., 204
Kettel, E., 304
Kezer, A., 550
Kindle, W. K., 251, 343
King, C. M., 499
King, W. J., 437
Kiseda, J. R., 438

Kislytsin, S. G., 342
Kiyono, T., 499
Klein, G., 369
Koeblitz, W., 343
Koerner, H., 174, 249, 368, 498
 (*See also* Burr-Brown Research Corp.)
Kogan, B. Y., 35, 73, 120
Konigsberg, R. L., 204
Kopp, R. E., 499
Korn, G. A., 34, 35, 73, 74, 120, 121, 171,
 249, 304, 305, 342, 343, 368–370, 497,
 501, 548, 552
Korn, T. M., 34, 73, 171, 304, 369, 370,
 552
Kovach, L. D., 251, 305, 548, 552
Kovatch, G., 303
Kozak, W. S., 437
Krasny, L. M., 500
Kruper, A. P., 250
Kuchlewski, T. R., 502
Kuh, E. S., 437
Kuntze, K., 73
Kusto, T. J., 497

Lambert, J. M., 369
Landauer, J. P., 437, 438, 550
Lane, R. Q., 205
Lange, A. S., 547
Langill, A. W., 370
Larrowe, V., 251
Lauber, R., 35
Lazarus, H., 342
Lee, R. C., 500
Leger, R. M., 499
Lehmann, J., 174
Leite, C., 369
Leondes, C. T., 550
Levenstein, E., 342
Levine, L., 35, 548
Levitt, J. R., 251
Levy, H., 499
Liban, E., 551
Lilamand, M. L., 250, 304
Litvin, F. L., 342
Liu, B., 438
Lofgren, L., 303, 433
Loopstra, B. J., 174
Loveman, B. D., 120, 341, 433, 497,
 498
Lucas, P., 206

McCool, W. A., 174, 303
McCoy, R. D., 306, 341, 342, 437, 497
McDonald, R. K., 205
McGrath, R. J., 550
McGregor, W. K., 35

Machol, R. E., 35
MacKay, D. M., 36, 306, 434, 502, 551
McLeod, J., 369
McMahan, M., 368
MacNee, A. B., 120, 251, 305, 502
MacNichol, E. F., 342
MacRae, D., 304, 341
McWhorter, M. M., 206
Maloy, R. W., 251
Mangels, R., 436
Marchant, H., 342
Margolis, M., 550
Margolis, S. G., 437
Marimon, R. L., 206
Markle, R., 435
Marshall, B. O., 548
Marsocci, V. A., 120
Maslov, A. A., 251, 302, 304, 305
Mason, M. S., 252
Massey, W. S., 205
Mathews, M. V., 34
Matsuno, S., 552
Matyaš, J., 73
Maybach, R. L., 305, 343, 368, 438, 501
Mayer, R. E., 253
Medkeff, R. J., 249
Meissinger, H. F., 119, 250, 252, 306, 547,
 548
Mengel, A. S., 174, 341
Meserve, W. E., 303
Meyer, R. A., 305
Meyer-Brötz, G., 175, 204, 250, 369,
 497
Michaelis, T. D., 34
Mickey, M. R., 550
Middlebrook, R. D., 205, 206
Milford, F. J., 35
Miller, F. C., 497
Miller, I. A., 304
Miller, K. S., 73, 119, 547
Miller, S. E., 173
Millman, J., 249, 304, 434
Mills, R. L., 305
Minorski, N., 73
Mishkin, E., 550
Mitchell, B., 250
Mitchell, B. A., 499, 501, 550
Mitchell, J. M., 500
Mitrovic, D. M., 438
Miura, T., 120, 205, 250, 251, 343, 435,
 499, 551
Moll, J. L., 250
Monastyrshin, G. I., 370
Moore, J. R., 343
Morrill, C. D., 249, 302, 304, 343, 368
Morrison, J., 368
Moser, J. H., 549
Munson, J. K., 550
Murari, E., 206

Murray, F. J., 119, 547, 548
Myers, G. H., 501
Mynall, D. J., 251

Nagata, M., 120
Nambiar, K. P., 205
National Semiconductor Corp., 206, 250
Navigation Computer Corp., 500
Nelson, D. J., 500
Nelson, J. K., 35
Netter, Z., 306
Nettleton, L. A., 120, 342
Neustadt, L. W., 548, 549
Noble, S. W., 205
Nothman, M. H., 435

O'Donnell, J. J., 437
O'Grady, E., 501
Ohlinger, L. A., 499
Okada, R. H., 204
Oliver, B. M., 369
Olsen, R., 436
Orlando, P., 547
Ornstein, G. N., 550
Osburn, P. V., 550
Owens, A. R., 250
Oxeni, J., 303
Ozdes, D., 175, 205

Page, J., 369
Palevsky, M., 500, 502
Palmer, J., 205
Palumbo, O. J., 369
Parent, R. J., 249
Parezanovic, N., 342
Paskman, M., 499
Paul, R. A. J., 304, 502
Paynter, H. M., 370
Pearman, C. R., 502
Pederson, C. N., 251
Peretz, R., 252
Perez, J. J., 436
Perry, K. E., 500
Petrenko, A. I., 174
Petrovic, R., 302
Petternella, M., 252
Pettit, J. M., 206, 249, 434
Pfeiffer, P. E., 249, 305
Philbrick, G. A., 206, 252, 305, 437, 438
Philco Corp., 205
Pierce, D. E., 497
Pike, H. L., 436
Piloty, H., 437
Pinckney, R. P., 251, 343
Platzek, R. C., 498

Polimerou, L. G., 251, 252
Polonikov, D. E., 174
Popodi, A. E., 502
Potts, T. F., 550
Price, R., 303
Puckett, T. H., 249
Purlov, Y. G., 251
Pyne, I. B., 548

Rademaker, J. R., 547
Radio Corporation of America, 502
  (See also RCA Laboratories Division)
Raggazini, J. R., 436
Rajaraman, V., 550
Rall, B., 498
Ramo, S., 35, 500
Rawdin, E., 433
Raymond, F. H., 343
RCA Laboratories Division, 304, 342
  (See also Radio Corporation of America)
Ream, N., 306
Reece, J. M., 35
Reed, C. O., 549
Reich, J. E., 436
Revis, J. T., 174
Rideout, V. C., 437, 550
Riebman, L., 303
Ritchie, C. C., 306
Rittenhouse, J. W., 174
Robichaud, J., 74
Rogers, A. E., 36, 73, 437, 548
Rogers, S., 497
Root, C. D., 249
Rosenkranius, L., 251
Rote, W. A., 205
Ruberti, A., 252
Rubin, A. I., 73, 368, 549, 550
Rubinoff, M., 250
Russell, D. W., 35
Rybashov, M. V., 548

Sack, H. S., 304
Sargent, R. S., 502
Saucedo, R., 436
Savet, P. H., 303
Savitt, A., 498
Sayre, D., 342
Scanga, W. A., 303
Schaefer, R. A., 502
Schenkerman, S., 204
Schmid, H., 249, 253, 302–305, 343, 501, 502
Schmidt, H. A., 341
Schmidt, W., 305
Schneider, W., 250, 304

Schreier, D., 251, 305
Schwartz, J., 205
Schwartz, S., 435
Schwent, G. V., 35
Scott, N. R., 36
Scott, R. E., 304
Seay, P. A., 342
Sebestyen, G., 250
Seegmiller, W. R., 502
Seening, Yee, 253
Seifert, W. W., 34
Sellars, H. C., 549
Sheinin, I. S., 253
Shen, C. N., 370
Sherchant, I., 342
Short, E., 252
Shubin, A. B., 549
Shumate, M. S., 436
Siliconix, Inc., 206
Siljak, D., 302
Silverberg, B., 251
Simulation Councils, Inc., 499
Single, C. H., 120, 437
Skiles, J. J., 499
Skramstad, H. K., 501, 549
Slaughter, D. W., 205
Smith, G. W., 34, 36, 250, 369, 437
Smith, R. E., 205
Smolov, V. B., 252, 500
Solomonoff, R., 205
Soltes, A. S., 304
Sommer, B., 205
Sommerville, M. J., 303
Sondack, A. C., 438
Soroka, W. W., 35, 548
Sosenskii, N. L., 120
Spencer, M., 251
Stakovskii, R. I., 549
Stanton, J. W., 204
Stein, M. L., 498
Steingroewer, H., 370
Stern, T. E., 252
Sternberg, S., 205, 304
Sternick, L., 305
Stewart, E. L., 502
Stone, R. S., 437
Storch, L., 437
Straehli, E. H., 250
Stranddorf, S. P., 249
Strassberg, D. D., 434
Strauss, L., 250, 434
Stubbs, G. A., 434, 551
Sunstein, D. E., 251
Susi, F., 343
Susskind, A. K., 498
Svechnikov, S. V., 174
Sykes, R. P., 120, 498
Systron-Donner Corp., 501
Sze, T. W., 436, 500

Tarpley, R. E., 174
Taub, H., 249, 304, 434
Taylor, A. D., 205
Taylor, R. M., 369
Tazkin, A. I., 549
Terasaki, R. M., 552
Terrazas, C., 370
Texas Instruments Inc., 204, 206, 343, 435, 498
Thaulow, P., 343
Thogersen, G. O., 433
Thornton, R. D., 205
Tomlinson, N. P., 249
Tomović, R., 36, 121, 252, 434, 436, 548, 551
Tompkins, J., 250
Truitt, T., 36, 498, 499, 502
Truxal, J. G., 341
Turner, R. M., 549
Turner, W. W., 433
Tuteur, F. B., 341

Ulbrich, E., 437

Vance, P. R., 497
Van der Schmidt, G. F., 35
Verster, T. C., 253
Vichnevetsky, R., 436, 438, 549–551
Volkers, W. K., 174
Vosteen, R. E., 35

Wadel, L. B., 434
Wagner, J. H., 434
Waha, J. P., 550
Wait, J. V., 434, 499, 501
Waldhauer, F. D., 206
Wallman, H., 174, 252
Walsh, J. B., 73
Walters, L. G., 304
Wang, H., 370
Warfield, J. N., 36, 437
Warner, H. R., 552
Wass, C. A., 36
Weinberg, L., 437
Wentzel, V., 252
West, J. C., 436
Weyrick, R. C., 343
Whigham, R., 501
Whitaker, H. P., 550
Whitman, G. B., 175, 501
Wierville, W. W., 438
Wilkinson, R. H., 253
Williams, A. J., 174, 205, 250
Williams, F. C., 205, 342
Williams, R. W., 342
Wilson, A., 499

Winkler, H., 36, 251, 305
Witsenhausen, H., 74, 369, 550–552
Wollard, S. B., 174
Wong, M. S., 370
Wood, R. C., 34, 36, 250, 369, 437
Wooldridge, D. E., 35, 500
Wright Air Development Center (WADC), 343, 501

Yee, Seening, 253
Young, R. W., 306

Zackon, D. L., 437
Zampino, J., 370
Zenner, R. E., 251
Zuzi, F. C., 497

SUBJECT INDEX

References in the subject index are to section numbers, not page numbers. Note that section numbers are displayed at the top of each page for convenient reference.

Absolute-value circuit, in digital voltmeter, **9**-4
  diode, **6**-13
  precision, **9**-2
  servo, **2**-11, Appendix Table A-2
A-c amplifier for chopper stabilizer, **4**-14
Acceleration limit, **8**-1, **8**-3, **8**-4
Accumulator, exponential, **10**-13
  track-hold, **10**-8
Accuracy, general discussion, **1**-18, **3**-1
A/D converter (*see* Analog-to-digital converter)
A/D/A converter/multiplier, **7**-6, **7**-22, **11**-16
Adaptive system, **12**-12
Adjoint method, **10**-11
Adjustment (*see* Calibration)
AGC· (*see* Automatic gain control)
Aircraft-Marine Products, **11**-1
Algebraic equations, **12**-8
Algebraic loop, **2**-18
Aliasing, **10**-15
All-pass delay approximation, **10**-18
Alpha cutoff, **5**-11
AM/FM multiplier, **7**-3, **7**-7
Amplification factor, **4**-4
Amplifier, servo, **8**-3
Amplifier delay time constant, **8**-2
Amplitude modulation, computer circuit, **9**-5
Amplitude scaling (*see* Scaling)
Amplitude-selection multiplier (*see* Multiplier, triangle-averaging)
Amplitude selector, **6**-3, **6**-17, **9**-3
AM/PWM multiplier (*see* Multiplier, time-division)
Analog comparator (*see* Comparator)
Analog-to-digital (A/D) converter, **7**-6, **9**-4, **11**-11, **11**-12, **11**-19
  partial, **11**-19

Analog subroutine in digital computer, **11**-16
Analog switch (*see* Electronic switch)
AND gate, **10**-10
APACHE code (*see* Programming automation)
Applied Dynamics, Inc., **1**-2, **11**-1
Arizona, ¡University of, **4**-23, **11**-1, **11**-7, **11**-9, **11**-10, **11**-19
  (*See also* ASTRAC I; ASTRAC II)
ARM terminal, **3**-4
Assembler program, **11**-15
Astable multivibrator, **9**-5, **7**-16
ASTRAC I, **3**-19, **3**-24, **7**-15, **10**-4, **11**-7
ASTRAC II, **11**-7, **12**-15
Astrodata (*see* Comcor, Inc.)
Attenuator (*see* A/D/A converter/multiplier; Coefficient-setting potentiometer)
Automatic balancing, **4**-13, **4**-14, **5**-8 to **5**-10
Automatic gain control (AGC), **7**-23, **8**-13, **9**-6
Automatic optimization (*see* Optimization)
Automatic scaling, **11**-4, **11**-15, **12**-6
Automatic setup, **11**-4

Back-to-back zener diode, **6**-3
Back resistance, of diode, **6**-2
  of switch, **6**-11
Backlash, in servo gears, **8**-1, **8**-3, **8**-4
  simulation of, **9**-7
Backward difference, **12**-19, **12**-21
BALANCE CHECK MODE, **10**-3, **11**-4
Balancing of d-c amplifiers, **4**-1, **4**-3, **5**-12, **11**-4
Barrier, simulation of, **9**-7, **12**-10

Base resistance, 5-2
BCD counter (see Binary-coded decimal counter)
Beckman/Berkeley Division, 4-23, 6-13, 7-12, 11-1, 11-2, 11-6
Bell function, 2-4
Bell Telephone Laboratories, 5-12
Beta cutoff, 5-11
Bias stability, 5-2
Binary-coded decimal counter (BCD counter), 10-10
Binary counter, 10-10
Binary-increment multiplier (see A/D/A converter/multiplier)
Binary variable, 6-1, 6-8, 10-6
Bistable circuits, 9-5
  in multiplier, 7-11, 7-12
  (See also Schmitt trigger)
Block diagram for computer setup, 2-3
Block-diagram symbols, 1-6, 2-4
  for digital circuits, 10-10
  for iterative computer, 10-7
Blocking capacitor, 4-13
Bode plot, 3-12, 4-15 to 4-21, 8-2
Booster resistor, 4-7
Bootstrap circuit, for high impedance, 1-19
  in transistor amplifier, 5-3, 5-11
Borg, George, Corp., 3-4
Bottle plug, 11-1
Boundary-value problem, 12-13, 12-14, 12-16
  (See also Partial differential equations)
Breakaway torque, 8-1, 8-4
Breakdown voltage, 6-2, 6-7
Breakpoint (see Function generator)
Bridge limiter (see Diode bridge)
Bucket-brigade delay, 10-19
Buffer, digital, 11-12, 11-13
Burr-Brown Research Corp., 5-12

CADDA (see Hybrid-code computer)
Calculus of variations, 12-16
Calibration, of coefficient-setting potentiometers, 3-5, 11-4
  of function generators, 6-13 to 6-15
  of multipliers, 7-20
  of tapped potentiometers, 8-8
Canonical equations, 12-16
Capacitance, distributed (see Parasitic capacitance)
Capacitor model, 3-9
Capcoder, 11-10
Carbon-film potentiometer, 3-4, 8-1, 8-5, 8-10
Carrier-type d-c amplifier, 4-13
Carry generation, 11-17, 11-19

Cascade encoder, 11-11
Catching diode, 6-3, 6-10, 7-16
Cathode follower, 4-1
  for low grid current, 4-12
  output stage, 4-7
  totem-pole, 4-7, 4-8
  "white," 4-8
Cathode-ray tube (see Display; Function generator; Multiplier)
Central difference, 12-19
Characteristics, transistor, 5-2
  vacuum-tube, 4-3
Charging time constant of track-hold circuit, 10-4
Check, digital, 11-15, 12-5
Checking, of computer accuracy, 11-5
  (See also Calibration)
  of computer setup, 2-8, 11-4
  of multiplier, 7-20, 11-5
  by resubstitution, 3-1, 12-5
  of solutions, 3-1, 3-11, 11-4, 12-5
Chemical reactions, simulation, 2-4
Chopper, 4-13, 4-14
  electronic, 5-8 to 5-10, 6-11
  (See also Electronic switch)
Chopper stabilization (see Automatic balancing)
Chopper stabilizer, plug-in, 4-23
Circle test, 3-24
  (See also Harmonic oscillator)
Clamping, 11-9
Clock-gated logic, 10-10
Clock motor, 1-4
Clutch, simulation, 9-9
Coefficient setting (see Potentiometer)
Coefficient-setting potentiometers, frequency response, 3-6
  loading effects, 3-5
  specifications, construction, 3-4
  three-terminal, 3-4
Coincidence multiplier, 7-3
Collector characteristics, 5-2
Combinatorial logic, 10-10
Combined simulation, 11-12, 11-13
Comcor, Inc., 5-12, 11-6, 11-20
Common-emitter stage, 5-2
Common-mode gain, 5-4
Common-mode rejection (see Differential amplifier)
Commutator stabilization, 4-13
Comparator, 6-1, 6-8, 7-11, 10-9, 11-2
  for automatic scaling, 12-6
  block-diagram symbol, 10-7
  in hybrid-code computer, 11-19
  in iterative computation, 10-6, 10-9, 10-12
  multiple, 9-2
  (See also Bistable circuits; Precision limiter)

Comparator/switch function generator, 6-18, 7-19
Compensation of power supply, 11-8
Complementary symmetry, 5-12
Complemented code, 11-10
Complex capacitance (*see* Dielectric absorption)
Complex roots, 12-8
Component accuracy, 3-1, 3-2
COMPUTE mode, 1-6, 10-2, 10-3, 10-5
COMPUTE-RESET switch, 1-12
Computer, general definition, 1-1
Computer Instruments Corp., 8-5
Computer Products, Inc., 1-2
Computer servomechanism (*see* Servomechanism)
Computer setup (*see* Differential equations; Scaling; Setup method)
Computer Systems, Inc., 10-4, 11-3, 11-6
Computer time, 2-5
Computing time, maximum, 1-12, 1-19
Conductive paper, 6-16
Conformity of potentiometer, 8-1, 8-5, 8-6
Conformity error, 8-5
Constant-temperature oven (*see* Oven)
Constraint, 12-7, 12-9, 12-10
  dynamical, 12-9, 12-16
  in mechanics, 12-9
  redundant, 12-9, 12-19
Control system, 10-3, 10-11
Control-system optimization, 12-13
Control variable, 10-6, 11-16
  (*See also* Binary variable)
Control-variable patchbay, 10-6, 10-11, 11-1, 11-6, 11-7, 11-13
Coordinate transformation, 8-9, 11-12, 11-17
Correction to solution, 12-1 to 12-5
Correction function, 2-4, 6-12, 6-15, 7-22
  (*See also* Perturbation)
Cosine computing circuit, Appendix Fig. A-3
Coulomb friction, simulation, 9-8
Counter, 10-10, 10-11, 11-13
Criterion function (*see* Optimization)
Cross-correlation, 12-11
Crossed-fields multiplier, 7-18
Crossplotting, 10-6
Crosstalk, 11-1, 11-9
Crystal clock, 10-11
Current balancing, 5-12
Current drift, 5-7
Current generator (regulator), 1-19
  for driving switches, 7-12
  for potentiometer calibration, 8-8
Current-source load, transistor, 5-3
Curve follower, 11-3
Cutoff of transistor, 6-11

D/A converter/multiplier (*see* Digital-to-analog converter/multiplier)
Damping of servomechanism, 8-2
Darlington circuit, 5-3
DAS, 11-15
Data reconstruction, 10-15
D-c reset of flip-flop, 10-10
D-c servo, 8-3
DDA (*see* Digital differential analyzer)
Deadspace circuit, 6-3
  applications, 7-22, 9-7 to 9-9
  precision, 7-16, 9-2
  as quadrant switch, 8-12
Decoder (*see* Digital-to-analog converter-multiplier)
Degenerative stage, 4-20
Delay networks, 10-18
Delay operator, 10-13
Delta modulation, 7-3, 7-7
Delta-sigma modulation, 10-20, 11-18
Demodulation in resolver, 8-11
DEPI, 11-15
Deposited-film potentiometer (*see* Carbon-film potentiometer)
DES-1, 11-15
Desk-top computers, 1-2, 11-6
Dials for potentiometers, 3-4
Diamond switch, 6-11, 10-4
Dielectric absorption, 3-8, 3-9, 3-20
  in amplifier design, 4-13, 4-14
Dielectrics, properties of, 3-8
Difference approximation for partial differential equation, 12-19, 12-20
Difference equations, computer solution of, 10-13, 10-14, 10-16
Difference operator, 10-14
Differential amplifier, in comparator, 10-9
  transistor, 5-4 to 5-6, 5-12, 5-15
  vacuum-tube, 4-6
Differential analyzer, 1-5, 1-6
  hybrid-code, 11-19
  (*See also* Differential equations; Digital differential analyzer; Iterative differential analyzer)
Differential difference equation, 12-19, 12-20
Differential equations, computer solution, basic method, 1-5, 2-7
  linear, 2-9, 2-10, 2-12 to 2-16
  nonlinear, 2-11
  systems of equations, 1-5, 2-7
  (*See also* Partial differential equations)
Differential gain, 5-4
Differentiation, electrical, 1-16
Diffusion equation, 12-17 to 12-21
Digital-to-analog (D/A) converter/multiplier, 11-10, 11-12, 11-16, 11-19, 12-14

Digital circuits, **10**-10
Digital computer, operational, **10**-13, **10**-14, **11**-17
simulation of, **11**-12
Digital control of analog computer, **10**-11, **11**-1, **11**-7, **11**-12, **11**-13
Digital controller, **11**-16
Digital differential analyzer (DDA), **11**-12, **11**-17 to **11**-19
Digital patchbay (*see* Control-variable patchbay)
Digital storage, **10**-20
Digital variable (*see* Binary variable)
Digital voltmeter (DVM), **9**-4
Diode, **6**-2
catching, **6**-3, **6**-10, **7**-16
high-frequency characteristics, **6**-5
(*See also* Electronic switch; Limiter)
Diode bridge, in comparator, **6**-8, **9**-5
limiter, **6**-6, **9**-2
switch, **6**-10, **8**-11, **9**-2, **10**-4
Diode function generator (*see* Function generator)
Diode multiplier (*see* Multiplier, quarter-square)
Diode switch, **7**-12
Direct-analog techniques, **1**-14
Direction cosines, **8**-16
Discrete-delay operator, **10**-13
Discriminator, **7**-7
Display, oscilloscope, **10**-11
Dissipation (*see* Dielectric absorption)
Distortion, **3**-16, **9**-16
Dither, **6**-13, **7**-14
Division, **1**-13, **2**-4, **7**-11, **7**-18, **7**-23
with automatic scaling, **12**-6
method for avoiding, **2**-4
by steepest descent, **12**-9
Donner Scientific Co. (*see* Systron-Donner Corporation)
Double chopper system, **5**-9
Double integral, computation, **10**-12
Double integrator, **1**-14
Douglas Aircraft Co., **6**-14
Drift, current, transistor, **5**-7
in d-c amplifiers, **4**-10, **4**-11, **4**-13, **5**-2, **5**-5, **5**-7
of diode breakpoint, **6**-4, **6**-13
effects of, **3**-2, **3**-15, **3**-21, **4**-10, **7**-20
in HOLD, **10**-4
power supply, **11**-8
in repetitive computer, **11**-6
specification of, **4**-1, **4**-10
(*See also* Automatic balancing; Low-drift circuits)
Dry-friction clutch, simulation, **9**-9
Dry-reed relay, **10**-10
Duodial, **3**-4
DVM (digital voltmeter), **9**-4

Dynamic error (*see* Calibration; Component accuracy; Frequency response; Phase error)
Dynamic load resistor, **4**-8
Dynamical constraint, **12**-9, **12**-16
DYSAC, **11**-15
DYSTAC (*see* Computer Systems, Inc.)

Earth-satellite trajectory, **12**-3
EASE (*see* Beckman/Berkeley Division)
Educational computer, **11**-6
Effectiveness (*see* Optimization)
Eigenvalue problem, **12**-13, **12**-14
Elastic stop, **9**-7
Electromagnetic fields, circuit for control, **1**-19
Electron-beam multiplier, **7**-18
Electronic Associates, Inc., **8**-8, **8**-13, **11**-1, **11**-6, **11**-8, **11**-13
Electronic chopper, **5**-8 to **5**-10, **6**-11
(*See also* Chopper; Electronic switch)
Electronic graph paper, **10**-11
Electronic resolver, **8**-14 to **8**-16, **12**-9
Electronic switch, **6**-8, **6**-18, **7**-11
block-diagram symbol, **10**-7
in D/A converter, **11**-10
diode, **6**-8, **6**-10, **10**-4
transistor, **6**-8, **6**-11, **7**-12, **10**-4
vacuum-tube, **6**-8, **6**-10, **7**-12
(*See also* Chopper; Diode bridge)
Embree Electronics Corp., **4**-23
Emitter follower, **5**-3
Emitter resistance, **5**-2
Encoder (*see* A/D converter/multiplier)
End resistance, **3**-4, **8**-5, **8**-7
Equal-coefficient rule, **2**-14
Equalization (*see* Frequency response)
Equations, solution of, **12**-8
Equivalent circuit, for capacitor, **3**-8
for operational amplifier, **3**-10
for potentiometer, **3**-6
for resistor, **3**-7
for transistor stages, **5**-2 to **5**-5, **5**-7, **5**-11
for vacuum-tube stages, **4**-4, **4**-16, **4**-17
Error, estimation of, **3**-1, **12**-1, **12**-4, **12**-5
in multipliers, **7**-13
in operational amplifier, **1**-14, **3**-12, **3**-19 to **3**-21
in solutions of linear differential equations, **3**-22 to **3**-24
(*See also* Phase error)
Error light, **4**-14, **11**-4
Error-rate equalization, **8**-2
Etched circuits, **5**-13
Euler-Lagrange equations, **12**-16
Euler rule, **10**-14, **11**-14, **11**-18
Event counter, **10**-11

Extended-scale integrator, 11-19
Extrapolation, 10-15
Extreme-value holding, 9-3

Failure report, 11-5
Feedback limiter, 6-3, 6-4
Feedback pair, transistor, 5-3, 5-11
Feedback ratio, 1-11, 1-14, 3-11, 4-15
Feedforward circuit, 4-19, 4-23, 5-12
Field-effect transistor (FET) as chopper, 5-10
Film potentiometer (see Carbon-film potentiometer)
Filter, notch, 1-19
  ripple, for chopper stabilizer, 4-14
    for multiplier, 7-13
    use of operational amplifiers, 1-19
First-order hold, 10-15, 11-12
  (See also Track-hold circuits)
Flip-flop, 10-10
Flow diagram, 10-6, 10-12, 12-14
Flow valve, linearization, 1-19
FM/AM multiplier, 7-3, 7-7
Folding error, 10-15
Follow-up potentiometer, 8-1, 8-2
Forcing function, generation of, 2-7
Forward difference, 12-19
Forward resistance, 6-2, 6-8
Four-quadrant division, 12-9
Four-quadrant multiplier, 1-13, 2-4, 7-2
Fourier analysis, 10-19
Free-running multivibrator, 7-16, 9-5
Frequency modulation, computer circuit, 9-5
Frequency response, of amplifiers, 4-15 to 4-20, 5-11
  of comparator, 10-9
  of digital integrator, 11-14
  of diode circuits, 6-5, 6-10, 9-2
  of function generator, 6-13 to 6-15
  of hybrid-code computer, 11-19
  of integrator, 3-20
  of multipliers, 7-13
  of operational amplifiers, 1-14, 3-12
  of phase inverter/summer, 3-19
  of precision limiter, 7-16, 9-2
  of ripple filter, 7-13
  of servomechanism, 8-1, 8-2
  (See also Component accuracy; Error)
Frequency-response measurement, 4-21
  weighting-function method, 2-16
Frequency sharing, 7-8
Friction, simulation, 9-8
Full scale, 1-18, 3-1
Function of two or more variables (see Function generator; Resolver)
Function generation, functions of time, 2-7

Function generation, with linear potentiometer, Appendix Table A-2
  nonlinear functions, Appendix Fig. A-2
  (See also Function generator)
Function generator, 1-13, 6-12
  block-diagram symbol of, 1-3
  cathode-ray-tube, 6-15, 6-19
  comparator/switch, 6-18, 7-19
  correction functions, 2-4, 6-12, 6-15, 7-22
  diode, 6-13, 6-17
  hybrid, 11-12, 11-20
  tapped potentiometer, 6-16, 8-8
  two or more variables, 6-16 to 6-19, 11-20
  varistor, 6-14
Function-generator setting, 11-2
  (See also Calibration)
Function memory, 10-17 to 10-20, 12-4, 12-21, 12-23
Function storage, 10-17 to 10-20, 12-4, 12-21, 12-23
Functionals, optimization, 12-13 to 12-16
Fuses for potentiometers, 3-4

Gain of servo amplifier, 8-2, 8-4
Gas-tube regulator, 11-8
Gate, 10-10
Gauss-Seidel iteration, 12-8
Gear ratio, 8-2, 8-3
General Electric Co., 11-17, 11-18
Generalized integration, 2-7, 8-16, 12-9
Germanium (see Diode)
Globar, 6-14
Goodyear Aircraft Corp., 6-13, 7-12
GPS Instruments, Inc., 7-15
Gradient method, discrete, 12-14
  continuous (see Steepest descent)
Grid current, 4-11
Ground currents, 1-2, 4-11, 4-14, 11-9
Ground system, 5-14, 11-9

Half-bridge (see Diode bridge)
Half-scale, 3-1
Hall effect, 7-6
Hamiltonian function, 12-16
Harmonic oscillator, simulation, 1-5, 2-9
  (See also Circle test)
Hazeltine Electronics, 11-17
Heat-conduction equation, 12-17 to 12-21
Heat-transfer multiplier, 7-6
Heated-pen recorder, 11-3
Helipot Corp., 3-4, 8-5, 8-6
HI terminal, 3-4
High-gain amplifier, block-diagram symbol for, 2-4
  equalization, 4-18
  (See also Implicit computation)

Hilbiber-Bénéteau circuit, 5-6
Hill climbing (*see* Optimization)
HOLD mode, 10-2 to 10-5
Hold relay, 10-2, 10-3
Hybrid-code computer, 11-19, 11-20
Hybrid function generator, 6-18, 11-12, 11-20
HYDAC, 11-13
HYDAPT system, 11-18
Hyperbolic-field multiplier, 7-18
Hysteresis, of comparator, 10-9
  dielectric, 3-8
  simulation of, 9-9
  (*See also* Bistable circuits)

I_{CBO}, 5-2
  temperature dependence, 5-2, 5-5
IBM 7094, 11-12, 11-14, 11-15
IC (initial condition) terminal, 1-12, 2-4, 10-2
Identification of system, 12-12
Implicit computation of sine and cosine, 8-16, 12-9
  (*See also* High-gain amplifier; Steepest descent)
Impulse response, 2-16
Incremental converter, 11-11
Incremental impedance, 4-4
Incremental transfer, 11-17 to 11-19
Independent linearity, 8-5
Induction generator, 8-2, 8-12
Induction resolver, 8-11
Inelastic stop, 9-7
Inequality constraint (*see* Constraint)
Infinite-impedance circuit, 1-19
Initial conditions, 1-5, 1-12
  for difference equations, 10-13
  for transfer-operator setups, 2-14
  (*See also* Integrator; Partial differential equations; RESET mode)
INITIAL-RESET mode, 10-8, 10-11
Input circuit of servo, 8-2
Input impedance, of d-c amplifier, 3-14, 4-1
  of operational amplifier, 3-14
  of transistor stage, 5-2, 5-4
Instrumentation, computer circuits for, 1-19
Integral equation, 12-23
Integrating network, 1-12
Integration (*see* Integrator)
Integration routine, 11-14
Integrator, block-diagram symbols for, 1-2, 10-7
  DDA, 11-17
  digital, 11-14, 11-17
  double, 1-14
  electrical, 1-4, 1-12

Integrator, error analysis, 1-12, 3-20, 3-21
  error sources, 3-20, 3-21
  extended-scale, 11-19
  generalized, 2-7, 8-16, 12-9
  hybrid-code, 11-19
  HYDAPT, 11-18
  scaling, 2-4
  stabilizing networks, 4-18
Internal impedance, of d-c amplifier
  stages, 4-4 to 4-8, 5-2, 5-3
  of operational amplifiers, 3-13
Interpolation, in function generator, 6-16, 11-20
  with tapped potentiometers, 6-16, 8-8
Interrupt line, 11-12
Interstage networks, 4-1, 4-16, 4-17
Inverse function, 6-12, 12-9
Inverse resolver, 8-9, 8-13
Inverted transistor, 5-8, 5-9, 6-11, 10-4
Inverter, logic, 10-10
Inverting amplifier (*see* Phase inverter)
Isolation transformer, 11-9
Iteration, 12-21, 12-22
Iterative differential analyzer, 10-6, 11-6, 11-7, 11-13
  amplifiers for, 4-23, 5-12
  frequency response, 3-24
Iterative optimization, 12-13 to 12-16

Keyboard, 11-3, 11-6

Ladder network, 11-10
Lagrange multiplier, 12-9, 12-16
Land camera, 10-11, 11-3
Latching comparator, 10-9
Lead network, 6-5, 7-13, 8-2
Leakage, capacitor, 3-9
  patchbay, 11-1
Leakage current, 5-13
  in amplifiers, 4-11 to 4-13
  diode, 6-2, 6-8, 6-10
  transistor, 6-10, 6-11
  (*See also* I_{CBO})
Legendre polynomials, generation of, 2-10
Legendre's differential equation, 2-10
Limit cycle, 2-11
Limit stops, for servo, 8-3
  simulation of, 9-7, 10-12
Limiter, 6-3, 6-4
  precision (*see* Precision limiter)
  series, with temperature compensation, 6-13
  for simulating saturation, 9-7
Linear operation (*see* Transfer operator)
Linear programming, 12-10
Linearity of potentiometer, 3-4, 8-5

Linearization, 12-2
  of transducers, 1-19
Link Division, General Precision, Inc.,
  6-16
Linkage system, 11-12, 11-13
LO terminal, 3-4
Load capacitance, 4-7, 4-17
Load line (see Characteristics)
Loading, of operational amplifier, 3-11,
  4-17
  of potentiometer, 3-5, 8-7, 8-8
  by rolloff network, 4-19
Logarithm network, 7-17
Logic circuits, 10-10
Loop gain, of operational amplifier, 1-10,
  3-10, 4-15
  of servo, 8-2, 8-5
Low-drift circuits, 4-12, 5-4 to 5-10
Low-pass delay approximation, 10-18

Machine equations, 2-3
Machine variables (see Scaling)
Machine unit, 2-2
  hybrid code, 11-19
Magnetic amplifier, 8-3
Magnetic modulator, 5-10
Magnetic storage, 10-20
Magnetoresistance, 7-6
Magnetostrictive delay line, 10-20
Maintenance, 11-5
Mark-space multiplier (see Time-division
  multiplier)
Mass-spring system, simulation of, 1-14
  (See also Harmonic oscillator)
Massachusetts Institute of Technology
  (MIT), 7-15, 11-16
Matched transistors, 5-5, 6-11
Matching, model, 12-12, 12-13
Mathieu's differential equation, 2-10
Max/min circuits, 9-3
Maximum-holding circuit, 9-3
Maximum principle, 12-16
Mean-square perturbation, 12-2
Measure of effectiveness (see Optimiza-
  tion)
MEI (minimum excursion indicator), 2-2,
  11-4
Memory, function (see Function memory;
  Function storage)
  point (see Track-hold operation)
Memory pair, 10-14
  (See also Track-hold pair)
Microphonism, 5-13
MIDAS, 11-15
Miller compensator, 4-12
Miller effect, 4-1, 4-6, 4-16
  transistor, 5-11
Minimal-phase network, 7-13

Minimum-excursion indicator (MEI),
  2-2, 11-4
Minimum-holding circuit, 9-3
MIT (Massachusetts Institute of Tech-
  nology), 7-15, 11-16
Mode control, by digital computer,
  11-12
  electronic, 10-4, 10-5
  integrator, 10-2 to 10-5
  iterative differential analyzer, 10-6,
  10-8, 10-11
Model matching, 12-12, 12-13
Modified adjoint system, 10-11
Modulation in resolver, 8-11
Modulator, 4-13
  for servo, 8-2, 8-3
  simulation of, 9-5
Moment of inertia, 8-2, 8-3
Monte-Carlo method, 10-6, 11-7
Motor (see Servomotor)
Motor damping coefficient, 8-2, 8-3
Motor gain, 8-2
Motor time constant, 8-2, 8-3
Multiaperture core, 10-20
Multiar, 10-11
Multicomparator, 9-2
Multiplexing, 10-6, 11-12, 11-13, 11-16
Multiplication, 1-13
  (See also Multiplier; Servomultiplier)
Multiplier, A/D/A converter, 7-6, 7-22,
  11-16
  block-diagram symbols for, 1-3, 2-4
  coincidence, 7-3
  digital, 11-17
  electron-beam, 7-18
  Hall effect and magnetoresistance, 7-6,
  7-21
  heat-transfer, 7-6
  hybrid-code, 11-19
  logarithmic, 7-17
  pulse-rate, 11-17
  pulse-width, 11-18
  quarter-square, 1-14, 2-4, 7-14, 7-15,
  7-21
  sampling, 7-6, 8-15
  scaling, 2-4
  time-division, 7-9 to 7-14, 7-21,
  10-20
  triangle-averaging, 7-16, 7-21
  (See also Servomultiplier)
Multitrace display, 10-11, 11-3
Multivibrator, simulation of, 7-16, 9-5
  (See also Flip-flop; Schmitt trigger)
Mylar, properties of, 3-8, 3-9

NAND gate, 10-10
Neon bulbs for interstage coupling, 4-1

Network, integrating, 1-12
  passive time-delay, 10-18
  (*See also* Filter)
Neumann series, 12-23
Neutral mode, 6-11
Noise, chopper, 4-14, 5-9
  in d-c amplifiers, 4-10, 5-9
  effects of, 3-21
  in potentiometers, 3-4
Noise generator, 6-19, 6-31, 11-7, 12-15
Nominal solution (*see* Perturbation)
Nonlinear oscillations, 2-11
Nonsaturating switch, 6-11, 10-4
Normal response, 2-14
Notch filter, 1-19
Nuclear reactor, 12-6
Null method, 3-2, 6-14, 7-20
  (*See also* Calibration)
Nyquist, 4-15

Objective function (*see* Optimization)
Oblique impact, simulation of, 9-8
Offset in transistor switches, 6-11
  (*See also* Drift)
One-shot multivibrator, 10-10
Open trapezoidal rule, 10-14
OPERATE mode (*see* COMPUTE mode)
Operating point, transistor, 5-2, 5-5
  vacuum-tube, 4-3
Operational amplifier, 1-10, 1-14, 1-15
  error analysis, 3-10 to 3-21
  frequency response and stabilization,
    4-18
  (*See also* Differentiation; Integrator;
    Limiter; Phase inverter; Summing
    amplifier; Transfer function)
Operational-amplifier circuits for time
  delay, 10-18
Operational digital computer, 11-17,
  11-18
Operational relay, 6-9, 10-10
Operator (*see* Transfer operator)
Optimization, continuous, 12-7 to
  12-12
  integral, 12-16
  parameter, 10-6, 12-12 to 12-15
  by random perturbations, 12-15
Optimum gradient method, 12-14
OR gate, 10-10
Orbit, 12-3
Oscilloscope display, 10-11, 11-3
Output stage, transistor, 5-3, 5-11, 5-12
  vacuum-tube, 4-7
Oven, 3-7, 3-8, 11-1
Overload alarm, 11-4
Overload hold, 10-3, 11-4
Overload light, 4-14, 11-4
Overload recovery, 4-14

PACE (*see* Electronic Associates, Inc.)
Packard-Bell, 11-17
Padding networks, 8-8
Padé approximation, 10-18
Parallel-feedback integrator (*see* Inte-
  grator)
Parallel-feedback operational amplifier
  (*see* Operational amplifier)
Parameter estimation, 12-12
Parameter-influence coefficient, 12-4,
  12-14
Parameter optimization (*see* Optimiza-
  tion)
Parameter perturbation, 12-11, 12-12,
  12-14
Parameter sensitivity, 12-4
Parameter-setting circuit, 12-14
Parameter stepping (*see* Accumulator;
  SCAN mode)
Parasitic capacitance, 3-7, 3-19, 3-20
Partial A/D converter, 11-19
Partial differential equations, 12-17 to
  12-22
Partial-fraction expansion, 2-15, 10-14
Partial system test, 2-5
Passivation, 6-2
Passive network, 10-18
Patchbay, analog, 11-1
  control-variable, 10-6, 10-11, 11-1,
    11-6, 11-7, 11-13
Patchbay/control module, 11-6
Patchbay oven, 11-1
Peak detector, 9-3, 9-6
Peltier oven, 10-4
Penalty function (*see* Constraint)
Penmotor, 11-3
Perturbation, parameter, 12-11, 12-12,
  12-14
  random, 12-15
Perturbation techniques, 3-1, 12-1 to
  12-4
Phase adjustment in oscillator, 9-6
Phase error, 3-2
  of digital integrator, 11-14
  of operational amplifier, 3-12
Phase inverter, 1-10
  block-diagram symbol, 2-4
  error analysis, 3-19
Phase markers, 9-5
Phase-plane plots, 2-11
Phase-sensitive demodulator, 8-11
Phase shift in potentiometers, 3-6
Phase-shift oscillator, 9-6
Phase shifter, 1-19
Philbrick (G. A. Philbrick Researches,
  Inc.), 4-23, 5-12, 6-17, 7-16, 10-11,
  11-8
Photoconductive cell for AGC, 8-13
Photoelectric chopper, 5-10

Photoformer, 6-15
Picard's method, 12-5
Plate characteristics, 4-3
Plate resistance, 4-4
Plotting table (see Servo table)
Plug-in d-c amplifier, 4-23, 5-12, 11-7
Plug-in networks, 11-1, 11-6
Point storage (see Track-hold operation)
Polar coordinates, 8-9
POLAR mode, 8-13, 8-14, 11-1
Polarity indication in digital voltmeter, 9-4
Polarized relay, 6-9, 7-6, 10-10
Polaroid Land camera, 10-11, 11-3
Polystyrene, properties of, 3-8, 3-9
Pontryagin's maximum principle, 12-16
POT SET mode, 3-5, 10-3, 11-1
Potentiometer, carbon-film, 8-1, 8-5, 8-10
  coefficient-setting, 1-9, 3-4 to 3-6
    block-diagram symbol, 1-3
  follow-up (see Servomechanism)
  servo-driven, 8-1, 8-5 to 8-8
    block-diagram symbols, 1-3, 2-4
    function-generating, 8-6, 8-7
    load-equalizing resistors, 2-4
    specifications, 8-5
    tapped, 6-16, 8-4, 8-8
    wirewound, 8-1, 8-5
Potentiometer setting, 11-2, 11-12, 11-13
Power ground, 5-14, 11-9
Power supply, 11-8
Precision (see Component accuracy)
Precision limiter, 9-2 to 9-4
  dual, 9-2
  in multiplier, 7-16
  patchbay connections, 9-2
  as quadrant switch, 8-12
Predictor-corrector, 11-14, 11-15
Preloading, 8-7
Preregulator, 11-8
PRESENT period, 10-14, 11-26
Preset counter, 10-11
Printed circuits, 5-13
Problem check, 11-4
  (See also Checking, of solutions)
Problem scaling (see Scaling)
Processing delay, 11-12, 11-18
Program check, 11-4
Programming, linear, 12-10
Programming automation, 11-4
Pseudo-random-noise generator, 11-7, 12-15
Pulse-count modulation, 11-18
Pulse-frequency modulation (PFM), 10-20, 11-18
Pulse modulation, 11-18
Pulse-phase modulation (PPM), 11-18
Pulse-rate multiplier, 11-17

Pulse-ratio modulation, 11-18
  (See also Time-division multiplier)
Pulse-width modulation (PWM), 6-19, 7-3, 11-18
  in resolver, 8-15
  (See also Coincidence multiplier; Time-division multiplier)
Pulsed analog computer, 11-16
Pulsed attenuator (see Time-division multiplier)
Punched tape (see Potentiometer setting)
Pushbutton switches, 10-3

Quadrant switch, function generator, 6-13
  resolver, 8-12, 8-14
Quadratron, 6-14
Quantization noise, 11-14
Quantized-gradient method, 12-14
Quarter-square multiplier (see Multiplier)

Racing problems, 10-10
Radioactive paint, 4-1, 11-8
Ramp/comparator converter, 9-4, 11-11
Ramp response, 2-16
Random-perturbation optimizer, 12-15
Rate feedback, 8-2
  (See also Rate servomechanism)
Rate limiting, in amplifiers, 4-7, 4-16, 4-17, 5-3
  effects of, 3-2
  in servomechanisms, 8-1
  in track-hold circuits, 10-4
Rate resolver, 8-12, 8-14, 8-16
Rate servomechanism, 8-1, 8-12, 9-6
Rate test, 11-4, 11-5
Rayleigh's equation, 2-11
RCA Laboratories Division, 7-12
REAC (see Reeves Instrument Corp.)
Readout switching, 11-3
Readout system, 10-11, 11-3
Recorder, 1-17, 11-3
  control circuit, 10-3
RECTANGULAR mode, 8-13, 8-14, 11-1
Reed relay, 10-10, 10-14, 11-10
Reeves Instrument Corporation, 4-23, 6-13, 7-15, 8-2, 11-4 to 11-6
REFERENCE OFF mode, 10-3
Reference voltage, 1-17
  supply, 1-19, 11-8
Refrigeration of computing elements, 3-8, 11-1
Regenerative amplifier, 4-9, 5-6
  frequency response, 4-20
  use for equalization, 4-20
Regulator, 1-19, 11-8

Relay, block-diagram symbol, 10-7
  control, 10-3, 11-1
  integrator, 1-4, 10-2 to 10-4
  operational, 6-9, 10-10
  polarized, 7-6
  protection of, 10-3
  readout selector, 11-3
  simulation of, 9-9
Relay logic, 10-10
REPEAT switch, 10-11
Repetition-rate selector, 10-11
Repetitive operation, 1-7, 2-6, 10-2,
  10-11, 11-6
  (*See also* Iterative differential analyzer)
RESET mode, 1-6, 1-12, 10-2, 10-3, 10-5
Reset relay, 1-6, 10-2, 10-3
Residual, 12-8
Resistance-coupled amplifier table, 4-5
Resistive paper, 6-16
Resistors, 3-7
Resolution of potentiometer, 3-4, 8-1,
  8-5
Resolver, block-diagram symbol, 2-4
  electronic, 8-14 to 8-16, 12-9
  servo, 2-4, 8-9 to 8-13
Resubstitution, 3-1, 12-5
REVERSE SCAN mode, 10-11
Reversible counter, 10-10
Ripple filter, 4-14, 7-13
Rolloff network, 4-14, 4-17, 4-18
Root-locus plot, 4-19, 4-20
Roundoff error, 11-14
Runge-Kutta method, 11-15

Sample-hold (*see* Track-hold circuits)
Sampled data, 10-13 to 10-15
Sampled-data system, simulation, 10-6,
  10-13 to 10-15
Sampling, 10-15
Sampling readout, 10-11
Sampling resolver, 8-15
Satellite trajectory, 12-3
Saturable reactor, 11-8, 11-9
  in modulator, 11-18
Saturation, simulation, 9-7
  of transistor, 6-11
Scale factor (*see* Scaling)
Scaling, 2-2, 2-3
  automatic, 11-4, 11-15, 12-6
  for DDA, 11-17
  for hybrid-code computer, 1-2, 1-3,
    11-19
  rescaling, 2-8
  small differences, 12-6
  time, 2-5, 2-6, 2-9
  for transfer operator setups, 2-14
SCAN mode, 10-11
Scanning readout, 10-11

Schmitt trigger, 6-18, 7-11, 7-12, 10-4, 10-9
Schottky effect, 6-2
Scientific Data Systems, Inc., 11-15
Second-order transfer operator, special
  circuit, 1-14, Appendix Table A-1
Selector, amplitude, 6-3, 6-17, 9-3
  readout, 11-3
Self-heating, of resistors, 3-7
  of transistors, 5-5, 5-12
Semibell function, 2-4
Semielastic stop, 9-7, 10-12
Sense line, 11-12, 11-13
Sensitivity equation, 12-4, 12-14
Separation of variables, 12-18
Sequential logic, 10-10
Sequential random perturbations, 12-15
Series limiter, 6-3, 6-10
Series regulator, 11-8
Series-shunt limiter, 6-3, 7-15
Service report, 11-5
Servo amplifier, 8-3
Servo plotting board, 11-3
Servo-set potentiometers, 11-2
Servo table, 11-3
  for functions of two variables, 6-16
Servo tester, 9-6
Servomechanism, computer, 2-4
  design, 8-4
Servomotor, 8-2, 8-3, 8-5
Servomultiplier, 1-11, 2-4, 7-1, 7-6, 7-8
  (*See also* Servomechanism)
Setting of potentiometers, 3-5, 11-2
Setup method, summary, 2-17
Shift operator, 10-13
Shift register, 10-10
Shift-register noise generator, 12-15
Short-circuit transfer impedance, 1-14,
  Appendix Table A-1
Shunt limiter, 6-3
Sign bit, 11-10, 11-11
Sign changer (*see* Phase inverter)
Sign multiplier, 12-9
Signal generator, multivibrator type, 9-5
  sinusoidal, 9-6
Signal ground, 1-2, 4-14, 5-14, 5-15, 11-9
Signed-magnitude code, 11-10
Silicon (*see* Diode)
Simulation, combined analog/digital,
  11-12, 11-13
  digital, 11-15, 11-17
Simulation board, 11-1
Simultaneous equations, 12-8
Sine-cosine generator, diode circuits, 8-14
  implicit computation, 8-16, 12-9
  potentiometer, 2-4, 8-10
  quadrant switching, 8-12, 8-14
  sampling techniques, 8-15
Sine wave, hybrid-code representation,
  11-19

Sine-wave oscillator, **9**-6
Single-pole-double-throw (SPDT) switch,
   electronic, **6**-10, **6**-11, **7**-12, **10**-5
Single-pole-single-throw (SPST) switch,
   6-10
Six-diode bridge, **10**-4
Six-diode switch, **6**-10, **10**-4
Slack variable, **12**-10
Slo-reset, **8**-3
Slope adjustment, **6**-13
Small-signal frequency response (*see*
   Component accuracy; Frequency
   response)
Smoothing oscillator, **6**-13, **7**-14
Soakage (*see* Dielectric absorption)
Solenoid, simulation, **9**-9
Sonic delay line, **10**-20
Space-vehicle simulation, **11**-12, **12**-2,
   12-3, **12**-16
Specifications, for computer servomech-
   anism, **8**-1
   for d-c amplifier, **4**-1
   for multiplier, **7**-21
   for track-hold, **10**-4
SPEDAC, **11**-17
Speed/torque characteristic, **8**-3
Spike (*see* Switching spike)
Square-card potentiometer, **8**-10
Square-root circuit, **2**-4, **12**-9
Squaring network, **7**-15
Stability, bias, **5**-2
   of circuit elements, **3**-7, **3**-8
   of computer setup, **12**-19
   of computer solution, **3**-1
   of division loops, **7**-23
   feedback amplifier, **4**-15 to **4**-19
   improvement of, **4**-17 to **4**-19
   of operational amplifiers, **4**-18
   resetting, **3**-4
   of servomechanisms, **8**-2
   of steepest-descent loops, **12**-9
Stabilization networks, **4**-15 to **4**-19
Stacked transistors, **5**-11
Stall torque, **8**-3
Starting friction, simulation of, **9**-8
Starting routine, **10**-11
   (*See also* INITIAL RESET)
Starting torque, **8**-1 to **8**-5
Static accuracy, **3**-2
   of servo, **8**-1
Static check, **11**-4
Static error (*see* Component accuracy)
Statistics, computation, **1**-8, **10**-6, **10**-11,
   11-7, **11**-12
Steepest descent, **8**-16, **12**-7 to **12**-14
Step function, integration of, **1**-12
Step multiplier, **7**-6
   (*See also* A/D/A converter/multi-
   plier)

Step response, of computing elements,
   3-2
   of feedback amplifier, **4**-17
   of multiplier, **7**-21
   of potentiometer, **3**-7
   of servo, **8**-2
   weighting-function method, **2**-16
Step-size control, **12**-14, **12**-15
Stepping switch, **7**-6
Storage time, **6**-5
Strip-chart recorder, **11**-3
Subroutine, **10**-6, **11**-16
Subroutine counter, **10**-11
Successive-approximation converter,
   11-11
Summing amplifier, **1**-11
   block-diagram symbol, **1**-2
   design, **3**-19
   error analysis, **3**-19, **3**-24
   scaling, **2**-18
Summing integrator (*see* Integrator)
Summing junction (summing point), **1**-10
   (*See also* Operational amplifier)
Summing-junction capacitance, **3**-19,
   3-20, **4**-18
Summing network, **1**-11
Surface passivation, **6**-2
Switch, electronic (*see* Electronic switch)
   transistor, **5**-8, **5**-9, **6**-11, **10**-4
Switch-timing errors, **7**-12, **7**-13, **10**-4
   (*See also* Timing errors)
Switched amplifier, **10**-5
Switched-capacitor decoder, **11**-10
Switched-capacitor memory (delay),
   10-19
Switching spike, **5**-8, **5**-9, **6**-11, **10**-4
Synchronous vibrator (*see* Chopper)
System design, **3**-24, **11**-6, **11**-7
System identification, **12**-12
Systron-Donner Corporation, **1**-2, **4**-23,
   5-12, **7**-12, **7**-15

Table-top computer, **1**-2, **11**-6
Tachometer, **8**-2, **8**-12
"Tail-switching" amplifier, **10**-4
Tapped potentiometer, function gener-
   ator, **6**-16, **8**-8
   for functions of two variables, **6**-16
   phase compensation, **3**-6
Teflon, properties of, **3**-8, **3**-9
Telefunken G.m.b.H., **7**-11, **7**-12
Television display, **10**-11
Temperature compensation, amplifier,
   5-5 to **5**-7
   function generator, **6**-13, **7**-15
   multiplier, **7**-15
Temperature dependence, of capaci-
   tance, **3**-8

Temperature dependence, of d-c amplifier
    performance, 4-11, 5-2, 5-5 to 5-7
  of diode breakpoint, 6-4, 6-13
  of resistance, 3-7
  of transistor parameters, 5-6
Terminal linearity, 8-1, 8-5
Test with artificial errors, 3-1, 11-19
Test circuits, 3-1, 4-17, 4-21, 5-12, 6-13,
    7-20, 8-1, 11-5
Testing of multiplier, 7-20, 11-5
Three-state mode control, 10-2, 10-7,
    10-8
Three-terminal potentiometer, 3-4, 3-5
Threshold gate, 10-10
Thyrite, 6-14
Time constant of integrator, 1-12
  (See also Charging time constant)
Time delay, 6-33, 10-18, 11-3
Time-division multiplier, 7-9 to 7-14,
    7-21, 10-20
Time-scale check, 3-1, 11-4
Time scaling (see Scaling)
Time sharing, 7-8
Timing, digital, 10-6, 10-11
Timing errors, 3-2, 7-12, 7-13, 10-2 to
    10-4
Torque/speed characteristic, 8-3
Total transfer, 11-17, 11-18
Totem-pole stage, 4-7, 4-8, 5-3, 5-11, 5-12
Track-hold circuits, specifications, 10-4
Track-hold operation, 10-8, 10-13 to
    10-15
Track-hold pair, 10-8
  applications, 10-12 to 10-15, 12-14
TRACK mode, 10-4
Tracking accuracy of servo, 8-1
Trajectory, 12-3
Transcendental equations, 12-8
Transconductance, 4-4
Transfer characteristic (see Function
    generator; Limiter)
Transfer function, of integrator, 1-12,
    3-20
  of operational amplifier, 1-14
  for sampled-data operations (numer-
    ical integration), 11-14
  of servomechanism, 8-2
  (See also Transfer operator)
Transfer impedance, 1-14, 9-45, 9-46,
    Appendix Table A-1
Transfer operator, computer representa-
    tion, differential-analyzer technique,
    2-12 to 2-16
  direct-analog technique, 1-14
  sampled-data, 10-14
  special operational amplifiers for,
    1-14, 1-15
Transistor chopper (see Electronic chop-
    per)

Transistor switch for analog data, 6-24,
    6-32 to 6-34, 7-6 to 7-9
Trapezoidal rule, 10-14, 11-14
Triangle-averaging multiplier, 7-16, 7-21
Triangle generator, 7-16, 9-5
Triangle-integration multiplier, 7-16,
    7-21
Triangle test, 11-5
TRICE, 11-17
Triggering, 10-10
Truncation error, 11-14
Tuning-fork oscillator, 11-3
Turn-counting dial, 3-4
Two-quadrant multiplier, 1-13, 7-2
Two-time-scale computation, 6-33, 10-6,
    10-11, 10-12

Unity-gain follower, 5-15
Unloading circuit, 1-19, 8-7, 9-4
Unperturbed solution (see Perturbation)
Up-down counter, 10-10

V_{BE}, 5-2
  temperature dependence, 5-5
Vacuum diode, 6-2, 6-10
Vacuum-tube switch (see Electronic
    switch)
Valves, linearization, 1-19
Van der Pol's equation, 2-11
Variable time delay, 10-18, 10-20
Variation, 12-16
Varistor, 7-14
Varistor multiplier, 7-22
Velocity limit, 8-1, 8-3, 8-4
Volt box, 1-12
Voltage regulator, 1-19, 11-8
Voltage-sensitive gate, 7-6
Voltage switches (see Transistor switches)
Voltage-to-time converter, 9-4, 11-11

Weighting function, 2-16
Wideband d-c amplifier, 3-24, 4-19, 4-23,
    5-12
Wien bridge, 9-6
Wire-wound potentiometer, 8-1, 8-5
  (See also Resolver)

xy recorder, 11-3

z transform, 10-13
Zener diode, 4-1, 6-3, 11-8
Zener voltage, 6-2
Zero-based linearity, 8-5
Zero error of multiplier, 7-15, 7-20, 7-21
Zero-order hold, 10-15
  (See also Track-hold circuits)